THE GREEK EXPERIENCE OF INDIA

The Greek Experience of India

FROM ALEXANDER TO THE INDO-GREEKS

RICHARD STONEMAN

PRINCETON UNIVERSITY PRESS
PRINCETON & OXFORD

Published by Princeton University Press
41 William Street, Princeton, New Jersey 08540
6 Oxford Street, Woodstock, Oxfordshire OX20 1TR

press.princeton.edu

Jacket image: The Buddha accompanied by Vajrapani, who has the characteristics of the Greek Heracles

LCCN 2018958249
ISBN 978-0-691-15403-9

British Library Cataloging-in-Publication Data is available

Editorial: Ben Tate and Hannah Paul
Production Editorial: Kathleen Cioffi
Jacket Design: Layla MacRory
Jacket Credit: Gandhara relief
Production: Jacqueline Poirier
Publicity: Jodi Price

This book has been composed in Arno

Printed on acid-free paper. ∞

Printed in the United States of America

10 9 8 7 6 5 4 3 2 1

To Aleksandra Szalc

Καὶ ἡμεῖς τοιαῦτα πεπόνθαμεν

'An Ordinary Person'

A stick under his arm, a pack on his head,
At dusk a villager goes home along the river.
If after a hundred centuries somehow –
By some magic – from the past's kingdom of death
This peasant could be resurrected, again made flesh,
With this stick under his arm and surprise in his eyes,
Then would crowds besiege him on all sides,
Everyone snatching every word from his lips.
His joys and sorrows, attachments and loves,
His neighbours, his own household,
His fields, cattle, methods of farming: all
They would take in greedily and still it wouldn't be enough.
His life story, today so ordinary,
Will, in those days, seem charged with poetry.

—RABINDRANATH TAGORE

CONTENTS

PART III. INTERACTIONS

ILLUSTRATIONS

PREFACE AND ACKNOWLEDGEMENTS

THIS BOOK HAS BEEN a long journey, since I first began to reflect on Alexander's encounter with the naked philosophers of Taxila in the early 1990s. Many other projects intervened before I felt ready to embark on the research for this book. It has benefited from a number of external stimuli. Al Bertrand agreed to publish the book, and both he and his successor in Princeton's Oxford office, Ben Tate, have shown admirable patience as I worked to complete it.

I must mention in particular my friend and colleague Richard Seaford, who shares my interest in the relations of Greece and India (though he stops where I start, in the fourth century BCE): we have had many conversations over the last few years about matters covered in this book, and I am grateful to him for reading parts of it as well. John Wilkins also gave valuable comments on portions of the book. A long conversation with Robin Lane Fox was also rewarding. I have also benefited from the expertise of Aleksandra Szalc, whose PhD from Wrocław is on the subject of Indian elements in the Alexander Romance. Sushma Jansari (British Museum) was kind enough to let me read her PhD thesis on Megasthenes. A lecture by Sushmita Basu Majumdar about the Ājīvikas, given at the conference organised by Richard Seaford in 2014, was a source of illumination, while her photographs galvanised me into organising a first trip to India in 2015.

Trailfinders provided a bespoke travel service and organised a smoothly run itinerary around a somewhat unusual list of places in India. They organised a second such trip in 2016. On both occasions we had excellent drivers and guides, and I must single out the guides to Patna and Sanchi for their knowledge and diligence, and the enthusiasm with which they responded as it became evident that I was determined to see everything. The guide at Ajanta (Amud) was equally thorough, and introduced me for the first time to the *Citra Sūtra* (see chapter 15).

Chance encounters also forward scholarship. At Mumbai airport I fell into conversation with Diane Tepfer, a student of Walter Spink, who set me on the way to his scholarly work on Ajanta. Three academic readers for Princeton University Press have expanded my horizons, bibliographical and otherwise, and helped me to clarify many of my ideas.

The University of Exeter continues to provide a background for my scholarly work, and I have benefited from access to its library, as well as those of the Institute of Classical Studies, the School of Oriental and African Studies, the Bodleian and Sackler Libraries and Oriental Institute in Oxford, and the London Library.

ABBREVIATIONS AND CONVENTIONS

CHI *The Cambridge History of India*

CIG *Corpus Inscriptionum Graecarum*

DI *Didyma Inscriptions*

FGRH F. Jacoby, *Die Fragmente der griechischen Historiker*

OGIS *Orientis Graecae Inscriptiones Selectae*

POXY *Oxyrhynchus papyri*

PSI *Papiri greci e latini* (Società italiana per la ricerca dei papiri greci e latini in Egitto)

RE *Paulys Realencyclopädie der Alterumwissenschaft*

SEG *Supplementum Epigraphicum Graecum*

Greek and Latin authors and their works are cited according to standard abbreviations, as specified in for example the *Oxford Classical Dictionary* and Liddell and Scott's *Greek–English Lexicon*. Classical journals are cited according to the conventions of *L'Année philologique*. The titles of Indology journals are normally cited in full.

The *Mahābhārata* is cited in the Chicago translation by van Buitenen and Fitzgerald where available (books 1–5, and 11–12, part I) and for the rest from the translation by Kisari Mohan Ganguli. The *Ṛg Veda* is cited from the Oxford translation by Jamison and Brereton.

Greek names are normally Latinised. Greek is frequently quoted in Greek, but individual words and short phrases are generally transliterated.

Sanskrit and other Indian languages are transliterated according to the standard system. (See, for example, *Teach Yourself Complete Sanskrit*.) Thus:

Long and short vowels are distinguished.

Consonants are sounded roughly as in English except that:

c represents the sound 'ch' as in 'church';
letters dotted below (ḍ ṇ ṛ ṣ ṭ) are retroflex;
ṁ represents a nasalisation of the preceding vowel;
ñ is palatal; ṅ is velar;
r and ṛ are semivowels;
ś (palatal) resembles English 'sh'
bh ch dh ḍh gh jh kh ph th ṭh are aspirated consonants: thus ch, th and ph are not pronounced as in English 'church', 'thing' or 'phantom', but separately as in 'clubhouse', 'church hall', 'madhouse', 'dog-house', 'barge-house', 'Okehampton', 'flophouse', 'hothouse'. (The retroflex consonants have no equivalent in English.)

THE GREEK EXPERIENCE OF INDIA

PROLOGUE

The Moon at Noon

IN INDIA, the curving moon lies on its back, and resembles a little boat sailing sedately across the heavens. The Greek hero Heracles sailed across the sky to the west in the boat of the Sun, a beneficent god. In India, the sun, Surya, is also a god, and the dawn, Uṣas, is a goddess, but the moon is not, like the Greek eye of night, a goddess.

Some of India's best light effects are achieved by moonlight, a cool light that is a relief from the burning heat of the day. The silvery white beauty of the Taj Mahal is like the light of the moon, and is a monument not only to mourning, but to love. When Chandni Chowk in Delhi was first built, it was a long boulevard with a rectangular pool down its centre, in which the light of the moon, Chand, was always reflected. The moon and stars are the diamonds of the night sky. When Babur first came to India, he wrote that 'all who visit India expect jewels to litter the sands as the stars do the sky at night'. He was disappointed in India, but he felt how India watches with the eye of night.

Amrit Lal Vegad, in his meditative account of a pilgrimage to the mouth and the source of the holy river Narmada, was struck by the behaviour of the moon.

> I suddenly noticed the sky and stopped, amazed. There was the moon, at high noon! Misty and low on the horizon but looming clearly over the open plain. Does the sun have the courage to show itself in the middle of the night? The moon is a wandering minstrel with no fixed home.

And again

> I went to the bank of the Narmada. The full moon had climbed over the hills and was pouring its glory into the valley . . . How strange it is, I thought, that the light of the moon is not its own. The moon is not the author, it is only the translator! It translates sunshine into moonshine.

> But what a divine translator the moon is! Where is the charm in sunlight that is in moonlight? I wondered whether I should call the moon a translator, a transposer or a transformer!
>
> However, my thoughts were only half correct. Translation may be in either direction. Sunlight may be translated into moonlight, but moonlight cannot be translated into sunlight.[1]

If Greece is represented by the sun and India by the moon, that is not to suggest any relation of inferiority one to the other. Each has its own style. If anything, there is an incommensurability; the one does not easily understand the terms of the other. Perhaps the Indian, like the moon, absorbs and transmutes the rays of the sun, while the Greek remains largely stupefied by the subtle emanations of the moon.

The translation of sunshine into moonshine is an alchemical process as strange as the translation of the words of philosophers through three interpreters into Greek; like trying to get water to run clear through mud.

In a sacred grove in India, according to the *Alexander Romance*, Alexander and his men encountered two trees which they understood to be those of the Sun and Moon respectively. One spoke 'in Indian', one in both Greek and Indian. Both told him the same mournful story of his approaching end. The Sun and the Moon in concert whispered a message of defeat and doom.

This book is about the encounter of two incommensurable civilisations that came face to face for two pregnant centuries.[2] What did they learn from each other? How did they share their wisdom? The poet Nonnus envisaged an Indian 'hamadryad' (that is, a *śalabhañjikā*, a tree spirit) welcoming the Greek invader god Dionysus and allowing him to be at home in her land, to bring the spirit of Greek humanism into a land where trees and rivers are sacred. (See chapter 3, *Dionysus*.) I hope to show that this encounter was more than an encounter between people and nature-spirits; that two peoples grew and learned as a result of their familiarity one with another.

1. Vegad 2008, 29 and 146–7.

2. Subrahmanyam 2017, 214 sees 'incommensurability' as one interpretative strategy among several, and does not find India more incommensurable for Europeans than other regions of the world. Perhaps he is right.

PART I

First Impressions

1

Writing a Book about India

In India everything is done differently from the rest of the world. This will never change.

—BABUR (CITED IN DALRYMPLE 1998, 173)

Everyone who wrote about India preferred the marvellous to the true.

—STRABO 15.1.28

Hindus differ from us [Muslims] in everything which other nations have in common.

—AL-BIRUNI (SACHAU 1910, 17)

India is the inner state of every man.

—BILL AITKEN 1992, 194

Drawing aside the Curtain

An outsider writing a book about India faces a formidable problem, which is even greater today than it was for Megasthenes. Centuries, indeed millennia, of familiarity, or should one rather say unfamiliarity, with India have erected a series of curtains through which it is difficult to peer clearly. As great a writer as Carlo Levi confessed that he found India 'impossible to describe'.[1] Every age has had its own picture of India, always from the vantage point of an observer who finds what he observes essentially alien. Yet the otherness of India exerts a pull, a fascination, which naturally results in a particularly

1. Levi 2007, 19.

strong distortion of reality to fit what the observer thinks he sees, wishes to see, or believes he ought to see. In order to understand how Greeks such as Megasthenes saw India, it is necessary to peel back these curtains or at least to be aware of the distorting, pixillating effect each separate one has on our field of vision.

I draw back, or at least identify, the curtains one by one, starting with the most recent.[2] I don't know what your mental picture of India is, but there are a few things I was aware of before visiting the country. As I grew up in the sixties India came into my consciousness when the Beatles went there, bringing back an aura of joss-sticks and sitar music that infested our teenage rooms. A never-forgotten experience was a Ravi Shankar concert in Coventry Cathedral (I came away with the great man's signature on a record sleeve), at which, after about a quarter of an hour, a friend leaned over to me and asked, 'Has he finished tuning up yet?' Growing maturity made me conscious of major political figures and events, and a general picture developed of a vast, crowded, untidy country, full of intellectuals and mystics, and bathed in startlingly brilliant colours.

This view of India can be traced as early as the 1930s. The central character of W. Somerset Maugham's *The Razor's Edge* sought enlightenment (and acquired the skills of hypnosis) in India. A modern-day saint and mystic, after visiting the Elephanta caves and seeing the colossal heads of Brahma, Viṣṇu and Śiva, he 'suddenly became aware of an intense conviction that India had something to give me that I had to have'. He enters a period of study with a swami given to such pronouncements as 'By meditation on the formless one I found rest in the Absolute'.[3]

Anita Desai's novel *Return to Ithaca* traces the experience of two lost Westerners trying to find meaning and their 'true selves' in India.[4] Amrit Lal Vegad describes meeting a young French couple on an island in the Narmada: 'what magical thread had drawn the young Frenchman and his wife across the seven seas to this deserted island in the Narmada? The hunger for beauty? Solitary

2. I find myself drawing inspiration from Sam Miller's book *A Strange Kind of Paradise* (2014), on the history of foreign responses to India, which proceeds in the normal chronological order from past to present. William Dalrymple's numerous writings on India also present an admirable model of how to look at India squarely and without blinkers.

3. Maugham 1944, 253.

4. 'to discover her true self', 199; 'she didn't care to have the real India', 271; 'her soul is waiting for her in India', 272.

meditation? Or an intense desire to escape the rat race of the West and immerse themselves in the peace of the East?'[5] Even Indians can fall for the clichés about 'escaping the West', as depicted in Upamanyu Chatterjee's novel *English, August*, where the disquiet of the protagonist caught up in the need for a career still allows him to satirise the Englishman for whom it is all too easy: 'John Avery ... had sensed a country through the books and films of other climes, and had been moved to take a passage, only to be a little bewildered, and perhaps feel a little foolish.'[6] Even *The Best Exotic Marigold Hotel* presents an India which catalyses spiritual change in all the characters.

Other writers become simply impatient with India. Arthur Koestler in 1960 devoted a journey to investigating the most extreme forms of mystical battiness, and judged all Indian thought by that measure. A tone of contempt suffuses his book. 'The genuine mystic is entitled to state experiences and affirm convictions which contradict logic, science and common sense. But he is not entitled to borrow words which have a precise meaning in science and philosophy and roll them around in a game of Wonderland croquet with mobile hoops.'[7] V. S. Naipaul seems to see nothing in India but human shit and tedious bureaucracy.[8] Allen Ginsberg ignores the bureaucracy but substitutes photographs of mutilated limbs which for him apparently represent the essence of India.[9] Undoubtedly more examples could be brought in to illustrate these and related reactions.

My studies of Alexander the Great increased my awareness of India, but only from the point of view of its would-be conqueror. This book is an attempt to see not just what Alexander saw, but also what his more studious companions had more time to see. Onesicritus, Megasthenes, Nearchus and the rest acquired a dubious reputation in antiquity as 'liars', as did their predecessors Herodotus and Ctesias, because no one in the Greek world could believe what they reported. This book aims to recover their observations and to test them against what we can know from an Indian point of view, as well as to identify the patterns in the curtains that prevented them too from seeing India clearly. They may, I hope, emerge as better reporters of what their informants told them than curmudgeons like Strabo took them for.

5. Vegad 2008, 117.
6. Chatterjee 1988, 229.
7. Koestler 1960, 49–50.
8. Naipaul 1964.
9. Ginsberg 1970/1996.

Curtain number two, for a British writer, must be the complex of attitudes associated with British imperial rule in India, which ended in 1947 (four years before I was born). It can be quite startling now to read the comments of some nineteenth-century writers, including major intellectuals like Thomas Macaulay and James Mill, on India as they saw it: the country was not fit for self-government, and so on. Even great thinkers like Hegel and Marx were blind to the qualities of India, defining the country as a place without history, because of its immersion in an immemorial 'oriental' stasis. It is true that historical works in India are hard to find: the distinguished scholar F. E. Pargiter wrote, quoting his predecessor Arthur A. Macdonell, 'Ancient India has bequeathed to us no historical works. "History is the one weak spot in Indian literature. It is, in fact, non-existent".'[10] Hegel went a step further and made a value judgment out of this fact. 'India has no history at all, at least no known history', he wrote; 'what we call its history is but the history of the successive intruders who founded their empires on the passive basis of that unresisting and unchanging society'.[11] Even Louis Dumont, author of the classic *Homo Hierarchicus*, doubts whether there is a history of India, a country and people immutable and indifferent to time.[12] Carlo Levi, more philosophically, saw India as a land of 'time without action': 'What I have seen, with its infinite brilliant and multiform faces, is nothing more than the tiniest fragment of a boundless, limitless reality. Time flows as slowly as the sacred rivers that coil back on themselves in these grasslands'.[13]

Such expressions of bafflement are by no means always as hostile as Hegel's comment sounds. But many of them are. Edward Said has collected plenty of examples of such attitudes, to which he gave the unfortunate descriptor 'Orientalism', in a casual insult to many scholars who are proud to call themselves orientalists.[14] Others found Indian art no better than the work of 'savages'; blinded by the classical ideal of Greek art, Sir George Birdwood wrote in 1910, à propos a Javanese statue of Buddha,

> This senseless similitude, by its immemorial fixed pose, is nothing more than an uninspired brazen image, vacuously squinting down its nose to its

10. Pargiter 1922, 2.

11. See Miller 2014, 260.

12. Dumont 1980, 195.

13. Levi 2007, 75. A more optimistic view of Indian historical writing is developed at length in Thapar 2013b.

14. Said 1978; Irwin 2006.

> thumbs, knees and toes. A boiled suet pudding would serve equally well as a symbol of passionate purity and serenity of soul.[15]

The 'boiled suet pudding' school of criticism had repercussions not only among his own people but among Indians of a nationalist bent. Even a serious art historian like Percy Gardner could write, 'The art of Asoka is a mature art; in some respects more mature than the Greek art of the time, though of course far inferior to it, at least in our eyes.'[16] This sort of thing, and the concomitant enthusiasm for Gandhara because of its patent influence from Greek artistic style, has enraged some Indian scholars, who throw out the baby with the bathwater and reject more than just the idea that any tradition other than Indian was involved in the development of Indian art. I have myself been told by a guide at Khajuraho that the temple as an architectural form was an exclusively Indian invention, going back several thousand years. (In fact the temples at Mamallipuram are generally agreed to be the earliest such structures in India, and they date from the ninth century CE. I would of course agree that they show no influence from the Greek temples of sixteen centuries before that date.) Hindu nationalism increasingly rejects not only Western scholarship on Hinduism,[17] but that on all aspects of Indian history, to which it prefers a strange construct known as 'Non-Jonesian Indology'.[18]

Such an approach denigrates the other main strand of nineteenth-century work on India, namely the extraordinary, dedicated and brilliant labours of those Western scholars (often amateurs) who recovered Indian history and created the disciplines of archaeology and philology in India. Nor should one forget the explorers, the botanists and naturalists, like Joseph Hooker, even if he did react to the flora of Ceylon with the reflection that 'all one longs for is the bracing air, and far more wholesome, though less attractive, beauties of an English country scene'.[19] It is important to remember that these men were working – on the ground, in India – simultaneously with those who, in distant Europe, came out with easy platitudes about suet puddings.

In India, too, of course, there were plenty who saw the brown race that surrounded them as other, beyond the pale socially, intellectually and morally.

15. Quoted in Smith 1962, 3. On Birdwood, see Bryant and Weber 2017, 16–20.

16. Quoted in Smith 1962, 16.

17. Wendy Doniger's *The Hindus* (2009) was banned in India.

18. Pal 2002; this book contains many interesting assertions including that Bagoas is really Chanakya, and that Palibothra is mentioned in the Persepolis tablets.

19. See Arnold 2005, 142.

Their attitudes have been explored in classic works of literature such as Forster's *A Passage to India* and Paul Scott's *The Jewel in the Crown*. A considerably more nuanced view is presented by Rudyard Kipling, who, at the end of a day's work on the *Lahore Gazette*, liked nothing better than to 'step down into the brown crowd' and disappear for an evening to immerse himself in the life that most Westerners never saw. The view that saw everything in India as 'heathen' exasperated him.[20] Kipling's view of India is complex and multi-faceted; a recent book distinguishes two strands in his stories about India, those that show a real sympathy and empathy, and those that pander to the jingoistic tastes of his readership.[21] With his evidently warm feelings for 'the flat, red India of palm-tree, palmyra-palm, and rice', Kipling held the view that an army of Indians, led by British public schoolboys, could easily defeat a southern European army:[22] lucky for Alexander that the British public school had not been invented in his day. Not a few found that the classics not only 'helped them cope' but were actually useful in India: Lord Dufferin remarked that they contained 'all that is worth knowing if you ever have to govern India'.[23] Kipling himself became a thoroughgoing jingo as he got older, but he had left India by that time. The masterpiece of the 'sympathetic' Kipling is *Kim*. I have found it illuminating to juxtapose Kipling and Megasthenes in approaching the latter's work, as will be seen. Kipling once told the Irish writer John Stewart Collis that the British 'did not travel to create empires but, like all islanders, to explore more of the world'.[24] Alexander might have half-understood that view.

The German Romantics

India has a special place in German romantic thought, though I can offer no more than a few pointers here.[25] Romantic poets and philosophers devoured the first Western translations of Indian texts, Anquetil du Perron's *Upaniṣads* and others, making of them what they could to develop a philosophy of their

20. Kipling 1987, 88.

21. Sergeant 2013.

22. Gilmour 2002, 99 and 178.

23. Hagerman 2013, 163–5. Also the important study by Vasunia 2013, esp. ch. 1.

24. Quoted in *Times Literary Supplement* 12 August 2016, 16; cf. Collis 1937, 126: 'wherever these men pitched their tents there was safety ... so for safety's sake more and more natives gathered round them. Finally the tiny circle of their influence spread over the whole country, and the English found themselves in possession of a continent.'

25. See Willson 1964; Sedlar 1982.

own. Their work represented a sharp break from that of late classicism. Goethe (1749–1832) regarded the gods as 'Indian monstrosities',[26] though he did touch on Indian themes a couple of times, notably in 'Der Gott und die Bajadere'. C. M. Wieland gave an Indian setting to his novel *Agathodaimon*, in which the protagonists encounter the great sage Apollonius of Tyana and arrive at an opinion shared by many scholars before and since, that Apollonius' alleged companion Damis had made up most of what he wrote about India. 'So dumpf und idiotisch Damis war, so wäre doch zu wünschen, wir hätten sein Buch noch gerade so von Wort zu Wort wie ers geschrieben'.[27]

The first great enthusiast for India was J. G. Herder (1755–1803), who thought that India represented 'the childhood of the human race'; Friedrich Schlegel thought ancient India was a 'Golden Age'.[28] Herder's enthusiasm for *Śakuntala* (translated by Georg Forster in 1789) was shared by Schiller, who thought it better than the Greek drama. Herder was fascinated by ideas of metempsychosis and wrote three 'Dialogues' on the subject; he also studied the visual arts with enthusiasm. Schlegel's brother August Wilhelm was one of the great scholars of the age, and in the 1820s and 1830s his *Indische Bibliothek* brought texts and information about India to any German reader who might be interested. Later in the century two more scholars made an impact on Indian studies. Friedrich Rückert (1788–1866) was not only a scholar but a poet; though best known as a source of some marvellous settings by Gustav Mahler, his *Weisheit der Brahmanen* is an attempt to convey a philosophy, loosely based on Indian ideas, in German verse. Friedrich Creuzer (1771–1858) may be best remembered as the object of the passion of young Karoline von Günderode (1780–1806), who failed to draw him away from his ageing wife and expressed her sympathy with the Indian practice of sati (widow-burning), and her love for Creuzer, in a moving poem, 'Die malabarischen Witwen', and subsequently by taking her own life in the Rhineland town of Bingen.

The culmination of German interest in India is Arthur Schopenhauer (1788–1860), who was much influenced by the idea of Brāhman as an immanent deity; his theory of the Will has much in common with Brahmanism.[29] All these studies no doubt fed directly into the later Western idea of the mystic East.

26. *West–östlicher Diwan* 195. Cf. Sedlar 1982, 40; Willson 1964, 63.

27. Wieland, *Werke* 5.857. See ch. 16 below for further discussion.

28. Sedlar 1982, 35–6.

29. Sedlar 1982.

Traders

Before the imperial rulers came the great commercial exploiters, who could see nothing in India but goods to make them wealthy. The East India Company laid the foundations of the British Raj; before them, the Portuguese led by Vasco da Gama in 1497 conducted a voyage of discovery described by João de Barros as a mission to 'conquistar e conservar', but which also had the purpose of cutting out the Arabs from the India trade, and of converting the natives to Christianity, a religion to which they were understood to be already close. On arrival in Calicut the men took a Vasihnava temple, which is accurately described, for a Christian church.[30] Luís de Camões's epic poem *Os Lusíadas*, about Gama's voyage, begins and ends with Alexander:

> You in such manner through the world shall spread,
> That Alexander shall in you repose,
> Without envying the Maeonian lyre.[31]

The Portuguese king Dom Manuel liked to be told that in this 'conquest' of India he had excelled Alexander.[32]

India as a source of wealth was a constant cynosure in the early modern period, as it had been in the Roman empire, when Pliny complained that the spice trade served no purpose except to encourage luxurious tastes in formerly hardy Romans. Putting pepper on your food was a direct index of moral decline. Horace Walpole took a similar line to Pliny, describing England as 'a sink of Indian wealth'.[33] Most of the traders did not write much about it, so their contribution to intellectual formations is limited; but they contribute to the sense of otherness, of India as a source of amazing wealth. Now, one of the first words that springs to mind in regard to India's population is the opposite, 'poverty'.[34]

If traders did not write about India, there were others who did; a great range of early modern writers is collected in the survey by Pompa Banerjee, from 1500–1723.[35] Many of them were diplomats dealing not only with the

30. Subrahmanyam 1998, 131–3, cf. 162–3, 194

31. Camões, *Os Lusíadas* 10.156, tr. Richard Fanshawe. References to Alexander thus both open the poem (at 1.3) and close it. See also 7.54.

32. Subrahmanyam 1998, 188 and 194.

33. William Dalrymple, *The Guardian* 4 March 2015, 27.

34. Miller 2014, 35.

35. Banerjee 2003, with a list at 251–4.

Abbasid court in Persia but with the Mughals in India. They include such famous names as Pietro della Valle, Thomas Coryat,[36] Peter Mundy, Thomas Herbert and many others, most of them interested especially in religious matters.

Muslim Visitors

Whoever comes from Iran to India imagines
That in India gold is scattered like stars in the evening sky.

—ASHRAF MAZANDARANI, SEVENTEENTH CENTURY[37]

Several centuries of Muslim rule have also drawn a veil between us and the perception of the India that the ancients knew. An earlier conqueror of most of India, the first Mughal emperor Babur (1483–1530), crossed the Indus into Hindustan in December 1525. He did not like India much, though he learnt, and wrote down, quite a lot about it, especially its climate and natural history. His description of Hindustan runs to some twenty-five pages. 'It is a strange country', he writes. 'Compared to ours, it is another world. Its mountains, rivers, forests and wildernesses, its villages and provinces, animals and plants, peoples and languages, even its rain and winds are altogether different.'[38] His descriptions of animals, birds and plants are detailed and accurate: he has observed the rhinoceros, elephant and monkey (in Begram he and his companions 'watched a rhinoceros with delight');[39] the peacock, parrot and partridge; the mango (not so good as the melons of Samarkand), myrobalan and citron (the sweet kind is 'sickeningly sweet and unsuitable for eating, though the peel is good for marmalade', while the Bajaur kind is 'nicely sour').[40] He is informed about divisions of time, weights and measures. But 'I always thought one of the chief faults of Hindustan was that there was no running water.'[41] Any Persian worth his salt wants a garden around him, a *chahar-bagh* with geometric rills and pools. Babur found it hard to discover a site for one.[42]

36. See Moraes and Srivatsa 2003.
37. Quoted in Dale 2004.
38. Thackston 2002, 332.
39. Ibid., 312.
40. Ibid., 348.
41. Ibid., 363.
42. Dalrymple 1993 remarks on the contrast of Persian formal gardens and the Indian 'neglect' of nature.

'There was no really suitable place near Agra, but there was nothing to do but work with the space we had.' And so, 'in unpleasant and inharmonious India, marvellously regular and geometric gardens were introduced'.[43] In the end,

> I deeply desired the riches of this Indian land;
> What is the profit since this land oppresses me?[44]

E. M. Forster sketches the essence of his response:

> His description of Hindustan is unfavourable, and has often been quoted with gusto by Anglo-Indians. 'The people', he complains, 'are not handsome, have no idea of the charms of friendly society, of frankly mixing together, or of familiar intercourse ... no good fruits, no ice or cold water, no good food or bread in their bazaars, no baths or colleges, no candles, no torches, not a candlestick' ... Nothing in his life was Indian, except, possibly, the leaving of it.[45]

Beside his son Humayun's bed of sickness, Babur watched and prayed until he 'bore away' the sickness from his son, and passed away in his stead. For Forster, Babur is a lesser conqueror than Alexander, who is 'mystic and grandiose', despite Babur's love of detail which far exceeds anything we find in the descriptions written by Alexander's entourage.

The great Arab traveller Ibn Battutah (1304–68) spent thirty years in motion, from 1325 to 1354, and arrived in India in September 1333. A network of Arabic-speaking contacts enabled him to travel in comfort and security, and his descriptions are matter-of-fact and vivid. The king of Delhi is 'never without some poor man enriched or some living man executed'.[46] Much of his account is about life, but he does go wandering alone and is taken prisoner by 'the blacks', an ordeal which ends only when he encounters another Muslim who is able to release him. He feels safe only in Muslim company. He does, however, have interesting reports on the wildlife, notably the rhinoceros, and on the custom of widow-burning.[47]

About the same time, Hamd Allah Mustawfi of Qazvin (b. 1281, fl. 1330–40), composed his *Nuzhat al-Qulub,* an extensive account of the known

43. Thackston 2002, 363–4.
44. Written on 28 December 1528; quoted in Dale 2004.
45. Forster 1940, 291.
46. Ibn Battuta 1929, 197.
47. Mackintosh-Smith 2002, 151 and 158–9.

world. It contains a long and interesting description of Persia, but a much briefer account of India. He makes use of Indian scholarship since he writes, 'The Indian Sages divide the habitable world into squares, these laid out three by three'.[48] Thus:

Bāyab Greeks & Franks	Ūtar Turks	Aysan Cathay/Khotan
Basjim Egypt, Berbers	Madwaysh Iran	Būrb China
Nayrit Copts, Berbers	Dakshin Arabia	Agnī Hindus

The diagram seems to betray some Persian influence since it places Iran at the centre, but is tolerably accurate geographically. Mustawfi's account of Hind occupies a mere two pages,[49] giving little more than the remark that it is hot and a list of major localities from the Delhi Sultanate to Ceylon and Coromandel.

Around the same time, Amir Khusraw of Delhi – 'the parrot of India' – in his *Nuh Sipihr* ('Nine Spheres') of 1318, poured out his enthusiasm for India. He regarded the country as much superior to Babur's beloved Khorasan, and gives seven arguments for its superiority over all other lands: it is a natural paradise since its climate is benign and it blossoms with flowers and fruits all year round; the Indians excel even the Greeks in science and philosophy, though in divinity they are inferior to the Muslims; they can speak all languages of the world; people come from all over the world to study in India, while no Indian ever feels the need to go abroad for study; *Kalila and Dimna* was composed in India; chess was invented in India; its music is better than anyone else's, and it has the best poets, including one Amir Khusraw![50]

Only a few years before this, another Arab writer known as al-Qazvini (d. 1283), purveyed a very different view of India. Writing in an entirely fabulous tradition, for him India is a 'land of wonders'.[51] He shares the tradition about the wonders of India that medieval Europe, likewise, inherited from Pliny's

48. Le Strange (ed.) 1919, 921–2.

49. Ibid., 255–6.

50. Mirza 1935, 182–4.

51. Berlekamp 2011, 170–4.

account of the monstrous races and from his late antique successors, Solinus, the *Physiologus*, and the Latin *Letter of Alexander to Aristotle about India*.[52] This is the focus of his interest and there is no attempt to write a description of India as it actually existed in his time. This is perhaps the more surprising since he makes use of what is definitely a travel account, the book of Buzurg ibn Shahriyar (see below), and shows no awareness of the scholarly work of al-Biruni (though, to be fair, that is not the kind of book he was trying to write).

Al-Biruni (973–1048) justly has the reputation of being the greatest writer on India of all time.[53] His book, *al-Hind*, in which he describes the country in which he spent many years as the companion of an earlier conqueror, Sultan Mahmud of Ghazni (d. 1030), emphasises the importance of eye-witnesses in describing the features of India. His introduction is philosophical; he is a great scholar who quotes Greek philosophers and other writers constantly, as well as Arabic authorities; he regards Indian science as on a similar level to that of ancient Greece; and he learned and liked the language;[54] yet even he has little good to say about the people to whom his book of more than six hundred pages is devoted.

> We can only say, folly is an illness for which there is no medicine, and the Hindus believe that there is no country but theirs, no nation like theirs, no kings like theirs, no religion like theirs, no science like theirs. [With Indians holding such views, who needs westerners to descant on 'otherness'?] They are haughty, foolishly vain, self-conceited, and stolid. They are by nature niggardly in communicating that which they know, and they take the greatest possible care to withhold it from men of another caste among their own people, still much more, of course, from any foreigner.

Still, his view is that, even if one does not like the Indians, one should still understand them, and make more of an effort than, according to him, previous Arab writers have done.[55] He is anything but colonialist.[56]

Captain Buzurg ibn Shahriyar's *The Wonders of India* (tenth century), one of the most delightful books from the oriental Middle Ages, takes us back into

52. On the latter, Stoneman 2011. In general, Wittkower 1942; Friedman 1981; Baltrušaitis 1981.

53. We still depend on the complete translation by Edward Sachau 1910. On al-Biruni's achievement, see Miquel 1967, 223–7.

54. Starr 2013, 35–79.

55. Ibid., 361–2.

56. Miller 2014, 86.

a world of fabulous tales and amazing phenomena. It consists of 'what was told me at Basra by Abou Mohammed el-Hosein ... who was at Mansoura in the year 288', so the author makes no claim to have witnessed the things he recounts. Not all of them belong strictly to India. Many of them clearly derive from Greek sources including the Alexander legends, such as the account of the gold-digging ants in the country of the Zindj, the island of women where the sun rises and sets, the Valley of Diamonds (situated in Kashmir), and various anecdotes about Indian ascetics, some of which sound plausible, some less so. Indian ascetics are said to pluck their hair, to go about naked and covered in ashes, and to drink from human skulls– which is perfectly true – while two others are said to have immersed themselves in pits of smouldering dung and continued to play draughts until they burned to death – which sounds scarcely possible.[57] He reports on diviners in India, and enchanters who can cast spells on crocodiles to make them harmless, as well as on a tree on every leaf of which the name of God is written. He reports that '[t]heft, among the Indians, is a very serious offence', for which the penalty is death,[58] which at least chimes with earlier reports on the justice of the Indians (see chapter 8 below). His book concludes with the famous story of the merchant of Basra and his escape from an island by hanging onto the feet of a giant bird, which is also incorporated in *The Thousand and One Nights*. Buzurg's book is a collection of travellers' tales which hardly expects to be taken quite seriously. Not all of its stories are set in India, but India certainly functions as a location for the amazing.

The Western Middle Ages

Writers like Ibn Battutah and al-Biruni probably did not penetrate the consciousness of the West before the nineteenth century. From the tenth century onwards in the West the prevalent view of India was formed by the various Alexander-texts, and these lay at the root of the observations of both the fictional traveller, Sir John Mandeville (ca. 1356), and that very real traveller, Marco Polo (1254–1324). The latter's journey back from his long sojourn in Cathay brought him to the East Indies, to Ceylon and to parts of India, where he reports on the nudity of the inhabitants – so that it is impossible to find a tailor there – on the Diamond Valley of Mutfili, on the Brahmans, of whom

57. Buzurg ibn Shahriyar 1928, 132–3 and 125.
58. Ibid., 137–8.

his account contains a good deal that is accurate, and on several other Indian kingdoms.[59] Polo's is one of the great books of the world, and his account of India is never less than intriguing; but it cannot be said to be a sober description of reality. (I leave aside the revisionist argument that Polo never went to any of the places he describes.)[60] Forster's strictures went further: 'It is not a first-rate book, for the reason that its author is interested in novelties, to the exclusion of human beings. Herodotus was interested in both, and he is a great traveller in consequence. Marco Polo is only a little traveller . . . He could not differentiate between men and make them come alive, and the East that he evoked is only a land of strange customs. . . . The East will not reveal itself wholly through a mind of this type, and we have to wait two hundred years more before we can see it in its full splendour, in the autobiography of the Emperor Babur.'[61]

Sir John Mandeville's *Travels* (1356) has been an immensely popular book, but no one has ever taken it for literal truth. His stories of India are taken from the Alexander legends, and Alexander's encounter with the 'Brahmans'; he reprises the story of the gold-digging ants which began its long journey in Herodotus; and he mentions the four rivers that flow out of Paradise (though of that land 'I cannot speak properly, for I have not been there' – unlike Alexander, according to one medieval account).[62]

'You should know that India is divided into three parts, that is to say, India the Greater, which is a mountainous and hot land; India the Lesser, to the south, a temperate land; and the third part, to the north, so cold that, because of the great cold and continual frost, water congeals into crystal. On the rocks of crystal good diamonds grow . . . they are so hard that no metal can polish or split them.'[63] (The confusion about India's relation to the equator goes back to the report of Megasthenes that in southern India the shadows fell to the south.)[64] Mandeville goes on to describe the river Indus: 'eels of thirty feet [9 m] long are found in that river. The people who dwell near the river are an ugly colour, yellow and green.' He revisits the old Arab tale that ships in this region are made with wooden pegs, not nails, because the magnetic rocks

59. Polo, ed. Yule and Cordier 1903, 331–406.

60. Wood 1995.

61. Forster 1940, 286–7.

62. 'Alexander the Great's Journey to Paradise', in Stoneman 2011.

63. Mandeville 1983, 118.

64. Str. 2.1.19 = Daimachos *FGrH* 716 F 3.

would pull out all the nails.[65] He then describes the island of Thana, whose king 'was once so great and powerful that he fought against Alexander the Great'. The identity of this island is obscure (modern Thana is a town near Mumbai), but the varied religions of the island lead the author on to a disquisition on 'idols – images made in the likeness of whatever a man wishes', such as animals with three heads, of a man, a horse and an ox, which is perhaps a distorted recollection of statues of the four-headed Brahma, or of gods with many arms. Further on is the land of pepper trees, and then the Fountain of Youth near the city of Polumbum, whose water runs direct from the Earthly Paradise. (Though the Fountain of Youth is a popular theme in medieval art,[66] it seems here to have become mingled with the Water of Life of the Alexander legends.) The reverence for the ox is reported in a somewhat confused form, and the account concludes with a description of sati, of St Thomas's mission in India and of the rites of Jagannath. Some of the same themes reappear in Gervase of Tilbury's *Otia imperialia*,[67] in which India is merely a Land of Wonders.

If we compare Mandeville's account with the portrayal of India on the Hereford *Mappa Mundi*, we find several of the same features. The shape of India is entirely lost in this representation, perhaps in order to fit it into the circular frame of the map as a whole: Taprobane (Sri Lanka) is located to the west of India on the map though the accompanying text explicitly states that it lies to the east of India (and has two summers and two winters per year, and many elephants and dragons). India is defined by the series of rivers known from the Alexander historians: Indus, Hydaspes, Acesines, Pasma(?) and Hypanis, directly beyond which is a depiction of Adam and Eve being expelled from Eden into a land of Giants. 'This side' (west) of the Pasma are a drawing of the altars of Alexander, a citation of Solinus' description of the parrot and a fine depiction of an elephant with a turret on its back. Pygmies and wyverns appear, as well as the Averion bird. Midway down the course of the Indus is the Corcina people, 'who live on a mountain whose shadow falls to the north in winter and to the south in summer'[68] (i.e., it is on the equator). Still nearer its mouth is the city of 'Pobbrota' (i.e., Palibothra) 'a powerful people, whose king

65. Mandeville 1983, 120; Hourani 1995; Lakhnavi and Bilgrami 2007, 220–4.
66. Stoneman 2008, 153 and plate 28.
67. Mandeville 1983, 122–5; Gervase *Otia imp*. 2.185–91.
68. Cf. Plin. *NH* 2.184 on Mount Maleus.

can muster an army of 600,000 infantry, 30,000 cavalry and 8,000 elephants'. To the left (north) the Ganges runs eastwards and to its north is a fine Sciapod and a citation from Solinus about the people who live on smells alone. The sources for this section, clearly, are a combination of Solinus and the Alexander legends.

Some years before Mandeville, about the time that the *Mappa Mundi* was being drawn, the Italian poet Fazio degli Uberti (1305 or 1309 to after 1367) composed *Il Dittamondo*, an attempt to do for the known world what Dante had done for the world beyond. Fazio, inspired by an allegorical vision of Virtue, sets off in the company of the Roman 'geographer' Solinus (playing the role of Dante's Virgil) to visit the whole of the known world. Taking Solinus as a guide was not a good start, for that author, writing probably soon after 200 CE, had selected many of the least likely bits of Pliny and compiled them into an account of the world that concentrated on the fabulous. India is one of the first places Fazio visits:

> India è grande, ricca e 'l più in pace;
> Dal mezzodí e suso in oriente
> Sopra il mare Oceano tutta giace.
> Indus la chiude e serra di ponente
> Monte Caucaso di ver settentrione:
> Queste son le confine dirittamente.
> Ed ivi d'animali e di persone
> Tante son novità, che spesso piange
> Quale va solo per quella regione.
> Idaspen, Sigoton, Ipano e Gange
> Bagnan la terra e con grossa radice
> Maleo vi par, che 'n su molto alto tange.
> Sotto scilocco, da quella pendice,
> La isola si trova Taprobana,
> Che quasi un altro mondo la si dice.[69]

Fazio revisits India in his account of Alexander, a passage which seems to place the Jews in India.[70] He briefly mentions the oracular trees and emphasises

69. *Il Dittamondo* 1.8.46–59.

70. Ibid. 4.2.85–99.

that a New World lies beyond. He alludes to Alexander's death by poisoning, with the comment 'Oh, mundo cieco, quanto se' fallace!'.[71]

For each of these witnesses, India is a place whose importance is defined by its appearance in the career of Alexander, and described by exotica from Solinus. Alexander's voyage of discovery not only opened up a new world of knowledge to the Greeks, but also imposed a veil of cliché on the vision of medieval writers. A few stereotypes come to define what the Greeks had tried to explore. We may think we do better now, but we must beware of our own sets of clichés.

Chinese Pilgrims

Before all these visitors from the west came those from the east, pilgrims and historians from China. Both Faxian (ca. 400 CE) and Xuanzang (602–64 CE) were interested in discovering the roots of Buddhism and collecting valuable Sanskrit Buddhist texts to bring back to their own nation. Xuanzang achieved fame as the hero, under the name Tripitaka, of the great Chinese novel variously known as *Monkey* and *Journey to the West*.[72] He spent fourteen years (630–44) on pilgrimage to India and back, travelling from Pataliputra as far as Gandhara, Pushkalavati and Takshasila,[73] and composed a detailed and dispassionate description of India and its people's beliefs and customs, which at many points is a valuable enhancement and corroboration of Megasthenes; for example, 'they swear on oath and keep their promise'.[74] An earlier Chinese visitor, Faxian in 400 CE, is also factual, and contains much hard detail in his description of Pataliputra; but he is sometimes prone to gullibility, as when he informs his readers that the royal palace of Pataliputra was built by King Aśoka with the assistance of demons, who piled up the stones for him.[75] The great historian Sima-Qian (Ssu-ma Ch'ien, fl. 108–90 BCE) is an important source for contemporary events in Bactria but does not touch on the subcontinent as such.

71. Ibid. 4.2.105.

72. Beal 1884; Devahuti 2001. For a historical account of Xuanzang, see Waley 1952, and more recently the lively Wriggins 2004.

73. See ch. 6 below for more detail.

74. Devahuti 2001, 132; Miller 2014, 66.

75. Beal 1884, lv. See further discussion in ch. 6 below.

The Classical Accounts of India

Our reverse chronological journey now brings us to the Romans and Greeks. Leaving aside for the moment the account of the *Life of the Brahmans* (*De gentibus Indiae et de Bragmanibus*; hereafter *De Bragmanibus*) by the fifth-century author Palladius of Helenopolis, and the interest of the third-century philosopher Plotinus in Indian philosophy, to both of which we shall return, as well as the staccato fourth-century description of Marcianus of Heraclea, which is a bald listing of points that might have been read off the relevant page of an atlas (in fact he epitomises the once important but now completely lost Artemidorus, ca. 150 BCE), the first notable writer to give an extended discourse about India is the second-century Philostratus, in his life of the sage and wonder-worker Apollonius of Tyana, who lived in the reign of Nero and into that of Domitian. Much of Philostratus' book is devoted to a narrative of Apollonius' travels in India and his encounter with fictional kings and philosophers. It makes use of earlier travel accounts but is determinedly fabulous in its approach, picking up some local colour and circumstantial details from the *Alexander Romance* and Alexander historians and focusing largely on philosophical conversations held by Apollonius in India. Philostratus' view of India is comparable in many respects to the mid-twentieth-century image of an exotic land, full of strange animals and a population devoted entirely to philosophical contemplation. It is much debated whether his book can be used as evidence for anything regarding India.[76] (See chapter 16 below.)

Slightly earlier than Philostratus is Arrian (ca. 86–160 CE), whose history of Alexander is the major source for his career and for ancient knowledge of India. As much of what he writes is based on sources contemporary with Alexander, and his description of India relies on no author later than Megasthenes (ca. 350–290 BCE),[77] it makes sense to consider him below among the representatives of the Greek view prevailing in Alexander's time.

Philostratus was preceded by the encyclopaedist Pliny the Elder (23/4–79 CE), whose Indian chapters preserve much from earlier writers, and who was in turn excerpted by the later Roman writer Solinus. Solinus wrote, probably about 200 CE, a *Collectanea rerum memorabilium*, a collection of geographical facts about parts of the known world, almost all lifted from Pliny and Pomponius Mela, whose book delineated the order of the lands and seas in the time

76. Smith 1914; Charpentier 1934; Bäbler and Nesselrath 2016.

77. Dihle 1964; Schwarz 1975.

of the emperor Claudius. Pliny is an important witness though sometimes uncritical, and his method means that different treatments of a topic occur at different places in his book, under different headings, and often with different and incompatible information. At book 6, 64–79 he provides a long litany of the peoples of India, apparently based on the Alexander historians and Megasthenes. He also cites Artemidorus (ca. 150–100 BCE), whose eleven books of *Geographoumena* are lost. The latter's itinerary seems to have been rather strange: he travelled down the Ganges, around the coast, and then successively down and up the Indus to the borders of the subcontinent at Kabul.[78] Pliny's is not a book about India, but an encyclopaedia, informed by a doctrinaire position on the decline of Roman morals as a result of luxury, exemplified in the trade with India.[79] However, his Indian place names can almost all be identified with Sanskrit originals,[80] and most are also in the classical sources, including Ptolemy; some that are now unidentifiable may derive from a source we cannot define – for example on the leaf-wearers, whose existence need not be doubted.[81]

Important but of less moment for the formation of a comprehensive view of India are the guides for traders: the *Parthian Stations* of Isidore of Charax (first century CE),[82] the anonymous *Periplus of the Erythraean* [*Red*] *Sea* (also first century CE)[83] and its predecessor Agatharchides' *On the Erythraean Sea* (second century BCE);[84] also the *Description of the World* by the poet Dionysius Periegetes (first century CE),[85] which gives a brief but colourful account of India. Eudoxus' account (120–110 BCE) is all but lost. Eudoxus of Cyzicus was sent by Ptolemy VIII Euergetes II of Egypt with a stranded Indian guide to find the sea-route to India; 'he returned with a cargo of perfumes and precious stones ... but Eudoxus was wholly deceived in his expectations, for Euergetes took from him his entire cargo.'[86] In the first

78. For Artemidorus, see *GGM* 1.556.31, and esp. 574ff.; Strabo 14.1.26; Settis 2008, 54–63.

79. Plin. *NH* 12. 83–4, 6.101; Beagon 1992, 191. Such complaints were echoed by nineteenth-century critics of the British activities in India, such as Edmund Burke in 1848: 'what, then, shall become of us, if Bengal, if the Ganges, pour in a new tide of corruption?' See Hagerman 2013, 114–16.

80. André and Filliozat 1980, 87–111.

81. Forsyth 1871, 15.

82. Schoff 1914.

83. Casson (ed. and tr.) 1989: *Periplus Maris Erythraei* [hereafter *Periplus*].

84. Burstein (ed.)1989. (Citations of Agatharchides below refer to this edition.)

85. Lightfoot 2014.

86. Str. 2.3.4.

century BCE Apollodorus of Artemita wrote a *Parthica* which contained a good deal about India and was used as a source by Pompeius Trogus,[87] as well as Strabo. None of these Roman-period writers, except Pliny, is substantial enough to pose any kind of veil to be drawn aside.

The Greek View of India

Predecessors of Alexander

Our journey back in time brings us now to the writers who will be the subject of this study: the Greek writers around Alexander and of the generation or two that followed. Sadly, these are mostly in a very fragmentary state, and what we have of them consists only of quotations or paraphrases made by later classical writers, notably the geographer Strabo, the historian Diodorus (both writing in the late first century BCE) and the encyclopaedist Pliny (about a hundred years later). These authors, important though they are, can be considered only in the context of the authors whose 'fragments' they transmit, since none of them was setting out to write a book about India as such.[88] Strabo had an uncharitable view of all of them, often unfairly, as we shall see.[89] Felix Jacoby's collection of the 'Fragments of the Greek Historians' (*FGrH*) assembles the fragments of sixteen writers on India (plus some further fragments which he regarded as dubiously attributable and relegated to an *Anhang*), to which should be added the relevant Alexander historians, Aristobulus, Onesicritus and Nearchus, and the *Alexander Romance*. Chief among them is Megasthenes, a younger contemporary of Alexander who spent time in the Maurya capital of Pataliputra. Megsathenes will be the lynchpin of this book, for he was the authority for all the later classical accounts of India.[90]

Here at last, do we have writers with an unmediated view of India? No, because even they were conditioned by the accounts of Scylax and Herodotus in the fifth century BCE and of Ctesias in the fourth, and furthermore Strabo, on whom we rely for our knowledge of much of their work, complained that

87. *FGrH* 779; Tarn 1951, 45ff.; Dihle 1960.

88. On Strabo: Roller 2014 (translation) and his forthcoming commentary. On Diodorus: Sacks 1990; Sulimani 2011; Muntz 2012 is valuable in disentangling what is what in his extensive use of Megasthenes. On Pliny: Beagon 1992 is a valuable overview of the author's aims and assumptions in his *Natural History*.

89. Str. 2.1.9, 15.1.28.

90. Dihle 1960.

all those who wrote about India preferred the marvellous to the true.[91] So here now, we must reverse our chronological telescope: instead of examining the veils and false perspectives that inhibit our own view of India, we must start to consider the clichés and stereotypes that were in place when the first Greek travellers to India began to compose their accounts.

Scylax of Caryanda

Neither Herodotus nor Ctesias had been, or claimed to have been, to India. Herodotus certainly, and Ctesias probably, knew that their chief predecessor in writing about India was the Carian author Scylax of Caryanda.[92] Caryanda is close to Myndus on the north shore of the Bodrum peninsula,[93] a bare nineteen miles (31 km) from Herodotus' home in Halicarnassus, but Herodotus does not seem to have known the text of Scylax's work but only that he had made a voyage, on the orders of the Persian king Darius I, in about 515 BCE, to Asia.

> As to Asia, most of it was discovered by Darius. There is a river Indos, which of all rivers comes second in producing crocodiles. Darius, desiring to know where this Indos issues into the sea, sent ships manned by Scylax, a man of Caryanda, and others in whose word he trusted; these set out from the city Caspatyrus and the Pactyic country, and sailed down the river towards the east and the sunrise till they came to the sea; and voyaging over the sea westwards, they came in the thirtieth month to that place whence the Egyptian king sent the Phoenicians aforementioned to sail round Libya. After this circumnavigation Darius subdued the Indians and made use of this sea. Thus was discovered that Asia, saving the parts towards the rising sun, was in other respects like Libya.[94]

91. Str. 15.1.28 and cf. 2.1.9. In fact Strabo proves the limitation of his own understanding of India, which he regards as small and homogeneous, not observing that differing reports may come from regions far removed from one another. Still, his aim is a noble one. Abolfazi Beyhaqi (995–1077) also remarks that 'most people are so constituted that they prefer the absurd and the impossible', and finds his mission in ferreting out the truth. See Starr 2013, 349.

92. *FGrH* 709. Essential reading are the three studies by Panchenko, 1998; 2002; 2003.

93. Cf. Str. 14.2.20. The site, and Scylax's voyage, are vividly evoked in Kamila Shamsie's novel *A God in Every Stone* (Shamsie 2014); but if Panchenko is right, Scylax never went to Peshawar, where most of the action is located. See below. Scylax is probably the same man as Scylax of Myndus, a ship's captain who was a friend of Aristagoras and was mistreated by the Persian Megabates: Hdt. 5.33.

94. Hdt. 4.44. Hdt. 3.98–116 are presumably derived from Hecataeus' summary of Scylax.

Some later writers seem to have been familiar with Scylax's book. Philostratus and Tzetzes[95] mentioned that he described Troglodytes, pygmies, men with enormous ears and sciapods, one-eyed people and those who used their ears as blankets when asleep. The same wondrous peoples appear in the ancient Persian text the *Videvdad*, presumably from the same source that Scylax used.[96] Athenaeus indicates an interest in rivers and plants, including the artichoke (*kynara*),[97] while Aristotle tells us that, according to his book, there was 'a great difference between the kings and those they ruled'.[98]

It is generally assumed that Scylax's voyage was down the Indus and around Arabia to a Red Sea port,[99] in which case his starting point of Caspatyrus should be Peshawar in Gandhara. But there is an obvious problem, which is that Herodotus clearly states that he followed the river in an easterly direction and then sailed westwards around India. (However, even Cleitarchus thought that the Ganges flowed north to south.)[100] Dimitri Panchenko has argued persuasively that *ho Indos potamos* in Herodotus need mean no more than 'the Indian river', and that the Ganges is meant. No sentence quoted from Scylax actually names the Indus: Hecataeus is the first to use the name.[101] There are of course crocodiles in both rivers – the gharial in the Ganges, the mugger crocodile in the Indus. Besides the eastward direction of the Ganges, a strong point in favour of Panchenko's view is the fact that Megasthenes stated that none of the tributaries of the Ganges is inferior to the Maeander, 'where the Maeander is navigable'.[102] We do not know where Megasthenes came from, but as Scylax grew up close to the Maeander it is highly likely that this comparison originated with Scylax, as it would be of little relevance for an author writing for the Macedonian King Seleucus in Babylon.[103] The report in One-

95. *FGrH* 709 F 7.

96. *Videvdad* 2.5: see Stoneman 2015, 53.

97. Scylax Ff 3 and 4 = Athen. 2.82 (70a–d).

98. Arist. *Pol.* 1332b12 = F 5. Parker 2008, 20 for the artichoke.

99. E.g., Jona Lendering, 'Scylax of Caryanda', www.livius.org.

100. Kienast 1965, 185.

101. Milns 1989, 356. Hecataeus' words (*FGrH* 1 F 299) are 'among them people live on the Indus [Indian] river, the Opiai; there is a royal garrison; as far as that (are) the Opiai, from there on is sandy desert as far as the Indoi'. Herzfeld 1968, 282, argues the sandy desert is the Thar desert, which lies east of the Indus, and that the Opiai must therefore be in Sind (cf. Plin. *NH* 6.21; McCrindle 1927, 112): therefore Scylax is reporting on the Indus, not the Ganges. But the fact that he reports this information does not prove that this is the route he followed.

102. *FGrH* 715 F 9.

103. Panchenko 1998, 222–3. Panchenko's additional argument, that the reference in Aelian *NA* 12.41 to islands as big as Lesbos in the Ganges (ὁ παρὰ τοῖς Ἰνδοῖς ῥέων) should be set

sicritus that Taprobane (Sri Lanka) is twenty days' sail from the mainland may come from Scylax,[104] since it is true only if the mainland starting point is the mouth of the Ganges.[105] A further point is that, if Scylax had sailed to the mouth of the Indus, and Alexander knew of his voyage, the latter could not possibly have arrived in India thinking, as he did, that the Indus was connected to the Nile.[106]

But if Scylax sailed down the Ganges, not the Indus, where is Caspatyrus? The identification with Peshawar was always uncertain and it is unusual to find no resemblance between an Indian and a Greek name: the Indian name for Peshawar was Purushapura.[107] An alternative spelling is Caspapyrus (in Hecataeus), which would seem to incorporate the Sanskrit ending *-pura*, meaning 'city', though other Indian names in *-pura* retain their feminine gender in Greek. Herodotus locates the city in Pactyice, Hecataeus in Gandarike. Pactyice is probably connected with the modern name Pathan, while Gandarike, though it sounds like Gandhara (where the Indus rises) is commonly attached to a people living in the eastern Punjab or on the Middle Ganges, where they sometimes bear the name Gangaridae.[108] (Their king was Xandrames or Aggrammes and they lived 'on the far bank of the Ganges'.) Panchenko canvassed the possibility that Caspapyrus is Pataliputra (which is on the south bank of the Ganges), but later discounted it, proposing instead, tentatively, the city of Hastinapura, capital of the Kurus or Kauravas and location of the action

alongside a similar statement in Hdt. 1.202 about the Araxes, and that 'Araxes' for Herodotus was simply a Persian word for 'river' and here refers to the Ganges, is imponderable. However, Herodotus does say that the people who live near this Araxes (which he locates in Scythia) 'have discovered a kind of plant whose fruit they use when they meet in groups. They light a bonfire, sit around it, and sniff the smoke rising from the burning fruit they have thrown on to the fire. The fruit is the equivalent there to wine in Greece; they get intoxicated from the smoke'. This sounds rather like the use of soma in Brahmanic rituals of Vedic times, and may explain the accounts in Greek writers of peoples in India who have no mouths and live on smells, for Brahmans too are supposed to do no more than inhale the smoke from sacrifices. See ch. 10 below.

104. *FGrH* 134 F 12.

105. As stated by Pliny, *NH* 6.82. The argument is that of Panchenko 1998, 225.

106. Bosworth's attempt (1993, 416–17) to explain away this problem – the Indus had more than one mouth – does not persuade me. But his emphasis on the importance of geographical theory for Alexander is valuable.

107. Beal 1884, 1.97: Xuanzang calls it 'Fo-lu-sha' (ibid., xxxii). Singh 2009, 389 accepts that Purushapura could be Caspapyrus, as does Naqvi 2011, 120.

108. Str. 15.1.30; Curt. 9.2.3; *Tabula Peutingeriana* 'Gandari Indi'; Panchenko 1998, 233–4. Also Sircar 1947/1971 on Gandaridae on the river Beas.

of the *Mahābhārata*.[109] The identification is not compelling – Hastinapura (Elephant City), or Hasanpur, is not on the Ganges but sixty miles (100 km) north-west of Delhi, close to Meerut – but nor is it crucial to the argument. However, other identifications have been canvassed. Toynbee proposed Multan,[110] and there is a resemblance of names with Kuśapura on the river Gumati, a western tributary of the Indus. I would like to propose yet another identification: Keśavapura, a district of Mathura on the Jumna/Yamuna.[111] The latter was Cunningham's candidate for Cleisobora, though Lassen made Cleisobora 'Krishnapura' and identified it with Agra. Mathura was a major crossroads as early as the sixth century BCE.[112] The resemblance of names is close, and if Cleisobora really represents Krishnapura the alternative name makes sense, since Mathura in later times (and still today) became celebrated as the birthplace of Kṛṣṇa. Keśava is a name of Viṣṇu, of whom Kṛṣṇa is one of the avatars, and it is likely that the name Keśava pre-existed the individuation of the Hindu gods as we know them.

If it was the Ganges that Scylax sailed down, the consequences are momentous. At the end of the sixth century BCE, a Greek in Persian service had already travelled to the east coast of India and circumnavigated the subcontinent. A further implication may be that Persian control in the reign of Darius extended right along the Ganges; this is hard to believe, and certainly did not last long, but the Achaemenid influence on the architecture of Pataliputra is unmistakable. No other Greek went so far, not even Alexander; and Herodotus and Ctesias had far hazier views of the country than this intrepid explorer achieved.

Herodotus of Halicarnassus and Ctesias of Cnidus

Herodotus mainly provides a list of tribes, sprinkled with delightful details.[113] He is impressed by the large numbers of the Indians, and is the first author to tell the unforgettable account of the giant ants that dig up the gold dust guarded by griffins, which reappears in every subsequent writer and has exercised the ingenuity of scholars to fathom what is really being described. He

109. Panchenko 2003, 293. In the *Mbh.* [= *Mahābhārata*] 12.39.1ff., Hastinapura is depicted as a city of great bejewelled mansions, overflowing with women.

110. Toynbee 1961, 171.

111. Law 1954, 107. It is also known as Keśavadeva: Thapar 1989, 15.

112. Eck 2012, 350; Srinivasan 1989.

113. Hdt. 3.94, 3.97–106, 7.65 and 7.86.

mentions the expedition of Scylax of Caryanda (4.44) but without any detail of what he said about it.[114]

Ctesias has a lot more to say about India;[115] in fact he wrote a whole book about it, in which he makes clear that his information comes from Indian visitors to the Persian court, where he worked as a doctor for seventeen years. (He returned to Greece in 398 BC.) Several times he refers to acquiring information from Bactrian merchants. (Bactrians and Indians are said to have reached the Black Sea according to Pseudo-Scymnus, writing in the second century BCE.)[116] One of the latter explained to him the miraculous properties of the *pantarbe* stone, which Ctesias seems to have fallen for, even though he was able to handle one;[117] and a Bactrian also gave him information about the silver mines of Bactria (which must include Tajikistan as well as north-east Afghanistan).[118] Bactrians spoke an Iranian language which was presumably intelligible to people at the Persian court, but they may have known no more Sanskrit/Prakrit than was necessary to buy the goods they imported from India at a market.

Ctesias probably had access to no written sources at all, and certainly in the case of India it is debatable whether there were writings to draw on. The emergence of writing in India is a controversial matter, but some indications suggest that it existed by the middle of the fifth century BCE.[119] The evidence is somewhat contradictory. The Buddha (d. 405) certainly did not make use of writing.[120] The first physical evidence for writing comes from some Brāhmī

114. Ibid. 4.44.

115. Ctesias, ed. Lenfant 2004, tr. Nichols 2011. The articles of Bigwood restore a good deal of Ctesias' credit.

116. Ps.-Scymnus 930–4 in Diller 1952, 165–76 (173). 'There is a Greek city of the Milesians called Phasis; it is said that sixty peoples, with different languages, descend on it, among whom it is said that barbarians from India and Bactria turn up here'.

117. There may be a connection with topaz, described by Agatharchides (F 84a).

118. Ctes. F 45 paras. 6 and 26; Nichols 2011, 24–5.

119. Goyal, in Falk 1993, 295, suggests that writing may have been in use as early as 483 BCE. Kant 2000, 107 goes so far as to say that writing was 'common by the sixth century BC'. Suggestions that writing is referred to in the Vedas may be rejected. *RV [= Ṛg Veda]* 1.164.39 does not refer to 'letters' but to 'syllables'; *RV* 10.71.4, referring to the goddess Vac (voice) whom man has never seen, and the 'blessed sign' of verse 2 of the same passage do not indicate script but 'marks of friendship'. *Mahābhārata* 13.23 states that the Vedas are not to be reduced to writing: there is no difficulty in supposing that writing was in use by the time the text of the *Mahābhārata* reached something like its present form.

120. Gombrich 2013, xiii, though he believes that numerals may have been in use.

graffiti on pottery associated with fifth-century BCE levels at Anuradhapura,[121] but thereafter there is nothing until the inscriptions of Aśoka in the third century BCE, which make use of both Brāhmī (left to right, sometimes thought to be derived from the Indus 'script' – if it is a script) and Kharoṣṭhī (right to left), which is based on Aramaic and is used in the region west of the Sutlej. Of the Greek writers, Nearchus, writing in the 320s BCE, states, in Strabo's words, 'that they write missives on linen cloth that is very closely woven, though the other writers say that they make no use of written characters'.[122] The remark occurs in a discussion of the Macedonian impact on Indian handicrafts, such as the making of sponges and the forging of strigils, so may imply that this is another instance of copying western skills. Quintus Curtius Rufus, too, refers to Indians writing on bark, or bast.[123] Megasthenes, by contrast, perhaps two decades later, states categorically that the Indians did not use writing: 'a people who have no written laws, but are ignorant of writing, and must therefore in all the business of life trust to memory'.[124] But in another place, according to Strabo, Megasthenes recorded that at the Great Synod at the beginning of the New Year, 'the philosophers, one and all, come together at the gates of the king; and whatever each man has drawn up in writing or observed as useful with reference to the prosperity of either fruits or living beings or concerning the government, he brings forward in public'.[125] But the verb here translated 'draw up in writing', συντάττειν, may not mean that. It is used by Polybius to refer to 'composing' a history, but its more general meaning is to compile or collect; so Megasthenes need not be saying that the philosophers brought written documents to the court; perhaps they brought, or told about, for example, new kinds of animal feed.

The passage has been used to corroborate the story that the grammarian Pāṇini travelled to Pataliputra to present his 'book' to the Nanda king. Pāṇini was certainly aware of writing. He uses the word for 'script', *lipi*,[126] and we are also told that several schools of rishis had proposed different forms of letters at some time prior to Pāṇini.[127] But Pāṇini's references to script may have

121. Coningham, Allchin, Batt and Lucy 1996.

122. Str. 15.1.67 = Nearch. F 23.

123. Curt. 8.9.15; Falk 1993, 296 and 310. Other materials that have been used for writing include palm leaves and birch bark, referred to by al-Biruni: Naqvi 2011, 79.

124. Str. 15.1.53 = F 27 Schw = F 32 J.

125. Str. 15.1.39 = F 33 Schw = F 19 J.

126. Pāṇini, *Ashtadhyayi* 3.2.21

127. Agrawala 1953, 16 and 20–1.

been based on familiarity with Greek writing (he refers only to *yavana lipi*), or with the Aramaic used for administrative purposes in the neighbouring Persian empire until its fall to Alexander in 330 BCE. Much depends on the date of Pāṇini. Thapar places him in the mid-fifth century BCE, and believes that writing may have been in limited use for communication with the Achaemenid bureaucracy, while Habib and Jha represent a perhaps commoner view that has him working around 350, shortly before Megasthenes but a generation or two after Ctesias.[128] Agrawala marshals strong arguments for a mid-fifth-century date, as follows.[129]

1. Pāṇini's reference to Yavanas (Greeks) does not entail that he is familiar with the events of Alexander's invasion, for Greeks were familiar in the empire of Darius I.
2. Pāṇini also refers to Parsus (Persians) who were not politically active after Alexander.
3. An argument that Agrawala rejects is Pāṇini's reference to a federation of the Kṣudrakas and Malvas, who were at loggerheads during Alexander's invasion and may only later have federated. However, Curtius refers to the two peoples squabbling over a choice of leader, implying that a federation already existed, though it was friable.
4. Pāṇini is also associated with Nanda kings, especially Mahānanda, who belongs to the mid-fifth century. The Nandas were overthrown by the Mauryas soon after Alexander's arrival in India.
5. A strong argument is from astronomy: the beginning of the year is determined by the rising of Sravishta from 1372 to 401 BCE, and this is the marker that Pāṇini uses; after 401 it was the rising of Sravana. In sum, there are good reasons for assigning a fifth-century date to Pāṇini.

The contradiction between the reports of Nearchus and Megasthenes is easily resolved by the consideration that the two authors are writing about regions distant from one another, Nearchus about the Punjab and Megasthenes about Magadha. It is easy to suppose that writing was more familiar in a region that had been ruled by Persia than in the Ganges plain.

But even if Pāṇini lived in the fifth century, and was familiar with and made use of writing, and he and others like him had written physical books, they

128. Thapar 2002, 163; Habib and Jha 2004, 146–9. See also Gombrich 2013, 17; Goyal 2006, passim.

129. Agrawala 1953, 455–74.

were no doubt few in number; they may not have reached Persia from India within the fifty years or less between their putative composition and Ctesias' time of writing; and there is no evidence that Ctesias, or any member of the Persian court, understood, let alone read, Sanskrit.

Oral literature did make some impact on Ctesias.[130] Early forms of the *Rāmāyaṇa* and *Mahābhārata* were in circulation. The Vedas and the Brahmāṇas and Purāṇas had taken shape, and the Upaniṣads were in process of formation. Some of Ctesias' stories of fabulous peoples, which were repeated by Megasthenes, had their origin, as we shall see, in Sanskrit traditions. The wondrous pool Silas may be an equivalent, by metathesis of l and r, of Sanskrit *saras* 'pool, water'; but Salila is also one of the 108 names of the Ganges. Magic springs feature several times in Ctesias, and *Mahābhārata* 3.80–155 is a long account of the sacred fords (*tirthas*) of India, and there are hot and cold springs at Yamunotri.[131] It appears that Aristotle made use of Ctesias' description of the elephant, and that the information he gained therefrom was of good quality.[132] Ctesias never mentions Scylax, but he may have made use of his report.[133]

The information Ctesias gives is often very circumstantial, and associated with precise numbers and quantities. Though some scholars have suggested that this circumstantiality is a ploy to create verisimilitude and a scientific appearance, or an arch joke,[134] more detailed study of his work has led to an improved assessment of his qualities. In general, Ctesias reported well what he was told, and his information is no more unreliable than much that is in Herodotus.[135]

These Greek writers were the source material for a variety of other writers in antiquity, who have further filtered what we know of the originals. Strabo was often polemical and could be more caustic than necessary about the failings

130. Nichols 2011, 22.

131. Haberman 2006, 46.

132. See Romm 1989; Bigwood 1993a. Nichols 2011, 96 finds Ctesias' information good on this point.

133. On Scylax, see Shipley 2011, 4–6; Panchenko 1998 and 2003.

134. Gómez Espelosín 1994 takes the former view, Auberger 1995 the latter. In antiquity, Lucian (*VH* 1.3) wrote that Ctesias described what he had never seen nor heard from any truthful witness.

135. Ruffing 2011, who provides a useful doxography of earlier views; Almagor 2012. Earlier scholars used such phrases as 'mass of absurdities' (Bunbury) and 'worthless' (Jacoby): Milns 1989, 358.

of his predecessors, giving Megasthenes a notably bad name. Diodorus is a writer who has elicited much scorn from modern scholars as an unintelligent and uncritical compiler, though recent work suggests that his procedures are more complex than simply copying out one author for a bit, then putting him aside and copying out another.[136] The historian Arrian, writing in the second century CE, is generally regarded as the most sober and reliable account of Alexander's campaign, and his excerpting of Megasthenes and other writers as trustworthy. More juicy morsels are found in Aelian, a writer of miscellanies about animal behaviour (the Persian king's amours are unfavourably compared to the marital constancy of the wrasse, an ungainly fish) and also random facts from history. Other outliers include writers with specific agendas, such as Clement of Alexandria. All in all, dealing with the classical writers involves peeling back some further curtains, not just of prejudice and particular interests, but those occasioned by the multiple layers of reporting and repeating of earlier accounts.

One might hope to set against the Greek writers of the fourth and later centuries BCE the testimony of their Indian contemporaries, as well as of Greeks who had become assimilated, like Heliodorus who erected a column in honour of Viṣṇu at Besnagar in the later second century BCE (see chapter 13 below). However, there are few such to draw on. The dating of Indian literature is notoriously problematic. The *Arthaśāstra* of Kautilya has often been regarded as a genuine work of Kautilya who was the chief adviser to the Maurya emperor Candragupta (or Chandragupta), in which case it would be a valuable counterpoise to the description of Megasthenes. However, the position has been assailed from all sides. Otto Stein thought that the many resemblances between Kautilya and Megasthenes were more apparent than real. Present scholarship would not agree, but there is an influential argument that the *Arthaśāstra*, though it may contain fourth-century material, is itself a work of compilation dating in its present form from many centuries later.[137]

Some of the Dharmaśāstras may also contain fourth-century material, though their dating too is problematic.[138] The most imposing of these, *The Laws of Manu* (*Manusmṛti*), though later, seems to codify many kinds of immemorial Indian customs.[139] Elements of the *Mahābhārata* certainly go back

136. Muntz 2012.

137. Stein 1921; Trautmann 1971. The matter is discussed more fully in ch. 6 below.

138. Olivelle 1999.

139. Doniger and Smith 1991; Olivelle 2004.

to the fourth century BCE, though its 'composition' belongs to the early centuries CE.[140] The *Kāma Sūtra* of Vatsyayana was probably written in the third century CE. It is not usually regarded as a book of historical information, but in fact it has a great deal to say about social as well as marital life.[141] Like the other works mentioned, it shows an interest in codification of custom, which is what Megasthenes was also engaged upon.

A rare fixed point is constituted by the inscriptions of Aśoka, which are firmly situated in the third century BCE. They are a remarkable document of a 'philosopher king'. (See further, chapter 13 below.) Aśoka even went to the trouble of having a version of his edict about the *dharma* inscribed in Greek for those living in his western dominions around Kandahar.[142]

Of historical works there is, indeed, a paucity. The epics *Rāmāyaṇa* and *Mahābhārata* only reached their present form maybe as late as the sixth century CE. The play, *The Rakśasa's Ring* by Visakhadatta, which is about the minster Kautilya and has done much to create the tralatician picture of that statesman as a Machiavellian crook, belongs to no earlier than the late fourth century CE. The only Sanskrit work to mention Alexander is the *Harṣacarīta* of Bāna, which mentions him only in passing as an inferior comparand for the great victories about to be achieved by the hero King Harṣa: Harṣa lived in the seventh century CE (he was also a patron of Xuanzang) and the work was probably written in his lifetime or soon after.

As will be seen in the following chapter, useful historical information can be gleaned from works with a different purpose such as those by the grammarians Pāṇini and Patañjali. The Purāṇas, Brahmanical accounts of ancient India written in prophetic form in the future tense, contain some illuminating passages,[143] as do the Sri Lankan chronicles the *Mahāvaṁsa* and *Dīpavaṁsa*.

Only the great religious works may predate the Greek writers: the *Ṛg Veda*, the Upaniṣads and some of the writings attributed to the Buddha. The Jātakas, stories of the Buddha's previous births, probably began to be compiled soon after his death, while the *Life of the Buddha* by Aśvaghoṣa probably belongs to the second century CE. While Megasthenes must have understood some Sanskrit, he is probably unique in this among the Greek writers, and in any case he cannot have consulted any written texts, since he says there were

140. Parpola 2015, 299; Prakash 1964.

141. Doniger 2016.

142. On Aśoka, Bloch 1950/2007; Allen 2012.

143. Pargiter (ed. and tr.) 1913; 1922.

none. I believe that Megasthenes did hear some of the stories from the *Ṛg Veda*,[144] and probably had some of them explained to him by Brahman informants; but he will not have found it easy to recall accurately everything that he heard.

Conclusion

Three main points emerge from this discussion.

1. Our own presumptions about India make it hard for us to see writers like Nearchus, Onesicritus and Megasthenes clearly, or to see India with their eyes.
2. Many of the authors who have formed our preconceptions can, often, be used as corroborative detail for what is in the classical authors. Among the most valuable are Xuanzang, al-Biruni, Babur and even Mandeville. But we must beware of the danger that we are looking for what they have taught us to expect.
3. Could our central authors – Nearchus, Onesicritus and Megasthenes – see India clearly, or did they look for what Ctesias and Scylax had taught them to expect? Because the earlier authors are lost to us this is very difficult to estimate. With this in mind, one should always test them against other available sources and their likely Indian informants.

Thus armed with protective self-awareness, we embark on the march into India.

144. See on Heracles and his daughter ch. 7 below.

2

Alexander in India

It is said that the Stagirite [Aristotle] received eight hundred talents from Alexander as his contribution towards perfecting his *History of Animals.*

—ATHENAEUS 9.58 (398E); CF. FRANCIS BACON, *ADVANCEMENT OF LEARNING* 2.11

King Alexander the Great being fired with a desire to know the natures of animals and having delegated the pursuit of this study to Aristotle as a man of supreme eminence in every branch of science, orders were given to some thousands of persons throughout the whole of Asia and Greece, all those who made their living by hunting, fowling and fishing and those who were in charge of warrens, herds, apiaries, fishponds and aviaries, to obey his instructions, so that he might not fail to be informed about any creature born anywhere.

—PLINY, *NATURAL HISTORY* 8.17.44[1]

Alexander's Aims in India

It is not easy to establish Alexander's motives for his expedition to India. The conquest of the Persian empire had been completed with the death of Darius III in summer 330. The consolidation of his position as King of Kings was complete with the elimination of the pretenders Bessus (spring 329) and Spitamenes (winter 328/7). At this point he and his men might have considered their mission accomplished: the war of revenge against the Persian em-

1. Cf. Reese 1914, 100. Pliny also states (*NH* 10.85.185) that one result of these researches was the discovery that mice copulate by licking each other, rather than in the usual way.

pire was over and Alexander could now settle down to enjoy his new role as 'King of Asia'.[2] Many reasons have been proposed for the continuation of the campaign over the Hindu Kush and into India. It is possible that the Punjab and Sind had been part of the Achaemenid empire at its greatest extent, under Darius I, though in his successor Xerxes' time it is certain that Achaemenid sway did not reach beyond Bactria. If that is so, Alexander still had another extensive territory to subdue before he could consider the conquest complete.[3] But if the Indian campaign took him into regions that had never been part of the Persian empire, other reasons must be sought. The one most commonly put forward is Alexander's *pothos*, his longing to go beyond, to see what was over the next hill – for in this case, he had been led by Aristotle to suppose that once he crossed the Hindu Kush the River of Ocean would be in sight and he could go on quickly to conquer the entire world.[4] The motivation is explicitly romantic, and is tied up with the idea of Alexander as an explorer rather than a conqueror. 'Alexander had a yen to sail along the whole expanse of sea from India to the Gulf'.[5] But his exploration also had a practical motive, as Arrian makes clear in his explanation of his commissioning of Nearchus' voyage, 'from a desire to explore the whole coastline along the route ... to gather information about all the coastal settlements, and to find out what land was fertile and what was desert.'[6] It was the king's duty to gain firsthand knowledge of as much of his empire as possible. Napoleon's expedition to Egypt, with its extensive scientific staff and research programme, was probably planned with the model of Alexander in India in mind.[7] Gonzalo Fernández de Oviedo's *Natural History of the Indies* was also a report to the

2. On the title, Fredricksmeyer 2000.

3. Chattopadhyaya 1974 surveys the evidence. See also Briant 2002, 139–40. According to Darius' Bisutun inscription (*DB* 1.6), his empire included Gandhara and Sattagydia. Did Cyrus conquer beyond the Indus? The name of the Kamboja people has sometimes been linked with Cambyses. Josephus *AJ* 11.33 refers to Indian toparchs at Darius' court. Xerxes also included Indian troops in his army – though these might have been Punjabi mercenaries – and Herodotus (3.89–95) specifies the tribute from India. Few darics have been found in India, though one hails from Rawalpindi: Chattopadhyaya 1974, 30.

4. Arist. *Mete.* 1.13.15.

5. Arr. *Ind.* 20.1.

6. Arr. *Ind.* 32.11.

7. The idea of Alexander as a 'scientific conqueror' (Said 1978, 58) goes back to Giovanni Domenico Cassini in the time of Louis XIV, who stressed the role played by Callisthenes: Briant 2016, 268–9.

Spanish king of everything that could be found useful about the West Indies – its flora and fauna, foodstuffs, and so on. If only we had such a book from Alexander's entourage!

Much of succeeding literature did indeed perceive Alexander in the light of an explorer, beginning with the fictional *Letter of Alexander to Aristotle about India* and continuing through Pliny to the Persian Middle Ages;[8] but there were also pragmatic reasons for maintaining an army in the field for a further time. Sabine Müller has argued that a Macedonian king's authority depended on his army, and that his best way to maintain authority was to be at war.[9]

Both the Romantic and the military interpretation gain support from the explicit aim of emulating certain ancient conquerors, including Semiramis and Dionysus (though both precedents may have been fabricated for the purpose). But the aim of exploration and discovery also receives considerable support from the sources. First, it is well known that Alexander was accompanied by a considerable scientific staff, from the bematists whose task it was to record the stages of each day's journey and the notable matters observed, to historians who would record the king's achievements and triumphs, to philosophers who would investigate the world they entered and would entertain the king with their speculations and discussions. These intellectuals included the philosophers Anaxarchus, Callisthenes and apparently Pyrrho; the memoirist Chares, the court chamberlain; and several officers who wrote significant works, both of history (Ptolemy, Aristobulus) and of an ethnographic kind (Nearchus, Onesicritus).[10] In addition, Alexander is frequently credited in the sources with an active interest in geography, strange races and matters of natural history going beyond a simple concern with stock breeding and food plants.[11]

8. 'Since I know that you are interested in philosophy [Alexander writes to Aristotle], I thought I would write to you about the parts of India, and the kinds of serpents, men and beasts that are to be found there': *Epistula* 1. Abu Taher Tarsusi's *Darabnameh* (tenth century CE) concentrates on Alexander's explorations and discoveries, to which his conquests are almost incidental, and in any case often carried out by his feisty wife Burandokht while Alexander is busy thinking.

9. Müller 2014.

10. On the use of the term 'ethnography', see Almagor and Skinner 2103 and the discussion in ch. 5 below.

11. The range of interest reminds one of that of the early antiquaries in India, such as the brilliant Sir William Jones, or Alexander Cunningham, or the seventeenth-century John Marshall, or Francis Buchanan. See, e.g., Keay 2001, 175–6; Singh 2004, 44.

Arrian provides many examples of Alexander's own 'researches' in India. At Arigaeum (Nawagai) he captured two hundred and thirty thousand oxen, and was so impressed by their quality that he sent a number back to Macedon;[12] he investigates elephants;[13] he is intrigued by the tale of 'Dionysus' told him by the chief of the people of Nysa, Acuphis, and visits the neighbouring Mount Meros;[14] he and his men 'disproved' many of the fables about India (while inventing some themselves);[15] reports of good quality elephants and brave farmer-warriors beyond the Hyphasis 'spurred in Alexander a desire to press on further';[16] Alexander believed that he had discovered the source of the Nile when he observed crocodiles in the Indus, and 'Egyptian beans' (lotus) along the banks of the Acesines, indicating that he was aware of the controversy over this matter that went back to Scylax's expedition – in fact, he was so excited that he wrote about it in a letter to Olympias, but then deleted the passage when he had better information;[17] the tides at the Indus estuary amazed Alexander and his men, though it may be a stretch to regard this turmoil as a scientific revelation; he went on to investigate the relative merits of two mouths of the Indus;[18] and he took a great interest in the Indian philosophers he encountered at Taxila.[19]

Plutarch likewise emphasises Alexander's intellectual interests: in medicine, philosophy and literature; his experiment with the qualities of naphtha; his giving of medical advice; his relations with Anaxarchus and Callisthenes; his letter about an unusual spring near the Oxus, which Alexander regarded as an 'omen', and about which he wrote a letter to Antipater; his relations with the Indian philosophers; his study of the ocean and coastline.[20] In his *De Alexandri fortuna* he even writes that Alexander 'lived like a philosopher'.

12. Arr. *Anab.* 4.25.4.

13. Ibid. 4.30.8.

14. Ibid. 5.1.1–2.1, 5.2.5.

15. Ibid. 5.4.4.

16. Ibid. 5.25.1–2.

17. Ibid. 6.1.2–3, 6.2.5. Bosworth 1996a, 70–1 points out that Alexander and the Greeks 'interpreted local data according to Greek categories' but concedes that the empirical research refuted the older theories by showing that the Indus and the Nile had no connection. Nevertheless the misconception persists that 'Alexander, on arrival in India, had no idea where he was going' because of the raising of this scholarly question: the canard was given currency by Sona Datta in a BBC TV programme, 'Treasures of the Indus' 1 on 31 August 2015.

18. Arr. *Anab.* 6.19.1, 6.20.2. But see Hamilton 1994 on Arrian's muddle about this matter.

19. Arr. *Anab.* 7.1.5, 2.2–4.

20. Plu. *Alex.* 7; 35; 41; 52–3; 57.5–9; 64–5; 66.

Presumably it was Alexander or a companion who sent back the citrons from central Asia ('Median' or 'Persian apples') that Theophrastus describes in such detail.[21] Notably, there is never any reference to research into Indian languages, despite the sophistication of Indian grammatical scholarship: but language was never included among the ethnographic topics pursued by the Greeks.[22]

The controversial 'Last Plans' also include missions to explore the Caspian Sea, to round Africa and to explore Arabia, to build roads in Libya, and so on; but apart from a mention of Heracleides of Argos' exploration of the Oxus, there is no record of anyone writing any reports.[23] Pytheas' mission to Britain may have belonged in this climate of exploratory frenzy, though it is impossible to find evidence that Alexander had anything to do with it.

Do these examples add up to a scientific mission? Scarcely. Yet one need not demand that Alexander himself be at the forefront of research for there to be a genuine scientific aspect to the expedition.[24] It was Friedrich Pfister who first broached the idea of Alexander's campaign as a 'proto-Smithsonian expedition', and the activities of Napoleon surely lay behind his idea.[25] The approach was developed by Hugo Bretzl in his important book *Botanische Forschungen des Alexanderzuges.* P. M. Fraser considers the origins of Theophrastus' botanical information, which undoubtedly came from Alexander's companions,[26] even though, as Pliny despairingly remarks, 'The Macedonians have given accounts of kinds of trees that for the most part have no names'.[27] Whether there was really an archive in Pfister's terms may be doubted, in the light of Callisthenes *FGrH* 124 T 3, where Simplicius in his commentary on Aristotle's *De caelo* 2.12 states that 'because the observations made by Callisthenes had not yet reached Greece from Babylon, Aristotle scolded him, as Porphyry records'. Nonetheless, there would not have been nearly so much

21. Thphr. *HP* 4.4.2.

22. Schmitt 1990.

23. Bosworth 1988a, 164–9. Libya: Diod. 18.4.1ff. The Caspian: Arr. *Anab.* 7.16.1–4. Arabia: ibid. 7.25.2; Tarn 1951, 394. Arr. *Anab.* 7.20.2 remarks that Alexander was incited by 'the prosperity of the country', with its valuable plants such as cassia, myrrh and frankincense, as well as cinnamon and spikenard. Africa: Plu. *Alex.* 68. Carthage: Curt. 10.1.16–18.

24. Molina Marín 2010, 152–4 points out that Alexander was seeking answers to old questions, rather than posing new ones.

25. Pfister 1961.

26. Fraser 1994.

27. Plin. *NH* 12.13.25.

scientific data – nor, for that matter, so rich a development of paradoxography in later Greek writing – without Alexander's expedition.[28]

One particular case in which it has been supposed that Alexander deliberately provided material for Aristotle's researches is that of the elephant. The story is so appealing that it was even developed into a novel, *An Elephant for Aristotle*, by L. Sprague du Camp, which charts the travails of the beast on its long journey from India to Macedon to become the object of scientific experiments.[29] One need not fall for the nonsense retailed by Pseudo-Plutarch about Alexander's encounter with a talking elephant near the river Hydaspes[30] – which the writer presumably invented, along with the author he cites[31] – to believe that Alexander was particularly struck by the elephant. Indeed, there is plenty of evidence for his fascination with the beasts (see chapter 4 below). But the story that he sent one back to Macedon, as he did the oxen of Arigaeum, may be too good to be true.

James Romm has argued that the whole story of Alexander's scientific patronage is a myth.[32] He points out that there is very little in Aristotle's works about the wildlife of India other than his information on the elephant, and that, even though he knew there were differences between the African and Indian elephants, the specimen he examined was actually an African. (Athenaeus 8.47–9 is an extended attack on the inaccuracy of much of Aristotle's biological information, though the elephant does not feature here.) J. M. Bigwood extended the argument, insisting that most of Aristotle's information is drawn from authors earlier than Alexander, notably Ctesias: anything in Aristotle that resembles something we know of from Nearchus or Onesicritus was probably already in Ctesias. Furthermore, there is no evidence that, as is sometimes stated, Aristotle actually dissected an elephant, though Galen, five hundred years later, certainly did. Even making allowance for a tendency in Bigwood to see Ctesias at the root of everything, the cumulative argument is strong. Most of Aristotle's scientific research took place on Lesbos and is

28. Alexander was not expecting 'wonders', but many appear in the *Letter of Alexander to Aristotle about India*, not least the river of flowing sand, which is also in Xuanzang and the fictional rewriting by Wu Ch'eng-en known as *The Journey to the West*. See Wu 2006, 286. Dragons: Ael. *NA* 15.21. On paradoxography and the *Alexander Romance*, see Stoneman forthcoming a.

29. Travelling elephants have inspired more than one novelist, Jose Saramago being another example.

30. Ps.-Plu. *De fluv.* 1.4.

31. And most of the other sources in his book: see the edition by De Lazzer et al., 2003.

32. Romm 1989.

determined by the landscape of that island.[33] Maybe even the grant from Alexander is a myth; for the source that tells us Alexander gave fifty talents to Xenocrates, the head of the Academy, makes no mention of this much larger grant to Aristotle. The latter never mentions India in either *De plantis* or *Problemata,* where unusual data might be expected to appear.

Alexander's Advance

Winter was turning to spring 326 BCE, and the melting snows from the mountains were filling the rivers of the Hindu Kush, when Alexander began his descent into the plain of the Indus.[34] He had been three full years in the Afghanistan region, the longest stay in any area of the whole campaign. Arriving in Areia (Herat) in spring 329, he left the Companion Stasanor to take over the region while he pursued the Persian pretender Bessus northwards to Uzbekistan, founding in the process the most distant of his cities, Alexandria-the-furthest (Khojend). Bessus' end came in the late summer, but the warlord Spitamenes was a thorn in the flesh and was not assassinated until winter 328/7. The army wintered at Bactra, and by summer 328 Alexander was besieging the Sogdian Rock, somewhere in the highlands bordering Uzbekistan and Tajikistan. Alexander's temper grew worse and that summer saw the murder of his loyal supporter Clitus during a banquet at Maracanda (Samarkand). In spring 327 he brought the Sogdian war to a close by marrying the daughter of the warlord Oxyartes, Roxane, who soon became pregnant though she lost the baby during the taxing advance to India.[35]

Embassies came from some of the Indian states, notably from the ruler of Taxila, whom the Greeks called Omphis (perhaps Sanskrit *Ambhi). The pledges of support to the invading army encouraged the king, as did the loyalty of a renegade Indian called Sisicottus (perhaps *Sasigupta?) who had deserted Bessus and supported Alexander throughout the Sogdian campaign.[36] He was already beyond the limits of the Persian empire he had conquered, since the satrapy of Gandhara had apparently ceased to adhere to the empire by now (n. 3 above), and needed all the help and logistical information he

33. Leroi 2014.

34. Arr. *Anab.* 4.22.8: 'the end of spring'.

35. *Epitoma RG Alexandri* 70.

36. Arr. *Anab.* 4.30.4. Allen's theory (2002, 58 and 365) that Sisicottus is Candragupta is unconvincing.

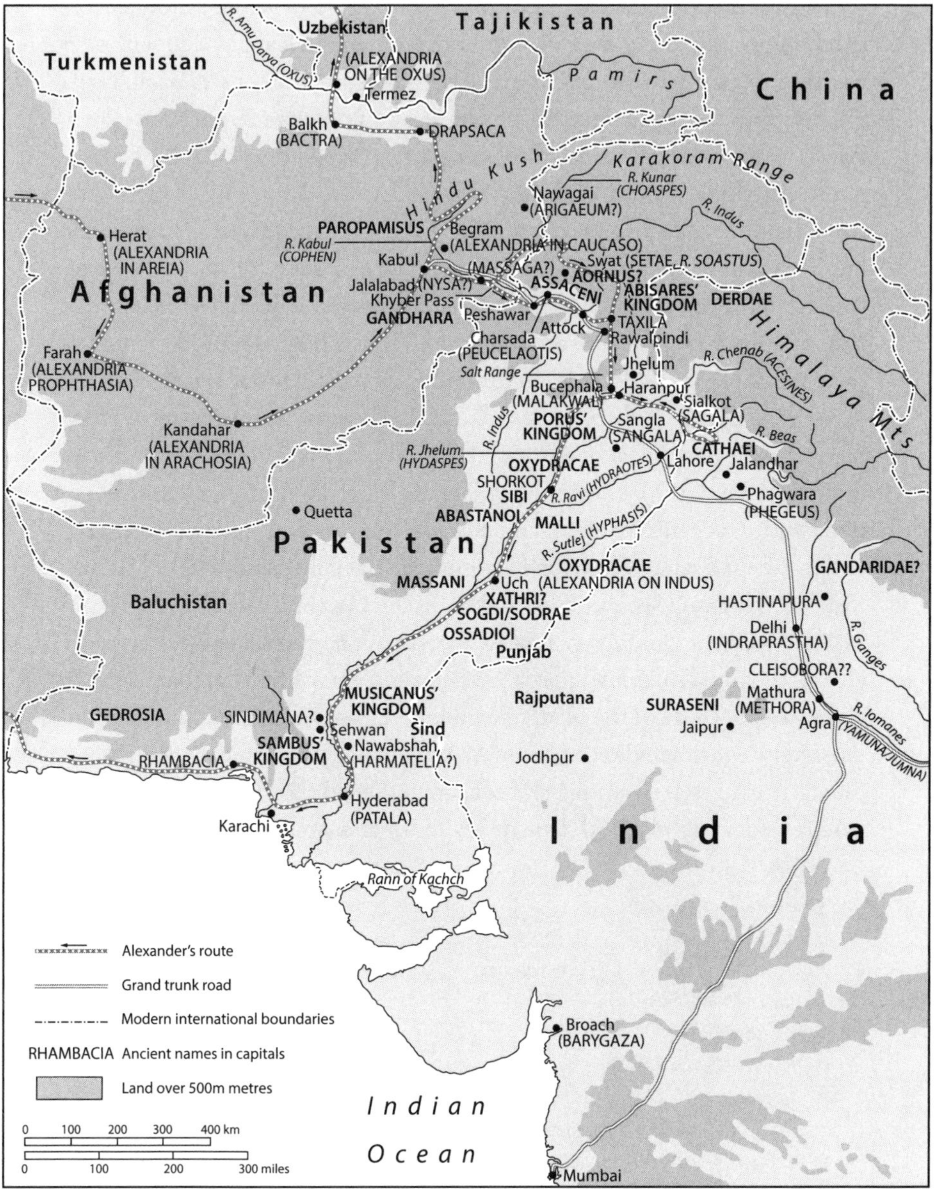

2.1 Alexander's India.

could get. The invasion force was divided into two.[37] Hephaestion led the main body along the main road into India, down the Kabul (Cophen) river and through the Khyber Pass.[38] He was accompanied by the ruler of Taxila on this journey. Almost immediately there was a revolt in Peucelaotis (Pushkalavati): the ruler Astis was killed, and was replaced by another prince, Sangaeus. Alexander characteristically chose the more difficult option, leading the remainder of the troops northwards along the river Kunar (Choaspes)[39] into Bajaur and Swat, once described by Queen Elizabeth II as 'the Switzerland of the East'. The next city, Andaca, capitulated while the tribals of the Kunar valley fled to the hills and vanished. (This was where Alexander found the prize cattle that he proposed to send back to Macedon.) Next came the Aspasioi (Aśvaka),[40] the Gouraioi,[41] and Arigaeum.[42] In the country of the Assaceni (perhaps Sanskrit Aśmaka)[43] he reduced the city of Massaga[44] with ferocious brutality. Next he made for Ora, on the Swat river, a walled city identified with Udegram by Stein, and close to Mingaora, the capital of Swat;[45] and thence to Bazira, whose fortification walls are still visible today.[46] He also fortified Orobatis (Shabazgarhi) and Embolima (Kabulgram).[47]

Somewhere in this region, representatives of one city, named Nysa, whose chief was named Acuphis, approached him and persuaded him that their city was sacred because of the birth of a god there, whom the Macedonians, impressed by the coincidence of names, immediately identified as Dionysus.[48] The fact that ivy grew at this altitude strengthened the connection, and the troops held a Bacchic revel, crowned with ivy and consuming plenty of wine

37. Bosworth 1988a, 119ff.

38. Arr. *Anab.* 4.22.7.

39. 'brown and fast-running between mud-flats and reeds, and up to three hundred yards across, but ice-cold': Levi 1972, 191. Peter Levi saw fortresses and fortified villages in this region, and orioles (226).

40. Arr. *Anab.* 4.24; Law 1954, 66.

41. The river Gouraios is identified with Panjkora by *The Landmark Arrian* 187.

42. Arr. *Anab.* 4.23.4, 25.6. Arigaeum may be Aligram, on the opposite of the river Swat.

43. Ibid. 4.25.5; Shastri 1996, 68. See the map in *The Landmark Arrian* 183.

44. Uncertain location, but it may be Churchill's Picket near Chakdara, which overlooks Wuch and the Swat valley.

45. Stein 1929, 60.

46. Arr. *Anab.* 4.27.5; Vajira, also known as Barikot: Stein 1929, 35–42.

47. Arr. *Anab.* 4.28.5, 7; Pollet 2014, 43.

48. On the identification, see ch. 3 below.

(which may not, unlike the ivy, have been local, though Martha Carter believes the Macedonians had stumbled on a local wine-festival and cult).[49] The city benefited and was granted its freedom under an aristocratic government of three hundred notables.[50] The location is unidentifiable, but it may be Jalalabad.

Indian States

Already the Macedonians had thus encountered examples of the varying types of polity that were characteristic of north-west India at this time. The period is known as the 'second urbanisation' (the first having been the long-forgotten Indus culture of the second millennium BCE).[51] During this period, in the Ganges plain and in Gandhara, growing agricultural surpluses,[52] the development of iron technology and the extensive trading networks that snaked across the whole subcontinent led to the coalescence of settlements into villages, towns and cities. Centralised irrigation may have been developed in areas subject to Achaemenid control or influence, and from the third century BCE through the activities of Buddhist monastic settlements.[53] Buddhism

49. Carter 1992; 2015, 355–76; see further ch. 3 below on Dionysus.

50. The exact location of Nysa is uncertain. Curtius (8.10.11ff.) places it high in the mountains in a wooded region, west of the Choaspes, and describes Alexander's arrival there before his conquest of Massaga. Arrian, however, locates Nysa 'between the Cophen and the Indus', therefore perhaps in the region of Peshawar. The cedarwood coffins hanging in the trees provide a powerful clue, for Lane Fox (1973, 342) describes seeing such coffins among the 'Kaffir' people of Nuristan (their name for themselves is Kalashas), who expose their dead in them. For some further references, see Stoneman 2004, 78–9.

51. For what follows, see Thapar 2002, 138–64. Continuity in such matters as building styles, religious practices, fire-altars, weights and measures and other practical matters is vigorously argued for by Danino 2010, 223–4 and passim, to the extent of denying any kind of Aryan invasion (256, 291). At 254–5 he proposes that the *Ṛg Veda* is a recollection of the Indus Civilisation before the drying up of the Sarasvatī; but whether the disappearance of this river was really a factor in the decline of the Indus Civilisation is still disputed: Possehl 2002, 239–40. See also the discussion in ch. 5 below, 'The India that Megasthenes Knew'. While there is likely to have been some continuity at the level of what Parpola calls 'village Hinduism', the second urbanisation has to be seen as a new beginning. The arrival of the horse is usually associated with the Aryan 'invasion'. The matter cannot be explored in detail here, but see, for example, Allchin 1995.

52. Probably rice in summer, wheat in winter: Shaw 2007, 251.

53. Ibid., 23–4 and ch. 2 esp. 29–30.

grew out of, and encouraged, urbanism, and in the period after Alexander a kind of Buddhist economy emerged as monastic settlements generated patronage and networks.[54] Some villages were communities of specialised craftsmen, located near their raw materials, and these could grow into towns as commercial centres. The craftsmen were organised in guilds: Buddhist texts mention woodworkers, smiths, leather-workers, painters and so on, perhaps up to eighteen different categories.[55] The terminology offers the *grama,* village, *nigama* and *putubhedana,* exchanges and markets, *nagara,* town, and *mahanagara,* city. Many towns and cities were protected by a rampart, against both floods and marauders, and provided with drains, houses of mud-brick and even some fired brick. These settlements were grouped into larger political units (*mahājanapadas*)[56] which divided into kingdoms, largely based in the Ganges plain, and *gaṇa-sanghas*, oligarchies, which were more characteristic of the north-west.[57] Much of India must have been tribal in character as parts of central India are now (especially Madhya Pradesh and Chhattisgarh), and tribal societies tend to be inherently democratic, until headmen acquire power and influence and turn themselves into rajas.[58] Thus there will have been considerable variety of local gods, languages, economies and customs.[59] Buddhism was readily able to absorb local cults, while Brahmanism was much more rigid.[60]

The religious difference was probably allied to regional divisions. Joannes Bronkhorst has argued persuasively, on the basis of observations by Patañjali (ca. 150 BCE) that Vedic, Brahmanical culture did not hold sway east of Allahabad (Prayag).[61] That is, the emerging region of Magadha, ruled in Alexander's time by the last Nanda kings, was defined by non-caste-based forms of

54. Ibid., 262.

55. Sharma 2009, 149 on the urban economy, and the Jain grading of cities.

56. Law 1954, 42 and 45. The standard number is sixteen, but the lists vary: Ghosh 1973, 35. A map in Allchin 1995, 116 indicates the usual candidates.

57. Sharma 1968, 237 specifies four types of aristocratic government. Republics persist into the fourth century BCE in the north-west, but show a tendency to move further east as the north-west becomes more monarchic (238–410); they also prefer rough terrain, perhaps because they are more tribal in character.

58. Fuchs 1973, 148–9.

59. Ibid., 40–74 and, on the north-west, 81–102.

60. Shaw 2007, 50–9, commenting on the prevalence of *nāgas* and *yakṣas* in Buddhist tales and iconography.

61. Bronkhorst 2007.

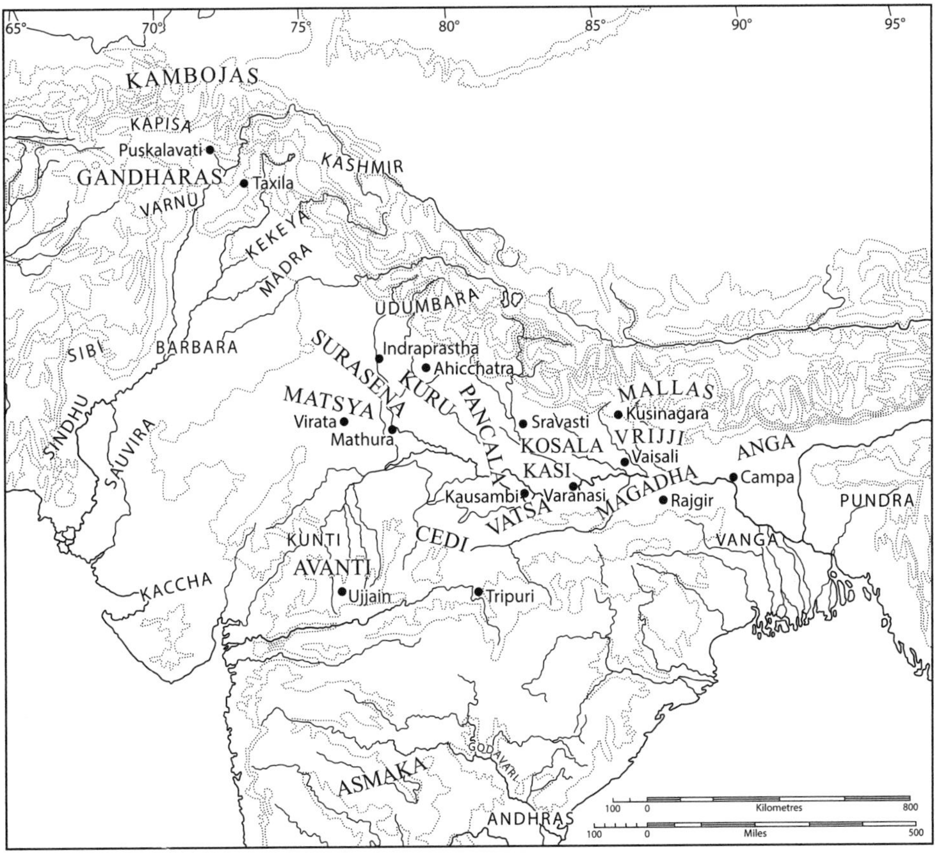

2.2 The *mahājanapadas* in the fourth century BCE.

asceticism, such as those of Buddhists, Jains and Ājīvikas. The *Śatapatha Brāhmaṇa* refers to the 'demonic people of the east',[62] who build round (i.e., Buddhist) stupas instead of square ones. This anti-caste tendency may have assisted the Mauryas (whose founder, Candragupta, was the son of a barber) in overthrowing the kṣatriya dynasty of the Nandas.

In the north-west it would seem that Vedic culture held sway at the time of Alexander's visit, and even the ascetics were predominantly Brahmins: Strabo mentions that the 'mountain-dwelling philosophers' are dressed in deer-skins and offer cures by the use of plants and spells, which defines them

62. *SB* [= *Śatapatha Brāhmaṇa*] 13.8.1.5.

as Brahmins.[63] (We shall have a great deal more to say about these people in a later chapter.) Thapar's distinction of kings in the east and oligarchs in the west cannot be applied wholesale, as we have already seen: though Nysa was clearly a *gaṇa-sangha*, the Assaceni apparently had a king, Assacenus (unless the Macedonians radically misunderstood the situation).

Across the Indus

Still I forded that river, entered that country.
The river was all I had come for, it waited for me.
It ran deep and still, I waded its waters.
Glycerine clear, they smelt of our Greek honey.
Had I held by them, they would have healed me . . .
Do not think that I am lonely. I retain some memories.
But I hear across distance that by my river
mothers tell children, 'Sleep or Iskander will kill you.'
I was never like that, scribe. The river could tell you.

—DOM MORAES, 'ALEXANDER'
(FROM *IN CINNAMON SHADE*, 1991)

The Assaceni retreated across the Shangri-La pass to the Rock of Aornos, where Alexander was again able to deploy mythology, as well as engineering skills, to assist his almost miraculous conquest of the apparently inaccessible stronghold.[64] The site was identified authoritatively by Aurel Stein as Pir-Sar, in a bend of the Indus five thousand feet (1,500 m) above the river, but the identification has been challenged in favour of Mount Ilam by Giuseppe Tucci: debate will continue. Alexander seized control and left Sisicottus in charge.[65] From here he began to return to the main road (the Trunk Road of its time) into India. If he came down the Choaspes he travelled via the city of Puśkalavati (Peucelaotis, modern Charsadda), which had been attacked and subdued by Hephaestion during Alexander's journey northwards.[66] There is a puzzle here, since Arrian states that Alexander himself received the

63. Str. 15.1.70; Bronkhorst 2007, 57. Contrast Buddhist medical practice: see ch. 8 below, *Medicine*.

64. Arr. *Anab*. 4.28.1.

65. Ibid. 4.28.5–30.4. Sisicottus remained loyal: 5.20.7.

66. Ibid. 4.22.8.

surrender of Peucelaotis, 'situated not far from the river Indus', on his way to Aornos.[67] Bosworth thinks that there must be two cities with the same name;[68] but in his *Indica* Arrian makes clear that they are the same: 'Assacenian territory includes the large city of Massaca, which is the regional centre of power, and another large city, Peucelaitis, not far from the Indus'.[69] It looks as if Arrian has imperfectly combined the narratives in two different sources. The ruins of Puśkalavati remain impressive. Barren grey walls tower to a height of eighty feet (25 m): today there remains of the City of the Lotus a 'Herculean block of mud' and a series of local legends of a city made of gold.[70] It seems, at least, that Alexander returned through the land of the Assaceni towards the Indus:[71] his exact route is impossible to extract from Arrian's words, but he presumably followed in the traces of Hephaestion, following the muddy, snow-swollen waters of the Kabul to the point where it joins the blue and sparkling stream of the Indus at modern Attock, already many hundreds of miles from its mountain cradle in the Himalayas. All around him on the march were the mountains that loom over Peshawar: 'dark green, almost black mountains; blue mountains; rose-coloured mountains; and away in the distance, snow-topped mountains'.[72]

On the way, Alexander had a first encounter with elephants. He found a herd abandoned by its people, who had fled to their king Abisares (*Abhisara?), located north of Taxila on the other side of the Indus.[73] Alexander had already engaged some elephant hunters, according to Arrian,[74] and captured most of the herd, whom he was able to provide with riders, either the hunters or others, and thus reinforced his army. He also found a forest with suitable timber for boat-building; the ships then sailed down river to the bridge which had been constructed in advance by Hephaestion. Curtius makes no mention

67. Ibid. 4.28.6.

68. Bosworth 1988a, 125 n. 307.

69. Arr. *Ind.* 1.8. Hammond's translation puzzlingly glosses 'Peucelaitis' as 'Gandhara', which is not a city.

70. Dalrymple 1998, 326–7.

71. Arr. *Anab.* 4.30.5.

72. Shamsie 2014, 92.

73. Stein 1929, 158 suggests this kingdom was the region of Hazara, centred on Abbottabad. Vārāhamihira puts Abhisara between the Chenab and the Jhelum, but this must be a different Abhisara: Shastri 1996, 67.

74. Arr. *Anab.* 4.30.7.

of a bridge, but only of boats which could be easily dismantled for transport by wagon.[75] This contradiction should alert us to a problem.

The Indus at Attock is some six hundred feet (180 m) wide, now dominated by the remains of the Mughal emperor Akbar's fortress; the railway bridge built in 1899 by Sir Guildford Molesworth had five spans totalling 1,385 feet (422 m). Before the building of the bridge the common method of crossing the river was by a bridge of boats. South of Attock, the Indus enters some one hundred miles of gorges and would have defeated even the legendary Alexander's bridge-building skills as celebrated in the *Romance*.[76] Many recent commentators have assumed that, both here and in the earlier crossing of the Oxus, Alexander's troops used the method described by Xenophon, of swimming across supported by animal skins stuffed with hay and similar lightweight material.[77] Robert Rollinger argues forcefully against this interpretation. First, putting a small group like Xenophon's across a river by this means would take long enough; for Alexander's army, many times the size, it would take an eternity. On the Oxus, according to Curtius, 'Alexander proclaimed that he would use rafts to transport the cavalry and phalanx; the lighter-armed troops he ordered to swim over on skins'.[78] Secondly, the common method in Mesopotamia and further east is to use inflated skins, not stuffed ones.[79] And thirdly, such skins are commonly bound together to form either rafts or pontoons. Rollinger provides many photographs explicitly showing the inflation of skins as floats in ancient Assyria, as well as of bundles of such skins ('keleks', Akk. *kalakku*) on the Huang-Ho.[80] Nonnus, too, imagined Dionysus' army

75. Curt. 8.10.3ff.

76. *AR* [= *Alexander Romance*] 2.37 γ. 'The plain was divided in the middle by a ravine, whose depth was immeasurable. There Alexander erected an arch to bridge the ravine; and on the arch he inscribed in Greek, Persian and Egyptian the following words: "Alexander came here and erected an arch over which the whole army crossed; his intention was to reach the end of the world, if Providence approved his plan".' On the problems of building bridges further south, on the flat alluvial plain through which the Indus spread with little idea of permanent banks, see Dewey 2014, 197–207.

77. X. *Anab.* 1.5.10.

78. Curt. 7.8.7.

79. Cf. X. *Anab.* 3.5.3–11. 'Till very recent times, inflated skins have been the normal means of crossing the Indus': Toynbee 1961, 27.

80. Rollinger 2013, 25, attacking Romm 2012 and Heckel 2008; 32–3 on small versus large contingents; 28 and 41–3 on keleks; 67 on pontoons. On p. 79 he quotes an extract from the late antique work *De rebus bellicis* on the methods of building an *ascogefyrus*. Inflated skins are depicted on an Assyrian relief in the British Museum.

2.3 A bridge of boats on the river Indus at Attock (photograph by William Henry Baker, 1870s).

swimming across the Hydaspes on individual goatskins: 'then the mass of combative footsoldiers, who had no boats, puffed their own wind into swelling goatksins; on air-filled hides they crossed the Indian Hydaspes, and the skins, distended with internal winds, were their vessels'.[81]

But a photograph taken at Attock by William Baker in 1863 shows the local technique that preceded the construction of the modern railway bridge, namely a bridge of boats, consisting of a pathway of logs, with a handrail, laid over what looks like about fifteen or twenty two-ended ferry-boats. British troops used precisely the same method of crossing in the 1840s.[82] There can be little doubt that this is the method Alexander and Hephaestion adopted: such 'boats', being inflatable skins, could not only be easily dismantled for transport, as Curtius says, but were very quick to build.[83] Arrian notes that neither of his main sources states exactly how Alexander crossed the Indus,

81. Nonn. D. 23. 147–50.

82. Dewey 2014, plate 55, and plate 56 for Baker's photograph.

83. Curt. 7.8.7: on the Oxus, as above, 'the boats were put together with such zest by the men that some 12,000 were completed within three days'. See also Singh 2004, 33 on Cunningham.

2.4 An Assyrian relief depicting troops crossing a river on inflated skins (British Museum, London).

but he himself surmises that a bridge of boats was used.[84] A broader point to be drawn from this is that the classical sources' treatment of Alexander as a resourceful inventor is grossly exaggerated (though not by Arrian):[85] he (or in this case Hephaestion) followed local custom, and no doubt drew on the advice of Ambhi who had surely crossed the Indus many times.

The next two states that Alexander encountered were also kingships: that of Taxila and that of Porus. Omphis (*Ambhi)[86] was also known as Taxiles, and in the case of Porus the only name we know is his dynastic name: the Puru tribe had been settled in the region since the middle of the second millennium.[87] Alexander received a warm welcome at Taxila and stayed there for

84. Arr. *Anab.* 5.7.1–8.2.

85. Rollinger 2013, 83.

86. The name is known to Pāṇini: Nilakanta Sastri 1950, 119.

87. Habib and Jha 2004, 8.

three months. Omphis gave him eighty talents of *argentum signatum*, which is probably our first reference to Indian punch-marked coinage.[88]

Taxila, close to modern Rawalpindi, was an important settlement at a position where three trade routes crossed, a true caravan city.[89] It was named either for Taksha, a Naga king, or for a people, the Takkas; *sila* means a hill or rock. It is flanked by a small stream, the Tamra-nullah which is probably the *Tiberios potamos* or *Tiberoboam* of Palladius' *De Bragmanibus.*[90] Though the apparent remains date from the sixth century BCE and later, there is evidence of habitation for more than two thousand years before this. It may have had a notably Achaemenid character still when Alexander arrived: no burials have been found, which may imply exposure of the dead in the Zoroastrian style or Indian-style cremation (perhaps less likely). Philostratus' *Life of Apollonius of Tyana* attributes to it the sun worship Greeks thought was the key feature of Persian religion.[91] It was also famous as a university centre (especially in Buddhist sources) and later become a major Buddhist monastery: Jivaka, the son of Bimbisara, a great physician of Rajagriha, the Nanda capital, was educated at Taxila. Pāṇini lived here, probably a generation or more before Alexander, and the *Mahābhārata* is said to have been composed here. Alexander was intrigued by the 'philosophers' of Taxila, and we shall have much to say of them in a later chapter. The evocative description of the city in Philostratus' *Life of Apollonius* may be largely fiction, though there are some intriguing correspondences to the archaeological remains.[92] Dar thinks that the reliefs depicting the exploits of Alexander and Porus which Apollonius observed were probably the reliefs depicting Mara's attack on Buddha, in which some of the figures wear Greek dress.[93]

While Alexander was at Taxila a mission came from Abisares, offering token submission. But Porus, the next king along, as it were, whose lands lay between the Hydaspes (Jhelum) and Acesines (Chenab), was more recalcitrant.

88. Curt. 8.12.15; Cribb 2005, 44.

89. See above all Dar 1984, though this does not entirely supersede Marshall 1960. Lahiri 1992, 378 on the trade routes.

90. There may be an assimilation to the name of the Brahmans' island, Tamrapani, i.e., Sri Lanka.

91. Bäbler and Nesselrath 2016, 86–8; exposure of the dead: Str. 15.1.62 = Aristob. F 42; sun worship: Philostr. *VA* 2.26.2, 2.32.2.

92. See ch. 16 below, and Bäbler and Nesselrath 2016.

93. Dar 1984, 61–2.

In May Alexander advanced to meet the king in the last major engagement of his campaign, the battle on the river Hydaspes. It had begun to rain during the stay at Taxila, and by the time the army reached the Hydaspes the rain was falling more or less continuously.[94]

Greek and Indian River Names

Greek	Modern Indian	Sanskrit
Kophen	Kubha	Nadistuti (RV)
Hydaspes	Jhelum	Vitasta
Acesines	Chenab	Candrabagha *or* Asikni
Hydraotes	Ravi	Iravati
Hyphasis	Beas	Vipasa
Zaradrus/Hesidrus	Sutlej	Śatadru

See Law 1954, 29–30. All the rivers of the Punjab are celebrated in *RV* 10.75. Aitken 1992, 163–4 evokes the fierce rapidity of the Sutlej.

Alexander was now following the immemorial route through India that later became the Grand Trunk Road, unforgettably evoked by Kipling in some of the most beautiful pages of *Kim*. Kim noticed everything as he walked

> as it were, a little above the country, along a stately corridor, seeing all India spread out to left and right. It was beautiful to behold the many-yoked grain and cotton waggons crawling over the country roads: one could hear their axles, complaining a mile away, coming nearer, till with shouts and yells and bad words they climbed up the steep incline and plunged on to the hard main road, carter reviling carter. It was equally beautiful to watch the people, little clumps of red and blue and pink and white and saffron, turning aside to go to their own villages, dispersing and growing small by twos and threes across the level plain.[95]

Can it have been so different when Alexander's army passed through? Nearchus noted the Indians' love of bright colours:

> This Indian linen is brighter in colour than other linens, or else it may just seem brighter by contrast with the people's dark skin. They wear a linen shirt down to mid-calf, another garment wrapped over their shoulders, and another wound round their heads. Some wear ivory earrings, but this

94. Str. 15.1.17.
95. Kipling 1987, 63.

> is only common practice among the very wealthy. Nearchus says that the Indians dye their beards in various colours: some go for whiter than white, others for dark blue, crimson, purple or green.[96]

There was plenty for Alexander and his companions to observe, and some of them may have been as observant as Kim. But Kim's companion, the lama, 'never raised his eyes ... He looked steadily at the ground, and strode as steadily hour after hour, his soul busied elsewhere'. Surely there were many in Alexander's army who trudged on, noticing as little, though their minds were less on the elevation of their souls than on the decaying state of their boots and armour.

The rivers were already swollen by the snow-melt from the Himalayas, and in June the spring thunderstorms would give way to the continuous rains of the monsoon season. Arrian mentions both these phenomena,[97] but it is unclear whether Alexander knew about the imminence of the monsoon, though one presumes that Taxiles, Abisares and the five thousand Indians who were now accompanying him[98] might have mentioned it.

The ford may have been at Haranpur,[99] or perhaps at Malakwal, or even at Jhelum, which lies on a major modern route from Rawalpindi to Lahore. The river in this region contains a number of islands, and there are several modern ferry crossings. The boats (Arrian is now clear about the boats) were dismantled and brought to the Hydaspes.[100] This last major battle of the campaign was fought in drenching rain, and was the Macedonians' first encounter with elephants on the battlefield.

It is no part of this book's purpose to rehearse the military details of Alexander's campaign, but rather to establish his experience of India, what he (and his companions) saw and learned, what opened their eyes and filled them wonder or, perhaps, enlightenment. In this battle there were two such elements: mud and elephants.

96. Arr. *Ind.* 16.2–4. Octavio Paz (1989, 116–17) likewise succumbed to the riot of Indian colour: 'a rose and green, yellow and purple undulation, wave upon wave of women.... The main courtyard seethed with sounds, smells, tastes, a gigantic basket filled to overflowing with bright yellow, ochre, pomegranate, cinnamon, purple, black' and so on.

97. Arr. *Anab.* 5.9.4.

98. Ibid. 5.8.5.

99. Bosworth 1988a, 126 n. 313, following Stein and Fuller.

100. Arr. *Anab.* 5.8.4.

The Battle on the Hydaspes

With incessant onslaughts the impetuous hero reaped the iron harvest of steely battle-lust; he fought with all, some on the banks, others down in the river, cutting them down with his warlike hand. The whole stream was filled with corpses. The white Hydaspes was incarnadined with the blood of staring cadavers.[101]

—NONNUS, *DIONYSIACA* 22.360–5 (DESCRIBING DIONYSUS' CAMPAIGN)

In dusk's red shimmer Jhilam's winding stream
Turned to dark in the dark, as a curved sword can seem
To hide away inside
Its scabbard. Night's high tide
After the ending of the ebb of day
Floated in on a dark water-way.

—RABINDRANATH TAGORE, 'GEESE IN FLIGHT'

The battle on the Hydaspes is more reliably described than any of Alexander's three other major battles.[102] Arrian's account is full, though not always easy to follow. Porus' army assembled on the east bank of the river, on the Karri plain.[103] Craterus with the heavy infantry was stationed at the major crossing point. Alexander was concerned to prevent the horses taking fright at the sight of the elephants as they plunged across the river, and accordingly he moved his cavalry about seventeen miles (27 km) upstream, opposite a wooded island (probably Admana), so that he could cross in concealment and surprise Porus from the north. Porus, anticipating this move, sent his brother Spitaces upstream to a point opposite. Fires burned in Alexander's camp all night to convey the impression that this was the main part of the force.

It rained heavily all night, but eased off around dawn, at which point Alexander embarked the horses on rafts to cross under cover of the island. Unfortunately they landed, not on the far bank, but on a second island, which occasioned some delay as it was hard to find the fords owing to the rain in the night, which had raised the water level. However, his forces made it across,

101. The word translated 'staring cadavers' is *mormurōn*: *mormuros* is a kind of fish noted for its fixed stare.

102. Arr. *Anab.* 5.10–17; Diod. 17.87–8 (brief); Bosworth 1988a, 126–9; Fuller 1960, 180–99.

103. Prakash 1964, 167. See maps in Majumdar 1960, 50–2.

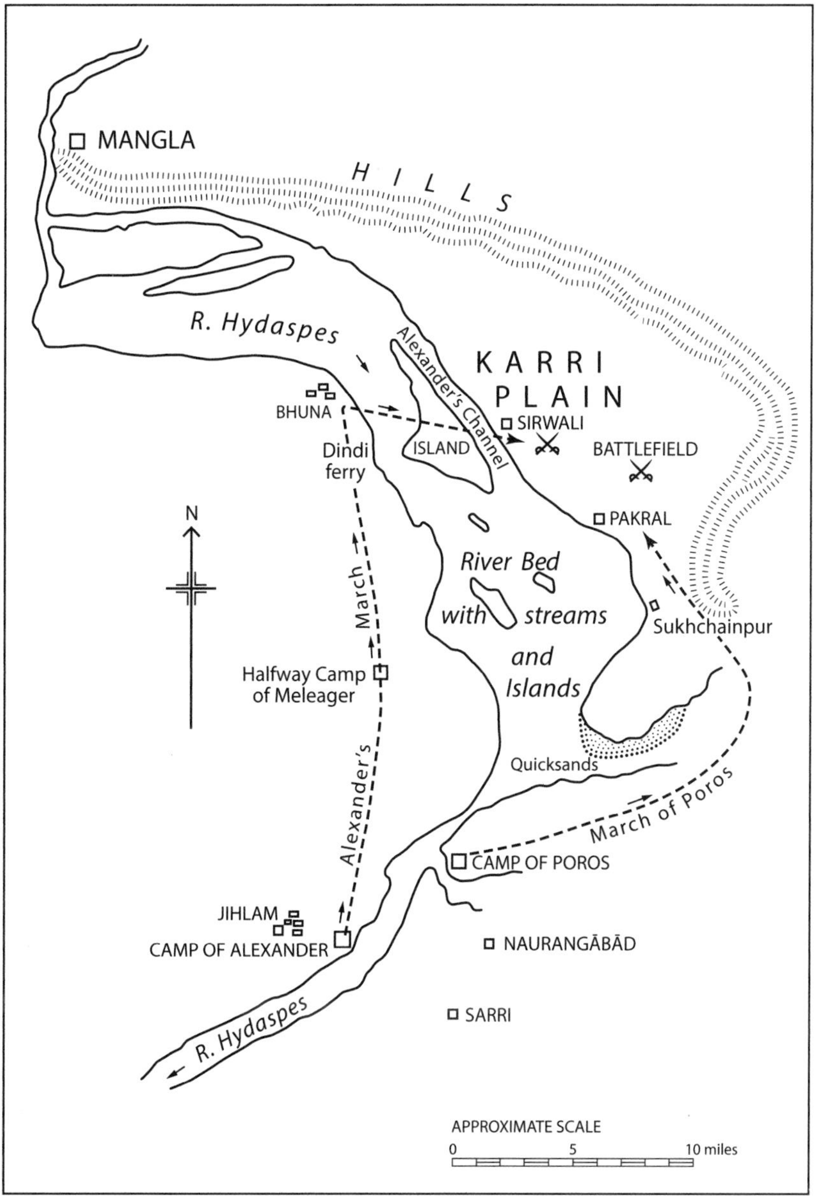

2.5 The battle field of the Hydaspes, BCE 326 (after R. C. Majumdar 1960).

since Porus' son, who had arrived with a force of chariots (either sixty or twice that number), overshot and failed to prevent them. Alexander's force then overwhelmed them and captured the chariots, but they were useless because of the deep mud. Bucephalas was apparently wounded in this fight.

Porus sought out a place by the river bank where there was sand rather than mud to draw up his elephants. Alexander commanded Craterus to keep his infantry static, while he swooped down with the cavalry. At the same time, another force under Coenus approached Porus' army from the south so that his cavalry 'had to face both ways' and he was caught in a pincer movement. Fuller calls this 'Porus' Dilemma'.[104]

Now that Porus' army was in confusion, a first wave of infantry crossed over and began to attack the elephants; javelins were used and most of the mahouts were shot down. Porus' infantry were crowded into a tight place, and the elephants began to back up 'like ships'. Craterus' forces also crossed (the exact order of events is somewhat unclear), and, as the Indians had already begun to retreat, pursued the fleeing and cut them down. (As so often, cavalry trumped elephants: the same happened when Babur's cavalry beat Rana Sangha's elephants in 1527.)[105] The Indians, according to Arrian, lost twenty-thousand foot soldiers and three thousand horsemen; all the chariots were broken to pieces; two sons of Porus died as well as his brother Spitaces, and all the surviving elephants were captured.[106] The greatest distress for Alexander was that his horse Bucephalas died, worn out, according to Arrian, by old age and not wounded by anyone.[107] Porus surrendered, and Alexander celebrated his victory with sacrifices and the foundation of two cities, Nicaea ('Victory'), and Bucephala, in memory of the horse. Presumably these two cities were on opposite banks: it is not known where.

Porus

The scene of Porus' surrender is one of the most famous moments in Alexander's career. As the towering Indian, at least six feet tall, was brought before the diminutive Alexander, the conqueror asked him how he expected to be

104. Arr. *Anab.* 5.16.3; the obscurity of Arrian's language is discussed in Brunt's note on the passage. Fuller 1960, 189.

105. Dale 2004, 350–1.

106. Arr. *Anab.* 5.18.2–3.

107. Ibid. 5.19.4.

I. Audran
A Messire Jules Hardouin Mansart, Conseiller du Roy en ses Conseils,
Chevalier de l'Ordre de S.t Michel, Comte de Sagonne, Sur-Intendant
et Ordonnateur general des Batimens, Jardins, Arts, et
Manufactures de sa Majesté
Par son humble et tres obeissant
Serviteur I. Audran.
VIRTUS TIMORIS NESCIA SORDIDI.
PORUS destitutus a pluribus tela in circumfusos ingerens,
multis éninus vulneratis Taxilis fratrem interemit. & hoc ultimo virtutis opere edito ipse novem vulneribus confossus ex Elephante dilabitur.

2.6 The battle with Porus (engraving by J. Audran after a painting by Charles Le Brun).

treated. 'Like a king', was the reply; and Alexander 'was pleased', and restored him to his kingdom under the suzerainty of Alexander, while extending his territory further than his present holdings. Porus remained loyal to Alexander's government until his murder in 317.

The encounter of the two kings became a defining moment of the Alexander story. It offered a structure and a moral; where the conspiracy of Philotas and his trial showed Alexander as a cruel tyrant, his generosity to Porus in restoring his kingdom was the mark of a benevolent despot. In addition, both episodes had the makings of a drama, as reactions in the seventeenth and eighteenth centuries show. Philotas became the theme of a political play by Samuel Daniel (1604),[108] while the Porus episode reappeared several times in French drama and Italian opera from 1648 onwards. The earliest treatment was Claude Boyer's *Porus, ou la générosité d'Alexandre*, soon to be eclipsed by Jean Racine's *Alexandre le Grand* (1687). In both of these a love interest is added to highlight the virtuous decision of Alexander.[109] While in Racine the virtuous king is intended to remind the reader or spectator of Louis XIV, the next reinvention of the story has a very different political bent. This is the libretto *Alessandro nell'Indie* by Pietro Metastasio (1729). This was dedicated by Metastasio's colleague Cavanna to 'James III of England', that is, the Old Pretender, currently living in Italy, and the implication was that George II might take the role of Alexander and forgive his adversary (or perhaps the other way around). In this version of the drama, Porus is in love with Cleofide; when she is prepared to leap into a burning pyre rather than see him defeated – introducing the titillating theme of sati into the drama – Alexander forgives Porus and restores him to his kingdom.[110] In all these rigmaroles the domi-

108. Stoneman 2013.

109. In Boyer, Alexander's general Perdiccas is in love with the captive daughter of Porus, while Porus' wife is in love with Alexander, and aims to save Porus by abandoning him for the conqueror. Porus plots against Alexander, but is forgiven, and Alexander restores him to power because he admires his virtue. Racine's plot is less involved but introduces Queen Cleofile, the sister of Taxiles, who persuades him to ally with Alexander. Cleofile, or Cleofide, now becomes a fixture in the plot; see next note.

110. This libretto was astonishingly successful, and was set to music by more than eighty composers following the first version of 1729 by Leonardo Vinci. They include two settings from 1731, by Porpora and by Handel (under the title *Poro*, using the same heavily adapted libretto as J. A. Hasse's *Cleofide* of 1730), as well as, to name only the better-known composers, Galuppi, Gluck, J. C. Bach, Paisiello, Cimarosa and Cherubini; nearly a hundred years later, it was set again by Pacini (1824). See Markstrom 2007, 287. In Handel's version, it is a fictional general of Alexander, Timagenes, who is in love with Porus' sister, who is in turn in love with

nant theme is of the clemency and generosity of the conqueror. This was a moment in the king's career when he could be celebrated as a 'good king'; one might then avert one's eyes from the history of slaughter that was soon to follow.

Porus has been deemed by some to be Alexander's greatest opponent, a more formidable king and warrior than Darius III. The territory he controlled was indeed much smaller, but his rise to power seems to have been rapid. Some parts of north-west India had been under Achaemenid control, counting as the twentieth satrapy according to Herodotus (3.94), who simply speaks of the 'Indians', the most numerous people of all.[111] But from the reign of Xerxes there is no evidence of Persian control further east than Bactria, and native dynasts move into the vacuum, Omphis in the case of Gandhara. Further to the south the Pauravas had begun to expand at the expense of Gandhara, so that Omphis was pleased to welcome Alexander as a possible ally against Porus and *his* ally Abisares.[112]

The Purus were an Aryan tribe of the migration into India;[113] in the words of Buddha Prakash,

> some remnants of them survived in the mountainous retreats of the North-West and emerged from there in the plains of the Panjab and set up a powerful state in the region between the Jhelum and the Chenab ... The *Bṛhatsaṁhitā* of Varāhamihira associates the Pauravas with the peoples of Takśaṣilā and Puṣkalāvati and locates them in the vicinity of the Mālavas and Madrakas. The *Mahābhārata* also refers to the city of the Pauravas, which was adjacent to the republics of the Utsavasaṅketas and the territory of Kaśmīra. The Purus were the leading tribe of the Parvatīya group, for, when Arjuna marched against the Pauravas, he encountered the stiff resistance of the Parvatīya warriors and, after defeating them in a battle, he proceeded towards the capital of that country, which was guarded by Paurava.[114]

Alexander. He plots with Porus against Alexander. In the end Alexander forgives Timagenes, and the conclusion is a celebration of the love of Porus and Cleofide.

111. See n. 3 above.

112. Prakash 1964, 152–64 is a stimulating account of events from an Indian perspective.

113. The *Ṛg Veda* however states that they dwelt on the banks of the Sarasvati, i.e., they had been there in hoary antiquity, since the Sarasvati dried up around 3000 BCE: *RV* 7.96.2; Danino 2010, 278. For the *RV* everything in India has been unchanged since the dawn of time!

114. Prakash 1964, 152–3. The *Mbh.* reference is 12.29.1; Prakash's reference to 11.27.14–17 seems to be erroneous.

Close to a thousand years later the Chinese pilgrim Xuanzang refers to Po-fa-to, that is, Parvata, as the designation of this country.[115] D. C. Sircar places Porus' dominion in the Pandya region west of Indraprastha (Delhi),[116] while a legend current in the seventeenth century made Porus the conqueror of Dilu, the legendary founder of Delhi.[117] So it is not impossible that Porus' influence stretched as far east as Delhi, which would have implications for Alexander's sources of information about that region. Porus also seems to have controlled the Cathaei, an intensely Vedic people.[118]

Alexander's alliance with Taxiles enabled him to send the latter as an envoy to Porus when he was defeated; but Porus saw this as an opportunity to settle scores with Taxiles and was about to run him through with his javelin when he retreated.[119] 'Even then Alexander did not show anger against Porus', but sent a series of envoys of whom the last, successful one was Meroes.[120] Bosworth, in his commentary on this passage, follows Berve in describing Meroes as an otherwise unknown Indian prince. It took the acuity of Buddha Prakash to make the intuitive leap that this man is the same as Candragupta Maurya, known as so often by the dynastic name rather than the personal one (like Taxiles, and, for that matter, Porus).[121] Plutarch tells us that Candragupta (whom he, or his manuscripts, call Androcottus instead of the usual Greek Sandrocottus) met Alexander when he was very young.[122] Since several sources inform us that Candragupta studied in Taxila under the tutelage of Canakya, there is a neat correspondence here.[123] It may be that Candragupta, and Canakya, were already engaged in the negotiations with Porus for an alliance against the Nandas that are referred to in Hemacandra.[124]

115. Beal 1884, 2.275.

116. Sircar 1947/1971, 101.

117. Singh (ed.) 2006, 88.

118. Prakash 1964, 160.

119. Arr. *Anab.* 5.18.6.

120. Ibid. 5.18.7–19.1.

121. Prakash 1964, 172. See also Schwarz 1968, 225; Karttunen 1997, 259–60 rejects the identification. Meroes is no. 518 in Berve.

122. Plu. *Alex.* 6.2.4, 9.

123. *Mahāvaṁsa Tika*: Mookerji 1966, 22. *Vaṁsatthapakāsini*: Prakash 1964, 171.

124. Hemacandra 1998, 8.298–312 (Parvataka). This also forms one of the themes of the later play about Candragupta's rise to power, the *The Rakśasa's Ring*. See further ch. 5 below. Allen (2012, 50) thinks that Candragupta is the same as Sisicottus, a deserter from Bessus whom Alexander made commander of Aornos, but the names do not seem to be the same and the identification is not convincing.

It was not just baroque and classical dramatists who were struck by the possibilities of the encounter of the two kings. Greek writers, too, soon began to turn the moment into legend. The *Alexander Romance* has Porus refusing Darius' desperate request for help and sending an extremely rude letter to Alexander on his approach.[125] The crisis gives Alexander the opportunity to employ two stratagems in quick succession: first, he visits Porus' camp in disguise, and secondly he finds a way to combat the elephants by fashioning a number of metal statues which can be made red-hot so that the elephants burn their trunks and turn tail. This story reappears in Ferdowsi's *Shahnameh*, when Iskandar defeats the elephants of Foor by having a wax model of an elephant made; after pondering its weak points for some time, he creates a number of iron horses, which can be filled with oil and then made to burst into flames at the moment of attack. In both these accounts, a duel to the death ensues, and Porus is killed. More soberly, Philostratus in his *Life of Apollonius* has his hero observe at Taxila a series of bronze panels depicting the deeds of Alexander and Porus, who have become friends and gone on to have adventures together.[126]

While none of these accounts resembles history, they are demonstrations of the power that Alexander's conquest of an Indian king held over western minds. In India, however, he is scarcely noticed.

Alexander now begins to move into what the *Romance* calls Prasiake, Sanskrit *Pracyaka*, the eastern region.[127] First he crosses the river Acesines (Chenab), while sending part of his army back to quell a revolt of the Assaceni. Here Arrian (following Ptolemy) is very explicit about the method of crossing: light-armed soldiers crossed on floating hides, with little difficulty, while those using boats were wrecked by the swift current, even though Alexander had chosen to cross where it was widest and the current therefore slowest.[128] Now he set off in pursuit of another ruler called Porus, 'the bad Porus', presumably the leader of a breakaway group of the Purus/Pauravas. (Prakash suggests that he was a junior king to the Elder Porus, and that his territory was

125. *AR* 2.12, 3.1–4. A similar letter is in the *Metz Epitome* (56–7), which also depicts Porus' moment of indecisiveness, when he thinks of flight, perhaps the moment of Meroes' intervention.

126. Philostr. *VA* 2.20–1. This is much expanded in the *Alexander Romance*: Stoneman 2008, 76.

127. *AR* 3.17. Sharma 1968, 136; there is an ethnological table in the *Aitareya Br.* 8.14.

128. Arr. *Anab.* 5.20.8–10.

between the Chenab and the Ravi.)[129] According to Diodorus, he retreated to the land of the Gandaridae.[130] The location of this people is a puzzle, as their location does not suit the obvious identification with Gandhara. Bosworth takes them as a people of the Ganges valley, dwelling beyond the Ganges,[131] who also turn up under the name of Gangaridae.[132] The late antique world map, the *Tabula Peutingeriana*, shows the Gandari Indi extending along much of the Middle Ganges on its left bank,[133] but Strabo puts the country of Gandaris in the eastern Punjab.[134] These two indications are contradictory. The picture is further confused by the datum that the city of Caspapyrus was a polis Gandarike.[135] Caspapyrus is often stated to be Peshawar, but Panchenko has shown that this identification is untenable.[136] He opts for a location perhaps at Hastinapura, which has the merit of having a vaguely similar name. Hastinapura is on the Upper Ganges, north of Delhi, and would thus be a reachable destination for the fleeing Porus. But if I am right in my surmise that Caspapyrus is Keśvapura, a communication hub from the sixth century BCE, this is further south, at Mathura on the Yamuna. It is possible that the Gandaridae later migrated further eastwards to the Middle Ganges, but the topographical distortions of the *Tabula Peutingeriana* makes its use for detailed topography questionable. I imagine Porus II falling back on the upper reaches of the Yamuna, either at Mathura or possibly at Hastinapura. Both destinations are a long way from the starting point, but not as far as the Middle Ganges.

Arrian's topographical indications now become extremely hard to accept.[137] He states that Alexander's pursuit brought him as far as the Hydraotes (Ravi), from whence he continued his advance against the Cathaei of Sangala. There are two possible candidates for this Sangala: the place now known as Sangala

129. Prakash 1964, 154.

130. Diod. 17.91.1.

131. Bosworth 1980–, 2.325; Romm 2012, 223 equates them with the Nandas.

132. Curt. 9.2.3.

133. In the atlas of Habib and Habib 2012, map 7, they are located around the mouths of the Ganges.

134. Str. 15.1.30. Panchenko 1998, 233; Habib and Habib 2012, map 5.

135. Hecat.Abd. F 295.

136. See ch. 1 above.

137. For another instance of topographical puzzlement in Arrian, see Hamilton 1994, on the two arms of the Indus estuary.

Hill,[138] almost due west of Lahore, which itself lies on the Ravi, or Sialkot, ancient Sagala, due north of Lahore and situated between the Chenab and the Ravi.[139] Neither destination is to be reached by a traveller from the west crossing the Ravi! Presumably Arrian means the Acesines. This is the location given for the Cathaei by Onesicritus.[140] Arrian sneers at Onesicritus for his claim to be an admiral when he was a steersman,[141] but here Onesicritus is right and Arrian has presumably misunderstood his source, or misread his map.

On the way to the stronghold of the Cathaei Alexander received the submission of a people called the Adraistae,[142] whose city he reached in two days march from what Arrian calls the Hydraotes. Their city was called Pimprama, but it is unidentifiable.

After a day of rest the army advanced on Sangala. The Cathaei were another group of 'autonomous' Indians: a *gaṇa-sangha*. The Indian name of this people is unrecoverable, though they have been tentatively identified with the Katthis of Kathiawar.[143] It was among them that the Greeks first observed the custom of widow-burning, or sati.[144] The Cathaei surrounded their sheer hill with a circle of wagons, but Alexander constructed a stockade around the city; when the defenders attempted to flee through a gap that had been deliberately left, Ptolemy and his troops cut them down.[145] Porus now arrived with a force of elephants and five thousand troops, while siege engines were brought up against the walls. The Macedonians stormed the city and in the course of the sack seventeen thousand Indians were killed. This terrified the neighbouring peoples into submission.[146]

It was after this, according to Arrian, that the army advanced to the Hyphasis but began to lose heart. However, Strabo and Diodorus place the encounter with the kingdom of Sopeithes immediately following the Cathaean

138. I take this to be the same as Prakash's (160) 'Sanglawala Tiba in the Jhang district', referred to in Pāṇini (4.2.75) as Sankālidi. Cf. 8.3.91 on the Kaṭhas of Kapisṭhala, presumably the Kambistholoi of Megasth. F 20.8 Schw: Agrawala 1953, 324.

139. Law 1954, 29–30 suggests that the place is near Fathgarh, but I have not been able to discover this latter town on any map.

140. Str. 15.1.30; Arora 2005, 80.

141. Arr. *Anab.* 6.2.3.

142. Ibid. 5.22.3; Diod. 17.91.2.

143. Karttunen 1997, 31 n. 60; he also hazards the Vedic school of Kathakas.

144. Diod. 17.91.3–4; Str. 15.1.30, citing Onesicritus (134 F 21).

145. Arr. *Anab.* 5.22.4–24.3.

146. Ibid. 5.24.4–5.

campaign.[147] 'Some put both Cathaea and the country of Sopeithes, one of the nomarchs, between these two rivers, but others on the far side of the Acesines and the Hyarotis [i.e., Hydraotes], as bordering on the country of the second Porus'.[148] Sopeithes (perhaps Skt. *Saubhuti or *Subhuti) ruled in the region of the Salt Range.[149] The Salt Range is actually on the right bank (west) of the Hydaspes, which should by Arrian's topography, but also by Diodorus', be behind Alexander by now.[150] It seems more likely that Sopeithes is one of the rulers 'terrified into submission' by the Sangala brutalities.

Diodorus enthuses about Sopeithes' kingdom, which he regards as extremely well governed. The people value physical excellence and destroy any children seen as inadequate, and marriages are contracted on the basis of physical beauty alone. The account seems to come from Onesicritus and is presumably one of his collection of 'ideal' states gathered by observation on the journey.[151] The magnificent Sopeithes himself welcomed Alexander and his submission ensured that he retained his kingdom. Perhaps he had realised that Alexander would not be staying long and a gesture of friendliness would pay dividends and entail no permanent subjection. Fourteen years later, it seems, this king was still on the throne and issuing coins, using the form of his name 'Sophytes'. The coins depict the king's imposing profile of a long, massive nose with a bulging bridge, and a jutting chin, wearing a helmet resembling that on the coins of Seleucus; the reverse shows a cock and a caduceus.[152] If this is a portrait, it may be the first royal portrait on a Hellenistic coin. Scholarly opinions have differed about the nature of this portrait. Jansari holds, rightly, that it is impossible to identify racial characteristics in such

147. Bosworth 1995, 336–7 remarks that Arrian is not interested in, or very selective regarding, events between Sangala and the Hyphasis.

148. Str. 15.1.30; Diod 17.91.4 puts the Sopeithes campaign immediately after the Cathaei.

149. Habib and Jha 2004, 9.

150. Arr. *Anab.* 6.2.2. Bosworth 1988a omits Sopeithes from his narrative altogether. Brunt, app. 17.20 regards the confusion as insoluble.

151. Str. 15.1.30; Arora 2005, 86–7.

152. Habib and Jha 2004, 17. Mørkholm 1991, 73 places him in Afghanistan. (See also his illusration no. 148.) I have been privileged to read Sushma Jansari's discussion of Sophytes and his coinage in her as yet unpublished PhD thesis (UCL 2016), in which she argues for the identity of Sopeithes and Sophytes, and discusses the problems of the coinage exhaustively. Why the cock? Is the man's face a portrait of the king? Is it the model for Seleucus' coins? Jansari surmises that the coinage began after Eudamus' murder of Porus in 315, and was produced in order to pay Greek mercenaries in the resistance against Peithon, or Seleucus, or even Candragupta. On Sopeithes, see also Bopearachchi and Flandrin 2005, 195–202.

a portrait. Narain thought the man's features quite un-Indian and supposed that he was a Persian satrap who had, presumably, broken free of Persian control, and that he was therefore an Iranian. Mørkholm regards him as a dynast of the early third century; this leaves the question of the identity with Sopeithes open. To me, for what it is worth, the features *do* look Indian: the name is not Greek, but it is hard to find a convincing Sanskrit equivalent. Cunningham's colourful argument that it means something like 'morning light' and that the cock and caduceus are therefore a kind of rebus for 'herald of the dawn' is quite fantastical.

Whoever Sopeithes was, he gave Alexander a friendly welcome and presented him with 150 magnificent dogs. (Perhaps they were easier to look after than the elephants, but the Macedonian army must have looked a bit like a travelling menagerie by now.)

The next people along, the kingdom of Phegeus or Phegelas, also gave Alexander a friendly welcome.[153] He was probably the ruler of a place called Phagwara, which is a few miles east of Jalandar.[154] If so, Alexander had now crossed the Beas. Phegeus also gave him information about the lands beyond the Indus, twelve days of desert before reaching the Ganges, where the predominant inhabitants were the Tabraesioi and the Gandaridai. The latter were ruled by Xandrames.[155] The information was confirmed by Porus, who was evidently travelling with Alexander's army. Alexander perhaps also sent out a scouting party, since Craterus sent a letter home to his mother telling her that he had reached the Ganges.[156] But Alexander himself did not see it.

The Turning Back

Was it
Fear of the mountains rising red from the plain,
Fear of the unknown tribes on the other side?

153. Diod. 17.93.12; Curt. 9.2.3–7 (calling him Phegelas). Phegeus is omitted by Arrian. His name may be Bhagala, according to Nilakanta Sastri 1967, 67.

154. Prakash 1964, 164 gives the name Bhagawara, and says it is a railway junction between Amritsar and Jalandar; but on my map it is east of Jalandar. Kipling seems to have known a legend that Alexander came to Jalandar: see Kipling 1987, 33.

155. For the continuation of this story, see ch. 5 below. Kienast 1965 and Romm 2008 think it uncertain that Alexander knew of the Ganges and the Nandas, but there is no reason to doubt Diodorus' report. On the location of the Gandaridae/Gangaridae, see Sircar 1947/1971.

156. *FGrH* 153 F 2 = Str. 15.1.35.

> No,
> However the legends go, or the histories patch it together,
> The place was not ready. Over the other side . . .
> was a possible paradise,
> Untouched, immaculate, the dreamt of place. . . .
> Then they turned back.
>
> —ANTHONY THWAITE, 'AT THE INDUS'[157]

The army now continued towards the Hyphasis, which was to be the turning point of the expedition. The soldiers were 'exhausted with their constant campaigns' and a spirit of mutiny began to infiltrate the troops. 'There had been many losses among the soldiers, and no relief from fighting was in sight. The hooves of the horses had been worn thin by steady marching. The arms and armour were wearing out, and Greek clothing was quite gone. They had to clothe themselves in foreign garments, recutting the garments of the Indians.'[158] In addition to this, the monsoon had begun two months before, at the time of the battle on the Hydaspes, and there had been heavy rain and thunderstorms for the past seventy days.

> Thousand-eyed Indra satisfied the earth with water and ripened the crops . . . Passing before mountains and trees with a deep, pleasing sound, the clouds released their water . . . Water-bearing clouds dark as blue-lotus petals darkened the ten directions.[159]

The deep sound was less pleasing to the Macedonians than to Rāma and Lakṣmaṇa. A modern writer evokes a commoner reaction. 'All through the months, the rains poured, waters running, rushing, and stagnating in pools . . . The sky was perpetually overcast. Winds blew cold and damp and drenched one's surroundings and person. For a few days, the change of season was fascinating, but, in course of time, the persistent gloom and wetness proved depressing.'[160] Eighteen centuries later, Babur found that weapons became unusable in the monsoon: bows could not be drawn, and broke because of the damp.[161]

157. *Selected Poems 1956–1996* (2000).

158. Diod. 17.94.1; cf. Arr. *Anab*. 5.25.2.

159. *Rām. [= Rāmāyaṇa] 4 (Kiṣkindhākāṇḍa)* 22–4.

160. R. K. Narayan (1972, 117) is describing the monsoon that confines Rāma to quarters in the *Rāmāyaṇa*, but the description is apposite here.

161. Dale 2004, 365–6.

Alexander had to revive his men's spirits if he was to persuade them to continue. He was simply excited by the prospect of taking on the army of the Ganges peoples, because 'the land beyond the Hyphasis was fertile, and the inhabitants good farmers and excellent fighting men, with their affairs under orderly government'.[162] (This contradicts Phegeus' statement about the twelve days of desert: perhaps Craterus had come back with better information about the conditions in Haryana, which is by no means desert, unlike Rajasthan to the south.) Some Indian historians have seen the great power of the Prasii as the main reason for Alexander's retreat, deriving support in this from Diodorus' comment that Alexander did not campaign against the Gandaridae because of the number of their elephants.[163] Jawaharlal Nehru dismissed Alexander's expedition as 'a minor and unsuccessful raid across the border',[164] while A. K. Narain summed it up in the epigram 'They Came, They Saw, but India Conquered'. India, said Nehru, does not 'bow low before the blast', but assimilates.[165] We shall see how true this is: Alexander's military impact, though ferocious and brutal, was short-lived, but Greek culture had a more subtle impact in the centuries that followed.

Arrian gives Alexander a great set-piece speech to the brigade commanders in which he attempts to revive the flagging spirits of his men.[166] As Curtius expresses it, 'he and his soldiers saw things differently: while his thought encompassed world-wide empire and his programme was still in its initial stages, the men were exhausted by the hardships of the campaign and wished only to enjoy what profits from it lay closest to hand, now that the danger was finally past'.[167] The speech is too long to quote in full, but Alexander begins by insisting that it is not far from here to the river Ganges – which is true, for if he had made it from Taxila to the Indus in two days, he could make it from the Sutlej to the spring of the Ganges at Haridwar in another four. He certainly knew about the Ganges, and Craterus in a letter to his mother even told her

162. Arr. *Anab.* 5.25.1.

163. Diod. 18.6.1; Majumdar 1960, 52.

164. Nehru 2004, 115.

165. Ibid., 144.

166. Arr. *Anab.* 5.25.3–26.8.

167. Curt. 9.2.11. Cf. Diod. 17.94, where Alexander simply recognises the troops' desire to return, and allows them to plunder freely as a reward for having come so far. Kienast 1965 thinks the speech is probably an invention by Arrian, which is no doubt true of the detail; but Diodorus (17.94.5) also refers to a 'carefully prepared speech', which cut no ice with the troops.

that they had reached it.[168] Presumably a scouting party, perhaps including Alexander, had gone that far, though they may have been unaware quite how long the Ganges was or how difficult it would be to descend in boats.[169]

A visit of this kind might explain the legend alluded to by Kipling: '"the last of the Great Ones [to come to the northern Punjab]", said the Sikh with authority, "was Sikander Julkarn (Alexander the Great). He paved the streets of Jullundur and built a great tank near Umballa. That pavement holds to this day; and the tank is there also".'[170] Even if Alexander did have a look at the headwaters of the Ganges, he hardly had to time to build anything at Jalandhar or Ambala, both of which lie on the direct route to Haridwar. The advance to the Hyphasis and the mutiny took place in high summer, and by November the army was back at the Indus beginning its descent to the ocean.

After the Ganges, Alexander recited from his geography book, they would reach the eastern sea, which would turn out to be continuous with the Hyrcanian [Caspian] Sea, the Indian Gulf (Arabian Sea) and the Persian Gulf, so the fleet would sail thence round Libya to the Pillars of Hercules and bring all of Europe and the west under Macedonian control. Turning back, he insisted, would leave too many hostile peoples beyond the Hyphasis and from the Hyrcanian Sea to the north. This account replicated the common view of the geography of the world that had prevailed since Hecataeus, but it was only in times much closer to Arrian's own that Roman traders had proved the feasibility of the voyage from the Red Sea to the eastern coast of India at Arikamedu.

The men and, more importantly, the officers were unmoved. Coenus responded to Alexander's speech point by point.[171] Alexander attempted to change their minds, and even retired to his tent for a three-day sulk; but when he offered sacrifices with a view to crossing the Hyphasis, they turned out un-

168. *FGrH* 153 F 2 = Str. 15.1.35. Bosworth 1996a, 186–200, is puzzled by Arrian's 'strange silence' about the Ganges, except in *Anab.* 5.25.1; but why should he say more? He apparently knew of the Nanda country, but while the Vulgate calls this a kingdom (which it was), for Arrian it is an oligarchy (194, 198). But there was more than one people beyond the Hyphasis, and indeed beyond the Ganges, and the two traditions may be making different selections. See also Hornblower 1981, 80–7.

169. Cf. Newby, *Slowly down the Ganges* (London: Hodder & Stoughton, 1966), on the tribulations of trying to get a small boat over the many series of rapids in the Upper Ganges.

170. Kipling 1987, 33. See also Kipling 1919, 55.

171. Arr. *Anab.* 5.27.1–9.

favourable and so he proclaimed to the army that they would be turning back. He erected twelve altars on the west bank of Hyphasis 'as thank-offerings to the gods who had brought him so far as a conqueror, and as memorials of his own exertions'.[172] These altars, which few from the west can ever have seen in subsequent centuries, became a fixed datum of Asian geography for two millennia: the *Tabula Peutingeriana* shows them to the east of the Caspian Sea, well to the north of the continuous chain of mountains that comprises the Taurus, Caucasus and Himalayas. The Hereford *Mappa Mundi*, with its equally non-naturalistic geography, places them just to the west of the river Pasma(?) which joins the Hypanis to flow into the eastern ocean; just over the river, an angel with a flaming sword guards the gates of Eden while giving Adam and Eve a firm push into the land of the giants who occupy the land opposite the altars. The altars are also described in the other ancient sources: Diodorus has them dedicated to 'the twelve gods', a natural extrapolation from the information that there were twelve of them. Plutarch just says 'the gods', while Justin just says 'altars'. Strabo says that Alexander set up altars in imitation of his predecessors Heracles, Dionysus, Cyrus and Semiramis.[173] According to Philostratus, his hero Apollonius visited them and saw that they were dedicated to Ammon, Heracles, Athena Pronoia, Zeus, the Cabiri of Samothrace, the Indus, Helios and Apollo.[174] This strange collection – which does not add up to twelve – is a little difficult to explain, though the inclusion of the rare cult of Athena Pronoia may echo the importance of Pronoia as a goddess in the *Alexander Romance*, with which Philostratus seems to have been familiar.

The retreat from the Hyphasis begins in Arrian with the death of Coenus from disease.[175] No doubt he was already sickening when he made his impassioned speech to Alexander arguing for a halt to the expedition, so it may have been some satisfaction to have won his point even though he did not live to enjoy the return. Alexander embarked on the Hydaspes on the boats that were already waiting there from the previous crossing, while Craterus led a division down the right bank and Hephaestion advanced down the left bank to the kingdom of Sopeithes. The cavalry from Nysa were sent home.

172. Ibid. 5.29.1. Curt. 9.3.19 also has twelve altars. Plin. *NH* 6.62 implausibly places the altars on the east bank. See Brunt, app. 16.5.

173. Diod. 17.95; Plu. *Alex.* 62; Justin 12.10.6; Str. 3.5.5.

174. Cf. the dedication of the altars on the Danube, including one for the god of the river, Istros: Arr. *Anab.* 1.4.5.

175. Ibid. 6.2.1.

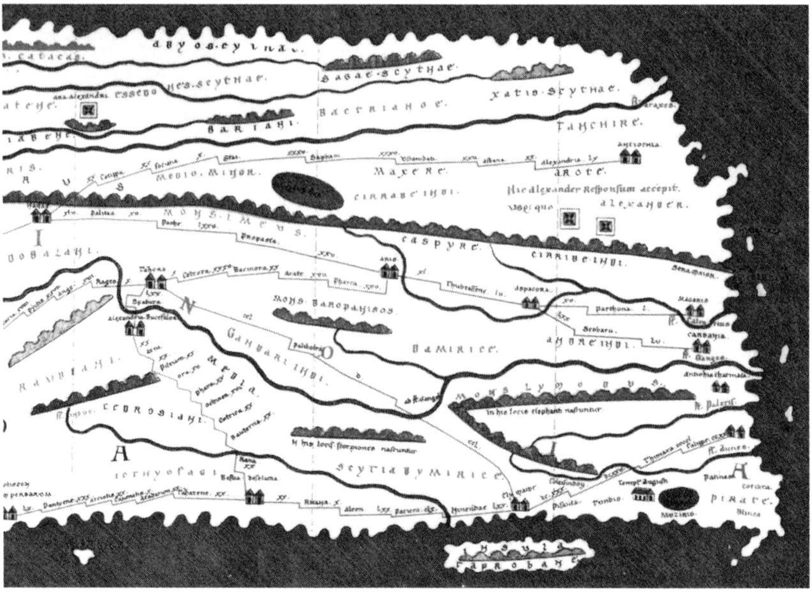

2.7 Eastern section of the *Tabula Peutingeriana,* a late antique map of the Roman empire. It shows India and the East in very elongated form, perhaps more like an itinerary than a topographical map.

The Voyage down the Indus

Straight in her course, mottled, glistening, in her greatness she holds encircled the expanses, the dusky realms –
The undeceivable Sindhu, busiest of the busy, dappled-bright like a mare, lovely to see like a beautiful woman
Sindhu has yoked her own well-naved, horsed chariot; with it she will gain the prize in this contest here,
For the great greatness of it invites admiration – it undeceivable, self-glorious, conferring abundance.

—*ṚG VEDA* 10.75.7–9

Alexander was looking forward to the voyage down the Indus, since, in one of the rare revelations about his intellectual interests in Arrian, he had formed the view that on reaching the Indus he had discovered the source of the Nile, since there were crocodiles in both, as well as lotuses (Egyptian beans). He even wrote to his mother about it but cancelled that part of the letter when the local Indians gave him more accurate information about the course of the rivers in the Punjab; by this time he knew that he could expect to sail, not into the Nile, but into the encircling ocean.[176] Though the evidence is slight, it is clear that there had been contact between the coast of Sind and the west, including Egypt, on the one hand, and the interior on the other hand, before Alexander.[177]

Nearchus was admiral of the fleet, while Onesicritus was steersman (κυβερνήτης) of Alexander's ship, though Arrian castigated him for claiming that he was its captain.[178] The term 'skipper', of course, would cover both, and Arrian may be being churlish. The fleet consisted of eighty triaconters, and many *kerkouroi* or skiffs. Particularly startling to the Indians were the horse transports, since, as Arrian observed, the Indians had quite forgotten that Dionysus had made his expedition against India with a fleet. (If they had really never seen horses on ships before, this may be a permanent legacy that the Greeks brought to India, since in the nineteenth century horse transports regularly plied the Indus, as is clear from many illustrations.)[179] The total number of vessels was around two thousand. Though many of the ships were built for the purpose, the army must surely have commandeered a good many local vessels and boatmen as well.

Arrian vividly describes the embarkation of the fleet, with the ships all keeping in tight formation. The banks of the river were often higher than the ships, and the noise of the oars splashing and the boatswains shouting reverberated around the gorges. The local people came running down to the shore 'singing barbarian incantations. For none have more love of song and dance than the Indians, ever since the days of Dionysus and of those who shared his revels in India'.[180]

The rain had finally ceased by this time. Aristobulus recorded the timings precisely. It had stopped raining when Arcturus rose, the voyage down the Hydaspes began a few days before the setting of the Pleiades, and during the voyage to the sea they saw no more rain, arriving about the time of the rising of the Dog Star.[181] The astronomical indications mean that the voyage lasted from approximately November 326 to July 325 BCE. Strabo calls this ten months,

176. Arr. *Anab.* 6.1.4–6.
177. Lahiri 1992, 396–7.
178. Arr. *Anab.* 6.2.3.
179. Dewey 2014, plates 53 and 54.
180. Arr. *Anab.* 6.3.3–5.
181. Str. 15.1.17.

but it is somewhat less than that even by inclusive reckoning. Plutarch says it took seven months.[182]

It took the fleet five days to reach the junction of the Hydaspes and the Acesines, which Alexander had been assured was 'not far away'. If they were at Sangala, this means they took five days to cover barely sixty miles (ca. 100 km), but if they were at Sialkot the distance would be more like two hundred miles (ca. 300 km). Progress was evidently slow.

Diodorus places a visit to the Sibi at this point;[183] Alexander got a good reception and gained the impression that these people were descendants of the army of Heracles that had attempted to besiege Aornos. But the next people was less hospitable. The Agalasseis had drawn up forty thousand infantry and three thousand cavalry against them. Alexander massacred most of them, enslaved the remainder, and pursued a rearguard into a large city which he set on fire, burning most of the occupants alive.

This hostile reception from the Agalasseis (who, like the Sibi, are not mentioned by Arrian), and the savagery it inspired in Alexander, seems to be the beginning of the descent of what should have been a steady voyage home into a reign of terror. It is hard to understand why Alexander felt it necessary to turn this voyage into a series of massacres: the need to raid the countryside for food must be part of the reason, and the army had to go further from the river as the countryside along the Indus became more arid, turning to desert on the east side below the Salt Range, while the western side was mountainous.[184] Aitken calls the Indus near Leh 'an emerald aberration in the folds of unending khaki'.)[185] But this hardly explains the ferocity. Bosworth, in a chapter entitled 'The Justification of Terror',[186] pointed out that the Malli, whom Alexander went hundreds of miles out of his way to attack (see below), had shown no indication of wishing to do so themselves. His conclusion is that their crime was not to have sent emissaries to greet him respectfully with signs of 'submission'. The victims became culprits, and, like Cortes, Alexander punished all those who showed signs of non-compliance.[187] The policy of

182. Plu. *Alex.* 661. See Hamilton 1969 ad loc., 161–2.

183. Diod. 17.96.1–2: the Śiva of Śivapura, near Shorkot (Patañjali 4.2.2).

184. Engels 1978, 107–8.

185. Aitken 1992, 191.

186. Bosworth 1996a, 133–65.

187. Vasco da Gama's comparable savagery in India – he burned a ship full of Arab traders, which included women and children – is more easily explained, since his aim was to eliminate trading competition from the Arabs. Subrahmanyam 1998.

terror is perhaps a sign of increasing megalomania in the king, and increasing frustration and desperation among the troops who had to fight their way out of a very large corner to get home: slaughter was a way to keep them motivated. By this time, to be sure, there was no sense in which this was a voyage of discovery or research. However, Onesicritus did manage to keep his eyes open, and Nearchus' account of the voyage through the Arabian Sea that followed the Indus voyage is invaluable.

At the junction of the Hydaspes and the Acesines the river conditions were formidable. Whirlpools in the narrows threatened to swamp the ships. Diodorus misplaces this crisis at the confluence of these two rivers with the Indus, and adds a dramatic story about Alexander having to swim ashore to escape his sinking ship, and then sacrificing to celebrate his success in, like Achilles, fighting a battle with a river.[188] But presently the river broadened out and Alexander brought the fleet to shore on the right bank.

Alexander's next target was the Malli people. According to Diodorus, they were waiting for him with a huge army of eighty thousand infantry, ten thousand cavalry and seven thousand chariots. But if we read Arrian aright, he had to go a long way to find this hostile army. He sent Nearchus ahead to the borders of their territory to prevent their neighbours coming to assist them, while he himself led the army eastwards through the desert. In a day and a night the army covered five hundred stades, or an astonishing fifty-six miles (90 km), to reach a city where the Malli had taken refuge. Actually the total distance as the crow flies from the junction of the two rivers to the Ravi is about sixty miles (97 km), so Arrian may have included the next night's march as well in the distance. The army broke through the defences of this town, slaughtered some two thousand people, and paused for dinner, while Perdiccas ran down the fugitives and massacred them. Marching again through the night, the army now reached the Hydraotes (in the right geographical position this time), and crossed it to reach the Malli town.[189] Here a fierce battle was followed by a brutal siege, in which the king himself scaled the walls with a ladder and found himself surrounded by angry defenders. The ladder broke under the weight of hypaspists coming to assist him, and he was left alone with a few companions in the midst of the enemy. He received a dangerous wound in the chest, from which, according to Ptolemy, both blood and breath spurted out. Peucestas stood over him and protected him until he could be got away.

188. Arr. *Anab.* 6.5.1; Diod. 17.97.1.

189. Arr. *Anab.* 6.8.4. Sircar 1947/1971, 42 identifies this with Malwa, which I cannot find.

Cleitarchus attributed this feat to Ptolemy, but Ptolemy himself denied it.[190] The wound sounds like a punctured lung, if Ptolemy's report is to be credited, but it is not clear that he was present at the crucial moment. It was without doubt severe and dangerous, and Alexander lay in a critical condition for many days, a condition which perhaps permanently weakened his constitution and contributed to his early death.

Arrian writes grumpily that 'many stories have been written by the historians about the misfortune, and tradition has received them as the first falsifiers told them, and still keeps them alive to this day, nor indeed will it ever cease handing on the falsehoods to others in turn, unless it is checked by this history'.[191] Unfortunately, as we have already seen, Arrian did not achieve a monopoly of accuracy in his account of this campaign so distant in place and time.

One of his complaints is that other historians placed this crisis among a different people, the Oxydracae (Kṣudrakas): this is certainly the case in Diodorus and Curtius.[192] Malavas and Kṣudrakas are mentioned in the same breath in the *Mahābhārata,* and seem to have been closely associated.[193] The Kṣudrakas' 'nomarchs' came in person to greet Alexander, offering gifts and submission, and thus were spared massacre. They diplomatically announced that their freedom dated back to the arrival of Dionysus in India, but that 'since the story prevailed that Alexander too was born to a god, they would accept a satrap whom Alexander might appoint'.[194] By this they probably denoted the arrival of the Aryans in India: see chapter 7 below for a discussion of the ancient history of India as reported by Megasthenes. Alexander duly appointed Philip.

Alexander's convalescence occasioned a delay of some time, during which many new ships were constructed. According to Diodorus, his recovery was celebrated with a great banquet marked by the curious incident of the combat of the Herculean Greek swordsman Dioxippus with a Macedonian of similar physique named Coragus.[195] This will be discussed in more detail in chapter 3.

Alexander was now able to sail on to the confluence with the Indus. Here he was joined by Perdiccas and the land army, who had stopped off to subdue

190. Arr. *Anab.* 6.11.8.

191. Ibid. 6.11.2.

192. Diod. 17.98.1; Curt. 9.2.26ff.

193. The Śudrakas (Hydracae) had supplied troops to Cyrus: Megasthenes F 46.6 Schw; Prakash 1964, 145; so Alexander was still within the erstwhile Achaemenid domains.

194. Arr. *Anab.* 6.14.2.

195. Diod. 17.100–1.

a tribe called the Abastanoi (Aṁbaṣṭha).[196] He now received the submission of two peoples called the Sodrae (Śūdra, the Zydri of Ptolemy: perhaps a surviving Dāsa tribe) and Massani (Ptolemy's Musarni?), 'who lived on either side of the river' (Diodorus), and the Ossadioi (Arrian: Vasātis), as well as a further supply of ships built by the Xathri (Kṣatriyas) and Sogdi.[197] One suspects that some of these people (particularly the Sogdi/Sodrae) may be the same under different names.[198] He built a city here and named it Alexandria: it is probably Uch. It may be the city referred to as 'Alexandria of the Yonas' in the *Mahāvaṁsa*.[199]

He moved his army and elephants to the left bank of the river, where the going was easier and the tribes less hostile, while he himself sailed on to the royal city of the Sogdians (unidentified), and appointed Peithon satrap of the region from the junction of the Indus and Acesines as far as the sea.[200]

The next stage of the voyage passed smoothly and quickly, and by the time he reached the kingdom of Musicanus the king had only just learned that he was coming.[201] Having no time to prepare an army, he received Alexander with gifts and submission, which he accepted graciously; nonetheless he stationed a garrison in the city. However, Musicanus later revolted in conjunction with the Brahmanes (see below); he was crushed by Peithon, his cities were razed, and he himself was hanged. Despite the obvious hostility between the invaders and the people of Musicanus, Onesicritus wrote an admiring account of their society, which is one of the earliest documents of the utopian idealisation of India (see chapter 9 below).

The next ruler, called Oxicanus by Arrian and Porticanus by Diodorus, was ordered to surrender. Alexander took away his elephants, and the neighbouring cities surrendered.

Next came Sambus, the self-appointed satrap of the hill men. Arrian implies a peaceable surrender, but Diodorus says that Alexander destroyed their

196. Law 1954, 61; they are in Patañjali: Shastri 1996, 67; associated with Śibis, Mālavas and Kṣudrakas, among many others (including bringers of gold excavated by ants), at *Mbh.* 2.48.1–15; Nilakanta Sastri 1957, 120–1 provides a number of these identifications.

197. Diod. 17.102.4; Arr. *Anab.* 6.15.1.

198. Shastri 1996, 94 lists the Sodrae as Śudras, who in Vārāhamihira's time lived in western Rajputana.

199. Rawlinson 1926, 35.

200. Arr. *Anab.* 6.15.4.

201. The name may reflect either the Mūshikas, on the west coast of south India (Lassen), or the Moghasis (Nilakanta Sastri 1957, 121).

cities and killed eighty thousand of the inhabitants. After all this the city, Sindimana, opened its gates and Sambus' relatives, with his elephants, came out to meet Alexander, apologising for the misunderstanding(!).

The next target was the city of a people called the Brahmanes, named Harmatelia. The Brahmanes had been the movers behind the revolts of Sambus (Diodorus) and Musicanus (Arrian). Arrian tantalisingly writes that he will explain 'the wisdom of these men, if such it is, in my Indian treatise'. There is no such discussion in the *Indica*, raising the suspicion that the work meant may be the part of the treatise *On the Life of the Brahmans* that is attributed to Arrian.[202] The name of the people is a puzzle, since Brahmanes should denote a caste not a people, but it is preserved in the older name of the ancient city of Harmatelia, which was Brahmanabad but is now the ruined site of Mansura, north-east of Hyderabad. Arrian also refers to a city of the Brahmanes much further north, in the region of the Malli town, but this looks like another confusion in his geography.[203]

A particular danger that the Macedonians faced here was the use by the defenders of Harmatelia of poisoned arrows. Diodorus has a vivid description of the preparation of the poison, from the bodies of dead snakes dried in the sun, and of its effects, which began with instant numbness, pain and shivering; the skin became cold and livid and a black froth exuded from the wound, quickly leading to death.[204] These are classic symptoms of snakebite, and one of the most prominent victims was Ptolemy, who came close to death. This crisis was the last occasion for some research on Alexander's part before leaving India. He had a dream vision of a snake carrying a plant in its mouth. According to Strabo search parties were sent out,[205] but in Diodorus Alexander just went and picked the plant itself, made an infusion of it, and cured Ptolemy with the drink. It seems quite likely, however, that he consulted a friendly, or captive, Brahman, since Brahmans were known for their skill with plant remedies (see chapter 8 below).[206]

202. Stoneman 2012, xxvi; 2008, 98; see also ch. 11 below.

203. Arr. *Anab*. 6.7.4.

204. Diod. 17.103.

205. Str. 15.2.7.

206. A Himalayan people, the Lepchas, poison arrows with aconite, for which the antidote is digitalis or atropine (nightshade). Koehler 2015, 65. Nicander, *Alexipharmaka* 13–30 describes the effects of aconite, comparing it with the madness caused by Dionysus; at 41–73 he discusses a variety of antidotes, both vegetable and mineral.

Another three days sailing brought Alexander to the city of Patala (Hyderabad), which had also sent a delegation and submission; but by the time he got there the people had fled the city. Alexander persuaded the fugitives to return, and they did so without molestation. Hephaestion fortified the city, and dockyards were constructed for the ocean voyage back to Persia. So Alexander leaves India. It was high summer 325.

The ready submission of so many of these peoples may be explained not only by the ferocity meted out to those who resisted, but also to the sense they must have had that Alexander would not be staying long. A lightning visit to instal a garrison was not going to be a long-term problem for the natives; and so it proved. Within months of Alexander's departure all the conquered peoples had revolted and regained their freedom. As Nehru wrote (see above), it was a short-lived border raid as far as India was concerned, though this view ignores the Indo-Greek kingdoms completely. Enough Greeks remained to establish a kingdom that survived in the north-west for two hundred years (see chapter 13 below). Brian Bosworth concluded that the reason for the impermanence of Alexander's conquest was that he did not *understand* India.[207] He 'rode roughshod over the deepest sensitivities of his new subjects'. But did Alexander ever intend it to be permanent, or was he just exploring with an army? A further point may be that India is self-sufficient: it does not need what others can bring it, though it will make use of what can be adapted. Alexander brought very little. Later conquerors left more of a mark, from the architecture of the Mughals to the railways of the British. But even one of the world's great religions, Buddhism, failed to endure in the land of its origin because the native tradition, and Brahman opposition, was too strong. And if the railways were a great success, steam ships were a flop.[208] What did Alexander have to offer? Nothing that India wanted.

207. Bosworth 1996a, 97.
208. Dewey 2014.

3

Heracles and Dionysus

Heracles

(Tiresias explained)
What Fate th'immortal Gods for Hercules ordain'd.
What fell despoilers of the land
The prophet told, what monsters of the main
Should feel the vengeance of his righteous hand:
What savage, proud, pernicious tyrant slain
To Hercules should bow his head...
Then shall his gen'rous toils for ever cease
With Fame, with endless life repaid.

—PINDAR, *NEMEAN* 1, TR. GILBERT WEST

How could this boy [Kṛṣṇa], at the age of seven, effortlessly lift up the biggest mountain with one hand, like the king of elephants lifts a lotus flower? The breast of the immensely powerful demon Pūtanā, along with her vital airs, was sucked by the infant with his eyes closed, just as the strength of the body is sucked out by the force of time... He killed with ease the demon in the form of a calf... he killed the donkey demon and his friends... he liberated the animals of Vraj and the *gopa*s from the forest fire. He forcibly subdued the chief of snakes... and cleared the poison from the waters of the Yamuna.

—*BHĀGAVATA PURĀṆA: THE BEAUTIFUL LEGEND OF GOD* 10.26.3–12

ALEXANDER CAME TO INDIA not just with a research project (if he did) but with a determination to stamp on the alien land a character that he and his fellow Macedonians could recognise. In the next generation, the ethnographic approach of Megasthenes to his subject is determined in many ways by Alexander's vision of India. One notable example is his treatment of the most prominent 'gods of India', Heracles and Dionysus. Scholars of the matter have generally tried to match each of the two Greek gods to one or another known Indian god, commonly Indra or Kṛṣṇa for Heracles, and Śiva for Dionysus.[1] However, Sir William Jones in his essay 'On the Gods of Greece, Italy and India' (1784) already resisted such identifications: 'In drawing a parallel between the Gods of the Indian and European heathens, from whatever source they were derived, I shall remember, that nothing is less favourable to enquiries after truth than a systematical spirit, and shall call to mind the saying of a Hindu writer, "that whoever obstinately adheres to any set of opinions, may bring himself to believe that the freshest sandal wood is a flame of fire": this will effectually prevent me from insisting, that such a God of India was the Jupiter of Greece; such, the Apollo; such, the Mercury'.[2] Strabo makes no mention of Heracles and Dionysus, but says that the Indians worshipped Zeus, Ganga and a number of local (ἐγχώριοι) gods.[3] Modern accounts of the gods of the tribes of India such as the Gonds make clear the variety of gods worshipped by them, ranging from hunting weapons and animals to deified human beings, and represented often by stones, or by such items as battle-axes and cows' tails suspended in trees.[4] These probably represent a form of Indian religion much more widespread before the crystallisation of Hinduism in the centuries following Alexander. Arrian and Plutarch both state that Alexander trained the Indians to respect the gods, among whom he included himself.[5]

1. E.g., Lassen 1847–61, followed by Dahlquist 1962; but see the scathing review of the latter by Kuiper 1969 and also Hartman 1965; Dahlquist's methodologically flawed approach is revisited by Puskás 1996.

2. Jones 1995, 349.

3. Str. 15.1.69.

4. See Russell and Hiralal 1916, 3.38–143 on the Gonds. James Forsyth (1871, 140–4), discussing the 'pantheism' and nonce gods of the Gond tribes: 'None of these powers of nature are represented by idols, nor have they any particular forms or ceremonies of worship. They are merely localized by some vague symbol; the mountain god by a daub of vermilion on some prominent rock; the tree god by a pile of stones thrown round the stem of a tree – and so on.' The observation shows how hard it is to record completely unfamiliar practices accurately.

5. Arr. *Anab.* 8.7.8; Plu. *de Alex. mag. fort.* 1.328c. Cf. Str. 16.1.11, where Alexander adds himself to the gods already worshipped by the Arabs, namely Zeus and Dionysus. See Sulimani 2011, 55–8.

Why was Alexander expecting to find these two gods there, and why did he attach such importance to them? The origin of their prominence lies in the role of both gods in Macedonian royal ideology, and hence in Alexander's mythologisation of his expedition in heroic terms. That is why Megasthenes expected to find them in India.[6]

The kingdom worshipped a relatively limited range of gods compared with the full Greek pantheon.[7] Prominent among them are Zeus and Athena, both of whom feature on the coins (of Philip and Alexander respectively), and the underworld gods Demeter and Kore, heavily represented in the archaeological record and providing a dominant motif for tomb adornment.[8] Heracles, though actual cults are poorly represented in Macedonia proper,[9] is central as the ancestor of the Macedonian royal house under the title Heracles Patroios, and from an early date his head dressed in the lion-skin occupied the obverse of Macedonian coins. Theocritus' *Encomium of Ptolemy* makes clear how important Heracles remained to the Macedonian rulers of Egypt, stating that both Alexander and Ptolemy 'trace back their birth to Heracles'.[10] The poem begins and ends with Zeus, but it is Heracles who receives the honour of a mythological excursus, and other gods appear only in passing. The mythological connection is expounded by Macedonian kings in Herodotus and Thucydides: Alexander I states that he is of Hellenic race, and Perdiccas avers that his ancestry is originally from Argos.[11] Heracles was born in Argos, and it is thither that the sons of Heracles are told to 'return' by the Delphic oracle, according to Isocrates.[12] The return of the sons of Heracles was commonly regarded as the beginning of history, as distinct from mythology, as Diodorus tells us.[13] The founder of the Macedonian kingdom, Temenos, the great-great-grandson of Heracles, then came to Macedonia from Argos.[14] Heracles was

6. Karttunen 1989, 210ff.

7. See the excellent survey of Fulińska 2014.

8. Palagia forthcoming.

9. For two examples, see *SEG* 48.836, Philippi and *SEG* 46.829, Vergina, with discussion and further bibliography by Koulakiotis forthcoming. There was also a cult of Heracles Patroios on the island of Thasos: Polyaenus *Strat.* 1.45.4. On Thasos there were in fact two separate cults, of Heracles as hero and as god: Hdt. 2.44.5, cf. Paus 2.10.1, with further details and discussion assembled in Bosworth 1980–, 2.82.

10. Theocr. 17.16–27.

11. Hdt. 1.56 and 9.45.1–2; Thuc. 5.80.2.

12. *Archidamus* 17–20.

13. Diod. 4.1.3, citing Ephorus, Callisthenes and Theopompus.

14. Hdt. 8.137.

thus part of the propaganda that enabled the Macedonian kings to claim a Hellenic origin for their race;[15] but this was not of prime importance to Alexander:[16] it was the exceptional achievements of the hero who had become god that provided him with a model. Already Philip had claimed land conquered by Heracles.[17]

One of Alexander's earliest exploits, as Lara O'Sullivan has shown, is modelled on a story about Heracles, when he raided the Delphic sanctuary and made off with the tripod.[18] When Alexander attempted to consult the Pythia during a closed season, she refused to prophesy for him; he then began to manhandle her, and threw her to the ground, so that she exclaimed, 'Young man, you are invincible!' – thus giving him the oracle he wanted.[19] The story may be modelled on a similar anecdote about an earlier visitor to the shrine, Philomelus,[20] but it is at any rate directly contributory to Alexander's myth, since it provides him with the epithet *aniketos*, 'invincible', which was also an epithet of Heracles.[21] So Alexander later recalled 'that the Pythia had named him invincible, and that Ammon conceded the rule of all the world'.[22] In the earliest version of the *Alexander Romance* Alexander threatens to steal the tripod 'as Heracles had done', and the priestess actually addresses the brutal king as 'Heracles Alexander'.[23] This text seems to preserve some element of Alexander's own propaganda, and O'Sullivan argues that the story was in fact contrived by the real Callisthenes, from whom the Pseudo-Callisthenes will thus have derived it. The title *aniketos* was that under which someone in 324 BCE proposed to set up a statue of Alexander 'the invincible god'.[24]

Once the expedition to the east had begun, the parallels between Alexander and Heracles began to multiply. In the early stages of the expedition, Achilles provided a convenient parallel, but after leaving the Greek western parts of Asia Minor Heracles takes over (except in the story of the dragging of Batis at

15. See also Huttner 1997, 102–3; Stafford 2012, 143–6.

16. However, in his fictional letter to Darius *PSI* 1285, ep. 14, he speaks of his descent from the Theban Heracles.

17. Antipater of Magnesia, *FGrH* 69 F 1; Bosworth 1996a, 64.

18. O'Sullivan 2015.

19. Plutarch (*Alex.* 27) places the event in 336 BCE.

20. Diod. 16.27.

21. Tyrtaeus F 11 West.

22. Diod. 17.93.4.

23. *AR* 1.45.

24. Hyp. 5.31–2; O'Sullivan 2015, 50.

Gaza). At Mallus he sacrificed to the oracular hero Amphilochus 'because Mallus was a colony of Argos, and he himself claimed descent from Argive Heracles'.[25] As early as the battle of Issus, Alexander (according to Curtius)[26] enthused his men by promising them that they would 'one day traverse the bounds set by Hercules and Liber to subdue not only the Persians but all the races of the earth'. After the victory at Issus, he set up altars on the banks of the Pinarus river, dedicated to Zeus, Heracles and Athena, the three gods that featured on his own coins when he began minting.[27] On arrival at Tyre the king *demanded* to be allowed access to sacrifice to Melqart, who was commonly identified with Heracles.[28] It was the refusal of the people of Tyre to admit him that precipitated the six-month siege. Perhaps this strengthened his determination to become as invincible as his ancestor. Heracles was also supposed to have visited Siwa, according to Callisthenes.[29]

Anaxarchus may have started the idea in the king's mind that he should be a god like Heracles. In an episode recounted by Arrian under the events of 328 BCE, the philosopher made a speech proposing that 'it would be far more just to reckon Alexander a god than Dionysus and Heracles, not so much because of the magnitude of Alexander's achievements, but also because Dionysus was a Theban, and had no connection with Macedon, and Heracles an Argive, also unconnected with Macedon, except for Alexander's family, for he was descended from Heracles'. Callisthenes responded by pointing out that 'even Heracles did not receive divine honours from the Greeks in his own lifetime, nor even after his death till the god of Delphi gave his sanction to honouring him as a god'. In short, Alexander should wait until he was dead if he wanted to be a god.[30]

The idea of outdoing Heracles seems to have settled into Alexander's mind from this point, even though no previous writer mentions exploits of Heracles east of the Caucasus. However, the identification of the Hindu Kush as the Caucasus assisted the extension of his adventures to this region.[31] The recollections of Heracles in the rest of the campaign may be summed up as fol-

25. Arr. *Anab.* 2.6.4.

26. Curt. 3.10.5.

27. Ibid. 3.12.27.

28. For the identification, cf. 2 Macc. 4.18–20.

29. *FGrH* 124 F 14a.

30. Arr. *Anab.* 4.10.6–11.7. See Bosworth 1980–, 2.78–9.

31. On the geography see, for example, Stoneman 1994b.

lows.[32] They are the capture of the Rock Aornos;[33] Alexander's sacrifice to Heracles *propatōr* ('the ancestor') as the fleet embarked for the voyage down the Indus;[34] his encounter with the army of the Sibi with their standard representing Heracles;[35] the curious episode when Dioxippus the wrestler, dressed as Heracles, fought a single combat with an armed Macedonian soldier and won;[36] the proposed voyage westwards to the Pillars of Heracles;[37] and Alexander's final illness brought on by drinking from 'the cup of Heracles' or 'in commemoration of Heracles'.[38] It was his *pothos* that drove him to outdo Heracles.[39] To this may be added the altars erected at the beginning of his career on the Danube, to Zeus Soter, Heracles and Ister (the god of the Danube),[40] as well as the twelve altars on the Hyphasis following the decision to turn back from India. The historians do not mention to whom these twelve altars were dedicated,[41] except that Diodorus attributes them to 'the twelve gods', and it is left to Philostratus, in his fictional *Life of Apollonius*,[42] to specify a group of Ammon, Heracles, Athena Pronoia, the Cabiri, the Indus, Helios and Apollo (which only adds up to eight).[43] It would be surprising indeed if Heracles were not one of these; the one requiring explanation is Athena Pronoia, a rare epithet though she is worshipped under that title at Prasiai in Attica and on Delos,[44] and Pronoia, 'The Providence Above' frequently directs Alexander's actions in the *Alexander Romance*.

32. Heckel 2015, 29–30 lists many of these, but omits Dioxippus.

33. Arr. *Anab.* 4.28.1–4 and 4.30.

34. Ibid. 6.3.2.

35. Diod. 17.96.1–2; Curt. 9.4.1–2; Justin 12.9.2.

36. Diod. 17.100.5–6; Curt 9.7.19–20; Ael. *VH* 10.22; Bosworth 1996a, 115–19.

37. Diod. 17.113.2.

38. Plu. *Alex.* 75.5; Diod. 17.117.1.

39. Arr. *Anab.* 4.28.4; Justin 12.7.13.

40. Arr. *Anab.* 1.4.5.

41. Ibid. 5.29.1; Diod. 17.95; Plu. *Alex.* 62; Curt. 9.3.19; Plin. *NH* 6.61.

42. Philostr. *VA* 2.43.

43. Lane Fox 1973, 370 mentions some of these – but not Heracles – and suggests that the Cabiri were included because they were 'wild gods who were favoured by his mother Olympias'.

44. Macrob. *Sat.* 1.17.55. Pronoia as a goddess is rare generally, though she gets a mention in *h. Orph.* Proem 30 and Artem. *Oneiro.* 2.39.59, and there is a Pronoia Sebaste at Aizanoi: *CIG* III 3831a [15] *add.* P. 1062. Pronoia as a Stoic deity is ubiquitous: Cic. *ND.* 1.8; Dragona-Monachou 1994.

The conquest of Aornos seems to be the point at which the myth of Heracles begins to infiltrate the myth of Alexander in a significant way. Aornos was convincingly identified by Aurel Stein with Pir-Sar.[45] Arrian writes that the story about it was that even Heracles had been unable to capture it, but in his opinion the story was invented 'as a boast', to magnify Alexander's achievement.[46] (In this he follows Eratosthenes, who lies behind Strabo's insistence that 'that these stories are fabrications of the flatterers of Alexander is obvious'.)[47] The defenders mocked him that he would never take it unless his soldiers grew wings; but some deserters showed him a route by which some skilled mountaineers were able to scale the rock and break the defences. The name means 'birdless' in Greek, but Stein assumed that it represented a Sanskrit word, later identified by Tomaschek in *RE* as *āvaraṇa*, 'defence-wall'. Robert Rollinger however has shown that a tradition of 'birdless rocks' conquered by great kings goes back to the Assyrian empire, and further that the Avestan expression *upāiri.saēna*, used to denote the Hindu Kush, means 'above the flight of birds'. The Avestan word was itself borrowed into Greek as *paropanisus*, so that the birdless rock is really no more than a rock in the Hindu Kush.[48] The Greeks took for a specific name what was offered to them as a general description, as Ctesias did in the case of the manticore (see chapter 4 below).

Bosworth was sure that the story about Heracles was invented by Alexander's propagandists, and that 'Alexander came to believe that he was following in the footsteps of his divine ancestors'.[49] He was simply repossessing territory that Heracles had once conquered (as Philip had followed the same hero in his conquest of Chalcidice, according to the historian Antipater of Magnesia).[50] If that is so, there is no need to suppose that there was a story about a similar exploit by Kṛṣṇa, as Bosworth had earlier accepted.[51]

45. Stein 1929. But see ch. 2 above regarding recent alternative suggestions.

46. Arr. *Anab.* 4.28.2. The narrative of the assault concludes at 30.4. See also Diod. 17.85.4–6; Curt. 8.11.3–19. It is also recounted in *AR* 3.4.8–10 (α only) and thence in *Itin. Alex.* [50] 112: possibly the source of this version was Cleitarchus.

47. Str. 15.1.9; Roller 2010, 137.

48. Rollinger 2014.

49. Bosworth 1996a, 121–4 and 164.

50. *FGrH* 69 F 1.

51. Bosworth 1988a, 123. Dahlquist (1962, 120–30) thought the name Aornos was a version of a rare epithet of Vrtra, Aurnavabha, who was a monster defeated by Indra (as Geryon's dog Orthros was tamed by Heracles), and that Heracles is always Indra.

The statement in Curtius that the army of Porus carried before it a statue of Hercules (Heracles) does not occur in the other authors, and Curtius' claim that 'to desert its bearers was considered a disgrace for a soldier' has a distinctly Roman colour.[52]

Kṛṣṇa may be more pertinent to the matter in the case of the Sibae or Sibi, a people of the northern Punjab,[53] who 'clothed themselves in skins … moreover, they carry cudgels and brand their cattle with the mark of a club'.[54] The Greeks took them for the remnants of Heracles' invading army. As the club was an attribute of Kṛṣṇa, and the practice is mentioned in the *Mahābhārata*, there may be something in the identification.[55]

The similarities of a Greek and a foreign god need not be that close for Greeks to identify them, as Lucian shows in his account of the 'Gallic Heracles' Ogmius, represented as a very old man who, besides his club, bow and lion-skin, has a chain bored through his tongue by which he leads his followers.[56]

Heracles raises his head again further south in the encounter with the Suraseni.[57] Arrian states that Heracles 'is chiefly honoured by the Suraseni, an Indian tribe, with two great cities, Methora and Cleisobora; the navigable river Iomanes flows through their country. Megasthenes says that the garb this Heracles wore was like that of the Theban Heracles by the account of the Indians themselves'. The people are clearly located in the vicinity of modern Mathura and the unidentified Cleisobora.[58] Mathura is today celebrated as the birthplace of Kṛṣṇa and it seems likely that the flute-playing cowherd-hero was already revered in the third century BCE, and that his name is garbled in the Greek form Cleisobora, perhaps representing an original Kṛṣṇapura or Keśavapura.[59] Kṛṣṇa's childhood as a killer of a series of monsters sent by the tyrannical demon-king of Mathura, Kansa (though Indra also kills monsters)

52. Curt. 8.14.11–12.

53. West of the Acesines, below the junction with the Hydraotes (McCrindle 1901, 14) . See Shastri 1996, 92, who places Sibipura at Shorkot, east of the Acesines, but also notes that Faxian places this people in the Swat valley.

54. Arr. *Ind.* 5.12; *Anab.* 5.3.4. Also Diod. 17.96; Curt. 9. 4.1–3; Str. 15.1.8.

55. *Mbh.* 3.240.5. See also Mairs 2014, 128 on the identification of Heracles with Vasudeva/ Kṛṣṇa.

56. Luc. *Her.* 1–3. See Parker 2017, 33–76 on *interpretation*, 38 on Heracles, 184–90 on India.

57. Arr. *Ind.* 8.4.7. Discussion: Thapar 1989, 14–15. The Suraseni constitute one of the sixteen *mahājanapadas*.

58. Eggermont 1993, 75, citing Sircar 1947/1971, 30; Shastri 1996, 94.

59. Karttunen (1989, 211) cautiously accepts the identification

is an obvious spur to an identification with Heracles.[60] Later Kṛṣṇa celebrated his defeat of the hateful king Naraka by taking to wife the sixteen thousand virgin apsaras that the king had taken captive, and improved on Heracles' record of fifty women in a night by satisfying all these girls simultaneously.[61] (The improbably large numbers are a leitmotif of Indian storytelling.) Being an avatar of Viṣṇu, Kṛṣṇa in due course ascended (or returned) to heaven, but only after being wounded (like Achilles) in his one mortal spot, his foot.

If we can securely identify the Heracles of the Suraseni with Kṛṣṇa, that is by no means an argument that every reference to Heracles in an Indian context refers to Kṛṣṇa. It should not be forgotten that in subsequent centuries the Paśupata hero Lakulīśa carries a club like Heracles,[62] and that Heracles found an independent life in India in the guise of Vajrapāṇi, the bearded, club-wielding companion of the Buddha, often represented in sculpture.[63] He appears on a medallion on the neck of a Gandharan sculpture of a prince.[64] We have no imagery from the period of Alexander's conquest, but it is possible that Indian artists found the figure of Heracles coalesced neatly with their earlier, now lost, conceptions of one hero or another. But the central point is that, for Megasthenes, Heracles (and Dionysus) had to be identified in India because Alexander had insisted they were there.

The last episode of the expedition concerning Heracles brings us back to Macedonian attitudes rather than putative identifications. After the battle at the Malli town, the historians Diodorus and Curtius (but not Arrian) recount a curious episode where a boastful Athenian boxer named Dioxippus was induced to fight a single combat with a Macedonian soldier, Corragus (Korragos: Curtius calls him 'Horratas').[65] The Macedonian appeared with an infantryman's weapons, shield and sarissa, lance and sword, while Dioxippus 'grasped a purple cloak in his left hand and a stout knotty club in his right'.

60. See for example *Bhagawata Purāṇa* 10, in Bryant 2003, 59 and 82. Bryant xvii–xviii takes the two gods to be the same and even links the names, Herakles and Hare-Krishna (Bryant's spellings).

61. Haberman 1994, 168.

62. See ch. 12 below on Cynics and Paśupatas.

63. E.g., Smith 1962, plate 51d. Dreyer 2011, plates 16 and 37 show Chinese and Central Asian versions of Heracles. Different classical models may also be used to represent the same Indian gods: Boardman 2015, 187; so Vajrapāṇi sometimes takes on characteristics of Zeus. Bowersock 1994.

64. Fischer 1987a, with plates 8–10.

65. Curt. 9.7.16–26; Diod. 17.100.2, 101.6; Ael. *VH* 10.22.

3.1 A statue of Lakulīśa (Government Museum, Mathura).

The resemblance to Heracles is made explicit by Diodorus. Despite the inequality of the weapons the Athenian masquerading as a god defeated the mortal Macedonian. According to the historians, Alexander was dismayed at the result, 'for he feared that a mockery had been made of the celebrated Macedonian valour'. Presumably the defeat of a Macedonian outweighed the victory of a 'Heracles'; or perhaps he was indignant that an Athenian should play the role of the quintessentially Macedonian hero. At all events, the king's supporters contrived to frame Dioxippus by planting a gold cup under the cushion of his banqueting couch, and the unfortunate athlete in shame committed suicide.[66]

66. See also the discussion in Bosworth 1996a, 115–17. Does this story resurface in the *Alexander Romance* 2.15 when Alexander is caught stealing cups from Darius' banquet?

3.2 A statue of Vajrapāṇi (Government Museum, Mathura).

Alexander probably regarded it as his sole right to masquerade as Heracles, as Ephippus tells us: besides dressing up at banquets as Ammon, as Hermes[67] and even as Artemis,[68] he 'often also wore a lion's skin, and carried a club, like Heracles ... and all the bystanders kept silence, or spoke only words of good omen, out of fear. For he was a very violent man, with no regard for human life'.[69] The other disguises may be deliberate misinterpretations of Persian attire, but that does not seem to explain the Heracles get-up. Alexander genuinely identified with the god.

Heracles' role as a tamer of savage nature may also have appealed to Alexander.[70] Curtius has a Scythian spokesman describe Alexander as making war

67. Wearing a petasus and carrying a caduceus, perhaps implying a Persian cap and sceptre.

68. The point seems to be that he went hunting dressed in a Persian robe, which Greeks regarded as suitable clothing for a woman.

69. Ephippus *FGrH* 126 F 5 = Athen. 12.54 (537e–38b).

70. Romm 1992, 69.

'on woods, on snow, on rivers and wild animals'.[71] At the Sogdian Rock he was 'bringing even nature to her knees',[72] at the Indus he was 'at war with the river' (perhaps recalling Achilles rather than Heracles).[73]

Dionysus

> From a wind-tossed branch a Hamadryad Nymph bent low, emerging womanly from her leafy flanks. Thyrsus in hand, she looked just like a Bacchant . . . and whispered in the ear of grape-draped Dionysus: 'God of Wine, lord gardener of the fruits . . . I am a Hamadryad of the beautiful leaves; and here, where fierce warriors lie in wait for you, I will reject my fatherland and save your army from death. I offer loyalty to your satyrs, although I am Indian, and I take the part of Dionysus.'
>
> —NONNUS, *DIONYSIACA* 22. 84–100

Dionysus was not an ancestor of the Macedonian house, though by the end of Alexander's reign somebody had managed to insert him there: 'the stemma was fully fledged in the Ptolemaic period, and there was every reason for its evolution at Alexander's court'.[74] His prominent role in the Grand Procession of Ptolemy Philadelphus is a result of his adoption by Alexander as a presiding deity of his reign.[75] Dionysus was, however, already an important Macedonian god, and is featured on the fourth-century Derveni crater as well as on the funerary couches from Potidaea (now in Thessaloniki Museum).[76]

Why did Alexander like to identify with Dionysus? One reason seems to be that the latter was a god who had a mortal mother, though his father was Zeus. Like Heracles, he was a latecomer to Olympus, but unlike Heracles he was a 'true god', because his mother Semele was also translated to Olympus.[77]

71. Curt. 7.8.13.

72. Ibid. 7.11.4.

73. Ibid. 9.4.14.

74. Bosworth 1996a, 125–6 n. 128, citing Satyrus *FGrH* 631 F 1 and *POxy* 2465, col. 2, 2–11. Euripides, *Cyclops* 38–40, perhaps hints that Althaea, the mother of Heracles' wife Deianeira, had once dallied with Dionysus.

75. Rice 1983, 83.

76. Palagia forthcoming.

77. Hes. *Thg.* 942. The Dioscuri were likewise halfway between mortals and gods; according to Arrian (*Anab.* 4.8.1) Alexander once replaced a sacrifice to Dionysus with one to the

3.3 A *śalabhañjikā*, or tree nymph, from the northern gateway of the stupa at Sanchi.

Alexander was thus predisposed to find signs of this god's presence in India. Born (or reared) in Nysa, which was traditionally localised in Arabia,[78] the god had conquered all of Asia including Bactria – in a play by Euripides surely known to Alexander – and India.[79, 80] The legend was widely current in Hellenistic times, no doubt as a result of Alexander's expedition, and Eratosthenes was at pains to declare it quite unfounded.[81] Albrecht Dihle has shown how the legend consolidated because of Alexander's expedition, even though a few references precede Alexander.[82] Later, Polyaenus even knew of a stratagem practised by Dionysus in the expedition.[83] Lucian was able to make fun of the legend in his usual way,[84] while Nonnus devoted a large section of his epic about Dionysus to the Indian expedition, in which Dionysus' campaign and image are modelled on key features of Alexander's expedition.[85]

The place-name Nysa seems to be the catalyst for Alexander's discovery of Dionysus in India.[86] Besides Arabia, there were places called Nysa in Euboea, Thrace, Lydia and Ethiopia. This new Nysa that the Macedonians came to, near Jalalabad, not only had a name that fitted, but vines and ivy grew there. The Macedonians and Greeks do not seem to have understood that it was simply a question of altitude whether such plants grew in 'India', but took it as a sign of the god's presence. The location was named Mount Meros by the expedition, probably from the name of the holy mountain Meru of Hindu cosmology which they will have encountered here.[87] Since the infant Dionysos had been concealed in the thigh (Greek *mēros*) of his father Zeus, the

---

Dioscuri, but he does not seem to have had any lasting affection for these gods, and repented of his disrespect to Dionysus. Perseus was another mortal son of Zeus but his place in the Macedonian ancestry is not emphasised despite the link it would provide to the Persian kings; but see *PSI* 1285, ep. 11 where Darius refers to Perseus.

78. Pi. F 85a = 247; Diod. 3.66.3 and 4.2.1.

79. E. *Ba.* 15.

80. Diod. 3.66.7 and 4.3.1.

81. Eratosth. F 23 = Arr. *Anab.* 5.3.4; cf. F 21 = Str. 15.1.7.

82. Dihle 1987, noting in particular the poet Antimachus' speculations about Nysa (writing ca. 400 BCE). See also Boardman 2014; 2015, 205ff.: at 217 there is a picture of an eastern Dionysus on a Bactrian camel.

83. Polyaen. *Strat.* 1.1.1–3.

84. Luc. *Dionysus.*

85. Djurslev 2016.

86. The most comprehensive collection of the evidence is in Otto 1965, 61ff. See the discussion of Dionysus in Bosworth 1996a, 119–30.

87. Lane Fox 1973, 341–3, in some brilliant paragraphs.

name was confirmation of the link.[88] Arrian noted that the Indians wore dappled clothing like Bacchants and banged drums and cymbals a lot,[89] both of which things could easily have been observed in India, and could be taken by the enthusiast as proving that they were devotees of Dionysus.

As the expedition progressed, several further signs of the presence of Dionysus were discovered.[90] The 'boundaries of Dionysus' or 'of Liber' are referred to several times.[91] As soon as Alexander entered the 'boundaries of India', he was met by the petty kings of the area, who 'welcomed him as the third son of Zeus to come that way', according to Curtius.[92] When the army reached the Oxydracae (Kṣudrakas), near the junction of the Hydaspes (Jhelum) and Acesines (Chenab), the people announced that 'they wished to retain the freedom which they had preserved for all time from Dionysus' arrival in India to that of Alexander.[93] Strabo even said that they claimed descent from Dionysus, which he must have got from one or other of the Alexander historians.[94] Further south, the people they called the Sabarcae (in the region of Multan) were so terrified by the sight of the Macedonian army that 'they believed an army of gods was approaching with a second Father Liber (a name famous among those peoples).[95]

Furthermore, there were signs of the wine-god everywhere. The Macedonians seem to have encountered a 'Dionysiac' wine-cult in north-west India.[96] A festival of Kama could take on Dionysiac overtones,[97] while even the Hindu festival of Holi may become a merry riot that the god would have loved.[98]

Is this all just happy supposition by the Macedonians, predisposed to find evidence of Dionysus' presence at the slightest hint? Or did they identify a particular Indian god with Dionysus, as they did Kṛṣṇa, in at least one case, with Heracles? The usual candidate proposed in scholarship has been Śiva.

88. Soma (the god of intoxicating drink) was concealed in the thigh of Indra: Collins 2014, 126.

89. Arr. *Ind.* 5.9.

90. See also the discussion of Dionysus in Bosworth 1996a, 119–30, as well as Boardman 2014; 2015.

91. Arr. *Anab.* 4.4.8, 5.1.6 and Bosworth ad loc.; Curt. 7.9.15, 9.4.21.

92. Curt. 8.10.1; Bosworth 1980–, 2.125–72.

93. Arr. *Anab.* 6.14.1–2.

94. Str. 15.1.8, cf. 33.

95. Curt. 9.8.5. Diod. (17.102.3) calls them the Sambastae, but makes no mention of their familiarity with the god.

96. Carter 1992; 2015, 355–76: see further ch. 5 below; Karttunen 1989, 210–19.

97. Parpola 2015, 251.

98. Daniélou 1992, 266–7.

There is no doubt that the gods Śiva and Dionysus have a lot in common;[99] what is more in doubt is whether Śiva existed in the form he is now known at the time of Alexander.[100] It would not in any case follow that when Greeks 'found' Dionysus they were observing Śiva. Śiva is never mentioned in the Vedas, nor in Pāṇini, though Patañjali refers to images of Skanda and Śiva.[101] (If Skanda had existed when Alexander reached India, could he have ignored this god who bore a name so like his own?) The gods of the Mauryas are *yakṣīs* and *yakṣas*, like the hamadryad of Nonnus' poem.[102] There are various 'proto-Śivas', not least the apparently ithyphallic horned figure on an Indus seal, though this is much debated and the present consensus seems to be that it is not any kind of Śiva;[103] Eck mentions a pre-Śiva, Kaśiśvara (Lord of Kashi, i.e., Varanasi), in a text of the fifth century BCE, as well as Rudra Śiva in the *Śatapatha Brāhmaṇa*,[104] and the characterisation of Rudra in the *Śvetāśvatara Upaniṣad*, probably of the fourth to third century BCE.[105] The oldest lingam may date from the second century BCE.[106] Śiva and the other members of the 'Hindu triad' (Brahma and Viṣṇu) emerge by the early centuries CE.

Śiva shares many characteristics with the Vedic god Rudra, who is in essence a storm-god.[107] Rudra's special animal is the bull (like Śiva and Dionysus); he is a lord of the animals (Paśupati),[108] a mountain-dweller who is by

99. O'Flaherty 1980. We may be looking at a Jungian archetype, or direct influence, or a common Indo-European source. There are many parallels, not least the legend of Soma being concealed in the thigh of Indra as Dionysus was in that of Zeus (Collins 2014, 126); the connection with the Bull, with Dance and Music, with drunkenness, and his phallic nature (Bhattacharji 1970/2000, 147, 144, 156–7, 179); as well as the resemblance to Zagreus and Enkidu (Bhattacharji 1970/2000, 115). Both are gods in whom contradictions meet (Bhattcharji 1970, 202). To O'Flaherty's list we may also add the satyrs. The story of Daksha, transformed into a goat as punishment for resisting the god, has many resemblances to that of Pentheus.

100. O'Flaherty 1973/1981, 83–110. Basu 1969, 193ff. and 202 also makes him post-Vedic.

101. Smith 1962, 10. Skanda-Kārttikeya originates as a central figure in the propitiation of Grahas, female deities who threaten childbirth and infant mortality. He comes to be seen as a son of Śiva in the fourth century BCE, but is only fully fledged in the *Mahābhārata* (e.g., 3.213–21, 9.43–5, 13.83–6) and is later supplanted by Ganeṣa. See Mann 2012.

102. Eck 1983/1992, 52–3.

103. Possehl 2002, 141–4: the most that can probably be said is that the figure sits in a yoga posture. Both the phallus and the three faces may be illusory.

104. *SB* 9.1.1.

105. Eck 1983/1992, 68.

106. At Gudimallam, Andhra Pradesh: Allchin 1995, 250.

107. Ions 1967, 39; Bhattacharji 1970/2000, 109–57 is exhaustive.

108. Bhattacharji 1970/2000, 140–1.

3.4 This seal from the Indus Civilisation (third–second millennium BCE) is often interpreted as depicting a prototype form of Śiva, with three faces, erect phallus, and horns. The identification is controversial.

turns benign and terrifying,[109] a protector and a destroyer;[110] he has wild braided hair (like Śiva);[111] he is associated with ascetics,[112] uses intoxicants (like Śiva and Dionysus)[113] and is also a god of healing who wields a bow and arrow: this last is not obviously characteristic of Śiva and not at all of Dionysus, but rather recalls Apollo in the Greek pantheon. Rudra is commonly accompanied by an army of Maruts, heroic ephebe demi-gods, sometimes said to be his sons but more commonly the sons of Indra. These warriors in golden armour ride on the backs of dappled deer,[114] and advance singing to their wars:

> Bring forward a brilliant chant for the singing, swift, self-strong
> Marut(-troop).

109. *Śvetāśvatara Upaniṣad* 3.3.1–6.

110. Ibid. 4.12.21–2.

111. *RV* 1.114.

112. Ibid. 10.136.

113. Ibid. 10.136, 2.33; O'Flaherty 1973/1981, 120; Bhattacharji 1970/2000, 156–7.

114. *RV* 2.34, 5.52. Cf. Megasth. F dub 57 Schw (not in Jacoby) = Polyaenus 1.1.1–3.

Those who overpower powers with power, before (those) combatants
the earth trembles, o Agni.
Flaring like the dart of the ceremony [= ritual fire], stirring thirstily
like tongues of fire,
Chanting like boisterous heroes, the Maruts with their flashing birth
are unassailable.
The Marut(-troop) grown strong, with flashing spears, the son(s) of
Rudra I seek to entice here with an invocation.[115]

It is not inconceivable that this was the vision that occurred to the Sabarcae when they saw the Macedonian army with its bright lances advancing towards them, and that the Macedonians took chants of this kind as evidence of a Bacchic-style revel accompanying an Indian god. But it needs to be emphasised that Alexander and his companions were not seeking to explain phenomena of Indian religion, but to find evidence for Dionysus in this unfamiliar land. When we come to Megasthenes, the purpose he had in view may be rather different.

G. O. Trevelyan, with a classical education at least as deep as Alexander's, found that an Indian religious procession reminded him of Dionysus.

> If it had not been for the colour of the faces around, I should have believed myself to be on the main road to Eleusis in the full tide of one of the Dionysiac festivals. The spirit of the scene was the same, and at each step some well-known feature reminded one irresistibly that the Bacchic orgies sprung from the mysterious fanaticism of the Far East. It was no unfounded tradition that pictured Dionysus returning from conquered India, leopards and tigers chained to his triumphal car, escorted from the Hyphasis to the Asopus by bands of votaries dancing in fantastic measure to the clang of cymbals. It was no chance resemblance this, between an Hindoo rite, in the middle of the nineteenth century, and those wild revels that stream along many a Grecian bas-relief, and wind round many an ancient Italian vase; for every detail portrayed in those marvellous works of art was faithfully represented here.[116]

Bacchic elements are plentiful in the later part of the expedition of Alexander. The author of the *Alexander Romance* emphasised the prominence of his mythology when his heroes arrived at the 'harbour of Lyssos' close to a high

115. *RV* 6.66.9–11.
116. *The Competition Wallah* (1864), 246, quoted in Hagerman 2013, 3.

mountain. In the temple on the mountain top 'was a circular temple ringed by 100 columns of sapphire. Within and without were carved images of almost divine artistry: bacchants, satyrs, maenads playing pipes and raving in trances, and the old man Maron sitting on his mule'.[117] The altars erected on the banks of the Hyphasis included dedications to Dionysus, according to Philostratus' *Life of Apollonius*;[118] the same author mentions a group of statues among the Indian sages that included Dionysus as well as Athena Polias and Apollo.[119] Alexander himself may have been the author of a satyr-play, *Agen*, that satirised the activities of his renegade treasurer Harpalus;[120] on arrival in Carmania after the Gedrosian disaster, the army (what was left of it) held a Bacchic revel.[121] This was criticised by Plutarch, on the grounds that trying to outdo a god was a bad idea.[122] Dionysus appears as a symbol of Alexander in the Grand Procession of Ptolemy Philadelphus.

After Alexander

Both gods remained popular in the Greek regions of Afghanistan, Pakistan and India in the centuries after Alexander. Heracles in particular enters Indian iconography in several guises.[123] The myth of Dionysus' expedition to India accelerated after Alexander's death, turning up in several lost Hellenistic epics, and culminating in the massive outpouring of Nonnus.[124] Both gods are prominent as culture-heroes in Diodorus, as Sulimani has shown.[125] So it is no surprise that the two gods, Dionysus and Heracles, were inescapable for any writer describing India, from Megasthenes onwards.

117. *AR* 3.29.
118. Philostr. *VA* 2.43; n. 39 above.
119. Philostr. *VA* 3.14.3
120. See ch. 14 below.
121. Curt. 9.10.20–8.
122. Plu. *Alex.* 67.6.
123. Above, nn. 58–60.
124. Dihle 1987; Bowersock 1994.
125. Sulimani 2011.

4

The Natural History of India

There are also many more [trees] which are different from those found among the Greeks, but which have no names.

—THEOPHRASTUS, *INQUIRY INTO PLANTS* 4.4.5

Some people praise the mango to such an extent that they prefer it to all fruit except the melon, but it is not so good as to warrant such praise.

—BABUR, *MEMOIRS* (THACKSTON 2002, 344–5)

They brought me this wild plant, its leaves
  A yellowish green, its flowers
Like crafted cups of a violet hue
  For drinking the light.
I ask, 'What's it called?'
  No one knows.
It belongs to the universe's infinite unfamiliar wing,
  Where the sky's nameless stars also belong.

—RABINDRANATH TAGORE, FROM *PATRAPUT* (1936), IN *I WON'T LET YOU GO* (2010), TR. KETAKI KUSHARI DYSON

The special feature of India's beauty is that its flowers blossom the year round and they are all fragrant.

—AMIR KHUSRAW, *NUH SIPIHR* (NATH AND FAIYAZ 1981, 39)

WHEN THE GREEKS in Alexander's entourage entered India, they knew that they were entering a land where everything in nature was different from in Greece, or at the very least larger. They had read the books on India by Scylax and Ctesias, perhaps with due scepticism, but they waited with curiosity to see how the reality would match up to the limited information with which they were equipped. Flora and fauna interested them at least as much as the customs of the people.[1]

Scylax of Caryanda had been sent by the Persian king Darius I (r. 522–486 BCE) to explore and report on the regions along and beyond the river Indus, which was the border of Persia's easternmost satrapy.[2] Scylax did as he was instructed, but it did him little good, though he did not suffer the fate of Sataspes who was despatched on a similar mission round Africa by Darius' son Xerxes; when his report failed to convince, Xerxes had him impaled. The extent of Scylax's voyage has been discussed in chapter 1: he sailed down the Indus (or more probably the Ganges); at its mouth his ship turned west and 'sailed for thirty months' until it reached a part of what Herodotus calls Libya. The tales he brought back of one-eyed people and people who used their single foot as an umbrella for sleeping under stretched Darius' credulity,[3] and perhaps also that of later readers since only a few fragments of his work survive. Apart from the references to the fabulous races, there is a remark about the artichoke (*Cynara scolymus*), which he stated grew in the mountains of Hyrcania (Gurgan, in Iran), in Chorasmia (Khwarezm, the region east of the Aral Sea), and furthermore along the Indus. Athenaeus, apparently quoting Scylax's words from Polemon, a later writer, states 'that land is well watered with fountains and with canals, and on the mountains there grow artichokes and many other plants'.[4] His lexicographical approach leads him next to draw attention to a reference in Sophocles to a plant called *kynaros*, by which he believes Sophocles is referring to the bramble.[5]

So, there might be some prickly plants awaiting visitors to India. A little more was to be gained from Ctesias. This author spent seventeen years at the

1. The major modern treatments for the subjects discussed in this chapter are Bretzl 1903; Reese 1914; Fraser 1994; Shastri 1996, 279–94; Menon 2000; Arora 2005, 55–63; Amigues 2011; Krishna and Amirthalingam 2014.

2. Hdt. 4.44.

3. Discussed in detail below, ch. 10. They are also in the Avestan book *Videvdad*, which presumably drew on the same sources as Scylax: Stoneman 2015, 53.

4. Athen. 2.82 (70ac) = Scylax *FGrH* 709 F 3.

5. S. Ff 348, 718. Sophocles' *Triptolemus* is a play about foreign plants.

Persian court as a doctor, which undoubtedly gave him an interest in diet and food plants,[6] and wrote two books based on the gossip he picked up there: the *Persica* and the *Indica*. Both have been much criticised from antiquity onwards. The first is often at odds with Herodotus and with what else we know of Persian history; the second is explicitly based on conversations with merchants and diplomats visiting Persia from India. One of the most notorious of the creatures Ctesias describes is the manticore, 'a beast which has a human face, is the size of the lion, and is red like cinnabar. It has three rows of teeth, human ears, and light blue eyes like a man's. It has a tail like a land scorpion on which there is a sting more than a cubit long . . . It can fire its stings as far as a *pletheron*. . . . The word *martichora* means man-eater in Greek'.[7] The last statement is more or less true, and casts light on Ctesias' method, since *mard-chor* is indeed the Persian for 'man-eater': presumably Ctesias was shown a tiger in a cage and told by his Persian hosts that it was a man-eater. He was, understandably, unwilling to check too closely whether it really had three rows of teeth, and the foot-long stings in its tail had no doubt all been fired at its assailants before it was put into the cage.[8] It was to be more than a thousand years before Europeans learnt the truth about the manticore.

The arrival of a tiger in Athens in the late fourth or early third century BCE does not seem to have led the Greeks to make the connection. King Seleucus sent the beast to the city as a gift, prompting an exchange in the comic dramatist Philemon:

A. Since Seleucus has sent us here this tiger that we saw, we ought to send him some beast from here in exchange.
B. Let's send him a Monty-Crane: they don't have those there.[9]

Probably Probably Seleucus was sent a tiger, or several, by Candragupta, as well as the aphrodisiacs and antaphrodisiacs that are mentioned by Phylarchus.[10]

6. Amigues 2011, 60 on his discussion of liquorice.

7. Ctes. F 45.15. See also Lenfant ad loc., 301–2 n. 810; Stoneman 2008, 69.

8. Karttunen in Arora 2005, though he does not make the point about the Persian language.

9. Philemon PCG F 49 (47 K). 'Monty-Crane' translates τρυγέρανον, in which the first part of the compound, 'tryg–' probably connotes something comic, though it could also be derived from a personal name, or a compound with *trygon*, another bird. Alexis PCG F 207 (204 K) also mentions the tiger, as well as the hippopotamus.

10. ap. Athen. 1.32 (18e); see Mehl 1986, 187–8. Aśoka, Rock Edict 2 also speaks of sending useful drugs to Greeks.

As far as these are concerned, Theophrastus quotes an authority he simply calls 'the Indian' regarding some kind of aphrodisiac:

> The most wonderful is the drug that the Indian had. They said that after, not swallowing it, but simply rubbing it on one's member, men could obtain an erection so powerful that they could have intercourse with as many women as they wanted – up to twelve, according to those who had made use of it. The druggist said he – a big strong man – had once managed it seventy times.[11]

Ctesias also writes about elephants, monkeys and parrots, horned asses (reindeer?), the *dikairon* bird which is poisonous to eat, serpents and several puzzling kinds of fruit, as well as recounting the details of the monstrous races. He also has something to say about the social mores of the Indians ('most just of people'): to all of these matters we shall return under their own headings.

Ctesias became a byword in antiquity for unreliability and improbability. The precision of his reports, with detailed numbers and so on, has been interpreted in modern times either as a 'strategy of verisimilitude',[12] or as a form of joke.[13] While there is much in both of Ctesias' books that cannot be believed, it may not always be his fault. He may often have reported faithfully what he was told; it is at the door of his informants that charges about 'untruth' must be laid, if at all. He has a way of describing things which makes them as outrageous as possible when in fact they can be reduced to existing phenomena, plus a little embroidery; the manticore is a case in point. Suzanne Amigues has demonstrated the case exhaustively in her discussion of his Indian flora. For example, the amber-tree is shown to be flame-of-the-forest, *Butea monosperma*, which is the favoured habitat of the lac insect, though it also produces a latex of its own.[14] It is not now found west of the Jhelum but Ctesias' informants may have been widely travelled in India. The tree that produces a beautiful red dye is probably the fire-flame,[15] while even the apparently fabulous magnetic tree that draws gold and silver to it may not be fantasy: an examination of the name suggests that it means something like 'ever-youthful', or 'flourishing alongside', which suits the pipal with its epiphytic tendencies and habit of 'perpetual renewal', particularly as its branches are used for divina-

11. Thphr. *HP* 9.18.9. Amigues (ed. and tr.) 2006 ad loc., 227.

12. Gómez Espelosín 1994.

13. Auberger 1995.

14. Amigues 2011, 36–44.

15. Ibid., 45–9.

tion of precious metals.[16] The *siptachora* – another clearly Persian name, like the manticore, this one meaning 'sweet to eat' – is identified by Amigues with the *Madhuca latifolia,* and the *karpion* with the pandanus.[17] In sum, even the data that seem most improbable, and were perhaps presented by Ctesias in such a way as to evoke a sense of wonder or incredulity, can be shown to be reliable, though sometimes with a little exaggeration. One is reminded of Herodotus' strategy of referring to something as a *thoma,* a wonder, when he wants his readers to pay particular attention rather than to disbelieve it.[18] This conclusion needs to be borne in mind when considering the similar charges that have been laid at Megasthenes' door by ancient and modern writers.

It is hard when encountering plants and animals that are completely unfamiliar to describe them accurately and judiciously, without misleading the reader. Theophrastus (see epigraph above) expresses the problem clearly: a tree may be quite different from anything known in Greece; even if it has a name, that name will be useless in explaining it to anyone who has not seen it, so in a sense it 'has no name'.[19] (His expression οὐδὲν θαυμαστὸν τῆς ἰδιότητος is mistranslated by Bretzl as meaning that there are no unfamiliar plants in India, and they all belong to genera familiar in Greece;[20] what it actually means is, 'there is nothing surprising in their having a special character': that is, Theophrastus emphasises the alien nature of Indian flora, not its familiarity.) The author of the Latin *Letter of Alexander to Aristotle about India* made the point equally forcefully: 'Truly marvellous is Mother Earth, who brings to birth so many things both good and bad, including plants and animals in so many different forms. Even if a man could see all those things it would hardly be possible for him to learn all their names, so many and various are they.'[21] Carl Linnaeus, however, refused to succumb to this kind of despair: 'If you do not know the names of things, the knowledge of them is lost too.'[22] Perhaps this indicates a limitation of Greek science, or any science: that it baulks at studying what it cannot name.[23]

16. Ctes. F 45.38 and 47; F 35, the *parebon* tree. See Amigues 2011, 27–34.

17. Amigues 2011, 50–4 and 62–9.

18. Munson 2001.

19. Plin. *NH* 12.13.25 says the same: 'The Macedonians have given accounts of kinds of trees that for the most part have no names'. Cf. Thphr. *HP* 1.14.4, on wild as against cultivated plants.

20. Bretzl 1903, 248.

21. *Epistula* 1.

22. Quoted in Crane 2013, 204.

23. This is an infinitely recurring problem for any taxonomic system, even Linnaeus', as John Wilkins has pointed out to me. Aristotle is defeated by the variety of crabs.

Flora

> A page of tangled plant calligraphy. A thicket of signs: how to read it, how to clear a path through this denseness? Hanuman smiles with pleasure at the analogy that has just occurred to him: calligraphy and vegetation, a grove of trees and writing, reading and a path.
>
> —OCTAVIO PAZ, *THE MONKEY GRAMMARIAN* (1989), 47

The Greeks with Alexander had to have their wits about them if they were to describe and report on what they saw. Nevertheless, it is surprising to note what they did not see, or notice. A visitor to India today is immediately struck (if my own experience is anything to go by) by the greenness of the landscape, flat around Delhi and to the east, but in the region that Alexander reached hilly, and even mountainous, but still fertile with trees and crops. The Greeks were interested in trees and crops, and Nearchus noted the Indian's love of bright colours which so immediately assails the senses in India, but they say nothing – in what we have of them – about (say) the lives of women, religious practice, music and dance, or even, most remarkably, food. You'd think they'd have mentioned curry![24] What could be more different from the typical Greek diet of bread and olives, barley gruel and onions?[25] Plants, trees and animals, as well as social customs, did indeed engage them to a greater or lesser degree, but none of the Greek writers seems to have been setting out to write a systematic account of Indian society or natural history. The approach is always Hellenocentric; it is assumed that any new society will have much in common with that of Greece, and they pass over in silence what seems familiar. Theophrastus regularly compares the plants he is trying to describe to known Greek plants,[26] while acknowledging peculiar properties like that of the Gedrosian 'bay', which is poisonous.[27] 'In general the lands of the East and South appear to have peculiar plants, as they have peculiar animals.'[28] One should also bear in mind the difficulty of gathering information from local people: E. M. Forster, having asked to be taken to a certain ancient building and ending up at a shed, writes, 'I asked the driver what kind of trees those were, and he answered

24. But see Athen. 2.39.153 = Megasth. F 28c Schw, 2 J, quoting Megasthenes on rice accompanied by 'ὄψα . . . Ἰνδικοῖς σκευασίαις'.

25. Some valuable evidence for diet in the Punjab at this period has been recovered from botanical remains: Singh 2009, 432.

26. Hardy and Totelin 2016, 109, discuss his trope of 'x looks like y'.

27. Arr. *Anab.* 6.22.4ff., from Aristobulus; cf. Plin. *NH* 12.18.33.

28. Thphr. *HP* 4.4.2.

"trees"; what was the name of that bird, and he said "bird"; and the plain, interminable, murmured, "old buildings are buildings, ruins are ruins".[29] Babur would not have settled for this. Always observant, even when he made clear how far he regarded the fruits of India as inferior to the melons of Samarkand, he seems to have noticed everything – not just fruit but elephants, rhinos, birds.[30]

Ctesias' botany has been discussed above. Megasthenes, in the surviving fragments, gives us even less: scarcely a plant is mentioned.[31] Most of what we know of what Alexander's companions observed of Indian natural history is collected by Arrian in the first chapters of his *Indica.* Apart from this, the most important source (of fragments as well as discussion) is Theophrastus.[32] Theophrastus began teaching his course, which became his book, in 314/13 BCE, but was collecting information for it up to 301.[33] For the earlier part of Alexander's expedition his main source was Callisthenes,[34] but after that scholar's death in Central Asia the picture is less clear. Amigues proposes that his main sources were Aristobulus and Androsthenes:[35] of the latter's work not a word survives. Theophrastus' achievements and limitations as a botanist are surveyed by Bretzl,[36] who notes for example that he was unaware of the sexual nature of plant reproduction. Pliny in his *Natural History* made use of most of the same sources as Theophrastus but must have gone back to the originals, as he includes quite a few plants that are not discussed by the Greek author.[37]

The Banyan (Ficus indica) *and the Banana*

Nearchus, who wrote an account of his voyage down the Indus and along the coast back to Persia, describes 'enormous trees whose shade extends for five hundred feet [150 m] all round; such is their size that ten thousand men could shelter under one tree'.[38] The same author is presumably one of the sources

29. Forster 1940, 297. I myself, encouraged by our Delhi guide's identification of the ashoka tree, pointed to another nearby tree and asked if he could tell me what it was. 'Tree', he said, and confessed with a twinkle in his eye that he was not omniscient.

30. Dale 2004, 361.

31. But Diod. 2.35.3 and 2.36.2 are probably from Megasthenes (F 4 J).

32. See the introduction by Amigues to her Budé edition of the *Historia plantarum*, vol. 1.

33. See Thphr. *HP* 4.84, 5.82.

34. D.L. 5.4, cf. Leroi 2014, 55.

35. Thphr. *CP* 2.5.5; Amigues, introduction to the Budé edition, xxvi.

36. Bretzl 1903, 303–4.

37. In general on Pliny: Beagon 1992; Stannard 1965 (not very detailed); Morton 1986.

38. Arr. *Ind.* 11.7.

4.1 A banyan tree with a splendid panoply of aerial roots. This one is in Aurangabad.

for the account of this tree in Strabo, Theophrastus and Pliny:[39] both Onesicritus and Aristobulus also described the tree and are paraphrased by Strabo. The authors vary on the size of the tree, for 'Aristobulus speaks of the trees that have their branches bent downwards and of such size that fifty horsemen – according to Onesicritus, four hundred – can pass the noon in shade under

39. Str. 15.1.21; Thphr. *HP* 4.4; Plin. *NH* 12.23; Amigues 2010, 20 and 140–1.

one tree'. Inflation continued over the centuries: Sir Monier Monier-Williams, writing in 1883, asserted that an army of seven thousand could take shelter under a single banyan tree.[40]

The most careful, and yet most puzzling, account, is that by the scientist Theophrastus, the pupil and successor of Aristotle, in his *Inquiry into Plants*: the tree 'drops its roots, not from the new branches, but from those of last year or even older ones; these take hold of the earth and make, as it were, a fence around the tree, so that it becomes like a tent, in which men sometimes even live ... They say that it extends its shade for as much as two stades; and the thickness of the stem is in some instances more than sixty paces ... The leaf is no smaller than a peltast's shield, but the fruit is very small, only as large as a chick-pea, and it resembles a fig. This is why the Greeks named this tree a "fig-tree"'. The description of the banyan's habit, and of its fruit, is tolerably accurate, but the statement about the size of the leaf is a puzzle. The banyan's leaves are about nine inches (23 cm) long, while a peltast's shield is big enough to cover the chest and commonly has a cutaway section at the top giving it the appearance of a fat crescent moon. (Onesicritus' own text compounds the problem by saying it the size of an *aspis*, a full-size shield.) Pliny gives more or less the same information, in effusive terms: 'the fruit is scanty and not larger in size than a bean; but as it is ripened by the rays of the sun shining through the foliage it has an exceedingly sweet taste, and is worthy of the marvellous tree that produces it'.[41] But he too tells us that the leaf is enormous: 'the breadth of the leaves has the appearance of an Amazon's shield' (*foliorum latitudo peltae effigiem Amazonicae habet*), which is the same as a peltast's.

Clearly Pliny and Theophrastus are both using the same source. Pliny often refers to the Alexander-writers but never to Theophrastus,[42] so it is unlikely that he is simply paraphrasing Theophrastus. One of Alexander's companions, then, was either a very bad observer or he muddled his notes on two different trees. In the circumstances it is perhaps not very fruitful to try to identify the tree with giant leaves. There are various possibilities: the arjuna has large oval leaves, the paulownia has leaves which may be as much as sixteen

40. *Religious Thought and Life in India* (1883), cited in Haberman 2014, 165. John Evelyn, using the same kind of analogy, describes a large tree (not a banyan!) that could shelter three hundred sheep under a single branch: Crane 2013, 196.

41. Plin. *NH* 12.11.23. At 7.2.21, a passage mainly about animals, he mentions in passing that 'squadrons of cavalry' can shelter beneath a single tree. He evokes its 'fresh offspring planted in a circle around the parent tree like the work of an ornamental gardener'.

42. Morton 1986.

4.2 An Amazon with a shield, as depicted on Attic vases.

inches (41 cm) across, and the teak also has very large leaves.[43] All of these might have been growing in the relevant region of India at this time. Bretzl, meanwhile, in the last detailed examination of Alexander's botanical legacy,

43. Pearson 1960, 101 suggests the teak, but notes that it probably did not grow in this region of India in Alexander's time. Catalpa may have leaves up to twelve inches (30 cm) long, which are also heart-shaped, but that is out of the question here as it is a New World tree.

developed a complicated argument to transfer the description of the leaf to the banana tree (*Musa sapientum*).[44] It runs as follows. The text containing Theophrastus' passage about the banyan continues thus:

> There is also another tree which is very large and has wonderfully sweet and large fruit; it is used for food by the sages of India who wear no clothes. There is another tree whose leaf is oblong in shape like the feathers of the ostrich; this they fasten on to their helmets, and it is about two cubits long.[45]

These sentences could both clearly be descriptions of the banana tree, suggesting that the repeated 'another' is an error of Theophrastus or his source. Although the Loeb translator asserts that the first sentence refers the jackfruit (*kathal, Artocarpus heterophyllus*),[46] it seems just as likely that it refers to the banana, as was clear to Linnaeus when he devised the name *Musa sapientum* for the banana tree on the basis of this description.[47] Bretzl suggests that the text is muddled, perhaps corrupt, and that the phrase 'as large [or 'wide'] as a peltast's shield' should simply be moved to the end of the description of the banana leaf. Pliny, he observes, took the phrase as describing the breadth of the leaf rather than its overall size.[48] The remedy seems too extreme for the problem, but it is an object lesson in the slipperiness of our sources for Alexandrine botany, and an example of the difficulties under which even a scholar close to the events in time, such as Theophrastus, would labour.

The only other trees mentioned by Strabo in his account of India are both from Aristobulus.[49] One is the 'wool-tree', which is apparently a misunderstanding of the cotton plant, and later came to be merged with the fabled tree of the Seres, from the branches of which silk was combed. Theophrastus also refers to the cotton plant as a 'tree':

> The trees from which they make their clothes have a leaf like the mulberry, but the whole tree resembles the wild rose. They plant them in the plain in rows, so that when seen from a distance they look like vines.[50]

44. Bretzl 1903, 195–200; the discussion of the problem begins on p. 171. He is followed by Arora 2005, 56.

45. Thphr. *HP* 4.4.5.

46. A. F. Hort, noted for the unreliability of his plant identifications.

47. Amigues 2010, 140–1.

48. Pliny's description of the banana is otherwise unexceptionable, *NH* 12.12.24: he says that it has leaves like a bird's wings and provides food for the sages, though he unfortunately goes on to give it the name *pala*, which is actually *Alstonia*, with glossy oval leaves.

49. *FGrH* 139 F 37.

50. Thphr. *HP* 4.4.8.

This information is repeated in Pliny and Mela.[51] Curtius refers to the fabric worn by Indians as 'linen'.[52] Cotton was already familiar to Greeks from the time of Herodotus and it is already in Onesicritus and Nearchus and thence Strabo, who mentions that it was used for stuffing saddle-cushions.[53]

The other tree mentioned by Strabo is a 'tree, not large, with pods, like the bean, ten fingers in length, full of honey; he says that those who eat it cannot easily be saved from death'. This is not the Indian bean tree (*Catalpa bignonoides*), as one might suppose, since that does not come from India (though it grows widely there now), but it might be the East Indian walnut (*shirish*; *Albizia lebbek*) or some other legume tree: the *shirish* has a sweet scent in flower, but the pods, though palatable to moth larvae, are not eaten by humans. If it is the banana, which Theophrastus, referring to a 'long, curved, sweet fruit', says Alexander forbade his troops to eat because it caused dysentery, then the Greeks had rather sensitive stomachs.[54]

Of the many species of tree native to northern India this is almost the entire account in the Greek writers. No mango, no ashoka with its crinkly leaves like a spear-blade; no semal with its startling red tulip-like flowers in February/March, no coconut (perhaps these occur too far south); nor any of the trees with useful timber like sissoo, cedar (too familiar?) and sandalwood. An exception is ebony, which Theophrastus does mention. Theophrastus adds several more kinds of tree, though we do not know which writer he was following. The 'Persian apple'[55] is identified by Hort as the citron: it has a leaf resembling the 'andrachne' (probably meaning *Arbutus andrachne*, the strawberry tree, though Linnaeus used *Andrachne* to designate a different genus), and thorns; the 'apple' keeps the moth away from clothes and also acts as an antidote to poison as well as being used as breath freshener. Babur attributes the quality of being an antidote to poison instead to the lime, not the citron, which he regards as good mainly for marmalade.[56]

51. Plin. *NH* 12.13.25; Mela 3.62.

52. Curt. 8.9.21. Arora 2005, 58 and n. 128; Arora proposes that the information derives from Androsthenes. He points out that the German name for cotton, *Baumwolle*, perpetuates this false datum.

53. Hdt. 3.106; Onesic. F 22; Nearch. F 19; Str. 15.1.20, 21.

54. Thphr. *HP* 4.4.5. The banana suggestion is offered by Pearson, 1960 174–5; Hort proposes the mango, which does not seem to fit the description.

55. Thphr. *HP* 4.4.2.

56. Thackston 2002, 348.

Aristobulus mentioned myrrh trees as well as mangroves and nard around the mouth of the Indus.[57] Nearchus also observed the mangroves, with their remarkable habit of growing in sea water,[58] and the lotus,[59] which, along with the crocodiles, induced Alexander to suppose that the Indus would run into the Nile. In fact the Indian and Egyptian lotuses are different plants. The Indian lotus is *Nelumbo nucifera*, and its rhizomes are eaten, sliced, and may be bought in oriental grocery shops; the Egyptian lotus is *Nymphaea lotus*; but the blue lotus, *Nymphaea caerulea*, also occurs in Egypt, and may have been present in Asia in antiquity.[60]

The jackfruit is mentioned by Theophrastus, and also by Babur, who says that its fruit has the appearance of stuffed tripe! Theophrastus also refers to jujube, to 'terebinth' with a fruit like almonds (i.e., the pistachio), and to dates.

Vines interested Greeks. According to Megasthenes, the vine was not cultivated in India. However, Onesicritus refers to its growing in the kingdom of Musicanus, and there is no doubt that it also grew in Gandhara, where there are plentiful signs of a kind of Dionysiac cult (see chapter 3 above, on Dionysus). Archaeological evidence includes the intriguing find from Gandhara of what appears to be a still, indicating that wine was not only made, but distilled into some form of brandy (Gandhy-brandy).[61]

Pipal and Neem

It may be possible to add to the list of trees observed by the Greeks the two that occur in the Latin *Letter of Alexander to Aristotle about India*.[62] After his conquest of India,

> Some of the wise men of the kingdom came to Alexander and said, 'Your majesty, we have something to show you which deserves your special attention. We will take you to the trees that speak with a human voice'. So they brought Alexander to a place where there was a sanctuary of the Sun

57. Aristob. Ff 49a, 49b7. Discussion in Pearson 1960, 177.

58. Plu. *NQ* 1.1.911ef: they bear no fruit, and are nourished by rivers; Plin. *NH* 13.135 and 139, cf. 2.226, notes that they do have berries.

59. Nearch. F 20.

60. See Thphr. *HP* 4.8.7–8; Hardy and Totelin 2016, 72 and 109. Dalby 2003, 199–200 takes it that Alexander saw *Nelumbo nucifera* in both rivers.

61. See the illustrations in Carter 2015, 159–61 and Allchin 1979.

62. The following discussion covers the ground also treated in Stoneman 2016a.

> and the Moon. The There was a guardpost here, and two trees closely resembling cypresses. Around these stood trees that resembled what in Egypt is called the myrrh-nut [this is the myrobalan tree, or *amala, ambla, amlaki* in Hindi],[63] and their fruits were also similar. The two trees in the middle of the garden spoke, the one with a man's voice, the other with a woman's. The name of the male one was Sun, and of the female one Moon, or in their own language, Moutheamatous.[64]

Offerings may have been made to the trees since they are surrounded by the skins of lions and panthers, though it is perhaps more likely that these are for sitting on to meditate, particularly as the skins are of female animals for the female tree, male for the male tree. (Sādhus, holy men, are normally exhorted to sit on animal skins for meditation.)[65] No iron is allowed to be brought into the sanctuary, and in the Latin *Letter* further elements of ritual purity are also required. Tree worship was conspicuous enough to impress the Alexander historians as well, since Curtius (though we cannot say which of Alexander's companions he got the information from) refers to the divine status of trees in India.[66]

Of the many sacred trees in India, two stand out for importance, the pipal and the neem. The pipal is perhaps the holiest tree in India, further sanctified by its association with the Buddha, who achieved enlightenment sitting under one at Bodhgaya, known as the bodhi tree. It is regarded as a masculine tree.[67] The neem is widely regarded as a beneficent and friendly tree, and is usually thought of as a feminine.[68] Many trees in fact have a feminine aspect, being the home of a *yakṣī* or (feminine) tree spirit. (*Yakṣa*s, masculine, are equally common.)

Haberman reports a conversation with two Hindu workers who were in charge of sweeping the temple at Bodhgaya:

> For us there are two sacred trees. One is a god [*devata*]; the other is a goddess [*devi*]. The first is the pipal; the second is the neem. The pipal is Vasudeva; the neem tree is Shervahani.[69]

63. The Latin *Letter* makes it opobalsamum, *Terminalia chebula*.

64. *AR* 3.17 β.

65. Hartsuiker 1993/2014, 125.

66. Curt. 8.9.34. On tree worship in the post-Vedic period, see Krishna and Amirthalingam 2014, 17–32. See also Singh 2009, 430 on ancient 'tree-huggers', about 300 BCE; Parpola 2015, 306.

67. Menon 2000, 105; Haberman 2014, chs. 3 and 4.

68. Krishna and Amirthalingam 2014, 209 note that it is often masculine in Rajasthan and the Punjab, so women conceal their faces when passing a neem tree.

69. Haberman 2014, 139; see also 103.

4.3 A pipal and a neem tree entwined ('married'),
near the Rock inscription of Aśoka at East of Kailash, Delhi.

The pipal is conceived as the form of one or other god, normally Viṣṇu. An informant told Haberman that the pipal tree is regularly conceived as being Vasudeva, or Viṣṇu.[70] It is either the residence or, more commonly, the embodied form, of Vasudeva.[71] 'The great wonder is that the gods take the form of trees ... Vishnu is the tree itself. It is the form of Vishnu.'[72]

'Shervahani', which means 'she who rides a tiger', generally refers to Durga, but in his conversation Haberman elicited that the neem (*Azadirachta indica*) could also be the goddess Shitala;[73] furthermore, an informant in Varanasi (Banaras) told Haberman that the neem tree growing in the middle of his sweet shop was Ma, the Mother, who might take the form of Durga or Shitala or indeed another goddess. Many people simply address the neem tree as 'Nima Mai, Neem Mother'.[74]

Sometimes the trees even intertwine, or are said to be 'married',[75] and in the eleventh-century Persian poem *Shahnameh* the trees visited by Alexander are said to twine together into a single tree, one trunk being male and the other female.[76]

I believe that the names Ma and Vasu(deva) – the 'deva' being simply a suffix meaning 'god' – may be concealed in the earliest Greek recension of the *Alexander Romance*, μουθου εμαουσαι. I am tempted to restore as an original text something like Μα θεα και Ουασου. The oracular trees would therefore be the (male) pipal and the (female) neem.

The *Alexander Romance* makes explicit not only that the trees are male and female but that they are trees of the Sun and Moon respectively. The pipal is sometimes said to be 'the abode of the Sun on earth'[77] and is associated with the sacred fire: in kindling the sacrificial fire 'the friction drill was made from pipal wood and was considered male, whereas the friction pan

70. Ibid., 103.

71. Ibid., 179.

72. *Skanda Purāṇa* 152.1, quoted in Haberman 2014, 31 and 51. The idea of the World Tree may also be present here: see *RV* 1.24.7. In a popular myth (Krishna and Amirthalingam 2014, 21), the gods are said to live in trees because of a curse laid on them by Parvati.

73. Sometimes, too, she is Kali, or Vana Durga, the 'forest goddess': Krishna and Amirthalingam 2014, 209.

74. Haberman 2014, 138; see also 186; Krishna and Amirthalingam 2014, 209–10.

75. Haberman 2014, 156.

76. Abolqasem Ferdowsi, *Shahnameh, the Persian Book of Kings*, tr. Dick Davis (Harmondsworth: Penguin, 2007), 517. Pliny's account (*NH* 16.66.162) of the two forms of bamboo, male and female, is probably irrelevant here.

77. Haberman 2014, 68.

was made from sami wood and considered female'.[78] The pipal tree is also often said to be the home of the god Shani, son of the Sun and brother of Death, though sometimes he only takes up his abode there on Saturdays, as otherwise the tree is Vasudev's.[79]

I have not been able to discover any corresponding match between the neem tree and the moon, though it is not hard to suppose that a Greek, with his inbuilt 'polar' habits of thinking,[80] on hearing that one of a pair of trees was that of the Sun, would instantly assume that the other was that of the Moon.[81] It is also possible that the motif has become combined with the report of Ctesias about a sanctuary of the Sun and Moon in India, though they are not said to take the form of trees.[82] Certainly the pipal is a tree of the daytime, which people often fear to approach at night because it is the home of ghosts (*bhut*s, an intriguing development of the Persian word for a pagan god, deriving from 'Buddha'). 'People only visit and worship the pipal tree during the day, especially during the morning hours'.[83]

The neem tree, on the other hand, is a friendly tree, which people love to have close to their houses. One common form of Ma is as Shitala, 'the smallpox goddess', whose functions extend much more widely to protection of children and health in general. The pipal is worshipped because it is beneficial to the soul, the neem for good health, and the banyan for long life.[84] 'To most Indians, the neem has for centuries been the symbol of good health and harbinger of good times.'[85]

Thus it seems highly likely that the author of the *Alexander Romance* was writing from first-hand knowledge acquired on a visit to a sacred grove

78. Ibid., 72. The sami (or shami/*śami*, or *khejari*; *Prosopis spicigera*), the Indian mesquite, also has a number of religious associations besides its importance in creating fire: Krishna and Amirthalingam 2014, 171–5. O'Flaherty 1973/1981, 284 notes that Agni, the fire-god, hides in a *śami* tree.

79. Haberman 2014, 113–14.

80. G.E.R. Lloyd, *Polarity and Analogy* (Cambridge: CUP, 1966).

81. Oppositions between sun and moon do occur in Indian religion: for example, the god Śiva, who wears the moon in his hair, is celebrated in the annual Shiva-ratri by night at the new moon in January/February, while Rāma, an avatar of the Sun god, is celebrated at noon in March or April. See Hartsuiker 1993/2014, 116–17.

82. Ctes. F 45.17. Karttunen 1989, 220, citing Gunderson 1980, 111–12. Nichols (2011, 106–7) thinks the report is 'probably authentic'; Lenfant (2004, 303–5) is dubious.

83. Haberman 2014, 107 and 125.

84. Ibid., 57.

85. Menon 2000, 94.

containing a pipal and a neem tree, identified to him as Vasu and Ma, and perhaps associated also with day and night *puja* respectively. Though the author was unable to describe the trees accurately, and said vaguely that they resembled cypresses, he was able to remember what went on around them. The passage is, then, a more vivid and complete recollection of an Indian sacred grove, and the customs pertaining to it, than any of the historians have left us.

Food Plants

The Macedonians recognised some of the plants that they came across. Finding ivy at Nysa was a particular delight, and persuaded them that this was the birthplace of Dionysus. As is well known, Alexander's renegade treasurer, Harpalus, spent some time trying to get ivy to grow in his garden in Babylon, so that, like his Athenian girl-friend, it would be a reminder of his native Greece.[86] (Times change; I spend much of my time trying to eliminate ivy from my garden).

Notably interesting to the Greek writers are, of course, food plants. Theophrastus discourses on the various legumes, which are similar to those of Greece but not the same; barley and sorghum; rice 'which resembles millet' and 'lentil' (*phakos* in Greek). This latter 'looks like *boukeras*', which according to *LSJ* (following Dioscorides) is a synonym for *telis* and means 'fenugreek' (*Trigonella faenum graecum L*).[87] Fenugreek is plentiful in India. Hort suggests that this is actually *Phaseolus mungo* (now *Vigna mungo*), which is the pulse normally sold in Indian shops as *urad dal*, or black lentils. It would be natural for Greeks to refer to this as a kind of lentil, though why anyone should think it looked like a fennel seed is beyond understanding. Perhaps, then, Alexander's men did enjoy the occasional plateful of spiced *dal* without succumbing to stomach trouble. (A few centuries later, the *Questions of King Milinda* lists the ingredients of a typical sauce: curds, salt, ginger, cumin, pepper and other spices – much like a modern curry.)[88]

86. Thphr. *HP* 4.4.1; Plu. *Alex.* 35.8; 2 Macc. 6.7; Callixeinus does not tell us whether ivy adorned the float representing the cave of Dionysus in Ptolemy Philadelphus' Grand Procession (Rice 1983, 136).

87. Diosc. *De mat. med.* 2.102.

88. *Milindapāñha* 1.97. The point Nāgasena is making is that the flavours cannot be separately tasted, just as the elements of sense-perception cannot be isolated.

Onesicritus refers to millet,[89] a broad term covering any kind of grain that is not wheat, oats or barley, and Eratosthenes to millet, rice and sesame, as well as flax, and also a mysterious grain called *bosmoron*. This seems to come from Megasthenes,[90] and may be a form of wheat,[91] but is identified by Dalby as bulrush millet.[92] Often these grains were simply made into a lumpy gruel (*ghughri*).[93]

Spices

Spices may indeed have been fewer than are known in modern Indian cookery, as many of them, including cloves, cardamom, nutmeg and black pepper, originate from south India or South East Asia. Ginger, garlic and coriander however were certainly known,[94] as well as basil, turmeric and cumin, which have been found in Indus-civilisation contexts;[95] cumin and fenugreek grow wild in northern India. Traces of cinnamon, which originates in the south of India, have been found in a seventh-century BCE context on Samos,[96] and Herodotus believed that giant Arabian birds built their nests with cinnamon sticks, and had to be tricked into damaging these nests with heavy cuts of meat so that the fragrant sticks would fall to the ground.[97] Nard is mentioned by Onesicritus and Aristobulus, whence Theophrastus.[98] Asafoetida (hing) grows freely in Iran and Afghanistan, and is related to the now extinct silphium of Cyrene, which the Greeks prized, so that it is surprising that Alexander's men

89. Onesic. F 15; Arora 2005, 61. Millet and rice were both introduced to India about 1300 BCE: Robinson 2015, 134, cf. 24. The tribal diet today consists largely of rice, millet and pulses. 'They scoop fish from the stream, and scour the forest': Moraes 1983, 173. They practise boiling and roasting, but never frying: Elwin 1955, 46.

90. Eratosth. F 74; Megasth. F 4: Roller 2010, 180.

91. Diod. 2.36.

92. Dalby 2003, 219. On the archaeological evidence from the Punjab, see again Singh 2009, 432.

93. Agrawala 1953.

94. Ibid., 99–119, 201–4.

95. Robinson 2015, 88.

96. Amigues 2011.

97. Hdt. 3.107–11. See also Dalby 2003, 87. Achaya 1998, 45–6 identifies cinnamon with Ctesias' cassia; but see Amigues 2011.

98. Onesic. F 22; Aristob. F 49a; Thphr. 9.2.7f: Dalby 2003, 229–30.

regarded asafoetida, when they met it in Afghanistan, as a poison.[99] The *Questions of King Milinda* remarks that the Himalayas are rich with hundreds of magical drugs.[100]

Pliny, some four hundred years after Alexander, is our most comprehensive source on Indian spices.[101] Some of them are hard to identify, and it is not certain where he got his information from, though much of it, as for trees and plants, must come from the Alexander historians: as he says, 'the Macedonians have given accounts of kinds of tree that for the most part have no name'.[102] Pliny kicks off with something that looks like a terebinth in every other respect, but has a fruit like an almond (probably pistachio).[103] The flax tree is a puzzle; Pliny says it has leaves like a mulberry and fruit like a dog rose. H. Rackham in the Loeb translation suggests the cotton-tree, but as cotton does not grow on trees this seems unlikely. Cotton plants do however grow relatively tall in India. König and Winkler suggest ramie, *Boehmeria nivea*, but this is a kind of nettle, in no way resembling a dog-rose.

Passing over the barren olive tree (Indian olive, *Olea cuspidata*),[104] Pliny's next offering is a tree like juniper which produces pepper, presumably long pepper.[105] This is followed by ginger (the name is Indian, Sanskrit *sṛngivera*, Pali *singivera*);[106] these two piquant spices prompt him to an outburst of moralising about the Roman obsession with hard-to-obtain flavourings.[107] Next comes the 'caryophyllon', which is presumably the clove (*Syzygium aromaticum*), native to Indonesia and still rare in Europe in medieval times. (It does not grow on lotuses!) The 'thorn bush resembling henna' (*Lawsonia inermis*),

99. Dalby 2003, 29; Kipling 1987, 196; Bretzl 1903, 285–92. Dalby 2003, 29 says it is probably a different species, but with similar properties. See Amigues 2010, 225–7, who suggests *Margotia gummifera.*

100. *Milindapāñha* 4.8.16.

101. Plin. *NH* 16.59.135. See also 12.13.25–12.19.36.

102. Cf. Thphr. *HP* 1.14.4. 'Pliny was very uncomfortable with anonymous plants' such as the Scythian *anonymus*: *NH* 27.31, Hardy and Totelin 2016, 96.

103. This is the opinion of R. König and J. Hopp in their commentary, 1994, 200.

104. Cf. Thphr. *HP* 4.11 – barren in India.

105. For an illustration of the pods (but not the tree or foliage), see Sen 2015, 24. The dry husks are called *bregma* = Skt. *vrkna*, 'dead'.

106. Dalby 2003, 159; Achaya 1998, 1 s.v. *adhrak*. It does not of course originate from Arabia, but is imported from there to Rome.

107. In the second millennium BCE the trade in spices from Melukkha (the Indus realm) to Akkad was also one way!: Robinson 2015, 103.

with bitter fruits and a root that can be boiled into a medicine, defies identification, even though it apparently grew also on Mount Pelion in Greece and might therefore have had a Greek name. As Pliny says that Greeks sometimes call it 'Chiron's buckthorn', it is presumably some kind of barberry (*rhamnus*). 'Macir', a tree with red bark, remains unidentified, though it may be mace. Dioscorides mentions under this name a yellowish and astringent 'foreign bark', beneficial in cases of diarrhoea.[108]

We are on firmer ground with sugar (Latin *saccharon*, Pali *sakkhara*), which originated in Papua New Guinea but migrated to north-west India many thousands of years ago. Nearchus saw it in the Punjab and referred to it as 'a reed tree that produced honey without the association of bees',[109] and this was reported also by Eratosthenes ('the large sweet reeds'),[110] though where he got it from is not made clear.[111]

Various poisonous plants in Pliny's next chapter are followed up by the honey-fig tree of Hyrcania, described by Onesicritus, and the bdellium of Bactria; he then moves on to Iran.

We may I think assume that this is a fairly comprehensive run-down of the spice plants observed by the Macedonians in the Punjab, though they probably do not constitute a complete conspectus of what there was at the period. Shastri shows, for instance, that other plants were known at this period, including the jujube, the rose-apple, the coconut and saffron, none of which were observed by Alexander's men.[112] Patañjali mentions several kinds of rice and pulses, many sorts of sweets, and fruits including bimba (*Momordica monadelpha*), which resembles women's lips, and pomegranate, vine and jujube.[113]

Dyes were not mentioned by the Alexander historians, though they noted the Indians' love of bright colours. Ctesias was familiar with purple and lac, Scylax with cinnabar.[114]

108. Diosc. *De mat. med.* 1.110.

109. Str. 15.1.20.

110. Eratosth. F 75 Roller. Also *Periplus* 14; Dalby 2003, 314–15

111. Also Lucan 3.237.

112. Shastri 1996, 279–94.

113. Puri 1990, 91–3.

114. Arora 2005, 61; *Jātakas* 71, 138, 157, 325.

Animals

In all animals there is something wonderful.

—ARISTOTLE, *DE PARTIBUS ANIMALIUM* 645A17

When Ptolemy Philadelphus held his Grand Procession in Alexandria some time in the 270s BCE,[115] several of the seemingly endless series of floats depicted Indian scenes associated with Alexander's expedition to India: the cave of Dionysus in Nysa, the god's return from India, and Alexander himself in solid gold, carried in a quadriga drawn by elephants with Nike and Athena on either side. Among the abundance of objects of solid gold and ivory, of women dressed to represent the islands of the Aegean, of groups of five hundred little girls here, three hundred lyre-players there, and the unforgettable golden thyrsus measuring 135 feet (41 m) and golden phallus of 180 feet (55 m), 'painted all over and bound with golden fillets, having at the end a gold star whose circumference was nine feet [2.75 m]', there were very large animals. There were two thousand bulls with gilded horns, two thousand four hundred hunting dogs, and many African birds and animals – oryxes, hartebeest, ostriches and onagers; 'twenty Ethiopian cows, one large white bear, fourteen leopards, sixteen cheetahs, four caracals, three cheetah cubs, one giraffe and one Ethiopian rhinoceros'. As Ptolemy's African domains were represented by their animals, so was the historical memory of Alexander's advance into India represented by its beasts. There was an eighteen-foot (5.5 m) statue of Dionysus in a purple cloak and a golden crown of ivy and vine, seated on an elephant and with a live satyr as a mahout. There followed the five hundred little girls, then 120 satyrs and behind them twenty-four elephant quadrigae—that's ninety-six elephants – and later on six bigae of camels and mule carts bearing tents in which sat Indian women. 'More camels carried three hundred minae of frankincense, three hundred of myrrh, and two hundred of saffron, cassia, cinnamon, orris, and other spices.' There were six hundred Ethiopian tribute bearers carrying six hundred elephant tusks and two thousand ebony logs among other things. 'Then there were borne along in cages parrots, peacocks, guinea fowl, pheasants and Ethiopian birds'.

Some of the details of this menagerie – which must in part have come from Ptolemy's own zoo – recall the gifts sent by Queen Candace of Meroe to Alexander in the *Alexander Romance*: ingots of gold, young Ethiopians, two hun-

115. Rice 1983, 4–5.

dred monkeys, elephants, panthers, bloodhounds and fighting bulls, as well as three hundred elephant tusks, three hundred panther skins and three thousand ebony wands.[116] The image is of the opulence and abundance of Africa, to which Ptolemy has added items that represent India, though it is surprising that no monkeys are included in the Indian cavalcade. Perhaps they were too hard to get hold of, or too difficult to control; or perhaps the 'satyrs' should be understood as monkeys. The elephants, too, were probably African ones, since it is unlikely that so many Indian elephants had reached the West by this time.[117] However that may be, there is no doubt that India is represented and brought to life by its animal denizens, not least the peacocks that Alexander admired above all: he was 'struck with amazement at the sight of these birds in India, and in his admiration of their beauty threatened the severest penalties for any man who slew one'.[118]

Ptolemy's concept of Indian wildlife represented an advance on the roll-call available from earlier writers, notably Ctesias. The latter had referred, soundly enough, to serpents, parrots, elephants and monkeys as well as sheep and goats (no pigs), but added to these the martichora (manticore), the poisonous dikairon bird and the unicorn, the dog-headed men and the 'giant worm' of the Indus.[119] Apart from the Dog-heads (on whom see chapter 10 below) and the implausible dikairon, these creatures can be reasonably identified with the tiger, the rhinoceros and the crocodile, though all have suffered some elaboration in the telling. 'There are wild asses in India the size of horses and even bigger. They have a white body, crimson head, and deep blue eyes. They have a horn in the middle of their brow one and a half cubits in length. The bottom part of the horn is bright white. The tip is sharp and deep vermilion in colour, while the rest in the middle is black. They say that whoever drinks from the horn (which they fashion into cups) is immune to seizures and the holy sickness and suffers no effects from poison'.[120] And the Indus river worm 'is seven cubits long. They say it is so wide that a ten-year-old child could hardly embrace it. It has two teeth, one above and one below, and eats

116. *AR* 3.18.

117. Rice 1983, 86 and 91.

118. Ael. *NA* 5.21. There were large numbers of these birds in the forest bordering the river Hydraotes (Ravi): Curt. 9.1.13.

119. Ctes. F 45.

120. Cf. Ael. *NA* 3.41 and 4.52: in the latter he gives Ctesias as his source. Rhinoceroses are now found only in Assam (Keay 2001, 206; Enright 2008, 139), but 'once roamed from Pakistan to Burma' (Enright 2008, 141). For more on rhinos, see ch. 10 below.

whatever it grabs with these teeth. Throughout the day they live in the mud of the river but come out by night. When it comes across an ox or camel on land, it bites it, then drags the beast into the river and consumes everything except the intestines'. Ctesias also says that these worms are captured with giant hooks and then hung up to produce a precious oil that is a fire accelerant.

The companions of Alexander have rather little to say in their surviving fragments about Indian animals. None of them, it seems, was trying to write a comprehensive account of the fauna, as Babur did.[121] There is virtually nothing in Onesicritus and Aristobulus except for some dubious statements in the latter about elephants' longevity (see below) and on the gigantic serpents that Abisares kept as pets.[122] Cleitarchus provides rather more, describing monkeys, serpents and some birds.[123] Nearchus provides information about the gold-gathering ants,[124] already known from Herodotus and due to reappear in Megasthenes. Aelian's vast compilation of snippets about animals cites Ctesias and Cleitarchus often, but not the other companions of Alexander.[125] Alexander himself, he tells us, was frightened by the monkeys he encountered – it is not often that Alexander is frightened by anything, except in the *Romance* – though apparently not by the snake, seventy cubits long, that had eyes like a Macedonian shield and lived in a cave.[126] The snakes are poisonous, he says, but if one kills a man it is never able to return to its lair, but dies a miserable and lonely death for its crime.[127] He has quite a lot of scraps of information about elephants,[128] as well as common animals like, dogs, sheep and goats, and the hunting of hares and foxes. I wonder if the 'dogs

121. Philostr. *VA* 3.4 mentions monkeys and pepper trees, perhaps simply to improve on his predecessors.

122. Aristobulus F 38 states that there are no huge animals in India, mentions crocodiles and dangerous snakes, as well as fish (F 39) and dogs (F 40); Onesicritus (F 14) speaks of elephants and (F 16ab) the serpents of Abisares.

123. Cleitarchus Ff 15, 18, 21, 22.

124. *FGrH* 133 F 8 = Arr. *Ind.* 15.4.

125. Aelian's information on Indian creatures is collected by McCrindle 1901, 136–49.

126. Ael. *NA* 17.25 (monkeys), 15.21, cf. 17.2. The snake is probably not the same as Abisares' pet one, though it had a long afterlife, reappearing in, for example, Nizami's *Iskandarnameh*, where Alexander devises a way to kill the savage creature by tempting it to eat a bull that has been stuffed with pitch, so that when the serpent swallows it its insides are burned up.

127. Ael. *NA* 12.32. The source for this moralising conclusion, so suitable to Aelian's temperament, is hard to guess; perhaps Cleitarchus.

128. Ibid. 3.46 (affectionate), 4.24 (hunting elephants), 5.55 (uprooting trees), 6.21 (elephant fights snake), 6.37 (loyalty of Porus' elephant), 4.44 (taming elephants), 13.7 (diseases of

bred from tigers' might be cheetahs (which no Greek ever mentions)?[129] The lac insect makes an appearance.[130] Some of Aelian's other Indian animal lore must come from Megasthenes, and will be discussed when we come to that author's account of India.[131] Lynxes are mentioned uniquely in the *Alexander Romance*.[132]

Aelian also mentions several birds, including parrots, peacocks and pheasants.[133] He quotes Cleitarchus for the orion bird,[134] a kind of singing heron which is unidentifiable to D'Arcy Thompson,[135] and the catreus, which may be a kind of pheasant.[136] In his *Varia historia* he mentions that 'Indian traditions report that yellow/green (μηλίνας) pigeons are found in India'.[137] This is not a mistake about parrots, well-known to Greeks and Romans, but a reference to the Indian green pigeon, *Treron sp.*:[138] there are several varieties. A woman in the throes of sexual intercourse, according to the *Kāma Sūtra* may 'according to her imagination', imitate the cry of the green pigeon, as well as of the dove, cuckoo, parrot, bee, nightingale, goose, duck or partridge.[139]

Aristotle gives accounts of a number of Indian animals in various works, especially of course the *Historia animalium*.[140] In *De generatione animalium* he rebuts the statement of Ctesias that the semen of elephants dries to the hardness of amber,[141] as well as the statement of Herodotus that the semen of Ethiopians is black (one wonders how he verified the latter discovery), and

---

elephants), 13.8 (their love of flowers and perfumes), 13.22 (they guard the king), 13.25 (use in warfare), 17.29 (Ctesias on elephants).

129. Ibid. 8.1 (dogs). Aelian's 'black lion' (17.26) is probably a panther.

130. Ibid. 4.46.

131. Ibid.: the electric eel (8.7); monkeys (17.39); the hoopoe (16.5); flying scorpions (16.41).

132. *AR* 3.17.20.

133. Ael. *NA* 16.2.

134. Ibid. 17.22.

135. Thompson 1936; but cf. Arnott 2007: perhaps a type of crane.

136. Ael. *NA* 17.23; Cleitarchus, *FGrH* 137 Ff 20–22; the catreus is also mentioned at Strabo 15.1.69.

137. Ael. *VH* 1.15; the information comes from Daimachus' *Indica*, as is made clear by Athenaeus 9.51, 394e.

138. Thompson 1936, 247.

139. *Kāma Sūtra* 2.7.7.

140. Reese 1914, 99ff. collects the passages, which include *Cael.* 2.14 (elephants in both Egypt and India), *SE* 5 ('if an Indian is black but has white teeth, is he black or white?'), as well as passages on non-zoological matters: e.g., *Pol.* 7.14 (Scylax on Indian kings).

141. Arist. *GA* 2.2.736a. Also *HA* 3.22.523a.

remarks that Indian dogs spring from the union of a dog with some wild dog-like animals.[142] He generalises from the case of the parrot that 'all birds with crooked talons are short-necked, flat-tongued, and disposed to mimicry. The Indian bird, the parrot, which is said to have a man's tongue, answers to this description; and after drinking wine, the parrot becomes more saucy than ever.'[143] Did Aristotle work with a parrot perched beside his desk, making saucy remarks the while? He quotes Ctesias for the lack of swine in India, while remarking that he is 'no very good authority',[144] and also mentions a deadly snake in India.[145] For all these facts his source must be one or other of the Alexander historians.

The star exhibit is of course Aristotle's account of the elephant, which has been much discussed. The companions of Alexander provided plenty of information about elephants and their habits, as well as the employment of them by the kings. Elephants love flowers and perfume, they can uproot trees, they are noted for loyalty and guard the king, they have to be captured by a method described in detail, and tamed, and are used in warfare.[146] Both Nearchus and Onesicritus described elephant habits, though Nearchus is the more reliable, for example in saying that elephants are excellent swimmers, whereas Onesicritus said they were poor ones, as did Aristotle.[147] The longest account of elephants is in Arrian and is surely from Megasthenes, as is the parallel passage in Strabo, describing the method of capture.[148] Aristotle's longest account of elephant behaviour is the following:[149]

> Elephants fight fiercely with one another, and stab one another with their tusks; of two combatants the beaten one gets completely cowed, and dreads the sound of his conqueror's voice. These animals differ from one another to an extraordinary extent in the way of courage. Indians employ these

142. *GA* 2.7.746a. They are tigers in *HA* 8.28, 607a. See also Ael. *NA* 8.1.

143. *HA* 8.12.597b.

144. Ibid. 8.28.606a.

145. Ibid. 8.29.607a.

146. Ael. *NA* 13.8, 5.55, 6.37, 13.22, 4.24, 12.44, 13.25.

147. Arora 2005, 51

148. Arr. *Ind.* 13; Str. 15.1.42–3.

149. *HA* 9.1.610a, 15–32. But there is information throughout the *HA*: Leroi 2014, 99–100. Aristotle describes their breasts, genitals, limbs, skull, gall, sperm, teeth and trunk; he believes they live in swamps and use their trunks as snorkels (137–9). He was wrong to say that elephants have no joints in their legs; this non-fact is also in Agatharchides and was repeated constantly into the Middle Ages: Trautmann 2015, 239.

animals for war purposes, irrespective of sex; the females, however, are less in size and much inferior in point of spirit. An elephant by pushing with his big tusks can batter down a wall, and will butt with his forehead at a palm until he brings it down, when he stamps on it and lays it on the ground. Men hunt the elephant in the following way: they mount tame elephants of approved spirit and proceed in quest of wild animals; when they come up with these they bid the tame brutes to beat the wild ones until they tire the latter completely. Hereupon the driver mounts a wild brute and guides him with the goad; after this the creature soon becomes tame, and obeys guidance. Now, when the driver is on their back they are all tractable, but after he has dismounted, some are tame and others vicious; in the case of these latter, they tie their front legs with ropes to keep them quiet. The animals are hunted whether young or full-grown.

This circumstantial account is very close to that of Ctesias,[150] though contains more details. The question that arises is whether Aristotle relied solely on this early source for his information about elephants, or whether Alexander and his men provided him with further information and perhaps even specimens. It was commonly believed in later antiquity that Aristotle had given Alexander a commission to supply him with scientific information. The *Letter of Alexander to Aristotle about India* begins with Alexander's promise to supply his teacher with information: 'since I know that you are interested in philosophy, I thought I would write to you about the parts of India, and the kinds of serpents, men and beasts that are to be found there: whenever a man learns something about a new subject, it increases his learning and his understanding'. Pliny states that Alexander was 'fired with a desire to know the natures of animals' and 'delegated the pursuit of this study to Aristotle as a man of supreme eminence in every branch of science'.[151] The result was some fifty volumes of zoology from Aristotle's pen. Athenaeus adds the further information that Alexander gave Aristotle eight hundred talents to support the 'perfecting' of his *History of Animals*.[152] Many subsequent scholars have supposed that this was true and that Alexander and his men provided the philosopher with information and specimens;[153] for, without funds, how could Aristotle have acquired so much knowledge? As Athenaeus says, 'I should

150. Ctes. F 45bα.
151. Plin. *NH* 8.17.44; Beagon 1992, 128 n. 7.
152. Athen. 9.58.398e.
153. Jaeger, for example: see Romm 1989; Scullard 1974, 37–52.

like to know when he learnt, or from what Proteus or Nereus who came up from the depths he found out, what fish do, or how they go to sleep, or how they live': the diatribe continues for a couple of pages.[154] The conduit for information is supposed to have been Callisthenes, who is certainly quoted by Theophrastus, Aristotle's pupil and successor, for botanical information. But Callisthenes was dead by the time the expedition reached India. Theophrastus must have drawn on the Alexander companions, but Aristotle never states that he himself did so. James Romm has argued forcefully that the philosopher and his pupil were no longer seeing eye to eye by this date, and that Alexander was likely to have had little interest in channelling information back to Macedon.[155] This is speculative, but the fact remains that Aristotle shows very little knowledge of Indian fauna – except the elephant. Keller proposed that Alexander had sent one home to Macedon after the battle of Gaugamela, and, as mentioned previously, L. Sprague du Camp even wrote a novel that described the tribulations of the poor beast on its long journey westwards. Aristotle certainly knew that elephants existed in both east and west, in India and Africa,[156] but Romm thinks that the specimen he examined was African. In fact it is not necessarily the case that he examined one at first hand, and certainly not that he dissected one: Galen was apparently the first scientist to do that.[157] Sadly, the evidence of Aristotle turns out to be a generation old;[158] the best and earliest first-hand account of the elephant will be that of Megasthenes.[159] Further discussion of Indian zoology will be reserved for chapter 10 below, on that writer and the natural world.

154. Quotation at Athen. 8.47.352de. Much of Aristotle's research was done on Lesbos: Leroi 2014, 32, deriving from Lee 1948, 61–7.

155. Romm 1989.

156. Arist. *Cael.* 298a.

157. Bigwood 1993a.

158. Similarly, on the 'Indian ass', his source is probably not even as recent as Ctesias, but Scylax: Panchenko 2003, n. 16.

159. Scullard 1974, 37–52 concludes that Aristotle had no first-hand knowledge of elephants, but (58–9) that Megasthenes' information is of good quality.

PART II

Megasthenes' Description of India

5

Introducing Megasthenes

MEGASTHENES (ca. 350–290 BCE) was the author of the most extensive description of India, its geography, peoples, customs and (to some extent) history written by a Greek author.[1] He was for many years associated with Sibyrtios, the satrap of Arachosia and Gedrosia, and therefore presumably lived in Kandahar (Alexandria in Arachosia). His particular importance stems from the fact that, according to his own testimony, he travelled to India as ambassador for King Seleucus to the court of Candragupta Maurya in Pataliputra. As a result of this experience, he knew India better than any other Greek, and was able to write from authoritative knowledge and deep experience.

Most of Megasthenes' work survives only in 'fragments' – short excerpts or longer paraphrases in later authors – and we know frustratingly little about him. Though he was certainly a Greek, we do not even know what part of the Greek world he came from. The only recorded instance of the name belongs

1. General accounts are few. The fragments were collected by Schwanbeck 1846 and translated by McCrindle 1926; they were re-edited, far more selectively, by Jacoby, *FGrH* 715, which is translated by D. Roller in *Brill's New Jacoby*. For a concordance of these two editions, see the Appendix below. Still fundamental is the hundred-column *RE* article by Stein; see also Stein 1921. Derrett's article in *Der Kleine Pauly* is also excellent. Timmer's book (1930) is thorough and judicious. Other wide-ranging treatments include Brown 1955 and Brown 1973, 141–51, who calls Megasthenes' book 'not a particularly distinguished performance', and opines that other Greeks could have made much better use of Megasthenes' opportunities; while Pearson 1960, 110 disparages his 'crude methods'; then Bosworth 1996a; Kosmin 2014; Majumdar 1958; Goyal 2000. Both Majumdar and Muntz (2012) minimise the presence of Megasthenes in Diodorus. Sachse 1981 (I rely on the German abstract of the Polish text) is reliable despite some fables, and good on the state. Arora 1991–92 is a clear statement of the standard views of the issues. A recent collection, Wiesehöfer, Brinkhaus and Bichler (eds.) 2016, contains a great many valuable articles, including Roller 2016.

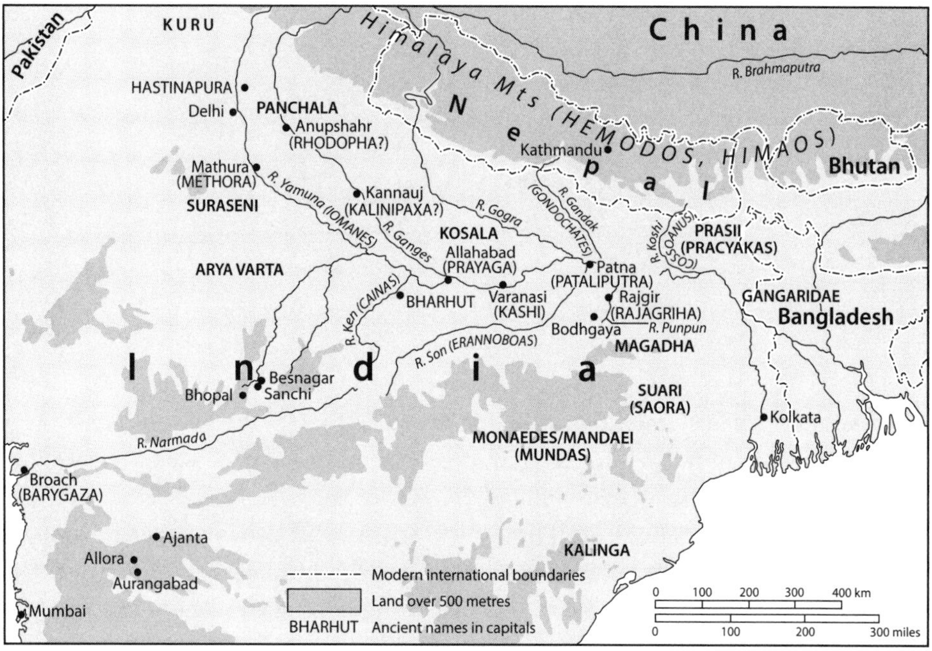

5.1 Megasthenes' India.

to someone from Chalcis in Euboea. When writing of the rivers Ganges and Indus, he compares them for size to the rivers of Asia Minor, the Caicus, Cayster, Maeander and Hermos. This might imply that he was familiar with these rivers because they ran near his native land. However, another author on India, Nearchus, who came from Crete, also chose these rivers for comparison; they are the only rivers of any size running into the Aegean basin apart from those of Macedonia, the Axius and Haliacmon, and of Thrace, the Hebrus and Strymon; neither of these regions was regarded as strictly Greek. Signs of Ionic dialect, the dialect of western Asia Minor, have also been detected in some of the fragments; but it would be very natural for dialect to be changed by an author quoting him, and other indications are for Attic. Furthermore, a writer in the Herodotean tradition might choose to adopt Ionic dialect, as Lucian did later. So no conclusion can be drawn from any of these pieces of evidence. We do not know where Megasthenes came from.

His date is just as difficult to determine, and more depends on the answer. The key passage is Strabo's sentence about him, which could be translated either 'he states that he repeatedly visited the court of Candragupta', or 'he repeatedly states that he visited the court of Candragupta'.[2] Seleucus also employed a second ambassador, Daimachus, presumably later than Megasthenes; according to Strabo in scathing mood, what Daimachus wrote about India was 'even worse' than Megasthenes. Since Seleucus died in 280, one should set Megasthenes' mission(s) well before this. But how much before? Candragupta's reign probably began in 321 (*CHI*: Stein prefers 316), and he reigned for twenty-four years, that is, till 295 or 290. Seleucus and Candragupta signed a treaty in 304 or 303, so a date after that seems the most natural context for those 'repeated visits'.[3] If we assume that Megasthenes was a mature man when he was given the role of ambassador, we might give him the dates ca. 350–290, which would chime with the statement of Clement that he was a 'contemporary' of Seleucus, who lived from 358 to 280.[4] He would have written his book about 300.

There is also the unanswerable question as to whether the 'repeated visits' were journeys to India from Kandahar, or journeys from a residence in India to the court at Pataliputra; the latter, implying an extended sojourn in India, would give Megasthenes the opportunity to penetrate Indian culture deeply, and perhaps learn a suitable language.

The date matters because Brian Bosworth has argued for a recalibration of Megasthenes' date, setting his visit (a single visit) in about 319/8 and the composition of his book around 310.[5] At this date he would be describing Alexander's world, when Porus had only just died, while in 300 he would be describing Candragupta's world.

Bosworth's key piece of evidence is a puzzling sentence of Megasthenes where he refers to his own visit(s) to 'Candragupta, the greatest king, and

2. I agree with Mehl 1986 that *pollakis* is best taken with 'visited' not with 'states'. But one cannot be certain.

3. Wheatley 2014, 516 remarks that the only irrefutable dates are those in the classical tradition, such as this one.

4. Clem. *Strom.* 1.72.5 = Megasth. T 1 J.

5. Bosworth 1996b, revisited in Bosworth 2003, 312–13. Wheatley 2014, accepting Bosworth's early dating of Megsathenes' mission, has added further arguments to suggest that Alexander's India collapsed immediately following Porus' death: first, that was no Macedonian control of the satrapies west of the Indus up to 304, as they had come peacefully under Maurya control as soon as Porus was dead; and second, that this is because we are told that Seleucus had to subdue the Bactrians on his way to India. (This simply means, however, that the Bactrians were independent, not that they were Maurya vassals.) Thus Megasthenes need have had no part in the signing of the treaty in 304. The points depend on acceptance of Bosworth's dating. See further the narrative below, this chapter.

Porus, who was still greater'. On any reading this is nonsense. What can he really have said? The text is generally emended to 'Candragupta, the greatest king of the Indians, one who was still greater than Porus'. Bosworth accepts the transmitted text and takes it that it refers to a time when Porus *was* a greater king than Candragupta, before the latter's empire was fully established. Megasthenes is thus describing conditions in India around 319/8, immediately before the death of Porus. But this still does not make sense of the superlative, which can only have been used when Candragupta *was* 'supreme' king in India, which would still mean that Megasthenes was writing under Candragupta's supremacy. The reference to Porus would then have to be a retrojection into the past, meaning that he also met Porus, who had at one time been still greater.

Bosworth continues his argument, that the India Megasthenes describes reflects conditions in the immediate aftermath of Alexander's expedition rather than those when Candragupta had already established his empire in northern India, with several further points. He argues, first, that many details reflect Alexander's 'Last Plans' for western conquests, notably the surprising information about the Pharaoh Taharka's western expedition (a fiction). Second, Megasthenes states that no one from the West, apart from Alexander, had penetrated India, which would have been a tactless thing to write at a time when Seleucus had done just that. In fact Arrian writes, 'Megasthenes says that the Indians had never attacked, or been attacked by, any other people'. But Arrian is excerpting what Megasthenes wrote, and is himself writing from the perspective of a historian of Alexander. He had no reason to excerpt what may perfectly well have been the conclusion of the sentence, the qualification 'before Alexander'. Third, according to Megasthenes, there were many local kings in India, and there were also *poleis*: independent cities and autonomous peoples. Bosworth's argument is that this was the case when Alexander arrived, but was not so under the Maurya empire. However, the *poleis* certainly did not evaporate as a result of Candragupta's rise to power, and the kings may have continued to function as vassals, as Porus had done for a short time under Alexander. It is characteristic of ancient ethnographic writers to describe conditions that are slightly out of date, as a result either of time-lag in information, or because their informants like to describe things as they were 'in the good old days' and ought to be now.

Richard Ricot, in an unpublished paper, has also argued for the traditional date, rejecting Bosworth's view on the grounds that it erects too powerful a superstructure of argument on an insufficient foundation of data. Indeed, the first argument above, about the reference to Taharka, is insubstantial, since there might have been many reasons for Megasthenes to refer to Taharka, as in the case of Nebuchadnezzar, mentioned in one fragment only. Paul Kosmin argues in detail against Bosworth's dating on the following grounds.[6]

1. The phrase 'still greater than', however it is interpreted, makes no sense and should probably be regarded as intrusive. I would myself suggest that it is a gloss by a scribe who thought he knew better than the author because he was thinking about the time of Alexander, not that of Candragupta.
2. The reference to Sibyrtius need imply no more than that Sibyrtius' court provided a 'base' for Megasthenes' repeated journeys to India.
3. An important point is that everything Megasthenes writes about India implies a unified state:[7] note especially Pliny *NH* 6.17.58, which makes no reference to either Porus or Sibyrtius, and categorises Megasthenes among diplomats, and not under military expeditions. Pataliputra is the epicentre of his world, and the end point of the Maurya 'Royal Road' (F 6c).
4. I would myself add here that the way Megasthenes refers to the philosophers who wait on the king reflects an increased understanding of their categorisation. While Onesicritus simply refers to 'naked philosophers', Megasthenes has 'Brahmanes and Sarmanes', i.e., *brahmanaśramaṇam* in the correct Sanskrit phrase.[8] He knows that there are two varieties of philosopher, both of whom have a role to play with kings. There is no hint of this in Onesicritus. The fact that Megasthenes' explicit distinction of the two kinds introduced an irredeemable confusion in later writers (from the Geneva papyrus onwards), who began to think of the naked philosophers as Brahmans, should not mislead us here. Megasthenes describes the conditions of the Maurya court.
5. Finally, Kosmin has an explanation for the startling fragment about Nebuchadnezzar (F 1), which acquires a context if Megasthenes' 'employer' is lord of the erstwhile city of Nebuchadnezzar, Babylon.

6. Kosmin 2014, 265–71.

7. So also Primo 2009, 55.

8. See Dihle 1964, 21: he comments that 'his translations and transliterations of Indian names are astonishingly correct'.

If this is accepted, there is no need to consider Bosworth's very hypothetical argument that Megasthenes' mission to India was to secure elephants for Eudamus' (and Sibyrtius') war against Peithon.[9] Even if he did, this may have been only the first of his 'repeated visits'. He may have come to prominence through negotiating the 'Treaty of the Indus' (as Kosmin calls it).[10] A further consideration is his possible connection with Hecataeus of Abdera, who was writing about 320–205 BCE: see below, this chapter.

In conclusion, I believe it is not necessary to abandon the traditional date for Megasthenes. He spent some time in India, either in Pataliputra or in an ambassador's residence from which he frequently visited the court, and wrote about the established Maurya empire.[11] (One wonders if he had an opposite number in Babylon).[12] For what it is worth, the depth and quantity of his information seems to me to suggest a residence over an extended period, particularly when we consider the inferiority of the material that Ctesias managed to gather in a residence of seventeen years at the Persian court! Though his account poses many problems, it is the work of a serious writer, and it was unfair of Strabo to brand him a liar; he recorded not only what he saw but what he was told, and sometimes what he was told was Indian tradition which we now know to be untrue, such as the existence of people with the heads of dogs. Herodotus, who was also sometimes branded a liar, did the same, and regularly invites his readers to reflect on whether the stories he transmits can actually be the truth. If we had Megasthenes' own words we would very probably find him doing the same. Only a few years later, another ambassador, Daimachus wrote a book about India which would be a valuable comparison if we had more than the exiguous snippets that remain.[13]

It is important to try to identify Megasthenes' informants, and indeed his hypothetical audience. The question of informants is an important one for

9. Bosworth 1996b, 120.

10. Kosmin 2014, 32–7. On this treaty see ch. 13 below. See also the amusing anonymous novella *Chandragupta and his Marriage with Alexander's Granddaughter* (Anon. 1904), which (in ch. 11) similarly makes this deduction.

11. Whether Megasthenes can settle the date of Kautilya, as argued by J.D.M Derrett, is a further question, which we will return to later when considering Megasthenes' descriptions of the Maurya state. Stein's view is that Kautilya is later; but others would allow for a Maurya core and the existence of a man called Kautilya even if much of the work was added later.

12. Wiesehöfer 1998, 230 thinks he must have done, since Aśoka's Rock Edicts 2 and 13 must have been erected courtesy of Antiochus II.

13. Schwarz 1968 pulls together what can reasonably be said about Daimachus.

modern anthropologists, who are aware that their data may be skewed by an unrepresentative choice of informants, as well as by the preconceptions they bring to the task.[14] Some are radically sceptical. As the African witch doctor says to the Jack Nicholson character, a journalist, in Michelangelo Antonioni's 1975 film *The Passenger*, 'Your questions are much more revealing about yourself than my answers would be about me.'

Megasthenes' Project

The discovery of a 'new world' could open up many new avenues for writers, as did the European discovery of the Americas in the sixteenth century. Responses to the Americas ranged through ethnographic accounts (Walter Ralegh), accounts of natural history (Oviedo), testimonies of violent conquest (Bernal Diaz) and poets' reflections on otherness (John Donne, Shakespeare's *The Tempest*).[15] What was Megasthenes setting out to do in writing a book entitled *Indica*? Felix Jacoby categorised him among those he defined as ethnographers, but then blurred the category by amalgamating it with local history, which to modern perceptions is a very different field.[16] The three authors who provide us with our largest number of fragments of Megasthenes – Strabo, Diodorus and Arrian – are, respectively a geographer, a historian and the author of another *Indica* (but otherwise known as a historian: at *Ind.* 17.7 he calls the subject of this first part τὰ Ἰνδῶν νόμιμα, which Hammond translates boldly and misleadingly as 'an Indian ethnography'). Some of Strabo's complaints about Megasthenes' unreliability can be understood in terms of his different scientific perspective.[17]

14. Dougherty 2001, 9: 'ethnography is a kind of hermeneutics, or "the comprehension of self by the detour of the comprehension of the other". The ethnographer aims to decode the target nation and to recode what he discovers for his own cultural fellows, his readers.'

15. See in general Greenblatt 1991.

16. Skinner 2012, 30–4. The project is different from that of the anthropologist, who aims to construct theories, probably on a comparative basis (like Levi-Strauss or Mary Douglas). Dillery 2015, 384, referring to Momigliano 1975, 92, remarks that Greeks expected their ethnographies to conform to certain models, whether written by Greek observers or by members of the people in question.

17. Strabo 2.1.9 is the author's most comprehensive attack on his predecessors: 'All who have written about India have proved themselves, for the most part, fabricators, but predominantly so Daimachus; the next in order is Megasthenes; and then Onesicritus, and Nearchus, and other such writers, who begin to speak the truth, though with faltering voice.'

In the generations before Megasthenes, Greeks had not written books of this nature. The roots of Greek 'ethnography' are commonly found in Homer (especially the *Odyssey)* and of course in Herodotus and his predecessor Hecataeus. But these authors, and also Thucydides, who includes a number of ethnographic observations,[18] embed their observations in the course of a wider narrative, in the latter two cases that of a war; and even Homer in his *Iliad* was mainly describing a war. The ethnographic monograph is something new in the age after Alexander. Alexander's companion Onesicritus does not seem to be an exception to this generalisation: though most of the fragments we have of his work relate to India, to the extent that it is impossible to be sure what his book really covered, it was certainly some kind of narrative of the campaign.[19]

In the case of Herodotus, much discussion has centred on the idea of 'the other': of ethnographic description as Greek self-definition.[20] V. S. Naipaul has said that 'the traveller is a man defining himself against a foreign background'.[21] Recognition of the relativity of cultural values in the age of the sophists led to an attempt to investigate the roots of Greekness. At its weakest, the ethnographic impulse is 'an interest in foreign peoples', something that could hardly be absent even in the most insular of communities. It is notable, however, that Megasthenes and the other writers on India do not customarily refer to the Indians as 'barbarians', in this doing better than, for example, Bartolomé de Las Casas writing about the inhabitants of the West Indies.[22]

The age of Alexander ushered in some different perspectives, particularly after Alexander himself blew apart the idea of the barbarian by his adoption of Persian dress, his employment of Persian staff and troops, and his creation of a multinational empire. Perhaps Aristotle's ideas and advice had some impact on this.[23]

There is a further way in which Aristotle is relevant to the ethnographic project. His approach to the understanding of the world, collecting and comparing data and attempting to classify these data, sometimes in ways that to

18. Thuc. 3.94.4–51; 2.68.5; 6.2.3,6; cf. 1.3.3 where he notes that there is no word for 'barbarian' or 'Greek' in Homer.

19. See Pearson 1960, 87–8, for discussion of the problematic title, πῶς Ἀλέξανδρος ἤχθη.

20. This began with the work of Francois Hartog and Edith Hall; it is reviewed by Dougherty 2001 and Skinner 2012; some counter-argument comes from Gruen 2011, who argues for a less hard-and-fast position; but he does not discuss India, except for some pages on Clearchus.

21. Quoted in Paul Theroux, *Deep South* (Boston: Houghton Mifflin Harcourt, 2015), 9.

22. See Nippel 1996 for an interesting discussion.

23. Stern 1968.

us are unconvincing, spawned a new kind of interest in the world. The extraordinary achievements of such works as the *Historia animalium* spawned numerous successors, many of them of the degenerate kind known as 'paradoxography', a genre generally regarded as beginning with Callimachus in the third century BCE.[24] Many paradoxographical works, including that attributed to Aristotle, are the merest hotchpotches of unlikely 'facts'; but in a rare moment of theoretical reflection, Aelian offers a rationale for the project:

> That dumb animals should by nature possess some good quality and should have many of man's amazing excellences assigned to them along with man, is indeed a remarkable fact. And to know accurately the special characteristics of each, and how living creatures also have been a source of interest no less than man, demands a trained intelligence and much learning . . . I have collected all the materials that I could . . . so if anyone considers them profitable, let him make use of them.[25]

As for ethnography, the impetus is a clearer understanding of the nature of humankind.

Ethnography can be many other things too. Philosophical ethnography can be used as criticism or satire of one's own society, as in the numerous utopias of the Hellenistic world, many of which made use of data first purveyed by Megasthenes: most Greek utopias are in India. Several authors have gone so far as to argue that Megasthenes' own work was intended as a portrait of an ideal society.[26] I do not think that this will wash, though one might perhaps argue it for part of Onesicritus' work. Like Onesicritus, Daimachus seems to show a particular interest in philosophical aspects of Indian culture.[27]

It is not even yet established that Megasthenes' book should be called an ethnography. There have been other proposals. Kuhrt and Sherwin-White proposed that the treatise was in effect a political report for Seleucus, designed to show what he was up against in a hypothetical project of conquest of the Maurya empire.[28] Similarly, Paul Kosmin has recently argued, following a hint from Bosworth, that the book was in effect an apologia for Seleucus, justifying his abandonment of the empire east of the Khyber Pass on the grounds

24. See Stoneman forthcoming (a), with extensive bibliography.

25. Ael. *NA* prologue.

26. Biffi 2000, 24; Zambrini 1982; 1985 ; Murray 1972; see Kosmin 2014, 50 and 285 n. 138.

27. Schwarz 1968 argues that even the *Poliorcetica* was mainly about India.

28. Kuhrt and Sherwin-White 1993, 97. Relevant to this interpretation would be Ff 25–7, 33 and 46, on manners and customs. Kuhrt and Sherwin-White's phrase is 'a legitimation of Seleucus' non-conquest'.

that India was in some sense unconquerable.[29] Furthermore, Maurya India is presented as a kind of analogue of the Seleucid state, with the king as the nodal point. Another possibility is a genre familiar from the present day, not so much a travel book as a diplomat's or amateur researcher's memoirs: Paul Scott's *The Jewel in the Crown* introduces Mr Cleghorn, 'an ordained member of the Church and an enthusiastic amateur scholar of archaeology and anthropology, and much concerned with the impending, never-got-down-to composition of a monograph on local topography and social customs'.[30] And could one imagine Megasthenes saying what Kipling says: 'one of the few advantages that India has over England is a great knowability'?[31] What this seems to mean is that it is easy (for Kipling) to delineate the civilisation with broad brush strokes: as an anonymous contemporary critic wrote of Kipling's India: 'correct or not, it is – surely it must be – true'.[32] Megasthenes insists on the truthfulness of the Indians, and thus presumably of his informants; but that does not make them omniscient, and his India must in some sense be packaged, not only for his readership, but by his informants. As I shall argue, these informants must be, in the main part, Brahmans. Vincent Smith asserts that Megasthenes certainly talked to courtesans;[33] but if he did, why is there nothing about women's lives in his book?

Other still more reductive categorisations, that nevertheless reflect part of what was in Megasthenes' book, might be: natural history; human geography (Ff 41–44, from Strabo, F 45 from Arrian, and the 'dubious' Ff 54 and 55); history (in part; this label only suits F 50c); mythography (Ff 46, 57–58); collection of folktales or local anecdotes; and paradoxography *avant la lettre* (Ff 19, 29–30, 31).[34] I shall settle for 'ethnography' as a shorthand description. The nature of Megasthenes' project can be better understood by setting him in the context of other contemporary writers who appear to be engaged in the same kind of enterprise.

29. Kosmin 2014, 37. Kosmin 2014, 51–2. shows how Megasthenes inverts the Herodotean view of nomadism: for Herodotus, the Scythians were unconquerable because they were nomads and had no cities; for Megasthenes, the Indians were unconquerable precisely because they did have strongly fortified cities.

30. Scott 2005, 21.

31. Sergeant 2013, 62, quoting 'The Phantom Rickshaw'.

32. Quoted by Sergeant 2013, 63, from R. L. Green, *Kipling: The Critical Heritage* (London: Routledge and Kegan Paul, 1971), 132.

33. Smith 1901, 75.

34. All the numbers are from Schwanbeck's numeration, not Jacoby's.

Onesicritus

The most important of Megasthenes' predecessors is Onesicritus, since the focus of his book seems to have been on India.[35] His origin is variously reported as Aegina or Astypalaea; if the latter, it is probably not the island of that name but the old (pre-Hellenistic) city on Cos, which was an intellectual centre in the fourth century.[36] If he was also, as we are told, a pupil of Diogenes, he must have spent time in Corinth or in Athens. His military role seems to have been minor (he was subordinate to Nearchus, who criticised his history and his judgment of maritime matters)[37] and he was perhaps primarily an intellectual. There is no knowing what became of him after the expedition ended.

Onesicritus' book had the puzzling title *How Alexander was Led*; such a title would suggest that it gave an account of his career as a whole, but, apart from F 2 on the resources that Alexander had at the beginning of his expedition, and Ff 34–36 on Cyrus, Darius and their tombs, every fragment concerns aspects of the expedition from Central Asia onwards, and most of those are about India.[38] There is in fact no evidence for his participation in the expedition before 331. One might surmise that the book was actually about Alexander's expedition to the East, taking his position as 'King of Asia' as a given. Who was it that 'led' Alexander? Could it be Providence, or Fortune? If that is so, Onesicritus could reasonably be regarded as having written a book about India, rather than simply discussing India in a book about Alexander's career. It may be right to regard his book as the first monograph on India since Ctesias', though it is hard to determine whether Megasthenes knew the book.

Strabo's comment about the excess of 'wonders' in Onesicritus' book derives from Strabo's acerbity, and is not evidence regarding the true content of the work,[39] though Onesicritus certainly made some mistakes, about trees

35. The major discussions are Brown 1955; Pearson 1960, 83–111; Arora 1991–92; Winiarczyk 2011, 73–115; Müller 2014, 58–65.

36. He mentions the dogs of Cos: Pearson 1960, 106.

37. Arr. *Ind.* 3.2.9–13; Arora 1991–92, 45–9. Possibly he commanded Alexander's ship while Nearchus was admiral of the fleet.

38. Ff 3 and 4 on Hyrcanian figs, F 1 and Tt 1 and 8 on the Amazon queen's visit in Zadracarta, F 5 on customs of Bactria and Sogdia. Ff 33–38 are about Persia but relate to the return there after the Indian expedition. I discount the doubtful F 39 which asserts that Onesicritus was an Assyrian and wrote about the Nectanebo story.

39. Müller 2014.

and the latitude of India. He betrays strong philosophical interests, in his account of the 'utopian' kingdom of Musicanus, of Cathaea, and of the meetings with the naked philosophers of Taxila. It may well be that these passages reflect interests deriving from his education with the Cynic philosopher Diogenes, though Winiarczyk urges caution regarding this shibboleth.[40]

Nearchus and Androsthenes

Nearchus, a childhood friend of Alexander, also wrote on India, but his book was about the homeward voyage from the mouth of the Indus to Carmania.[41] However, he entered into dispute with Onesicritus, who seems to have published first, about some details of his account. The remains of his work indicate a rational writer with a positive view of Alexander.

Androsthenes wrote a 'Circumnavigation of India', but no fragments survive. It may have been a source for Theophrastus. (See chapter 4 above.)

Contemporaries of Megasthenes

At the end of the fourth century BCE, writing ethnographic and historical accounts of the remoter parts of the Greek world became quite a common pursuit.[42] Much of the impetus came from Alexander: if he did not commission these studies, he certainly had an interest in learning more about the regions he proposed to conquer, or had conquered, and those who wished to become more at home in the wider world he created were eager for information about its less familiar parts. In addition, the strange information coming back from distant parts offered opportunities to those of a philosophical bent to compose utopian texts in the form of ethnographic accounts. Indeed, many of the works we are about to consider could be called 'philosophical ethnographies'.[43]

Two of these writers had Indian connections and it is tempting to suppose that they were acquainted with Megasthenes in person: Clearchus of Soli and Hecataeus of Abdera. If, as seems likely (though not all agree), the philosopher Clearchus, pupil of Aristotle, is also the Clearchus who erected at

40. Winiarczyk 2011, 75–9.

41. The main discussions: Pearson 1960, 112–49; Müller 2014, 65–9.

42. Historians: Hieronymus, Dicaearchus, Duris, Phylarchus and Aristoxenus.

43. Many are usefully discussed by Primo 2009.

Ai Khanum the inscription enshrining the Delphic maxims, then he travelled at least as far as Afghanistan. Perhaps he also had something to do with the philosophical dialogue of which a few fragments survive on papyrus at Ai Khanum.[44] Since, further, we know that he took an interest in the Brahmans, and compared their philosophy with that of the Jews,[45] it is quite likely that he went on further down Alexander's route, through the Khyber Pass and into Taxila, perhaps talking to Megasthenes as he went about the nature of Indian philosophy.

Clearchus' works are lost, though he wrote books on sleep, on riddles, on proverbs, on various scientific topics and on love, friendship and education.[46] We have only a modest number of fragments, a very large number of them coming from Athenaeus' *Deipnosophists*, especially from book 12 which is devoted to the topic of luxury. Many of these are from his περὶ βίων, a title which is difficult to translate in the absence of more evidence for its contents. It could mean 'On Lives', and have been a collection of 'Lives' of individuals, but it seems more likely that the phrase means 'On Lifestyles', and that it was a philosophical discussion of various ways of life, as evinced by both peoples and individuals. The fact that most of the fragments relate to one particular kind of lifestyle is a result of the filter through which Athenaeus has put the work: luxury is exampled by the Persians, Lydians, Sicilians, Tarentines, Milesians, Scythians, but also by Polycrates the tyrant of Samos, Dionysius of Syracuse (rolling about in beds of flowers with naked girls), Parrhasius the painter and the abominable Phalaris of Syracuse eating babies.[47] Though Clearchus' interests were clearly wide and scholarly (his exposition of the philosophical value of riddles is particularly interesting),[48] the *Lives*, though we have no idea how extensive it was, seems to be his most-quoted work. It displays an interest in distant peoples, both within the Greek world and outside it (Persians, Scythians), and suggests that he was influenced by the information filtering back from distant lands.

44. Lerner 2003.

45. Clearchus = Jos. *cAp* 1.179, ἀπόγονοι τῶν ἐν Ἰνδοῖς φιλοσόφων; see Bar-Kochva 2010, 59–62 and 146–57; Gruen 2011, 312–14. Megasthenes makes a very similar comment, F 3a = Clem. *Strom*. 1.15.72.5.

46. Fragments, ed. Wehrli 1969.

47. Athen. 12.9 (514 C), 11 (515 C), 15 (518 C), 23 (522 C), 26, 27 (524 C) (Persians etc.), 57 (540 C) (Polycrates), 58 (541 C) (Dionysius), 62 (543 C) (Parrhasius); 9.54 (396 C) (Phalaris).

48. Athen. 10.86 (457ce); see also Clearchus Ff 84–95 Wehrli.

Hecataeus of Abdera was a pupil of Pyrrho of Elis, who travelled to India in Alexander's entourage and took an interest in Indian philosophy (see chapter 12 below). We have a total of fourteen fragments surviving from his works.[49] Eight of these are from his book about the Hyperboreans, the fabulous people of the far north who reflect the Indian traditions about Uttarakuru (the Sanskrit word is cognate with the Greek): these will be discussed in chapter 9.[50] A mere six fragments survive from his *Aegyptiaca*,[51] on the topics of Egyptian philosophy, priests, the gods (at which point Clearchus on the gymnosophists is brought into the discussion), sanctuaries, Moses and wine. Little can be divined of the structure of Hecataeus' book from this information, though it probably began with geography and customs,[52] and one might suppose that it is more than just accident that results in most of the fragments relating to religion. Oswyn Murray argues that the whole of Diodorus' book 1 reproduces the structure of the *Aegyptiaca*.[53] If so, we we can be more confident about its content. Religion is indeed a natural subject for a book about a remote people (religious customs are the bread-and-butter of modern ethnographers), and it is surprising that Megasthenes has so little to say about Indian religion. It is possible that Megasthenes knew Hecataeus' book.[54]

A little more can be said about two further writers, Berossus and Manetho.[55] These differ in one obvious respect from Megasthenes: they are natives of the countries they write about, writing in Greek, whereas Megasthenes is a Greek outsider. Their work has been defined as 'apologetic historiography',[56] whereas Megasthenes' motivation must be different. Momigliano once observed that

49. *FGrH* 264.

50. Bridgeman 2005, ch. 7.

51. This must have been composed before 300, since Ptolemy is not called 'king'; probably it was composed between 320 and 306. Murray 1970, 143.

52. Moyer 2011, 105.

53. Sacks 1990, 91–3 accepts this, though he believes that Diodorus was not a mechanical copyist, and made additions of his own. Similarly, Diodorus book 2 has been supposed to be largely a paraphrase of Megasthenes; Sacks 1990, 67–9; but see Muntz 2012.

54. Bosworth 1973, 145. Arora 1991–92, 312 thinks that Hecataeus was a 'model' for Megasthenes, while Bosworth 2003, 313 suggests that Megasthenes may have influenced Hecataeus. Murray 1972, 208 suggests that Megasthenes' book was a 'reply' to Hecataeus, and Murray 1970, 167 n. points out that Megasth. F 15 J seems to be a rejection of Hecataeus on Sesoösis. I am not persuaded by Murray's position, in the 1972 article, that Megasthenes is presenting India as a Platonic ideal state.

55. Dillery 2015 is a comprehensive study of both authors.

56. G. Sterling, quoted in Moyer 2011, 96. Dillery 2015 follows this interpretation.

all the nations in contact with the Greeks produced books about themselves, in Greek.[57] But the Indians did not!

Berossus, the author of *Babyloniaca*, was a contemporary, he states, of Alexander, so was born about 350 BCE; his book was written in 281.[58] His account of Babylonian legend and history was in three books and seems to have contained a strange mixture of material. Book 1, devoted to origins ('Procreatio') begins with an account of Babylon's geographical location between two rivers, and of its crops, fruit, fish and birdlife; it describes a state of nature in which men lived without laws until the emergence from the sea of the monstrous Oannes, who functioned as a kind of culture-hero and revealed the nature of the cosmos to men. Book 1 also contained a description of the walls of Babylon, and its festivals.

Book 2 consisted largely of a list of kings, interrupted by the account of the Flood and the role of Ziusudra (Xisouthros in Greek), familiar to us also from the Epic of Gilgamesh. Both Noah and Gilgamos were mentioned somewhere by Berossus, presumably in this book. After the Flood, Berossus gives a list of a further eighty-six kings who ruled until the conquest by the Medes in 539 BCE. Book 3 gave plentiful detail about the great historical kings, Tiglath-Pileser, Sennacherib, Marudach and Nebuchadnezzar II, with quite a lot to say about the latter's buildings and waterworks. In this book Berossus also said something about the Persians, who 'worshipped fire and water, like the philosophers' until Artaxerxes II introduced the cult of images.

In sum, the book seems to have been a well-ordered historical account, beginning with geographical coordinates and including legendary traditions as the early stages of the history. If there was extensive discussion of society, customs and daily life, evidence of it has not survived. Again, one wonders whether Megasthenes and Berossus ever met, or at least whether Megasthenes knew the other's work; the reverse seems less likely, on the basis of the evidence. It is possible that Megasthenes' mention of Nebuchadnezzar was inspired by something in Berossus.[59]

Manetho, an Egyptian priest, writing a generation or so later, during the third century BCE, wrote an *Aegyptiaca* in three books.[60] This appears to have

57. Moyer 2011, 98.

58. *FGrH* 680.

59. Jos. *cAp.* 1.143–4, cf. *AJ* 10.227–8. Perhaps Nebuchadnezzar was invoked as a parallel for Seleucus by one or other author: Dillery 2015, 290–2; cf. 311–12 where Dillery proposes that Manetho had read Berossus.

60. *FGrH* 609.

covered 'Gods, demigods, spirits of the dead, heroes and thirty dynasties of mortal kings until Darius I'. The order of these is the same as in Herodotus, whom Manetho had presumably read.[61] He also wrote a *Sacred Book* on the subject of Egyptian religion, as well as books *On Sacred Doctrines, On Ancient Ritual and Religion* and *On Festivals*. These titles evince a strong interest in religion, and the *Sacred Book* is the source for the myth of Isis, Osiris and Typhon in Plutarch's *De Iside et Osiride*; but the bulk of the fragments are preserved for us by chronographers and consists of dry king-lists. (They may be dry, but they are the indispensable armature of our chronology of the Egyptian dynasties.)[62] Such king-lists are the basis also of the Brahmanic Purāṇas, early versions of which Megasthenes must have had access to when they were still being transmitted in oral form. But unlike the Indian texts, Manetho's, in as much as he is creating an Egyptian past for Greek readers, shows some evidence of syncretism with Greek history.

Another writer visited the opposite end of the known world and brought out a book just about the time that Alexander died: this was Pytheas of Massalia (Marseille). His book *On the Ocean* described his visit to Britain, and his account of a Scotch haar, 'where sky and sea merge into a kind of jelly', has provoked as much incredulity as some of the tales of the writers on India, and with as little justification. His book was completed in about 320 BCE and it has even been suggested that he may have had a commission from Alexander to explore these northern regions in preparation for a possible future expedition.[63] Be that as it may – and we have no alternative explanation for his voyage, though trade may be presumed – his expedition shows that writing about distant parts was already a fashion by the time Alexander reached India.

We do know that Alexander commissioned another explorer, Heracleides of Argos, to make a voyage through the Caspian Sea. If he had completed it, he would have learnt that the common assumption that the river Oxus flows into that sea was false, and maybe Alexander would thus have become aware of the existence of the Aral Sea (into which the Oxus actually does, or into modern times still did, drain).[64] Alexander's 'Last Plans' also included an ex-

61. Moyer 2011, 103–4.

62. King Osorohu is identified with Heracles. Manetho differs from Herodotus on the identification of Sesonchosis with Heracles; and he makes use of the *Königsnovelle* about Amenophis: Moyer 2011, 123, citing also Dillery, *ZPE* 127 (1999), 93–116.

63. Michael Wood, *Evening Standard* 20 Oct. 2001, reviewing Cunliffe 2001.

64. Arr. *Anab.* 7. 16.1–4.

pedition to Arabia,[65] a circumnavigation of Africa (by Euthymenes) and the building of a road through North Africa as far as Carthage.[66] But there is no mention of his asking anyone to prepare written reports on these regions.

A couple of other writers of whom we have no more than names and book titles are Palaephatus of Abydos (working ca. 336 BCE),[67] who wrote *Cypriaca, Deliaca, Attica* and (beyond Greece) *Arabica*; and Rhianus of Bene (ca. 300 BCE),[68] who wrote some histories of Greek states (*Achaica, Eliaca, Thessalica*) which may have been more in the nature of *patria*, another genre now coming into its own. Asclepiades of Myrleia wrote a book about Turdetania, and Demetrius one on the kings in Judaea;[69] Artapanus in the second century also wrote a history of the Jews.[70] Amometus,[71] whose work was known to Callimachus in the third century BCE, wrote a *Voyage out of Memphis* which mentioned India and the people called the Attacorae (i.e., Uttarakuru, the northern Kurus). Demodamas of Halicarnassus,[72] a general of Seleucus, wrote a history of Halicarnassus and also one of India, which seems to have been limited to an account of his own military incursion and perhaps of the cities he saw.[73]

Strabo refers to a very large numbers of writers in his account of India.[74] Some of these are the producers of literary classics, such as Homer, Pindar, Sophocles and Euripides; some are philosophers, including Democritus and Aristotle; some are later than Megasthenes by several centuries, and include the geographers Eratosthenes and Artemidorus as well as the historian Nicolaus of Damascus, themselves important preservers of fragments of earlier writers. He mentions several of the Alexander historians – Nearchus, Cleitarchus, Onesicritus and Aristobulus, as well as Alexander's general Craterus, who is said to have written a letter to his mother saying he had reached the Ganges – and of course those who wrote before that date, such as Scylax and

65. Bosworth 1988a, 168–9.

66. Arr. *Anab.* 7.25.2, and Tarn 1951, 394; Curt. 10.1.16–18; in general Bosworth 1988a, 164–5.

67. *FGrH* 263, end.

68. Ibid. 265.

69. Dillery 2015, 357–87: a rewriting of the Septuagint in Greek historical style.

70. Clarke 1999, 318–323.

71. *FGrH* 645.

72. Ibid. 428.

73. Primo 2009, 81. F 2 = Plin. *NH* 6.29 says only that he crossed the Jaxartes or Silis (?= Syr Darya), but according to Stephanus (F 3) he referred to a town called Antissa in India.

74. Gathered together in Clarke 1999, 376–7.

Ctesias. In the generation after Megasthenes was Daimachus of Plataea,[75] who was ambassador to Candragupta's son Bindusara/Amitrochates. His history consisted of at least two books.[76] Strabo scorned him, even more than he did Megasthenes, for mentioning (like his predecessor) the fabulous peoples of Sanskrit tradition,[77] but quoted him for distances and for the latitude of India, on which he disagreed with Megasthenes.[78] He is probably the source for the anecdote that Bindusara sent a request to Antiochus (probably Soter) for 'wine, figs and a philosopher'.[79] He also mentioned that there were apple-green pigeons in India.[80] His book was called *Indica*, but Strabo calls it (and Megasthenes' book) *hypomnemata*, 'notes' or 'memoirs'. Lesser-known names are Orthagoras, Patrocles (the military commander of Babylon in 312–11, who seems to have focused on Central Asia), Androsthenes of Thasos, Theodectes and Apollodorus (author of *Parthica*), Megillus, Gorgus and 'other mythographers'. Diodorus' account of India after Alexander probably derives from the Hellenistic historian Hieronymus of Cardia.[81] Other writers of relevance, but later than Strabo, are Eudoxus, the anonymous author of the *Periplus* and Agatharchides, whose *On the Erythraean Sea* includes a history with an ethnography in its fifth book.

Such a list only serves to remind us how much we have lost and how little we can know of the ethnographic enterprise in the last decades of the fourth century and in the third. In this perspective, Megasthenes is well represented, and the fact that he bulks so large suggests that his centrality is not altogether imaginary.

The India that Megasthenes Knew

If we are to assess Megasthenes as a writer on India in the period of Candragupta, it is important to be clear what we know about the India that he was describing. It is hard to avoid circularity in this enterprise since most modern historians, Indian writers included, find it necessary to draw on Megasthenes to flesh out their picture of the Maurya state, with varying degrees of accep-

75. *FGrH* 716.
76. F 1.
77. T 1, F 5.
78. F 3.
79. F 6 = Athen. 14.67 (652–3 C); Primo 2009, 83–4.
80. F 4: see ch. 4 above.
81. Diod. 18.5–6; see Hornblower 1981, 80–7.

tance of his data.[82] It is also important to try to identify the type of informant that Megasthenes could have used.

Substantial work has been done in recent decades to reconstruct the history of India from about 600 BCE, and to establish what connections should be made with the legendary record and with the first developed civilisation of the subcontinent, the Indus Civilisation of ca. 2600–1900 BCE. The Mature Harappan period in the Indus valley and neighbouring regions is notable for its sophisticated planned cities and towns, ruled by priest-kings similar to those known also from contemporary Mesopotamian civilisation. There were certainly links between the two regions, and in Mesopotamia, where writing was already in use, the Harappan world seems to have been known as Meluhha. The language of the Indus valley is unknown and the characteristics of its script are much debated: Asko Parpola has developed a number of intriguing but inevitably speculative arguments on a linguistic basis, interpreting the ideograms, or whatever they are, of the Indus script in relation to known Dravidian languages of the subcontinent.[83]

The linguistic argument can be combined with analysis of the mythology of the *Ṛg Veda* to construct a picture of Aryan invaders arriving, with horses, in about the ninth century and pushing the aboriginal Dravidian inhabitants deeper into the subcontinent, establishing a society and ideology that can be linked with the western branch of the Aryan invaders who came to dwell in Iran. The main god of the *Ṛg Veda* books 2–7, generally regarded as the earliest stratum, is Indra.[84] Indra, the storm god and battle leader, who wears a beard, carries a mace and is a lusty consumer of the sacred drink soma – and thus might recall to a Greek the characteristics of Heracles more than Zeus – is a culture-hero: he destroys the serpent Vṛtra,[85] whose world is the Sapta Sindhu or 'Seven Rivers',[86] makes war on the Dasas and suppresses the Asuras. Both

82. Thapar 1997 and Singh 2004 are the most reliable guides. See also the excellent study Goyal 2000. Kalota 1978 does not dig very deep. Megasthenes scarcely makes an appearance in the book of Paranavitana (1971), who relies instead on some remarkable inscriptions which no one else has ever seen, or is likely to see: Weerakkody 1997.

83. Parpola 2015.

84. Ibid., 95ff.; Prakash 1964, 28. In Philostr. *VA* 2.9.2, Dionysus as conqueror of India is the son of the similarly-named god Indos; but it does not seem possible to find earlier references to this connection. See ch. 7 below.

85. The name has been linked by comparatists with Heracles' dog Orthros, though this dog is Heracles' companion, not his opponent. It is more certainly the same as the Iranian monster Verethragna.

86. Prakash 1964, 42–7.

these names deserve some comment. Dasas, the 'black-skinned enemy' whose home is Arachosia, are the same as the Dahae referred to by Curtius:[87] Prakash plausibly links the word to the Iranian root *deh*, which in Persian means 'village'.[88] Later, Dasas are the 'barbarians' who are beyond caste. The Asuras are cognate with the Iranian Ahuras; in the Indian tradition it is the virtuous *deva*s who defeat the Satanic Asuras,[89] while in Iran the boot is on the other foot, and the Ahuras are the celestial gods (later, only one god) who suppress the *daeva*s, or demons. But it is also possible that the name of the Asuras is related to that of the Assyrians. If these references recall a defeat of invading Assyrians in the early stages of the Aryan conquest of north-west India, this might provide a reason why Megasthenes thought it reasonable to connect the conquering range of Heracles with that of Nebuchadnezzar.[90]

The mythological reflection of the Aryan invasion continues in the structure of the *Mahābhārata*, in which the pale-skinned Pandavas (the word means 'pale') become masters of the Kurus/Kauravas. (In Ptolemy they are the Πανδοουοι.)[91] The epic seems in a sense to have been composed to impose Brahmanism on the kings of the east.[92] The non- or pre-Aryan customs of the Kurus, a hill people, are represented in the practices of polyandry (Draupadi marries five brothers, who in turn represent five tribes) and sati (widow-burning).[93] A number of other institutions that are also characteristic of later Indian society, even up to the present, include the establishment of ghats and tanks, and the practice of yoga.[94] The origins of the *Mahābhārata* war can probably be placed in the period ca. 700–350 BCE, since a number of the names associated with it are known to Pāṇini (ca. 350 BCE), though it did not develop its final form until the fourth century CE.[95]

The 'Aryan invasion' need not, however, be a literal invasion. Allchin describes the Aryan hypothesis as 'a dead end'.[96] There is no archaeological evi-

87. Curt. 8.3; Parpola 2015, 97.

88. Prakash 1964, 28ff.

89. E.g., *RV* 10.124.5.

90. Megasth. F 48 Schw.

91. Prakash 1964, 90 and 115.

92. McGrath 2013, 43, following Bronkhorst's arguments.

93. Prakash 1964, 90–2. On sati, note *Mbh.* 1.125.25–31, where it is seen as a strange act.

94. Parpola 2015, 209.

95. Ibid.; McGrath 2013, 100.

96. Allchin 1995, 89, cf. Danino 2010, 256–7 and 291.

dence to support the idea of an invasion. The emergence of the Aryans may rather be a power shift of indigenous populations, accompanied by a re-defining of cultural categories. Danino associates it with the drying up of the river Sarasvati in the third millennium BCE, a river of memory in the *Ṛg Veda*. But there may be no direct connection with the disappearance of this river; this too may be a constructed memory relating to a cultural shift, and perhaps reflects instead a sharp change in the course of the river Sutlej some eight thousand years ago.[97] However, there seem to have been no horses in the Indus Civilisation, whereas they are a pre-eminent Aryan animal. Here is a tangible, archaeological change. What actually happened in north-west India in 2000 BCE is still not certain.

The conflict between the pale-skinned Aryans and the dark-skinned Dravidians seems to be expressed in a more extreme form in the characterisation in Sanskrit sources of the Mongoloid Toto people of north-west Bengal as eaters of carrion, pigs and flies, and even as cannibals;[98] the Nagas of the north-eastern hills, meanwhile, known in living memory as head-hunters, also bear the name of the demonic Nagas or serpents of ancient myth.[99]

Thus by the seventh century the Aryans were established in the north-west of India and the Punjab, which became their home and the locus of Vedic culture.[100] As Arrian remarks, not even Cyrus was able to conquer the region,[101] though it does appear that the region came under Achaemenid control later, as the 'twentieth satrapy' of their empire.[102] Gandhara was certainly Iranianised to some degree: Taxila has Achaemenid levels, exposure of the dead seems to have been practised,[103] and Pāṇini was familiar with

97. The research has been carried out by Sanjeev Gupta. See for example the article by Caroline Brogan, 'Scientists Show how Himalayan River System Influenced Ancient Indus Civilization', http://www3.imperial.ac.uk/newsandeventspggrp/imperialcollege/newssummary/news_28-11-2017-11-54-48?hootPostID=f8132514907cf420e8c08683526eb580. See also Possehl 2002, 239–40.

98. Sanyal 1971 provides the information that Totos today eat carrion (21), are unwashed (22, 25), and bury their dead (40). Perhaps stories of the Totos' unattractive habits influenced the portrayal of the 'Unclean Nations' in the *Alexander Romance*.

99. On the Nagas, see Jacobs 2012 (a detailed anthropological study) and Glancey 2011.

100. Prakash 1964, 81.

101. Arr. *Ind*.9.10.

102. Hdt. 3.128.

103. Karttunen 1989, 224.

aspects of Persian culture.[104] The north-west is the home of 'bad habits' from a Brahman point of view, as the *Mahābhārata* makes clear.[105] The upper Indus valley and Gandhara became prosperous from wool and Taxila developed into a major educational centre, where Candragupta was educated, and may have been there when Alexander arrived.[106] By that time the Pauravas/Purus were in the ascendant in the Jhelum region, and the Paurava king whom Alexander encountered, whom the Greeks called Porus, was expanding his sphere of influence at the expense of the king of Taxila, Omphis/*Ambhi. The memory of this dynasty was long-lasting, for when Xuanzang visited in the sixth century CE the region was still known as Parvata.[107] In the form 'Parvataka' the name also appears in the classic Sanskrit play about the intrigues of the reign of Candragupta, the *Mudrarakśasa* (*The Rakśasa's Ring*). It was a land of many cities, as indicated by both Strabo and Pāṇini.[108]

Further to the east, in the land of the Prasii ('Prachyakas', or easterners), where the major city was Palimbothra/Pataliputra,[109] the Vedic imprint seems to have been less intense. For Patañjali, writing about 150 BCE, the region of the eastern Ganges, east of Allahabad – Magadha – was non-Brahmin territory.[110] Vedic texts in general avoid mentioning Magadha, except in tones of disapproval.[111] The *Śatapatha Brāhmaṇa* refers to 'the demonic people of the east' (*āsuryaḥ prācyaḥ*), who build round stupas (i.e., Buddhist ones) instead of square ones.[112] The *Mahābhārata* speaks with contempt of the east-

104. Goyal 2000, 30.

105. *Mbh.* 8.40 Ganguli; discussed by Karttunen 1989, 216–17, who gives the reference in the critical edition as 8. 30.9ff. He sees the north-west as being characterised by Dionysiac qualities.

106. *Chand. Upan.* 6.14

107. Beal 1884, 2.275.

108. Prakash 1964, 74.

109. Cf. Plin. *NH* 6.21.8–23.11 = Megasth. F 56 Schw.

110. Bronkhorst 2007, 1–9. But Arora 2005, 89 takes an opposite view, that the north-west was more open to trade and travel, even by Brahmans, which is why Calanus felt free to travel with Alexander. (He cites Karttunen 1989, 228–30 for this point.) His further inference, that the Ganges region was more rigid, is based on Megasthenes' report that Brahmans he met criticised Calanus. But the fact that Megasthenes met Brahmans in Magadha in 310 or so does not entail that the region was predominantly Brahman in pre-Maurya times. Rather the reverse: Candragupta's inclusion of Brahmans at his court is a gesture of inclusiveness towards his new north-western dominions.

111. Allchin 1995, 91.

112. *SB* 13.8.1.5.

erners' 'worship of charnel houses'.[113] It is noteworthy too that the language of Magadha (including Aśoka) replaces the phoneme /r/ with /l/, thus *laja* instead of *raja*. This is referred to in Brahmanical texts as 'asura' speech, and is another marker of non-Vedic culture.[114]

The kings of Magadha are all non-Brahmanical. The first Magadha kings, Bimbisara and Ajataśatru, ruling in Rajagriha (Rajgir) were Buddhist or Jain; the Nandas who ruled from about 350 were also Jains. Candragupta is a Jain hero, playing a large role in the *Lives of the Jain Elders* of Hemacandra. His son Bindusara supported ascetic sects including the Ājīvikas, and his grandson Aśoka's preaching of the *dharma* is couched in strongly Buddhist terms; he also gave further support to the Ājīvikas. The Śungas, who overthrew the Maurya dynasty in 187 BCE, were the first Brahman rulers in Magadha.

Northern India, then, was by no means a homogeneous culture in the years of Alexander and Megasthenes. Both of them arrived in a period of religious revolution. The rise of Buddhism, associated with urbanisation and trade, may be either a response to, or a driver of, social change.[115] The various kinds of wandering mendicant characterised as 'śramanas' had not yet become clearly differentiated. The forest life was still important for ascetics, and Brahmans idealised the forest and avoided cities, where Buddhists made their mark as holy men and mediators.[116] One should imagine a great variety of available choices of religious lifestyle in Magadha as well as the north-west.

Candragupta unified the regions politically, but that is another matter.[117] Brahman or Vedic culture was firmly entrenched in the north-west, but further east along the Ganges its sway was much more limited and the immemorial traditions of 'Hindu village religion' and asceticism were more prominent. 'Hindu village religion' is the phrase used by Parpola, following Sir John Marshall, who published his account of the excavation of Mohenjo-Daro in 1931, to characterise the practices of the Indian countryside that seemed to go back to pre-Vedic times, including, for example, tree-worship and reverence for crocodiles.[118] Such practices were more happily absorbed into the Buddhist way of life than into Brahmanism. 'Hinduism' is a contested term today, but it is used in this instance without prejudice to describe a set of practices

113. *Mbh.* 3.188.64.
114. Thapar 2013b, 324.
115. Bailey and Mabbett 2003, 259.
116. Ibid., 161–74, and 185 on forest life.
117. Nilakanta Sastri 1967, 171.
118. Parpola 2015, 306.

historically known in the religion of India. (However, in my view the term is better avoided when referring to any period before that of the Gupta empire around the fifth century CE.)

One should not exaggerate the divide: the Alexander historians encountered naked ascetics, possibly Jains and/or Ājīvikas, in Taxila, though later sources mistakenly called them Brahmans; Megasthenes on the other hand makes clear that Brahmans were prominent at the royal court of Candragupta, while saying nothing about the latter's religious inclinations. His education in Taxila must have had some impact.

The extent to which the gods known from the present-day Indian pantheon had emerged at this date is also unclear: the ethnographer James Forsyth in 1871 was ready to call Śiva and the rest 'non-indigenous' because they were not worshipped by the tribal people, the Gonds.[119] Undoubtedly much more of India was 'tribal' in Alexander's day than it is now, and thus not only non-Hindu but non-Vedic. There is a famous image of a 'proto-Śiva' from Mohenjodaro, a horned ithyphallic personage seated in a yogic posture, but Śiva himself is not a Vedic god. The Vedic god Rudra exhibits many of the characteristics that are later attached to Śiva. Diana Eck is clear that Śiva only emerges in about the first century BCE, though elements of his worship, including the lingam, can be traced earlier.[120] Maurya religion and Maurya art depict divine beings such as *yakṣa*s and *yakṣi*s (tree-spirits, male and female), *ganesha*s (protecting deities, but not in the form of elephants), river-goddesses and the like. The most famous image from Maurya art is the 'yakṣi' or fly-whisk bearer in the Patna Museum (if she is Maurya: see chapter 15 below): not a tree-spirit as such, but a bounteous female with improbably swelling breasts, the very essence of fruitfulness and nourishment. These nature deities predominate in the Buddhist art of Sanchi in the second century BCE and later.[121]

The 'second urbanisation' of around 500 BCE, focused on Magadha,[122] is essentially independent of Vedic civilisation. This tension of the two Indias needs to be borne in mind whenever interpreting a statement by one of the Alexander historians or Megasthenes: their data will differ according to the region they are familiar with. (The same is equally true of botanical remarks,

119. Forsyth 1871, 144. On the Gonds, see Russell and Hiralal 1916, 3.38–143.

120. Eck 1983/1992, 52–3; 68 (pre-Śiva); 69 (lingam). See also ch. 3 above.

121. Shaw 2007, 177–88.

122. Bronkhorst 2006, 249.

since the lower Indus and *a fortiori* Gedrosia are quite different from Gandhara and the upper Indus.)

By the time Alexander arrived in the Indus valley, there were many identifiable 'cities' in the region, though Arrian and other authors refer to several more that were built, or ordered to be built, by Alexander.[123] There was a 'royal city of Sogdia' on the Indus, the city of Musicanus,[124] Nagara Dionysopolis (probably Gandhara near Jalalabad),[125] Nysa (somewhere between the Cophen and the Indus, possibly Begram),[126] Puṣkalavati/Peucelaotis, Sagala/Sialkot and – the most famous of the region – Takśasila/Taxila. Cohen's inventory does not extend beyond the limits of Alexander's expedition, but urban settlements were emerging along the middle and lower Ganges from 'the midst of teeming villages' in the sixth century BCE.[127] These ranged from fortified towns and market towns to large cities: among the latter the Pali canon names, in the middle Ganges region, Kauśambi, Vaiśali, Varanasi and Rajagriha/Rajgir. On the upper Ganges, Hastinapura and Mathura were well established and later to become famous in legend as, respectively, the scene of the action of the *Mahābhārata* and the home of Kṛṣṇa.

The later survey of Varāhamihira refers to settlements in other parts of India which might be categorised as cities,[128] including Baladevapattana/Balipattam,[129] Bharrukaccha/Barygaza, Murucipattana/Muziris, Mathura,[130] Paraloka (where pearl fisheries were located, perhaps the Paralia of the *Periplus*),[131] Tāpasāśrama ('hermitage of the sages, perhaps Ptolemy's Tabasoi),[132] Ujjihana (Ujjain, probably Ptolemy's Ozoana)[133] and Yaśovati, 'the city of the elves', sadly in an unidentified location.[134] Many of these were certainly in existence many centuries earlier than Varāhamihira. Megasthenes also knew

123. Arr. *Anab.* 6.15.2 and 6.15.4; Curt. 9.10.3; Cohen 2012, 291 lists six Alexandrias, as well as Bucephala, Nikaia and Xylinepolis (Plin. *NH* 6.96), plus one Alexandropolis, built by Seleucus.

124. Arr. *Anab.* 6.15.4 and 6.15.7.

125. Ptol. 7.1.43.

126. Arr. *Anab.* 5.1.1.

127. Singh 2009, 278–85; the quotation is from 278.

128. Shastri 1996.

129. Ibid., 14.16.

130. Ibid., 4.26.

131. Ibid., 80.2.4.

132. Ibid., 14.15.

133. Ibid., 14.2.

134. Ibid., 14.28.

of Pandaea and its chief city of Madurai, vividly evoked some centuries later in the *Periplus*,[135] as William Dalrymple reminds us:

> The *Periplus* gives a wonderful picture of the courtly lifestyle of the time when it records that the area around Madurai imported Mediterranean eye-shadow, perfume, silverware, fine Italian ware and beautiful slave-girl musicians for concubinage; in turn the town exported silk, ivory, pearls and, curiously, pepper.[136]

Megasthenes sees the emergence of cities as central to India's impregnability. Dionysus had been able to conquer it because it was a land of nomads (in a reversal of Herodotus' account of the Scythians, who could not be defeated because they were nomads); but now conquest from outside is impossible.[137] The other Greek hero, Heracles, was said to be the founder of Pataliputra.

While Varanasi lays claim to being the oldest city in the world, founded by the god Śiva in about 9000 BCE,[138] Rajagriha is of direct relevance for our story.[139] Lying on a main trade route, it was the capital of the kingdom of Magadha; massive fortification walls around the old city date from the time of Bimbisara in the sixth century BCE, while his son Ajataśatru was responsible for the circuit around 'New' Rajagriha in the fifth century BCE (and, allegedly, for the 'prison' in which he confined his father). The expansion of Magadha continued under Ajataśatru (492–460 BCE),[140] who defeated the king of Kosala and subsequently conquered the Lichchavis, who were based on the northern bank of the Ganges in the region of Vaiśali, around 484–468 BCE. In the course of his campaign Ajataśatru constructed a fort at Pataligrama on the Ganges, which became the nucleus of the great city of Pataliputra. Both kings are said to have been followers of ascetic spiritual leaders, Mahavira in the Jain tradition and Buddha in the Buddhist. Four further kings, variously named, followed, the last of them being expelled and replaced by a popularly elected king, Śiśunaga (413–395), who established a second capital at Vaiśali. His son, Kalaśoka, moved the capital to Pataliputra, but was presently murdered by a man variously called Mahapadma (Purāṇas) or Ugrasena (Buddhist texts), who established the Nanda dynasty.

135. *Periplus* 54–6.

136. Dalrymple 1998, 183–4.

137. Kosmin 2014, 39–41 and 44.

138. Eck 1983/1992 is an unparalleled evocation of the history of this extraordinary place.

139. Singh 2009, 284.

140. For the Indian sources in what follows I rely largely on Singh 2009, 272.

This man was the son of a barber by a courtesan, according to the Jain *Pariśiṣṭaparvan*,[141] while Curtius and Diodorus tell us that he was himself a barber who became a lover of one of the queens and murdered her husband at her instigation.[142] The Purāṇas also make the Nanda king a low-caste śudra, while Buddhist texts describe him more discreetly as 'of unknown lineage'. There were nine Nanda kings, who ruled for a century, and it was the last of these, Dhana-Nanda, who was on the throne when Alexander arrived in India. The stories that the Indian texts tell of the founder's low birth are transferred in the classical writers to the last of the Nandas, perhaps from garbling of the information Porus gave directly to Alexander. If we are to believe Plutarch,[143] Candragupta himself came face to face with Alexander when young and 'he often said in later times that Alexander narrowly missed making himself master of the country, since its king was hated and despised on account of his baseness and low birth'. If the first Nanda was low-born, by definition his last successor should also be, so perhaps the more general statement has become involved with the barber story that applied to the earlier king.

Diodorus gives this man's name as Xandrames, and the people he ruled over are the Gandaridae; for Curtius, he is called Aggrammes,[144] and he rules the Gangaridae and Prasii. Justin gets closer to his name, with Nandrus (by emendation), and the people are the Praesidae and Gangaridae.[145] Gangaridae is presumably the better form, meaning people who dwell on the Ganges, and has been assimilated to the more familiar name of Gandhara in Diodorus.[146] The Prasii (etc.) are simply Prācyakas, 'easterners'. The Nanda dynasty seems also to have controlled Kalinga, as is made clear by the Hāthigumphā inscription of King Khāravela of Orissa (first century BCE).[147] The enthusiasm of these kings for ascetic sects seems consistently reported and may explain the prevalence of the story of their low origins: origins which would have shocked the Brahmans – who, as the learned elite, were probably the informants of the Greek writers – as well as King Porus, who ruled in the Vedic heartland.

The Nandas commanded a large army, whose numbers are variously reported: Curtius gives their king twenty thousand cavalry, two hundred

141. Hemacandra 1998.

142. Curt. 9.2.6–7; Diod. 17.93.3.

143. Plu. *Alex.* 62.9.

144. Perhaps the equivalent of Ugrasena, one of Nanda's names: Kumar 2013, 68 and 73.

145. Justin 15.4.16, 12.8.9; cf. Plu. *Alex.* 62.3.

146. Sircar 1947/1971 is a thorough account.

147. Line 12: Kant 2000, 29; Habib and Jha 2004, 13.

thousand infantry, two thousand chariots and three thousand elephants. It may be noted that this is a properly constituted Indian *caturaṅga* army.[148] The dynasty's wealth may have depended on access to iron ore mines, but also on fertility and extensive forests for timber and elephants; there is no information on its administrative structures.[149]

Candragupta

And euer lik of his condiciouns
Was Sandrococtus, set up in hih estat;
Vexed peoples, troubled regeouns,
Set cites and touns at gret debat:
Whose gouernaunce was infortunat,
As it was seyn and founde at alle preues,
Cherished no man but robbours & fald theuys.

—JOHN LYDGATE, *FALL OF PRINCES* 4.3165–71

Soon after Alexander's departure from India, the Nanda dynasty was overthrown by Candragupta, who may have been connected by birth to the dynasty.[150]

> Then did the Brahman Cāṇakya anoint a glorious youth, known by the name Candragutta, as king over all Jambudīpa, born of a noble clan, the Moriyas, when, filled with bitter hate, he had slain the ninth (Nanda) Dhanananda. Twenty-four years he reigned .... [151]

Some Indian writers say that his name, Maurya, means 'son of Mura', who is supposed to have been a concubine of the king; the Pali *Mahāvaṁsa* makes him a member of the Śakyas from whom the Buddha was also descended,[152] while the name seems most likely to be a tribal one, 'Moriyas' in the Pali books,

148. Trautmann 2015, 108: 'a full army is like a beast with four legs'.

149. Singh 2009, 273.

150. Lassen 1847–61, 2.205ff.; Mookerji; 1966; more in Kumar 2013. Alexander had been told of the Nanda king Agrammes in 326, which is a testimony that Candragupta's rise to power came later. Candragupta's story is prettily retold in Hilda Seligman's novel, *When Peacocks Called* (1940).

151. *Mahāvaṁsa,* tr. Geiger 1950 [1912], 27. See also *Viṣnupurāṇa,* tr. Wilson 1840, 468: 'Upon the cessation of the race of Nanda, the Mauryas will possess the earth, for Kautilya will place Chandragupta on the throne'. (The work is written in the form of a prophecy.)

152. F. W. Thomas in *CHI* 470; Mookerji 1966, 16.

'Morieis' in the Greeks ('a people who live in wooden houses').[153] There may be a connection with the word Mayura, a peacock: some traditions say that his family were peacock-tamers. This might explain the use of the peacock as an emblem in Maurya sculpture.[154]

The rise of Candragupta is the subject of various legends which certainly contain a kernel of historical truth, though one cannot be sure how much. The two main sources are Hemacandra, *Lives of the Jain Elders* (*Pariśiśtaparvan*) and *The Rakśasa's Ring* (*Mudrarakśasa*), a play by the fifth-century author Visakhadatta about the king.[155] In the former, the fall of the Nanda is the result of scheming by the Brahmin Canakya, who considers himself insulted by the king.[156] Recognising that he is 'destined to be a king hidden in a shadow',[157] he contrives, in the guise of a wandering ascetic, to satisfy the longing of a peacock-breeder's wife, who is pregnant, to 'drink the moon'. He places a bowl of water under a hole in the roof, and in it at midnight the moon is reflected. In due course she gives birth to a son and names him Candragupta, *candra* being the Sanskrit word for 'moon'. The young Candragupta shows himself a natural king even in play,[158] and his playmates inform Canakya that he is 'the son of a wandering ascetic, adopted by the ascetic while he was still in his mother's womb'.[159] Canakya takes the boy and mounts an assault on Pataliputra; but his paltry forces are quickly defeated. Canakya does all he can to protect Candragupta, including killing a Brahmin and cutting him open to feed the boy on the rice pudding that the Brahmin had just eaten.[160] Canakya then enlists the aid of King Parvataka (Porus of the Greek texts) and mounts a successful assault on the Nanda capital. As he is going into exile on a waggon with his wife and daughter, the daughter espies Candragupta and falls in love with him.[161] When the two kings enter the palace to share out the treasure, Parvataka falls in love with a girl; Canakya arranges a marriage, without explaining that she is in fact a poison-maiden, whom he has fed on poison

153. Thomas, *CHI* 470: *Digha Nikaya* 2.167; Euphorion F 168 Powell: Μωριεῖς. ἔθνος Ἰνδικόν, ἐν ξυλινοῖς οἰκοῦντες οἰκοῖς (from Stephanus Byz). Cf. Hesychius: Μωριεῖς. Οἱ τῶν Ἰνδῶν βασιλεῖς.

154. Kumar 2013, 59; but there are many other animals in Maurya art besides the peacock.

155. The conclusion of the play seems to allude to King Candra Gupta (ca. 376–415 CE).

156. So too in *Mudrarakśasa* (*The Rakśasa's Ring*) 1.11.

157. *Pariśiśtaparvan 8.227.*

158. A similar story is of course told of Cyrus, Sargon of Akkad and many other rulers. See Kumar 2013, 79 and 80. Cyrus was perhaps deliberately adopted as a model by the kings of Magadha: Amigues 2011, 71.

159. *Pariśiśtaparvan 8.250.*

160. Ibid. 8.281–9.

161. Another story prevalent in Persian and Greek literature: Stoneman 2012.

from infancy: so as soon as Parvataka kisses the bride, he is poisoned and dies. Thus Candragupta becomes sole heir to the kingdom, '150 years after the liberation of holy Mahavira'.[162]

The story in *The Rakśasa's Ring* involves most of the same dramatis personae but revolves around the withdrawal, after the death of Parvataka, of the Nanda minister Rakśasa from Pataliputra, and Canakya's campaign to win him over to the Maurya side.[163] Rakśasa joins forces with Parvataka's son Malayaketu, but Canakya, who in this text bears the name Kautilya, contrives to frame Rakśasa for the killing of Parvataka. The rebel Nandas thus lose credibility with Malayaketu and his campaign falters. Furthermore, Rakśasa's ring has fallen into the hands of a jeweller, his friend, from whom a spy obtains it for Kautilya, who uses it to embroil Rakśasa in further suspicions. While in Act IV the Brahmin courtier Bhaguryana contrives to alienate Rakśasa from his prince by trickery, in Act V a letter from Rakśasa to Candragupta, forged by Kautilya and sealed with the minster's own seal, drops him finally in the soup. In Act VI Rakśasa is prevented from hanging himself by Kautilya. In Act VII the jeweller is about to be executed for his loyalty to Rakśasa, but the latter gives himself up to save his friend. The minister, with his inability to be disloyal, has been outsmarted by the ruthless and Machiavellian Kautilya. In the end Kautilya's aim is achieved: Malayaketu is forced to accept terms from Candragupta, by which he is reinstated in his kingdom as a subordinate ruler, while Candragupta becomes the supreme ruler.[164] The plot is more involved than any eighteenth-century opera's; and is predicated on the traditional view of Kautilya, the author of the *Arthaśāstra*, as a figure of Machiavellian cunning and unscrupulousness, which has in ancient times as well as modern been read out of his masterwork. The play is a textbook demonstration of the arts of dissimilation, disinformation, duplicity and corruptibility, and would leave one in no surprise if the Maurya state created by Kautilya turned out to be a police state.[165]

162. *Pariśiśtaparvan 8.339.*

163. The author makes use of Buddhist and Jain sources, and the Purāṇas, and surely knew the *Arthaśāstra* well: Thapar 2013b, 359–60. The ring motif is probably borrowed from Greek drama, but in other respects the play is quite unlike a Greek play: ibid., 370.

164. The same general course of events is understood in the anonymous novella, *Candragupta's Marriage to Alexander's Granddaughter*, mentioned above.

165. Thapar 2103b, 368 sees the play as a study of the transition to imperialism. But the hero is certainly not a role model for Candra Gupta II, since Kautilya is a villain, and Candragupta a śudra: ibid., 372.

Of course, to rely on a play of the seventh century CE as evidence for events of the third century BCE is as risky a proceeding as to rely on, say, Schiller's *Mary Stuart* for knowledge of the historical fate of Mary, Queen of Scots. Both involve invented characters (Rakśasa; Mortimer) and both shape events to suit plot. However, the position is not so much worse than that pertaining to many of the sources for Greek history. The author of *The Rakśasa's Ring* is well informed about historical details of the period. Perhaps the most striking detail is the statement by the courtier Bhaguryana that 'at that time, when Rakśasa wanted Sarvartha-siddhi to be Emperor, it was His Majesty King Parvataka of glorious memory who, being even more powerful than Candragupta, was the most awkward obstacle in Rakśasa's path and his greatest enemy'.[166] The author is clearly familiar with the opinion recorded by Megasthenes that Porus was greater than Candragupta (see the beginning of this chapter). It would be too optimistic to hope that he was familiar with more of the text of Megasthenes than we have now, and thus to conclude that other details are drawn from the Greek writer (although Greek writings were certainly known to Sanskrit authors by this time, as witness the account of Apollonius of Tyana and Damis: see chapter 16 below). However, a few other details bear mentioning. Another character, Viradha-gupta, informs his master Rakśasa of events in Pataliputra since Candragupta's entry into the city: 'With Pataliputra now besieged on all sides by the great horde of Scythians, Greeks, hill tribesmen, Kambojas, Persians, Bactrians and all the others, numberless as the ocean waters at Doomsday, that make up the forces of Candragupta and Parvataka under Kautilya's guidance . . .' (Act II). The list of allies is plausible since it consists of the republics of the Punjab as listed by Panini.[167] The involvement of *mlecchas* and hill-tribes is discussed by Kautilya.[168] Perhaps there is a hint here of the source of Candragupta's power, and support for the idea that Eudamus, who the Greek sources tell us was the assassin of Porus, participated in the events between 323 and 317 as an ally of Candragupta. Eudamus was left by Alexander at the court of Taxiles, presumably to keep an eye on things,[169] and according to Diodorus he controlled a force of horse and foot as well as 120 elephants which 'he had secured after the death of Alexander by treacherously slaying King Porus'.[170] He took part in the conflict with

166. *Mudrarakśasa* 251–3.

167. Mookerji 1966, 23–4.

168. *Arthaśāstra* 9.2.6–8, 9.2.10.

169. Arr. *Anab.* 6.27.2. On Eudamus see Lane Fox 1996.

170. Diod. 19.14.8.

Eumenes on the side of Peucestas, who had an army that included ten thousand Persian archers as well as Greek, Thracian and Persian cavalry. Other commanders brought troops from Carmania, Arachosia, Paropamisadae, Areia and Drangiane and Bactria. The line-up is not dissimilar to that that the *Mudrarakśasa* places in the siege of Pataliputra, and perhaps Candragupta's diplomatic contacts with the huge forces massed on his frontiers were sufficient to enable him to sequestrate a few for his own campaign. The Buddhist sources inform us that Candragupta was brought by Canakya to his native city of Taxila for his education, where it was customary, according to the Jātakas, to send kings' sons to be educated.[171] This is a natural context for the meeting of the student prince with the conqueror Alexander that is alluded to by Plutarch.[172]

At all events, the rise of Candragupta resulted directly in the end of Greek power in north-west India. Justin states simply that 'India, following Alexander's death, had shaken from its shoulders the yoke of servitude and put to death his governors. The man responsible for this liberation was Sandrocottus. After his victory, however, he had turned the so-called liberty he had gained back into servitude; for on seizing power he began himself to enslave the people he had championed against foreign domination. He was a man of low birth, but he was called to royal power by divine authority'.[173] Justin's few sentences in his epitome of Trogus raise the question of who Trogus' source might have been. Probably it was an Indian source; Bussagli suggested that he derived his information from a Jain,[174] which is not implausible since, if Candragupta ended his life as a Jain, there may well have been a number of them at his court. Perhaps, then, the ultimate source is Megasthenes, with his familiarity with Candragupta's court. Daimachus is also a possibility. Justin goes on to tell a legend of Candragupta's being licked by a lion as he slept, after which he gathered 'a band of outlaws and incited the Indians to revolution' against King Nandrus. An elephant, too, made obeisance to Candragupta.

The major element of Candragupta's campaign was the elimination of the kingdom of Porus. Porus had been reinstated in his kingdom by Alexander after the battle of the Hydaspes, with extended territory. Taxiles was also restored to his kingdom, while Abisares had control of what is roughly modern

171. Only these Buddhist texts treat Taxila as a 'university city': Ghosh 1973, 57.

172. Plu. *Alex.* 62. So Mookerji 1966, 15–17. Chanakya is even seen as 'Chandragupta's Aristotle' by Kumar 2013, 41.

173. Justin 15.4.12–15.

174. Bussagli 1996; cf Wheatley 2014, 312.

Kashmir.[175] Alexander put Nicanor in control of the territory of the Assaceni (Asvakayanas), but the satrap was murdered while Alexander was en route to the Chenab, in 326, and the land was pacified by Philip, the satrap of the upper Indus, and the territory added to his own.[176] The land between the Hindu Kush and the Indus was under the control of Alexander's general Peithon. Philip was assassinated before Alexander had completed his journey back to Babylon. His replacement, Eudamus, had probably a purely military command; but very soon he had Porus murdered (319/8), seized his war-elephants and joined, with Peithon, in the war against Antigonus. Candragupta stepped into the vacuum thus created. The statement in Arrian (from Megasthenes) that no Indian had ever launched a military expedition outside their own country may perhaps support this view that the takeover was peaceful.[177]

Whether there is much historical truth in the stories of his and Canakya's plots against Porus' heir, there is no doubt that this was the first stage in Candragupta's rise to power. The *Arthaśāstra* is insistent in condemning foreign rule,[178] *vairajya*, and one might see in this a reflection or a justification of the steps Candragupta took to eliminate Greek power in the subcontinent. At some time in the next twenty years he reached an agreement with Seleucus – the Treaty of the Indus, probably 304 BCE – by which he obtained control of all the region as far west as Kandahar,[179] and presented Seleucus with five hundred elephants. There was also an agreement regarding *epigamia*: this has been interpreted as meaning that one of the rulers married the daughter of the other – in which case it would be possible for Aśoka's grandmother to have been Greek! – but it seems more likely that what is referred to is an agreement regarding intermarriage between the Arya people of Candragupta and the *mleccha* Greeks.[180]

The Indian king could consider that he had eliminated the opposition. A story in the *Mahāvaṁsa* recounts that 'a woman baked a chapatti and gave it to her child. He, leaving the edges, ate only the centre and, throwing the edges away, asked for another cake. Then she said [to Candragupta's spy, who was

175. Mookerji 1966, 28 notes that 'Alexander could not venture to post Greek governors to the east of the Indus'.

176. Arr. *Anab.* 5.20.7.

177. Arr. *Ind.* 9.12.

178. *Arthaśāstra* 82.

179. But never as far west as Herat: Wheatley 2014.

180. Wiesehöfer 1998, 225 raises the question of whether Candragupta was being treated as a vassal, since the gifts go only one way. The question of 'who won the peace' has been very variously answered: cf. Wheatley 2014, 510.

present], "This boy's conduct is like Candragupta's attack on the kingdom" . . . So Candragupta, in his ambition to be a monarch, without beginning from the frontiers, and taking the towns in order as he passed, has invaded the heart of the country; and his army is surrounded and destroyed.'[181] The story is a striking inversion of the parable presented to Alexander by an Indian ascetic, who took an ox-hide and showed that it could only be held flat by standing firmly in the middle of it, not on the edges. One wonders whether Candragupta had been present at this little demonstration in Taxila and had gone home to put it into practice, before discovering that, in his case, it would not work.[182]

Jawaharlal Nehru waxed eloquent about this triumph of Indian nationalism: 'Alexander's invasion of India in the fourth century BC was, from a military point of view, a minor affair. It was more of a raid across the border, and not a very successful raid for him.[183]. . . News came of Alexander's death at Babylon in 323 BC, and immediately Chandragupta and Chanakya raised the old and ever-new cry of nationalism and roused the people against the foreign invader. The Greek garrison was driven away and Taxila captured. The appeal to nationalism had brought allies to Chandragupta and he marched with them against north India to Pataliputra. Within two years of Alexander's death, he was in possession of that city and kingdom and the Maurya Empire had been established.'[184]

In the famous lines of Matthew Arnold,

The East bowed low before the blast
In patient, deep disdain;
She let the legions thunder past
And plunged in thought again.[185]

Candragupta extended his rule into southern India, but in about 298, at the age of about fifty, he abdicated and handed power to his son, Bindusara.[186]

181. *Mahāvaṁsa* p. 123; Mookerji 1966, 33. Cf. Hemacandra 1998, 8.91–301, a similar parable about rice pudding.

182. Elwin 1964, 147 recounts the myth of Nanga Baiga, who nailed down the four corners of the earth like a chapatti on the ocean. Getting a chapatti – or an ox-hide – to succumb looks like an indigenous piece of Indian folk wisdom.

183. Nehru 2004, 115.

184. Ibid., 123.

185. From 'Obermann Once More'.

186. See Mookerji 1966, 44 for chronology. We should know a lot more about this period if any credence could be given to the text presented by Paranavitana 1971, which is however

The Maurya state that Candragupta established was a new kind of political entity in India. The three major sources, the *Arthaśāstra*, Megasthenes' *Indica*, and the inscriptions of Aśoka, all imply a highly centralised state with control by the king reaching to every corner of his lands. Prakash speaks of the 'Achaemenian étatisme' of the *Arthaśāstra*,[187] while Rostovtzeff argued that Candragupta 'hellenized' India.[188] Nilakanta Sastri, by contrast, thinks that the prescriptions of the *Arthaśāstra* are more suited to a small state than to an empire.[189] The centralised view was the picture that Thapar originally presented of the political organisation of the empire,[190] while retreating from this view somewhat in later work.[191] Fussman has argued for a yet more decentralised view of the empire, simply on the grounds that communications would not allow of tighter control, and this has view has been preferred by Mookerji and Kumar.[192] Thapar's later view is of an empire divided into metropolitan, core and peripheral areas.[193] Ray 2011 sees the empire as decentralised, with poor techniques of central control, and argues that it was Buddhist trading networks that brought India gradually together.[194] It remains to be seen how Megasthenes' reports mesh with one or the other view of the empire, and whether Kautilya and Megasthenes are compatible.

Pataliputra

> On the southern and most excellent bank of the Ganga, that Rāja-ṛṣi (royal sage) will cause a pleasant city to be founded, filled with people and flower-gardens. And that pleasant city, the City of Flowers (Puṣpapūra), the son of Pāṭalī, will endure for 5000 years – there is no doubt of that: and for 500 years, and for five months, and for five days and *muhūrtas*.
>
> —*YŪGA PURĀṆA* 41–3, TR. MITCHINER, 2002, 103

---

certainly a forgery: see the review by Rocher 1975, as well as Weerakkody 1997 and Kosmin 2014, 276–7.

187. Prakash 1964, 185.

188. Quoted in Nilakanta Sastri 1967, 54. R. S. Sharma (2009, 151) is another supporter of the centralised view (against Heesterman).

189. Nilakanta Sastri 1967, 51.

190. i.e., in the first (1984) edition of *Aśoka and the Decline of the Mauryas.*

191. Thapar 1987; 1997.

192. Fussman 1987–88; Mookerji 1966; Kumar 2013, 135.

193. The state of the argument is valuably summarised by Singh 2009, 340–1.

194. Ray 2011.

How full how strong,
Her trembling panting surges run,
Where Patali's immortal son
To domes and turrets gives his awful name
Fragrant in the gales of fame!

—WILLIAM JONES, *HYMN TO GANGA*

One clear piece of centralisation is the creation of a new imperial capital at Pataliputra, inspired in part by Achaemenid models. Arrian writes, 'The greatest of the Indian cities is Palimbothra, in the district of the Prasioi'.[195]

The site of Pataliputra today is a pleasant park in the Patna district of Kumrahar, separated by a gateway from the main east–west thoroughfare of the city with its constant melee of bicycles, laden with bananas or pulling rickshaws, tuk-tuks – their windshields adorned with portraits of Bollywood stars and blue-skinned gods – cars, vans, tractors, trucks of malodorous rubbish and giant lorries all obeying the injunction painted on the vehicle in front in the snarl-up, 'Blow Horn'. (In Patna even the juggernauts' horns seem to announce 'Pa-ta-li-pu-tra'.)

The remains of the imperial palace of Candragupta lie concealed under a green open field; adjacent to this lawns are planted with trees – jamun, mango, banyan and ashoka – many of them bound with sacred red-and-yellow threads as prayers for good fortune. A tiny on-site museum evokes the splendours of the ancient city in an effective diorama, but the real treasures are in Patna Museum, with the largest collection of Maurya art to be found anywhere. At the edge of the park lie the substantial remains of the walls of a Buddhist monastery of the fifth century. A little to the south is the hill associated from Aśoka's time with the sage Upagupta, and a number of relic stupas.

According to the *Vinaya Pitaka*, it was the Buddha himself who prophesied the future greatness of Pataliputra,[196] and Buddha himself is quoted as saying, 'with my godlike vision that is purified, surpassing that of men, I have seen deities occupying the sites of the village in their thousands … As far as the Ariyan sphere extends, as far as merchants travel, this will be the chief city: Pāṭaliputta – where "the seed sacks are split open". But Pāṭaliputta will

195. Arr. *Ind.* 10.2.5. This is the only time that Arrian uses the term 'Prasioi', Skt. *prācya*, though it is common in the other historians, including in the *Alexander Romance* (3.17, etc.).

196. Singh 2009, 284.

5.2 View of the site of Pataliputra today (2015).

suffer from three hazards – fire, water, and dissension among its people'.[197] Greek tradition tells us that the city was founded by Heracles. Most probably it was founded by the Nanda king Udayi in 438 BCE,[198] while the *Yūga Purāṇa* says it was founded by Puṣpapura, son of Pāṭalī 'the charming', who are obviously legendary characters, and that it would endure for 5,505 years, five months, five days and five hours. (Pāṭalī is the name of the tree *Bignonia stereospermum/suaveolens.*)[199]

Megasthenes states that the city was located at the junction of the Ganges and the Erannoboas. The latter name was hard to identify with any modern river name, and until Sir William Jones, the father of Indology, made a breakthrough in 1793, it had been assumed that it probably referred to the Jumna, and that Candragupta's capital, which Megasthenes calls Palibothra, must be

197. *Mahāparinibbāṇa-Sutta* 88; in Gethin 2008, 49. Cf. Kalota 1978, 66–9, who mentions the last king, Buddha Gupta, who probably saw his city overwhelmed by floods in 340 CE.

198. Kumar 2013, 66–7, quoting the Purāṇas.

199. Slusser 2010, 136–7.

at Allahabad. The name of ancient Patna, Pataliputra, seemed to echo the Greek version; but no river now joins the Ganges at Patna. In a Eureka moment, Jones came across a reference to the river Son by the name of Hiranyabahu, the 'golden-armed'. Surely this was the same name?[200] Combined with the fact, established by James Rennell in the 1770s, that the Son had once joined the Ganges much further east, the identification of the site was assured, and, incidentally, provided testimony to the generally accurate recording by Megasthenes and other Greeks of Indian toponyms.[201] Nowadays the Son joins the Ganges some twenty miles (30 km) to the west, and a much smaller river, the Punpun,[202] also joins it from the south, some twelve miles (20 km) to the east. Though the original course of the Punpun is unclear, the Son was a major artery leading from Madhya Pradesh to the Ganges. The Ganges itself now runs further to the north than its ancient course: in antiquity the city of Pataliputra was on its southern bank.

Pataliputra was well placed to be a hub of long-distance routes, including what Eratosthenes calls 'the Royal Road'.[203] This is in fact the more southerly of two major roads, the Dakshinapatha, which ran from Lahore through Hastinapura, Varanasi and Allahabad (the junction of the Yamuna and the Ganges) to Pataliputra and Rajagriha, with an extension to the river Godavari.[204] The northern route, the Uttarapatha, followed a trajectory from Lahore to Bengal.[205] Besides these royal roads, *rajagraha*, there were also merchant roads, *baṇikpatha*, traceable by the spread of Buddhist sites referred to in the Jātakas

200. Plin. *NH* 6.64 mentions both the Eramonombua and the Sonus but erroneously treats them as separate rivers.

201. The story is attractively told by Keay 2001, 35–6.

202. Jha 1998, 219 calls the Punpun 'minor but highly menacing'.

203. Arr. *Ind*.3.4. Beyond (i.e., to the east of) Palibothra, he says, there is no accurate information available. His judgment seems accurate: Plin. *NH* 6.69 refers to peoples called the Monaedes and Suari, who live beyond Palibothra, around Mount Maleus; these cannot be identified, and at 2.184 Pliny places Mount Maleus among the Oreitae, while Solinus 52.13 places the mountain upriver from Palibothra.

204. Singh (ed.) 2006, xxvi. Cf. Rawlinson 1926, 42. Ctesias (F 33) provided a list of stages from Ephesus to Bactria and India; see the comment of Lenfant ad loc., which notes that the stages are confirmed by clay tablets from Persepolis. These routes have remained largely constant over millennia: Singh 2004, 149 and 151. The Dakshinapatha can already be identified in the chalcolithic period: Lahiri 1992, 404.

205. The route is a land one, though it closely follows the line of the Yamuna and the Ganges: Lahiri 1992, 395. Thus: Taxila, Sanghol, Mathura, Kausambi, Sarnath, Pataliputra, Chandrakutegarh; Xuanzang calls Sanghol 'She-to-t'u-lu', which must be Śatadru.

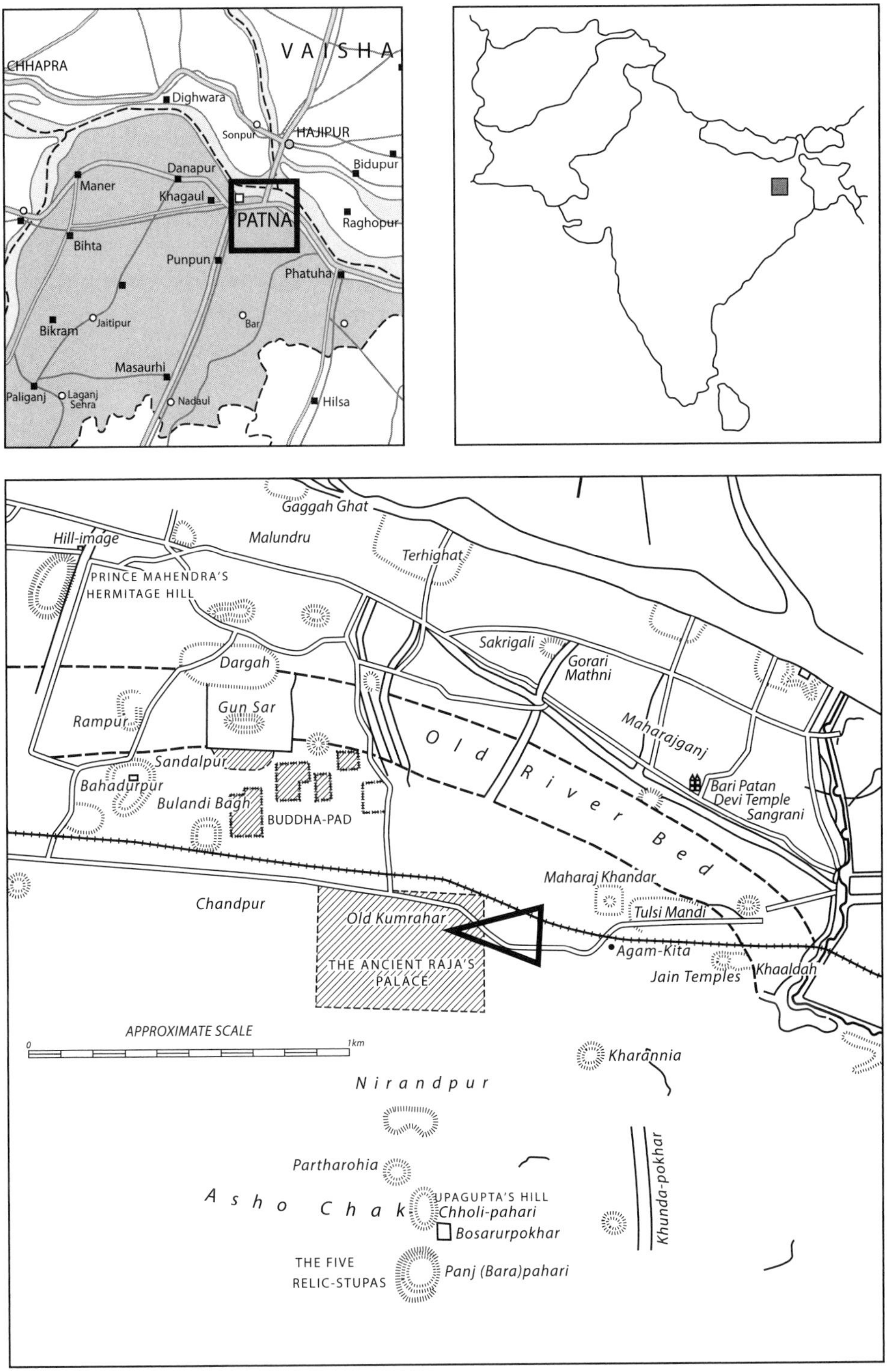

5.3 Plan of Pataliputra (Patna), Candragupta's capital.

and evidenced by archaeology: Sanchi is pivotal for these.[206] No doubt this royal road was the one followed by Iambulus at the end of his seven years of adventures in a utopian Indian land; he was 'shipwrecked, and brought by the natives into the presence of the king at Palibothra, a city which was distant a journey of many days from the sea. And since the king was friendly to the Greeks and devoted to learning, he considered Iambulus worthy of cordial welcome; and at length, upon receiving a permission of safe-conduct, he passed over first of all into Persia and later arrived safe in Greece'.[207]

Megasthenes' description[208] is precise. After mentioning the number of cities in India, which are impossible to count, he goes on,

> Those on the rivers or on the coast are built of wood; if they were built of brick, they could not last long because of the moisture due to rain, and to the fact that the rivers overflow their banks and fill the plains with water. Only where the cities are situated in commanding and lofty places and these are bare, are they built of brick and clay.[209] The greatest of the Indian cities is called Palimbothra, in the district of the Prasians, at the confluence of the Erannoboas and the Ganges; the Ganges is the greatest of all rivers, while the Erannoboas may be third of the Indian rivers but it is still greater than the rivers of other countries, though it yields precedence to the Ganges after joining it. And Megasthenes says that the length of the city on either side, where it is longest, extends to eighty stades [9 miles/14.5 km], its breadth to fifteen stades [1½ miles/2.5 km], and that a ditch has been dug round the city, six plethra [200 yards/183 m] wide and thirty cubits (45 feet/13.7 m] deep; the wall has five hundred and seventy towers and sixty-four gates.

S. K. Jha has calculated that these dimensions (14.4 km x 2.8 km: 3,000 hectares) would accommodate a population of 0.4 million, making Pataliputra the largest city in India of its time.[210]

The wooden buildings of the Ganges plain differed little from those that are still common there now. Reliefs at Bharhut and Sanchi, dating from the

206. Lahiri 1992, 385; Shaw 2007.

207. Diod. 2.60.

208. Ff 18 J, 25 and 26 Schw = Arr. *Ind.* 10.4–7 and Str. 15.1.35–6 In F 56.10 Schw = Plin. *NH* 6.22.4 (not in Jacoby), the Andarae (Andhra) of the Deccan are stated to have thirty fortified towns (*oppida*) as well as numerous villages.

209. The *Yūga Purāṇa* 48 confirms the 'famous mud walls' of Pataliputra.

210. Jha 1998, 184–5. See also Allchin 1995, 202: whether it was 1,200 ha or 4,500 ha, it was the biggest in south Asia.

time of Aśoka, depict circular and rectangular thatched huts closely resembling those that one may still see in the villages. Close to the river, nothing is permanent and dwellings are made of brushwood, bamboo and straw; when swept away by floods, the fragments are salvaged and the structure resurrected. 'On higher ground', writes an authoritative author on Indian architecture, 'it is possible to build with greater permanence. Here, the walls are of sun- or kiln-baked bricks, or are built up in courses of mud or dung. In the east the roof is pitched, or thatched with paddy straw. In Punjab and Haryana it is generally flat, surrounded by a low parapet'.[211] Again, the information given by Megasthenes, though truncated in Arrian's quotation, is seen to be quite accurate.

Other cities offer little comparable material. The ancient site at Delhi, which was Indraprastha, Ptolemy's Indapat, is within the Purana Qila, and was excavated in the 1950s.[212] It offers no structural remains, but the Painted Grey Ware would normally be associated with wooden architecture. The *Mahābhārata* describes the walls of Indraprastha as furnished with moats, walls and gates,[213] but the description is more likely to reflect the time of composition, several centuries later, than early historic times. However, a reference to 'bastion-battering tuskers'[214] implies that anti-elephant spikes had not been introduced in the imagined time of the action.

Strabo adds some further details.[215]

> The city is of the shape of a parallelogram,[216] and is girded with a wooden wall, pierced with loopholes for the discharge of arrows. It has a ditch in front for defence and for receiving the sewage of the city.

Allchin gives a good description of the archaeological record at Pataliputra. The timber rampart was excavated in 1927–28: it consisted of a double line, four metres (13 ft) wide, with an earth infill.[217]

The city walls of Pataliputra were identified by Rennell in 1783, excavated by Waddell (1903), though the contribution of Mukharji should not

211. Cooper and Dawson 1998. (The text is by Cooper, the photographs by Dawson.)

212. Singh (ed.) 2006, xvii, 30–2, 47.

213. *Mbh*.1.199.29ff.

214. Ibid. 2.54.10–11.

215. Ff 17 J, 25 Schw = Str. 15.1.35.

216. The *Arthaśāstra* says that cities should be square, but few are, apart from Śiśupālgarh: Allchin 1995, 206–7.

217. Allchin 1995, 200–8. The description of Manu's Ayodhya in *Rām*. 2 *(Bālakāṇḍa)* 5 conforms to this general model.

be forgotten,[218] and Spooner conducted the excavations at Kumrahar that exposed the remains of the central area of the city (1913). Pataliputra went beyond other contemporary Indian cities in including stone in its architecture, though most probably not before the reign of Aśoka.[219] The roof of the huge audience hall was supported by eighty sandstone pillars: the surviving one exhibits the beautiful 'Maurya polish'. Most of the other structures were of wood, including the column bases, and a passageway over eighty yards (75 m) long. The wooden drains were particularly advanced![220] Nehru exclaimed on the 'incredible state of preservation' of the massive wooden pillars sunk beneath the water-table but remarked that, despite resemblance in layout to the *apadana* of Persepolis, a 'characteristically Indian artistic tradition is visible'.[221]

The question of the architectural antecedents of Pataliputra, raised here by Nehru, is a matter of debate.[222] Spooner observed the resemblance of the audience hall to the hundred-column hall of Persepolis.[223] He also thought that the polish on the pillars was an Achaemenid technique, but the lustre of a Maurya sculpture is beyond that of anything at Persepolis, or indeed of any subsequent achievements of Indian art. If Persepolis was at the other end of the royal road that Eratosthenes refers to, Persian craftsmen, and even Greeks, may have moved back and forth on it. Some of the mason's marks at Pataliputra resemble those at Bisutun.[224] Nilakanta Sastri accepts Spooner's judgment

218. Singh 2004, 317–19.

219. The question of whether there was any stone architecture before the Greek period was generally answered in the negative before Cunningham: see Singh 2004, 88 and 91. The double line of stone walls at Rajgir, which have been dated to the sixth century BCE, would be the most notable example if this date is correct. Jha points out (1998, 210) that this is two centuries before any other evidence for stone walls; Ghosh 1973, 63 also finds no evidence for stone walls before the end of the first century BCE, and dates the walls of Rajgir after this, as well as those at Rajghat (Varanasi). He dates the mud walls of Ujjain and Sravasti to the third century BCE. There is a romanticised description of Rajgir at *Mbh.* 2.19.1–20, which mentions a gate and a massive ancient tower. Kausambi had an earth rampart by 400 BCE: Allchin 1995, 106–8. The walls of Pataliputra were still effective in the third century CE: Jha 1998, 273. Jacobs 2016 would place the stone buildings at Pataliputra in the reign of Aśoka.

220. Jha 1998, 236.

221. Nehru 2004, 136–7.

222. A valuable extensive discussion of the art of Pataliputra is Nilakanta Sastri 1957, 356–91.

223. So also Falk 2006, 139–41, on the possibility of Achaemenid architects.

224. Furthermore, Thapar 1997, 127 takes the view that the form of the edicts of Aśoka is comparable with those of Darius.

and states that 'there is good reason to believe that Aśoka consciously adopted the plan of the Achaemenid hall of public audience to proclaim the glory of his empire to his subjects'.[225] Aelian, in a passage for which he gives no source – but who can it have been but Megasthenes?[226] – makes a direct comparison with the Persian palaces: 'in the royal residences in India where the greatest of the kings of that country live, there are so many objects for admiration that neither Memnon's city of Susa with all its extravagance, nor the magnificence of Ecbatana is to be compared with them ... In the parks tame peacocks and pheasants are kept, and they live in the cultivated shrubs to which the royal gardeners pay due attention. Moreover there are shady groves and herbage growing among them, and the boughs are interwoven by the woodman's art ... There too parrots are kept and crowd around the king.' Quintus Curtius, too, remarks on the extravagance of the king's style, 'lounging in a golden litter fringed with pearls, and dressed in linen clothes embroidered with gold and purple. The litter is attended by men-at-arms and by his bodyguard amongst whom, perched on branches, are birds which have been trained to sing in order to divert the king's thoughts from serious matters. The palace has gilded pillars with a vine in gold relief running the whole length of each of them and silver representations of birds'.[227] The resemblance to Achaemenid palace architecture is notable, though the parrots and peacocks are an Indian idiosyncrasy.[228]

Megasthenes' description gives the opportunity for a first confrontation with the *Arthaśastra*. In this text, the ideal capital city is described in some detail.[229] It is to be built in the centre of the country, on both land and water routes and with a lake or tank in the vicinity. The fort is to be surrounded by three moats, full of lotuses and crocodiles (pretty as well as dangerous! – like a poison-maiden), and by a rampart planted with thorny bushes and poisonous creepers, and broad enough for chariots to drive along the top. All this is to be of stone or brick, not wood, as a precaution against fire. A removable bridge over the moat will lead to a gateway with a tower and a hall within. (Various designs are permitted.) Within the city there are to be three east–west

225. Nilakanta Sastri 1957, 88–9.

226. Ael. *NA* 13.18.

227. Curt. 8.9.24–6. Atkinson ad loc. opines that Curtius is also using Megasthenes for this information. Nilakanta Sastri 1957, 358 claims fragments of golden vines were found in the excavations, recalling those of Susa and Ecbatana.

228. See also Michell and Martinelli 1994, 68.

229. *KA* [= Kautilya's *Arthaśastra*] 2.3.3–32 and 2.4.1–31 (Kautilya 1992, 184–94).

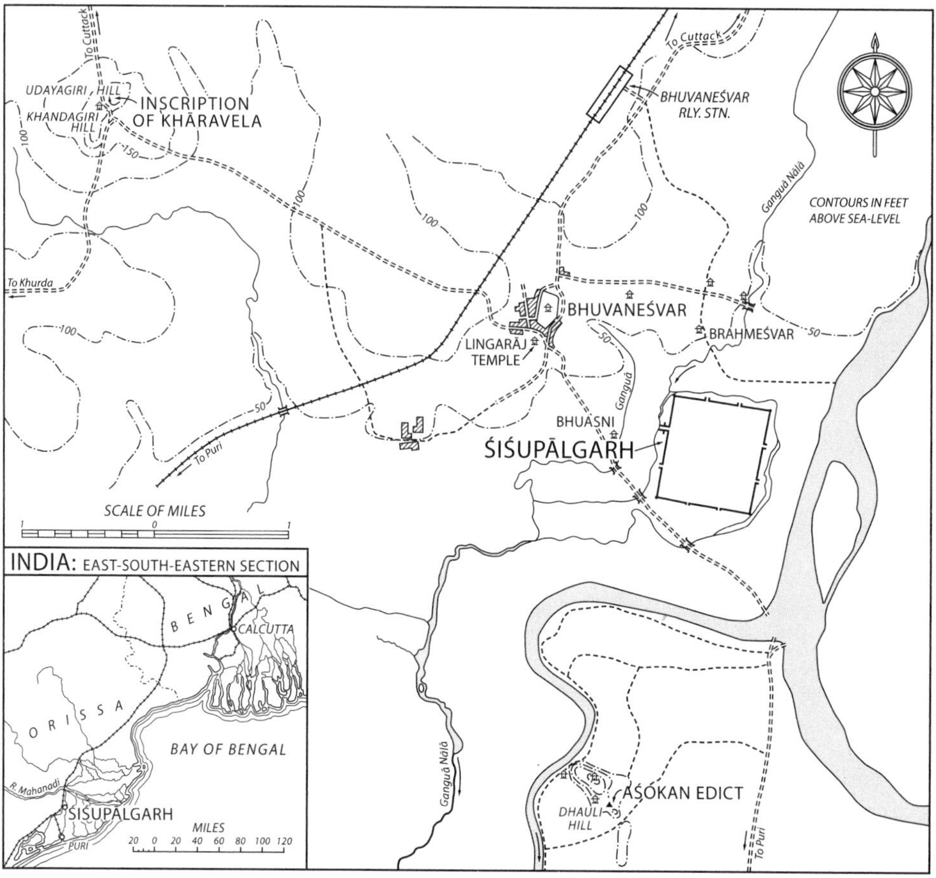

5.4 Plan of Śiśupālgarh, a rare example of a square city-plan, with stone ramparts. The city is probably pre-Maurya.

'royal roads' and three north–south ones; the palace in the centre and the *varnas* (castes) distributed by locality. Temples are to be in the centre of the city and at each of the four main gates. All workers with fire (e.g., blacksmiths) are to be concentrated in a single area, and crematoria are to be situated outside the city. 'Heretics' and Caṇḍālas (who dispose of corpses) are to live beyond the cremation grounds. It appears that the city is to be square in shape: apart from what Megasthenes tells us of Pataliputra, only the third-century foundation of Śiśupālgarh fits this ground plan.

The description is tidy-minded to the point of obsession, and would have done credit to the architects of such modern structures as the Berlin Wall. Such a city plan obviously requires a completely blank canvas to be put into

5.5 These reliefs at Sanchi depict typical architectural forms of the Maurya period.

effect, though certain provisions, such as making the untouchables live beyond the cremation-grounds, are observable in present-day India. But it is not at odds with what Megasthenes tells us about Pataliputra, except for the number of gates: one or four in Kautilya, sixty-four in Megasthenes. The insistence on stone may point to a later date however, in the light of the discussion above. The only cities where there seems to have been an opportunity to create a grid plan such as that recommended by the *Arthaśastra* are Śiśupālgarh and Taxila. Kautilya's ideal city does, however, look not unlike what we know of Pataliputra as described by Megasthenes. Paul Kosmin has suggested that Megasthenes interpreted the city he knew as if it were a Hellenistic one.[230] But he may not have been wrong to do so if the links between Magadha and the Achaemenid world were as significant as I have suggested. Both traditions fed into the cities of the Hellenistic East.

230. Kosmin 2014, 45 and 47

In about 400 CE the Chinese Buddhist pilgrim Faxian visited Pataliputra, which was by now in ruins. He regarded the palace as the work of Aśoka, 'the different parts of which he commissioned the genii (demons) to construct by piling up the stones. The walls, doorways and the sculptured designs are no human work'.[231] Most of the other structures belonged to a later era, including the alleged eighty-four thousand stupas constructed by Aśoka. He identified a pillar with an inscription by Aśoka stating 'the king presented the whole of Jambudvipa to the priests of the four quarters'. Three or four hundred paces north of the 'pagoda' (stupa), is another pillar, topped with a lion, with a detailed historical record of his reign'.[232] Clearly fantasy has mingled with observation in this description. No pillar is known to have stood at Pataliputra, though there is a fine lion-column at Vaiśali, some twenty-five miles (40 km) to the north. Some of those genie-fashioned sculptures have been recovered and are in the museum in Patna.

The later pilgrim Xuanzang (seventh century CE) found Pataliputra deserted but its foundation walls still surviving, and a small town of about a thousand houses lying to the north of it on the banks of the river, which had already evidently begun to run further north. It was known as 'city of the scented flowers' (Kusumapura), and later as Pataliputra because a Brahmin sage sat under a patali tree (*Bignonia suaveolens*) there. Xuanzang also observed the palace of the king, and 'to the north of it', a stone pillar several tens of feet high, marking the place where Aśoka built his 'hell', in the days before his conversion. He regards Aśoka as the great-grandson of Bimbisara and as the builder of the rampart around the city. He also observed those numerous stupas, as well as the Buddhist *vihara* (monastery: probably that of which the foundation walls survive), a stone with the footprint of Tathagata, the pillar with the inscription giving Jambudvipa to the Buddhists, and a large house built by the genies for Aśoka's brother.[233]

The description has little of substance, and is embedded in a much longer account of Aśoka's reign, most of it legendary; it adds nothing, apart from the pillar, to what could be observed by the excavators of the site. The city which Megasthenes visited remains elusive in its detail, though his writing, as well as the texts of Kautilya and the Chinese pilgrims, give some hint of the scale and impressiveness that it once displayed.

231. Beal 1884, lv.
232. Ibid., lvii–lviii.
233. Ibid. 2.82–92.

One may envisage something of Megasthenes' life in Pataliputra from the details given in the *Arthaśastra* about the duties of an envoy. He must be clear about his mission, treat his opposite number with respect (which must be reciprocated) and must be 'friends with the enemy'. He should avoid women, and strong drink, and sleep alone, in the interests of security, but make a point of talking to beggars, drunks and watchmen, and of paying attention to those who talk in their sleep.[234] If this sounds rather austere, one should recall that Megasthenes' position was not that of an envoy to an enemy but, as far as we can tell, an intermediary between two friendly courts.

One text that may give us some insight into the society of Pataliputra in the late fourth and early third centuries BCE is the *Kāma Sūtra* of Vatsyayana. Most scholars would date this to the third century CE, around six hundred years after the death of Megasthenes,[235] but the life of the man-about-town it describes is not incompatible with the splendour that is attributed to the Maurya court. The only city mentioned in this work is Pataliputra, the Maurya capital: in the opening chapter the author writes that the original *Kāma Sūtra* consisted of a thousand chapters, which were then cut down to 150 by Babhrayva of Panchala; from this, 'Dattaka made a separate book out of the sixth part of this work, about courtesans, which the courtesans de luxe of Pataliputra commissioned.'[236] Dattaka, we are told, was the son of an old Brahmin of Mathura who lived in Pataliputra: when his mother died, his father gave him to another Brahmin woman for adoption, and she named him 'Little Gift'. So Dattaka was able to describe the Pataliputra of his childhood and youth, presumably a generation or so before Vatsyayana. Vatsyayana's touchstone of proper behaviour is the city of Pataliputra: 'the men of the city do not indulge in oral sex themselves, but the people of Surasena do everything, without the slightest hesitation.'[237] Vatsyayana gives a vivid description of the life of the man-about-town of his day:

> He settles down in a city, a capital city, or a market town, or some large gathering where there are good people, or wherever he has to stay to make a living. And there he makes his home in a house near water, with an orchard, separate servant quarters, and two bedrooms.... [in the outer

234. *KA* 1.16; see Kumar 2013, 199–200.

235. Doniger and Kakar 2002, 11.

236. *Kāma Sūtra* 1.1.11. Doniger's note indicates that 'Pataliputrikas' could also be interpreted as 'Daughters of the Trumpet-Flower'.

237. *Kāma Sūtra* 2.9.31.

> bedroom] there is a grass mat and an altar ... a spittoon ... a lute, hanging from an ivory tusk; a board to draw or paint on, and a box of pencils. Some book or other, and garlands of amaranth flowers ... a board for dice and a board for gambling. Outside, cages of pet birds ... In the orchard, a well-padded swing in the shade, and a bench.[238]

Vatsyayana goes on to describe the daily routine of ablutions, parties, on certain days 'an assembly of invited guests at the temple of the goddess Sarasvati',[239] salons, picnics and swimming 'in pools built to keep out crocodiles'. If this was Megasthenes' life as a highly-regarded diplomat, he was having a wonderful time.

> The man who tells stories in society,
> neither too much in Sanskrit
> nor too much in the local dialect,
> becomes highly regarded in the social world.[240]

238. Ibid. 1.4.1–26, abridged.
239. The name of the goddess seems anachronistic for Maurya times.
240. *Kāma Sūtra* 1.4.37.

6

Megasthenes' Book

The Structure of Megasthenes' Book

Megasthenes' description of India acquired the status of a classic. His book became the primary, and often the only, source for all later imaginings of India, so that even when Rome had been in trading contact with India for two centuries, Pliny was still describing a world essentially as it had been evoked by the Greek author.[1] The observations of the author of the *Periplus,* and of Agatharchides, have little impact on later writers. Somehow Megasthenes' India was the sort of India that the Hellenistic and Roman worlds found it comfortable to imagine. There was no critical attempt to evaluate what he had written and to compare it against later observations.

The case reminds one of the impact of Kipling's India in the Britain of the late imperial years. Even though India was a country ruled by Britain – whereas it was never ruled by any Greek or Roman after the decline of the Indo-Greek kingdoms, which produced no descriptive works – Kipling could be confident that his India would carry conviction. 'One of the few advantages that India has over England,' he wrote in *The Phantom Rickshaw,* 'is a great knowability'. As David Sergeant has observed, Kipling tells his readers what they believe must be the truth about British India. 'Correct or not, it surely must be true', wrote an anonymous critic about Kipling's work in 1896. Edmund Gosse lauded the 'persuasiveness' of Kipling's writing. A captivating style will take an author a long way, even one who, like Kipling, is 'suspicious of texts, attributions and sources', and aspires to be 'scientific'.[2]

1. Dihle 1964; Schwarz 1975.
2. Sergeant 2013, 63.

How scientific is Megasthenes? Strabo was the first ancient writer to criticise him for including implausible stories such as that of the men with faces in their chests. In modern times, this lead has been followed by many who have not studied Megasthenes himself, and by some who have. The fact is that, if one is to say anything at all about Maurya India, Megasthenes' evidence is inescapable, and must be treated to a proper evaluation. This is the conclusion of the most recent Indian historians to discuss his work closely, Romila Thapar and Upinder Singh, as well as of many Western scholars – notably in the fine work by Barbara Timmer,[3] though there have been divergent voices in both groups.[4] As Brown observes, 'without Megasthenes' *Indica* Eratosthenes would have failed to write an intelligible account of Indian geography'.[5]

We looked in the previous chapter at some of Megasthenes' contemporaries and immediate successors in the field of ethnography, the structure of whose books seems to follow a recognisable pattern. If we look at the three main witnesses – Diodorus, Strabo and Arrian – for Megasthenes' content, a similar pattern can be observed. Of these, Diodorus is a straight epitome of information about India, citing no previous authors. Both Strabo and Arrian, by contrast, explicitly cite a great many authors besides Megasthenes, including both Eratosthenes and the Alexander historians Onesicritus, Nearchus and others. Nevertheless, all three accounts have a broadly similar structure, one which was, to some extent, determined by the conventions of ethnographical writing.

First comes a geographical description of India, with a lot of emphasis on its rivers. Strabo adds some information about Taprobane after the rivers section. Then comes the narrative about the expedition of Semiramis, and the gods Heracles and Dionysus in India. (Both Arrian and Strabo interrupt the section about Heracles with an account of pearl-fishing.) Strabo next discourses on trees and plants and then returns to the topic of rivers. He also speaks of Taxila and various Indian rulers at this point. The other authors go straight from the account of Heracles and Dionysus to discussion of the gov-

3. Timmer 1930.

4. Thapar 1987; 1997; 2002, and elsewhere; Singh 2009. Sharma 2009 uses Megasthenes' work critically. In favour of Megasthenes: above all, the magisterial Stein 1932; then Brown 1955; Sachse 1981; Derrett in *Kleine Pauly* s.v. Megasthenes; Dahlquist 1962 (though Dahlquist's own views will not stand scrutiny). Against Megasthenes: Basham 1954; Majumdar 1960.

5. Brown 1955, 33. More recently, Arora (1991–92, 329) has added his support to this view: 'Despite the unreliable character of certain fragments, the *Indica* of Megasthenes may be placed among one of [*sic*] the best literary sources of ancient Indian history'.

ernment of India, and the city of Palibothra, at which point Strabo rejoins the itinerary, as it were. He slips in here some information about tigers, taken from Megasthenes. Then all three authors continue with a discussion of the seven so-called castes of India which Megasthenes described, and move to the description of elephant-hunting. At this point the three witnesses diverge: Diodorus writes of Indian magistrates and Arrian writes of tigers, parrots and the ethnic characteristics of the Indians, while Strabo has a much more extensive description of beasts (taken from Nearchus) and then goes on to talk of the fabulous races and of the Brahmans. There are good reasons why Arrian would have broken off his account without including either of these two topics: he would have no patience with the fabulous races, and he had already written about the Brahmans in his *Anabasis*, where, furthermore, he promised a monograph on them, which alas we do not have, unless it is incorporated in some way in the first part of Palladius' *De Bragmanibus*.[6]

The similarities in the order of topics suggest both that the three authors are following a single source, Megasthenes, and that their accounts represent a more or less complete epitome of the kind of material that Megasthenes covered. Charles Muntz has argued that Diodorus is much more eclectic (or discriminating) in his use of sources than has previously been supposed: he proposes that Diodorus' main source was Eratosthenes, supplemented by direct use of Megasthenes for the portion on Heracles and Dionysus.[7] Even if this is so, it must be admitted that Eratosthenes was largely reliant on Megasthenes. Muntz finds evidence of direct use of Onesicritus, and of Daimachus (a slippery customer). Where Bosworth wrote that Diodorus' account of the Ganges was 'grafted on to a digest of Megasthenes',[8] Muntz finds that Diodorus regularly 'selects and combines'.[9] Muntz's close examination of Diodorus' procedures is valuable, but it does not, in the end, eliminate the primacy of Megasthenes. The latter's book was, then, mainly about geography and political structures, with an excursus early on about the Greek gods in India, and probably rather more at the end than either Arrian or Diodorus troubles to summarise about beasts and fabulous peoples. It is surprising that

6. Stoneman 2012, and cf. Derrett; but Stadter 1980, 228 n. 42 is sceptical, citing the refutation by Hansen 1964.

7. Muntz 2012; also, briefly, Muntz 2017, 73–4.

8. Bosworth 1996a, 188.

9. A similar view is presented by Sulimani 2011, e.g., 59: Diodorus uses one key source, with interpolations.

only Strabo gives us what may be, to some scholars,[10] the most extensive and interesting passage, about the Brahmans and other philosophers.

All the extant fragments of Megasthenes can easily be fitted into this structure. Compare Photius' summary of Ctesias, an author who probably did not visit India but only picked up stories from travellers. Photius no doubt picked out the bits he found striking as he read through, rather than making a systematic précis, but the structure is comparable: he starts with rivers and springs, interspersed with elephants and monkeys; then comes the manticore, then some ethnographic remarks and a passage about Indian weather; pygmies; more water features; griffins, goats and trees; more springs; the health of the Indians; serpents and various poisonous creatures; rivers again; a long passage on the dog-headed people; more strange beasts; yet another spring; and the long-lived Indians. Photius concludes that 'these are the stories that Ctesias writes . . . and he asserts that they are completely truthful'.

Apart from the strange obsession with springs and rivers, and the obviously fantastical character of much of the information, the overall structure is not unlike Megasthenes', except for its patent lack of anything plausible about the real inhabitants of India, their way of life, beliefs and government, and its treatment of the data he conveys as essentially amazing wonders. It is remarkable, however, that both these Greek Indologists say absolutely nothing about so many topics that would interest us, such as mythology, religious practices, women, the life of the people, sanitation, sex, food. The contrast with Ctesias should not lead us to suppose that Megasthenes provided what we would regard as a comprehensive ethnography of India. Already the genre had its own implicit rules.

Perhaps the most vivid extended description of India in a Roman writer is the excursus by Quintus Curtius in his *History of Alexander*, a 'digression' occurring just before Alexander advances to the conquest of India.[11] Like the Greek writers, he begins with geography:

> Almost the whole of India faces eastward, and it is a country greater in length than width. The areas exposed to the south wind are of higher elevation, but the rest of the country is flat, and the many rivers that rise in the Caucasus [i.e., the Himalayas] are afforded a gentle course through its plains. The Indus is colder than the others, and its waters are little different

10. E.g., Stoneman 1995.

11. Curt. 8.9.

> from the sea in colour. The Ganges, greatest of all rivers of the east, flows in a southerly direction and, taking a direct route, skirts the great mountain ranges, after which it is diverted eastward by some rocky mountains which bar its course. Both these rivers flow in to the Red Sea [i.e., the Arabian Sea – clearly false].

And so it continues, sober geography written in a lively and colourful style, and with some egregious errors. The pattern is Megasthenic, but what can his source have been for the following bit of 'information'?

> In that part of the world the earth inverts its regular seasonal changes, so that when other places are baking in the heat of the sun, India is covered with snow; conversely, when everywhere else is frozen, the heat there is intolerable.[12]

Certainly not from anyone who had ever lived in India: the passage derives from geographical speculation about the Antipodes, believed to lie just beyond the southern limits of exploration. One cannot use Curtius' description as firm evidence for what was in Megasthenes' book, but on the other hand it is hard to know what his alternative source might have been for certain passages (for example, that on the king's palace, also described by Aelian, discussed at the end of the previous chapter).

Another author who structures a description of India by beginning with rivers is Dionysius Periegetes. Indeed his account of India consists of little besides rivers and mountains – nothing on the people, diet and customs, law and polity. Rather he uses the description of the mountains of Nysa as a lead-in to a reappearance of one of the dominant deities of the poem, Dionysus. Jane Lightfoot in her edition shows how most of Dionysius' descriptions conform to a standard order of ethnographic topics, though not all may appear in every case.[13] They begin with *situs*, that is geographical location and disposition, or orientation; rivers are important in this context; then climate and natural resources; crops and livestock; human population, including origins and customs.[14] Dionysius' India is particularly elaborate. He starts from the 'southern

12. Curt. 8.9.13. Atkinson's commentary offers no remarks on this passage at all.

13. Lightfoot 2014, 139–41, and 142–3 on India. See also Timmer 1930, 35ff. Murray 1970 draws attention to the similar structure of Hecataeus of Abdera's work, except that the latter begins with religion.

14. Dion. Perieg (line) 1158.

Scythians', who 'live by Indus' streams':[15] the river rises in the Caucasus and passes through desert lands to Patalene; though crops are hard to raise, the wealth of coral and sapphire provides the people with a livelihood. Then 'Eastwards the Indians' lovely lands extend'.[16] The inhabitants' skin colour is first noted, then their exploitation of gold-bearing sands, of elephant tusks, and the precious stones hidden in the rocks.[17] Millet also gets a mention. The orientation of India comes next (not at the beginning as one might expect). The rivers are recounted, and then Dionysius moves on to speak of the Rock Aornos. His final tableau is the beautiful portrait of Nysa 'beside fair-flowing Ganges' (which is a bit off course), where Bacchus set up his rites, slew his Indian enemies and began his progress 'back' to the river Ismenus (in Thebes). Dionysus is the most prominent god in the *Periegesis*, as he is, along with Heracles, in Diodorus.[18] These two civilising gods are the makers of the known world.

The disposition of material in all these authors prompts consideration of the organisation of Megasthenes' book, and of the fragments in the collections of Schwanbeck and Jacoby. Can we extrapolate from Strabo, Arrian, Curtius and Dionysius to a putative order of the fragments of Megasthenes? There seems to be a difference from some other authors of local histories: when writing a history, gods, religion and human origins seem to come first. This is the case with Hecataeus of Abdera, Berossus and Manetho.[19]

Barbara Timmer proposes the following 'contents' for Megasthenes:

1. Borders and extent, nature
2. History and customs, society and urban life
3. Religion and philosophy. (Should Taprobane be tacked on here?)

Josephus (Jacoby F 1Δ) mentions a fourth book, but Jacoby emends Δ to A; the content, a comparison of Heracles to Nebuchadnezzar, is remarkable in any case, but if it fits anywhere it is with the account of Heracles.

The problem is that there are very few fragments suitable for book 2. The bulk of the fragments concerns the natural world, religion and philosophy, though the long passages on kingship and caste would fit book 2. There ap-

15. Ibid. 1088.

16. Ibid. 1107–65.

17. Gems have a function as 'paragraph markers', as Lightfoot remarks (2014, 152).

18. Sulimani 2011.

19. Murray 1970; Dillery 2015.

pears to be no history in Megasthenes, though perhaps the ancient history about Heracles and Dionysus fills that slot, along with the brief mention of the list of succeeding kings. King-lists are certainly an integral part of most regional histories, notably in Berossus and Manetho,[20] and they are also the armature of the later Brahmin Purāṇas, which presumably extend an oral tradition of past times; so perhaps the excerptors of Megasthenes simply recorded the total with no details. A list of 130 strange names could seem rebarbative. This topic should most naturally appear in book 1: that is where it belongs in Berossus, and that is where Arrian seems to position it. Many obvious topics that would fit under 'customs and society' do not appear: women and their lives (and deaths), music and arts, food, religious practices. Should we assume that those who used Megasthenes' book for their own purposes never showed an interest in these topics, which thus have not survived?

Geography is probably over-represented in the fragments because that is Strabo's primary interest, though he does also give us the fullest account of the philosophers. Arrian's interest is primarily in society, and he is hard-headed about religious and mythological matters.

We long to know how big Megasthenes' book was. Several topics, including ones that are certainly from Megasthenes, are difficult to place in the template: I instance Taprobane, the fable about the hoopoe, the long account of elephants. The latter is strangely positioned in the middle of the discussion of caste in Strabo, though after it in Arrian. And the disquisition on pearl-fishing is oddly positioned in the middle of the account of Heracles and Pandaea.

I tentatively propose the following new order of fragments, which seems to provide the most logical disposition of the material within the ethnographic template:

Book 1. Geography and natural resources; ancient history; human populations

4 J	general account
6 J	size of India
3 Schw.	boundaries
7 Schw.	Hipparchus controversy
7 J	shadows
9 J	rivers, with *Anhang* 16
20B Schw.	rivers

20. Dillery 2015.

9 J	Silas (spring)
57 J	Dionysus
58 J	Heracles and Pandaea [maybe 1J here, if this was not in 'book 4']
51 J	Pandaea
Anhang 7	Alexander, distances
Anhang 10	Taprobane
15B Schw.	kartazon
13 J (part)	pearls
26 J	Palaeogoni; pearls
25 J	sea-trees
24 J	fish
21 J	monkeys etc. [or in 2?]
22 J	serpents
Anhang 18	the hoopoe
23 J	ants [or in 2?]
56 Schw.	peoples
27 J	fabulous races
28 J	reverse-feet
29 J	[more of the same]
30 J	[more of the same]

Book 2. Political structures, society and customs

19 J	castes
16 J	tombs

2 J separate tables (Athenaeus tells us this is from book 2)

17 J	cities
18 J + 26 Schw	Palibothra
31 J + 34 and 35 Schw	archontes and astynomoi
32 J + 27 Schw	Sandrocottus' conquests; truthfulness; marriage; exercises
27bcd Schw	usury
20 J	elephants
35 Schw	horses and elephants
52 and 53 Schw	elephants
21 J	monkeys [or in 1?]

Book 3. History (hardly to be distinguished from mythology), religion and philosophy

33 J + 42 Schw	philosophers
34 J	suicide; Calanus
55 Schw	Calanus
Anhang 20	Brahmans
Anhang 21	Brahmans
3 J	Brahmans and Jews (Clement tells us this is from book 3)

I shall have rather little to say about the purely geographical topics, and Strabo's treatment of the technical aspects. I shall treat first the matters of politics and society, and in the two subsequent chapters I shall turn to, respectively, the natural world, and the discussion of the philosophers, which had the longest resonance by far in ancient and later literature.

7

Geography and Ancient History

The Geography of India; or, Why Diodorus Disagrees with Strabo about what Eratosthenes Got from Megasthenes about the Dimensions of the Subcontinent

Arrian explicitly bases his account of the geography and hydrography of India on Eratosthenes, who must have used Megasthenes, while Strabo incorporates his references to Megasthenes into the general discussion of these matters in which he takes issue with all his predecessors, referring also from time to time to Daimachus and Patrocles. The closest approach to Megasthenes' original has usually been taken to be Diodorus 2.35–42. But Muntz argues for a more complex relationship.[1] Regarding the boundaries of India, Diodorus overlaps with Megasthenes, but the latter is not necessarily his sole source; and in fact he may be following Eratosthenes in the first instance. He also follows Eratosthenes on the Sacae. Diodorus however differs from both Strabo and Eratosthenes (and Megasthenes) on the matter of the dimensions of India, and may, Muntz suggests, be following Daimachus here.[2] On physi-

1. Muntz 2012.

2. Diodorus: 28,000 stades east–west, 32,000 north–south; Strabo: 16,000 east–west, about 16,000 north–south. Strabo says that the east–west distance is derived from Eratosthenes, based on the register of the stages on the Royal Road, and that Megasthenes agrees with him; however. Arrian (*Ind.* 3) quotes Megasthenes for the dimensions 22,300 north–south and 16,000 east–west. It is hard to argue with confidence from these varied figures. Nonetheless, Alexander Cunningham in 1871 was impressed by the accuracy of the information provided by the Alexander historians: see Eck 2012, 69. The Purāṇas also gave detailed measurements for India: Eck 2012, 507 n. 57, so Megasthenes may have been able to draw on earlier versions of these data.

cal geography, Diodorus resembles Strabo, who cites both Megasthenes and Eratosthenes.

Apart from the (not unimportant) matter of the dimensions of India, there is a general correspondence between Diodorus and Megasthenes, if we assume that he was mediated through Strabo. Diodorus moves on to describe the two harvests enjoyed in India, and then to an account of the rivers. Arrian goes directly to rivers, with nothing on crops; he cites Megasthenes several times here, for the size of the Ganges in relation to the Indus, for a comparison with the navigable stretch of the Maeander, and for the navigability of other Indian rivers. This is much more detailed than Diodorus, who moreover says that Alexander reached the Ganges,[3] whereas both Megasthenes and Arrian knew that he did not. Apart from this piece of Diodoran misinformation, the passage on rivers looks to me like a mere abbreviation of an account reproduced more fully by Arrian.[4]

Both Arrian and Diodorus mention the wondrous spring Silas, though Arrian dismisses it as a fable.

Muntz has shown that Diodorus' procedure is less mechanical than has been supposed,[5] but in my opinion his evidence can stand as a précis of Megasthenes, perhaps through the intermediacy of Eratosthenes. But what of the following section, on Dionysus and Heracles? According to Strabo, Megasthenes considered the stories of their 'wanderings' trustworthy, whereas Eratosthenes did not.[6] So the detailed account of these gods is more likely to be direct from Megasthenes. Though Diodorus is not identical with Arrian, Muntz has no better candidate to offer and writes that Diodorus here 'reworks' Arrian. Sulimani shows how Dionysus and Heracles are the prime civilising heroes of the 'pagan mission'. Placed in this position by Alexander, they are inescapable in later generations.

Arrian took Megasthenes' account of Indian geography very seriously. 'Megasthenes does in fact give the names of many other rivers besides the Ganges and Indus which flow into the eastern or southern ocean, and concludes that the total number of Indian rivers is fifty-eight, all of them navigable. But I do not think that even Megasthenes visited much of India, though

3. Also implied at Diod. 18.6.1–3. Muntz thinks this may be from Hieronymus of Cardia.

4. So also Bosworth 1996a, 188, noted above: 'grafted onto a digest of Megasthenes'.

5. Also, in the case of Ctesias, Bigwood 1980 shows that Diodorus does not just summarise Ctesias in book 2: he adapts, adds material of his own and – presumably – from other authors.

6. Str. 15.1.7; Eratosth. F 21.

he certainly saw more of it than the men who invaded with Alexander'.[7] Megasthenes' credit as a geographical witness remains intact, as far as his competence lay.

The Ancient History of India

Arrian follows his précis of the geography of India with a few comments on weather and on the skin-colour of the natives. In the next paragraph he moves on, again citing Megasthenes explicitly, to inform us that the total number of Indian tribes is 118. Arrian believes Megasthenes could have no adequate grounds for so precise a figure; presumably he had been told it by native informants. He then moves on to ancient history.

> Originally, he says, the Indians were nomads, like those non-farming Scythians who move about in their wagons from one part of Scythia to another, without any permanent settlements or centres of worship. In the same way the Indians at first had no settled communities or edifices for worship of the gods, but simply clothed themselves in the skins of the wild animals they killed, and ate the bark of trees ... They also fed on the animals they caught, eating them raw – at least that was their practice before the arrival of Dionysus in India.[8]

The first part of this could be any classical account of the primitive state of humankind, but the arrival of Dionysus, who founded cities, established laws, introduced wine and taught the Indians agriculture as well as religious worship with cymbals and drums, dances and the wearing of long hair, marks a new level of specificity to the Indian case.[9] When Dionysus left India, Arrian goes on, he appointed his companion Spatembas as king; he reigned for fifty-two years, and in due course his son Budyas succeeded to the throne and reigned for twenty years.[10] Budyas' son Cradeuas continued the line, which passed by heredity as long as sons were available: 'if the family succession

7. Arr. *Ind.* 5.2–3. The *Ṛg Veda* regards India as a land of seven rivers, those of the Punjab plus the Sindhu and Sarasvati, or alternatively the Ganga, Yamuna, Narmada, Godivari, Krishna and Kaveri: Eck 2012, 167–8.

8. Arr. *Ind.* 7.2–3.

9. Cf. Sulimani 2011, 248–99.

10. Budyas can hardly be intended for Buddha, and Biffi 2000, 146 suggests an identification with Budha, the planet Mercury.

failed, kings of India were appointed on merit'.[11] Later, Arrian adds that from Dionysus to Sandrocottus (Candragupta) the Indians reckoned 153 kings, over a period of 6,042 years, interrupted by three periods of democratic government.[12] The lapse between Dionysus and Heracles was fifteen generations.[13]

Pliny gives a long account of the people of India which corresponds in structure to what is in Arrian and Diodorus, though he enumerates a great many of the races by name.[14] He emphasises the importance of the Maurya capital Palibothra – a clue to his source – but does not mention the series of kings. By my count he names ninety-nine tribes, as well as a good many cities including the capital of the Galingae, Parthalis. So Megasthenes' 118 tribes may not have been so far from the truth.

Can we correlate Megasthenes' account of the ancient past of India with any independent evidence? It seems, for example, to be in contradiction of the statement in the *Mahābhārata* that the land is the home of the descendants of King Bharata.[15] Plainly, too, he exhibits no knowledge of the civilisation of the Indus that flourished in the third millennium BCE. The arrival of nomads from Scythia looks like a recollection of the Aryan 'invasions', remembered in India as Indra's suppression of the Dasas.[16] But what is the role of the culture-hero Dionysus here?

In another part of his history, Diodorus discusses the theory that there may have been several gods called Dionysus,[17] of whom the most ancient was an Indian one; he introduced the cultivation and use of the vine (and figs), he wore a long beard, and he travelled through the world founding cities that bore his name. In book 1 Diodorus says that Osiris travelled to India and

11. Arr. *Ind.* 8.1–3. There is a similar account in Plin. *NH* 21.4–5 (and Solinus 52.5, and Dicuil 7.36): in the 6,451 years preceding Alexander, there were 153 kings.

12. Diodorus says instead that after many generations the Indians turned to democratic governments. He may have based this assertion on his knowledge of the Alexander historians' descriptions of such polities, though he cannot have supposed that they had become universal in India.

13. Arr. *Ind.* 9.9–10.

14. Plin. *NH* 6.21.8–23.11.

15. *Mbh.* 6.9; Eck 2012, 64.

16. Kosmin 2014, 44 notes that, for Megasthenes, Dionysus' invasion was successful because the people were nomads, while now it would be impossible because the people are settled in cities. Thus urbanisation enhances security and civilisation.

17. Diod. 3.62.2–5, with parallel versions at 3.63.1–66.1, 67.1–74.6 and 4.2.1–5.4: Sulimani 2011, 167ff. Cf. Plu. *IsOs* 29 (*Mor.* 362bc), who asserts that Dionysus brought two bulls, called Apis and Osiris, from India to Egypt.

established the city of Nysa, and that the Indians of the present day claim that he was born in India.[18] Syncretism is running rife here: clearly Diodorus or his sources had an idea of the character of Dionysus, which they set out to establish in India. It is sometimes argued that this Dionysus is a form of Indra as first king, culture-hero of the Aryans, warrior-leader and bringer of agriculture.[19] Martha Carter produces some compelling evidence that Alexander's expedition may have wandered into the Indrakun festival in the Kafir lands, in November or January, which involved a dancer dressed as a horned goat, behaving lewdly, while wine was pressed and drunk.[20]

An extension of this argument, first proposed by S. R. Goyal and followed by Carter,[21] is that Indra is represented in Greek by the name 'Indos'.[22] But the most natural reading of Diodorus' Greek, *καί φασι τὸν μὲν ἀρχαιότατον Ἰνδὸν εἶναι*, is that 'the most ancient [*sc.* Dionysus] was *an Indian*'. The loss of this piece of parallelism does not, I think, destroy the argument as a whole. Dionysus may well represent Indra here, though there have been plenty of other candidates, usefully summarised by Goyal.[23] They include Kṛṣṇa, the god of the Mundas, and Goyal's own candidate, the legendary King Pṛthu who was born from the arm of his father (after a dwarf had already been born from the thigh). Pṛthu's father Vena was deposed because he was opposed to the performance of sacrifices, so that in his reign the gods did not partake of soma. When Pṛthu came to the throne he restored the Vedic sacrifices. In the same way Dionysus is said to have introduced religious practices to the godless non-Aryans. Furthermore, Pṛthu was a founder of cities and a proponent of agriculture: he introduces the plough,[24] as well as being a *cakravartin*, a king who conquered the whole earth. 'The valiant Pṛthu traversed the universe, everywhere triumphant over his foes'.[25] Unfortunately there is no mention of wine in his legend. However, K. D. Sethna, who also argues forcefully for Prithu (as he styles him), emphasises the connection of the god with soma. When the earth surrenders to him, he 'milks' her, and this milking is in effect

18. Diod. 1.9.7.

19. See, e.g., Bhattacharji 1970/2000, 249–83.

20. Carter 1992.

21. Goyal 1985, 107–8.

22. So Indos would be the last king of India before rule by humans, as Horus was of Egypt in Dicaearchus F 58a.

23. Goyal 2000, 62–4.

24. *Atharvaveda* 8.10.24.

25. *Viṣṇu Purāṇa*, quoted in Sethna 1989, 84.

'the production of a wondrous drink from earth-products'.[26] Sethna goes on to argue that Vena himself is a form of soma, and that the patronymic form, Prithu Vainya, will have reminded Greeks of their word for wine.[27] This begins to stretch credibility, but in any case the search for aural parallels seems unnecessary: all that is required is a correspondence of functions. It is perhaps more likely that Megasthenes would have heard a Brahman legend about Pṛthu than news about a festival in Gandhara, but he must have got the vine cultivation from somewhere. What does become clear from this discussion is that Megasthenes' aim was not to seek one-to-one correlations between Greek and Indian gods, but to convey ancient history as he heard it in terms that would be intelligible to Greeks. In the same way Herodotus had explained Egyptian gods by giving them Greek names.

There may even be a candidate for Dionysus' successor Spatembas, though neither Sethna nor Goyal puts this forward, in the first legendary king of the earth, Svayambhuva. Here there is an aural parallel and function fades into the background. The succeeding kings and their reigns do not match Indian records,[28] since Megasthenes mentions that there were 153 kings from Dionysus to Sandrocottus, whereas the Purāṇas give a total of 113 from Viṣṇu to Candragupta. The numbers game is not worth playing, but the general principle of long lists of kings and generations is common to both the Indian and Greek traditions.

Megasthenes was, then, familiar with lore that attributed the coming of settled civilisation to India to the activities of a culture-hero who, to him, resembled Dionysus. As this is subsequent in his account to the arrival of Scythian-like nomads, should we postulate a second 'Aryan invasion'? Parpola finds many references in the *Ṛg Veda* to an assault by Indra against the Dasas (the non-Aryan 'indigenous' inhabitants of India); the bearded god is thirsty for the intoxicating soma, and with his *vajra* (his mace, which is a lightning-bolt) he also quells the Asuras (enemy gods, or demons).[29] He shreds their fortresses, he 'chastises those who follow no commandment', he smashes and crushes 'those of no intelligence', who show no hospitality and carry out no sacrifices. This resounding celebration of the arrival of Aryan culture in a benighted India has points of resemblance to Megasthenes' description of

26. Sethna 1989, 86. Sethna's book needs to be used with caution; for example, his theory that the Imperial Gupta dynasty originates in the fourth century BCE is clearly unsustainable.

27. See Konaris 2011, 471, who traces this idea to Kuhn in 1859.

28. Sethna 1989, 124.

29. Parpola 2015 94–7, 107. *RV* 10.124–5 for the Asuras.

Dionysus' arrival, though the Greek author makes his hero much more peaceable. There is no mention of wine in the *Ṛg Veda*, but Megasthenes might have interpreted the soma of Indra as wine on the analogy of Dionysus. There is no need to seek exact correspondence, any more than Herodotus did. What matters is that Megasthenes has some conception of an Indian (Brahman) tradition about the arrival of Aryan, Vedic culture in India, presumably from Brahman informants. These Brahmans will have been the origin of the king-list to which he alludes; in later centuries such king-lists formed the armature of the Purāṇas, texts created by Brahmins to codify the Indian past in terms that supported their claims to authority.[30] An important point here is that genealogies stop time from being merely cyclical, or a dream-time, as it is in 'tribal' consciousness, and create an authority for the Brahman view of the world over that of the tribal Dasas.[31]

Next Megasthenes went on to speak of Heracles. As I argued above, there is no one-to-one correspondence to be sought, though the Heracles who appears at the beginning of his account, particularly revered in Methora (Mathura) and Cleisobora (Kṛṣṇapura?), does look a lot like Kṛṣṇa.[32] But the story he tells about Heracles is *sui generis*. It involves the origins of the southern Indian kingdom of Pandaea, and is interrupted by a digression on pearls.[33]

> As for Heracles, commonly said to have visited India, the Indians themselves hold that he was born from their earth. This Heracles is particularly revered by the Suraseni, an Indian tribe whose territory includes two large cities, Methora and Cleisobora, and is traversed by the navigable river Iomanes (Yamuna) Megasthenes says that by the Indians' own account this Heracles wore the same sort of outfit as the Theban Heracles. This Heracles too married many wives, and fathered a very large number of male chil-

30. Dillery 2015, 96–7 discusses the importance of king-lists as a way of creating a past. Thapar 2013 (e.g., 50) sees such lists as one of the elements that go to create 'historical thinking' in India. On the practical aspect of such long lists, Peter Levi (1972, 187) mentions meeting a man in Chitral who was able to recite his own genealogy for fifty-four generations.

31. Elwin 1947, 225–65 notes the contrast of genealogical with tribal time.

32. Arr. *Ind.* 8.4–5. Mathura is today celebrated as the birthplace of Kṛṣṇa; I have visited the cave, complete with a kind of manger and devotional images of the holy family, where he is said to have been born. It is now underground and reached by a tunnel, since the Mughal emperor Aurangzeb maliciously built a mosque directly on top of the sacred site.

33. The following discussion modifies a paper I wrote in 2013, published in Howe, Müller and Stoneman (eds.) 2016.

> dren in India, but only one daughter. The girl's name was Pandaea, and the country in which she was born and over which Heracles made her queen was called Pandaea after her: here her father endowed her with some five hundred elephants, four thousand cavalry, and a hundred and thirty thousand foot-soldiers. [There follows a story about Heracles's discovery of pearls, which he collected from every sea and brought them to India for the adornment of his daughter. Megasthenes' disquisition on pearls is omitted.] . . . In this country where Heracles' daughter was queen the girls are ready for marriage at age seven, and the men live for forty years at most. The Indians have a story they tell about this. Heracles' daughter had been born to him late in life, and when he realized that his own end was near, in the absence of any potential husband for her of a distinction comparable to his, he slept with her himself when she was seven years old, so that he and she could leave a line of progeny to rule India. So Heracles made her marriageable at that age, and ever since then the whole nation over which Pandaea was queen has enjoyed this privilege as a legacy from Heracles.[34]

Scholars have speculated vigorously about this Heracles and made various proposals to identify him with one or another Indian god.[35] The most popular candidate has been Indra, who carries a club and is known for having killed a lioness (though he did not wear the skin) as well as other monsters, including the dragon Vṛtra:[36] the latter's name has been linked etymologically with that of the dog Orthros, killed by Heracles when he stole the cattle of Geryon, as well as that of Verethragna, the Persian lion-wrestler. Heracles with his club is depicted on coins of the Indo-Greek king Demetrius. There is also a cattle connection, since in *Indica* 5 Arrian mentions the Sibae (between the rivers Indus and Acesines), who carry clubs and brand their cattle with the mark of a club: Alexander's propagandists argued that the Sibae were the descendants of Heracles' army. Indra's case has been argued most vigorously by Allan Dahlquist,[37] but dismissed without argument by Klaus Karttunen.[38] In the Gandhara period the iconography of Heracles is adapted

34. Arr. *Ind.* 9, tr. Martin Hammond. Cf. Plin. *HN* 6.76.

35. Kṛṣṇa: P. A. Brunt in his Loeb translation of Arrian 2.437, following *CHI*. Bala-rama: Biffi 2000, 147, following André and Filliozat 1986, 340 n. 8.

36. *RV* 1.32, 10.28.7, etc.

37. Dahlquist 1962.

38. Karttunen 1989, 210 ff.

for Vajrapāṇi, the frequent companion and protector of the Buddha, often so depicted in art, but the right mythology does not seem to attach to him.

The problem with Indra is to find a story comparable to that of Heracles' incest with his daughter Pandaia that can be attached to him.[39] Other gods are more promising. One story was that given by James N. Tod in his *Annals and Antiquities of Rajasthan*, first published in 1829. He found in the Purāṇas the following legend. Vyasa was the illegitimate son of Santuna, the sovereign of Delhi, who belonged to the race of Hari, namely the Hari-kula. When the legitimate successor, Vichitravirya, died, Vyasa became guardian and preceptor of his three daughters, one of whom was named Pandaia or Pandya, because she concealed herself from public eyes with a covering of yellow ochre. Vyasa married his 'spiritual daughter' Pandaia, and their son Pandu became king of Indraprastha. The names seem to fit neatly, and Pandaia's descendants ruled, we are told, from 1120–610 BC, so were already ancient history by the time Megasthenes arrived. The iron pillar of the Pandavas remained as their monument, and inspired the eloquent author to a Gibbonian meditation on the fall of empires and the duty of the British rulers to leave as great a monument. The syncretism is possible, except for the problem that Pandaia is not Vyasa's daughter.

Dahlquist presents a completely different argument, that Pandaia is Uṣas (whose name, cognate with Greek Eos, marks her as the goddess of the dawn).[40] He thinks that Megasthenes knew enough Sanskrit to realise that the root of Uṣas' name, meaning 'fiery or burning bright' had the same meaning as 'pan-daie', all-blazing. Few will be convinced by this. But let us not drop the story just yet.

Dahlquist also cites a passage of the *Ṛg Veda* which he describes as one of 'the most obscure and unpleasant of all the texts in the *RV*' (it is omitted in the complete translation of the text by Griffith),[41] concerning the incest of an unnamed god with his daughter. The passage is graphic:

> The manly one then pulled away (his penis, which had been) 'attending on' (her) … As they were going apart, the two left behind a little semen sprinkled down on the back and in the womb of the well-performed (sac-

39. There is probably no connection with the story of the Indian poison-maidens, discussed by Stoneman 2008, 88.

40. Dahlquist 1962, 111–12.

41. Ralph T. H. Griffith, *The Hymns of the Rg-Veda* (5th edn, Varanasi: Chowkhamba Sanskrit Series Office, 1971). The passage in question is *RV* 10.61.5.

> rifice). When the father sprang on his own daughter, he, uniting with her, poured down his semen upon the earth

The verses go on to describe how from the semen 'the gods, very concerned, begat the sacred formulation, and they fashioned out (of it?) the Lord of the Dwelling Place, protector of commandments.'[42] In some versions, the father is then pursued by an archer, usually identified as Rudra.[43] It is at once clear that this is not a story about the origin of a race of queens.

Furthermore, there is an alternative candidate for the incestuous father. In fact the story concerns the creator god Prajāpati, the 'Lord of Creatures', and his daughter, and is frequently told or alluded to in Brahmanical literature.[44] Since all creatures are Prajāpati's creation, the only way he can procreate is through one of his own progeny. This daughter is variously identified as Uṣas (the dawn), Vāc (voice), Dyaus (sky) and Sarasvatī, in the Purāṇas the river goddess and goddess of wisdom.[45] In the Purāṇas, the god is Brahma and the daughter is Sarasvatī, among several other names.[46] He then marries her (now called Śatarūpā) and she bears a son, Manu, the primal man.[47]

Besides the incest, this complex narrative has a couple of points of contact with our story: the violated daughter flees to the south and one of the names of the hunter who shoots the violator is Pandu. As previously mentioned, the *Ṛg Veda* never tells a story straight, and I am not as confident as Dahlquist that Megasthenes' knowledge of Sanskrit was up to working out the tale from the chanting of the hymns by the Brahmans. Much more likely is that he asked his Brahman friends to explain what was going on. Given the variability of names and details, he might well have become a little confused. It looks as if he has

42. Sometimes it is the spilled seed that makes the earth fruitful, or it turns into cattle: *Pañcaviṁśa Brāhmaṇa* 8.2.10. Also *Maitrāyaṇī Saṁhitā* 3.6.5, 4.2.12: 'Prajapati went on top of his daughter Uṣas. His semen flew away. It was poured on this one [the earth]. He made it perfect, [thinking]: "let this [semen] of mine not be spoiled". He made it [something] real, namely, cattle.' Translated in Ludvik 2007, 70.

43. See the account of the episode in Bhattacharji 1970/2000, 323; it is also discussed in Collins 2014, 71–2. Roberto Calasso gives a synoptic and poetic narrative in *Ka* (London: Cape, 1998), 43+53+55–6.

44. It is not only in *RV* 10.61.5–10, cited by Dahlquist (1962, 101–2), but also in 1.71.5, 3.31.1. Also *Maitrāyaṇī Saṁhitā* 4.2.12; *SB* 1.7.4.1–3; *Aitareya Br.* 3.33; *Pañcaviṁśa Br.* 8.2.10; *Jaiminiya Br.* 3.262; *Kanṣītakī Br.* 6.1.1–12.

45. The seminal(!) discussion is Jamison 1991, 289–302. See also Ludvik 2007, 60–72.

46. Ludvik 2007, 118–21. Sarasvatī is Brāhma's daughter in *Mbh.* 12.330.10cd.

47. *Matsya Purāṇa* 3.44cd.

combined two separate stories, about Indra the protector of humanity and about the incest of a god with his daughter, which involved an archer-hero (like Heracles) who bore the name Pandu. Combine that with the name of the people, the Pandavas, and you have Megasthenes' version. But it is the nature of myths to fluctuate, especially when related in oral form. There was no Indian Apollodorus to systematise these tales.

However, this is by no means the only instance of father-daughter incest in the *Ṛg Veda*. Another example is *RV* 3.31.1,[48] referring to Indra, and here are some more: [49] Brahma and Uṣas; Brahma and Upas; Brahma and many others; Dyaus and his daughter; Prajapati and Upas; Dakśa and Satī;[50] Vivasvant and his daughter.[51] There are in fact many Prajapatis.[52]

Here we may mention two other theories that have been proposed, by Jean Filliozat and by Asko Parpola, to explain Megasthenes' story of Heracles and Pandaea.[53] Filliozat adduces a story of the king of the southern Mathura who marries a daughter of Śurasena; he offers a sacrificial fire to be blessed with a son, but in the fire there appears a girl of three years old, who is given the name of Panti, or Tatatakai. 'In the legend, the king of Mathura is not the father and does not become the spouse of Tatatakai.' Panti does indeed become the ancestor of the people of Pandaea, but I fail to see any other similarity between this legend and that told by Megasthenes. Parpola brings in the story of King Aśvapati of Madra, who 'fails to marry off his daughter in time, and therefore sends her to search for and choose a husband on her own. The texts do not directly indicate that the king had had an incestuous relationship with Princess Savitri, but they do quote in this context a *smṛti* stating that 'if a girl sees her first menses in her father's house, the father incurs a great sin'.[54] Parpola then goes on to discuss the parallelism of the human Savitri with the goddess Savitri, whom he then identifies with the daughter of Prajapati, who can also take the names Vāc or Uśas or Sūryā; and so we are back to the Pra-

48. Doniger 1981,152.

49. O'Flaherty 1973/1981, 40, 74, 93–4, 113, 115–16, 150, 266.

50. Cf. also Eck 2012, 342.

51. *RV* 10.17.1; Doniger 1999, 52.

52. O'Flaherty 1973/1981, 74, Incest pops up in other combinations too: for example, the brother and sister Yama and Yami (*RV* 10.10), which may be not just a story of improper lust, but a reflection of the need to populate the earth.

53. Filliozat 1980, 156–7; Parpola 2002.

54. Parpola 2002, 366.

japati story from the *Skanda Purāṇa*.[55] In a cosmos where more or less everything can stand for everything else, this story might hang together, but to me it smacks of desperation.

A different tack is taken by S. R. Goyal,[56] who proposes an identification of Heracles with the legendary Manu, the first man.[57] In the *Ṛg Veda* Manu is the establisher of sacrifice. Escaping the Great Flood after being warned by a fish, he had sexual relations with his daughter and thus procreated the human race,[58] rather like Lot after the destruction of Sodom and Gomorrah. In the later Purāṇas, Manu is the lord of the Dravida country, that is, south India (where the Pandya kingdom lay), and he is said to have flourished 135 generations before Candragupta Maurya.[59] He had many sons and divided the kingdom among them. This corresponds remarkably to Megasthenes' figure of 138 generations.[60] The connection of Manu with Madurai (Mathura) in south India, the capital of Pandaea, and that of Kṛṣṇa with Mathura in north India may have strengthened Megasthenes' inclination to identify Heracles in both places.

A point which Goyal does not mention is that the *Laws of Manu*, a text attributed to the legendary Manu though it was probably compiled in the early centuries CE, includes the provision that a man of thirty should marry a girl of twelve, and a man of twenty-four should marry a girl of eight.[61]

The case for Manu being the origin of the Heracles of Arrian's story is compelling.

55. *Skanda Purāṇa* 3.1.40ff.

56. Goyal 2000, 75–79.

57. There are many Manus: Doniger 1999, 53. Note that Manu is also the son of Brāhma by Brāhma's own daughter Śatarūpā (see Ludvik, quoted above). Thus father-daughter incest seems to run in the family.

58. *SB* 1.8.1.1–10.

59. Goyal 2000, 77.

60. Arr. *Ind.* 9.9–10. He puts Heracles 15 generations after Dionysus, who is 153 generations before Sandrocottus.

61. *Manusmṛti* 9.84. Miller 2014, 190, mentions a seventeenth-century novel, *The English Rogue*, which purveyed the view that girls of seven in India are 'extreamely salacious and leacherous as fit, nay, as prone to enjoy man at that age, as Europeans at fourteen'.

8

Culture and Society

Indian Society: The Question of the *Arthaśāstra*

The great question that arises here is the relation between Megasthenes and the *Arthaśāstra* of Kautilya.[1] According to tradition, Kautilya is to be identified with the apparently historical personage Canakya, who is known from Jain traditions as the king-maker of Candragupta; he wrote the *Arthaśāstra* as a guide for the king in the administration of his empire. The probably fourth-century CE play *Mudrarakśasa* (*The Rakśasa's Ring*), uses the names Kautilya and Canakya indiscriminately for this person. In 15.1.73 of the *Arthaśāstra,* the author is identified as one Viṣnugupta, and later scholars who commented on it in the sixth and eighth centuries CE identified all three names as belonging to the same man. As with all Indian writings, its date is intensely disputed, since no texts were written down until several centuries after the date of Megasthenes. Alongside the problem of the identity of the author is that of the dating of the content of the text. Some scholars regard the work as belonging in essence to a much later period; others presume a core that dates back to Maurya times, with later accretions.

The earliest scholarship saw the book as a description of the Maurya polity – an exciting find given the paucity of material, let alone Indian material, for the history of early India. Breloer went so far as to call the work 'Candragupta's Magna Carta'.[2] The view remains attractive, and many Indian scholars have been glad of a straw to cling to in the ocean of uncertainty, and perhaps of an Indian text that reduces their dependence on a Greek outsider's information, particularly if they are dazzled by Strabo's attack on Megathenes for

1. Stein 1921; Goyal 1985, 2000.

2. Goyal 1985, 1, with extensive further doxography.

unreliability, and his one or two obvious mistakes (as on slavery). R. Shama Sastry's 1922 edition of the work presents this view most forcefully, as does R. P. Kangle's of 1965, and it underpins Mookerji's book on Candragupta.[3] Kalota (1978) also takes it as axiomatic that Megasthenes and Kautilya both provide evidence for the same period and polity.

Stein in 1921 was already doubtful of the possibility of a match between the two texts, and observed that if anything conditions in Megasthenes are closer to those implied by the Dharmasūtras.[4] The most trenchant recent treatment is that of S. R. Goyal, who builds on the work of Thomas Trautmann:[5] both of these argue for a late date for the *Arthaśāstra* in its entirety.[6] Trautmann's argument is based on stylistic analysis, showing that not all of the work can have been written at the same time or by the same author. This argument offers no absolute conclusion about the date of any individual element; so in principle parts of the work could date back to the time of Candragupta. The first external references to the *Arthaśāstra* date from the fifth century CE.[7]

This has prompted a number of scholars, including the great Romila Thapar, to try to save parts of the *Arthaśāstra* as evidence for the Maurya period, alongside a discriminating use of Megasthenes. 'Borrowings and similarities in other works throughout the centuries can be explained by the fact that only the original text was written at the end of the fourth century BC'.[8] The danger that lurks here is circularity: you may decide that a particular element looks Maurya, and then argue that that portion of the *Arthaśāstra* must be early and that it provides evidence for that detail. Goyal helpfully points out that the two texts are not congruent in their purposes. Megasthenes' account is a description, whereas Kautilya's is normative: it describes how things

3. Mookerji 1966, 4 and passim. See the brief survey in Habib and Habib 2012, 38. Majumdar 1960, 60 is typical: 'the picture given in the book may be looked upon as the one representing the age of Magadhan imperialism, especially when we remember the fact that the account of the Maurya administrative system, as outlined by Megasthenes, tallies substantially with that laid down by Kautilya'.

4. Stein 1921, 175, 202.

5. Goyal 1985; Trautmann 1971.

6. See also the judicious summary by Singh, 2009, 322–3. Brinkhaus 2016 surveys the history of the discussion and cites McClish's view that it is to be dated in the second/third century CE, and that it influenced the *Kāma Sūtra*.

7. Goyal 1985, 7.

8. Thapar 1997, 225 (the conclusion to her appendix 'The date of the *Arthashastra*', which surveys the history of the argument.) Allchin 1995, 187 and ch. 10, is also determined to use the *Arthaśāstra* as evidence for the Maurya period.

should be, not necessarily how they are. Thus the problem of the wooden walls: Megasthenes states that the walls of Pataliputra were built of wood; Kautilya states that city-walls should not be built of wood, but of stone. Thapar deduces that Kautilya's precept was not always followed, because stone was hard to get hold of and expensive. But if Kautilya's book is advice not description, there is no reason why it should match reality. He might be *criticising* the structures at Pataliputra. Or he might be writing in the context of a different historical period altogether, when it was natural to build walls of stone (as from the Gupta period onwards).[9]

A similar clash occurs as regards metallurgy and mining. Megasthenes and archaeology concur in indicating that these techniques were in their infancy in the Maurya period, while the *Arthaśāstra* lays great stress on the importance of mines, and of the control of mines.[10]

The administrative system described by Kautilya is different from that of the Aśokan inscriptions.[11] R. S. Sharma raises the question of whether the state control of production envisaged by Kautilya 'suits the Maurya state',[12] and proposes that 'the Maurya model may have continued with modification under the Satavahanas and the Kushanas' up to the third century CE. Thus he both has his cake and eats it. Goyal comes to a different conclusion, that this level of state control is not evidenced in Megasthenes, and reminds us that Kautilya's account should be seen as normative not descriptive.[13]

Kautilya also seems to reflect a different religious world from that of the Maurya kingdom. There are large temples with large estates, and the gods include several who are not in evidence at the earlier date, notably Śiva.[14]

Several larger considerations suggest that the world of Kautilya is different from that of Candragupta. Among the more subjective is the assessment of the kind of kingdom implied by the *Arthaśāstra*: is it designed as a blueprint for a large empire like that being established by Candragupta, or for a smaller-scale state beleaguered on every side by other small-scale states, as in the period of Kushan decline? Both cases can be argued.[15] More specific points in-

9. The third-century stone walls of Śiśupālgarh seem to provide some rare support for Kautilya.

10. Goyal 1985, 58; cf. Kumar 2013, 126.

11. Goyal 1985, 11, following Sharma 1959.

12. Sharma 2009, 135–6.

13. Goyal 1985, 58–9.

14. Ibid., 31–3.

15. The cases are summarised by Singh 2009, 340–4.

clude the many items that appear in the *Arthaśāstra* but for which we have no independent evidence in Megasthenes; for example, the elaborate network of spies, including prostitutes.[16] Megasthenes does mention that he had talked to prostitutes, but this is not sufficient corroborative detail for the existence of a Kautilyan spy-network in his period. Further, the elaborate and often ferocious range of punishments detailed by Kautilya is at odds with the Greek authors' observation of the minimalism of law in the lands they visited. Then again, the prominent role given to Brahmans in the state seems to imply a state run on Brahmanical principles. Megasthenes refers to the regular appearances of the 'philosophers' at court, but they do not seem integral to the running of the kingdom. If Bronkhorst is right to regard Magadha as a less Brahmanised region than the west and north-west, one would expect their role to be weaker. The tradition that Candragupta was a śudra, and in later life a Jain, would lead one to expect he would be less receptive to Brahman dominance.

Thus both specifics – wooden walls and mines – and more general considerations – the nature of society – suggest that the *Arthaśāstra* belongs to a different world from that of the Maurya. However, as Trautmann showed, the book must belong to many different periods. Scholars commonly favour a date for its final form in about the third century CE. (Wendy Doniger has even argued that the *Kāma Sūtra*, also dateable about 300 CE, specifically echoes details of the *Arthaśāstra*; certainly both works are written in the same dispassionate, neatly structured, encyclopaedic and – to use Goyal's word – 'amoral' style.)[17] Olivelle would favour a somewhat earlier date, between 100 BCE and 100 CE, not least because the text refers only to silver and copper coins, never to gold, which was prolifically minted by the Kushan kings from the end of the first century CE.[18]

Can the *Arthaśāstra* be used as corroborative evidence for the reliability of Megasthenes, even though it postdates him by two or more centuries? The procedure may easily become circular, but it would be foolish simply to reject the evidence of the later work where it provides a parallel for something in the earlier. Two pieces of evidence are better than one. What it is unsafe to do

16. A recurrent feature of Indian diplomacy. Dalrymple 1993, 176 mentions the use of hijras and eunuchs as spies for the king, and at 292 refers to evidence from the Tughluq dynasty for employing palace slave girls as spies in the house of the amir.

17. Doniger 2016. Cf. Goyal 1985, 9 on the parallels of 'plan, language, style and basic attitude to life'.

18. McClish and Olivelle 2012, xiii–xiv with xx.

is to use the *Arthaśāstra* to *fill out* the outlines derived from Megasthenes – for example, by assuming that Megasthenes' chats with loose women imply the Kautilyan spy network. I would not wish to add to the series of works entitled something like 'Kautilya and Megasthenes' a new one, to be characterised as 'Kautilya *versus* Megasthenes', but the only reasonable procedure is to examine each individual topic in turn and see whether there is a fit or a mismatch.

Kingship

In Mulk Raj Anand's novel *The Private Life of an Indian Prince*, the semi-hysterical Maharaja of Sham Pur, desperate to preserve his independence against the newly-founded Republic of India that wishes to absorb all the former petty kingdoms, recites at length from the 'ancient Hindu' litany on the duties of a king:[19]

> To thee this stew is given, thou art the director
> And regulator; thou art steadfast and will
> Bear this responsibility of the trust so
> Given for agriculture, for well-being, for
> Prosperity and for development.[20]

The narrator, the westernised and democratically-inclined Dr Hari Shankar, observes sardonically, 'I was thinking that you defined the powers and privileges of a monarch, but did not say anything about the limits and responsibilities of kingship.'[21] The raja's response is to call on the authority of Plato and his philosopher-kings and, in the same breath, on the *Laws of Manu*: 'I think there should be some kind of legislature of men chosen for their good sense. As the sage Manu says: "Learned men who know the traditional history and the customary law of the land, men who will be alike to foe and friend, distinguished for their rectitude and fearing God and religion".'[22] The narrator becomes exasperated, and clearly the reader is meant to feel the same way.

19. General studies: Basham 1954, 81–93; Sharma 2009, 57–8 and 65–6 on kingship and polity; Heesterman 1985 discusses kingship with a high degree of abstraction which is not easy to relate to actual historical behaviour. Roy 1994 also takes an anthropological and theoretical approach, and links the rise of kingship to the replacement of the *Ṛg Veda*'s *ṛta* by *dharma* (in the Upaniṣads).

20. Compare, for example, Bhīṣma's instructions in *Mbh.* 12. 45–59.

21. Anand 1953/2008, 107–8.

22. Ibid., 108.

The prince is being somewhat disingenuous in quoting Manu to support his vision of absolute rule, since the ancient Indian writers on statecraft all lay considerable emphasis on the duties and responsibilities of kings, as well as their rights and privileges. The *Laws of Manu*, for example, includes the following discussions (as neatly collected in the index to Wendy Doniger and Brian Smith's Penguin translation): 'duties: to protect and not to oppress subjects; to punish the wicked; to honour, support and make gifts to learned priests; to be humble; to study the Veda and sciences; to shun the eighteen vices; to appoint ministers and other officials; ... to wed a queen; ... to make conquests; ... to consult regarding state affairs and to follow the principles of state policy; ... to decide lawsuits, either personally or through judges', and much more. The *Arthaśāstra* of Kautilya, commonly regarded as more or less Machiavellian in its elevation of policy over ethics, states not only that 'the king and his rule encapsulate all the constituents of the state', but also that 'a king who observes his duty of protecting his people justly, according to law, goes to heaven, unlike one who does not protect his people, or inflicts unjust punishment'.[23] The Rani of Jaipur observed of her husband that 'everyone in the city recognised his Bentley and his jeep, and knew that they could stop him on the street, or the polo-grounds, or at the gates of the palace – anywhere – if they had a complaint, or wished to bring some problem to his attention, or simply wished to ask after the welfare of his family and tell him about their own'.[24]

Kingship as a phenomenon – indeed, the state itself, or *mahājanapada* – emerged in India in the sixth to fifth centuries BCE.[25] States were divided into two kinds, monarchies (*rajyas*) and *gaṇas* or *sanghas*, commonly interpreted as 'tribal republics', since that is how the Greek writers saw them,[26] though it would be more correct to describe them as oligarchies. At the same time theoretical discussion of political structures began to emerge, and is reflected in the *Arthaśāstra,* parts of which, as discussed above, may go back to the time of Candragupta Maurya (r. ca. 324–ca. 300, a reign of twenty-four years), as well as in the *Laws of Manu*.[27] In the *Mahābhārata,* the contract theory of kingship prevails, while Manu approves of the appointment

23. *KA* 8.2.1.(12?), 1.19, and 3.1.41. The king is the state: 8.2.1.

24. Devi 1976, 171.

25. Thapar 2002, 150–4; Singh 2009, 160–1.

26. E.g., Arr. *Anab.* 5.22.1, *autonomoi Indoi.*

27. On the use of *Manusmṛti* for interpreting data from the fourth century BCE, see Stoneman 1995.

of kings.[28] The *Arthaśāstra* has an extensive section on the duties of kings: they are to be trained in study and self-restraint, and care for the welfare and wealth of their kingdoms.[29] However, it entirely ignores the sacral aspects of kingship which are prominent in Vedic texts.[30] Candragupta was a new kind of king, since his rise to power exemplified the 'law of the fish' in a big way:[31] the Maurya big fish swallowed up many smaller neighbouring fish/states. It was the first foundation of a 'state transcending the limitations of the tribal clan monarchy or oligarchy'.[32] Scholars differ as to whether the *Arthaśāstra* reflects the conditions of a still circumscribed kingdom or the later conditions of an extensive empire.[33] Whichever view one takes, it reflects a debate that began with the emergence of kingship, about the morality and desirability of that institution. The Maurya kingdom itself, as it developed, exemplified both tendencies in the nature of kingship, from the straightforward will to power of the founder Candragupta to the self-recrimination, repentance and near-renunciation of Aśoka barely a century later (r. 269/8—ca. 232 BCE). James L. Fitzgerald interprets the immensely long twelfth book of the *Mahābhārata*, which includes the sermon of Bhīṣma to Yudhiṣṭhira on the nature and duties of kingship, as a reflection of the debates about the subject that characterised the Maurya empire of the mid-fourth to mid-second century BCE.[34] Yudhiṣṭhira, the Brahman, constantly expresses a desire to renounce the kingship and go to the forest;[35] Bhīṣma, the kṣatriya, has to argue for the maintenance of authority. Arjuna too has to try to argue Yudhiṣṭhira out of it, insisting that killing and other hard acts are necessary to proper rule: the king must use his rod (*danda*), though of course he must use it rightly.[36] The discussion reflects the tension present in the *Mahābhārata* between the heroic world and the Brahmanical, as well as that between the ascetic impulse to 'go to the forest' and the world of duty.[37] (The *Bhagavad-gītā*, the most fa-

28. *Mbh.* 5.34.38; *Manusmṛti* 7.1–2 and 35; Heesterman 1985, 114ff.

29. KA 1.6.

30. Heesterman 1985, 131.

31. KA 1.13.5–12; Thapar 2002, 176–7.

32. Heesterman 1985, 132.

33. Khilnani 2016, 38, for example, goes for the latter.

34. Fitzgerald 2004, 128–32.

35. *Mbh.* 12.7.

36. Ibid. 12.14–15.

37. This is discussed interestingly in McGrath 2013.

mous section of the entire poem, is a much more complex exploration of the same tension, and is certainly to be dated much later than the third century BCE, probably in the first to third century CE).[38]

A similar tension is apparent, incidentally, in the *Rāmāyaṇa*: when Rāma is banished to the forest for fourteen years and his brother Bharata is instructed to become king in his stead, the latter insists that he too will renounce the kingdom for fourteen years, and it takes the assembled company of philosophers some time to persuade him to do what his dying father had wished.[39]

If I am right in treating Magadha as a region less in thrall to Vedic thinking and more receptive to Buddhist, Jain and other ascetic attitudes (see previous chapter), there is a particular tension inherent in the emergence of a mega-kingdom or empire in Prācyaka. All the Greek writers make it plain that the king is surrounded by 'philosophers' as advisers, but one must be careful (as Strabo was not) to distinguish the region and date which each of the writers is describing. Strabo quotes Nearchus for the information that 'the Brachmanes engage in affairs of state and attend the kings as counsellors; but that the other sophists investigate natural phenomena; and that Calanus is one of these'.[40] Nearchus did not travel east of the Indus and his information must be based on one or more of the kingdoms the Greeks visited in Punjab and Sind: those of Porus, Taxiles or Musicanus. Arrian and Diodorus both reproduce information from Megasthenes.[41] The former distinguishes between members of his sixth and seventh 'castes', respectively inspectors appointed by the king and an advisory council, from whom administrators of all kinds are selected. The matter of Megasthenes' 'castes' will be discussed below; here we need only note that these advisers are not said to be Brahmans.

None of the kings of Magadha were strongly Vedic in their approach, and they were receptive from the sixth century onwards to ascetic orders of śramanas who could include both Jains and Buddhists.[42] (Thus Gore Vidal may be displaying an uncharacteristic lapse of historical imagination when, in

38. Fitzgerald 2004, 140–1. Khilnani 2016, 144 and 152 is eloquent on the conflict of rule and renunciation.

39. Narayan 1972, 63–4.

40. Str. 15.1.66.

41. Arr. *Ind.* 12.5–6; Diod. 2.40–1.

42. See Fines's introduction to Hemacandra (1998), xxviii.

Creation, he imagines the king of Rajagriha, Bimbisara, expressing anger at the rise of the ascetic orders.)

Comparison with a passage from the *Mahābhārata* is illuminating:

> Bhīṣma said: ... Just as a peacock's tail has feathers of many colors, so should a king who knows the Laws display many different forms – sharpness, deviousness, indomitability, truthfulness and rectitude; standing in the middle of all of them, relying upon his mettle, he reaches a comfortable position. He should take whatever coloration would be good for some particular affair ... He should stand sentry in the gateways of crisis, as the peacock does at waterfalls; and as the peacock relies upon the water from rain showers and mountain streams, so he should rely upon Brahmins and accomplished ascetics.[43]

The *Arthaśāstra*, too, states that a king 'should decide on the affairs of person learned in the Vedas and of ascetics with due respect to them'.[44] In general 'Kautilya' seems more disposed to give a dominant role to Brahmans.

If Candragupta's dominance emerged in a region strongly influenced by the ideas rather of ascetics than of Vedic specialists, it is perhaps no surprise that Buddhist tradition attributes even to Aśoka, the most 'virtuous' of kings, an early life of spectacular cruelty and violence. John Strong suggests that 'the inclusion of these acts reflects an underlying Buddhist apprehension toward the institution of kingship as inherently, perhaps inevitably, prone to such actions'.[45] (The *Questions of King Milinda* exhibits a similar suspicion of kings). The *Lotus Sutra* identifies three levels of kings.[46] Later Buddhist thought developed the idea of the *cakravartin*, the 'wheel-turning king' who maintains a kind of permanent Golden Age on earth;[47] but this is scarcely relevant to the Maurya empire, least of all to Candragupta.

Buddhist texts do take some interest in the relations between kings and monks. Is it proper for the king to summon the ascetic, or should it be the other way around? Aśoka, for example, wishes to consult the sage Upagupta in his forest hermitage: he is quite willing to make the pilgrimage to visit the hermit, but his advisers insist that the king ought to send a messenger and

43. *Mbh.* 12.120.1–9; Fitzgerald 2004, 465–6.

44. *KA* 1.19.31; Doniger and Smith 1991, 149.

45. Strong 1983, 41–2.

46. Ibid., 54.

47. Ibid., 44–5; Tambiah 1976.

summon him to Pataliputra.[48] In the end the king defers to the monk. One is reminded of the encounter of Alexander with the naked philosopher Dandamis in the *Alexander Romance*, when the sage refuses to visit the king and demands the king come to him.[49] Similarly, the king should give extravagant gifts to the *sangha*, as Aśoka does in the *Aśokāvadāna*, and as the seventh-century King Harṣa is known to have done.[50] The fact that Alexander tries to give gifts to the naked philosophers, but they are rejected, perhaps suggests that these are not Buddhists. Another Buddhist (or ascetic) reflection on kingship seems to be present in the philosophers' reply to Alexander's question in the *Alexander Romance*, 'What is kingship?': 'Unjust power used to the disadvantage of others; insolence supported by opportunity; a golden burden.'[51]

There is no evidence that Candragupta's relations with his advisers were of this kind. Most of our information about his rule, in fact, comes from the Greek writers, and there are only limited opportunities to test what they say against Indian evidence. We may begin with what Strabo has extracted from Nearchus' book. Strabo reports two items about Indian kings which he attributes to Nearchus: first, he tells us that 'the Brahmans engage in affairs of state and attend the kings as counsellors, but that the other sophists investigate natural phenomena; and that Calanus is one of these'.[52] Given the mention of Calanus, Nearchus is presumably referring to the philosophers who attend the court of the king of Taxila. Thus Ambhi/Omphis is a king within the Vedic sphere. In the next section, Strabo quotes Nearchus for the statement that 'it is the custom, instead of making obeisance (προσκυνεῖν), to offer prayers to the kings and to all who are in authority and of superior rank'.[53] The statement is imponderable, but not as puzzling as the third piece of information about

48. Strong 1983, 79.

49. The scene is replicated in the 'Collatio Alexandri et Dindimi', in Palladius' *De Bragmanibus*, and a millennium thereafter in Amir Khusraw's *Mirror of Alexander*, where the king invites the hermit Plato to his court, but the sage insists that the king must come to him: see Khusraw 1999, 126–8.

50. Strong 1983, 91–2. The festival of giving (*dāna*) is described by Xuanzang: Devahuti 2001, 144.

51. *AR* 3.6. The response does not occur in the parallel but much longer colloquy of Yudhiṣṭhira and the *yakṣa* in *Mbh.* 3 (the drilling sticks), 313, which includes a few of the same questions. Nor is it in the version of the *Mahābhārata* by Jean-Claude Carrière, which borrows a number of the questions from the *AR* for the *yakṣa*'s catechism.

52. Str. 15.1.66 = Nearch. 133 F 23.

53. Str. 15.1.67. On gifts to kings, Ael. *NA* 15.14 (see McCrindle 1901, 144), and 13.25, on birds as gifts.

kings, given in a random collection of facts about India attributed to 'the historians': 'when the king washes his hair, they celebrate a great festival and bring big presents, each man making rivalry in display of his own wealth'.[54] There is no way of knowing what state this was supposed to be true of, or why it is singled out as important. It may perhaps be a reference to the Vedic coronation ritual (*abhiśeka*), which included bathing,[55] and cutting of the hair after a raiding expedition;[56] but this is not a repeated event. The passage in Strabo is preceded by a remark about the Indians worshipping Zeus Ombrios and the Ganges, and followed by one about the gold-mining ants and another about elephant parades, which might suggest that the information relates to a kingdom on the Ganges and thus might derive from Megasthenes; but the section ends with a number of facts about trees and birds from Cleitarchus, which must therefore relate to the western regions. The fact is that Strabo makes no distinction between different regions of India, or between the different dates of his various sources; so it is not surprising if he sometimes finds them inconsistent with one another. Strabo has done a great service in preserving so many extracts from the writers on India, but one wishes he had been more critical in his treatment and less driven by the impulse to find fault with his predecessors.[57]

The information deriving from Megasthenes is more substantial and easier to relate to Indian sources. We can be sure that the longest passage from Strabo describes the court of Candragupta.[58] He starts by mentioning the king's female bodyguards, who are also alluded to in the *Arthaśāstra*.[59] Strabo continues with the information that 'a woman who kills a king when he is drunk receives as her reward the privilege of consorting with his successor; and their children succeed to the throne'. Curtius is eloquent on the luxury of the Indian king's life: 'women prepare the king's meals and they also serve him his wine, which is drunk in copious quantities by all Indians. When a drunken drowsiness comes over him, the concubines carry him to his bed-

54. Str. 15.1.69.

55. Khilnani 2016, 208.

56. Heesterman 1985, 120. Hair-cutting is also the final stage of initiation as a priest: *Manusmṛti* 2.65.

57. Cf. Dihle 1964, 18.

58. Str. 15.1.55 = *FGrH* Megasth. 715 F 32.

59. *KA* 1.21.1 (Kautilya 1992, 152). Akbar had them too, mostly Russian and Abyssinian – in addition to three hundred wives: Gascoigne 1971, 85.

room, at the same time chanting a traditional hymn to the gods of the night'.[60] No such statement occurs in the *Arthaśāstra*, which does however devote a good deal of discussion to arrangements for succession, while the detailed programme for the king's day does not include any mention of strong drink. One wonders why Strabo picked this particular fact to report, and whether Megasthenes did not provide a more ordered account of the king's routine (and whether Curtius is making it up). The following sentences, about the king's security and constant changes of sleeping place, depict a situation closely similar to that expounded by Kautilya, where the price of safety is constant vigilance.[61] One is reminded too of Alexander's lament to Dandamis in Palladius' *De Bragmanibus*: 'What shall I do, seeing that I live with incessant fears, and drowning in continuous disturbance? . . . By day I torment the nations, but when night comes on I am tormented by my own reflections, my fear that someone may come at me with a sword.'[62] If, as has sometimes been suggested,[63] Candragupta was inspired to empire-building by the example of Alexander, he may have discovered that its disadvantages remained constant too.

Strabo continues by discussing the king's 'non-military departures' from his court: his progresses to the courts, to sacrifices, and to 'a kind of Bacchic chase'. Regarding the first of these, the *Arthaśāstra* allots the second hour and a half after sunrise to the hearing of petitions, but there is no mention of simultaneous massage.[64] The hour and a half before sunrise are specified for 'religious, household and personal duties', as well as discussions with ritual specialists and astrologers. The reference to sacrifices is almost the only mention in Megasthenes of any kind of religious practice, and one longs to know more, given the importance of sacrifice in the life of later Indian kings.[65] The 'Bacchic chase' seems to be a hunting expedition, in which, as in the Moghul court, he is accompanied by women, which must have been surprising to Greeks: it is presumably their presence that inspired the thought of Dionysus and his maenads, thus strengthening the inclination to find traces of Dionysus everywhere in India.

60. Curt. 8.9.28–30.

61. *KA* 1.21 with 1.17: see the passages collected in Kautilya 1992, 152–67.

62. Pall. *De Brag.* 2.33.

63. Plu. *Alex.* 62.

64. *KA* 1.19.6.9–24 (Kautilya 1992, 147–8).

65. See Heesterman 1985.

The next major piece of information about the king comes from, closely corroborated by Diodorus.[66] This concerns the 'inspectors' who report to the king, and the 'seventh caste', who act as advisers to the king, and weather forecasters, and provide the king's administrators. Leaving aside the fraught terminology of the 'seven castes' for the moment, we may note the extensive sections of the *Arthaśāstra* devoted to the selection of councillors and ministers, and the various officials, enumerated one by one.[67]

The most problematic statement about the king comes almost in passing in the middle of Diodorus' discussion of the 'castes': 'for the land they [the farmers] pay rent to the king, since all India is royal land and no man of private station is permitted to possess any ground; and part from the rental they pay a fourth part into the royal treasury'.[68] Timmer, in a careful discussion, noted that all our Greek sources say the same thing, that landholders pay tribute plus rent of one quarter. *The Laws of Manu* allows for the levying of a tribute of one quarter *in an emergency*.[69] Sometimes it has been thought that the account simply reflects the situation in Egypt, or has been overwhelmed by the Seleucid institution of the *chora basilike*. Timmer concludes that in India, in theory, all land is ultimately the king's, and that Megasthenes did not understand that there were also landowners, which there certainly were. Kumar, for example, hypothesised a distinction between two types of *janapada*: there were 'free cities', which were taxed, and king's land, which was under direct control.[70] Sir William Jones rejected the idea that the king in India was ever the owner of the land – a doctrine 'unjust, unfounded, and big with ruin'.[71] Louis Dumont regarded the problem as a false one: 'far from a given piece of land being exclusively related to one person individual or corporate, each piece of land was the object of different rights relating to different functions, expressed in the right to a share of the produce or to some due from the cultivator. The king's share in particular, far from representing a kind of salary for the maintenance of order, expressed an overall right over all land, but limited to this levy in each case.'[72] More recently, U. Singh has returned to

66. Arr. *Ind.* 12.5–6, from Megasthenes; Diod. 2.40–1.

67. Kautilya 1992, 195–228 collects passages from various parts of the *KA*, including 1.8–9, 1.15, 5.4–5, etc.

68. Diod. 2.40.5.

69. *Manusmṛti 10.118.*

70. Kumar 2013, 152–3.

71. Trautmann 1998, 118 n. 27.

72. Dumont 1980, 157.

the problem, in a way that clarifies this discussion considerably.[73] She makes clear that the institution of private property in land emerged by the sixth century BCE; the law books contain a wealth of detail on issues of possession, ownership and title. There may also have been some form of corporate and communal ownership, as suggested by epigraphic and other evidence, in the fourth century BCE.[74] It seems fairly clear that the king did own (some) land,[75] and probable that his overlordship of the land was regarded as the justification for taxation, conceived as a kind of rent – or a combination of rents and fees, as suggested by R. S. Sharma.[76] (Some thinkers disagreed, regarding taxes as the king's wages for providing protection to his subjects.) 'The *Katyayana Smriti* (16) states that the king is owner of the soil and hence can claim 1/4th of the farmers' produce.' This statement is almost exactly parallel to what Megasthenes tells us, and one could almost imagine that Megasthenes had copied it from the author! Over the next few centuries this view crystallised into the position that 'from c. 300 CE onwards, the king was considered the lord of all the land, but not the 'owner' in the legal sense'.[77] This splendidly confusing conclusion is probably the best explanation of the puzzling statement of Megasthenes.

The situation was no less complex in the nineteenth and twentieth centuries. Forsyth in 1871 found it a grey area in central India: 'it was found, too, on inquiry, that there had never really existed any clearly recognised right of property, in our sense of the term, which would give the agricultural classes a real interest in the improvement of their lands, while many classes of persons had been allowed to exercise very undefined powers over the whole of this immense area of unreclaimed land'.[78] A century later, the Rani of Jaipur states of Jaipur, 'there was no income tax, and all farmers were allowed to graze their herds on state land without payment'. And again, 'the land of Cooch Behar, as

73. Singh 2009, 491–2.

74. Sharma 2009, 77 and 144: land may be communal in the *Ṛg Veda*. Heesterman (1985, 139) states that the king is not 'owner' of the soil, but there are differential rights in its productivity, the 'division of the grain heap'.

75. *KA* 2.1.17–18 (Kautilya 1992, 179–80) on *sita* land.

76. Sharma 2009, 162, cf. 124–5.

77. In the Gupta period, the kings frequently made grants of land, or villages, to individuals, or groups of Brahmans: Gaur 1975, especially charters 11, 20, 36. The *Sāmaññaphala Sutta* 37 (Bodhi 1989, 27–8) takes the hypothetical case of 'a farmer, a householder, who pays taxes to maintain the royal revenue': if he becomes a renouncer, he cannot return to his land.

78. Forsyth 1871, 20.

in most Indian states, was organized on a feudal basis and divided into crown lands, or *khalsa*, and fiefs held from the crown, some of which were sublet a second, third, or fourth time. The revenue from the *khalsa* came directly to the Maharaja, while the taxes from all the other lands were held separately, but the money from both sources was gathered by officials on elephants, setting out from the five district headquarters.'[79]

And that brings us to the end of what the Greek (and modern) authors can tell us about kingship in Maurya India.[80]

Caste

In February 2016 rioting broke out in Haryana state among the Jats, who were demanding quotas in government jobs and educational institutions on the grounds that in most states (but not in Haryana) they are classified as a 'backward community' or 'backward class'. The Jats are 'an agricultural caste group', and in 1881 Sir Denzil Ibbetson defined the Jat as 'the husbandman, the peasant, the revenue-payer par excellence'.[81] Without going into the rights and wrongs of the Jats' case, one may see in the agitation a marker of the complexity of the questions of caste, community, status and class in present-day India, and the continuing echoes of the Brahmanical contempt for the indignity of labour. An analytical article in the *Indian Express* for February 22, 2016 noted that 'out of 80 castes, only 16 – Ahir, Arora/Khatri, Bishnoi, Brahman, Gossain, Gujjar, Jat, Jat Sikh, Kalal, Mahajan/Bania, Meo, Muslim, Rajput, Ror, Saini and Tyagi – do not find mention in the lists of Scheduled Castes and Backward Classes notified by the Haryana government'. Such a list indicates how involved social categorisation can become in India, and how the fluctuating terminology of 'caste' and 'class' can include not only occupational groups but religious communities. Louis Dumont's classic discussion of caste saw in it a state of mind, a system of ideas encompassing birth, endogamy, and a hierarchy in which status is defined in terms of purity, and has no correlation with power. Sub-castes are key to this complex classification system.[82]

79. Devi 1976, 198 and 73.

80. For what else can be gleaned from the Indian sources, Nilakanta Sastri 1962, 173–81 is a reliable basic summary. See also Mookerji 1966, 54ff.

81. Quoted in the *Indian Express*, February 22, 2016. See also Fürer-Haimendorf 1967, 165 on the dominant status of Jats.

82. Dumont 1980, 33, 61, 66–7. See also Fürer-Haimendorf 1967, 151–79, 'Conformity as a moral ideal'.

As Piers Moore Ede puts it, 'by the rules of Indian caste social classes are defined according to thousands of hereditary groups'.[83] This might give us pause when we try to consider the account Megasthenes gives of the seven μέρη (*merē*, literally 'parts') of Indian society.[84]

Megasthenes' detailed account of the social division of the Indian population obviously impressed his readers, so that both Strabo and Arrian reproduce it at length in paraphrase. Here is Strabo.[85]

> The first in status (*timē*) are the philosophers, though fewest in number. These philosophers are used, each one individually, by those who make sacrifices to the gods or offerings to the dead, but as a group by the kings at the so-called Great Synod, at which, at new year, all the philosophers gather at the gates of the king; and whatever each one has assembled (συντάξῃ)[86] or observed as useful for the prosperity of crops or animals, or for the state, he brings it forward in their midst . . .
>
> The second *meros* is that of the farmers, who are the most numerous and the most practically capable (*epieikestatoi*), and are exempt from military service and untrammelled in their farming . . . [87]
>
> The third is that of the shepherds and hunters, who alone are permitted to hunt, to breed cattle and to sell and rent out beasts of burden; and in return for freeing the land from wild beasts and birds that steal seeds, they receive a grain allowance from the king, while living a wandering life in tents.

Strabo now inserts a long passage about elephants. This is not in the corresponding passage of Arrian (who writes about elephants *after* his account of

83. Ede 2015, 13–14. He mentions the Doms, who include the managers of the burning ghats, scavengers, weavers of ropes and baskets, magicians and jugglers; and (110) the Mallahs who are boatmen, as well as (126) the Julakas, Muslim weavers. Cf. Gold 2015, 99–100: 'literally thousands of specific castes and sub-castes'.

84. Ff 19 J, 33 Schw.

85. Str. 15.1.39–41 and (following elephant digression) 46–9. Essentially the same account is given by Arr. *Ind.* 11.1–12.9 = F 32 Schw, except that Arrian uses the word γένεα, *genea*, 'kinds'.

86. Both H. L. Jones and D. Roller translate this as 'written'. This interpretation is certainly legitimate in Hellenistic Greek (Polybius for example) but begs an important question about the existence of writing in India in the period under discussion: see ch. 1 above. Cf. *Milindapañha* 4.3.36, on the duties of Brahmans regarding all intellectual matters.

87. Some details are omitted here including the problematic passage about land ownership, which states that 'the whole of the country belongs to the king and the farmers cultivate for a rental in addition to paying a fourth part of the produce': see above.

caste) and must have been brought in by Strabo from another part of Megasthenes' book or perhaps another author, though it is difficult to see why he chose to put it here. At the end he writes 'let us now return to Megasthenes and continue in order from where we left off', which seems to imply that the elephant passage is not from Megasthenes.[88]

> The fourth *meros*, after the hunters and shepherds, is that of the craft workers, the tradesmen and the manual workers. [Armour-makers and shipbuilders are specifically noted here.]
>
> The fifth *meros* is that of the warriors, who spend much of their time at leisure and in drinking, at the expense of the royal treasury . . .
>
> The sixth are the overseers (*ephoroi*), whose role is to keep an eye on what is done and to report secretly to the king, using the courtesans as colleagues, the city overseers employing the city courtesans and the camp overseers the camp ones. The best and most reliable men are appointed to this status.
>
> The seventh are the advisers and councillors of the king, in whose hands are the chief offices of state, the courts and administration of everything.
>
> It is not legal for a man either to marry a wife from another *genos*, nor to change his pursuit or type of work from one to another; nor may one man take part in several <pursuits?>[89], unless he is one of the philosophers; this is permitted because of his superiority (*aretē*).

Strabo now goes on to discuss the various different kinds of official, who are all presumably subdivisions of the seventh kind.

The passage is not easy to interpret. Arrian paraphrases the same portion of Megasthenes' book,[90] though the information he gives within the sections is not entirely the same: for example, he does not mention that the soldiers spend peace time at drinking parties, which may be Strabo's extrapolation from complaints about the Roman legions in his time. He also adds that the first group, the philosophers, go naked and sit under enormous trees. A more serious problem is posed by the terminology, *merē* or 'parts' in Strabo, *genea* or 'kinds' in Arrian. Is this just literary variation (*genea* being the Herodotean word, proper for Arrian's model in this work)? What word did Megasthenes

88. So also Timmer 1930, 76.

89. The word used, πλείους, is masculine/feminine, which precludes it being a reference to the *genea* or *merē*, since these words are neuter.

90. Arr. *Ind.* 11.1–12.9. Also Diod. 2.40–1; Plin. *NH* 6.18.66; Sol. 52.7; see Stein 1921, 122.

use? And what Indian word was he translating (if any)? In modern terminology, caste is *varna* (which means 'colour'), while occupational status is *jati*.[91] It is notable that neither author makes any mention of untouchables.

Scholarly reactions to Megasthenes' account of these *merē* range from outright dismissal – there are four castes or *varnas*, not seven![92] – to a variety of more subtle criticisms. Stein did not believe that Megasthenes had talked to an Indian about the matter.[93] One view is that he is trammelled by the conventions of Greek ethnography: because Herodotus said there were seven population classes (the word is *Stand* in Dutch [Timmer] and German [Stein]) in Egypt,[94] and Aristotle said the same about Crete; in Philadelphia, too, there were supposed to be seven *phylai* (divisions).[95] Though Timmer discusses this view, she does not in the end accept it, preferring the more subtle view that Megasthenes has confused different categories.[96] His list of seven seems to combine both *varna* and *jati*: Brahman, kṣatriya, vaiṣya and śudra are all there, though there is no mention of untouchables; but the seventh group seems to reprise certain aspects of the first, while the sixth class, the overseers, consists of men who are appointed to a post, not a hereditary group (though they are selected from the *aristoi*). For Timmer, Megasthenes has obtained his information about four *varnas* from theorising Brahmans but has confused the picture by adding to it some of his own observations regarding guilds and occupations.

Upinder Singh observes that this division into seven 'strata' seems to be Megasthenes' own invention.[97] An interesting variant of this view is that of Falk, that is, that Megasthenes has actually got hold of an account of the tripartite taxation basis of Candragupta's India, which Falk regards as being recorded in the *Arthaśāstra* 5.2, where special levies are specified for the various classes of farmers and livestock owners, merchants and professionals, and

91. But see Singh 2009, 293, quoted below n. 100.

92. Majumdar 1960. *RV* 10.90.12 describes the creation of the four *varnas* from the primeval man.

93. See Falk 1991, 48–56. Stein 1921, 119–24 and whole chapter: he regards it as 'out of the question that M. spoke with an Indian about caste relations' (123), because he places the kṣatriyas in fifth place.

94. Hdt. 2.164–8; Plat. *Tim.* 24. Cf. also Isoc., *Busiris* 15 and Diod. 1.73–4: the latter's ἱερεῖς, μάχιμοι, νομεῖς + γεῶργοι, τεχνῖται seem to match the four *varnas*. See Karttunen 1997, 82–7.

95. Timmer 1930, 66–7.

96. Ibid., 59–69.

97. Singh 2009, 339–40.

temple personnel.[98] WhatMegasthenes is enumerating is thus tax categories, not castes, and the distinction is a tripartite one, first of 'philosophers' (non-governmental and not taxed), second of non-governmental and taxed, and third of governmental and not taxed. However, three does not equal seven, and it is hard to see this theory as a solution.

A question that arises is whether the caste system indeed existed in its present form in the third century BCE. Bronkhorst is categorical: 'no one seems to have stated what seems now obvious, viz. that Megasthenes spent time in Magadha during a period when this region had not yet been brahmanized . . . brahmanization means, first of all, the imposition of the brahmanical vision[99] of society, typically into four *varnas*.'[100] Not everyone shares this view: Mehl remarks, perhaps in passing, that the four castes existed already in Candragupta's time,[101] while Basu states that the four castes are clearly established in the Brāhmanas,[102] and Agrawala (1953, 75–79) finds them clearly established in Pāṇini in the fourth century BCE.[103] The strength of Bronkhorst's position is that one may admit the existence of the Brahmanical theory of caste at this period, but not its applicability to the region Megasthenes knew.

Prakash sees a collapse of the ancient system of caste in the north-west following the Achaemenid and Macedonian invasions:[104] the fourfold system could not apply to Yonas, Kambojas and Gandharas. He cites the *Mahābhārata* for the remark that 'there, a person becomes Kshatriya after being a Brahman; a Vaisya becomes a Sudra and then becomes a barber. Again from the position of a barber he rises to that of a Brahman. Having become a Brahmana he

98. Falk 1991.

99. Or 'division'?

100. Bronkhorst 2011, 73. The same view is taken by McClish and Olivelle 2012, and by Brinkhaus 2016, 33–4. There is certainly no caste in the *Ṛg Veda*: Jamison and Brereton 2014, 57. See Singh 2009, 293: 'one of the great triumphs of the Brahmanical tradition is that, even today, many people persist in thinking that Indian society was for centuries divided into four groups – Brāhmanas, Kśatriyas, Vaiśyas and Śudras – and consider *varna* to be the basis of *jati*. This was not so.' This is a splendidly succinct discussion.

101. Mehl 1986, 175. Similarly, Allchin 1995, 84, is of the opinion that the four *varna*s were in place by the sixth century BCE. He quotes *RV* 10.90, but Jamison and Brereton (2014, 1528) regard this passage as likely to be a later insertion.

102. Basu 1969.

103. Agrawala 1953, 75–9.

104. Prakash 1964, 229.

again turns a slave.'[105] However, it may be not so much a collapse of an ancient order as the observation of a more flexible situation in the past, reinterpreted through the Brahmanical lens of the later writing in the *Mahābhārata*.

Romila Thapar has discussed the issue in her usual trenchant manner.[106] For her, Megasthenes is talking not about caste but about categories of production, *jati* not *varna*.[107] He has heard of the political term *sapta-prakṛti*, referring to the seven limbs of the body politic, which is in the *Arthaśāstra*.[108] But he has misapplied the number to the *merē* category which he remembered from his own background.[109] The question of whether *varna* prevailed in his time thus becomes beside the point. But it is important that Megasthenes did identify the two key aspects of the system: hereditary occupation and endogamy. Thapar insists however that society was more flexible in his day than Brahmanism wished it to be, or than it later became.

In summary, then, Megasthenes has derived from his conversation with Brahmans an idea of the ideal division of society into four *varnas*, but also of the seven limbs of the body politic. This classification, however, cannot be tidily applied to the Maurya state, which was not Brahmanical. In addition, any discussion of caste and class soon becomes complicated by the very large number of 'castes' that are differentiated in Indian society.[110] Thus Megasthenes has imported some occupational designations into his account, but by and large he has reproduced the emergent Brahmanical system; and he has identified the key points of hereditary occupation and endogamy.

Slavery

> ... that my countrymen may take [the abolitionists'] noble example as their guide in the emancipation of their Sudra brethren from the trammels of Brahmin thraldom.
>
> —JYOTIRAO PHULE (1827–90), 'SLAVERY IN THE CIVILISED BRITISH GOVERNMENT UNDER THE CLOAK OF BRAHMANISM' (QUOTED IN KHILNANI 2016, 261)

105. *Mbh.* 8.45.6–7.
106. Thapar 1987, reprinted in Thapar 2013a, 296ff.; Thapar 2002, 190–3.
107. See also Kak 1996. For Stein 1921, 121, *Beruf* is the key category.
108. *KA* 6.1.
109. Thapar 1987, 50 = 2013, 315.
110. Sharma 2009, 183: this process gained pace in the seventh century CE.

Megasthenes states that there was no slavery in the India of his time, a notable point of difference from contemporary Greece.[111] 'The Indians have this in common with the Spartans, except that the Spartans have helots as their slaves to perform all servile functions. In India, though, there are no slaves of any kind, let alone Indian slaves.' The statement seems patently false in view of the evidence of such early texts as the *Arthaśāstra* and the *Laws of Manu*, both of which give detailed prescriptions for dealing with slaves, and their legal position. What did Megasthenes mean? Or was he simply mistaken, or, worse, making up a 'utopian' feature of Indian society? According to Diodorus, Megasthenes went on to say 'it is foolish to make the laws apply to all on an equal basis, and yet to establish inequality of status'.[112] The word here translated status is *ousia* (which usually means 'essence' or 'substance') but it has been subject to various emendations: *sunousias* (Capps), 'association' or 'intercourse', and *exousias* (Dindorf, Bekker), 'property' or, more generally, 'capability'. I cannot get much sense from the former, while the latter would have essentially the same implication as *ousias*. Following Timmer, Thapar follows the MS reading and 'sees in this passage an attempted criticism of the Greek system. Megasthenes is suggesting that the Greeks cannot see that an equality of laws and slavery are incompatible.'[113] However, the comment may be Diodorus' not Megasthenes'; furthermore, it is risky to base such an important conclusion about Megasthenes' views on such an uncertain basis. The best that can be said is that this could be seen as an element of a utopian vision of India.

Megasthenes presumably wrote with knowledge of Onesicritus' description of the kingdom of Musicanus in Upper Sind. According to Onesicritus, there was no slavery in that kingdom, but people made use of the young men to carry out the work of slaves, in the manner of the helots in Sparta and the Aphamiotae in Crete. Onesicritus' Cynic credentials might well make him opposed to slavery, but it is difficult to see that he would then be neutral about helotage.

Megasthenes, however, seems to imply that there was nothing corresponding to Onesicritus' 'helotage' in Magadha, either. As he also says – according to Strabo, a sentence later – that 'the care of the king's person is performed by

111. Arr. *Ind.* 10. 8 = F 26 Schw = F 18 J. See also Str. 15.154, 'Megasthenes says that no Indian uses slaves', Diod. 2.39.

112. Diod. 2.39.

113. Thapar 2013a, 286.

women who themselves have been bought from their fathers', the position is not clear-cut.[114] He also informs us that artisans had to work for the state for a certain number of days each year in lieu of paying tax, which is in effect forced labour even though the men were technically free.[115]

It is probably true that India did not know slavery on the Greek model.[116] The word translated 'slave' in the following passages of the *Arthaśāstra* is *dāsa*, fem. *dāsī*, which is also the term for a person of the lowest caste, or aboriginal. *Dasa* was not the same as *doulos*, since the former could own property and earn money; it is primarily a racial distinction, connoting 'non-Aryan',[117] and in many contexts may be better interpreted as 'serf' or 'peon'. This leads to the suspicion that the line between slave and śudra, or person of the lowest caste, is very blurred: this would support Onesicritus' characterisation of slaves in the kingdom of Musicanus as a kind of helot. However, the Spartans famously treated their helots with great and arbitrary cruelty: it was no crime to kill one at any time.

The differences from Greek slavery are marked. There were no industrial slaves, for example. Workers on the land were not invariably slaves. R. S. Sharma epigrammatically states that 'ancient India can be called a slave owning society in the sense that people employed domestic slaves, but it cannot be characterized as a society based on the slave mode of production'.[118] The *Arthaśāstra* specifies 'slaves are of four kinds – born in the house, inherited, bought or obtained in some other way'.[119] These other ways might include capture in war, gifts and purchase. *Manu* states that there are seven types of slave: capture in war, 'becoming a slave in order to eat food', born in the house, bought, given, inherited from ancestors, or enslaved as a punishment.[120] A key point is that a slave, though lacking property, continued to have 'human rights' and was to be treated with dignity; a slave could buy his or her way out of slavery at any time, and temporary slavery to earn money was not uncommon. Gosaala, the leader of the Ājīvikas, was of servile origin, which suggests considerable freedom of possibility for self-determination in life.[121] A man should regard his

114. Str. 15.1.55. Stein 1921, 114 has no doubt that these are slaves.
115. F 19b J = Str. 15.1.46, Thapar 2013a, 285.
116. Thapar 2013, 284–8. The *Arthaśātra* insists that an Arya can never be a slave.
117. Hale 1986. *RV* 2.12 concerns Indra's conflict with the *dasyus*.
118. Sharma 2009, 137.
119. KA 3.13.20.
120. *Manusmṛti 8.415*.
121. Chanana 1960, 75.

slave 'as his own shadow', while wife and son are 'his own body'.[122] 'Becoming a slave in order to eat food' does not sound much different from 'taking a job' in the modern world, with its attendant loss of freedom and self-determination.

Undoubtedly slaves were also sometimes treated with cruelty, as several Jātaka stories make clear.[123] The *Arthaśāstra* details many punishments for the abuse of slaves, especially those on the point of redemption. Rape of a female slave attracted various kinds of monetary punishment, including gifts of clothes and jewellery,[124] or 'just a very small fine';[125] it was a much less serious offence than sex with a female *svapaka* (dog-cooker), which led to branding and exile.[126] A woman who had sex with slaves, however, was put to death.[127] Agriculture made use of slaves: the 'Superintendent of Agriculture' should have the sowing done by 'slaves, workers, and men paying off their fines'.[128] As usual one cannot be sure whether these tidy-minded prescriptions are a bureaucrat's dream or a reflection of reality.

Megasthenes may have been led into error on this matter by the fact that slaves in India were treated kindly.[129] Aśoka (e.g., Rock Edict 11) requires 'proper behaviour towards servants and employees'. But it would be rash to suggest that he is simply wrong. He may be a victim of the summarising of Arrian and Strabo, since he cannot have imagined that the women 'bought from their fathers' by the king were not slaves in some sense. The *Periplus*, written in the first century CE and thus having some claim to be earlier than the Indian texts discussed above, describes the ruler of Barygaza's readiness to purchase fair-skinned slave girls from traders from the West.[130] Candragupta's son Bindusara famously assumed that a Western king would be able to sell (or give) him a philosopher, and had to be disabused of the notion.

Was it just the kings who could own people? That would seem to be too simplistic. The key to understanding the Greek reports on Indian slavery must lie in the peculiarities of the caste system as it existed at that time. In important ways the śudras fulfilled the role of slaves. R. S. Sharma studied the emer-

122. *Manusmṛti* 4.184–5.

123. Thapar 2013, 287.

124. *KA* 4.12.23, 28.

125. *Manusmṛti* 8.363.

126. *KA* 4.13.34, 35.

127. Ibid. 4.13.31.

128. Ibid. 2.24.2–4.

129. R. C. Majumdar, cited in Chanana 1960, 102.

130. *Periplus* 49.16.25–8.

gence of this class in India in detail, raising the question of how far the ritual status of śudras corresponded to their economic status: was the community formed in order to act as slaves to the three higher orders? At one point he declares that śudras and slaves are 'identical',[131] while asking in the next sentence whether śudras 'can … be categorised as slaves'. The position is complicated by his wish to interpret the classes in terms of Marxist economic ones, a procedure difficult to apply to pre-capitalist conditions. 'A work on the origin, growth, nature, and extent of slavery in ancient India still remains a desideratum.'[132]

If Onesicritus was aware of the slave-like status of the śudras, it seems odd that Megasthenes did not observe it too, unless the caste system, of which the śudras are an integral part, was not as fully developed in Magadha as in Sind. Perhaps this is further evidence for the relatively weak grip of Brahmanism on Maurya society. The fact that the king owned slaves, then, could be seen as simply an aspect of the unique status of the king and not something characteristic of society as a whole. I would be tempted to say that Megasthenes was describing what he saw, a society where people did not lose their freedom and become the property of others. When they worked for others, it was as free agents (just about).

Administration

Megasthenes says disappointingly little about other aspects of Indian society, though he has a little on city administration and on the army. It is surprising that a man who worked as an ambassador has nothing to say about policy, either domestic or foreign,[133] and this militates against the view that his book was a report for Seleucus to help him formulate his own policy and weigh up the pros and cons of attempted conquest. It is piquant to imagine what he would have made of the detailed instructions in the *Arthaśāstra* regarding the duties of an envoy: inveigling himself into the good graces of the king (whom Kautilya calls 'the enemy'); showing respect while keeping a watchful eye open; being required to 'avoid women and liquor, and sleep alone', but to hold conversations with beggars, intoxicated persons and the insane.[134] Both the

131. Sharma 2009, 88.
132. Ibid., 101. Sharma notes that Chanana's study is based mainly on the Pali texts.
133. For the *Arthaśāstra*, there is no real difference between an ambassador and a spy.
134. *KA* 1.16.

Arthaśāstra and Megasthenes refer to the use of prostitutes as spies.[135] Buddhist monks were also useful as go-betweens, and many stories in the Jātakas concern interactions between monks and prostitutes.[136]

The councillors are the highest rank in Megasthenes' description of Maurya society.[137] 'Kings depend on counsellors as cattle do on rain', says the *Mahābhārata*.[138] As Kautilya puts it, 'a single wheel does not turn': the *cakravartin* or 'wheel-turning king' needs his advisers. Basham suggests that the array of secretaries and clerks and red tape that make up this class for Kautilya show that 'no later state developed the same degree of control as the Mauryas'.[139] The conclusion is based on the assumption that the *Arthaśāstra* is a Maurya text, but in a general way the picture can no doubt be read back to that earlier period. Stein, however, thinks that the subdivisions of officialdom cannot be recognised in India, and that Megasthenes' description is based on Plato's *Laws*.[140] If one does not require Megasthenes' description to match Kautilya, it is easier to take it as straightforward reporting of the Indian state administration.

Legislation is in the hands of the seventh *meros*, the *sumbouloi kai sunedroi*, counsellors/councillors.[141] These look very like the counsellors of the *Arthaśāstra*,[142] but they are certainly not a caste. Laws were unwritten, according to Nearchus.[143] (If the laws were unwritten in the west of India, that Nearchus was describing, it is even less likely that they were written in Magadha at this time.) Onesicritus says that there were few lawsuits, but that the penalties were severe for murder and other brutal crimes.[144] Both the *Arthaśāstra* and the *Laws of Manu*, however, have detailed and elaborate lists of penalties for every kind of crime, reflecting a later, or more Brahmanical, or more bureaucratic, caste of mind.

135. Str. 15.1.48. This has become generally accepted in modern writing (e.g., Thapar 1997, 117), though *KA* 4.4.3 only specifies brothel-keepers and 'performers' in its litany of suitable secret agents. Nuns may also be so employed. See also *KA* 1.12.20–3, and n. 152 below.

136. Bailey and Mabbett 2003, 224.

137. Basham 1954, 98–101.

138. *Mbh.* 5.34.38; also 12.112–17 on the need to choose virtuous advisers.

139. Basham 1954, 101.

140. Pl. *Lg.* 760b; Stein 1932, 281; cf. also Arist. *Ath. Pol.* 50.2.

141. Megasth. F 19 J = F 33 Schw = Str. 15.1.49.

142. Basham 1954, 112–21.

143. Nilakanta Sastri 1957, 108; cf. Agrawala 1953, 16 and 20–1, discussing the evidence of this passage of Megasthenes regarding writing. See above, ch.1.

144. Arora 2005, 97–9.

Megasthenes says nothing about 'provincial' or local administration: nothing about, for example, viceroys (*uparajas*), such as were in post later in Taxila and Ujjain, nor about village headmen.[145] On city administration, he tells us that the *archontes*, who are drawn from the sixth *meros* of society (below the councillors), include market inspectors and city inspectors (*agoranomoi* and *astynomoi* – the latter in Modern Greek denotes the police), as well as the army chiefs. The distinction between the first two seems to correspond to that between country and city. 'The market inspectors [rather surprisingly] are responsible for river works and measurement of the land, as in Egypt, and are also in charge of the small canals from which the water is distributed into the conduits, so that all may make use of the water on an equal basis. The same men are in charge of hunters and have the power of reward and punishment over those who deserve it. They also collect the taxes and oversee the crafts connected with the land – woodcutters, carpenters, brass-workers and miners. They build the roads and place markers every ten stades to indicate the turnings and the distances.' None of this information calls for much comment. The *Arthaśāstra* does not provide any essentially different information, though it has more subdivisions,[146] and specifies a Ministry of the Interior, Ministry of Works and Ministry of Letters (which obviously would not have existed in a pre-literate state). *Manu* too emphasises the importance of water-supplies, and adds the information that anyone who destroys a pond is to be executed, preferably by drowning.[147] The seriousness with which the Maurya kings took matters of water-supply is evident from the later inscription of King Rudradaman (r. 130–50 CE) at Junagadh: in this partially obliterated text, he describes his own works to repair a lake and other water-works 'ordered to be made by the Vaishya Pushyagupta, the provincial governor of the Maurya king Chandragupta; adorned with conduits for Aśoka the Maurya by the Yavana king Tushaspha while governing; and by the conduit made by him, constructed in a manner worthy of a king (and) seen in that breach, the extensive dam.'[148]

145. Basham 1954, 102–7.

146. Timmer 1930, 184ff.: overseers for customs and tolls, alcohol, butchers, courtesans, leopards and elephants among others.

147. *Manusmṛti* 9.279.

148. *Epigraphica Indica* 8 (Calcutta, 1905–6), 36–49, quotation at 46–7; available at https://archive.org/stream/in.ernet.dli.2015.69971/2015.69971.Epigraphia-Indica-Vol---Viii-1905---1906#page/n57/mode/2up. This is the first inscription of any length in Sanskrit.

Megasthenes continues: 'The city inspectors are divided into six colleges of five. One group is in charge of the artisans, another of the accommodation of foreigners: they assign lodgings, follow their behaviour closely, provide them with attendants and send them on their way, or forward their property if they should die; they also care for them when they are sick and bury them if they die. The third group are registrars of births and deaths – when and where – both for the sake of taxation and in order that the births and deaths of both the better classes and the worse shall be known.[149] Fourth are those in charge of retail trade and barter, who are responsible for measures and for seasonal produce, to ensure that it is sold as marked.... The same man may not barter more than one thing without paying taxes twice. The fifth group are those in charge of the products of craftsmen, and their sale according to the mark, keeping the old and the new separate: there is a penalty for mixing them. The sixth and last group are those who exact a ten per cent sales tax: the penalty for theft is death.'

These details are very precise and circumstantial, and suggest a level of bureaucracy that would appeal to the author of the *Arthaśāstra*. There is nothing in Megasthenes' information that is in conflict with the later work, though Kautilya's text is in fact more abstract and less punctilious than Megasthenes'.[150]

The Greek must have been well aware of the arrangements for the supervision of foreigners. One of the most striking parts of the *Arthaśāstra* is that dealing with the elaborate secret service, involving the employment as spies of, among many other categories of person, courtesans and ascetics.[151] Did Megasthenes talk to individuals of either type? Kautilya adjures the envoy to be careful of women.[152]

The third 'ministry' described by Megasthenes is the military, also consisting of six colleges of five men. 'Of these, one is stationed with the naval commander, a second with the managers of the ox-teams, by which the materiel of war, food for the men and fodder for the beasts, and all other necessities are transported. These also provide the servants: the drummers and bell-carriers, as well as the grooms, the engineers and their assistants. They send out foragers to the sound of bells, and compel both speed and safety by re-

149. Also Diod. 2.57–8.

150. Timmer 1930, 225.

151. Basham 1954, 121–2; Thapar 1997, 112; McClish and Olivelle 2012, 98–110.

152. *KA* 1.20.14–21; McClish and Olivelle 2012, 26–7. See also *Mbh.* 12.130.36.

wards and punishments. The third group is in charge of the infantry, the fourth of the cavalry, the fifth of the chariots and the sixth of the elephants.'[153] Megasthenes thus describes a classic *caturaṅga* army. Arrian provides a little more detail about the army,[154] a subject on which one would expect Megasthenes to have been expansive if he was writing a report for Seleucus. The passage of Arrian in question does not mention Megasthenes, however, but rather follows on from several bits of information stated to come from Nearchus; so we cannot be sure whether it describes the Maurya army or one in Sind. Pliny's description of Palibothra, which is probably based on Megasthenes, mentions that its king maintains a standing army of six hundred thousand infantry, thirty thousand cavalry and nine thousand elephants: 'whence may be formed some conjecture as to the vastness of his resources'.[155] Arrian mentions the bow the height of a man used by the foot-soldiers, with arrows a yard and a half (1.4 m) long, with considerable penetrating power; and the shields nearly the height of a man but rather narrow and made of rawhide. Others use javelins.[156] The bow and arrow, however, are the supreme weapon of the heroes in the *Ṛg Veda* and in the epics, and are shown also in the siege scenes on the reliefs at Sanchi. All foot soldiers carry a broad 'cutlass', also a yard and a half long, which is used in hand-to-hand combat, though this is a thing the Indians prefer to avoid. However, it is 'an essential part of knightly equipment', and can be used not only for slashing in hand-to-hand combat, but for hurling.[157] The weapons were probably of bronze, though some iron may have been used.[158] The cavalry carry two spears and a smaller shield; they ride bareback and instead of a bit they have a band of rawhide bound around the muzzle, with a band of iron inside the mouth to control the horse.[159]

153. On the importance of the horses and elephants, see also Ael. *NA* 13.25.

154. Arr. *Ind.* 16.

155. Plin. *NH* 6.22 = Megasth. F 56 Schw (not in Jacoby).

156. Cf the depiction on the 'Porus tetradrachms' of an elephant rider with a javelin; e.g., Holt 2003 plate 5. Plates 6–7 depict archers on elephants.

157. Singh 1965, 109–10.

158. Ibid., 100 – from 600 BCE.

159. The Greek bit resembled a modern bit, with rings at either end attaching to the bridle; commonly there was also a link in the middle. The Indian bit was apparently not articulated in this way. Xenophon's *On Horsemanship* is the *locus classicus* on ancient horses. See Singh 1965, 66–7 on training to obey the bit. See also Willekes 2016, 17–18.

This very general information is not in conflict with our other sources on Indian warfare, and there is not much to surprise us.[160] Arrian shows an interest especially in the cavalry, though Singh suggests that chariots were usually the key in battle.[161] However, the Sanchi reliefs show the chariot being used for ceremonial processions, not as a weapon. Arrian also says nothing about the use of elephants in battle; perhaps he felt he had covered that in writing about the battle of the Hydaspes. The *Arthaśāstra*, by contrast, has a detailed discussion of warfare in books 9 and 10: the planning of a campaign, troop mobilisation, how to tell a strong army from a weak one, and many other categories; how to deal with losses and gains, and the dangers of rebellions and treachery; a section on the practicalities of a campaign follows, including battle arrays and the division of an army into units.[162] None of this appears in our Greeks, so it is not possible to say that there is any conflict between the Greek and Indian sources.

The Navy

It is a bit of a surprise to find that the landlocked Maurya kingdom requires a naval commander. No further information is offered by Megasthenes, though the *Arthaśāstra* gives more detail about this 'Superintendent of Shipping'.[163] The *Arthaśāstra's* provisions all relate to civil shipping – ferries, trading vessels, and ports and tolls – but it may be that there was also a military aspect. The *Mahābhārata* envisages a kingdom having a navy,[164] for control of pirates and for communications with Sri Lanka. Given that the Maurya empire at its greatest extent (under Aśoka) reached from sea to sea, it may be that Candragupta was already building up a fleet for conquest. But Megasthenes does not say so. Alexander's fleet used an Indian guide on its journey to the ocean, and Majumdar has suggested that he may also have made use of Indian ships, though we know that he had a number built as well.[165] Megasthenes regards the shipping command as a military role and not a civil one, but we can only speculate as to what it entailed.

160. On Indian warfare, see Singh 1965; Trautmann 2015.

161. Singh 1965, 66.

162. See also *Manusmṛti* 7.90ff., also155ff. on foreign policy.

163. KA 2.28.1–26; McClish and Olivelle 2012, 56–8; Majumdar 1960, 55–6.

164. *Mbh.* 12.59.41–4.

165. Arr. *Ind.* 271; Majumdar 1960, 56.

Morality

Megasthenes, in what survives of his work, shows more interest in the moral qualities of Indians than in such practical matters. He descants on the frugality and simplicity of the Indians, and their honesty.[166] On their insistence on telling the truth he is probably right. There are many references to this subject in the Dharmasūtras,[167] and it is hardly irrelevant that the motto of the present Republic of India is 'Truth Alone Triumphs' (*Satyameva Jayate*), from the *Mundaka Upaniṣad*.[168]

Indian justice was famous among the Greeks: Ctesias states that 'the Indians are very just people', a characteristic they share with the Dog-heads.[169] Though the description 'most just' is attached by various Greek authors to other peoples as well,[170] many other writers too have emphasised the justice of the Indians, from Xuanzang in the sixth century to Amrit Lal Vegad in the twentieth: the latter writes, 'The law says, "Don't commit crimes", whereas religion says, "That is not enough – do some good deeds." … The law is necessary, but it isn't enough. We shouldn't stop at the level of the law. We should go beyond it and scale the peak of religion.'[171] This quotation from Vegad shows how close justice and religion lie in Indian thought, and both may be encompassed in the word *dharma*, the 'first foundations' as they are called in *Ṛg Veda*.[172] When the British ruled India they took *dharma* to be the equivalent of Law and attempted to introduce the laws of Manu (*Dharmasūtra*) as a law-code for the country. It seems to have been *dharma* that the Greeks were observing when they extolled the 'justice' of the Indians.

Some further scraps of information have to be taken in isolation as there is little supporting documentation from the *Arthaśāstra* or other texts.[173]

166. Megasth. Ff 27 Schw, 32 J.

167. E.g., A.1.7.11.

168. 3.1.6; see the discussion in Timmer 1930, 253–4.

169. Ctes. Ff 45.16 (cf. 45.30), 45.43.

170. Homer and Aeschylus: the Abii/Gabii; Agatharchides: the Fish-Eaters. See the fuller discussion of the justice of the Indians in Stoneman 2016b.

171. Vegad 2008, 178 and 180. Xuanzang's observation is quoted in Stoneman 2016b, 254, from Beal 1884, 1.83: 'With respect to the ordinary people, although they are naturally light-minded, yet they are upright and honourable. In money matters they are without craft, and in administering justice they are considerate … They are not deceitful or treacherous in their conduct, and are faithful to their oaths and promises.'

172. *RV* 10.90.9–16.

173. Ff 27 Schw, 32 J.

Megasthenes tells us that Indians tended to have many wives, that they drank little alcohol and that their tombs were inconspicuous. (The absence of tombs is noted too by the Alexander of the *Romance*.)[174] He refers to the king going hunting, and here one may compare the several depictions of the hunt on the reliefs at Sanchi, as well as frequent references in narrative texts including the Purāṇas and the Jātakas. He is also intrigued by the Indians' forms of exercise, especially massage: the *Arthaśāstra* requires that when the king is visited by prostitutes they must cleanse themselves by bathing and rubbing.[175]

Pearl-fishing

One curious glimpse of everyday life is Megathenes' account of pearl-fishing,[176] which is inserted into the middle of Arrian's disquisition on Heracles and Pandaea. The reason for its position here is in one sense obvious, since Pandya is one of the main regions for pearl-fishing, as is known from both Greek and Indian texts.[177] Greeks had never seen pearls before Alexander's expedition, as is clear from Theophrastus' reference to 'that which is known as the oyster';[178] Athenaeus quotes several of the Alexander historians for information on oysters and related shellfish:[179] Androsthenes details the varieties of pearl and their values, and Chares refers to an 'oblong oyster'; later, Isidore of Charax in the *Parthian Stations* describes the pearl fisheries of the Arabian Sea. A curious feature of Megasthenes' description is that he tells us that the oysters are caught with nets rather than being brought up by divers: this is possible because oysters have a king and a queen, and once you can catch the king, the rest of the oysters will follow obediently. The story seems to have come straight out of Lewis Carroll rather than a serious historian,[180] but Paul Kosmin has argued that there may be a political point to this extraordinary claim: Me-

174. *AR* 3.6.

175. *KA* 1.20.20.

176. Arr. *Ind.* 8.11.13 = F 13 J.

177. *KA* 2.11.2, see Singh 2009, 401; Shastri 1996, 317; Shimada 2013, 122. Other ancient sources include *Bṛhatsaṁhitā* 81; *Periplus* 59 (located in the kingdom of Pandion); Ptol. 7.1.10; Plin. *NH* 6.81, 9.106–7. Most of these specify that the biggest and best pearls come from Taprobane (Sri Lanka).

178. Thphr. *De lapidibus* 6.36, ὁ μαργαρίτης καλούμενος.

179. Athen. 3.45–6 (93 C).

180. 'But four young oysters hurried up, / All eager for the treat / … Four other oysters followed them, / And yet another four; / And thick and fast they came at last, / And more, and more, and more.' 'The Walrus and the Carpenter' in *Alice through the Looking Glass.*

gasthenes has simply invented it as an example of ideal kingship, since this is one of his themes.[181] I am not sure that I buy this. It seems more likely that it was one of those things that he was told: an old salt explains to the inquisitive Greek the secret of his bumper haul: 'you treat the boss real sweet, and the rest of the little perishers follow along'. It is still surprising that Megasthenes fell for it. The story is repeated by Aelian,[182] presumably deriving from Megasthenes, though as this chapter also contains references to the Bactrian king Eucratides, the Fish-Eaters and the island of Britain, it cannot all be from him, and others may have repeated it before Aelian. Megasthenes also provides the information that a pearl is worth three times its weight in gold, which is not in conflict with the high valuation placed on pearls by other Greek writers and the *Bṛhatsaṁhitā*, which gives a detailed breakdown of prices for different kinds: this states that the pearls from Pandya are 'like neem-leaves, or coriander-seeds, and fine as grit'.[183]

The fact that the value of pearls is mentioned suggests that Megasthenes was aware of the trade in them, both within India and abroad. Madurai in the Pandya region was one of the main centres for the later trade in pearls (and in other items), as the *Periplus* makes clear.[184] The extensive finds of Roman coins in the region show how important it later became as an import–export centre: 'Mediterranean eye-shadow, perfume, silverware, fine Italian wine and beautiful slave-girl musicians for concubinage' arrived in abundance in the first century CE, but the net gain was India's, as it exported high-value goods such as silk, ivory, pearls and pepper.[185] Thapar is confident that the same conditions prevailed in Megasthenes' time;[186] but it seems more likely that the trade was entirely internal, as no pearl had yet been seen in Greece (as Theophrastus makes clear). There are however some indications that the trade in spices had got under way already in the time of Seleucus.[187] Wiesehöfer notes that this king sent gifts to Didyma of frankincense, myrrh, cassia, cinnamon and costus in the year 288/7 BCE; but these seem to be Arabian spices, apart from the cinnamon, which was known to Greeks from the time

181. Kosmin 2014, 52.

182. Ael. *NA* 15.8.

183. A neem leaf is nothing like a coriander seed.

184. *Periplus* 59.

185. Dalrymple 1998, 183–5, a beautiful evocation of the second-century city.

186. Thapar 1997, 86.

187. Plin. *NH* 16.135; *OGIS* 214.59ff.; translation in Welles, 1934 no. 35, pp. 33–40; discussion: Wiesehöfer 1998, 228–9; Faure 1987, 197.

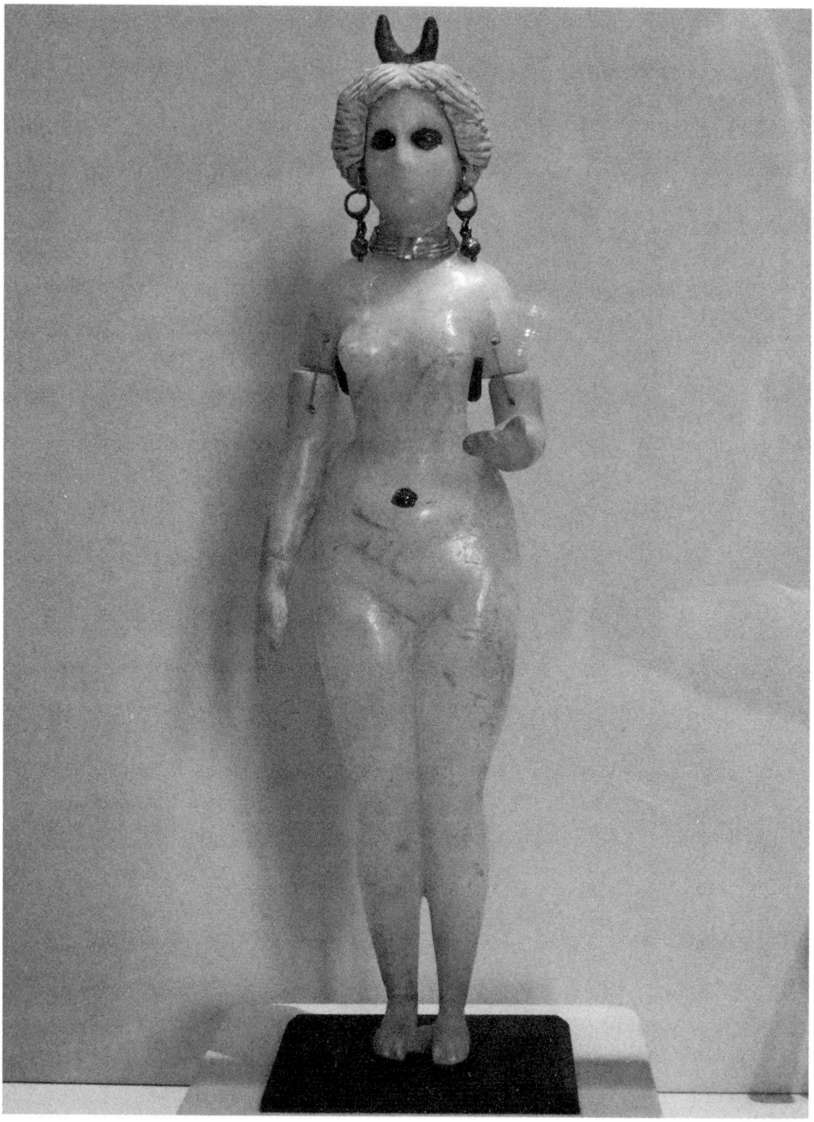

8.1 This Hellenistic figurine of Ishtar, from Babylon, has a ruby in her navel; this can only have come from India. (Musée du Louvre, Paris).

of Herodotus. This was perhaps another of Seleucus' attempts to impress the Greeks on his western fringe with the exotica of his realm, like the tiger he sent to Athens.[188] Rubies were reaching Babylon in the third century BCE, as witnessed by an ivory figurine of Ishtar with eyes of rubies and a ruby in her navel, now in the Louvre.

Medicine

Megasthenes' information about physicians is of interest. Strabo's summary states that physic is a function of the Hylobioi, the forest-dwelling ascetics, who are probably proto-Buddhists.[189] 'They are able by the use of drugs to cause women to have numerous children [or, multiple births?], and to bear males or females; their medicine is done mainly with cereal products, not with drugs; of drugs they mainly employ ointments and poultices, while other things have bad side-effects'. There is a sharp divide in the Indian medical tradition between the practices of the Vedas, carried out by Brahmans, which rely mainly on magical practices and incantations, and those of the ascetics, which grew into Buddhist medicine or Ayurveda, reliant as stated on herbal remedies, but also on the balance of elements in the body, regulated by diet and also ointments.[190] Brahmans (sādhus?) seem to be the 'Pramnae' of Strabo,[191] who 'carry wallets full of roots and drugs, making claims to medical expertise in spells and incantations and amulets'; they invoked the healing gods Kustha (for fever) and Arundhati, who presided over herbs, so infusions could be proffered; but the work of a healer (*bhisāj*) was not open to a Brahman, because contact with another body, especially a sick one, would pollute him. There is no evidence for anything resembling Greek 'rational medicine' until much later in the Greek period, and the only place in India where ancient surgical tools have been found is Taxila.[192] (What is now called Yunani medicine, relying in the Hippocratic manner on herbs and balance of humours, came

188. See ch. 4 above.

189. Str. 15.1.60.

190. Zysk 1998; Naqvi 2011. The three humours are wind, bile and phlegm. The triad is possibly pre-Vedic, but see *Chāndogya Upaniṣad* 6.2.5; King 1999, 169–70. However, *Sāmaññaphala Sutta* 61–2 (Bodhi 1989, 37–8) includes the administration of medicine as something from which the good renouncer should abstain.

191. Str. 15.1.70.

192. Naqvi 2011, 132.

in with the Muslims in the eleventh century CE.) When Ayurveda became dominant, Brahmans laid a claim to its origination, but it began with the ascetics.[193]

The word got around among the Greeks that Indian doctors could cure snakebite, a thing which defeated the Greeks.[194] Arrows smeared with poison caused much distress among Alexander's army during the campaign against Sambus,[195] and Ptolemy received a dangerous wound which Alexander eventually cured, he said, after dreaming of a plant which was an antidote to the poison. A large party was sent out to search for the herb, which the king described in detail, and it produced the desired effect.[196] The dream, one suspects, may in fact have been a quiet word with a friendly native, or maybe a memory of something learned from the naked philosophers in Taxila.

Eating

Megasthenes observed that the Indians 'always eat alone', whenever they feel like it. 'The contrary custom', he remarks, 'would be better for the ends of social and civil life'.[197] The practice is enjoined by caste purity, for which the rules are neatly laid out by Dumont: '[the Brahman] eats alone or in a small group in a pure 'square' (*caukā*) in the kitchen or a nearby part of the house carefully protected from intrusion. Any unforeseen contact, not only with a low caste man (sometimes going as far as his shadow) or an animal, but even with someone from the house (woman, child, or man who is not purified for eating) would make the food unfit for consumption.' [198] This practice was also observed by Babur and al-Biruni.[199]

Sexual Behaviour

It seems that Megasthenes probably did not try to give a comprehensive portrait of Indian society in the way that al-Biruni did. Instead, he noted things that struck him as worthy of attention, which is the manner also of Babur.

193. Zysk 1998, 118.

194. Arr. *Ind.* 15.11–12; Aelian *NA* 12.32.

195. Curt. 9.8.20–7 and Cic. *Div* 2.135 and 141.

196. Curt. 9.8.26–7.

197. Str. 15.1.53 = Megasth. F 27 Schw = F 32 J.

198. Dumont 1980, 138–9.

199. Dale 2004, 370; Sachau 1910, 180.

One of the things that presumably did not strike him as requiring specific attention was the lives of women.

Sadly it is impossible to get a connected picture of the lives of women from what remains of Megasthenes.[200] He mentions the duty of the royal spies to talk to 'public women' to gain information, but makes no suggestions that he did so himself.[201] He does tell us that women can join the ranks of the philosophers:[202] these are most probably Buddhists or proto-Buddhists, but note also the role of the female disciple Gargi in the Upaniṣads. The marriage practices of Brahmans are referred to, which is outlined in detail by Manu.[203]

Arrian says that Indian women are very moral and not corruptible at any price 'except that a woman will have sex with anyone who gives her an elephant'.[204] Megasthenes says, however, that wives will prostitute themselves quite openly if given a chance.[205] Both he and Onesicritus, and Herodotus,[206] also say that it is customary, at least in some parts of India, for couples to have sex in the open, in public.[207] The allegation sounds like some hippie fantasy (Woodstock-on-the-Indus), but a pious Brahman in the *Mahābhārata* says the same thing about the Bahlika (Bactrian) women of Sakala (Sagala, Sialkot):

> The women, intoxicated with drink and divested of robes, laugh and dance outside the walls of the houses in cities, without garlands and unguents, singing while drunk obscene songs of diverse kinds ... What man is there that would willingly dwell, even for a moment, amongst the Vahlikas that are so fallen and wicked, and so depraved in their practices?'[208]

Sexual licence is allied to gluttony, the eating of meat and the use of impure plates and bowls, as well as neglect of religious rites. Elsewhere, Pāṇḍu admonishes his queen Kuntī,

> In the olden days, so we hear, the women went uncloistered, my lovely wife of the beautiful eyes: they were their own mistresses who took their

200. Cf. Thapar 1997, 87.

201. Smith 1901, 75 took it for granted that he did.

202. Str. 15.1.60 end = F 41 Schw = F 33 J.

203. Timmer 1930, 270. See also *Manusmṛti* 3.23 and 24–6, 36–42.

204. Arr. *Ind.* 17.3–4.

205. Megasth. F 32; Arora 2005, 83ff.

206. Str. 15.1.56; Hdt. 3.101.

207. See also Sextus Empiricus, *PH* 3.200, who compares the practice with that of the Cynic Crates.

208. *Mbh.* 8.44, tr. Ganguli.

> pleasure where it pleased them. From childhood on they were faithless to their husbands, but yet not lawless, for such was the law in the olden days. Even today the animal creatures still follow this hoary law, without any passion or hatred. This anciently witnessed law was honored by the great seers, and it still prevails among the northern Kurus.[209]

The custom is associated with the north-west, exactly where polyandry remained customary until comparatively recent times. The peculiar freedom of the women of this region may also have contributed to the growth of the belief in a Kingdom of Women, or Amazons, in these parts, which is known in Indian literature as an aspect of Uttarakuru, the Northern Paradise, and reaches the Greeks in the *Alexander Romance*.[210]

The perceived 'promiscuity' of Indian women of the north-west is entailed by the custom of polyandry. This persisted in the Himalayas up until Independence,[211] and to the present day in Ladakh and Tibet. Many tribal peoples still practise polyandry (or did in the 1970s), as detailed by Stephen Fuchs in his survey.[212] Al-Biruni in the eleventh century observed that it was prevalent from Afghanistan to Kashmir, and Rudyard Kipling in *Kim* referred to 'the land where the women make the love'.[213] Thomas Coryate in 1616 described the practice in more detail, at

> a mountain some ten days journey between Lahore and Agra ... : the people that inhabit that mountain have a custom very strong, that all the brothers of any family, have but one and the self same wife ... the like whereof I remember I have read in Strabo, concerning the Arabians that inhabit Arabia Felix.[214]

The practice seems also to be depicted in some of the cave paintings at Bhimbetka near Bhopal, where scenes appear of sex between two men and a woman:[215] the artists will have been the ancestors of the tribal peoples of the historical period. Women might marry several brothers, as did the Pandavas

209. Ibid. 1.113, tr. A. B. van Buitenen.

210. See further ch. 9 below, on 'Utopia'.

211. For this paragraph, see Parmar 1975; also Karttunen 1989, 202–7.

212. Fuchs 1973, 90–4. See also Nevile 2006, 66 for anecdotal evidence on polyandry and bride sale in the region of Lahore.

213. Albinia 2008, 262–4.

214. Quoted in Moraes 2003, 104–5; cf. Strachan 1962, 226.

215. Moraes 1983, 4.

in the *Mahābhārata* (who are perhaps the same as the Padaioi referred to by Herodotus in another chapter),[216] or a succession of husbands: the latter practice is known as *reet*. The custom results from four factors: an excess of male births; the example of the Pandavas; the need to keep estates intact; and the need for manpower on those estates.

Parmar's data are drawn mainly from the region of Sirmur, south of Shimla in southern Himachal Pradesh; but the picture is confirmed for antiquity by the above passages, as well as the allegations of the practice of free love among the Madras,[217] the assumption by the *rakṣasa* Virādha in the *Rāmāyaṇa* that Sita is shared by Rāma and his brother Lakṣman,[218] and even some passages in the Vedas.[219] Though there is no explicit account of promiscuity in the *Ṛg Veda*, a widow is said to take her dead husband's brother as husband (*niyoga*, in this case levirate marriage);[220] while the dawn goddess seems to be married to both of the Aśvins (the Indian 'Dioscuri'), and they ride together in a chariot made for three.[221] Promiscuity belongs to the region beyond the Indus, which is also beyond *dharma*. It is regarded as non-Aryan by righteous Brahmans, though they have tacitly to accept it in certain places.[222] The idea that such practices are non-Aryan chimes with the location in the north-west, the link with the pale-faced Pandavas, and perhaps also with the connections of the pre-Aryan Harappan civilisation with Mesopotamia, where Inanna presided over the erotic life of the city, a Woodstock-on-the-Tigris: 'Copulation in the streets was apparently a normal and joyful event, and young people sleeping in their own chambers is singled out as a most worrying state of affairs.'[223]

Verrier Elwin writes that 'pre-nuptial sexual freedom is nothing unusual in the "primitive" world'.[224] The Bhotias of the 1970s, according to Fuchs,

216. Hdt. 3.99. The Padaioi, however, are eaters of raw meat, and they also eat their dead relatives, which the Pandavas certainly do not.

217. *Mbh.* 8.27.5–6. Singh 1978 surveys the evidence.

218. *Rām.* 3 (*Araṇyakāṇḍa*) 2.11cd–12ab: 'How is it that two ascetics are living with a young woman? You are evil men impersonating sages.'

219. Jamieson and Brereton 2014, 48 and 49.

220. *RV* 10.40.2, cf. *Atharvaveda* 14.1.46, 5.17.8.

221. *RV* 1.119.54.43.2, 8.69.3–4; Singh 1978, 43.

222. Singh 1978, 111 and 120.

223. Leick 2001, 59. Aitken 1992, 42, mentions that he observed the unusual sight of a couple openly kissing in the fields at Yamunotri. Perhaps this would be regarded by Greeks as 'sex in public'.

224. Elwin 1947, 271. See also Sugiyama 1969, 130: Munda youth are free of control, and 'such sexual relations are not exceptional cases among the young village boys and girls'.

practised a form of free love, which was even institutionalised in a kind of partying club known as the Rangbang.[225] The Murias of Madhya Pradesh had, up until at least the 1990s, an institution known as the *ghotul*, a kind of youth club whose members paired off to enjoy each other's bodies for three or four days before being compelled by custom to change partners. Privacy was not essential.[226] If the Murias extended further north in antiquity, or other tribes had similar customs, this would certainly have struck the Greeks as noteworthy.

Megasthenes also describes a completely different, plainly patriarchal, custom of marriage. There is no bride price or dowry but the fathers of marriageable women offer them as prizes for the victors in contests of running, wrestling and boxing. This latter information is in fact from Nearchus, as is made clear by its repetition in Strabo;[227] there is no reason to suppose that the same remarkable custom prevailed in Magadha, though it may have done. Something like it remains in force among the Bhils, where a brave youth may take his chosen girl without a bride price ('marriage by trial').[228]

Whatever the conditions in pre-Aryan or tribal India, the rise of agricultural civilisation required control of women for provision of labour resources Thus in more hierarchical societies, marriage was carefully controlled, and forms of marriage ranged from gift to exchange (dowry) to 'rape'.[229] As James Forsyth observed in 1871, the Gonds 'differ from the Hindus chiefly in the contract and performance [of marriage] both taking place when the parties are of full age. Polygamy is not forbidden; but, women being costly chattels, it is rarely practised. The father of the bride is always paid a consideration for the loss of her services, as is usually the case among poor races where the females bear a large share in the burden of life'.[230]

225. Fuchs 1973, 94.

226. Elwin 1964, 163–7. Refined by Gell 1992: a girl on entering the *ghotul* is asked 'with whom will you take place?' (175). In Gell's interpretation, it is a matter of sharing a sleeping mat, often no more (209), while the rarity of pregnancies suggests that not much sex is actually taking place (226).

227. Str. 15.1.66.

228. Fuchs 1973, 145. The Sauras also practise 'marriage by capture', according to Elwin 1955, 55; see also 56 on polygamy. Moraes 1983 discusses courtship and bride-seizing (86), as well as the different customs of the Baigas (89).

229. Roy 1994, 253 and 260.

230. Forsyth 1871, 148.

Trautmann does not comment on the statement that a woman will have sex for an elephant, but he does point out that the information indicates that in Nearchus' time and place a private individual could own an elephant, whereas in Megasthenes' day in Magadha, only a king could own one.[231]

One may conclude that Megasthenes made some pertinent observations of marriage customs, but offered nothing like a comprehensive account of the variety of practices prevailing in different parts of India. Much of his work is indeed lost, but any author interested enough in the subject to excerpt these pieces of information would be likely to excerpt the whole range. Greeks, both as visitors to India and as readers, were not unsurprisingly intrigued by unusual sexual practices.

Megasthenes, or his excerptors, took no interest at all in the minutiae of Indian polytheism, however. A bluff British consul once remarked to Verrier Elwin that an anthropologist is a person interested only in 'tits and temples'.[232] If Megasthenes did indeed take an interest (less prurient than the consul's) in sexual behaviour, he appears to have said nothing about the other part of the apophthegm, religious practices. A modern anthropologist would find this strange, but it does not diminish the magnitude of Megasthenes' achievement.

231. Trautmann 2015, 130–1.

232. Elwin 1964, 204.

9

The Question of Utopia

But even if I find my way out of the forest
I shall be left with the inconsolable memory
Of the treasure I went into the forest to find
And never found, and which was not there
And perhaps is not anywhere? But if not anywhere,
Why do I feel guilty at not having found it?

—T.S. ELIOT, *THE COCKTAIL PARTY*

Me seemeth that what in those nations we see by experience doth not only exceed all the pictures wherewith licentious Poesy hath proudly embellished the golden age and all her quaint inventions to feign a happy condition of man but also the conception and desire of philosophy.

—MICHEL DE MONTAIGNE, 'OF THE CANNIBALS', TR. JOHN FLORIO

SCHOLARS HAVE SOMETIMES SEEN some or all of the Greek writers, including Megasthenes, as using India as the location for a utopian fantasy of an ideal world. For example, Oswyn Murray, after arguing in 1970 that Hecataeus is wrongly seen as a Utopian, asserted in 1972 that Megasthenes was offering a description of a Platonic ideal state.[1] In this he followed the influential statement of Otto Stein, who saw Megasthenes as an idealising writer.[2] Onesicritus found the kingdom of Musicanus to be a happy land without

1. Murray 1972, 208.

2. Stein 1921. See Karttunen 1989, 97. Stein's 'ideal' traits include honesty and justice, no alcohol or slavery, and the exclusion of the farming classes from military duties. Zambrini 1985, 782 and 825 also sees Megasthenes as a utopian, but Kosmin 2014, 50 cogently rebuts him.

slavery, its inhabitants living a simple life according to nature; Megasthenes generalised the absence of slavery to the whole of India.[3] Undoubtedly the Greeks were impressed by certain aspects of the Indian way of life, but one must be wary of characterising their entire way of life on the basis of specific examples.

To begin with, the concept of Utopia needs some definition.[4] The term goes back to Thomas More, whose *Utopia* was a kind of thought-experiment to criticise the prevailing mores of his own society. Though such a tendency can be seen in the later Hellenistic writers such as Euhemerus, Theopompus and Iambulus, as well as the fifth century CE writer Palladius, the ideal society as envisaged by earlier Greeks more commonly takes the form of a Golden Age (Posidonius F 284 being the *locus classicus*). A Golden Age is normally set in the past, and our present state represents an irreversible decline from a lost ideal world.[5] The Hebrew variant of this is the story of the Garden of Eden, which entered Christian tradition as the myth of the lost earthly paradise. A variant on this, which envisages a Land of Cockaigne or Never-Never Land in some distant but unattainable place, seems to become current only in the Middle Ages.[6] A Golden Age, like what I shall call a 'Golden Land', can be characterised either by ease and pleasure of life, or by moral purity, or (but not necessarily) by both. It is a type of 'soft' primitivism, distinct from the 'hard' primitivism of Greek writers who saw human development as an advance from a more bestial to a better present state.[7]

India also believed in a Golden Age, which lay in the past but will return in the cycle of the ages. The *Atharvaveda* describes the rivers of Paradise and

> The full lakes of butter with their banks of honey,
> Flowing with wine, and milk and curds and water –

3. Arora 2005, 93.

4. See the essay by Stoneman 2015 and the comprehensive survey by Winiarczyk 2011, as well as the older book Ferguson 1975. The literature on utopias is considerable: see in the main Lovejoy and Boas 1935; Manuel and Manuel 1979; Carey 1999.

5. Mahatma Gandhi was a utopian in this sense, according to Octavio Paz 1997, 113: 'his social utopia was an idealization of ancient Hindu civilization that had no more reality than Rousseau's natural man'.

6. Pleij 2001.

7. Epicurus is something of an exception, in that he idealised the primitive world because of its anti-civilisational qualities. The idea of the 'noble savage' starts here. See Campbell 2003, 13–15. Primitive people are seen as 'philosophers' by Posidonius, F 284 – attacked by Seneca *Ep.* 90.5–32. Elwin 1955, 21 notes that Somadeva makes the Saoras of Orissa into 'noble savages'.

Abundant with their overflow of sweetness, these
Streams shall reach thee in the world of *Svarga*,
Whole lakes with lotus-blossom shall approach thee.[8]

This Golden Land is also the one that the blessed will reach after death, as revealed in the *Ṛg Veda*:[9]

Where the inexhaustible light is, in which world the sun is placed,
In that one place me, o self-purifying one, in the immortal,
imperishable world.

Onesicritus quotes the philosopher Calanus as saying that in olden times the world was full of barley-meal and wheat-meal, and there were fountains of water, milk, honey, wine and olive oil. In that blessed past, men and gods lived together on earth, according to the *Āpastamba Dharmasūtra*.[10] Buddhist thought, too, conceived of a Golden Age which was followed by decline as a result of karma left over from a previous world cycle; anarchy ensued, until kingship was introduced to reimpose order.[11] The cycle of ages is also expounded in the *Mahābhārata*.[12] Greeks, apart from Pythagoreans, did not generally believe in such world cycles, so a Greek utopia is more in the nature of a thought-experiment.

The aims of the later Hellenistic writers need disentangling from the approach of the ethnographers. As usual, the first hints at a distant ideal society come in Homer, who speaks of the 'blameless Ethiopians', and of the Abii;[13] the latter reappear in the *Prometheus Bound* attributed to Aeschylus as the Gabii, 'a people of all mortals most just and hospitable'. Herodotus follows up an account of Indian cannibals by describing another Indian tribe who

> do not kill any living thing or grow crops, nor is it their practice to have houses. They eat vegetables, and there is a seed, about the size of a millet seed, which grows by itself in a pod without being cultivated and which they collect, cook – pod and all – and eat. If any of them falls ill, he goes

8. Quoted in Drew 1987, 168.

9. *RV* 9.113.7, addressed to the sacred drink *soma*.

10. *Āpastamba Dharmasūtra* 2.16.1.

11. Strong 1983, 44–5. The idea reminds one of Empedocles, whose points of resemblance to Buddhist ideas are discussed in ch. 12 below.

12. *Mbh*. 3.148.10–39. Cf. *Yūga Purāṇa*, ed. and tr. Mitchiner, 2002, 6ff.

13. *Iliad* 13.6.

> and lies down in some remote spot, and no one cares whether he is dead or ill.[14]

In the next chapter he mentions that all Indians have sexual intercourse in public (and that their semen is black like that of Ethiopians). Here, then, is another variant of the life of ease, which is the life according to nature, much praised and developed by Cynic thinkers. It has elements that seem harsh and demanding, alongside the freedom from labour and trouble.

Of the writers who focused on India, the earliest is Ctesias. Almost nothing of what he said about customs and society survives.[15] But, according to Photius' summary, 'Ctesias claims that the Indians are very just people; he also describes their customs and manners'. Later he refers again to the Indians' justice, the kindly care of their king for his people, and their contempt for death. He then notes that 'the Dog-heads ... are just men who enjoy the greatest longevity of any people'.[16] Here already are three key elements of an ideal society: justice, honourable treatment of the fellow-man, and longevity. (The abundance of precious stones might also be seen as a sign of happiness, if one were not inclined to interpret wealth as a corollary to greed.)[17] I have argued that the 'justice of the Indians' is not really an idealising concept, since it can be shown that Indian society was, in Greek terms, very 'just', and Indian thinkers in general valued justice, which may be equated with *dharma*, very highly.[18] It may be that the same can be said of other apparently ideal traits identified in the Greek accounts of India.

There is a regular repertoire of utopian traits in ancient writers, and I can hardly do better than summarise the main headings of Winiarczyk's exhaustive catalogue, which covers writers from Homer to late antiquity (though he omits the *Letter of Alexander to Aristotle about India*).[19] These are (I have added some expansions in square brackets):

1. The Natural World: mild climate; eternal spring; fruits grow without human effort [implying vegetarianism]; springs and rivers of wine, milk, honey, nectar and soup.

14. Hdt. 3.99–100.
15. See, for example, Ruffing 2011.
16. Ctes. F 45.16, 30, 43.
17. Idem F 45.6, 11.
18. Stoneman 2016 b, and see ch. 8 above.
19. Winiarczyk 2011, appendix 1, 231–59. A similar table is in Campbell 2003, 336–53.

2. Human Characteristics: longevity;[20] tall stature [also in Arr. *Anab.* 5.4.4, *Ind.* 17.1]; enduring good health; piety; gods dwell among men; justice. [Add non-violence to animals].
3. Human Way of Life: community with the gods; community of women [or other distinctive sexual behaviour, such as the Brahmans' mating season]; absence of slavery; simplicity of life [according to nature]; peacefulness.

Almost all of these can be found attributed to India by one or more writers, though eternal spring seems to be an exception, and piety is attributed only to the Brahmans. (However, Britain is noted for its 'mild climate' by Julius Caesar, which is a bit surprising.) The mingling of gods and mortals is also a feature of Indian descriptions,[21] but not attributed to India by Greeks. All the other items are attributed to Indians by one or other of the 'ethnographic' writers, so the fact that they reappear in 'utopian' writers' like Euhemerus and Iambulus indicates that these writers found them useful to develop their image of an ideal land; it does not mean that the 'ethnographers' were applying an already-formed notion of an ideal to the land they actually visited. That is, the 'ethnographers' are reporting what they actually observed – or were told.

And in that last little clause is an important point. For Indians also had a long-standing tradition about ideal lands, usually located far to the north like the land of the Hyperboreans in Greek mythology.[22] For India this land was called Uttarakuru, 'the land beyond the north', and the name was known to the classical writers as the land of the Attacorae or Ottorocorae.[23] Pliny locates them somewhere in Central Asia, towards the Seres (China), though that is incompatible with his assertion that they are adjacent to the sea; Ptolemy and Ammianus Marcellinus put them somewhere in the Himalayas (*Emodus mons*),[24] though they are probably conceived in India as being even further

20. This is attributed to a great many peoples by Pliny (*NH* 7.2.25–6), including the Locust-eaters of Agatharchides, but Photius says that these are notably short-lived, so there is some confusion in the transmission.

21. *Āpastamba Dharmasūtra* 2.16.1.

22. There was also a fountain of youth associated with the legendary river Sarasvati: *Jaiminiya Br.* 3.20–9: see Doniger 1999, 134.

23. Amometus *FGrH* 645 F 2 ap. Plin. *NH* 6.20.55: *sinus et gens hominum Attacorum, apricis ab omni noxio adflatu seclusa collibus, eadem qua Hyperborei degunt temperie.* Also Mela 3.5; Solinus 51.1.

24. Ptol. 6.16.5; Amm. 23.6.64.

away, probably in the Tien Shan mountains.[25] (Pliny put the Hyperboreans 'north of Scythia'.)[26] In the *Aitareya Brāhmaṇa* it is stated that 'in the lands of the Uttara Kurus and the Uttara Madras, beyond the Himavat, their kings are anointed for sovereignty'.[27] Many of the references to Uttarakuru in Sanskrit texts are collected by Willibald Kirfel, who draws together a characterisation of the land as lying north of Mount Meru, and inhabited by people who are tall, graceful, free of passions, and long-lived. In the eastern part lies the golden Jambu hill, and in the middle of that grows the jambu (rose-apple) tree, with its leaves of beryl and its flowers of gems.[28] 'Above the stretch of mortal ken, / On bless'd Cailasa's top, where every stem / glow'd with a vegetable gem'.[29] This must be set in the context of the Indian conception of the world as a lotus set in the centre of seven concentric seas and seven circular islands.[30] The lotus is called 'Jambudvipa' ('Rose-Apple Island'). There are four petals of the lotus, with Mount Meru in the centre – possibly to be identified with the 'Pamir Knot'.[31] The southern petal is Bharata (India) and the northern is Uttarakuru. If one were to penetrate to the north beyond the very last sea, the sea of pure water, one would reach the land of Lokāloka and then the Land of Darkness, just inside the shell of the egg that is the world. Mount Meru is the centre of Jambudvipa, and of the whole universe. As one advances through the outer rings, the people become more long-lived and the bliss of their lives increases. 'On the outer rim of the universe, people are all healthy, powerful, happy, long-lived and equal . . . "Pushkara is in fact a terrestrial paradise, where time yields happiness to all its inhabitants, who are exempt from sickness and decay"'.[32] And again, 'in Ketumala, Uttarakuru and Bhadrashva, people are said to have golden complexions, their skin as lustrous as seashells.

25. This is the location of the Garden of Eden in Satyajit Ray's story 'The Unicorn Expedition'. See also Bolton 1962, 99 for a Chinese location. Later recreations of Ptolemy's map, up to the eighteenth century, place Ottaracorra Mons in northern China. On the Hereford *Mappa Mundi*, the Hyperboreans are located on a promontory projecting into the ocean beyond the Rhipaean mountains, the cannibals and the Essedones, not far from one of the two locations of the Altars of Alexander; but the whole of north-east Asia is very constricted in this representation, so no geographical coordinate can be extracted from it.

26. Plin. *NH* 4.26.

27. *Aitareya Br.* 8.14.

28. Kirfel 1967, index s.v. Uttarakuru (p. 346); and for the description, 235.

29. William Jones, 'Hymn to Ganga'.

30. Eck 2012, 106–20, with 504 nn. 19–25.

31. Ibid., 119–20.

32. Ibid., 117, quoting *Vishnu Purāṇa* 2.4.

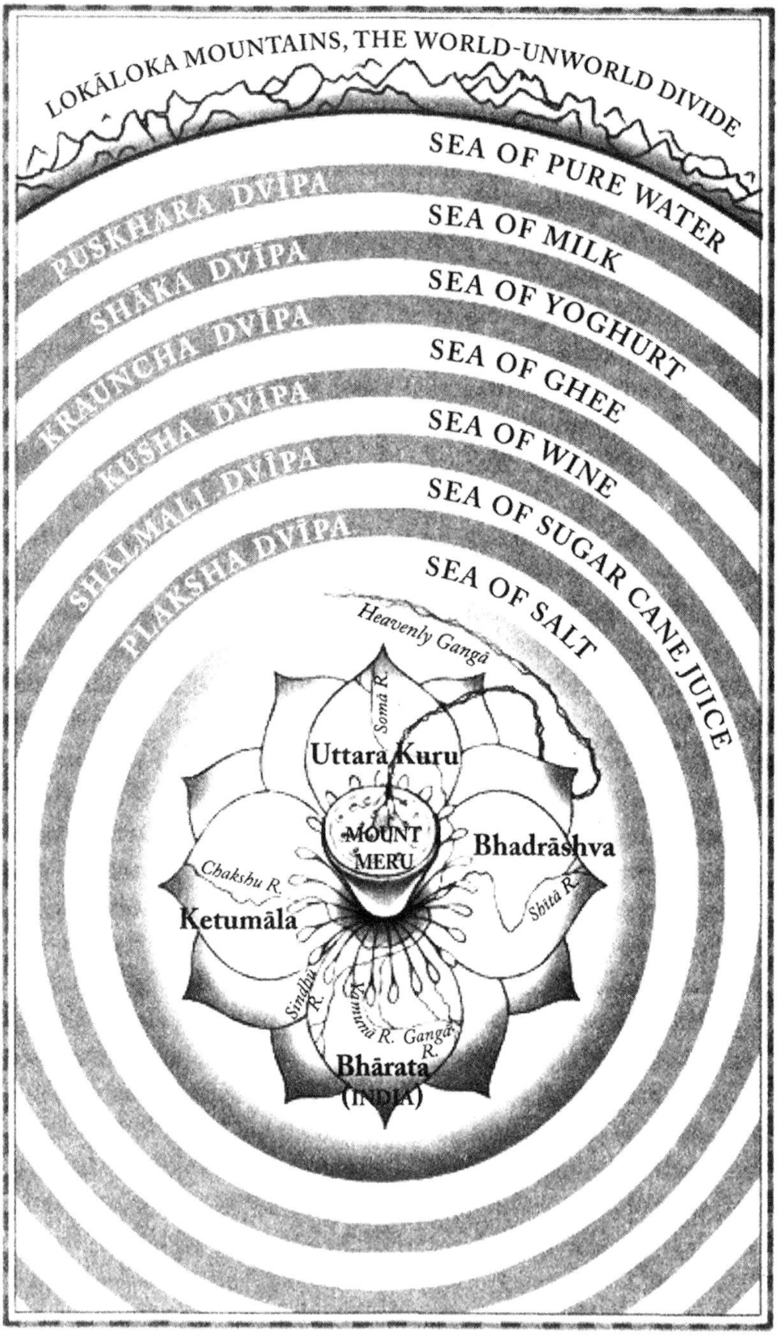

9.1 The mythological geography of Jambudvipa ('Rose-Apple Island') (based on Eck 2012, 106).

They live lifetimes of one thousand or ten thousand years.[33] They suffer no sickness or selfishness, no old age or decay. All are equal in strength and stature. Their lands are filled with rivers of cold, clear water and ponds of white lilies.... the wish-granting trees and the delicate waters seem to bestow their own perfection on the inhabitants of these lands'.[34] We also learn that 'whatever is placed is not taken back',[35] which sounds as if one can rely on the absolute honesty ('justice') of the inhabitants. In the *Rāmāyaṇa*, the *locus classicus* of the legend,[36] Uttarakuru is a land of bliss and comfort with every kind of fruit and flower, trees of gems and beautiful women, continuous music and laughter, and all the virtuous live there with three wives each—a Land of Cockaigne and definitely an example of soft, not hard, primitivism. (Some versions also have community of property, including of women, and even hierarchy and kingship.) Beyond it one may not go, for there is the land of eternal darkness.

The twelfth-century Sanskrit *Rājatarangiṇī* placed Uttarakuru in Ladakh, where it was ruled by beautiful Amazons.[37] This rather wayward version of the legend seems to be contaminated by the legend of the 'kingdom of women' which lay, according to Xuanzang, on an island south of Persia.[38] The story recurs in Marco Polo's account,[39] where there is one island of women and one of men; like the naked philosophers of the *Alexander Romance*, the men spend three months a year with the women, and male children go to live with the men while female ones remain with the women.[40] Three different legends are thus blended in Polo's version. The kingdom of women, like Paradise, was a place that Alexander was unable to enter, as the seventh-century writer Bāna observes – the only reference to Alexander in Sanskrit literature.[41]

Megasthenes was well aware of the Indian tradition about Uttarakuru (though not of the kingdom of women), for he reports that 'with regard to the Hyperboreans, who live a thousand years, they give the same account as

33. Cf. *Mbh.* 6.264: see Lassen ap. Schwanbeck 70.

34. Eck 2012, 127–8, quoting the *Markandeya Purāṇa*.

35. *Bhāgavata Purāṇa* 5.20.35.

36. *Rām.* 4 (*Kiṣkindhākāṇḍa*) 39 and 42, quoted in Bhattacharya 2000, 194–5. Also *Mbh.* 6.4.7.8–13.

37. Kalhana 1900, 4.173–5.

38. Beal 1884, 2.278–9. Noted by Albinia 2008, 262–3.

39. Polo 1903, ed. Yule and Cordier 3.31.

40. Ibid. 2.404.

41. Bāna, *Harṣacarīta* 7.

Simonides, Pindar and other writers of myths.'[42] Schwanbeck, followed by McCrindle, provides a long note on this passage, spelling out the connection berween Uttarakuru and the Hyperboreans.[43] Given that this sentence of Strabo follows his account of the monstrous races, it should be clear that we are in the land of legend and fable throughout.

The congruence of the legends of the Hyperboreans and Uttarakuru is a remarkable item of comparative mythology. Some time after Megasthenes (but perhaps very soon after), the poet Simmias of Rhodes, whose date is estimated as around 300 BCE, described the Hyperboreans living near the 'wondrous stream of the ever-flowing river Campasus'.[44] The river is unidentifiable, but its name recalls that of the city of Cambassu in northern China, east of the Lop desert; that is, in very much the same region as the Indian texts place Uttarakuru.[45] Bridgeman remarks that, in relocating the Hyperboreans from the north, where Herodotus placed them, to east of the Caspian Sea, Simmias may represent a version intermediate between Herodotus and Megasthenes It seems more probable, however, that he is using an Indian version as transmitted through Megasthenes. (Maybe Daimachus also mentioned the Hyperboreans? We do not know.) Simmias continues the itinerary of his narrator from the land of the Hyperboreans to that of the Dog-heads, which suggests that he is following some ethnological account that mentioned both.

Simmias may have been indebted to Hecataeus of Abdera's book *On the Hyperboreans*.[46] In this, their land was situated on an island called Elixoea, which Bridgeman surmises might be Britain: their sanctuary of Apollo would thus be Stonehenge.[47] The few fragments that survive do not suggest a utopian account of a real place, however, but rather a fantasy land inhabited by a blessed race.

42. Megasth. F 27 Schw = F 32 J.

43. McCrindle 1926, 77–9. Schwanbeck proposed that the Greeks borrowed the legend from India, which is unlikely.

44. Simmias F 1 in Powell, *Collectanea Alexandrina* 109. Bridgeman 2005, 77. Pliny (*NH* 6.51) refers to a river Caspasus somewhere in Scythia, but this is no reason for changing the text of Simmias.

45. The name somewhat resembles that of the river Carambyca, beyond which is the island of the Hyperboreans, according to Hecataeus of Abdera (*FGrH* 264 F 11): Bridgeman 2005, 131. The latter, following Jacoby, considers that this river, and the Carambycae people, were located somewhere around Jutland. When the same road leads both to China and to Denmark, one must recognise that the game of geographical identifications is fraught with pitfalls.

46. Diod. Sic. 2.47–8.

47. Bridgeman 2005, 133–7.

Every 'ideal' trait that is attributed by the Greeks to Indians can thus be found in Indian texts. It is worth repeating here that, although the Purāṇas in their written form date from the first three centuries CE, there is no doubt that they are a codification of Brahmanic oral traditions that are many centuries older.

India also believed in a past Golden Age, which is evoked in Bhiṣma's instructions on the duties of kings in the *Mahābhārata*.[48] Today represents a decline from that paradisaic past, and the Kaliyuga ('Age of Kali') in which we live reminds one in some ways of Hesiod's Age of Iron.

The Greek writers arriving in India found many things that impressed them. Onesicritus' account of the kingdom of Musicanus does seem to contain important 'utopian' traits.[49] In addition to its banyan trees, he noted 'things some of which are reported as common also to other Indians' as Strabo says: long life, health and simple diet; public communal eating, no use of gold or silver, no slavery, no scientific study except medicine, and no judicial procedures except for murder and assault, since the observance of contract is something for which a man must look out for himself. The location of the kingdom of Musicanus is uncertain, but from Onesicritus' coordinates it seems to be on the lower Indus.[50] He is therefore describing a real society, not that of Uttarakuru/Hyperborea. Not only does some of his description sound idealising, but parts of it may be actually mistaken, since there was slavery in ancient India – though not necessarily in this area.[51] The Spartan-type dining arrangements sound like a Greek invention, but Arora suggests that the reference is to Yajurvedic communal dining.[52] Onesicritus may have been prone to interpret Indian conditions in light of his own predisposition to Cynic philosophy,[53] but he does not invent wholesale. Lionel Pearson calls it 'a very commonplace type of ideal state, showing the anti-democratic prejudices that are so familiar in Athenian authors of the fifth and fourth centuries'.[54] There is some truth in this, but the fact is that 'ideal states' had not really become

48. *Mbh.* 12.59.

49. Ff 22 and 24, Str. 15.1.21 and 34. Brown 1949, 59–66; Arora 2005, 90–5.

50. Arora 2005, 91 locates it in Upper Sind and speculates that Musicanus may represent Skt. 'Muṣika', perhaps to be identified with modern Moghshi.

51. Ibid., 94.

52. Ibid., 93. It could also perhaps be a description of a tribal *ghotul* as described by Elwin 1947: see previous chapter.

53. Brown 1949, 60; Stoneman 1995.

54. Pearson 1960, 103. Arora 2005, 99–100 follows this interpretation.

current when Onesicritus was writing. Plato's ideal state in the *Republic* has little in common with the life of ease and gentleness that Onesicritus describes, and the reign of Cronus in the *Statesman* remains in the realm of myth. Onesicritus is the beginning of a utopian tradition, and later writers built on his attitude.

Onesicritus also described the kingdom of Cathaea, where kings were elected for their beauty, marriages were made for love, babies were scrutinised to decide whether they should live or die, and people dyed their beards in bright colours. This seems to be located somewhere in the Punjab, and is perhaps to be identified with the Katthis of Kathiawar.[55]

Whether Megasthenes followed Onesicritus' utopian lead is however a big question. Though he has been accused of utopianism, I hope the evidence I have assembled so far shows that this is inappropriate. Climate, fertility and abundance of precious metals are not inventions, the honourable behaviour of Indians is a reality, the hierarchical social structure (if that should even be regarded as utopian) is also a reality. Megasthenes seems to have been mistaken about the absence of slavery, perhaps adopting this unthinkingly from Onesicritus. There are enough dark shadows in the picture to assure us that this is a realistic portrait, not a fantasy one. As Kosmin elegantly puts it, 'the sense of reality and recognisability in Megasthenes' India is achieved – what an indictment! – through war, violence, corruption, and law'.[56]

However, Onesicritus really had started something. In the generations after Megasthenes, several Greek writers devised utopian societies which they located in India or, more commonly, just beyond India on the island of Taprobane (Sri Lanka: the name seems to correspond to Sanskrit 'Tamrapani', but has also been analysed as 'Dvipa Ravana', the island of Ravana).[57] Chronologically, the first of these utopias is that of the fourth-century historian Theopompus (ca. 378/7–after 320 BCE), who died before Megasthenes' book was written and who may have been aiming to set up a counter-example to Plato's Atlantis.[58] Theopompus called his happy land Meropis:[59] it was described by the satyr Silenus to the legendary Phrygian king Midas, and it appeared in the digression on 'Marvels' in book 8 of the *Philippica*. (The encounter is familiar from Vergil's sixth Eclogue.) Meropis was located on the island that surrounds

55. Karttunen 1997, 31 n. 60. See ch. 2 above, n. 121.

56. Kosmin 2014, 51.

57. Arora 2005, 42.

58. Ael. *VH* 3.17 = *FGrH* 115 F 75c.

59. *FGrH* 115 F 75d.

the encircling Ocean, and in it were located two large cities, called 'Warlike' and 'Pious'. The inhabitants of the latter obtain the fruits of the earth without labour, live healthy and disease-free lives and die happy. They are so just that the gods regularly visit them. The inhabitants of Warlike have, as you would expect, all the opposite characteristics; when they tried to invade our world, they were so disgusted at the simplicity of the Hyperboreans that they forbore to advance further.

Theopompus' Happy Land is not a 'realistic' utopia or political programme like Plato's Atlantis, for it contains supernatural elements. It does however resemble the Land of Cronus in the *Statesman*,[60] in which the period of bliss when the earth brings forth its fruits without labour gives place to a harder time: the world goes into reverse. Michael Flower regards Theopompus's account as no more than an 'entertainment'.[61] Several of the traits of a Golden Age type of existence are already present in this fantasy.

Epicurus (341–270 BCE) may also have believed that, in an Epicurean world, a new Golden Age would arrive, if Diogenes of Oenoanda is evidence for the master's teaching.[62]

Onesicritus must have been startled to find such features as long life and a concern for justice really present in the kingdom of Musicanus. The fertility of India was well known, though no one could really imagine that no labour was required to get the soil to give of its best.

Euhemerus was writing a little later, while in the service of Cassander (r. 311–298 BCE) but was probably active until 280 BCE. Paul Kosmin suggests (after Droysen) that Seleucus had sent Euhemerus to Candragupta on a mission similar to Megasthenes', and that his – very different – book was one of the results.[63] His account of a fictional voyage to a group of islands in the Indian Ocean, of which the chief was Panchaea, is preserved in Diodorus.[64] The island turns out to be a paradise, watered by the Fountain of the Sun, and in its centre a column of gold records the deeds of Uranus, Cronus and Zeus. In large part this place is a *locus amoenus*, full of marvellous trees and fruits – vines are mentioned several times – but also of fierce wild animals. It furthermore has rich resources of precious metals. The people are not peaceable, but warlike, and make use of chariots in warfare. Their society is divided into

60. Pl. *Plt.* 268d–275b.

61. Flower 1994, appendix 1, 214–17.

62. Diog.Oen. F 56.

63. Kosmin 2014, 286 n. 148.

64. Diod. 5.41–6, 6.1.

three *merē* (the Loeb translator gives 'castes'): priests (including artisans), farmers and soldiers; in addition there are the herdsmen. (This seems to make four, but Diodorus says three.) There is no private property, since everything has to be brought to the priests, who enjoy every luxury, including clothing of wool and of linen, interwoven with gold. The soldiers are kept busy keeping down the lawless robber bands that infest the country. This social structure is said to have been laid down by the gods who came originally from Crete.

Euhemerus's name is best remembered for his proposition that all stories of the gods are faded memories of ancient human benefactors; this, combined with the idealisation of the Cretan polity, seems to determine the outlines of this society. Panchaea may be a utopia, but it is by no means a land of bliss. Agriculture and warfare are both necessities, the society is strictly controlled and hierarchical in a rather Platonic way, and there is nothing about health, longevity and gentleness. Nevertheless, some details seem to be borrowed from descriptions of India, notably the 'caste' system, which here can hardly be seen as conducing to the shared happiness of all, since the priests are on top. If this is a disguised version of India, it is not a Golden Land (to coin a phrase on the analogy of the Golden Age).

The next writer of a utopia is Iambulus, who cannot be dated with certainty but probably belongs to the third century BCE. His account of his voyage to the Island of the Sun is preserved in Diodorus.[65] The coordinates of this island look very like Taprobane.[66] Iambulus (or his fictional narrator) was travelling in the spice lands when he and his party were taken captive by Ethiopian robbers, who brought them to this island. Here they were welcomed by the natives, who are all over six feet tall and very bendy, with no body hair, ears that open and close, and double tongues that enable them to carry on two conversations at once, as well as imitate birdsong. The climate is temperate, the days are all equal to the nights and there is no shadow at midday, and fruits ripen throughout the year. (This would fit a location on the equator.) The inhabitants live in clan groups and gather food in abundance, apparently without the need for cultivation. They catch fish and snakes, and cook their meat. But they are temperate in their consumption. Children are held in com-

65. Diod. 2.55–60.

66. Schwarz 1975, 183–7 and Schwarz 1982–83; Weerakkody 1997, 173 is dubious. The fact that Udaipur is referred to in Kipling's *Letters of Marque* as a 'City of the Sun' seems to be a coincidence; a cult of Surya (the Sun) is not evidenced for the third century BCE.

mon. They live long and healthy lives, but at the age of 150 are sent off to die, and are then buried by the seashore. Iambulus spent seven years there before being expelled for evil practices (unspecified) and returning home via India, on the shore of which they were shipwrecked. Iambulus' companion died, and the hero went on alone until he reached the court of the king at Palibothra, where he was looked after and given a safe-conduct pass to return via Persia to Greece.

This entertaining story clearly owes a good deal to the data provided by the writers on India, as well as something to discussions of social theory in the Hellenistic age. But it comes across mainly as a good adventure story. It has been thought that it may have influenced Aristonicus, who tried to set up a utopian state in the late second century BCE. Utopian ideas were also current in the circle of Cassander of Macedon (d. 297 BCE), since his younger brother Alexarchus tried to set up a utopian community on the Athos peninsula: he called it Ouranoupolis ('City of Heaven') and styled himself King Sun.[67]

These three authors were clearly doing something very different from Onesicritus and Megasthenes. The latter two may have found features in India that reminded them of descriptions of legendary lands more luxurious than Greece, but they were not presenting India as a whole as a Golden Land. Conversely, the three 'utopian' writers discussed used a kind of loosely-imagined India as the setting for their various fantasies, and (in Theopompus' case, perhaps) 'programmes'. In some later writers, India becomes a simple paradise. Dio Chrysostom describes a land running with rivers of milk and honey, where fruits grow spontaneously, and the people live a life of laughter and no labour; they are beautiful, they enjoy warm baths and a temperate climate, and live for four hundred years. They are wealthy with the gold brought by the gold-mining ants, and yet the Brahmans leave all this behind for a life of asceticism.[68]

The situation is somewhat different with the descriptions of ideal communities within the wider setting of India and elsewhere. Here again the trail begins with Onesicritus and his encounter with the naked philosophers of Taxila. This, as I have tried to show elsewhere,[69] is the beginning of a long development that includes the account of the same philosophers (sometimes called Brahmans) in the *Alexander Romance*, in the Geneva papyrus, in the

67. Ferguson 1975, 108–9 (Alexarchus) and 125–7 (Aristonicus).

68. D.Chr. *Or.* 35.18–24.

69. Stoneman 1995; 2012; 2015; 2008, 91–106.

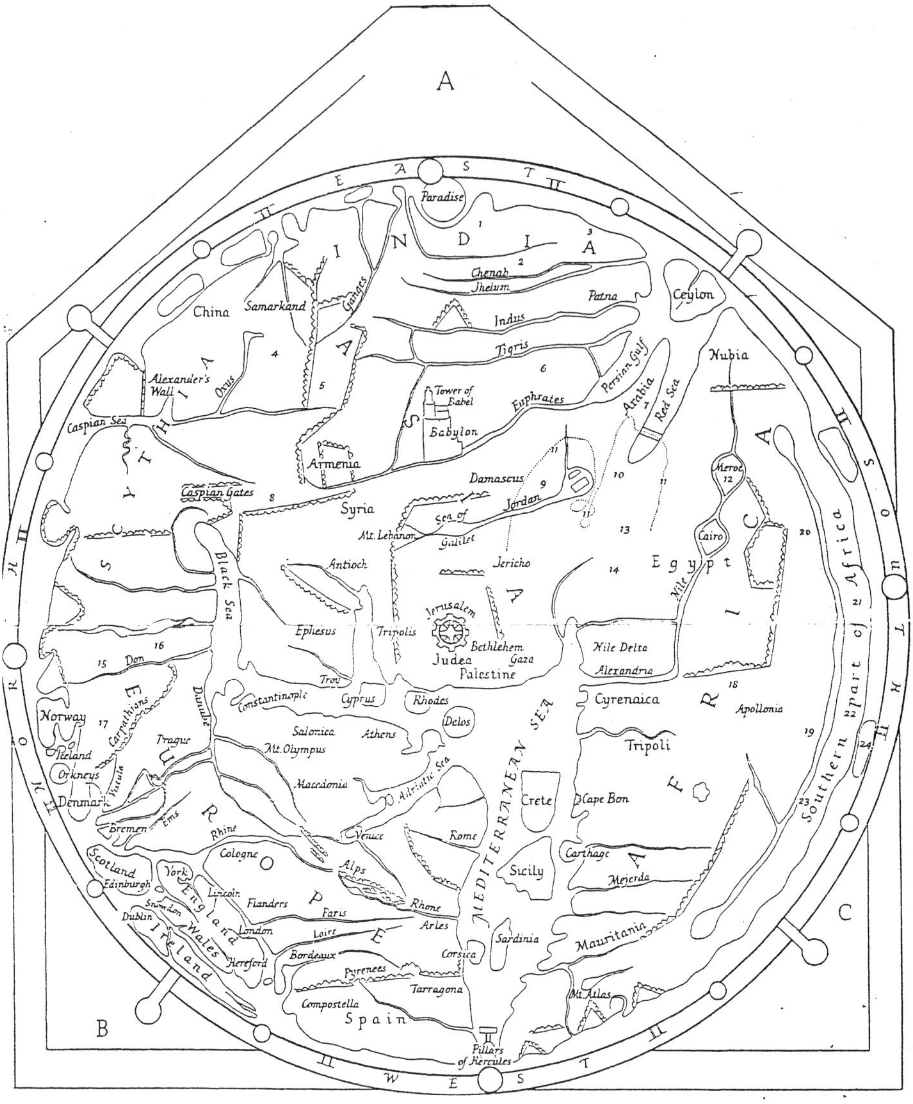

9.2 The Hereford *Mappa Mundi* (ca. 1300) is a symbolic depiction of the world with Jerusalem at the centre and the Garden of Eden in the east (at the top); its content is heavily dependent on the geography of the Alexander legends.

description of the Therapeutae in Philo's *De vita contemplativa,* and in the life of the 'Sons of the Blessed' in *The History of the Rechabites* which was later rewritten in Christian form as 'the Narrative of Zosimus'. The way that this story turns into a Christian parable is very notable, and it had a significant influence on the development of the Christian idea of the earthly paradise. It appears in several works of late antiquity, including the *Expositio totius mundi et gentium* (359 CE), the *Itinerary from Eden, the Paradise* (probably fourth or fifth century), and the *De Bragmanibus* of Palladius, bishop of Helenopolis.[70] Isidore of Seville's brief description of Paradise also uses the motifs of fruitful abundance, temperate climate and beautiful rivers borrowed from the idea of the Golden Age, though of course his paradise has no inhabitants, since the human race is excluded from it by an angel with a flaming sword.[71] I suggested further that these tales were influential upon the development of Christian monasticism, but this is not the place to revisit that subject.[72] The topic of the naked philosophers/Brahmans, and of philosophical contacts of Greece and India in general, is large enough to require a separate chapter.

In conclusion, the information about India that percolated back to the Greek world was very influential in the construction of several later utopias, but that does not mean that those who wrote books about India, notably Onesicritus and Megasthenes, were importing pre-existing ideas of utopia into the societies they observed. First, such ideas – in distinction to that of the Golden Age, which was common to both cultures – had scarcely yet evolved; and second, close examination suggests that these writers – and Nearchus – did their best to describe what they actually saw, even when they had to make use of Greek categories, like 'slavery', that did not really fit the Indian case.

70. This last work was also inserted into the oldest MS of the *Alexander Romance,* namely A, the unique witness of the alpha-recension.

71. Isid. *Etym.* 14.3.2–4. The next section describes India and Taprobane.

72. Stoneman 2015.

10

Megasthenes on the Natural World

The Elephant

India doth yield
So many elephants with snake like hands,
Their thousands like an ivory rampart stands
To bar the entrance of those wealthy lands.
Such multitudes of wild beasts are bred there,
Whereof we see but few examples here.

—LUCRETIUS, *DE RERUM NATURA* 2.536–40,
TR. LUCY HUTCHINSON

Megasthenes' account of the elephant is reproduced at length by both Strabo and Arrian:[1] most of it concerns the method of hunting, but at the end there is also some information about the breeding cycle, and the inaccurate information that elephants may live two or even three hundred years.[2] (The normal lifespan of an elephant is about sixty years.) Both say that the gestation period is sixteen to eighteen months, though Strabo adds that Onesicritus stated that females remained pregnant for ten years. Strabo also criticises Megasthenes implicitly for stating that horses and elephants could be owned by kings alone, since he knows that Nearchus, whom he cites, had said that an

1. Str. 15.1.42–3; Arr. *Ind.* 13–14.

2. Besides Romm 1989 and Bigwood 1993a, discussed in ch. 2 above, major discussions of elephants in the Greek period include Scullard 1974, 37–52 and 58–9, who notes that Megasthenes is good on elephants, Lane Fox 1973, 337–8; Trautmann 1982 and 2015; Arora 2005, 50ff. There are also interesting accounts in Abu'l Fazl and in Marco Polo, as well as a very large literature on modern elephant lore, including the works of 'Elephant Bill' (J.H. Williams) and the highly enjoyable Mark Shand.

elephant would be a possession of which anyone would be proud, and that 'a woman is highly honoured if she receives an elephant as a gift from a lover'. Strabo ignores the fact that Nearchus is writing about the Punjab in the 320s, where many of the states were republics, while Megasthenes is describing a kingdom in Magadha, a thousand miles (1,600 km) to the east and twenty or more years later.[3] The hyper-critical attitude of Strabo has done much to damage later views of Megasthenes' work. Several references in the Upaniṣads deploy elephants as one of many forms of wealth, not exclusive to kings.[4]

Megasthenes had various predecessors in writing about the elephant, who have been discussed in chapter 4: Scylax, Ctesias, Onesicritus and Nearchus. By the time he wrote, Aristotle had probably composed his passages on the elephant. In the years and centuries following, elephants became quite well known to the Greco-Roman world, as a result of the employment of elephants in warfare by the Hellenistic kings. This began when Candragupta made Seleucus a present of five hundred elephants as part of the 'Treaty of the Indus'. As we have seen, in Ptolemy's Grand Procession the elephant was the representative animal for India, and Lucretius regarded India as being, in effect, protected by an 'ivory wall' consisting of serried ranks of elephants.[5] Pliny knew quite a lot about elephants,[6] some of which came from a book on the subject by King Juba of Mauretania;[7] they had first been seen in Italy in 280 BCE and in Rome five years later. Besides fighting the ones brought by Hannibal, Romans had fought with them in the arena and had also set them to performing tricks like modern circus elephants. Plutarch describes some of the tricks he had seen them perform, and even Arrian inserts into his paraphrase of Megasthenes a few remarks about elephants he had seen dancing and playing the cymbals.[8]

The importance of the elephant is not explicitly stated in the passage of Megasthenes, which concentrates on the method of capture. It is of course implicit in this description that they were important to the kings: in fact their

3. Trautmann 1982; 2015, 131.

4. *Cāndogya Up.* 7.24.2 lists elephants among several forms of wealth, along with wives, gold and slaves. *Kaṭha Up.* 1.23 refers to a man with 'plenty of livestock and elephants'.

5. Lucr. *De rer. nat.* 2.536–40. Cf. Singh 1965, 82: elephants can be drawn up in blocks or in lines for battle.

6. Plin. *NH* 8.1–12.

7. *FGrH* 275 F 47.

8. Plu. *De sollertia animalium* 17.972b; Arr. *Ind.* 14.5–6.

10.1 A war-elephant, as depicted in Samuel Pitiscus' edition of Q. Curtius Rufus' *Historiae Alexandri magni* (Utrecht, 1693).

10.2 An elephant (ridden bareback) from the eastern gateway of the stupa at Sanchi (third–second century BCE).

prominence in India coincides with the rise of kingship.[9] Elephants do not appear in the *Ṛg Veda,* in which the gods universally ride on chariots. Nor do they become royal beasts as such until relatively late: neither the *Arthaśāstra* nor the *Mahābhārata* regard them as such, but in the *Rāmāyaṇa* they are the conveyance of kings.[10] Rather, elephants are an essential component of the royal army, the *caturaṅga.*[11] The word is the origin of 'chess' and the chessboard represents the four (*catur*) components of the Indian royal army: the elephants (rooks or castles), cavalry (knights), chariots ('bishops') and infantry (the pawns). Alexander's inquiries about the Nanda forces produced the information that the Nanda king had twenty thousand horse, two hundred thousand foot, two thousand chariots and three or four thousand elephants.[12] Where did all these elephants come from?

9. Trautmann 2015, 68 and 101. This book is an indispensable discussion of the topics of this paragraph.

10. Ibid., 128.

11. Singh 1965, esp. ch. 4, 72–84.

12. Curt. 9.2; Diod. 17.93. Plutarch has bigger numbers, and Pliny gives the Mauryas an incredible nine thousand elephants.

The terrain in which elephants can thrive is almost the inverse of that suitable for horses: their habitat is jungle, which can be anything from dense forest to open scrub with trees. Nowadays this kind of habitat is found in the more easterly parts of India, but in Alexander's time even the Punjab was thickly forested. The *Mahābhārata* describes the forests around Delhi (Indraprastha), and even Abu'l Fazl, in the reign of the Mughal emperor Akbar, speaks of rhinos, tigers and elephants roaming in this region. One reason that this habitat is preferred is food supply: elephants eat for eighteen hours a day to consume the two hundred kilos of green stuff needed to keep them going.[13] Keeping an elephant requires the employment of three or more leaf-cutters to provide them with fodder,[14] to which can be added a sack or two of rice daily.

Elephants take a long time to grow to maturity. Strabo's information is that the mothers nurse their young for six years. This is an exaggeration, but elephants do take sixteen years to reach adulthood. For this reason it is uneconomic to breed them – they need to be fed at considerable expense for sixteen unproductive years – and the only way to acquire a herd is by capture of wild ones. This is what Megasthenes describes. A number of Sanskrit treatises, of as usual uncertain date, describe the capture and care of elephants.[15] Several of these are attributed to the sage Palakapya, who is sometimes placed in the sixth century BCE. He was sent by the gods, according to the legend, to be born of a mother who had previously been cursed and had become an elephant, but had then been restored to human form; once adult, he in turn ministered to the elephant species, who had once been able to fly, until one day several of them perched on a branch and caused it to break and fall on the head of a hermit, who promptly cursed them to become earthbound. (Like the hoopoe tale, below, this is a candidate for the first 'Just So Story'.) The earthbound beasts became prey to sickness and disease until Palakapya came to restore them to health.

Another elephant manual, by Nīlakaṇṭha,[16] lists five methods of catching elephants: by trap pen, by enticement with cows, by pursuit, by assault and by pits – the last two being undesirable as likely to destroy the elephants. (The

13. Bosworth 2002, 108 is a vivid account of elephants' food requirements. There are amusing details also in Shand 1991. See too Williams 1950.

14. Cf. *KA* 2.32.16.

15. Trautmann 2015, 145–9. Elephants are divided into four kinds, with differing physical characteristics, by the treatises and also by Varāhamihira: see Shastri 1996, 295.

16. Nīlakaṇṭha 1931.

pit, covered by twigs, is not only the method favoured by Winnie-the-Pooh in the construction of his heffalump trap, but that described by the Mauretanian king Juba, as transmitted by Plutarch.)[17] The pen should be about one and a half miles (2.4 km) across, fenced around with stout trees and a ditch on the outside; into this pen a lane is constructed from bamboos.

> Raising aloft and fastening a great door-panel, (sharp-)edged, at the entrance inside the trap pen, making it very stout with wooden pillars on this side and on that, he shall deposit sugar cane, etc, there, and then, rounding up the elephants with drums etc, he shall drive the frightened animals in there (by the bamboo pathway leading to the gate), and then quickly cut the cords holding the top of the bolt (so that it shall drop and fasten the door).[18]

The huntsmen then wait two or three days until the elephants are weakened before going in with fetters and goads to bind them. Nīlakaṇṭha then goes on to describe how to catch elephants by 'cow-seduction', anointing the cows with fragrances including aloes and perhaps cardamom, as well as applying honey and other fragrances mixed with cows' urine to the cows' hindquarters. 'Likewise with seeds produced by the wood-apple tree,[19] kukkuṭāṇḍaka (kind of rice), and *Pongamia glabra*,[20] and with the fruit of *Grewia elastica*,[21] mixed together, this ointment (applied to cows)[22] will bring noble elephants into subjection.'

Megasthenes describes a combination of these two methods in terms very close to those of Nīlakaṇṭha. A deep ditch is dug, about four or five stades – something under two miles (3.2 km) – in circumference, with a narrow bridge leading into the enclosure. The hunters position three or four tame females inside the enclosure and then lie in wait in huts. When the wild elephants arrive by night, the men close the entrance on them and then lead in tame males to fight the wild ones until they are exhausted. The men then bind the

17. Plu. *De sollertia animalium* 17.972b. Juba also says that elephants pray to the sunrise, while Plutarch also mentions one at Alexandria which was a rival in love to Aristophanes the grammarian; it used to bring the beloved flower-seller fruit, and caress her breasts, inside her garments, with his trunk.

18. Nīlakaṇṭha 1931, 88.

19. The name is applied to several different species of wild fruit trees.

20. Sometimes known as Indian beech, *pungai* or *karanja*.

21. A member of the mallow family.

22. One must be grateful that he specified that.

wild elephants' feet together and tie them to the tame ones with leather thongs inserted through incisions in the wild ones' necks. They reject the very old and young and lead the rest to the stables, where these are tied and left to starve until they are subdued, after which they are fed on grass and sugar cane (a treat). After this they are trained by music and drums to obey commands.

Did Megasthenes observe all this? It seems more likely that he was given a detailed account by a native informant, on which he took notes, with the result that his own account bears an uncanny similarity to that in the Sanskrit handbook (though he, or perhaps Strabo and Arrian alike, omits the details of the scent applied to the female elephants' posteriors). Aelian gives more details of the music that elephants like: that of the four-stringed *skindapsos*.[23] This might very well be from Megasthenes, as might the next of Schwanbeck's fragments, on the method of treating wounds received by elephants in battle: warm water and butter for the wound, plus a pork steak laid over the top; cows' milk for ophthalmia, and red wine for other ailments.[24] Schwanbeck's fragment 52 may also be from Megasthenes, since the passages both preceding it and following it are explicitly so: it expatiates on elephants' love of wine and of perfumes and scented flowers; while fragment 53 is a romantic but not implausible story of the mutual love between a trainer and an elephant calf: when the king attempted to seize the elephant for himself, and bring back the man for punishment, the elephant protected his friend and carried him off to safety.[25] The lack of specifics in this story makes one hesitate to attribute it to Megasthenes, unless his book was more expansive than the surviving fragments indicate. Where then did Aelian get it? Ctesias? Or Cleitarchus (the joker in the pack when a source is needed)? The moral seems to be that only kings ought to have elephants, so was it in Nearchus when he wrote about private ownership of elephants? The question seems unanswerable.

Elephants today are labouring animals, excelling in such tasks as tree-felling and timber-transport;[26] but they do not seem to have been so used in antiquity, where they are always described as part of a royal army. Only a king's treasury had the resources to maintain armies of elephants. They were apparently ridden bareback, as the 'Porus medallion' of Alexander and the reliefs at Sanchi indicate, and howdahs were only introduced in the Hellenis-

23. Ael. *NA* 12.44 = Megasth. F 37b Schw, excluded by Jacoby.
24. Ibid. 13.7 = Megasth. F 38 Schw, also excluded by Jacoby.
25. F 52 Schw = Ael. *NH* 12.8; F 53 Schw = Ael. *NH* 3.46; both excluded by Jacoby.
26. Numerous fine illustrations in Williams 1950.

tic period, perhaps by King Pyrrhus around 300–280 BCE.[27] As weapons of war they could be very effective: the twelfth-century *Hariharacaturaṅga* states that one fully-armoured elephant can destroy 160 horses.[28] They could naturally strike terror into an opposing army by their sheer size, and horses would be especially alarmed.[29] However, they also had disadvantages. Elephants are easily panicked,[30] though not necessarily by the inventive trick that Alexander is said in the *Romance* to have devised, namely creating red-hot statues of soldiers to burn the elephants' trunks.[31] Timur the Lame, in 1398, panicked an opposing army of elephants by driving at them camels and buffaloes with burning grass tied to their tails, a trick he seems unlikely to have learned from the *Romance*, where Alexander creates the impression of a vast army advancing at night by tying torches to the tails of goats. (According to Ctesias, the stratagem went back to the legendary queen Semiramis.)[32]

Alexander had acquired elephants before he reached the Hydaspes, but he did not use them in battle, now or at any time; his men had learned how to respond to enemy elephants, however, and thus his army was able to outmanoeuvre the beasts by savage methods such as hamstringing and cutting off their trunks.

Elephants could always be something of a liability, but they became very fashionable in the Hellenistic world, partly as a result of Candragupta's princely gift of five hundred elephants to Seleucus to mark their treaty.[33] Tarn thought that the number was impossible, describing it as Megasthenes' 'talent for learned fantasy exquisitely wrought'. He argued that Megasthenes had got the figure from a Buddhist informant, and that Buddhists always deal in large round numbers. As Trautmann rightly observes, Megasthenes is more likely to have got the figure from the memorandum of agreement between the two kings, between whom he was the intermediary; probably he wrote it down himself in whatever document was taken back to Babylon.[34] It is not impossible that Candragupta had as many as two thousand elephants, if Porus in

27. Trautmann 2015, 230–1. In twentieth century Cooch Behar, the seats of the howdahs could be lifted up to expose a secret supply of chocolate biscuits: Devi 1976, 65.

28. *Hariharacaturaṅga* 1.28.

29. Arr. *Anab.* 5.10.2.

30. Trautmann 1982, 272.

31. *AR* 3.3.

32. Ctes. F 1b.16.8–10 = Diod. 2.16.8–10; Trautmann 2015, 222.

33. Str. 15.2.9; Grainger 1990, 109–11. See ch. 5 above.

34. Tarn 1940b; Trautmann 1982, 269; 2015, 233–4.

his little kingdom had two hundred, and now that his wars were reaching an end the Maurya king may have been glad to reduce the size of his herd and save considerable expense.[35] The five hundred elephants may have been a tongue-in-cheek gift, a white elephant indeed. Be that as it may, the elephants set a fashion among Hellenistic kings, and the elephant scalp became part of the iconography of Alexander,[36] and also of the Indo-Greek king Demetrius.[37] But that is another story.

Other Beasts

> As you wake from one India into another,
> The dream-animals shimmer and swim into new shapes.
> Yet they are real. God made them. They must mean something.
>
> —MATTHEW FRANCIS, *MANDEVILLE* (2008), 35

Megasthenes has much less to say about other beasts of India. Strabo speaks of the size and ferocity of tigers.[38] (Nearchus had only seen their skins,[39] as he had also seen those of the gold-digging ants, which resembled those of leopards: see below.) He describes the monkeys whose faces are black and tails a yard (1 m) long, as large as large dogs: that is, the black-faced langurs common further south and east in India,[40] while the north-west (and, in modern times, the region of Delhi and Agra) is characterised by the smaller, less aggressive pink-faced rhesus macaque. He does not go into the catching of monkeys, which Cleitarchus dilated upon.[41] He writes of flying serpents with wings like bats (just possibly flying foxes: our driver in Delhi pointed out these 'bat-birds', as he called them, roosting in the arjun trees in Janpath),[42]

35. Grainger 1990, 110.

36. The unique gold medallion of Alexander in an elephant-scalp from Afghanistan has occasioned much debate, since the iconography is otherwise first known from Ptolemaic Egypt. Art historians are inclined to see it as genuine, because of its beauty and insight into character ('the sneer of cold command'), while numismatists are sceptical. See Bopearachchi and Flandrin 2005; a forgery: Callatay 2013.

37. Tarn 1951, 131.

38. Str. 15.1.37 = F 12 Schw.

39. Nearch. F 7.

40. Cf. F 13 = Ael. *NA* 17.39, where the tails have grown to five cubits and the colours of face and body are reversed.

41. *FGrH* 137 F 19.

42. 12, also F 14; Ael. *NA* 16.41.

and huge winged scorpions, as well as large savage dogs. He also mentions enormous snakes, probably boa constrictors, though a connection has also been made with the mythical Nagas of the north-west.[43]

Our view of Megasthenes' account of Indian fauna must depend on what we make of Aelian's *De natura animalium* 16.2–22. Some of this is certainly from Megasthenes, but how much of it? Schwanbeck included it as a 'doubtful' fragment of Megasthenes, for reasons given in his commentary,[44] while Jacoby excluded it. It begins with accounts of several birds. First comes the parrot, of which he distinguishes three species: Nearchus mentioned only one and Ctesias describes a parrot with a red face and a black beard, that is 'dark blue as far as the neck ... like cinnabar', presumably the macaw.[45] Then pigeons and peacocks are mentioned, and what is obviously the guinea-fowl; the mynah bird, which Ctesias calls *kerkion,* the unidentifiable *kelas,* and the hoopoe, about which Aelian tells a long and fascinating story (see below). Then come the pangolin, sea-snakes and wild horses and asses.

There follows an account of monkeys, with red faces and tips to their tails, about the size of Hyrcanian dogs. This is treated by Schwanbeck as F 13b of Megasthenes because it discusses monkeys, as does F 13a, which is also from Aelian,[46] but in which Megasthenes is mentioned by name. It should be noted, however, that the latter fragment describes black-faced langurs whilst the former describes red-faced macaques. In both cases the animals are said to live in the country of the Prasii, and the red-faced monkeys are especially common in Latage, an unidentified place. Does this mean that the two fragments come from different authors, familiar with different parts of the country? Or did Megasthenes describe both kinds? If so, why has Aelian excerpted this discussion in two different places in his book?

The giant horse follows, which is hunted for its beautiful tail. What can this be? Aelian goes on to describe whales, various kinds of fish, and turtles from the sea surrounding Taprobane. He dilates upon the monsters of the deep surrounding Taprobane, which begin to sound rather implausible: fish with heads like lions and rams, and others resembling women but with prickles instead of hair, as well as amphibious creatures that eat dates. After all this, the sea-hare which is as deadly poisonous as the basilisk sounds almost

43. Arora 2005, 55; Karttunen 1997, 223.

44. Translated at McCrindle 1926, 164 n.

45. Nearch. F 9; Ctes. F 49.7. See Bigwood 1993b.

46. Ael. *NA* 17.139.

normal. Whales are the subject of Nearchus' fragments 1.30–31, which might make one think that he is Aelian's source here, since Megasthenes does not seem to have gone anywhere near a coastline. But the hard-headed Nearchus is not likely to have come up with the preceding aquatic creatures.

The next creature, the *kartazon*, was described by Megasthenes, because Strabo mentions him by name; the much longer description in Aelian is therefore likely to be also from Megasthenes.[47] (I discuss this creature more fully below in the section on the unicorn.) Aelian moves on to 'satyrs', which again sound like an elaboration of the stone-rolling monkeys of Megasthenes' fragment 15.

At the end of Aelian's chapter come the people called the Skiratai, a snub-nosed people who live beyond India, among whom live giant serpents. The Skiratai were described by Megasthenes, and the giant serpents that eat cattle have already made their appearance.[48]

All in all, there is a lot in this chapter of Aelian's, as Schwanbeck noted, that could well have, or probably did, come from Megasthenes. Did all of it? What was Aelian's method in his book? Did he, as has been said of Diodorus, stick to one source for long stretches at a time before switching to another one? Or did he pick bits from different books and interweave them? Recently Muntz has argued for a more discriminating procedure in Diodorus, taking apart his account of India and showing that not all can have come from Megasthenes.[49] There is no reason to suppose that Aelian's working methods were anything like Diodorus'; but his whole book is the product of a process of excerpting, so it would not be unreasonable to imagine that the chapter discussed above is based on more than one source. I have suggested Nearchus as a possible alternative at a few points, but he cannot be responsible for all. The other usual suspect is Cleitarchus, who wrote at length about monkeys and also some birds.[50] That Cleitarchus should have written about some creatures does not preclude Megasthenes from having written about them too, and I would say that the kind of information given in the 'Megasthenic' sections of Aelian is different from that in the 'Cleitarchan' sections. Probably most of the sober information is from Megasthenes.

47. Str. 15.1.56 = F 15 Schw; F 15b Schw.

48. F 30 Schw = Ff 28 and 29 J; F 16.

49. Muntz 2012.

50. F 19, Ff 21, 22.

What about the sea-monsters of Taprobane? Certainly Megasthenes never went there, any more than Nearchus did. He might have heard about the place from his informants, who told him a few tall stories.[51] However, Onesicritus describes Taprobane in very similar terms: 'amphibious monsters are found round it, some of which are like kine, others like horses, and others like other land-animals'.[52] This sounds like a Strabonian summary of the longer account in Aelian: I suggest that this portion of Aelian's chapter is from Onesicritus, but that the rest is based on Megasthenes.

The Hoopoe: The First *Just So* Story

Megasthenes may be the source of a remarkable story about the hoopoe in Aelian's *De natura animalium*.[53,54]

> The hoopoe of India was a bird twice as big as we know in Greece, and more beautiful in appearance; and Homer says that while the bridle and trappings of a horse are the delight of a Hellenic king, this hoopoe is the favourite plaything of the king of the Indians, who carries it on his hand, and toys with it, and never tires of gazing in ecstasy on its splendour, and the beauty with which Nature has adorned it. Therefore the Brachmanes even make this particular bird the subject of a mythic story, as follows:
>
> > To the king of the Indians there was born a son. The child had elder brothers, who when they came to man's estate turned out to be very unjust and the greatest of reprobates. They despised their brother because he was the youngest; and they scoffed also at their father and their mother, whom they despised because they were very old and grey-haired. The boy, accordingly, and his aged parents could at last no longer live with these wicked men, and away they fled from home, all three together. In the course of the protracted journey which they had to

51. There may be an allusion to creatures like this in the *Arthaśāstra* 2.26.5 (Kautilya 1992, 320), which includes among protected species 'sea fish which have strange or unusual forms' – and apparently in the Jātakas also: see Arora 2005, 44. (The whole discussion there of Onesicritus' description of Taprobane, at 41–4, is valuable.)

52. F 12 = Str. 15.1.15.

53. I discussed this hoopoe story in Stoneman 2016c: the present pages offer several modifications of my earlier views.

54. Ael. *NA* 16.5 = Megasth. F 59 Schw. The fragment is excluded by Jacoby.

> undergo, the old people succumbed to fatigue and died, and the boy showed them no light regards, but buried them in himself, having cut off his head with a sword.[55] Then, as the Brachmanes tell us, the all-seeing sun, in admiration of this surpassing act of piety, transformed the boy into a bird which is most beautiful to behold, and which lives to a very advanced age. So on his head there grew a crest which was, as it were, a memorial of what he had done at the time of his flight. The Athenians have also related, in a fable, marvels somewhat similar of the crested lark . . . [56] It seems, accordingly, probable that the fable, though with a different bird for its subject, emanated from the Indians, and spread onward even to the Greeks. For the Brachmanes say that a prodigious time has elapsed since the Indian hoopoe, then in human form and young in years, performed that act of piety to its parents.[57]

This story, told by Aelian, with its echoes of several tales including Joseph and his brothers, and the Phoenix, does not seem to occur elsewhere except in the passage of Aristophanes quoted by Aelian. Where did Aelian get it from? He cites no sources for the story other than the Brachmanes; on the strength of this, Schwanbeck included it among the fragments of Megasthenes, but only as 'doubtful'. His reasoning was no doubt that Megasthenes is the first author to mention the Brachmanes – indeed he writes about them in some detail; and furthermore that Megasthenes attributes to 'Brachman' informants (actually, 'philosophers') another fanciful tale, about the Swift-footed men (Ὠκυπόδες) who can run faster than horses.[58]

What are the chances that Aelian's source was Megasthenes? He cites the latter in three other places, always for stories about the natural world: on poi-

55. Filliozat 1967 assembles examples (with illustrations from art) of legendary sages who achieved this apparently impossible feat.

56. Ar. *Birds* 470–5, attributing the story to Aesop, though it does not appear in the latter's extant works. Dunbar (ad loc.) thinks that the Greek story arose independently of the Indian one, but this seems unlikely. According to *Birds* 114 the hoopoe was a man at first. The Greek hoopoe myth about Tereus is quite different, first appearing in the exiguous fragments of Sophocles' *Tereus.* For the confusion with larks, cf. the Latin name for the lark, *alauda*, which seems to derive from the Arabic name for the hoopoe, *al-hudhud.* Some Greeks believed that hoopoes turned into hawks in autumn: Dunbar, *Aristophanes: Birds* (Oxford: OUP, 1995), 141.

57. Megasth. F 59 Schw, tr. J. W. McCrindle; from Aelian *NA* 16.5; printed by Jacoby as *FGrH* 721 (*Anhang*) F 18. Thompson (1936, 167–8) regards the story as a solar myth: the Sun is buried when the bird's crest closes.

58. Megasth. F 29 Schw; Str. 15.1.57.

sonous fish, on snakes and scorpions, and on monkeys.[59] Of the twelve authors collected by Jacoby as writers of *Indica*,[60] Aelian cites only two by name, Megasthenes (three times) and Orthagoras, whose information is channelled through Nearchus (twice). From Jacoby's *Anhang* there are eight Aelian passages, including that under discussion. One should also consider the authors whom Jacoby collects elsewhere: Ctesias, Nearchus, Onesicritus and Cleitarchus. Of these, Aelian never cites Nearchus directly; he cites Ctesias ten times, Onesicritus twice and Cleitarchus three times. He also draws some information from Aristotle's *Historia animalium*, but only of a bare zoological kind. Cleitarchus is in general known as a source of information about wonders and *paradoxa*, but not of stories as such. The only other writer who actually tells stories or fables of this kind – such as the story of how the Indians hunt the hare and the fox[61] – is Ctesias. But the Brachmanes are never mentioned by Ctesias, and he does not seem to have spent time to talking to philosophers either. Ctesias may never have gone to India and perhaps drew all his information from Indians – diplomats and merchants, for example – visiting the Persian court. Nichols thinks his fragments display both autopsy and familiarity with Indian oral traditions such as those found in the *Rāmāyaṇa*, but does not explain this opinion.[62]

There is no proof, but I regard Megasthenes as the most likely candidate to have picked up this interesting story about the hoopoe. Unfortunately I have not managed to find any independent evidence for the tale's existence in Indian literature. The animal fable is well known to have originated in India,[63] which was no doubt one of the reasons that Rudyard Kipling thought of writing the *Just So Stories* (1902) and the *Jungle Books* (1894 and 1895). The *Pañcatantra*, the most likely source, does not contain any story of this kind about the hoopoe or any other creature. One element of the story, the removal of the boy's head, has a distant cousin in a Muria legend which recounts that, in

59. Ael. *NA* 8.7, 16.4.1, 17.39.

60. Megasthenes, Scylax, Tauron, Androsthenes, Patrokles, Orthagoras, Sosandros, Daimachos, Dionysius, Basilis, Bardaisan (who does not come into question as he is centuries later than Aelian) and Kaimaron; the fragments collected in the *Anhang* may constitute a thirteenth author.

61. F 45g = Ael. *NA* 4.26.

62. Nichols 2011, 22.

63. See also Macan's commentary on Herodotus (1895), vol. 2 appendix 14, 304–11, on Hippocleides and the peacock. The story seems to be echoed in *Pañcatantra* 1.150: 'Who can see the anus of the peacock . . . if the foolish cock himself does not dance?'

antiquity, men could remove the tops of their heads (to pick off lice) and as a result(!) they never died. So the god of the dead, Mahapurub, made a paste to glue their pates on, in order to populate his kingdom.[64]

Hoopoes in fact make very few showings in Indian literature (though they are rather widespread in Islamic lore),[65] but some of the information given about the hoopoe prompts one to question whether it really is this bird that is being talked about. The bird is said to be the plaything of kings, and to be very long-lived: both these features are more characteristic of another bird with a crest: the parrot or parakeet. The hoopoe is never, to my knowledge, domesticated. (Indeed its dirty habits would make it an unattractive pet.) As parrots were unfamiliar in classical Greece, Ctesias being the first to mention them,[66] the tale could have been retold to describe this more familiar crested bird.[67]

Parrots appear quite frequently in the Jātakas (Buddhist tales about the previous births of the Buddha which illustrate the eons-long path to Buddhahood), as do peacocks, geese, ospreys and other birds, as well as many animals of all kinds. In *Jātaka* 484, some wise men are reborn as parrots, to look after their parents and feed them. The Bodhisattva is said to be the son of the parrot king; when he is snared by a Brahman, the captor is impressed by his piety and offers him gifts, which the captive refuses. (The son of the parrot king reappears in *Jātaka* 503.) The theme of filial piety is quite common in the Jātakas, as is the propensity of the Bodhisattva in his animal form to offer protection to others.[68] (The Brahmans are usually the villains, too, in these highly partisan fables.) In *Jātaka* 521 a childless king adopts birds as his children; they preach wisely and honour their parents, and once again 'the Buddha was Jambu the parrot'.

Jātaka 518 introduces a previous birth of the Buddha as another bird, the Garuda or mythical king of the birds, who finds himself at odds with the king of the snakes, the Nagas. The eleventh-century author Somadeva, in his *Ocean of Story*,[69] has a tale about the Garuda, king of the birds, exhibiting filial piety to his mother, who has been captured by snakes: he fetches the nectar of immortality from the ocean of milk and gives it to the snake-men to free her. The god Indra then grants the Garuda a boon, and a tribute of one snake per day

64. Elwin 1947, 264–5.

65. Stoneman 2016c assembles some examples.

66. Bigwood 1993a: Ctes. F 45.8.

67. Levi 1972, 41 remarks that wherever there are Greeks, there seem to be hoopoes.

68. E.g., in *Jātaka* 486 the osprey, king of the birds, defends a hawk couple.

69. Penzer 1924, 2.152. See also Mallinson (tr.) 2007–09, 2.125–6.

for his food.[70] The combination of the themes of filial piety, the crested bird and the sun- or sky-god in this story is quite striking, though it is not 'the same' as Aelian's tale. But there is enough here to suggest that a story of this kind, attached to some bird or other (Aelian hints that it was not originally a hoopoe story), was part of Indian animal lore from a long way back. It could well have begun as a Brahman tale which was then adapted by Buddhist authors to the purpose of the Jātakas, before reappearing in its original Hindu form, more than a thousand years later, in Somadeva.

The Unicorn

Did Megasthenes mention unicorns? Strabo mentions 'one-horned horses with the head of a deer'.[71] Aelian states,

> There exists in India a one-horned animal, called by the natives the *Kartazon*. It is of the size of a full-grown horse, and has a crest, and yellow hair as soft as wool. It is furnished with very good legs and is very fleet. Its legs are jointless and formed like those of the elephant, and it has a tail like a swine's. A horn sprouts out from between its eyebrows, and this is not straight, but curved into the most natural wreaths, and is of a black colour.
>
> The animal has a very loud voice and is quarrelsome with its own species, and prefers to wander in solitude to pasture. They are sometimes captured and taken to fight for the entertainment of the king of the Prasii.[72]

Karttunen argues that the combination of the topic of the one-horned ass with tame animals living wild in India shows that Aelian got this account from Megasthenes.[73] Ctesias describes a creature that is plainly the same (see ch. 4 above). The name attributed to the beast is perhaps a giveaway: *kartazon* is very close to *karkadann*, the name of a mythical unicorn-like creature well known in medieval Persia, though it is also the word for a rhinoceros.[74] Sachau in the index to al-Biruni suggested that it represents *khadgadanta*.

70. Bhattacharji 1970/2000, 232 observes that all sun gods fight and conquer serpents; cf. 230. There is at least one other Garuda story in Somadeva: Penzer 1924, 5.160. Penzer 1.103–5 n. provides an informative note on the wonder-birds of every nation.

71. Str. 15.1.56 = F 27b J.

72. Ael. *NA* 16.20–1 = F 15b Schw (excluded by Jacoby).

73. Karttunen 1997, 185.

74. E.g., in Ibn Battutah: see Mackintosh-Smith 2002, 151–2; Ibn Battutah saw them several times in Sind.

10.3 A seal from the Indus Civilisation (third–second millennium BCE) depicting a 'unicorn'.

Monier Williams's dictionary does not give the word, but has *khadga* with the meanings 'sword, rhinoceros': so 'sword-tooth' might be a reasonable interpretation of the term.[75] Ctesias is very likely to have known the Persian name for an Indian beast. Al-Biruni describes the *karkadann* in almost the same terms as Aelian,[76] and illustrations of the *karkadann* in MSS of Qazvini closely resemble the rhinoceros.[77]

Alexander's men saw rhinoceroses in north-west India,[78] as did Ibn Battutah and Marco Polo, but they seem rarely to have been seen by the other classical writers, and lent themselves easily to mythologisation. Babur was able to give a detailed description of them, which makes it the odder that his descendant Jahangir is said to have maintained two unicorns at his court.[79] The plot is complicated by the existence of seals from the Indus Civilisation depicting a unicorn-like creature quite unlike the rhinoceros, which is also re-

75. Karttunen 1997, 185 reaches a similar conclusion on the etymology.

76. Al-Biruni, Sachau 1910, 1.204.

77. On rhinoceroses in Ctesias, see Karttunen 1989, 168–71.

78. Curt. 8.9.17 and 9.1.1. They are now close to extinction in India except in the Brahmaputra valley: Enright 2008, 139–43.

79. Dale 2004, 361; Moraes 2003, 24–5.

alistically represented on such seals.[80] This is the only non-naturalistic beast on Indus seals, and one wonders where it has come from. Its front resembles a horse's, its rear a bull's. It may be identifiable with the Vedic *ekashringi* ('one-horn').[81] Megasthenes' terminology suits the rhinoceros, and there is probably no need to suppose that he is thinking of the mythical animal.[82]

The Gold-digging Ants

As when a Gryfon through the wilderness
With winged course oer hill or moarie dale
Pursues the Arimaspian, who by stelth
Had from his wakeful custody purloined
The guarded gold.

—JOHN MILTON, *PARADISE LOST* 2.943–7

Strabo follows his expression of scepticism about Megasthenes' statement on the ownership of elephants with a completely matter-of-fact presentation of the information given by Nearchus and Megasthenes about gold-digging ants.[83] These mysterious creatures were already hallowed by their appearance in Herodotus,[84] according to whom the ants, which are bigger than foxes but smaller than dogs, make their nests underground and in the process excavate sand which contains gold dust. The Indians gather the dust, but they have to move fast, using the swiftest camels, as otherwise the ants, with their keen sense of smell, will come in pursuit. Later Herodotus writes that the one-eyed Arimaspians also steal gold from griffins, but he is sceptical about the existence of such people and confesses ignorance as to the origin of the gold from the north.

80. On 15 April 2015 BBC news reported the discovery of a figurine of a unicorn from Harappa.

81. Some intriguing links between the Harappan creature and the myth of the single-horned beast-man ṛṣyaśṛṇga are drawn by O'Flaherty 1973/1981, 50. (His birth is depicted on the north gate at Sanchi, front, right end of lowest architrave.) Robinson 2015, 110–11 thinks the seals may represent clan totems. A charming children's story by Satyajit Ray (2004 [1987]) describes a scientific expedition to Tibet to find the unicorn; the explorers get magic boots from a dead lama and fly over the wall of the Garden of Eden, 'where all the imaginary creatures live'.

82. Arora 1991–92, 317 proposes rather that Megasthenes took the mythical beast from Ctesias.

83. Str. 15. 1.44.

84. Hdt. 3.102, 105; cf. 116.

Ctesias too gives a version of the story, on the authority of Bactrian informants, of how the Indians collect the gold on moonlit nights from a 'dreary wilderness'; but here it is not ants that have to be eluded, but griffins: he describes the appearance of the griffin, with its neck of variegated feathers of dark blue, its feathers black on the back, red on the front, and its white wings, its head like an eagle's and its eyes like fire (something between a parrot and a Jabberwock).[85]

There seem to be two separate stories here, one about Indian gold from a hot desert, the other about gold from Central Asia or further east. Both Nearchus and Megasthenes referred to the Indian gold that was gathered by ants. Strabo simply cites the former for the information that 'the skins of gold-mining ants are like those of leopards',[86] but Arrian is a little fuller: 'Nearchus says that he himself did not see one like those which some other authors have described as existing in India, but that he saw many skins of these animals which had been brought into the Macedonian camp.'[87] (He had also seen skins of tigers).[88] Strabo continues,

> Megasthenes says about these ants that among the Derdae, a large tribe of Indians living towards the east and in the mountains, there is a plateau about three thousand stadia in circumference; below this are gold mines, and the miners are ants, beasts no smaller than foxes, which move at great speed and live by hunting. In winter they dig up the soil and pile it up at the entrances, like moles; and there is gold dust in it which requires little refining. Those who live nearby go after it stealthily on beasts of burden, for if they go openly the ants put up a fight and chase them away, and then, catching up with them, destroy them and their beasts. In order to escape being seen by the ants, they lay out pieces of flesh of wild beasts here and there, and when the ants have been lured away they gather up the dust and dispose of it to traders for what they can get, since they do not know how to smelt it.[89]

This unforgettable tale reappears many times in classical and later literature, including writers as diverse as Philostratus[90] and Buzurg ibn Shahriyar, as well

85. Ctes. F 45h = Ael. *NA* 4.27. Bolton 1962, 65–6.
86. Str. 15.1.44; Nearch. F 8b.
87. Arr. *Ind.* 15.8 = Nearch. F 8a.
88. Arr. *Ind.* 15.1.
89. Str. 15.1.44 = Megasth. Ff 39 Schw, 23 J. Cf. Arr. *Ind.* 15.5–7; D.Chr. *Or.* 35.23–4.
90. Philostr. *VA* 6.1; Mela 2.1.

as Ogier de Busbecq's letters from Constantinople.[91] Agatharchides has a puzzling reference to Arabian 'lions that are called "ants" ', which are much like other lions except that their genital organs face in the opposite direction.[92] The story has occasioned an enormous amount of scholarly discussion over the centuries, with rationalising explanations of the ants including actual Mongolian giant ants, mastiffs, leopards, Tibetan miners and marmots.[93] One scholar averred that Herodotus had simply made it up, a view which will not withstand a moment's scrutiny of the parallel evidence.[94] The story of the one-eyed Arimaspians and the griffins has also proved stimulating, and is of interest because it locates the source of gold much further north-east than Herodotus or Megasthenes did.[95] Bolton is especially interested in the Arimaspians, while Mayor puts forward a persuasive argument that the origin of the griffin legend lies in discoveries of Protoceratops skeletons in western Siberia.[96] Scythian artistic representations of men (in profile!) wrestling with griffins are plentiful, and are on the same model as the many Persian representations from Persepolis and elsewhere; these might therefore be the origin of the Arimaspian tale. But it is the ants that are the real problem.

Tarn pointed out that the ants are always located just beyond the regions known to the writer in question: in the Thar desert for Herodotus, in Dardistan for Megasthenes and in Siberia for the Indians.[97] For 'ant-gold' is indeed an Indian term, *pipīlika*, from *pipilī*, 'ant'; it is found in the *Mahābhārata*, where

91. Letter 4. Schiern 1873 surveys Islamic versions of the story.

92. Agatharch. F 70. Later writers interpreted these as a version of the gold-guarding ants, now localised in Aithiopia: Philostr. *VA* 6.1; Heliod. 10.2.6.

93. Rawlinson 1926, 23 (mastiffs); Laufer 1908, 449–50 (giant ants in Mongolia, in Chinese sources), quoted by Bolton 1962, 81–2, mentioning 'red ants as huge as elephants, and wasps as big as gourds', and followed by Nesselrath 1995, 36 n. 27; Bali 1879–88 (Tibetan miners, accepted by McCrindle 1926, 94); Lassen 1847–61, 1.850, Hennig 1930 and Peissel 1984 (marmots, a theory ridiculed by Tarn 1951, 107 for no stated reason). Wilford in 1822 and Humboldt in 1847 plumped for leopards. Later discussions include Pearson 1960, 124–5; Arora 2005, 63–4 (gold from Ladakh); Parker 2008, 22 (marmots). Karttunen 1989, 171–6 provides a fairly comprehensive list. The most exhaustive recent discussion is Nesselrath 1995, esp. 23–6, nn. 7 and 8.

94. Fehling 1989.

95. Also in Mela 2.1; Plin. *NH* 6.67, see Andre-Filliozat ad loc.; Tzetzes *Chil.* 12.330–40. Karttunen 1989, 177–80.

96. Bolton 1962; Mayor 2000, 38–53: see also A. Erman, *Reise um die Erde ... in 1828* (1833), 708–13, cited in Nesselrath 1995, 25.

97. Tarn 1951, 107.

the gold is brought by the northern nations to Yudhiṣṭhira.[98] Tarn also refers, sceptically, to the theory advanced by Laufer that the story might arise from the confusion of the name of a Mongolian tribe, *Shiraighol*, with the Mongolian word for an ant, *shirghol*. He rightly regards this as quite imponderable.

The contribution of Michel Peissel is worth attention.[99]

> In September 1982 ... the informant told me, in Ladakhi (an archaic form of Tibetan ...) that his grandparents and forefathers used to travel to the Dansar flats or plains (*thang*) to collect there the sandy earth from the burrows of the local marmots (*Arctomys himalayanus*) as it contained a high concentration of gold dust. This account, confirmed by two other residents in Dartzig ... is, I believe, the first local oral account to be recorded which confirms the story of Herodotus, which many believed to be merely a fable.

This circumstantial statement fits most of the data – the sand mixed with gold, the desert, the plateau. The general location, Dardistan, fits well for Ladakh. As for the ants, I wonder whether the Sanskrit term 'ant-gold' might in fact refer to the size of the grains,[100] and in being communicated from an Indian informant to a Greek this was misunderstood as referring to the creatures that dug it up? It may be worth noting that the Greek word for an ant, *myrmex*, somewhat resembles the Persian word for a marmot, *moushkhormā*. The skins Nearchus saw might well have been marmot furs.[101]

The Monstrous Races

Strabo's tetchiness towards his predecessors, including Megasthenes, turns to exasperation when he comes to consider the 'monstrous races' situated in India by authors from Scylax onwards. He eases us in with the 'unusual' customs of those who eat their dead relatives,[102] and then continues,

98. *Mbh*. 2.48.4: 'The kings who live by the river Śailodā between Mt Meru and Mt Mardara and enjoy the pleasing shade of bamboo and cane, the Khasas, Ekāśanas, Jyoghas, Pradavas, Dīrghaveṇus, Paśupas, Kuṇindas, Tanganas, and Further Tanganas, they brought the gold called Pipīlaka, which is granted as a boon by the pipīlaka ants, and they brought it by bucketsful and piles.' Addiitonal gifts included yak-tail plumes and Himalayan honey.

99. Peissel 1984: this information was not known to Karttunen when he reached his pessimistic conclusion at 1989, 176.

100. Cf. Puskás, quoted by Karttunen 1989, 175.

101. Bunbury 1879, 257.

102. Str. 15.1.56.

> Megasthenes, going beyond all bounds to the realm of myth, speaks of people five spans and three spans tall, some of them without nostrils but having two breathing holes above their mouths;[103] and he says that it is the people three spans tall that carry on the war with the cranes (which is referred to by Homer) ... Like this, also, are the stories of the Ear-sleepers, and the wild men, and other monstrous creatures. These wild men could not be brought to Sandrocottus, because they would starve themselves to death; they have their heels in front, and their soles and toes behind.[104] But some mouthless people were brought to him, gentle folk, who live around the sources of the Ganges, and sustain themselves by the smells of roast meats and the scent of fruits and flowers; however, they suffer when they breathe bad smells, and for this reason they can hardly survive, particularly in a camp. He says that other peoples were described to him by the philosophers, who spoke of the Okypodes (Swift-feet), who can run faster than horses; Ear-sleepers, who have ears that reach to their feet, so that they can sleep underneath them: they are very strong, and can uproot trees and break bowstrings. Then there are the One-eyes, who have dogs' ears and their eye in the middle of the forehead, hair that stands on end and shaggy chests.[105] And the Noseless Ones are omnivorous and eaters of raw meat, but they are short-lived and die before they are old.[106] Concerning the Hyperboreans he says the same as Simonides, Pindar and other retailers of myths.[107]

Megasthenes' is the fullest Greek repertoire of these legendary peoples, though most of them appear in one or other of the earlier writers on India.[108] Homer, as mentioned by Strabo, spoke of the pygmies who were at war with the cranes, though they were not specifically located in India, and his one-eyed giants likewise were not in India but in the fantasy-Mediterranean where Odysseus' adventures take place. But both Scylax and Ctesias put the

103. The latter appear also in the *Periplus* (62), under the name of 'Kirradai'.

104. Also in Baeton, *FGrH* 119 F 5.

105. Cf. Bolton 1962, 82, quoting Sayce (ed.) 1883 on Hdt. 1.201.

106. Pliny calls these the Sciritae, *NH* 7.2.25; cf. Ael. *NA* 16.22.

107. Str. 15.1.57.

108. Reese 1914, 49–50. They have, of course, an enormously long afterlife in classical literature, where Pliny (*NH* 7.2.21–30) gave them their defining form, and especially in the Middle Ages: Friedman 1981 is the classic account. Megasthenes does not have the Macrocephali, located in India by Scylax though not by Hesiod.

10.4 Hairy women, from the *Alexander Romance* MS D, fol. 100r (Hellenic Institute, Venice).

One-Eyes in India. Scylax described the Shadow-feet, those with a single foot they use as an umbrella, and they reappear in Antiphon, in Ctesias and in Philostratus.[109] The Ear-sleepers are also in Scylax and Ctesias. The latter also describes the Otoliknoi, who have eight toes on each foot, bear one child only and have white hair which becomes dark with age.[110]

Some of the peoples appear again in Agatharchides, a century after Megasthenes: the Dog-milkers, the Troglodytes, the Locust-eaters, who Agatharchides says are very short-lived, though Pliny says the opposite, and the Dog-heads.[111] The fullest list of 'monstrous races' is in Pliny,[112] who gave them their defining form for antiquity and the Middle Ages. He cites a great many authors, some otherwise scarcely known, as sources for his list. It comprises (Megasthenic races in bold): **Reverse-feet**, **Dog-heads**, **Monocoli** (i.e., Shadow-feet),[113] men with faces in their shoulders, Satyrs who can run on either two or four feet [*sc.* apes], screaming hairy men (from Tauron), people with very big and very small feet (from Eudoxus), **Sciritae** (in Megasthenes under the name of Noseless Ones), **Mouthless Ones**, **Pygmies** (citing Ctesias 58.11), Long-lived people (various kinds, from Isigonus, Crates and Ctesias, Agatharchides et al.), **very tall** and **very short people** (citing Onesiritus for the latter), and the Calingi (cf. Pliny *NH* 6.64). Most of these are repeated in Solinus, whose work essentially derives from Pliny. Given the large number of early Greek authors who treated of these races, one wonders why Strabo singled out Megasthenes for scorn.

Various stratagems have been adopted to save the credit of Megasthenes and to defend him against the charge of writing a fantasy. Robert Garland lists about forty 'monstrous races' and offers explanations for some of them by reference to actual deformities:[114] for example, the horse-footed people are based on a hereditary mutation in which the sufferers have two giant toes; the Amazons are from real one-breasted peoples; the Shadow-feet are based

109. Antiphon F 117 Blass; Ctesias ap Plin. *NH* 7.2; Philostr *VA* 6.25, locating them in Ethiopia. Their latest appearance seems to be in the guise of the 'Monopods' in C. S. Lewis's *Voyage of the Dawn Treader* (1952).

110. Ctes. F 45.50.

111. Agatharch. Ff 61, 62, 59, 75.

112. Plin. *NH* 7.9–30. Friedman 1981 is the classic account. For the Islamic world, see Berlekamp 2011.

113. He cites Ctesias for these.

114. Garland 1995, 159–77.

on observation of people practising a yoga position standing on their heads; others are due to seeing apes in the distance; the headless men are people with faces painted on their chests; and so on. It is true, as he says, that it is 'hard to articulate what one has witnessed' when it is quite unfamiliar, as India was to the Greeks; but these rationalising explanations do not seem to deal with the full impact of these strange races. As Italo Calvino has written, 'the human race is a zone of living things that should be defined by tracing its confines'.[115] The idea goes back to St Augustine, who was concerned as to whether the Antipodean races, lying outside the human cosmos, could be part of God's plan for salvation, and regarded the monstrous races as 'a demonstration of God's power'.[116]

However, Strabo himself gives us the clue, when he says that Megasthenes mentions being told by 'the philosophers' about certain of these races. Megasthenes was not describing his own observations, but retailing what he was told by Brahman informants. Most of the peoples described appear in Sanskrit literature, and we can assume that the traditions go back to a period well before Megasthenes. Otto Stein assembled the data nearly a century ago in his hundred-column *Realenzyklopädie* article (especially cols. 241ff. and 304, with a firm conclusion at 325: 'the "wonders" are from Indian sources').[117] Besides the *Ṛg Veda* and the epics, a valuable conspectus is given by Vārāhamihira, whose *Bṛhatsaṁhitā* was written in about 505 CE and was translated into Arabic by al-Biruni, who admired it.[118] Shastri has compiled from it a gazetteer of the peoples and places of the India of his time: many of the real peoples encountered by Alexander can be identified in it, and many of the fantastic races appear in the classical authors, but others do not.[119]

115. Calvino, 'Man, the Sky and the Elephant', in *The Uses of Literature* (1986), 323, quoted in Murphy 2004, 84.

116. Aug. *Civ. Dei* 16.8 and 21.8.

117. Stein 1932. See also Rawlinson 1926, 65–6.

118. Shastri 1996. They are also in the *Jaimini-Aśvamedha*, a little-known work that retells the *Mahābhārata*, written perhaps in the seventeenth century: Derrett 1970, 30.

119. Real peoples: Abisares, Assacenoi, Darada, Gandhara, Mālava, Paurava, Sibi, Sudras, Vasātis. The fabulous peoples are as follows: Aśvamukha, horse-faces; Bhadraśva, blessed ones; Cipiṭrnāsika, flat-nosed people (flat-nosed people appear again as the Kirata, who seem to be the Cirrhadae of classical accounts); Ekacarana or Ekapada, one-footed; Ekavilocana, one-eyes; Gandharva, centaurs(?); Kravyāda, raw-eaters; the Kuru-people, who seem to imply the region of Uttarakuru, Pliny's Ottorakorra; Nārimukha, feminine-faces; Parna-śabana, clad in

Cannibals are also mentioned by Herodotus and Strabo, and in the *Periplus,* which states that they have the faces of horses; this equates them with the *Aśvamukha* of Vārāhamihira.[120] The Noseless Ones,[121] mentioned also in the *Periplus* under the name of Kirradai, in Pliny as Scyrites, and by Aelian as Skiratai,[122] are certainly the Kirata of Sanskrit literature, who appear in the *Rāmāyaṇa,* and indeed in the *Ṛg Veda,* as well as in the *Bṛhatsaṁhitā.*[123] They can be identified with the pre-Aryan inhabitants of the subcontinent, the *dasyus* or Dasas, whose flat Mongoloid features characterise the peoples of the north and north-east, including the Nagas.[124] The name may survive in that of the Kirantis of present-day eastern Nepal.[125] The Swift-feet or Okypodes of Strabo/Megasthenes are probably a mistake for Sanskrit *ekapada,* which means one-footed, that is, the Sciapods. These occur frequently in Sanskrit literature.[126] The long-eared people are in the *Mahābhārata* under the name of Karnapravārama, and are mentioned by Vārāhamihira, as well as in the Purāṇas.[127] Stein also quotes a Chinese source. The One-eyes (Skt. *ekāksha*) and the pygmies[128] again occur in Chinese literature, appearing in illustrations to a book of the fifth century BCE.[129] The Reverse-feet are in the *Mahābhārata* as *paścādanigulayah.*[130]

---

leaves (cf. Ptolemy's Phyllitae); Puruṣāda, cannibals; Sabara, hunters and thieves (cf. the Suari of Pliny and the Sabarai of Ptolemy); Strīrājya, the kingdom of women in the north-west; Śūrpakarna, people with ears like winnowing-baskets (i.e., the Ear-sleepers); Svamukha, dog-faces; Turaṇgānana, horse-faced people; Ūrdhvakaṇṭha, those with high throats; Vyāgramukha, tiger-faced; Vyānalagriva, serpent-necks,

120. Hdt. 3.38, 99; Str. 4.5.4. Casson (ed and tr.) 1989, 234 mentions a horse-faced tribe who eat people, familiar in the folklore of Orissa.

121. Plin. *NH* 6.195 and 187f.; Agatharch. F 62. This identification is accepted by Chanana 1960, 18.

122. Ael. *NA* 16.22.

123. *Rām.* 4 (*Kiṣkindhākāṇḍa*) 40.28; *RV* 5.29.10; *Bṛhatsaṁhitā 14.26.*

124. Jacobs 2012, 10 on the connection with Sanskrit Kiratas.

125. Casson (ed. and tr.) 1989, 234.

126. E.g., *Mbh.* 1.114.57; *Rām.* (*Kiṣkindhākāṇḍa*) 20–6; *Bṛhatsaṁhitā* 14.7

127. *Mbh.* 2.28.44–50; *Bṛhatsaṁhitā* 14.18; e.g., *Mārkaṇḍeya Purāṇa* 346a.

128. Filliozat on Pliny *NH* 6.70.2; cf. Ctes. F 46ab, *AR* 2.44 γ.

129. Sayce (ed.) 1883, note on Hdt. 1.201.

130. *Mbh.* 10. 8.136.

The Mouthless Ones

Two of these fabulous races demand longer discussion: the Mouthless Ones[131] and the Dog-heads. There seems to be no parallel for the Mouthless Ones in the Sanskrit sources,[132] unless they are the same as the wearers of leaves who are mentioned by Vārāhamihira, but without allusion to their more striking characteristic.[133] The Mouthless Ones are not just the subject of something Megasthenes was told, for he says that some 'were brought' to Sandrocottus in his 'camp'. It seems he must have seen them. What did he see? One parallel that is sometimes deployed is Herodotus' description of a people dwelling on the Araxes who sniff the smoke of their bonfires in order to get intoxicated;[134] but these people are in the wrong place, and the purpose of their sniffing is quite different from that of the Mouthless Ones. Sushma Jansari and Richard Ricot have argued that the reference is in fact to Jains, who, though not strictly mouthless, do cover their mouths and restrict their diet to a very limited range of foods.[135] However, they certainly do not make use of roasted meats! Intriguing is the detail that Candragupta had these people 'brought' to him; Jansari and Ricot link this to the tradition that Candragupta later in life abdicated and became a Jain: this then would be the beginning of his investigation into the requirements of the Jain life. The suggestion is attractive but not compelling. I am drawn to another possibility, the practice of Brahmin priests who are supposed to gain their nourishment by sniffing the fumes of sacrifices.[136] It is possible to imagine Candragupta summoning Brahmans to his court for their usual functions of performing sacrifices, during which they would not eat but only sniff the sacrifice, which would of course include at

131. Note also the curious allusion of Plutarch, who, discussing the way in which the moon provides nourishment and moisture in desert places, writes, 'How could that Indian root which, according to Megasthenes, those who neither eat nor drink, for they have no mouths, kindle and cause to smoulder and feed on its aroma, grow there if it were not watered by the moon?': Plu. *De facie in orbe lunae* 24, *Mor.* 938c = Megasth. F 31 Schw, F 30 J. See also Plin. *NH* 7.2.25.

132. Stein 1932, 239.

133. Pliny (*NH* 7.25) says that the mouthless people are clad in leaves: see also West 1964, who prefers an alternative reading, feathers. The Gonds go clad in leaves: Forsyth 1871, 15.

134. Hdt. 1.202.

135. Jansari and Ricot 2016.

136. Doniger 2009, 116. Stein 1932, 306 suggests ascetics, who are referred to as 'smoke-drinkers' in the *Mahābhārata*.

this date roasted meat. Megasthenes can hardly have failed to observe, however, that these were normal people with mouths.

A suggestion made in 1912 by H. Horten seems to have been forgotten: that the reference is to a Himalayan people who are accustomed to sniff frequently at onions and garlic as a way of averting mountain-sickness. They could thus be described (loosely) as 'living on smells'; but still they had mouths.[137]

The Dog-heads

People with dogs' heads are located on the fringes of India from the earliest times and constitute one of the most persistent strands of 'monstrous' neighbours to India's people.[138] Ctesias records that they traded with the Indians, were noted for their justice and inhabited inaccessible mountains 'as far as the Indus', which from his perspective should presumably mean 'north-west of the Indus', though one cannot be sure.[139] The name he gives them, Kalystries, has proved unidentifiable in any language.[140] It bears no resemblance to any of the ethnic names in Vārāhamihira's *Bṛhatsaṁhitā*, for example, or in the Purāṇas, though dog-headed people appear in the Sanskrit texts under various names, including *śunamukha, svamukha.*[141] Megasthenes puts the Dog-heads 'in the mountains', while the Reverse-feet are localised on the mountain called Nulus: they 'wear a covering of wild beasts' skins, their speech is a bark and they live on the produce of hunting and fowling, for which they use their nails as weapons; he says that they numbered more than 120,000 when he published his work.'[142]

For Herodotus, the Dog-heads were North African baboons, and this seems to be the case also for those of Agatharchides,[143] but it seems fairly clear that the later writers are describing an actual race of human beings whose features evoked remark as different. The picture is further confused by the existence of another race known as 'dog-cookers' or 'dog-milkers' (*śvapāka, śvapaca).*[144]

137. A kind of *yakṣa* called Sūcīmukha, 'Needle-mouth', who is always hungry, is probably not relevant here. See Slusser 2010, 175.

138. The fullest study is White 1991.

139. Ctes. F 45.37–41.

140. Karttunen 1989, 181–85; Amigues 2011, 35.

141. *Mbh.* 9.44.54–100 for various animal-headed races.

142. Plin. *NH* 7.2.23. Cf Solinus 52.27; Megasth. Ff 30 Schw, 28 and 29 J.

143. Agatharch. F 75.

144. Karttunen 1984 places both races in Ethiopia and regards them as African tall stories.

These are generally seen as Indians of low caste and often identified with the Caṇḍālas.[145] (Nagas also eat dog).[146] But these were located within India, whereas the Dog-heads were always beyond the borders. The dog seems often to be a marker of the outcaste in India.[147]

Furthermore, demons are sometimes represented with dogs' heads. One example is a relief from Hadda showing dog-heads among Mara's demon army.[148] Two thousand years later, dog-heads appear in a relief from a Burmese Buddhist temple, now in San Francisco's museum of Asian art.

The *Alexander Romance* (gamma-recension) brings the hero in contact with Dog-heads,[149] though they do not appear in the earliest recensions of the work. However, their appearance in the Latin *Letter of Alexander to Aristotle about India*, as one of the many bizarre opponents of Alexander's army,[150] suggests that they may have belonged to the earliest, lost version of the *Letter* which was abridged in the Greek alpha-recension (and is now lacunose). The priest of the trees of the Sun and Moon in the *Letter* also has the head of a dog. Unlike Ctesias' Dog-heads, those of the *Romance* are ferocious, and they are described as cannibals when they are included in the list of Unclean Nations in the *Alexander Romance*.[151] Thus the origin of these stories about Alexander should be roughly contemporary with Megasthenes. The *Romance* seems to situate these adventures in the plains rather than in the mountains. But the latter is surely where they belong.

In later classical literature, and then in the Middle Ages, Dog-heads are everywhere. Although they are treated as creatures of fable in medieval literature, most visitors to India spotted a few of them. Ibn Battutah says that he saw them, and al-Biruni mentions them among the lands of the north.[152]

David Gordon White shows that while Greek sources place the Dog-heads somewhere in India, Indian sources place them in the north and west, while

145. *Mbh.* 12, p. 499; KA p. 323.

146. Sen 2015, 270.

147. White 1991, 87–9.

148. Ibid., 118 and plate 12.

149. *AR* 2.34 γ.

150. *Epist. Alexandri* 13.

151. *AR* 3.29. Cannibals are mentioned in the same breath as Ear-sleepers in *Mbh.* 2.28.44.

152. Al-Biruni, Sachau 1910, 1.302, along with not a few others of the races mentioned by Vārāhamihira.

10.5 Dog-headed demons (members of Mara's army) from the Temple at Bajo, Myanmar, 1470–80 CE (Asian Art Museum, San Francisco).

10.6 Alexander enters the grove of the Trees of Sun and Moon;
from the *Alexander Romance* MS D, fol. 139r (Hellenic Institute, Venice).

Chinese sources place them in the south and west.[153] The point of intersection for all these three traditions should thus be Central Asia.[154] White focuses on the region from Afghanistan to Tibet, but later narrows it down to the region where Ctesias seems to put them, in the far reaches of the Hindu Kush, perhaps around the Iron Gate south of Samarkand, which is one of the candidates for the legendary gate built by Alexander against the unclean races Gog and Magog. This localisation would combine the two traditions, of dog-headed people and of outcaste people who eat unclean food. Dogs feature also in the diet of the Unclean Nations in the *Alexander Romance,* along with vermin, worms, aborted foetuses and so on. Some of the 'primitive' tribes described in John Forbes Watson and John William Kaye's eight-volume study *The People of India* (1868–75), such as the Sonthals of Bihar, are 'quiet, inoffensive, cheerful, intelligent and obliging . . . and do not refuse to eat even snakes, ants, frogs and field rats'.[155] The legend of the creation of the Gonds recorded by Forsyth also makes them eaters of all kinds on non-Hindu foods: 'Everywhere they filled the country, / Killing, eating every creature; / Nothing knowing of distinction; / Eating clean and eating unclean; / Eating raw and eating rotten; / Eating squirrels, eating jackals, / Eating antelope and sambar; / Eating quails and eating pigeons, / Eating crows and kites and vultures; / Eating Dokuma the Adjutant, / Eating lizards, frogs and beetles, / Eating cows and eating calves, / Eating rats, and mice and bandicoots. / So the Gonds made no distinction.'[156]

Though Megasthenes has been made to take the blame for this long tradition of a race of dog-heads, it is clear that here too he, like Ctesias, was only reporting information derived from native sources. The people of Central Asia, with their un-Aryan features, were seen as beyond the pale. What started as a metaphor turned into a legend.

153. See White 1991, 130–1 on the Dog Jung of Chinese tradition. Bolton 1962, 81–2. notes that the Chinese associate them with the One-eyes and the giant ants.

154. White 1991, 115 and 184.

155. Miller 2014, 289.

156. Forsyth 1871, 182.

PART III

Interactions

11

The Indian Philosophers and the Greeks

Philosophy: 'First, then, I went to the Indians, the mightiest nation upon earth. I had little trouble in persuading them to descend from their elephants and follow me. The Brahmans, who dwell between the Oxydracae and the country of the Nechraioi, are mine to a man: they live according to my laws, and are respected by all their neighbours; and the manner of their death is truly wonderful.'

—LUCIAN, *THE FUGITIVES* 6

No doubt, the learning of Rum is widely admired, and it is well-known to the world. But India is not devoid of this wealth, as philosophic concepts of an excellent order abound here ... The Brahman of India is such a learned man that, as far as knowledge and learning are concerned, he has far excelled Aristotle.

—AMIR KHUSRAW (1251–1325), *NUH SIPIHR* 162;
IN NATH AND FAIYAZ 1981, 54

In the end, however naked, tall, there is still
The impossible possible philosophers' man,
The man who has had time to think enough ...
Who in a million diamonds sums us up.

—WALLACE STEVENS, 'ASIDES ON THE OBOE'

The Naked Philosophers

The word 'philosophy' was invented by a Greek, but Greeks were entranced by Indian philosophy from early times. Pythagoras, who has the credit for inventing the word, was said to have longed to go to India but never made it. Philosophy in the Greek sense was a great deal more than is connoted by today's academic discipline, concerned as it is with definitions and meaning. Philosophy, 'the love of wisdom', was a guide to life, and could even be applied to the way of life that was informed by wisdom. That is what Pythagoras meant by his coinage of the word: a life determined by the search for true understanding; and that is what the Greeks in Alexander's entourage seem to have thought they found in the Indian philosophers they met.

Onesicritus is our earliest witness. On arrival in Taxila, Alexander was intrigued by a group of naked ascetics he observed in a grove outside the city, practising various yoga postures, and sent Onesicritus to interview them and find out something about them.[1] Rebuffed by the first Indian he tried to approach (Calanus: see further below), Onesicritus turned to a more amenable fellow, whom he calls Mandanis, 'the oldest and wisest of the philosophers', who expressed admiration for Alexander as a 'philosopher in arms' and apologised for the fact that what he could impart to Onesicritus, through the medium of three interpreters, would be 'like expecting water to flow pure through mud'. What Onesicritus managed to grasp of his teaching, as paraphrased by Strabo, is that 'the best teaching is that which removes pleasure and pain from the soul … man trains the body for toil in order that his opinion may be strengthened, whereby he may put a stop to dissensions and be ready to give good advice to all, both in public and in private; and that he had advised Taxiles to receive Alexander'. Strabo goes on to state that Mandanis asked Onesicritus whether such doctrines were taught among the Greeks. Mandanis seems scarcely to have presented a 'doctrine' at this stage, but Arrian makes clear that Dandamis (as he calls him) had stressed his need for nothing, since he lived on what the earth offered freely, and expressed his opinion that Alexander's wanderings were pointless. He also spoke of death as a release from the body. In Strabo, Onesicritus answered that 'Pythagoras taught such doctrines, and also bade people to abstain from meat, as did also Socrates and

1. Str. 15.1.63–5 = Onesic. F 17. Cf. Arr. *Anab.* 7.2.2–4.

11.1 Alexander meets the naked philosophers; from the *Alexander Romance* MS D, fol. 114r (Hellenic Institute, Venice).

Diogenes, and that he himself had been a pupil of Diogenes.'[2] Mandanis goes on to assert that the Greeks are 'sound-minded in general, but wrong in one respect, in that they prefer custom to nature; for otherwise they would not be ashamed to go naked, like himself, and live on frugal fare'.

Vegetarianism is characteristic of all renouncers, whether Brahman (today Hindu) or Buddhist, though living on fruit alone is a step further. The *Sāmaññaphala Sutta* offers the reason: 'whereas some recluses and brahmans, while living on food offered to the faithful, continually cause damage to seed and plant life – to plants propagated from roots, stems, joints, buddings and seeds –

2. Keith 1909 is a level-headed discussion of the question of Indian influence on Pythagoras, primarily in relation to the doctrine of metempsychosis. He concludes that there is no influence of Indian ideas on Pythagoras, and that this is surprising, since the idea itself is not all that common worldwide. Its distribution is wider than Keith knew. Obeyesekere 2002 considers some parallels also with American Indian ideas, where influence does not come into question. Most beliefs in reincarnation are confined to reincarnation within the lineage. Empson 2016, 112 presents the common non-specialist assumption, that Pythagoras visited India.

he [the true ascetic] abstains from damaging seed and plant life'.[3] Though Vedic civilisation is founded on animal sacrifice, śramanas rejected this; the Bhāgavata religion then adopted the Buddhist approach in order to win people back to what has become Hinduism. A hymn to Kṛṣṇa expresses the transition:

> Moved by deep compassion, you condemn the Vedic way
> That ordains animal slaughter in rites of sacrifice.
> You take form as the enlightened Buddha, Kṛṣṇa.
> Triumph, Hari, Lord of the World![4]

The vegetarianism of the naked philosophers is a fundamental feature of all later Greek descriptions of them, and is adduced in several discussions of the ethics of meat-eating and sacrifice, including those of Plutarch and Porphyry.[5]

Onesicritus also reports that the philosophers are experts in natural phenomena, including 'prognostics, rains, droughts, and diseases'; and that they from time to time visit the city where they receive fruit from passers-by as a free offering; or they may receive gifts of oil, with which they are anointed. They also enter houses, including the women's apartments, and share in meals and conversation. 'They regard disease of the body as a most disgraceful thing; and he who suspects disease in his own body commits suicide through means of fire'.

The passage offers a vivid portrait of a recognisable type of Indian sādhu, intent on spiritual enlightenment by ascetic means. 'The Munis girdled with the wind, wear garments soiled of yellow hue. They, following the wind's swift course, go where the gods have gone before.'[6] Like modern ascetics (and Buddhist monks) he lives on the alms of others and practises various forms of yoga that resemble penances to the untutored eye. There are several naked sects at the present day, and to identify the one Dandamis adhered to is probably impossible.[7] There are obvious elements of Greek terminology in the description, from the opposition of 'nature and culture' to the references to Diogenes and to Pythagoras. It is notable that what we are told of Mandanis' teaching, at the point where Onesicritus compares it to that of Pythagoras, is very little. Neither the elimination of pleasure and pain nor the use of toil

3. *Sāmaññaphala Sutta* 46 (Bodhi 1989, 31).

4. Jayadave, *Gītagovinda*: Miller 1977, 71.

5. Stoneman 1994a.

6. *RV* 10.136.3. They follow the way of *brahmacarya*: see Drew 1987, 149; Gandhi cited in Stoneman 1995.

7. Arora 2005, 76.

11.2 Sādhus in modern India. These naked ascetics are in the same tradition as those whom Alexander encountered.

to make one's advice useful to others are prominent Pythagorean practices, while it is Onesicritus himself who adds the point about Pythagoras' vegetarianism.[8] Mandanis' exclusive consumption of, apparently, fruit, is only mentioned later. It may be that Strabo is reporting Onesicritus' account in a jumbled form, but the suspicion has also arisen that Onesicritus, as a pupil of Diogenes, eagerly attributed Cynic ideas to the man he encountered under the trees of Taxila.

When I wrote about this subject in 1995 I inclined to the view that much of what Onesicritus wrote was actually his own ideas, based on his own Cynic doctrines, but I have since come to believe that a good deal of what he reported is genuine Indian material.[9] After all, the style of Mandanis is recognisable to any visitor to India. But what of his doctrines? Nudity, vegetarianism, the receiving of alms do not get us very far. It is interesting that Mandanis is described as giving advice to rulers and as knowing about prognostics and weather, for these are skills attributed to the Brahmans who surround the king in Megasthenes' account, which we shall investigate in detail later.

There is a good deal more 'doctrine' in the other major source on the naked philosophers, the *Alexander Romance*.[10] The date of composition of this much-rewritten work is a controversial question, but there can be no doubt that the essentials of this passage go back to an early date and are based on a first-hand account of the visit to the philosophers, perhaps one written by Onesicritus himself. Here the naked philosophers are explicitly identified with 'the Brahmans or Oxydorkai'. The Oxydracae and the Brahmans are the objects of two completely different campaigns by Alexander in the Punjab, and neither of them has anything to do with the naked philosophers of Taxila. The source of the confusion is unidentifiable, but there may be some Buddhist influence here, since the Buddha was given to using 'the true *brahmaṇa*' as a designation for true religious seekers, despite his contempt for the philistine ritual-obsessed traditionalism of actual Brahmans.[11] On the other hand, Plutarch may be the origin of the confusion: see below.

8. This became an important issue in later Greek ethical thought, notably Plutarch and Porphyry, and the Indian 'Brahmans' were always cited. Bronkhorst 2016, 245–6 doubts whether such a diet as Dandamis' is sustainable and regards it as an imaginary ideal. But this text seems to show it as a reality before the resurgence of Brahmanism that followed the spread of Buddhism.

9. Stoneman 1995; Stoneman 2008, 94–5. Woodcock 1966, 33 is a clear statement of the Cynic interpretation.

10. *AR* 3.5–6.

11. *Dhammapada* 141–2: 'Neither wandering about naked, nor matted hair, nor mud, / Neither fasting, nor sleeping on hard ground, / Nor dust and dirt, nor austere acts in the crouch-

Here the philosophers invite Alexander to come and learn about their way of life: 'we are naked and we have devoted ourselves to the pursuit of wisdom'. Alexander finds the philosophers living in a woodland setting, surrounded by a river, and there are fruiting palm trees and grape vines. In the distance the philosophers' wives and children can be seen tending the flocks.[12] These sages resemble the mendicant homeless wanderers whom Prince Gautama meets in Aśvaghoṣa's *Buddhacarīta*, or the anchorites dwelling in a grove also described there:[13] some of the anchorites are grazing like deer.

Dwelling in groves is highly characteristic of Indian ascetics, often in groups, for they are not hermits. Octavio Paz's description is vivid and may help to envisage the group that Onesicritus interviewed:

> At the foot of the banyan tree a dozen *sādhus* had congregated, all of them advanced in years, with shaved heads or long tangled locks coated with red dust, wavy white beards, their faces smeared with paint and their foreheads decorated with signs: vertical and horizontal stripes, circles, half-moons, tridents. Some of them were decked in white or saffron robes, others were naked, their bodies covered with ashes or cow dung, their genitals protected by a cotton pouch hanging from a cord that served as a belt. Lying stretched out on the ground, they were smoking, drinking tea or milk or bhang, laughing, conversing, praying in a half-whisper, or simply lying there silently.[14]

Many ancient Indian texts describe such assemblages of ascetics. For example, the story of the king-seer Sumitra in the *Mahābhārata* describes the arrival of the king at the retreat of some ascetics in the 'great forest'. They pay their respects to the king and ask why he has come there. He explains that he is hunting deer:

> I am protected by a large army, and my advisors and my wives are with me.... I have come to this forest by chance while following the running deer. And now I am before you, good men, my Royal Splendor gone, my hopes dashed, faint with fatigue ... You men are highly blessed, so I will

ing posture, / Cleanses a mortal who has not transcended doubts. / Though well adorned, if one would move with tranquillity, / At peace, restrained, assured, living the higher life, / Having put down the rod toward all beings, / He is a *brāhmaṇa,* he, a recluse, he, a bhikkhu.'

12. *Buddhacarīta* 8.62: kings take their wives 'to the forest'.

13. Ibid. 5.17, 7.3.

14. Paz 1989, 150. See also the photographs in Hartsuiker 1993/2014.

ask you something I am not sure of. In this world, which one seems to you more vast, a man full of hope or the sky?[15]

The echoes of Alexander's encounter are numerous: the king's large army, his loss of confidence in his own position, his asking of questions, the first of which takes the form of 'this or that?' This is an Indian conception of an event that might frequently occur in legendary or ancient India.

Again in the *Harṣacarīta*, the ninth-century biography of King Harṣa by Bāna, there is a lengthy description of a peaceful grove where the ascetics dwell. 'The grassy glades were all bright with the antelopes skipping about without fear ... the deodars were spangled with their clusters of flowers, while the lines of rose-apples and *Jambhīras* were studded with patches of flowering betel-vines; the air was kissed by clumps of *Dhulīkadamba*-trees white with the powder of their flowers, while the ground was moist with the dropping honey'.[16] Into this *locus amoenus* the king enters and sees 'various Buddhists from various provinces seated in different situations, – perched on pillars, or seated on the rocks or dwelling in bowers of creepers or lying in thickets or in the shadow of the branches or squatting on the roots of trees – devotees dead to all passion, Jainas in white robes, white mendicants [*sc.* Hindus], followers of Kriṣna, religious students, ascetics who pulled out their hair, followers of Kapila, Jainas, Lokāyatikas, followers of Kaṇāda, followers of the Upaniṣads, believers in God as Creator, assayers of metals, students of the legal institutes, students of the Purāṇas' – the list goes on. Even the monkeys and parrots are engaged in rituals, while some owls are reciting the births of the Bodhisattva. (The company also includes a few vegetarian tigers.) The king approaches this group with reverence, leaning on the shoulder of a courtier and 'attended by a few tributary kings', to pose his questions, not this time in the form of a quiz.[17] (Many pleasantries later, he asks for news of his sister, to be told that she is even now ascending a pyre. He sets off to rescue her).[18]

In these two texts, written centuries later than the *Alexander Romance*, but in the case of the *Mahābhārata* probably going back in essentials to a century or more before Alexander's visit, we find scenes that resemble Alexander's encounter with the naked philosophers in striking ways. It is worth remarking that Bāna is the only author in the whole of Sanskrit literature to make

15. *Mbh.* 12.125.25–30; p. 486 in Fitzgerald's translation, vol. 7.

16. Bāna 1897, 234.

17. Ibid., 235–6.

18. Ibid., 240 and 249.

any reference to Alexander (as a model of prowess whom Harṣa will easily excel); but we need not assume that Bāna lifted his story from a reading of the Alexander historians. Both texts describe a familiar Indian reality. Does the fact that the *Alexander Romance* tells a similar story mean that it is drawing directly on Indian modes of narrative?

Not only Bāna made the hermits' grove into a classical *locus amoenus*. The orator Dio Chrysostom (ca. 40–120 CE), drawing on Ctesias and other fabulous accounts of the mysterious East, developed this aspect of the scene in his Thirty-Fifth Discourse:

> A gentle breeze is ever blowing, and the climate is nearly constant throughout the year, and it resembles most closely that of early summer ... And these people live more than four hundred years, and during all that time they are beautiful and youthful and neither old age nor disease nor poverty is found among them. So wonderful and so numerous are these blessings, and yet there are people called Brachmanes who, abandoning these rivers and the people scattered along their banks, turn aside and devote themselves to private speculation and meditation, undertaking amazing physical labours without compulsion and enduring fearful tests of endurance. And it is said that they have one special fountain, the Fountain of Truth, by far the best and most godlike of all, and that those who drink their fill thereof have never been known to lie.[19]

But the literary model changes in the next section where Alexander asks the philosophers a series of questions about their way of life. An independent version of this question-and-answer session existed and is partly preserved on a papyrus dating from about 100 BCE.[20] It was known to Plutarch, who incorporated it in his *Life* of Alexander. This story relates to the rebellious Brahmans of Brahmanabad, though Plutarch calls them 'gymnosophists'. Plutarch's conflation of the two groups seems to be at the root of the later, universal use of the word 'Brahmans' to denote the naked philosophers.[21] This version takes the form of what folklorists call a *Halsrätsel*, a riddle on the answer to which one's life depends. The papyrus begins in mid-sentence: '[whoever] I command to judge, he shall be your moderator; if I decide that he has

19. D.Chr. *Or.* 35.21–2. Less idyllic is Octavio Paz's description of a modern group of sādhus: Paz 1997, 150–1, quoted above.

20. Berlin papyrus 13044; translation in Stoneman 2012, 77–8.

21. Bichler 2016, 16.

judged well, he alone shall be let off alive'. At the end of the excerpt, Alexander asks the tenth philosopher to state which of them had given the worst answer; but 'the Indian did not want anyone to perish as a result of his answer, so he replied that each had answered worse than the other'. Alexander then says he will put them all to death, but the philosopher points out the logical fallacy and Alexander lets them all off.

The head-wager is not alien to Indian tradition. Indian sages who entered into debate with Tripitaka, the fictional version of the monk Xuanzang in the famous Chinese novel *Journey to the West*, showed themselves willing to forfeit their heads if they lost the argument. These Hindu thinkers seem to have been Lokāyatas, famous for their captious arguments. The get-out clause in this story is that Tripitaka, as a Buddhist, will not take life, and thus the sages do not die.[22]

It amused someone to turn this dialogue with philosophers into a philosophical puzzle – a form of the liar paradox – but that has little to do with the content of the questions and answers, which contain genuine information about the philosophers' way of life. Alexander, oddly, begins by asking them whether they have no graves, to which the reply is that the ground where they dwell is their grave. (Apparently they do not burn their dead as Hindus do.)[23] Further tricky questions follow: 'Who are more numerous, the living or the dead?' 'Which is stronger, death or life?'[24] 'Which came first, day or night?'[25] 'Which side is better, the left or the right?' The series of opposites may seem to recall the Pythagorean tables of opposites, but Śiva, for example, is a god who combines opposites in himself, so the fascination is equally Indian.[26] The questions and answers seem less than profound, but in the midst are two that relate to Alexander's own situation: 'Which is the wickedest of all creatures?', to which the answer is, 'Man', with Alexander as the prime example; and 'What

22. Waley 1952, 54–5 and n. 271. Śiva, in the form of a clever Dalit, made use of questions to confound a Brahman interlocutor: Dalrymple 2009, 40.

23. Cf. Megasth. Ff 15 J, and 32.54. The same question occurs in the dialogue with the Elders of the South in the Hebrew version of the *AR*: see Kazis 1962, 13–14 and 133–43. Present day sādhus are not always cremated, but their bodies weighted with rocks and thrown into a river: Hartsuiker 1993/2014, 138. It is also possible, since the encounter is supposed to take place in Taxila, that the strong Achaemenid component in the city's population favoured exposure of the dead.

24. Cf. perhaps *Bṛh. Up.* 1.2, where Death creates everything.

25. Cf. *SB* 13.5.2.17, 'What was the first conception? The sky': Basu 1969, 229–30. Also *Bṛh. Up.* 1.1.2.

26. O'Flaherty 1973/1981, 210ff.

is kingship?': 'unjust power used to the disadvantage of others; insolence supported by opportunity; a golden burden'.

The dialogue has sometimes been thought to be a thoroughly Greek confection, and Tarn was of the opinion that it influenced the *Questions of King Milinda*, a Greek version of which then further influenced the *Letter of Aristeas*.[27] In 1995 I assembled a good many examples to suggest that the dialogue takes a largely Indian form. I return to this topic in more detail in the following chapter.

The narrative moves on from these home truths to a short sermon by the leader of the philosophers, here (and in all subsequent versions of the encounter) called Dandamis. This is presumably the correct form of the name, related as it is to the Sanskrit *dānda*, 'rod'.[28] Dandamis describes a life without possessions, a diet of fruit that comes from the trees, presumably without cultivation, and a marital regime in which each philosopher mates with his wife once a month until she has borne two children.[29] They then ask Alexander for immortality, to which Alexander replies that that is not his to give. This may be just a feint, since immortality does not seem to be a typically Indian aspiration; but in the *Buddhacarīta* the ascetics describe their diet to Prince Gautama, and do go on to say that they are seeking Paradise.[30] The Upaniṣads are also frequently concerned with immortality (rather than nirvana). The mention of immortality enables the philosophers to make their next point: 'Since you are a mortal why do you make so many wars? When you have seized everything, where will you take it? Surely you will only have to leave it behind for others?' (The point gets emphasised in all the Islamic representations of Alexander, who instructs that he shall be placed on his bier with one hand exposed to show that he leaves the world empty-handed.) The topos of the sage reproving the king appears also in *Bṛhadāraṇyaka Upaniṣad*, and elsewhere.[31]

27. See Stoneman 1995, 111 with further details. Kubica 2016, 146 also emphasises the Indian quality of the *Milindapañha*.

28. *Manusmṛti* 4.36: 'the priest who is a Vedic graduate … should carry a bamboo staff, a gourd filled with water, the initiatory thread, a broom made of sacrificial grass, and two bright gold earrings'. The rod survives when the ascetic has renounced all else. The *dānda* is especially associated with Ājīvikas: Bhagat 1976, 141.

29. The detail may surprise a reader familiar with the prevailing image of the gaunt renunciant of India, but at the present day a significant proportion of sādhus do marry and raise children: Hausner 2007, 38 and 40. See also *Buddhacarīta* 8.62.

30. *Buddhacarīta* 8.12ff.

31. *Bṛh. Up.* 4.1. Janaka in the *Viṣṇu Purāṇa* is another example: Drew 1987, 148.

Alexander is moved, and responds that his own way of life, of conquest and rapine, is ordained by Providence above, and that action is as necessary to the world as quietism. He ends by offering Dandamis gifts of gold, bread, wine and olive oil. Dandamis laughs and accepts the oil, but instead of anointing himself with it, as we might expect, he pours it into the fire. His action is perhaps less shocking to Alexander than that of the old woman whom Allen Ginsberg encountered near the burning ghats of Calcutta: he offered her some coins, but 'she accepted them and flung them away, forward into the next fire-pit where a bearded Saddhu crouched toasting his pancakes'.[32] But the message is the same: possessions are worthless.[33]

The second part of Alexander's encounter with the naked philosophers has more philosophical content. I have considered its later literary developments in previous publications:[34] here I would like to try to relate it more closely to its possible Indian roots, by recounting an anecdote of my own visit (with my wife) to Varanasi in 2015.

The Brahmin Priest

As we walked down to watch the evening ceremony of launching leaf-lanterns on the Ganges, we were introduced to a Brahmin priest. Taking us aside into the cow-shed which seemed to be the base of his operations, he favoured us with an eloquent disquisition on the Hindu religion and its multiplicity of gods, as well as its ethical imperatives. A short, stocky man of sixty in a stained white *kurta*, his refined features framed by a grey beard and his forehead marked with a broad vertical red stripe, he was an arresting presence, and his speech held us riveted to the spot for a quarter of an hour. His English was excellent – no problem here of trying to conduct an interview through a series of interpreters like Onesicritus – and his remarks reminded me frequently of what Dandamis is said to have said to Alexander. A Brahmin and not a naked ascetic or *nāgā-bābā*,[35] he nevertheless insisted that all peoples worshipped the same divinity in their own way, whether Hindu, Christian, Jewish or Mus-

32. Ginsberg 1970/1996, 116. Aitken 1992, 81–2 mentions a sādhu who burns a gift of (paper) money.

33. In the version in Palladius, *De Brag.* 2.37, Dandamis accepts only the edible items. Cf. Hartsuiker 1993/2014, 94.

34. Stoneman 1994a and 1995; 2008, 97–106; 2012 (including translations of the texts).

35. Hausner 2007, 85 for this term.

lim. Though Śiva is the god who dominates Varanasi, the multiplicity of Hindu gods was, for him, ethicised in the same way as the monotheistic religions. Compassion, concern and good action were as important for him as ritual observance. The influence of Christianity may be felt in this ethicisation of the Indian gods: blue-skinned Śiva, with his matted locks and trident, able in his rage to destroy whatever he creates, is now commonly portrayed with an almost simpering expression of benevolence that surely owes something to Victorian and later representations of Jesus.

But there was nothing soft about this priest. His work was to maintain a hospice for the destitute elderly. At any one time there were some forty old people in his care. He and his fellow charitable workers provided them with basic rations, and furthermore roused them every day at 4.30 a.m. to go to the temple, where they could spend the day praying. It's not a regime I'd look forward to in my eighties or nineties, but it was well meant. And death, when it comes, is the same for all of us, he insisted. Possessions are worth nothing in the end, for we all leave the world empty-handed.[36] I remembered the persistent theme of the Persian Alexander texts, that the king insisted he be buried with one hand hanging outside his winding-sheet to indicate that even the greatest achievers leave the world empty-handed. This lesson, or something like it, is one that Alexander repeatedly learns in his conversations with the naked philosophers, especially after they have become redefined as 'Brahmans', in the Cynic Geneva papyrus and in Palladius. It seemed to me that here was an idea that presented itself to Alexander and his men when they came face to face with the great renouncers of India.

When the priest spoke of the poverty of the men and women in his charge, my hand moved towards my pocket, but he stayed me. There was something more he wished to show us. Stepping out of the cow-shed, he led us down among the fires burning on the cremation ghats. At six o'clock in the evening there were several families gathered to bid farewell to their loved ones, whom they had brought, clothed in white and garlanded with marigolds, to be immersed in Mother Ganga, left to dry out for some hours, and then placed on a pyre of ironwood logs, covered high with more logs, and ignited from an eternal flame of Śiva that was tended by priests in a nearby lean-to. He led us among the blazing piles, pointing out here a leg, there a head, blackening

36. As Raymond Chandler put it, 'In a little while we shall all be dead. Therefore let us behave as if we were dead already.'

rapidly in the consuming heat. The property of the ironwood was such that it burned hot and strong,[37] and, remarkably, no odour of burning flesh or hair mingled with the acrid smoke from the pyres. (We still had to send all our clothes to the laundry the next day.)

The ironwood, he explained, had to be imported many hundreds of kilometres and was very expensive: 750 rupees per kilo, and it could take up to fifteen kilos (if my notes are correct) to burn a medium-sized body, an expense that had to be met by the families when there were such, and in the case of his destitute veterans by charitable donations. This was the moment at which we were expected to dip into our pockets for the price of a kilo or two of logs.

When Alexander was impressed by Dandamis he attempted to give him gold, but was laughingly spurned, on the grounds that the ascetics had no use for wealth, or even for food other than that which hung on the trees. But Dandamis did accept some oil, which he used to feed his holy fire. So our donation too went to advance a sacred fire or two, and to promote the purity of the inevitable disposal of the remains of a life that had ended.

We had not a lot of money to give, but gained the impression that whatever we had given would not be enough for the insatiable requirements of human mortality. The words we had listened to certainly deserved a gift and we went away both educated and, a little, persuaded that, in a city as old as Varanasi, said to be the oldest continuously functioning city in the world, human constants were apparent, and that Alexander or Onesicritus, if they had stood where we did, might have received the same instruction.

A Pyre in Persepolis

Alexander's involvement with the philosophers of India did not end with this encounter in Taxila and its literary elaborations. A very real naked sādhu, Calanus, attached himself to Alexander's retinue and accompanied him to the end of his own life, which concluded in a spectacular fashion.[38] Sometime in February 324 BCE, seven months after the army and the fleet had departed

37. Pradip Krishen's marvellous *Trees of Delhi* (2005) merely remarks discreetly that it 'makes good charcoal'.

38. Lassen 1847–61, 2.695–6 is a clear account. See Plu. *Alex.* 69, and the sources cited in the next note.

from the mouth of the Indus, the army arrived back at the burnt-out city of Persepolis.[39] One of Alexander's friends, the Indian philosopher Calanus, fell ill at nearby Pasargadae and met a spectacular end – *en Persais*, says Plutarch, which strictly means 'at Persepolis'. A man of seventy-three, he had been suffering from stomach pains and sought to die, since his disease was incurable: 'having received the utmost limit of happiness both from nature and from Fortune', he insisted on death by fire, and requested that Alexander build him a pyre.

> At first Alexander tried to dissuade him from this plan, but when he was unsuccessful, he agreed to do what was asked. After the project had become generally known, the pyre was erected, and everybody came to see the remarkable sight. True to his own creed, Caranus [as Diodorus calls him] cheerfully mounted the pyre and perished, consumed along with it. Some of those who were present thought him mad, others vainglorious about his ability to bear pain, while others simply marvelled at his fortitude and contempt for death.[40]

Strabo adds more details about the pyre, saying that according to one account it was surmounted with a golden couch on which Calanus lay down to die. 'But others state that a wooden house was built, and that it was filled with leaves and that a pyre was built on its roof; being shut in as he had bidden, after the procession which he had accompanied, he flung himself upon the pyre and, like a beam of timber, was burned up along with the house'.[41]

As often, Strabo is not very clear. Was Calanus inside or on top of the house? The traditional image of a classical pyre has the dead hero placed on top of a great heap of timber. But at the burning ghats in Varanasi the dead are placed in the middle of the pile of logs, and it is clear from illustrations of both witch-burnings and sati-suicides that death ensues more rapidly if the victim is surrounded by the combustible material. Jean-Baptiste Tavernier, the seventeenth-century traveller, describes the method of widow-burning he

39. Strabo is specific, but Diodorus 17.109.1 merely says 'the frontier of Susiana'. The army then reached Susa after a further twenty-four days' march, in March 324: Plin. *NH* 6.100 = Onesic. F 28.

40. Diod. 17.107.2–5.

41. Str. 15.1.68. Ael. *VH* 5.6 lists the fragrant woods of which the pyre was constructed – cedar, citron, cypress, myrtle and laurel – and maintains that Calanus stood erect on the pyre as it blazed up.

had observed in Gujarat: 'on the margin of a river or tank, a kind of small hut, about twelve feet square [1.1 m^2], is built of reeds and all kinds of faggots, on which some pots of oil and other drugs are placed in order to make it burn quickly. The woman is seated in a half-reclining position in the middle of the hut, her head reposes on a kind of pillow of wood and she rests her back against a post to which she is tied by her waist by one of the Brahmins, lest she should escape on feeling the flame.'[42]

The procession – which Strabo only mentions after his account of the philosopher being shut in the 'house' – is described in more detail by Arrian:

> Some say that he also had a great procession formed, horses and men, some in full armour, others carrying all sorts of incense for the pyre; others again say that they carried gold and silver cups and royal raiment. For Calanus himself a horse was made ready, since he could not walk because of his illness; and yet he could not even mount the horse, but was borne on a litter, lying down, crowned with garlands in the Indian fashion and chanting in the Indian tongue. The Indians say that these chants were hymns of praise to gods . . . He climbed the pyre and lay down with decorum in the sight of the whole army . . . when the fire was lit by those detailed for the task, the trumpets (says Nearchus) sounded, as Alexander had ordered, and the whole army raised the shout they would raise when entering battle, and the elephants trumpeted their shrill war-cry, in honour of Calanus.[43]

In modern times the procession of a widow to the pyre has been accompanied by drums and other musicians, so Calanus was doing things in the proper style.[44] Calanus bade farewell to Alexander, remarking that they would meet again in Babylon.[45] The flames leapt high, and Calanus, like a good Hindu widow, remained motionless as the flames consumed him.

Calanus (Plutarch says his real name was Sphines, but that he was known as Calanus from the Indian word for 'greetings', *kale* – see below)[46] had become acquainted with Alexander at Taxila in spring 326. He was the only one of the ascetics who deigned to visit Alexander, and he had impressed the king

42. Quoted in Narasimhan 1990, 109. There is an illustration of such a hut in Hawley (ed.) 1994, 42.

43. Arr. *Anab.* 7.3.3–6.

44. According to Aelian (*VH* 2.41), contests took place after the burning, and included a traditionl Indian drinking contest 'in honour of Calanus'.

45. Plu. *Alex.* 69.6.

46. Ibid. 64.6.

with his parable about the ox-hide: he threw down a dry and shrivelled hide, and showed how, if he pressed down on one edge of it, the other edges rose up; the only way to make the hide stay flat was to stand in its centre. Thus, Calanus concluded, Alexander ought to have a care to maintain the middle of his empire in order to keep the edges under control.[47]

The illustration seems entirely characteristic of Indian thinking, since a similar story is told of Candragupta – but with an opposite moral. When the greedy child tried to bite into the middle of a hot chapatti, his nurse adjured him to nibble first at the edges. Thus, he learned, the way to conquer the Nanda empire was to pick off the edges first and gradually work to the centre. (See chapter 5 above.)[48]

Alexander was slow to heed the advice, perhaps because he did not yet know where the centre of his empire, which might yet encompass the whole world, was to be. However, he found Calanus a stimulating companion and the philosopher joined his entourage – for which he was much scorned by the other ascetics of Taxila. Megasthenes described him as 'a man without self-control, and a slave to the table of Alexander'.[49] He goes on to say that for this he was censured, while Mandanis (or Dandamis) is commended. The hostility of the other ascetics to Calanus is emphasised in the later retellings in the *Alexander Romance* and in Palladius' *De Bragmanibus.* Nearchus states that Calanus was not a Brahman,[50] but Aelian calls him such, since he is writing at a time when the word had come to mean simply 'Indian philosopher'.

Suicide and Sati

The black log crashed above the white,
    The little flames and lean
Red as slaughter and blue as steel,
That whistled and fluttered from head to heel,
Leaped up anew, for they found their meal
    On the heart of – the Boondi Queen!

—RUDYARD KIPLING, 'THE LAST SUTTEE'

47. Elwin 1955, 147 recounts a Baiga myth, in which the hero Baiga nails down the four corners of the world like a chapatti on the ocean.

48. Plu. *Alex.* 65.5.

49. Str. 15.1.68. = Ff 33 J, 41 Schw. Also Arr. *Anab.* 7.2.4, μάλιστα δὴ αὑτοῦ ἀκράτορα.

50. Nearch. F 23.

The manner of Calanus' suicide evidently became known among the philosophers back in Taxila, since their opinions of this act are also recorded, and Megasthenes a couple of decades later was able to report what they thought:

> Megasthenes says that suicide is not a dogma among the philosophers, and that those who commit suicide are adjudged guilty of the impetuosity of youth; that some who are of a hardy constitution rush to meet a blow or over a precipice, while those less tolerant of pain plunge into deep water; others, who can endure pain, hang themselves, while those of a fiery temperament hurl themselves into fire. Such was Calanus.[51]

There are two matters of historical interest in this narrative: first, the suicide by fire and the Macedonians' reaction to it; second, the judgment on suicide by fire that was offered by the other philosophers.

The dramatic bonfire at Persepolis, or Pasargadae, clearly made a tremendous impression on the onlookers, and on the historians who were present. By contrast, the expedition's first encounter with the custom of suicide by fire is passed over quite briefly by our sources. It was Onesicritus, with his interest in local customs, who observed that among the Cathaeans (between the rivers Ravi and Chenab) it was customary not only for bride and groom to choose one another, rather than entering arranged marriages, but also for wives to be burned alongside their deceased husbands. Onesicritus was told that this custom was established because of the propensity of wives to fall in love with other men and to poison their husbands in order to free themselves; but he is sceptical of both the practice and the reason.[52]

Suicide by fire became associated with Indians in subsequent centuries. The most striking account, from the years after the death of Alexander, is the case of the wife of the general Ceteus.[53] Ceteus died in the first major battle between the two successor generals, Antigonus and Eumenes, in late 317 BCE, which took place somewhere in the desert of central Iran. He was in charge of the Indian troops, and had two Indian wives, both of whom vied for the hon-

51. Str. 15.1.68.

52. Onesic. F 21 = Str. 15.1.30; also Diod. 17.91.3. Diod. 19.33 repeats this information. It became generally accepted in early modern writers on sati: Banerjee 2003, 138 and 142. The legendary example of Evadne, wife of Capaneus, who hurled herself into her husband's pyre, was not mentioned by the Greek writers in this connection. Herodotus (5.5) speaks of widow-sacrifice among the Crestones, in the region of Thrace – but not by fire.

53. Diod. 19.33–4. Bosworth 2002, 173–87.

our of being burned alive with his corpse. The younger asserted that the elder was pregnant and therefore could not be burned, while the elder demanded that as the senior wife she should have the right to carry out the sacrifice. Midwives were fetched to determine that the elder was indeed pregnant, on which she 'departed weeping, rending the wreath that was about her head and tearing her hair'. The younger wife rejoiced, and advanced on the pyre dressed as if for a wedding, with ribbons in her hair; she gave away her jewellery – rings set with precious stones, necklaces and a circlet for her head, of golden stars studded with jewels – mounted the pyre, assisted by her brother, and, after the army had marched three times around the pyre, submitted calmly to the flames. The reactions of the onlookers were the same as on the occasion of Calanus' immolation: some were moved to pity, others to extravagant praise, while some were appalled by the cruelty of the custom.

In the reign of Augustus an Indian whose name is reported as Zarmonochegas or something similar – the 'Zarmono' element is surely the Sanskrit *śramana*, an ascetic (see discussion below) – came from Bargose (Barygaza) to Rome and burnt himself to death.[54] The mode of death was adopted by the philosopher Peregrinus who wanted to make a spectacle of his end, as described by Lucian in a famous essay. The Indian practice of widow-burning was also well known to Roman writers.[55] Both Cicero and Propertius regarded it as a signal mark of female virtue.[56] Later writers often interpreted the act as one of devotion to the husband,[57] or simply as 'admirable' endurance.[58]

By contrast, Indian sources make no clear reference to widow-burning before the Gupta period.[59] It is never mentioned in the *Ṛg Veda*, both the *Arthaśāstra* and the *Laws of Manu* forbid the suicide (of any kind) of widow, and the first explicit statement seems to come in the *Viṣṇu Smṛti* (dated to about 700–1000 CE): 'When a woman's husband has died, she should either practise ascetic celibacy or ascend (the funeral pyre) after him.'[60] But the first

54. Nic. Dam. *FGrH* 90 F 100 in Str. 16.1.73, Dio 54.9.8.

55. The evidence is assembled in Yardley and Heckel 1981.

56. Cic. *TD* 5.78, Prop. 3.13.15–22: Banerjee 2003, 91. So also Montaigne, 'On Virtue'.

57. Banerjee 2003, 143.

58. Nicholas Worthington in 1613, quoted in Banerjee 2003, 118.

59. Narasimhan 1990, 17–18. See also Jamieson and Brereton 2014, 34. *RV* 10.18.7–8 seems to refer to a temporary ascent of the pyre before being recalled to the land of the living.

60. *Viṣṇu Smṛti* 25.14: cited from the Wikipedia article on sati, which should be used with caution.

11.3 A medieval sati-stone (commemoration of a sati) at Vidiśā (Besnagar).

sati-stones (monuments to the virtuous widow) date from about 40 CE, and there seems little doubt that the practice goes back earlier than the attested literature. Diodorus' account is enough to prove that.[61]

There are occurrences of self-immolation of both men and women in the epics. The *Mahābhārata* cites a bogus reference from the *Ṛg Veda* for the practice of sati,[62] but more than one episode revolves around it. In the first book of the *Mahābhārata*, Pandu, already married to Kunti and the father of five sons (the Pandavas), while wandering in the forest one day, is overwhelmed by the beauty of the nubile Madri, who has come out to follow him 'wearing one pretty piece of clothing'. 'He forced himself on Madri by the Law of copulation', but had forgotten the curse laid on him when he killed a deer (who was an ascetic in disguise) in the middle of mating with his doe. The deer cursed Pandu, that he would die 'while lying with a woman you love, blinded by passion'.[63] As Madri held the dead king in her arms, Kunti arrived and began to rage at Madri, who is described as 'a Bactrian woman'. The two of them vie for the honour of following Pandu into death, but it is Madri, 'Pandu's glorious wife by the law, [who] hastened after the bull among men on his funeral pyre'.[64] Prakash notes that the act is regarded as strange by the other participants in the drama, and that perhaps it should be seen as a Bactrian rite, characteristic of the north-west.[65] The widows of the Kurus, their opponents, do not commit suicide.

In the *Rāmāyaṇa* there is also a case of self-immolation, this time by a sage. The anchorite Śarabangha, who dwells in the Dandaka forest, wishes to depart from life once he has beheld the hero Rāma, and does so by ascending a pyre.[66] Again, at the end of the epic, Rāma's brother Bharat is about to burn himself to death when Rāma arrives by his magical air transport in the nick of time to resume his role as king.[67] A related case is that of Sita herself, whose

61. It is cited by Narasimhan, but does not deflect her from her insistence that the rite is not pre-Gupta.

62. Narasimhan 1990, 16.

63. *Mbh.* 1.109.

64. Ibid. 1.116.

65. Prakash 1964, 91–2.

66. *Rām.* 3 (*Araṇyakāṇḍa*) 2. The ashram may apparently still be visited, eight miles (13 km) from Chithara Station, MP.

67. In an episode set in the Nanda period, the pilgrim Faxian describes how Ananda burned himself in the middle of a river in order to enter parinirvana, in the presence of Ajataśatru and the Licchavis. See Li 2002, 190.

chastity falls under suspicion after her long captivity in the company of the demon king Ravana. In order to prove her purity, she steps into a fire and is unharmed. In the *Bhāgavata Purāṇa* the wives of Kṛṣṇa enter the fire on the news of his death.[68]

The original sati in Indian mythology is, of course, the goddess Sati, the daughter of Daksha.[69] Sati moved heaven and earth to persuade Śiva to take her as his wife. When Daksha subsequently refused to invite Śiva to his sacrifice because he was disgusted by his ascetic's appearance and habits, Sati stormed into the centre of the proceedings, quarrelled with her father, and created from her own ascetic heat (*tapas*) a huge pyre, by which she was consumed. Śiva's terrible revenge on Daksha, beheaded in a scene of carnage for his insolence, is a story that strongly recalls the fate of Pentheus at the hands of Dionysus in Greek mythology. When Śiva's anger subsides, Daksha's head cannot be found, and in order to restore him to life it is replaced with that of a goat.[70]

Burning as a marker of wifely loyalty is thus at the heart of Hindu mythology. As Amir Khusraw noted in the thirteenth century, 'A Hindu woman burns herself for her husband willingly. A Hindu man sacrifices his life for his deity or his chieftain. Although it is not allowed by the religion of Islam, it is a great and noble deed.'[71] The long story of its continuance in India, especially among the Rajputs of Rajasthan, makes startling reading for a Westerner.[72] Between 1815 and 1829, for example, there were 7,941 cases of sati in Bengal. Many widows in the nineteenth century were child brides, and girls as young as eight ascended the pyre. Controversy has always raged as to the degree of coercion involved, as observers speak of the women being forced into position with long bamboo poles (which are slow to burn), or being drugged and dragged, while others speak of their ecstasy and nobility on the pyre. (Kipling's fine poem 'The Boondi Queen' emphasises the latter, as does Goethe's 'The God and the Bayadere', where the prostitute with a heart of gold hurls herself

68. *Bhāgavata Purāṇa* 11.31.19–20; Bryant 2003, 418.

69. There is an eloquent retelling of the story in Eck 2012, 26.

70. The story, from the *Śiva Purāṇa*, is beautifully retold by Eck 2012, 195–7.

71. *Nuh Sipihr* 194: Nath and Faiyaz 1981, 99.

72. The thorough article 'Suttee' in Yule and Burnell's classic Anglo-Indian glossary *Hobson-Jobson* focuses mainly on the period from 1200 CE onwards. A large number of early accounts from the sixteenth to the eighteenth centuries are collected by Banerjee 2003. One of the most vivid descriptions is that of the traveller Ibn Battutah, who fainted at the sight: see Mackintosh-Smith 2002, 158–60.

11.4 A widow undergoes sati (from Houtman, *Verhael van de Reyse naar Oost Indien*, 1597).

on her lover's pyre, and is rescued, purified, by the resurrected lover who turns out to be Kṛṣṇa.) Karoline von Günderode's poem 'Die malabarischen Witwen' romanticised the devotion of the Indian widows – *zu süssem Liebesfeyer wird der Tod* – and one wonders if it ran in her mind when she took her own life in 1806, in despair over her love for the Orientalist professor Friedrich Creuzer.

Attempts to outlaw sati began with the Mughals. The series of abolitions in the nineteenth century – in British India in 1829, throughout India by Queen Victoria in 1861, and in Nepal in 1920 – and the agitation of Rammohun Roy and Fanny Parks are signal episodes in the fight against it, but nonetheless certain sectors of the population insist on maintaining it, and prosecutions are few. Mahatma Gandhi, commenting on a sati incident in 1931, recalled the account of Ceteus' wife in Diodorus, and supported his indignation by citing the hideously patriarchal account given there of the origin of the practice as a rite devised by men to discourage their wives from poisoning them.[73] If this

73. Narasimhan 1990, 57. See n. 38 above; the practice was apparently described by Onesicritus, though Bosworth 2002, 183–4 suggests that it first appeared in Cleitarchus, whence it was picked up by Hieronymus of Cardia, Diodorus' source. He cites *KA* 2.17.12 on the methods of poisoning that might be used; cf. 1.20.16.

story is strictly unbelievable, it nonetheless lays bare the patriarchal purpose of the rite, which of course also ensures the maintenance of family property intact. Since 1947 there have been some forty cases of widow-burning, twenty-eight of them in Rajasthan. The one that hit the headlines was the case of the eighteen-year-old widow Roop Kanwar in 1987, which galvanised scholarly, feminist and activist movements of all kinds, and resulted in the passing of a further law forbidding the practice.[74]

Self-immolation of wives is one matter; self-immolation of sages and ascetics is another. Curtius says death by fire is general among the philosophers of India (though he does not refer to Calanus): he seems to be exaggerating.[75] I used to arouse my students to attention when discussing Calanus by reminding them of such cases as the Buddhist monks who set fire to themselves in protest at the Vietnam war, and of Jan Palach, the student who did the same thing in Wenceslas Square, Prague, in reaction to the Russian invasion of Czechoslovakia in 1968. Today (summer 2016) one might mention some cases of refugees who preferred burning to be sent back to their war-torn countries. The case of Calanus is not one of protest, however, but of a considered exit from life. There are a few Brahmanical references to self-immolation: one enters the fire to reach the world of Brāhman.[76]

Megasthenes, as noted above, drew attention to a divergence of opinion among the philosophers, for whom 'suicide is not a dogma', and also to the variety of methods that were employed in seeking death. The difference of method is important and will help us in defining what kind of 'philosopher' Calanus was.

Who Was Calanus?

To define Calanus' philosophical stance more clearly will help us to understand the naked philosophers as a group. Onesicritus is our primary witness for Calanus, since it was he who, as described above, was sent by Alexander to

74. For accounts that are both scholarly and committed, see Narasimhan 1990; Hawley (ed.) 1994. The bibliography on the subject is very extensive. A large number of early accounts from the sixteenth to the eighteenth centuries are collected by Banerjee 2003.

75. Curt. 8.9.31–2.

76. *Vaśiṣtha Dharmasūtra* 29.4; *Taittiriya Saṁhitā* 7.4.9: Bronkhorst 2016, 37–8. Onesicritus (n. 38 above) refers to widow-burning among the very Brahmanical Kāthas, if that is who the Cathaei are: Bronkhorst 2016, 41 n. 126.

interview the philosophers at Taxila.[77] 'He found fifteen men at a distance of twenty stades [about 2½ miles/4 km] from the city, who were in different postures, standing or sitting or lying naked and motionless till evening ... Calanus was lying on stones when he first saw him'. Onesicritus approached politely and explained that he had been sent to interview the philosophers about their beliefs. Calanus responded rather rudely, telling him to take off all his clothes and sit down on the hot stones if he wanted to learn anything, backing up his admonition with a summary discourse on the decline of human history from the Golden Age,[78] and the need to maintain virtue. But another of the philosophers, Mandanis (elsewhere called Dandamis) 'rebuked Calanus as a man of arrogance', and suggested that he should be more accommodating to a king who wished to learn wisdom. Mandanis then offered a doctrine on how to eliminate pain and toil from the soul, and stated that he had advised Taxiles to cooperate with Alexander.

Strabo continues to summarise Mandanis' way of life, which involved frugality, investigation of natural phenomena and portents, and the receipt of food as alms. Disease the philosophers regard as disgrace, and if afflicted they seek death by fire. What is immediately clear here is the difference between Calanus and Dandamis. The former is much more extreme, practising mortification of the body, 'seeking pain', while Mandanis is more moderate. It should also be noted that the word 'Brahmans' is nowhere used in this description. It is however used in the short extract from Nearchus that Strabo gives later: 'Nearchus speaks of the sophists as follows: that the Brachmanes engage in affairs of state and attend the kings as counsellors; but that the other sophists investigate natural phenomena; and that Calanus is one of these; and that their wives join them in the study of philosophy; and that the modes of life of all are severe'.[79]

Nearchus thus makes a distinction between two groups, the royal advisers and the seers, who are treated as the same in the Onesicritus passage. Megasthenes too attributes to his 'Brahmans' this dual role, and distinguishes them from a varied group called 'Sarmanes', among whom the most honoured are the forest-dwellers.[80] Nearchus says that Calanus is one of the seers, but Onesicritus places him in a different group from the advisers-and-seers. There

77. Str. 15.1.63–5 = *FGrH* 134 F 17a; cf. Plu. *Alex.* 65 = F 17b.

78. The details here match *Atharvaveda* 4.34.6: Drew 1987, 167–8. The passage about the Golden Age was quoted in ch. 9 above.

79. Str. 15.1. 66 = *FGrH* 133 F 23.

80. Str. 15.1.58–60 = F 33 J = F 41 Schw.

is an echo of a controversy here: according to the *Sāmaññaphala Sutta*, renouncers are supposed to abstain from prophecy and fortune-telling, which are 'a wrong means of livelihood'.[81] Thus Calanus seems to be an example of a 'bad' renouncer. The two sophists (both Brahmans) described by Aristobulus also acted as counsellors, sitting in the market place and pursuing various mortifications, such as one of them standing on one leg for several hours while holding a heavy log above his head.[82] The older of the two gave up his way of life, having completed his forty years of renunciation, and followed Alexander to the end. It has often been assumed that this man is the same as Calanus, but Bosworth points out that this is not a necessary deduction from Aristobulus' words; nothing is said of the old man's mode of death.[83]

In Arrian, however, Dandamis is regarded as the master of the philosophers, while the others are his disciples.[84] Dandamis responds to Alexander with haughty arrogance (as he does later in the *Alexander Romance*), while Calanus is won over by the king: 'Megasthenes represents [Calanus] as a man utterly wanting in self-control, while the sophists themselves spoke opprobriously of Calanus, because, having left the happiness among them, he went to serve another master than God'.[85]

I envisage a group of fifteen men in their grove, each pursuing his own way to ascetic fulfilment. All are renunciants, but they need not be regarded as a 'school',[86] despite the implication of Strabo's summary of Nearchus (who did not interview them personally). Each of them probably thought the other fourteen were on the wrong path. However, we are told that as a group they disapproved of Calanus. Not only was he arrogant, but he was seduced by the pleasures of Alexander's table. At this point there is no objection – how could there be? – to his chosen manner of death. In fact Mandanis is said to state that suicide by fire is allowed in cases of sickness. It is Megasthenes who first brings this into his discussion, though he does not adduce it as a reason for condemnation by the other philosophers.[87] The much later *De Bragmanibus* by Palladius is the first text to bring Calanus' self-immolation into the reasons

81. *Sāmaññaphala Sutta* 56 (Bodhi 1989, 35): they should not predict eclipses either, ibid. 37. On the diversity of the philosophical schools, see Puri 1971, 29; Singh 2009, 301–2.

82. Str. 15.1.61 = Aristob. 139 F 41.

83. Bosworth 1998.

84. The *dānda* ('rod') is the mark of authority, as well as of an Ājīvika: Bhagat 1976, 141.

85. Arr. *Anab.* 7.2.9.

86. Though they may constitute a 'society': Hausner 2007, 52.

87. Megasth. F 34.

for disapproval.[88] The narrative here is adrift from the original sources, since Alexander comes to visit Dandamis on the advice of Calanus; Calanus is a wealthy man, greedy and vain; and 'terrible fire blazed within him, turning him away from wisdom towards pleasure. None of us rolls on red hot coals, and no pain wastes our bodies; our way of life is the recipe for our health.' Pleasure-seeking and rolling on red hot coals seem incompatible, though the latter may be a metaphor: but we are reminded of Calanus' position on burning hot stones when Onesicritus sought him out.

There seems no doubt that Calanus changed his way of life when he met Alexander; but how should we characterise him at the first encounter? He presents as a fairly typical Indian sādhu, using mortification as a way to enlightenment.[89] Such ascetics can be from any caste or sect. The usage that became common in Greek writers by which 'Brahman' was synonymous with 'philosopher' is misleading.[90] However, asceticism is commonly seen as a pre-Aryan tradition to which the Aryan Brahmans were opposed. This included an opposition to suicide, by fire or by any other means, though fire-suicide is allowed in cases of sickness, as Mandanis states, and he has the support of several Indian texts.[91] But *Manu*, for example, proposes throwing oneself head-first into a fire *three times*(!) as a punishment for the extreme sin of killing a Brahmin.[92] There is only one sect in ancient India that systematically favours suicide by fire as an ascetic practice, and that is the Ājīvikas.

Suicide is not uncommon as the conclusion of an ascetic existence.[93] Jains commonly seek death, but by passive means such as self-starvation (*sallekhana*), or, allegedly, stopping the breath.[94] The Buddha, meanwhile, famously tried extreme self-mortification as a road to enlightenment, but rejected it as a false trail; thereafter he was opposed to it, and Buddhist doctrine is opposed to suicide. Both Buddhists and Jains found themselves in disagreement with other kinds of ascetic in the still-fluid world of ascetic practice in fourth- and third-century BCE Magadha. Chief among the targets of their ire were the Ājīvikas, with the result that the latter died out by the seventh century CE,[95]

88. Pall. *De Brag.*2.2, 4, 11.
89. The rules are outlined in Olivelle 1992, for example.
90. It is, e.g., in Aelian: *VH* 2.41.
91. Bosworth 2002, 182 n. 40; Stoneman 1994a, 505.
92. *Manusmṛti* 11.74.
93. Filliozat 1963; 1967.
94. Strong 2001, 82 and 85. Dalrymple 2009, 5 notes that fasting is not regarded as suicide.
95. Singh 2009, 303.

while Buddhism and Jainism continued to flourish. What we know of the Ājīvikas we mainly know from hostile sources, both Buddhist and Jain.[96]

The sect traced its origin to Makkhali Gosala, who was older than the Buddha and died before Mahavira (the founder of the Jains, who possibly died in 468/7 BCE). He broke away from the Jains with whom he had begun, to found another equally extreme sect. He was one of six 'heretical teachers' summoned by the Buddha to the court of King Ajattasattu/Ajataśatru to offer spiritual guidance when the king was perplexed as to the path he should follow.[97] In later years, Aśoka favoured the Ājīvikas, providing them with caves in the Barabar hills where they could pursue their way of life. The inscriptions on three of the caves referring to this gift have been later vandalised by the obliteration of the word 'ājīvikas' by Jain hermits who came to occupy the caves when the Ājīvikas were no more.

The name 'Ājīvika' has sometimes been interpreted as meaning 'lifelong', but could perhaps also be read as 'anti-life'. Ājīvikas are to be distinguished from forest hermits, as they not only practise renunciation, but actively seek pain. A vivid passage of the Jātakas describes their practice, of course from a strongly Buddhist point of view:

> This story was told by the Master while at Jetavana, touching the false austerity of the Ajīvikas, or naked ascetics. Tradition tells us that behind Jetavana they used to practice false austerities. A number of the Brethren seeing them there painfully squatting on their heels, swinging in the air like bats, reclining on thorns, scorching themselves with five fires, and so forth in their various false austerities –, were moved to ask the Blessed One whether any good resulted therefrom. 'None whatsoever', answered the Master. 'In days gone by, the wise and good went into the forest with their birth-fire, thinking to profit by such austerities; but finding themselves no better for all their sacrifices to Fire and for all similar practices, straightway doused the birth-fire with water till it went out. By an act of Meditation the Knowledge and Attainment were gained and a title won to the Brahma Realm'.[98]

Many other details support this account of their 'false austerities'. In addition to habitually going naked, they commonly committed suicide; one drowned

96. The standard work remains Basham 1951.

97. Buddhist texts include many stories showing up the inadequacy of Ājīvikas: see, e.g., Strong 2001, 107.

98. *Jātaka* 144: Cowell 1895–1913, 1.307–8.

11.5 Doorway of the Lomas Rishi Cave in the Barabar caves complex, near Gaya, Bihar.

himself in public at a miracle contest.[99] But Buddhists accused them of hypocrisy: they were said to have meeting places where they would sing and dance, but would also feast in secret; and Jains accused them also of sexual licence.[100] They also acted as fortune-tellers.[101]

All these qualities and accusations interestingly echo the objections of the naked philosophers of Taxila to Calanus. In addition, the Ājīvikas had a veritable handbook of possible forms of suicide.[102] Most Ājīvika books were destroyed by the Jains because of their popularity with fortune-tellers, but the Jain accounts list forty-eight different forms of death that Ājīvikas might seek, from drowning and jumping off cliffs to leaping into a fire. Death by self-torture was admired by them, since pain was pursued for its own sake; the caves in the Barabar hills that were dedicated to the Ājīvikas by Aśoka were known as 'the forest of pain'. This sits rather oddly with the pursuit of luxury and self-indulgence of which the Jains also accused the Ājīvikas, but the endurance of various forms of discomfort is familiar from any account of Indian asceticism, including Aristobulus' description of the two 'philosophers' he saw at Taxila. Voluntary death is not an exclusive 'property' of the Ājīvikas, and suicide is enjoined for the sin of killing a Brahman: the sinner may seek death by fire, or plunge into the midst of a battle of arrows.[103] It is also acceptable for those who are very old, or incurably sick. The essence of the practice is the denial of the real existence of the body: it is a form of release.

Quite where one should situate Calanus on this spectrum is difficult to decide, but the criticisms levelled at him by the other 'naked philosophers' resemble those directed at the Ājīvikas by the Jains, and his final suicide by fire, though allowable because of his illness, is also one of the methods that were habitual with Ājīvikas. If he abandoned his austerities to join the court of Alexander, he returned to them in his last act.

There may be a clue in his name. Plutarch says that his real name was Sphines, but that he was called Calanus because he greeted everyone with the word *kale*.[104] The Suda goes so far as to say that 'the Indians call all *sophoi*

99. Basham 1951, 84.

100. Ibid., 115, 124. Also Singh 2009, 302–3. Ājīvikas were not unique in this: Kapālikas, or skull-wearers, were also regarded as dissolute men, users of strong drink and prostitutes: Daniélou 1992, 102; Hartsuiker 1993/2014, 21–3 refers to human sacrifice.

101. Basham 1951, 127.

102. I owe this information to Sushmita Basu Majumdar, in a lecture given in Exeter in July 2014.

103. Filliozat 1963, 35–6.

104. Plu. *Alex*. 65.

"kalanoi" ', and Clearchus makes a connection between the Jews and the Indian Kalanoi.[105] It is true that the Sanskrit word *kalyana* means 'greetings'.[106] But it also has a number of other meanings, including 'noble', 'beautiful', 'good fortune'; and it is the title of one of the fourteen legendary Jain scriptures, the Purvas, which have not survived, if they ever existed. (According to tradition, the first Purva was so long that it required a quantity of ink equal to the volume of an elephant to write it down. Each succeeding Purva took twice as much ink as the last, so that the *Kalyana Purva,* the eleventh in the series, would have required ink equivalent to 1,024 elephants. One may be glad it has not survived.) The use of the title suggests that Kalyana was a suitable name for a Jain, and thus that Calanus may have been a renegade Jain who chose Ājīvika self-indulgence and, finally, an Ājīvika form of death. Furthermore, if Calanus was an Ājīvika with Jain elements, and Dandamis was a Jain with Ājīvika elements, we have here a window on a dispute within the sect, on a doctrine in formation.

Why did Calanus join Alexander's expedition? Was it simply that the two men got on well and found each other interesting to talk to? He must certainly have been useful to Alexander as an interpreter, even if he was not one of the śramanas who habitually advised the kings. This brings us to the classification of the philosophers offered by Megasthenes.

Megasthenes on the Philosophers

Megasthenes' discussion of the Indian philosophers is the most extensive of his fragments.[107] The text we have is Strabo's paraphrase or summary, and as usual we remain uncertain how much Strabo has compressed his original, whether he has rearranged the material and how accurate his précis of the details may be. He begins with the information that the philosophers who live in the mountains are worshippers of Dionysus while those in the plains are worshippers of Heracles. This is rather difficult to match plausibly with the habits of any known group of ancient Indian 'philosophers', and would seem more intelligible as a description of the practices of the *peoples* of these

105. Jos. *cAp* 1.179.; cf. D.L. *Proem* 9 (Jews and gymnosophists). Bar-Kochva 2010, 60 n. 68. Another wise man, called Callaneus (perhaps the same man) is referred to, in a *parapegma* from Miletus of the mid 80s BCE, as an authority on the relation of weather to the stars: Diels and Rehm 1904, 1–20; see Lane Fox 2011, 11. The name recurs, e.g., in the author of *Rājataraṅgiṇī,* Kalhaṇa: Thapar 2013b, 602.

106. See Monier-Williams's Sanskrit dictionary, 263 s.v.

107. Megasth. F 41 Schw = F 33 J = Str. 15.1.58–60.

two opposed regions. The information could then be aligned with that of the Alexander historians about the alleged worship of Dionysus in the mountains west of the Indus, and that of Heracles among the Surasenoi (see chapter 3 above). The 'Dionysians' are said to dress in muslin, wear turbans and clothes of bright colours, use perfumes and accompany their kings with the sound of gongs and drums.

The information becomes more circumstantial in the next chapter of Strabo (59), which begins with the words 'Megasthenes makes a different division of the philosophers'. This cannot mean 'different from the previous writer quoted', since the previous paragraph is explicitly attributed to Megasthenes. It must, I suppose, imply that Megasthenes offered a second account of the philosophers, arranged under different categories. The need to unpack the sentence shows how tricky it is to be sure just how Strabo's words relate to what Megasthenes actually wrote. In any case the information in the next paragraphs of Strabo is coherent and seems to describe people we can recognise from other sources.

There are two groups of philosophers, the Brachmanes and the Sarmanes. The grouping of the two as a single category – *brahmaṇaśramanam* – is also found in Aśoka's Rock Edict 13 (in Kandahar).[108] It seems to imply that the two groups constitute the entire class of religious 'philosophers'. Pillar Edict 7 makes a slightly different categorisation, of 'the saṁgha, Brahmans and Ājīvikas'. The saṁgha is the normal name for the Buddhist community, so that this passage could imply that the class of śramanas includes both Buddhists and Ājīvikas (but apparently no others, not even the Jains who were admired by Aśoka's grandfather).

The Brachmanes of Megasthenes are brought up from infancy (indeed, from before birth!) by learned men, a description that fits very well the education of Brahman priests up to the present day. They dwell in groves on rushes and deer skins, abjuring meat and sexual relations, for a period of thirty-seven years, and then retire to their own property, after which they do eat meat, but not spicy food. They have many wives and devote themselves to preparation for death. This information seems to combine facts about Brahmans in general with details specific to ascetics or renouncers.[109] The description thus applies

108. Falk 2006, 244–5; Allen 2012, 413–14.

109. Dihle 1964 praises the accuracy of Megasthenes' picture of the philosophers, and thinks that they are Jains, which may be too neat a view. See also my discussion in Stoneman 1995, 105–6, though I would now dissociate myself from my remark in that paper about the suspect reliability of Megasthenes.

to Brahmans who have withdrawn from the role of householder for life in the forest, as prescribed by the *Laws of Manu*, which details four stages of the Brahmanical life: the chaste student of the Veda, the householder, the forest-dweller, and the ascetic.[110] They are often called *vānaprastha*, 'forest-dweller'.[111] The stated term of thirty-seven years in the forest corresponds well to the prescription of *Manu* that recommends thirty-six years study with one's guru, 'or half of that, or a quarter of that, or whenever the undertaking comes to an end'.[112] Dwelling in groves on rushes and deer-skins belongs specifically to the life of the renouncer: the ultimate renouncer, Śiva, is always portrayed with his deer-skin over his shoulder, ready to settle into meditation. The apparent contradiction between the assertion that the Brahmans abstain from sexual relations and their stated polygamy can be resolved by regarding these as separate stages of the life span. Strabo appears to have compressed a text that probably made the distinctions clearer.

Strabo says that the Brahmans do not share their philosophical speculations with their wives. In general it is true that women were and are excluded from such practices, though there clearly were female students, since our oldest philosophical text, the *Bṛhadāraṇyaka Upaniṣad*, introduces a clever female participant in debate in the person of Gārgī. Renouncers today include a small proportion of women in their ranks, though male sādhus are far more numerous.[113]

Strabo continues,

> They converse more about death than anything else, for they believe that the life here is, as it were, that of a babe still in the womb, and that death, to those who have devoted themselves to philosophy, is birth into the true life, that is, the happy life; and that they therefore discipline themselves most of all to be ready for death; and that they believe that nothing that happens to mankind is good or bad, for otherwise some would not be

110. *Manusmṛti* 6.87.

111. Bronkhorst 2016, 245–6. 'Countless hermits must have lived in the nearby forest, meditating on religion, searching out the fundamentals of life and spreading enlightenment. Our culture has grown out of the forests. And yet, we have cut down those sacred forests, and driven away or killed the animals, betraying the earth's trust': Vegad 2008, 111.

112. *Manusmṛti* 3.1. Hausner 2007, 101 notes that twelve or fourteen years of wandering is common. According to the *Bodana Dharmasūtra*, Brahmans are never to visit the cities.

113. Hausner 2007. Puri 1990, 140–9 surveys Patañjali's description of Brahmanical education, from which women are excluded, but notes a few exceptions. *Manusmṛti* 2.66 asserts that it is all right for women to be educated.

> grieved and others delighted by the same things, both having dream-like notions, and that the same persons cannot at one time be grieved and then in turn change and be delighted by the same things.

The concern with death and the view of the world as illusion are recognisable Indian philosophical tenets. In the *Bṛhadāraṇyaka Upaniṣad,* Death is the first thing that existed in the nothingness, and Death created other beings in order to supply himself with food. Death as a 'birth into a real and happy life' meshes not only with the surprising demand of the sages in the *Alexander Romance* that the king give them immortality, but with such passages as this from the *Bṛhadāraṇyaka Upaniṣad* : 'the unreal is death, and the real is immortality – so, when he says "From the unreal lead me to the real", what he is really saying is "From death lead me to immortality"; in other words, "make me immortal".'[114] According to Hausner, one of the hardest disciplines of the sādhu is to learn that everything that surrounds him in the physical world, including his body and its sensations and passions, is illusion.

Strabo moves on to outline briefly the physical doctrines of the Brahmanes. Megasthenes apparently stated that these ideas were crude and largely based on fables, yet that their views resemble those of the Greeks.[115] Indeed, if he was told about any ideas that did not resemble Greek ones (karma, for example), he does not mention them. The instances he gives relate to cosmology: the world had a beginning, and will end, and god is diffused throughout – a recognisable rendering of the Vedic accounts of the creator-god and the idea that Brāhman permeates the universe.[116] (This may remind one of Chronos in Pherecydes F 51 DK.) Bernabé and Mendoza compare the Pythagorean cosmogony with that of *Ṛg Veda* 10.129 and, despite differences, are driven to the conclusion that the two accounts must be connected, coming from thinkers at opposite ends of the Achaemenid empire.[117] They do not refer to Megasthenes. In the *Śatapatha Brāhmaṇa* the world begins as a golden egg, floating on the waters, from which Prajāpati emerges.[118] Megasthenes might have compared this with Pherecydes, or with the Orphic Egg described in Aristo-

114. *Bṛh Up.* 1.3.28. Cf. *Bṛh. Up.* 2.4.3. It is therefore not necessary to suppose, with Beckwith 2015, 81, that Strabo has misplaced a Buddhist section here.

115. This is also reported by Clem. *Strom.* 1.72.4 = Megasthenes F 3a J. *RV* 10.129 describes Creation.

116. E.g., *Manusmṛti* 1.5–13.

117. Bernabé and Mendoza 2013.

118. *SB* 11.1.6.3. Basu 1969, 229; Jurewicz 2016, 53.

phanes' *Birds*.[119] Megasthenes also notes that the world is spherical, which puts one in mind of Parmenides' notion that the universe is spherical; but for Parmenides it is uncreated and unchanging.[120] There are four elements plus a fifth, which produced the heaven and stars: this corresponds to the *ākāśa* of Sanskrit terminology. The earth is at the centre of the universe.[121]

To Strabo's testimony may be added the remarks of Clement and Eusebius that 'all that has been said regarding nature by the ancients is asserted also by philosophers out of Greece, on the one part in India by the Brachmanes, and on the other in Syria by the people called the Jews'.[122] Bar-Kochva observes that Strabo presents a Stoicised view of Megasthenes' analysis, which is expressed in pre-Socratic terms.[123] B. K. Matilal writes, 'I believe that anyone who wants to explain and translate systematically from Indian philosophical writings into a European language will, knowingly or unknowingly, use the method of "comparative philosophy". In other words, he cannot help but compare and contrast the Indian philosophical concepts with those of Western philosophy, whether or not he is conscious of so doing'.[124] This is as true of a fourth-century or first-century Greek as of a twenty-first-century Oxford professor. It is an interpretative strategy, not a testimony of direct influence of either culture on the other.

Strabo's summary of his next topic runs, 'Concerning generation, and the nature of the soul, and many other subjects, they express views like those maintained by the Greeks'.[125] This is beta-plus stuff, and one longs to ask *which* other subjects (it's basic office discipline never to have a file called 'miscellaneous'), and, 'What do you mean by "like"?'. Views of the afterlife, he says, are 'wrapped up in allegories' like those of Plato: this presumably refers to the myth of Er in the *Republic* and the use of the idea of reincarnation by both Indian philosophy and Plato. We shall return to the doctrine of reincarnation in chapter 12.

A Brahman is a Brahman is a Brahman. Trickier is to determine what is connoted by the term 'Sarmanes'.[126] There can be no doubt that this is the

119. Cf. DK1B 13 (Kirk and Raven no. 38).

120. Xenophanes' God is also spherical: 21A1 DK.

121. Cf. Anaximander T 26 = 125 KR.

122. Megasth. Ff 42 and 42b Schw = F 3 J = Clem. *Strom.* 1.72.4 and Eus. *PE* 9.6.

123. Bar-Kochva 2010, 152–4.

124. Matilal 2005, xiv.

125. Str. 15.1.59 (cont.).

126. The name appears as 'Garmanes' in the MSS (presumably a scribal error), and in variant forms in other authors, including 'Samanaioi' in Bardaisan.

Greek version of Sanskrit *śramaṇa*,[127] meaning a seeker, or ascetic. One of the earliest occurrences of the term is in the *Bṛhadāraṇyaka Upaniṣad*.[128] Ascetics of the present day fall into a great variety of categories – of doctrine, of practice, of dress, of attitudes to suffering and death – and in antiquity there were probably no fewer, though the categories were probably less differentiated. Nonetheless, we know of several kinds of ascetic, both Vedic and non-Vedic, mostly mendicant, prevalent in Magadha from the sixth century BCE onwards. Buddhists, Jains, Ājīvikas were all to be found, and a number of distinct schools of philosophy (whose adherents were not necessarily ascetics or renouncers) were also active.[129] It would be risky to assume that the practices of the sects were neatly compartmentalised. The fruit diet and nudity of Dandamis and his companions comes closest to the customs of present-day Jains (of the Digambara, or air-clad, variety),[130] but it is probably otiose to seek to label the naked ones too neatly, particularly since the information about their doctrines is so scrappy.

The term may thus be of fairly broad application. Megasthenes' information, filtered through Strabo, is somewhat heterogeneous: the most honoured among them are the Hylobioi, or forest-dwellers, who abstain from sex and wine and live on fruits and leaves. Thus far they resemble Alexander's 'naked philosophers', or present-day sādhus. But they also maintain close contact with the kings, and the kings perform their religious duties through the Hylobioi. These sound more like Brahmans, since it is the role of Brahmans to carry out the religious rituals that kingship requires: this is in fact stated by Nearchus.[131] 'Next in honour to the Hylobioi are the physicians': these live by begging (rice and barley) and can influence the sex of births by the use of *pharmaka* (drugs); but in the next clause Megasthenes states that most of their cures do not involve *pharmaka*, but are reliant on diet, as well as using salves and poultices (ἐπίχριστα καὶ καταπλάσματα). These sound more like Buddhists or their ilk, since these practices are known to be characteristic of Buddhist medicine, and could not be practised by Brahmans because of the danger of

127. Pali *samaṇa*. Khilnani 2016, 14 for the meaning.

128. *Bṛh. Up.* 4.3.22.

129. King 1999.

130. Cf. Dihle 1964, 21

131. Megasth. F 23 = Str. 15.1.66: 'The Brachmanes engage in affairs of state and attend the kings as counsellors; but the other sophists investigate natural phenomena; and Calanus is one of these.' See in general Heesterman 1985 and 1993 on the rituals related to kingship: his treatment is very theoretical and hard to relate to any particular historical period.

pollution by physical contact.[132] (The kingdom of Musicanus, too, gave honour to physicians.)[133] Both classes of Hylobioi are said by Strabo to practise asceticism (*karteria*, endurance), and to remain fixed for a whole day in a single posture.

To these Megasthenes adds diviners and *epōidoi*, performers of incantations, who travel from village to village begging – a description applicable to any serious sādhu, as well as to Buddhist monks. Even the most cultivated of them, he says, purvey 'superstitions' (θρυλουμένων) about the afterlife to instil piety and holiness. Though not very explicit, this could imply the notion of karma, and the need to do good acts in the present life for the sake of one's future lives: if so, it would be the only reference to karma in any Greek writer. He also mentions that some women pursue philosophy with the men. Again this is true of present-day sādhus; Nearchus asserts that the philosophers' wives join them in study,[134] and Strabo (from Megasthenes) asserts that women study with the 'Garmanes'. We have already met Gārgī the female philosopher in the *Bṛhadāraṇyaka Upaniṣad*;[135] but the inclusion of women in philosophical groups seems to be more characteristic of the Garmanes/śramanas.

Clement too speaks of the Hylobioi,[136] who are connected with the Sarmanes, and who do not live in cities or even in houses; they clothe themselves with the bark of trees and subsist on acorns and water; they neither marry nor beget children. This looks like a précis of the same text as Strabo was summarising, and may plausibly be regarded as another report of Megasthenes: it may indicate the kind of elisions and omissions that Strabo inclined to.[137]

Clement's next sentence plunges us straight into a matter of scholarly controversy. He writes, 'Among the Indians are those philosophers also who follow the precepts of Boutta, whom they honour as a god on account of his

132. Zysk 1998; Naqvi 2011; Arora 2005, 95–7, referring to Aśoka's boast in Rock Edict 2 that he had founded medical establishments in various places. See also ch. 8 above.

133. Onesic. F 22 = Str. 15.1.22.

134. F 23 = Str. 15.1.66.

135. *Bṛh. Up.* 3.6.1ff., 3.8.

136. Megasth. F 43 Schw, omitted by Jacoby. Clem. *Strom.* 1.71.5–6: διττὸν δὲ τούτων τὸ γένος, οἵ μὲν Σαρμᾶναι αὐτῶν, οἵ δὲ Βραχμᾶναι καλούμενοι. Καὶ τῶν Σαρμάνων οἱ ὑλόβιοι προσαγορευόμενοι οὔτε πόλεις οἰκοῦσιν οὔτε στέγας ἔχουσιν. Δένδρων δὲ ἀμφιέννυνται φλοιοῖς καὶ ἀκρόδρυα σιτοῦνται καὶ ὕδωρ ταῖς χερσὶ πινοῦσιν, οὐ γάμον, οὐ παιδοποιίαν ἴσασιν, ὥσπερ οἱ νῦν Ἐγκρατῖται καλούμενοι. Εἰσι δὲ τῶν Ἰνδῶν οἱ τοῖς Βούττα πειθόμενοι παραγγέλμασιν.

137. Dihle 1964 emphasises the 'classic' nature of Megasthenes' account for all later classical writers on India.

extraordinary sanctity.' Or the sentence may mean, 'the Hylobioi are those among the Indians who follow the precepts of Boutta . . . .' This is the first reference to the Buddha in a Greek or Roman author: was it in Megasthenes, like the observations preceding and following, or is Clement adding a comment of his own?[138] There may be another reference to Buddhists in Clement. At *Stromata* 3.60.2–4 he speaks first of the Brahmans, who eat no living thing, nor drink wine: some of them eat daily 'like us', others every three days. He cites Alexander Polyhistor's *Indica* for this information,[139] and continues that they despise death, regard life as 'nothing', believe in rebirth (*palingenesia*) and revere the gods Heracles and Pan. 'But those who are called *Semnoi* among the Indians go naked their whole lives long; they cultivate truth, make predictions about the future, and pay reverence to a certain pyramid, under which they consider the bones of a certain god to lie.'[140] Neither these Semnoi nor the gymnosophists take wives, but there are also female Semnai, who maintain virginity. 'Semnoi', which seems to be another transliteration of *śramana* or perhaps of the Pali form *samana*, is also the Greek word for 'holy', so there is some uncertainty as to which meaning Clement intends, if not both. Two things point strongly to this being a reference to Buddhists: first, their reverence for 'pyramids', obviously stupas containing relics of the Buddha; and second, the reference to female Semnai, who could be Buddhist nuns. However, nudity is not a characteristic of Buddhist monks and nuns. If all this is from Alexander Polyhistor, who was writing in the first century BCE, and was referring to his own times, it describes a period, unlike that of Megasthenes, in which Buddhist monasteries had long been established in India. But it cannot be excluded that Alexander's source was Megasthenes.

Does this mean that we should conclude that 'śramana' simply means 'Buddhist' in these and other contexts? Christopher Beckwith has recently argued strongly that 'the remarkably unanimous testimony of all non-Indian sources, most of which are far earlier than the actual dates of any Indian sources, is

138. Beckwith 2015, 100 believes that Clement is simply piling up a list, 'and clearly has no idea that any of them are the same or are not the same as any others'; this is because Clement's specification conflicts with Beckwith's view that the term 'śramana' is simply co-extensive with 'Buddhist'.

139. *FGrH* 273 F 18, the only fragment of this work.

140. Οἱ καλούμενοι δὲ Σεμνοὶ τῶν Ἰνδῶν γυμνοὶ διαιτῶνται τὸν πάντα βίον. Οὗτοι τὴν ἀλήθειαν ἀσκοῦσι καὶ περὶ τῶν μελλόντων προμηνύουσι καὶ σέβουσί τινα πυραμίδα, ὑφ' ἣν ὀστέα τινὸς θεοῦ νομίζουσιν ἀποκεῖσθαι.

that the term 'śramana' meant exclusively "Buddhist practitioner" in all early languages in which it is attested'.[141]

The dates of the Buddha are very uncertain and a matter of scholarly dispute, with the dates of his death currently being set anywhere from 486 to 360 BCE.[142] Most scholars would probably regard his teaching as belonging to the fifth century BCE rather than the fourth. The Buddha began as a prince, Siddhartha Gautama, who was so appalled by his first exposure to suffering, in the world outside the palace, that he embarked on a quest for the way to eliminate it, and for enlightenment. The awareness of suffering is a key motivator in Buddhist thought, as for example in the well-known story told by Buddhaghoṣa, that Buddha promised to bring a woman's sons back to life if she would bring him a mustard seed from the house of one who had never known sorrow: a version of this story reappeared in the Alexander tradition, in the king's letter to his mother Olympias warning her of his impending death.[143] An attempt to attain enlightenment by extreme austerities ended in failure, after which he followed a different path, based on philosophical understanding of the nature of existence. He quickly gathered around him disciples and acolytes, and over the subsequent centuries these followers formed themselves into communities, 'saṁghas', much resembling the later monasteries of the West. These clustered around cities and trade routes, in contrast to the forest-dwelling ascetics.[144] So there is every likelihood that the Buddha's teachings were known, and his followers in evidence, in Magadha at the time Megasthenes was there.

The Buddha's followers are, as Beckwith rightly observes, often referred to as 'śramanas'. One of his main pieces of evidence is Aśoka's Pillar Edict 7, in which the term 'saṁgha' appears to connote the same group as the previously mentioned śramanas. Al-Biruni in the eleventh century could still refer to Buddhadana and his adherents, the 'shamanians'[145]. In the *Questions of King Milinda* too, 'śramana' seems to be used to denote 'Buddhist'.[146] This need

141. Beckwith 2015, 102. See also, e.g., 69. However, Richard Seaford has pointed out to me that there are references to śramanas in the *Taittiriya Aranyaka* 2.7 and *Bṛh. Up.* 4.3.22, both of which must be dated earlier than any of the Greek references.

142. Strong 2001, 1. Gombrich 2013, xiii, says that he 'must have died round 405 BC'.

143. *AR* 3.33; Stoneman 2008, 191–3.

144. *Dhammapada* 14.188–9 states that saṁghas are better than the forest.

145. Sachau 1910, 1.40 and 158, 2.169.

146. *Milindapāñha* 1.230, 251.

imply no more than that the term 'Buddhist' had not yet been devised. An important testimony is that of Bardaisan of Edessa (154–222 CE, a Christian writer),[147] who describes the Samanaioi and Brahmans as two groups among the gymnosophists. While the Brahmans live on fruits and abstain from meat, devote many hours to worship, observe silence and fasting, the Samanaioi are described as living in an 'order' (εἰς τὸ τάγμα ἐγγράφεσθαι) and living outside the cities in houses and precincts built for them by the king (οἴκους καὶ τεμένη ὑπὸ τοῦ βασιλέως οἰκοδομηθέντα); they are summoned to meals by a bell, at which each has his own bowl, and they end their lives by suicide by fire. This all sounds very Buddhist except for the routine use of death by fire. Beckwith expounds the Buddhist qualities of this description in a well-taken polemic against a recent article proposing that the Samanaioi here are Jains.[148] There are various possible interpretations of this congruence of the Samanaioi with Buddhists besides the conclusion that the words are interchangeable. It could be that by Bardaisan's day the Buddhists were the only kind of Samanaioi left. But we know that there were Jains,[149] and even Ājīvikas survived a few centuries longer. Perhaps Bardaisan simply did not know about them. It is simpler to suppose that, for him, 'śramana' meant Buddhist.

Bronkhorst has directed an impassioned critique against Beckwith's argument, comparing him to a drunk man who has lost his house-keys and looks for them only under the street lamp because that is where he can see, or indeed believes that whatever he finds in the light of the street-lamp must be his keys.[150] 'A fundamental general weakness of Beckwith's arguments is that he is not willing to consider that there can be undated sources that yet contain historical information'.[151] In other words, Beckwith's reliance on the 'earliest' evidence prevents a balanced judgment.

Bronkhorst goes on to re-state the commoner view, that 'Buddhism arose in the same region as Jainism and Ajivikism, approximately at the same time. Buddhism and Jainism (and to some extent Ajivikism) are generally looked upon as responses to a shared problem, linked to the belief in rebirth and karmic retribution'.[152] It is true that Beckwith pushes his case too far on many

147. His words are quoted, seemingly verbatim, by Porphyry, *Abst.* 4.17.1–9.

148. Beckwith 2015, 97–9.

149. Beckwith's contention that Jainism arose centuries later than Buddhism is unlikely to win acceptance: Bronkhorst 2016, 484–5.

150. Ibid., 483–9.

151. Ibid., 489.

152. Quotations from ibid. 484.

occasions.[153] However, the case for regarding 'śramana' as, at least very often, referring to Buddhists, is a strong one. But śramanas do not occur in the Alexander historians, and it is unlikely that the latter were aware of Buddhists.

It seems that there was a continuum of ascetic styles, of which the Buddhists rapidly became the dominant mode. As Ludvik Skurzak describes it, the śramanas are 'pre-Brahman ascetics';[154] that is, Brahmanism had as yet made few inroads in Magadha. The way of life represented by the śramanas preceded the attempt by Brahmans to define and rearrange it in their own terms. Bailey and Mabbett present a persuasive picture of the situation: 'there were many groupings of ascetics who sought spiritual enlightenment by wandering from place to place and living on alms ... the Jains and the Ājīvikas were two groups which practiced severe asceticism. The Buddha's followers similarly lived as wandering mendicants but ... preferred a middle way, cutting ties with society and preferring simplicity and poverty to active self-mortification.'[155] Thus Megasthenes' Sarmanes may well be Buddhists, but the naked philosophers of the *Romance* have more in common with Jains. Megasthenes himself never mentions the Buddha (if we assume that Clement's remark is his own contribution and not a snippet of Megasthenes). The movement was more important than the master.

Here we enter on the major question regarding the relation between Indian and Greek thought that has stood at the forefront of scholarly investigation since the beginning of Indology.[156] The interaction of Greek and Indian ideas became inevitable after Alexander's visit and the settlement of many Greeks and Greek-speakers in Bactria and north-west India. I have discussed before the relation between Greek and Indian elements in this episode of the *Romance*, and would now argue that much of the content of the episode is Indian in nature.[157]

153. Cf. my review, Stoneman 2016e. O'Leary 1949, 125 seems to hold a similar view, that all śramanas are Buddhists.

154. Skurzak 1954.

155. Bailey and Mabbett 2003, 162.

156. Singh 2004, 54. See further ch. 12 below, opening section.

157. See Stoneman 1995; 2008; 2012, xxv. Cynic influence, perhaps inserted into the tradition at its outset by Onesicritus, has been proposed by Dudley 1937, 39–40; Brown 1955, 47–8;

A notable feature of the encounter of Alexander and the naked philosophers is the dialogue form of the interaction. The first section consists of questions and answers, before the narrative moves on to a sermon by Dandamis. The latter takes pride of place in the later rewritings of the episode, the Cynic diatribe in the Geneva papyrus, and the *De Bragmanibus* by Palladius which is based on the diatribe; but the latest rewriting from antiquity, the *Correspondence of Alexander and Dindimus*, reverts to the dialogue or debate form. Some have argued that the question-and-answer section betrays the influence of Greek literature, since the dialogue is held to have been invented by Plato; a corollary is that some later Indian dialogues, such as the *Questions of King Milinda*, are also held to be essentially Greek in spirit. (It is even been suggested that the Pali *Milinda* is a translation from Greek.) Debate and dialogue are integral to Indian philosophy from the beginnings. Many of the Upaniṣads take a dialogue form, and even the content of the interchange between Alexander and Dandamis in the *Romance* is paralleled in the *Mahābhārata*.[158] The use of tricky or logic-chopping questions, such as Alexander's devious threat to the philosophers to kill whichever of them has answered worst, is indeed a feature of the style of the Megarian philosophers, who had links with the Cynics;[159] but the materialist Lokāyata school also made use of paradoxes and quibbles, so one need not see this aspect of the story as a Greek contribution.

The debate of philosophers as a public spectacle, before a king or the general public, is a well-established form in Indian philosophy.[160] The Upaniṣads and the *Questions of King Milinda* have been mentioned. Kṛṣṇa's teaching to Arjuna in the *Bhagavad-gītā* is another example.

My conclusion, then, is that the passage of the *Alexander Romance*, fiction though it is, describes a perfectly plausible Indian scenario. There is no need to seek for Greek influence to explain its details. Is it therefore possible to define precisely what kind of philosophers the naked ones were?

As Buddhism became more familiar to the Greeks there was a tendency to mention the Indian philosophers in the same breath with Buddhists (Clem-

---

Muckensturm 1993; Stoneman 1995, 13. Indian influence on Cynics has also been canvassed by, e.g., Brown 1955, ch. 2; Ingalls 1962. See Stoneman 1994a, 505 n. 24.

158. *Mbh.* 3.297 in van Buitenen's translation, Stoneman 2008, 94–5; Stoneman 1995, 111 provides further examples of Greek and Indian dialogues.

159. Stoneman 1995, 113.

160. Bronkhorst 2011, 176–87.

ent is the first to do so),[161] but in Palladius the 'Brahmans' (as they are now called) are not Buddhists. Dandamis states, 'If Alexander takes away my head he will not destroy my soul, but only my head which will fall silent. My soul will depart to my lord ... I shall become breath and ascend to my lord, who enclosed us in flesh.'[162] The language here is more in tune with Brahmanical belief in the union of individual *ātman* with Brahman than it is with Buddhist ideas of no-self and extinction. But it is also assimilated to Christian ideas, and this is the dominant mode of Palladius' treatise. The movement was more important than the master.

161. Clem. *Strom.* 1.72.4 = Megasth. F 43 Schw.

162. Pall. *De Brag.* 2.17.

12

Two Hundred Years of Debate

GREEK AND INDIAN THOUGHT

THE EVIDENT FASCINATION that the Greeks felt for the Indian 'philosophers' they encountered reflects the fact that both peoples had a strong tradition of speculative thought. Greeks were frequently explicitly concerned to identify the 'sources' of their own ideas, customs and religious practices. Herodotus is full of such speculations, and many Greek philosophers, including Pythagoras and Democritus,[1] are said to have travelled widely in the east – Egypt, Babylonia, Persia, India – as part of their intellectual development. A thousand years after Pythagoras, Porphyry was still ready to assert that his master Plotinus had been anxious to visit India to learn from the philosophers there.[2] Modern scholars, too, have often been keen to suppose that there was a direct line of influence, and that many key doctrines of Greek philosophy could not have been developed without the input of ideas from India. The approach is as old as the beginning of Indology. The Royal Asiatic Society was founded by Sir William Jones in 1823 with the purpose of tracing the connections between the two traditions.[3] As Jones himself wrote in 'The Third Anniversary Discourse',

> The six philosophical schools, whose principles are explained in the *Dersana Sàstra,* comprise all the metaphysicks of the old Academy, the Stoa, the Lyceum; nor is it possible to read the *Védánta,* or the many fine compositions in illustration of it, without believing, that PYTHAGORAS and

1. Ael. *VH* 4.20.
2. Porph. *Vit. Plot.* 3.
3. Singh 2004, 54.

> PLATO derived their sublime theories from the same fountain with the sages of *India*.[4]

One should note that the Advaita (non-dualist) Vedanta, often seen by modern connoisseurs as the essence of Indian philosophy, is only one school, though it is given prominence by the push to dominance of the Brahmins, and of its exponent Śankara.[5]

Though it takes my discussion outside its chronological limits of the fourth to second centuries BCE, it is impossible to assess the interactions of Indian and Greek thinkers in the period without considering the possible antecedents from the sixth century BCE, and, to some extent, the later echoes of Indian ideas in Neo-Platonism.[6] Accordingly this chapter consists of a series of case studies, either of possible philosophical common ground, or of known personal interactions of Greeks with Indian thought. They are a heterogeneous group, but the cumulative effect will, it is hoped, be a nuanced view of the Greek experience of Indian thought.

Reincarnation

> He saw,
> By light which shines beyond our mortal ken,
> The line of all his lives in all the worlds
> Far back, and farther back, and farthest yet,
> Five hundred lives and fifty . . .
> Thus Buddha did behold
> Life's upward steps long-linked, from levels low
> Where breath is base, to higher steps and higher
> Whereon the ten great Virtues wait to lead
> The climber skyward.
>
> —EDWIN ARNOLD, *THE LIGHT OF ASIA*, BOOK 6

> For soules are free from death. Howbee't, they leaving evermore
> Theyr former dwellings, are receyv'd and live ageine in new.
> For I myself (right well in mind I beare it to be trew)

4. Jones 1995, 362–3. Aurobindo 1947, 59 sets out to demonstrate that the thought of Heraclitus resembles that of the Veda, but observes that 'the west cannot see spiritual beauty'.

5. Haberman 2006, 26.

6. Emphasised by Drew 1987.

> Was in the time of Trojan warre Euphorbus, Panthewes sonne,
> Quyght through whose hart the deathfull speare of Menelay did ronne.
> I late ago in Junos Church at Argos did behold
> And knew the target which I in my left hand there did hold.
> All things doo change. But nothing sure dooth perish. This same spright
> Doth fleete, and fisking heere and there dooth swiftly take his flight
> From one place to another place, and entreth every wyght,
> Removing out of man to beast, and out of beast to man.
> But yit it never perrisheth nor never perrish can.
>
> —PYTHAGORAS'S SPEECH, OVID, *METAMORPHOSES* 15, 176–88, TR. ARTHUR GOLDING

> Already I have been a boy and a girl, a bush and a bird and a dumb sea fish.
>
> —EMPEDOCLES, 31B117 DK/111 INWOOD

> It really wasn't until my incarnation as a courtier to Queen Nefertiti that I began to see the importance of a sense of self-esteem.
>
> —BOOPSIE, IN THE *DOONESBURY* CARTOON STRIP, 1987

Belief in reincarnation is relatively uncommon, globally speaking, as a component of a world-view, but it does occur in widely separated parts of the world including, at the present day, South Asia, West Africa and among the Inuit people, as well as the native peoples of western Canada.[7] Clearly such beliefs can arise autochthonously, as it were, since diffusion between such widely separate areas is unlikely in the extreme. It has always seemed remarkable that a similar belief should have assumed a position of particular importance in both Indian philosophy and in the doctrines of Greeks including Pythagoras, Empedocles, Plato and Plotinus. It is, however, totally absent in the thought of the geographically intervening peoples, the Babylonians and the Persians. Influence of one on the other (normally of India upon Greece) has been supposed since the time of Sir William Jones. The supposition needs to be examined very carefully; given the varying details of the belief as it occurs in the far-flung cultures where it occurs, are the forms of Indian and Greek belief so close that influence is the only explanation for the parallels?[8]

7. Burley 2016b.

8. Recent valuable discussions of the issues include O'Flaherty (ed.) 1980; Obeyesekere 2002; Burley 2016b; Ducoeur and Muckensturm-Poule 2016.

In India, a belief in rebirth is closely associated with the idea of karma; by its actions in one life, the soul accumulates a load of positive or negative karma which determines (by an unspecified agency) in what form it will reappear in its next incarnation: bad deeds lead to reincarnation as an inferior being, good deeds will ensure ascent to higher forms of life and eventually to a paradisaic world or, in the case of Buddhism, nirvana. According to most scholars there is no trace of this doctrine in the *Ṛg Veda*, though Joanna Jurewicz has argued at length that there are traces (of reincarnation, though not of karma).[9] Those she finds are all in the tenth book, which is generally agreed to be of much later date than the rest.[10] The first unambiguous appearances of the doctrine are in the Upaniṣads:

> Citra continued: 'When people depart from this world, it is to the moon that they all go. By means of their lifebreaths the moon swells up in the fortnight of waxing, and through the fortnight of waning it propels them to new birth. Now, the moon is the door to the heavenly world. It allows those who answer its questions to pass. As to those who do not answer its question, after they have become rain, it rains them down here on earth, where they are born again in these various conditions – as a worm, an insect, a fish, a bird, a lion, a boar, a rhinoceros, a tiger, a man, or some other creature – each in accordance with his actions and his knowledge'.[11]

There are two ways of looking at the emergence of this doctrine or belief. One is that early man looks around him and seeks an explanation of his misfortunes; not finding himself conscious of any obvious sin, he supposes it must have been something he did in a previous life. That is, the sense of culpability is primary.[12]

9. Jurewicz 2016.

10. *RV* 10.14.8, 'having left behind imperfection, come home again. Unite with your body in your full luster'. As so often, the words of the Veda are less than perspicuous. See also *RV* 10.16.5. The view that there is no rebirth in the Veda is forcefully presented by Bronkhorst 1999.

11. *Kauṣītaki Up.* 1.2. See also the earlier *Bṛh. Up.* 4.3.35–8; also *Manusmṛti* 12.18, 12.53–8. There is a similar account, in which the soul makes its choice of next life on the moon, in *Jaiminīya Upaniṣad Brahmāna* 3.27.18, 3.28.1–4, quoted in Jurewicz 2016, 626–7. The first part of this trajectory is referred to in a song transcribed in Manjapur by S.M.S. Gell (1992, 37): 'Your kind of people and my kind of people / will go to the upper world, by and by. / When it is time to go, we will go to / the Moon (or Silver) City / Grandfather and uncle, all will be there / But they will not recognise / or speak to us.'

12. Burley 2016b, 102.

An alternative approach is argued forcefully by Gananath Obeyesekere, who begins from a typological distinction of reincarnation. He distinguishes between ethical and non-ethical types, karmic or cyclical, suggesting that the random succession of lives (as typified by Boopsie in the epigraph to this section) develops into a more ethical form in which the individuals' actions in this life determine their states in the next.[13] In many non-Indian traditions, and in some tribal eschatologies, reincarnation is a matter of lineage: an ancestor is reborn in a new individual. In this case what is reborn is not an individual but a package of soul-substance.[14] Consonant with this view is the suggestion of Daniele Maggi (2016) that the doctrine of karma is a Brahman response to a long-standing kṣatriya belief in this kind of cycle.[15] Mikel Burley has criticised the (Whiggish) suggestion of progress from metaphysics to ethics in this model, and makes use of the work of Catherine Osborne to argue for, perhaps, a reverse development – from ethical stance to metaphysical buttressing. He also quotes Wittgenstein in another anthropological context:

> Where that practice and these views occur together, the practice does not spring from the view, but they are both just there.[16]

No doubt there was a conspectus of beliefs. Ājīvikas, for example, believed in a cycle of continuous reincarnation, prompting Buddhists to criticise them for their extreme ascetic practices: what good could these do if they had no impact on the form to be assumed in the next life?[17]

Though Buddhism adopted the doctrine of karma it posed an obvious philosophical problem for the school. Since for Buddhists there is no 'self', no 'soul', what is it that survives to be reborn and punished or rewarded? King Milinda posed the question straight to Nāgasena, and the sage struggled to find an answer.[18] One way to deal with the question is to conceive of the 'soul'

13. Obeyesekere 2002.

14. Parkin 1992, 203.

15. Maggi 2016.

16. Wittgenstein 1993, 119, quoted in Burley 2016a, 231.

17. The conceptual difficulty involved in the idea of a 'next life' for an individual in a philosophy, namely Buddhism, which determinedly denies the existence of a 'self' may be left aside here.

18. *Milindapāñha* 2.2 para. 40, p. 63: 'he who is born, Nagasena, does he remain the same or become another?'. Cf. 2.1.1. para. 25: 'if there be no permanent individuality ... who is it that lives a life of righteousness?' (The metaphor of the chariot is now introduced to deal with the question). See Burley 2016b, 78 and 108; Gokhale 2015, 195, Verpoorten in Ducoeur and

in a materialist way, as consisting of 'soul-stuff' or 'soul-atoms', which are dispersed on death and come together to make new souls. But this does not seem to meet the requirement that there should be a continuing 'person'. According to 'bundle' theories, the soul or person is just a function of the never-ending stream of consciousness. This is the conception that is tested in Derek Parfit's famous thought-experiment of the replica self: a person enters a teletransporter which destroys his original body at the same time as it creates a replica with all the same physical and psychological data in another place.[19] Can that person feel that he thus survives death? Can he be held responsible for the original's past misdeeds? Jonardon Ganeri has found an interesting parallel in a Buddhist tale in the *Mahāprajñāpāramitāśāstra*, in which a demon in a rage tears off the limbs of a man, one by one, while a second demon reattaches each limb to the torso of a corpse; both demons then devour the body of the original man. The man reflects, 'The body that was born of my father and mother, I have seen with my own eyes being entirely devoured by these two demons. Now my present body is entirely constituted by the flesh of someone else. Do I quite clearly have a body, or do I no longer have a body?'

On meeting a group of Buddhist monks the following morning, who ask him who he is, he expresses his uncertainty: 'I don't really know, not even whether I am a person or I am a non-person.' From the Buddhists' point of view this is an excellent answer: 'this man recognizes for himself the non-existence of the "I". He will easily attain the state of liberation.'[20]

The story may seem to help with the conundrum of 'self', but the fact is that the man's consciousness is continuous from the original form, that was devoured by the demons, to the new construction. He remembers his former existence in the body that has been destroyed. And this is the key to any hard-hitting theory of reincarnation: one should be able to remember one's previous life or lives. Such recall is presented as an exercise in meditation in the *Sāmaññaphala Sutta*: 'when his mind is thus concentrated ... he directs and inclines it to the knowledge of recollecting past lives ... He recollects his numerous past lives in their modes and their details.'[21] The Buddha was able to recollect his previous lives, as was Pythagoras, and many people seem to have

---

Muckensturm-Poule 2016. Gokhale 2015, 195 quotes B. R. Ambedkar: 'If there is no soul, how can there be karma? If there is no soul, how can there be rebirth?'

19. Parfit 1984, 199–201.

20. Ganeri 2012, 212–13.

21. *Sāmaññaphala Sutta* 95 (Bodhi 1989, 47).

inklings of this kind (like Boopsie), but in general we do not. We do not even remember life in the womb, though it would be nice to know whether the butterfly remembers its life as a caterpillar. So there must be some kind of continuity which does not (necessarily) include memory.[22]

This sketch of some Indian ways of conceiving of reincarnation may show how difficult it is to pin down any single belief as typically 'Indian'. If we say that a Greek thinker learnt a doctrine from an Indian, what doctrine are we looking at? Among the Greeks, Pythagoras was famous for his belief in the transmigration of souls. Herodotus seems to be referring to Pythagoras (among others?) when he writes,

> The Egyptians were also the first to claim that the soul of a human being is immortal, and that each time the body dies the soul enters another creature just as it is being born.... This theory has been adopted by certain Greeks too – some from a long time ago, some more recently – who presented it as if it were their own. I know their names, but I will not write them down.[23]

But no Greek in any surviving writing before Porphyry ever states that he has been influenced by an Indian thinker. There might be other explanations, such as parallel socio-economic development, or the observable fact that two people can have the same idea independently at the same time. Proof of influence depends not just on individual elements (memes?) but on structure and system. Magnone has proposed, in addition, that a principle of textual criticism can be employed here: when there are, not common errors, but common *peculiarities*, in a particular set of ideas, dependence of one (manuscript or system) is likely.[24]

Pythagoras, whom William Jones regarded as a prime candidate for Indian influence, has left no writings, and we must deduce his views from stories told by later writers, such as the famous anecdote that he begged a man to stop beating a dog because he recognised in the beast the soul of an old friend.[25] There is no way of knowing whether this implies any moral judgment about the friend; it may just be that it was his turn to be a dog. Other questions – such as 'Did the dog know?' – are not broached in the tradition.

22. Burley 2016b, 120, reviews the arguments of Bernard Williams and John Hick in this regard.

23. Hdt. 2.123.

24. Magnone 2016, 152.

25. D.L. 8.136. Also Xenophanes DK21B7.

Not many ancient authors refer to Indians and Pythagoras in the same context. A rare case is Strabo's summary of Onesicritus' meeting with the naked philosopher Mandanis (elsewhere Dandamis). Here Mandanis utters what seem to be little more than platitudes about living well; it is Onesicritus who answers that 'Pythagoras taught such doctrines, and also bade people to abstain from meat, as did also Socrates and Diogenes, and that he himself had been a pupil of Diogenes'.[26] There is nothing here about reincarnation, and it is Onesicritus who contributes the information about Pythagorean abstention from meat, though he had presumably observed that Mandanis' diet was a vegetarian one without it having to be spelt out to him.

Later writers, including Empedocles,[27] were aware of Pythagoras' recall of former lives, and of his doctrine of metempsychosis,[28] but without linking it to Indian ideas. The first writer to make a connection with India is Pausanias, in the second century CE, though he does not mention Pythagoras by name:

> The Chaldaians and the Indian wizards are the first people to my knowledge who ever said the soul of man is immortal, and one of the most important Greeks they convinced was Plato.[29]

About the same time, Philostratus had his hero Apollonius of Tyana, who is explicitly a Pythagorean philosopher, associate with Indian Brahmans and Egyptian naked philosophers. He stops short of associating Pythagoras with India, but the Indian Iarchas tells Apollonius that his belief about the soul 'is what Pythagoras transmitted to you Greeks, and we to the Egyptians', which may be taken to imply that Pythagoras acquired it from India.[30]

It was then in modern times, with William Jones, that the assertion became explicit that Pythagoras must have been influenced by Indian thought, and it was developed at length by Leopold von Schroeder in a book of 1884 which became highly influential.[31] Hellenists such as John Burnet rejected the connection, however, and indeed proposed that the direction of influence was all from Greece to India. (This entailed denying that the Upaniṣads and

26. Str. 15.1.63–5 = Onesic. F 17. Discussed at the beginning of ch. 7.1 above.

27. Emp. F 6/129 Inwood.

28. E.g., Arist. *de An.* 407b23.

29. Paus. 4.32.4.

30. Philostr. *VA* 3.19.1.

31. *Pythagoras und die Inder.* Coleridge, for example, was impressed: Drew 1987, 121–2. Drew claims that Schroeder's argument 'has not been refuted'. Yeats called Yajñavalkya 'the Indian Pythagoras'. See also Singh 2004, 47 on Alexander Cunningham.

the writings of the Buddha could be described as 'philosophy'.) A. B. Keith subjected the arguments for Indian influence on Pythagoras to a thorough examination.[32] He was able to deal with most of them quite briefly. He showed that there was no real evidence for Pythagoras' alleged journey to India. The mathematics (developed later in India), the theory of five elements (not the same five in the two traditions) and the taboos on certain foods (paralleled in many cultures worldwide) are all easy to set aside.

Reincarnation is the subject on which the parallels are most intriguing. But what we know of Pythagoras' views is really very slight, and goes back to an account by the third century BCE philosopher Heraclides of Pontus. This is then summarised in the *Life* written by the Neo-Platonist or Neo-Pythagorean Iamblichus, nearly a thousand years after Pythagoras:

> He aroused in many of those he met a most clear and vivid remembrance of an earlier life which their souls had lived long ago, before being bound to this present body. He gave indisputable proofs that he himself had been Euphorbos son of Panthoos, the opponent of Patroklos [in the *Iliad*].[33]

The fuller account by Heraclides of Pontus is preserved in Diogenes Laertius. This adds the information that Euphorbos, given the gift of recollection of former lives by Hermes, 'recollected the number of plants and animals he had been, and the things his psyche had suffered in Hades and what the other psyches endured'.[34]

What Pythagoras, or his previous incarnation Euphorbos, is describing here is a succession of lives without any stated ethical content. However, it is implied that his soul had 'suffered' (presumably bad things) in Hades before being reincarnated. This may be set alongside what can be gleaned of the teaching of Empedocles, who lived about a hundred years later than Pythagoras, about his own previous lives (see epigraph to this section) and the principles of reincarnation:

> There is an oracle of Necessity ... : whenever one of those demigods [*daimones*], whose lot is long-lasting life, has sinfully defiled his dear limbs with bloodshed, or following strife has sworn a false oath, thrice ten thousand seasons does he wander far from the blessed, being born throughout

32. Keith 1909.

33. Iambl. *Vit. Pyth.* 14.63.

34. D.L. 8.4.

> that time in the form of all manner of mortal things and changing one baleful path of life for another.[35]

The sin of bloodshed seems to be that of eating flesh;[36] and where 'a father lifts up his dear son, who has changed his form, and prays and slaughters him',[37] he seems to imply that a dead son might be reborn as an animal and thus be sacrificed.

Empedocles seems to present a modified version of the belief in immortality of the soul, since his cosmic cycle involves the complete dissolution of all things into their constituent four elements at the end of a period of (perhaps) thirty thousand years. But during the cycle, the soul keeps returning through different incarnations.[38] He seems also to refer to a place of torment visited by the soul.[39] This may simply be a version of the 'Homeric' idea of the gloomy home of the dead where the sun never shines and post-mortem torments are applied to the great sinners; but in Empedocles' account the succession of lives is ethicised: it is a punishment for meat-eating and false speech.[40] But there is no way out until the thirty thousand years are over – a stage which Empedocles is sure he has now reached.[41] It is a primal sin that can only be expiated over an entire cycle of the cosmos, and behaviour in successive lives is not stated to make any difference. The dissolution of personal identity is a happy event, as argued by Inwood,[42] a kind of entry into immortality, but it may also seem more comparable to nirvana. The *daimon* is very long-lived, but ceases to exist when its cycle of reincarnations is over. Such is the picture painted by Cebes in Plato's *Phaedo*:[43] the soul wears a man as a man wears a cloak, and the cloak wears out before the man. Likewise the soul outlives many clothings of flesh.

In Buddhist teaching, by contrast, behaviour in each life influences the status of one's rebirth in the next. It is possible that Pythagoras believed something similar, if we may rely on the recreation of Pythagorean doctrine

35. Emp. F 31b 115 DK = F 11 Inwood.
36. Ibid. Ff 124/139, 126/136.
37. Ibid. F 128/137.
38. Ibid. Ff 111/117, 7/113.
39. Ibid. Ff 115/118, 116–17/121.
40. But the idea of ancestral guilt is absent from Pythagoras: Zhmud 2012, 231–2.
41. Emp. F 1/112.
42. Inwood 2001, 54.
43. Pl. *Phd.* 86e–88b; Inwood 2001, 55.

in Plato's *Phaedrus* and *Republic*. Plato states explicitly, 'In all three incarnations he who lives righteously has a better lot for his portion, and he who lives unrighteously a worse.'[44] But the soul must go through a cycle of ten thousand years before it can return 'to the place whence it came'. For Empedocles, as we saw, it was thirty thousand years, and it is unclear whether each life was conditioned by the ethical behaviour in the previous life. (Can a bush be virtuous?) For Plato, each succeeding life is conditioned by the previous one. At the end of the ten or thirty thousand years, the soul returns to its home. In Buddhism, by contrast, the soul can be freed at any time and no fixed cycle seems to be envisaged.

In the *Republic*, the model is somewhat different.[45] Souls are judged in Hades (again, a familiar Greek idea) and punished tenfold for their evil deeds over a period of one thousand years. Thereafter they proceed to the allocation of lives, which takes place somewhere in the heavens (reminding one of the setting on the moon in the *Kauṣītaki Upaniṣad*), and have to choose lots for what they will be next time around. 'The blame is his who chooses', pronounces Lachesis, the Fate: 'God is blameless'. They are then offered a further choice, of many kinds of animal and human lives, from beggar to tyrant: 'but there was no determination of the quality of soul, because the choice of a different life inevitably determined a different character'. The task for a man (or a dead soul) is thus to know how to make a reasoned choice between the better and the worse life.[46] The choice made, the souls have to drink of the River of Forgetfulnes before returning to their new life.

While reincarnation is clearly central to this myth, far more of it is based on a traditional Greek idea of judgment after death. The ethical dimension is to the fore, but the crucial moral choice is made in the world of the dead; the tenor of one's earthly life is then determined in advance, and all we can do in this life is to seek the knowledge that will enable one to choose wisely in the hereafter (618c).[47] There are also clear echoes of what is described as Orphic doctrine, as evidenced in the Gold Plates and the Derveni papyrus, the texts in which are designed to enable the departed souls to navigate safely the hazards and choices of direction that face it in the underworld.[48]

44. Pl. *Phdr.* 248e.
45. Pl. *R.* 10.614–21.
46. Ibid. 10.618b, d.
47. Ibid. 10.618c.
48. Graf and Johnston 2007 is a dependable discussion.

One is never sure with Plato how far he is expressing doctrine and how far he is speaking in metaphors. But Plotinus seems to take all these ideas very seriously in his development of the Descent of the Soul in the *Enneads*,[49] where he tries to reconcile various doctrines of earlier thinkers, including Empedocles. However, he does not mention Indians, and it is reasonable to assume that his thought was developed entirely on the basis of Greek predecessors. The enthusiasm for India comes from his biographer, Porphyry.[50]

Keith rejected influence of India on Pythagoras and stressed the differences of the Platonic passages from the elements of Buddhist succession of lives. He argued that Plato's version is quite unlike those of the Upaniṣads, which stress the need of knowledge in order to attain enlightenment. The similarities seem to me greater than Keith allows.

In the *Kauṣītaki Upaniṣad*, for example, departed souls go to the moon, which swells up with their lifebreaths for a fortnight, and then wanes as it propels them back to new births, where they are reborn in various conditions – 'as a worm, an insect, a fish, a bird, a lion, a boar, a rhinoceros, a tiger, a man, or some other creature – each in accordance with his actions and his knowledge'.[51] The departed soul arrives first at a lake: 'He crosses it with his mind, but those who go into it without a complete knowledge drown in it'. The emphasis on finding the way through Hades with reliable knowledge recalls the instructions given to Orphic adepts, as in the gold plates and the Derveni papyrus. The soul is burdened with deeds both good and bad, but he 'shakes them off' and they fall upon his relatives, while he himself enters the world of *brahman*[52]

However, the question remains whether Pythagoras, or Empedocles, or Plato were, or even could have been, 'influenced' by Indian thought. As Keith says, there is a native tradition ready at hand to explain most elements of Plato's myth in the *Republic*; only the actual idea of reincarnation of souls seems to be Pythagorean. And this too looks much more like a shamanic idea of the wandering soul, which in any case would be rooted so far back in Indo-European antiquity as to precede both the Upaniṣads and Pythagoras. Two further considerations militate against the idea of influence. First, the Buddha's system depends in essence on moral behaviour, while Empedocles' and

49. E.g., 3.4.2, 4.3.12, 4.8.5.
50. Edwards 2006, 92–3.
51. *KaU* 1.2.
52. Ibid. 1.4a.

Plato's are conceived in terms of fixed cycles. These are essentially different concepts of salvation, and Buddha might have been as critical of Empedocles as he was of the Ājīvika insistence that destiny is fixed. Second, it is extremely hard to envisage any channel of communication by which Pythagoras might have learnt about the Upaniṣads, or Plato about the Buddha. Tales in later authors of Pythagoras' travels to the East are likely to be fantasy, while Aristoxenus' account of some Indian philosophers turning up in Athens to talk to Socrates is imponderable.[53] In any case, if there was transmission it is likely to have been in rather general terms – 'Oh yes, they believe that souls are constantly reincarnated' – and the Greeks built the detail of their systems independently. (It is very notable that they are all slightly different.) In sum, Onesicritus' response to Mandanis – 'Oh yes, Pythagoras said something like that' – is the only level at which exchange of ideas could take place unless there was a systematic programme of study with a guru. The Greek and Indian beliefs in reincarnation, like the Inuit and the West African, are independent developments in the human psyche.

The Tripartite Soul and the Soul-Chariot

> Know the self as a rider in a chariot,
> And the body, as simply the chariot.
> Know the intellect as the charioteer,
> And the mind, as simply the reins.
> The senses, they say, are the horses,
> And sense objects are the paths around them . . .
> When a man's mind is his reins,
> Intellect, his charioteer;
> He reaches the end of the road,
> That highest step of Viṣṇu.
>
> —*KAṬHA UPANIṢAD* 1.3.3–4, 9

> Let the soul be likened to the union of powers in a team of winged horses and their winged charioteer . . . it is hard, by reason of the heaviness of the horse of

53. Aristox. F 53 Wehrli = Euseb. *Praep. Ev.* 11.3.8; discussed by Bar-Kochva 2010, 74. The Indian reproves Socrates for concerning himself with human affairs when he has not yet understood the divine.

wickedness, which pulls down his driver with its weight, unless that driver has schooled him well.

—PLATO, *PHAEDRUS* 246A

The striking image of the soul is developed at length in the *Kaṭha Upaniṣad*. The charioteer, the rational intellect, must be in control in order to escape the tyranny of the senses, represented by the horses, and to reach the heavenly contemplation. Subjugation of the senses is also the theme of Kṛṣṇa in the *Bhagavad-gītā*.[54]

Plato's chariot is an image of the tripartite soul, consisting of intellect, passions and desires. It is spelt out in more detail, but without the chariot imagery, in the *Timaeus*.[55] The question presents itself, whether this very striking parallelism of imagery is due to influence.[56] It is notable, for one thing, that the image is rather intrusive in the *Phaedrus*, rather than an integral part of the argument. Again, the two principles apply: are the two passages close enough *in detail* to compel belief in influence; and what channel of transmission is to be supposed?

The main element that both passages have in common is the idea of the intellect as charioteer. In the *Kaṭha Upaniṣad*, the body is the chariot and the horses are the senses, and similarly in *Buddhacarīta*, where Aśvaghoṣa states that the Buddha 'with firmness overcame the rebellious horses of the senses'.[57] In Plato, the chariot as such is not part of the allegory, and the horses are 'the spirited' and 'the appetitive' parts of the soul – spiritual energy, which is good if rightly directed, and desire which has to be kept under control. These are significant differences.

Furthermore, chariots occur repeatedly as images in both Indian and Greek poetry. The *Bhagavad-gītā* (later, be it noted, than Plato) is delivered to Arjuna by his wise charioteer Kṛṣṇa, who shows him the path of virtue that a kṣatriya must follow. Parmenides' revelation about the nature of the universe is received as the conclusion of a journey in a 'soul-chariot' to the presence of the Goddess. In both Indian and Greek epic, chariots are crucial as means of transport and weapons of war; they continued to be such in India up into

54. *BG* 3.37–41.

55. Pl. *Ti.* 69–72.

56. Magnone 2016 argues forcefully for direct influence of the *Kaṭha Upaniṣad* on Plato.

57. *Buddhacarīta* 2.34.

historical times. A famous argument for no-self in *Questions of King Milinda* is based on the 'deconstruction' of a chariot into its component parts: it is their assemblage that makes a chariot, and it is the assemblage of the parts of a man that makes the putative 'self'.[58] The chariot was ready to hand, as it were, in both cultures, for the construction of metaphors.

The two passages can perfectly well have been conceived independently, just as, say, the divine apparatus in the *Nibelungenlied* need not be derived from that of Homer: both are Indo-European *Gemeingut.* It would hardly be necessary to pursue this further, but that the tripartite soul of Plato has been brought into relation with the threefold division of Indian society into Brahmans (wisdom), kṣatriyas (temper) and traders (desire). John Ferguson averred that Plato had got this idea from Pythagoras, following the latter's travels in India.[59] (The śudras, left out in this scheme, are supposed to match up with slaves for Plato.) The philosopher-kings of his ideal society, embodiments of wisdom, would be the equivalent of the Brahmans. If this were true, it would turn the Indian structure on its head since the kings in this scheme are supposed to be drawn from the kṣatriya caste and the Brahmans are their advisers. The idea cannot be seriously entertained, though Plato's threefold division might imply some awareness of the kind of tripartite division of Indo-European society argued for by Georges Dumézil.

The derivation of Plato's tripartite soul from any Indian source seems even less secure than that of reincarnation.

Pyrrho and the Buddha

All a person is, you see,
Is a hook to hang a lifetime on.

—IMTIAZ DHARKER, 'VITAL SIGNS',
IN *LEAVING FINGERPRINTS* (2009)

The possibility of influence is much more pertinent in the case of Pyrrho, who was a younger contemporary of Megasthenes. He was considered by his successors the founding father of Sceptical philosophy, and it has frequently been argued that his ideas exhibit the influence of Buddhist thought.[60]

58. *Milindapāñha* 2.1.

59. Ferguson 1975, 63–4.

60. Frenkian 1957 (1958); Sedlar 1980; Flintoff 1980; Kuzminski 2008; Beckwith 2015. In general terms, also O'Leary 1949, 120–30.

Not all scholars agree,[61] and the question brings us to the heart of an issue of principle. Could the Greeks have understood enough of what they heard from Indian philosophers to convey its essence to readers in their own language?[62] It will already be evident that my answer as regards the naked philosophers who spoke with Onesicritus is 'Yes'. Megasthenes probably understood a good deal of what was said to him, though his account is obscured by Strabo's method of paraphrase. In the case of Pyrrho, the answer hangs on two main items of technical philosophy: the tetralemma, an argument specifically used by the Buddha, and arguments about the fallibility of perception (mistaking a coiled rope for a snake), as well as the doctrine that every statement can be controverted by an opposing one,[63] which occur in many Indian texts but are also significant in Buddhist philosophy.

Pyrrho, a Greek from Elis, is himself an elusive figure. He probably lived from about 365/60 to 275/70 BCE (or maybe ten years later),[64] and was one of several philosophers and intellectuals who accompanied Alexander to India: he studied with Anaxarchus, with whom he 'travelled everywhere'.[65] Perhaps he knew Megasthenes, who may have been a little younger. Pyrrho wrote a poem in praise of Alexander, and was ticked off by Anaxarchus for pandering to kings, as a result of which he 'withdrew from the world and lived in solitude'.[66] But he remained with the expedition until its end, and 'even foregathered with the Indian Gymnosophists and with the Magi. This led him to adopt a most noble philosophy, to quote Ascanius of Abdera, taking the form of agnosticism and suspension of judgment.'[67] Returning to Greece after Alexander's death, he became a teacher of ethics, specifically of the way to escape suffering, *pathē*, and to achieve *apatheia*, 'freedom from suffering', and

61. Bett 2000 argues forcefully against any such influence. McEvilley 2002 devotes a chapter (450–84) to 'Pyrrho and Mādhyamika': he notes the congruence, but comes down against influence, insisting that Pyrrho arrived in India primed with such ideas from his Greek educators: see Kuzminski 2008, 48. Bronkhorst 2016, 247, denies that the Buddha held the view of no-self that Pyrrho is said to derive from him. See further below.

62. Cf. Bett 2000, 176–8, quoted below.

63. D.L. 9.75, Kuzminski 2008, 40.

64. Beckwith 2015, 13.

65. D.L. 9. 61.

66. Ibid. 9. 63. Anaxarchus is hardly innocent of the crime of 'pandering to kings', in view of his consolation to Alexander after he murdered Cleitus (Plu. *Alex*. 52) and his enthusiasm for declaring Alexander a god (Arr. *Anab*. 4.10.6; but see Plu. *Alex*. 28).

67. D.L. 9. 61.

hence *ataraxia*, 'untroubledness'.[68] He is thus perhaps the first of the long line of Hellenistic philosophers – Epicurus, who admired Pyrrho,[69] being the most prominent – who practised and preached 'philosophy' as a therapy to lead to a more untroubled life.[70] The desire to escape from suffering echoes the mission of the Buddha, but that in itself is hardly enough to establish influence. There was plenty of suffering in the Hellenistic world, which underwent forty years of warfare after Alexander's death; this might well prompt a philosopher to escapism, or, in Greek, *apragmosyne*.[71] One thinks here of the *Dhammapada*'s injunction, 'cherish disengagement' (5.75). Timon, Pyrrho's most notable disciple, was 'very fond of gardens and preferred to mind his own affairs' (the Greek word is *idiopragmon*), and Epicurus' school was situated in a 'garden', a symbolic representation of retirement from the world. No earlier Greek philosopher had sought anything like 'so negative a goal' as *ataraxia*.[72]

Nothing that Pyrrho wrote has survived, though he was regarded by the later Sceptics as the originator of their school of thought. The most detailed testimony to his views is a passage deriving from the dialogue *Pytho*, by his pupil Timon of Phlius. The passage is preserved in a chapter of the history of philosophy by Aristocles of Messene, and is quoted verbatim by Eusebius in his *Preparation for the Gospel*.[73] Timon states that 'whoever wants to be happy must consider three questions: first, how are *pragmata* (things, matters) by nature; secondly, what attitude should we adopt towards them; and third, what will be the outcome for those who have this attitude?' He goes on to (apparently) quote Pyrrho directly:

> As for *pragmata*, they are all *adiaphora* ('indifferent', 'undifferentiated by a logical differentia'), and *astathmēta* ('unmeasurable'), and *anepikrita* ('inarbitrable' [Long and Sedley], 'not susceptible of judgment, decision'). Therefore, neither our sense-perceptions nor our *doxai* ('opinions') either tell us the truth or lie to us. Therefore, for this reason one should not trust

68. Beckwith 2015, 16.

69. D.L. 9.64.

70. Nussbaum 1994; the main discussion of Pyrrho is at 312–15. Despite the apparent implication of her title, the name of the Buddha does not appear in the index.

71. D.L. 9.64.

72. Flintoff 1980, 94. Democritus' *athambia* (T A 1 (45), A 167, A169 DK) which became Horace's *nil admirari*, is on the way there.

73. Eus. *PE* 14.18.1–5; Long and Sedley 1987, 1.14–15.

in them, but should be *adoxastous* ('without opinions'), *aklineis* ('uninclined') and *akradantous* ('unwavering'),[74] saying about each single thing that it no more is than is not, or it both is and it is not, or it neither is nor is not.

Aram Frenkian in 1957 seems to have been the first to notice the congruence of this teaching with a crucial part of Buddhist philosophy, the tetralemma. Now the tetralemma as a form of argument was certainly known before Pyrrho:[75] it occurs, for example, in Plato's *Republic*, in the course of Socrates' argument to Glaucon that any beautiful thing may sometimes appear its opposite, what is now light may at another time be heavy, and so on: 'for these things too equivocate, and it is impossible to conceive firmly any one of them to be or not to be or both or neither.'[76] The passage is making an epistemological point that tends towards the eventual establishment of the Theory of Forms, a world of absolutes. This could not be more different from Pyrrho's, or Buddha's, use of the argument. Buddha used the recognition that things are beyond the firm judgment of humans (Pyrrho calls them *anepikrita*; the Buddha's term is *avyākrta*, 'insoluble or inexpressible')[77] to reject all forms of dogmatism. Megasthenes, it will be recalled, says that the Brahmans teach that nothing is good or bad (by nature).[78] Kuzminski quotes Nāgārjuna: 'Everything is real and is not real, both real and not real, neither real nor not real. This is the Lord Buddha's teaching.'[79] Nāgārjuna applies this form of words to the Buddha himself following his *parinirvana*: 'Having passed into Nirvana, the Victorious Conqueror / is neither said to be existent / nor said to be non-existent. / Neither both nor neither are said.'[80] To put it another way, 'when all alternatives are exhausted, only zero, śūnya, emptiness remains.'[81] In the hands of the Greek Sceptics this developed into the radical suspension of judgment outlined by Sextus Empiricus.[82]

74. Beckwith 2015, 23 interprets this as 'unwavering in our refusal to choose.'

75. Kuzminski 2008, 45–6.

76. Pl. *R.* 5.479c.

77. Flintoff 1980, 91.

78. Str. 15.1.59, Kuzminski 2008, 46–7.

79. Nagarjuna, *Mūlamadhyamakakārikā* 18.8.49; Kuzminski 2008 83. See Siderits and Katsura 2013, 200, whose translation has small verbal differences.

80. Ibid. 25.17: Garfield 1995, 75; Strong 2001, 163.

81. Matilal 2005, 122.

82. See Garfield 1990 for a detailed exploration of Eastern and Western 'skepticism.'

The form of argument can be traced back close to the time of the Buddha, appearing, for example, in the *Sāmaññaphala Sutta*,[83] when Ajāttasattu is portrayed as telling the Buddha what Sañjaya Belaṭṭhaputtua said to him: 'I do not say, "It is this way", nor "It is that way", nor "It is otherwise". I do not say "It is not so", nor do I say "It is not not so".' It was soon well known: in the *Questions of King Milinda* Nāgasena rejects the tetralemma as pointless.[84]

The tetralemma's radical rejection of certainty is of a piece with the famous doctrine of 'no-self', which holds – against, for example, the Upaniṣads – that there is no continuous identity to any thing or person. (Some ascetics, such as the Aghoris, deny the distinction between the soul and the Absolute, and insist on the identity of opposites, such as bad and good, and act accordingly.)[85] Bronkhorst insists that 'no-self' is *not* part of the earliest Buddhist doctrine, but a later development; he is however in a minority. Strong, for example, notes that no-self is clearly expounded in the Buddha's Second Sermon in Benares.[86]

William Empson thinks, by the way, that this instability of identity is represented in many of the earliest sculptural representations of the Buddha; by slicing photographs down the middle and reassembling two left and two right halves, he created images with different characteristics, often more contemplative on the left and more active or even aggressive on the right. In this view, the distinction between the rope and the snake is not merely imponderable; they are actually the same. Empson makes the stance into a mystic one: 'so far as he has achieved his state of ecstasy he combines them, he is "neither conscious nor not conscious", like the seventh Buddhist state of enlightenment'.[87]

There may be truth in this, but here we are considering the Buddha as a philosopher, not as a mystic, though both aspects may have co-existed. (Certainly Nāgārjuna's position is very supportive of mysticism, implying that only vision will suffice when words fail.)[88] The difference from earlier Indian ascetic positions is that Buddha does not seek, like the Brahman, to merge his

83. *Sāmaññaphala Sutta* 31 (Bodhi 1989, 24).

84. *Milindapāñha 1.206.*

85. Hartsuiker 1993/2014, 49.

86. Bronkhorst 2016, 247; Strong 2001, 110–11. The latter quotes *Mahāvastu* 3.328–9. Gombrich 2013, 60–2 also treats no-self as integral to the Buddha's own teaching.

87. Empson 2016, 85 and n. 88.

88. Matilal 2005, 130. One can hardly fail to be reminded of Wittgenstein: 'Whereof one cannot speak, thereof one must be silent.' Nehru 2004, 130 puts it thus: 'Where knowledge is not possible, we must suspend judgment'.

individual soul (*ātman*) in the universal Brāhman, but rather to be liberated from the world altogether.[89] The centrality of this is emphasised in the *Mahābhārata* when Panchasikha attacks the sceptical position and specifically states that it is Buddhist.[90] The Buddha famously uses the image of the chariot to demolish the view that there is any essence to the chariot apart from its pieces; similarly the human person consists only of his parts: there is no soul or self.[91] How different from Plato's use of the image of the chariot to represent his tripartite soul! Beckwith goes so far as to suggest that Pyrrho's *adiaphoron,* 'indifferent', can be seen as an equivalent to Buddha's *anātman,* 'no innate self-identity'.[92] Things in themselves, *pragmata,* have no identity, but are differentiated only by human observers: this is the epistemological problem of the Criterion.[93]

Richard Bett writes forcefully, 'it is extremely difficult to believe that anything as abstruse as a quadrilemma can possibly have been communicated in any remotely intact form from the Indian "naked wise men" to Pyrrho'.[94] I completely disagree. What is so hard about the concept? Pyrrho had two years to exploit and enjoy the company of Calanus, to improve his (and Calanus') linguistic skills, and to explore any questions that interested him. He was not dependent simply on an afternoon with Dandamis. In any case, the influence of Indian thinkers on Pyrrho is a question not exclusively of doctrine, but one of attitude, which could be established in a moment's illumination.[95]

Something not altogether different is characteristic of Jaina thought. Jains, like the Buddha, reject dogmatism and hold that reality is both manifold in nature (*anekantavada*) and that knowledge is relative (the doctrine of *syadavada,* or 'Maybe'). They do not, however, reject the idea of the self or soul, the *jiva.* The *jiva* can move 'through a transformation of consciousness and behaviour' from bondage to liberation.[96] Relativism is thus not a means to the

89. The lama in *Kim* seems to have forgotten that he is a Buddhist when he announces, in the closing pages of the novel, that his soul is ready to merge with the universal soul.

90. *Mbh.* 12.218–19 (pp. 15–16 and 18 in the Ganguli translation). See Gokhale 2015, 178.

91. 'Personal identity' is the product of a nexus of functionally integrated sources of psychophysical events bearing high degrees of continuity, writes Panaioti (2013, 33), summarising Parfit's view (Parfit 1984).

92. Beckwith 2015, 29–31.

93. Ibid., 26–7.

94. Bett 2000, 176–8.

95. Kuzminski 2008, 37–8.

96. Singh 2009, 314–15.

end, liberation, for it does not prevent the Jain from holding certain opinions and beliefs about right behaviour. It just means that he is aware that they are opinions and beliefs.

For the Buddha, this understanding of the relativism of everything is a liberating moment: once one understands that nothing has an essence, nothing is permanent, one is on the road to liberation and enlightenment. It can be reached through meditation.[97] The 'ten modes of perplexity' are key to the sceptical abandonment of the search for an abiding reality or self: they include the variability of perception, the evident and the non-evident, the recognition of the criterion and rejection of the apparent (interpretation of a sense-perception depends on the viewer: so is it a coiled rope or a snake?).[98] For the Buddha's philosophy has above all a moral purpose: liberation from *dukkha*, 'suffering'.[99] An eristic stance has an ethical aim, as was the case also for Socrates. It issued too in a particular way of life. Though the Buddha became a teacher, his followers led the lives of wandering ascetics, and this is a way of life that Pyrrho also adopted: his *apragmosune* is congruent with the *saṁnyāsa* mode of existence.[100] Both are 'non-dogmatic soteriological practices'.[101]

A key tenet of Buddhism is the need to eliminate desire in order to obtain release from attachment.[102] This aim it shares with other Indian schools of thought,[103] but the method is different. Ascetic practices are designed to en-

97. Hamilton 2000, 176.

98. Kuzminski 2008, ch. 3, explores these matters, noting that appearances are *skandhas* (78). This well-honed example was used by Buddhists as an example of erroneous cognition, by Nyāyas as an example of incorrect inference. Buddhists, like Lokāyatas, are suspicious of inference, and focus on the particulars: Matilal 2005, 103–4.

99. Gombrich 2013, 164 in fact suggests that the Buddha did not aim at presenting a systematic philosophy, but only at arguments that would serve the ethical purpose. Hermann Hesse, in *Siddhartha* (32) saw the Buddha's mission as 'not to explain the world but to deliver from suffering'. Actually it was both; but consistency of metaphysics is probably secondary to the moral purpose. A contemporary philosopher, S.R.L. Clark, once wrote (1977, 186), à propos vegetarianism, 'I am very much more interested in achieving a practical issue than in the details of abstract philosophy, and am willing to argue on almost any basis to achieve that end'!

100. Olivelle 1999 collects the sources and provides a long introduction on *saṁnyāsas*; see also Hausner 2007.

101. Kuzminski 2008, 35.

102. E.g., *Dhammapada* 16.215–16. Schopenhauer wrote that 'the will is like gravity, it is never satisfied': Panaioti 2013, 68–9. Bhagat 1976, 28: 'the extinction of desires is for Indian philosophy the indispensable ethical desideratum for all spiritual achievement'.

103. O'Flaherty 1973/1981, 255–60: the Śaivite principle is not sublimation, as in Tantra, where sexual activity is regarded as a 'cure' for desire (*Linga Purāṇa* 1.86.23) but resistance: 'desire is increased by desire'.

able the practitioner to get free of the body, which is regarded as a nuisance,[104] reminding one of Plotinus' remark that he was 'ashamed to have a body'. The Stoic Epictetus, though not an ascetic, also saw the body as an undesirable possession, inimical to freedom, and his thought was echoed and developed by Gandhi: 'perfect non-violence and love can be exercised only by being prepared to renounce the body in death for the service of humans'.[105]

Some extreme ascetics hang heavy weights from their penises, for example, not simply as a spectacle, but in order to destroy the erectile tissue and thus the possibility of (sexual) desire.[106] There are different ways of eliminating desire, which can be summarised into 'destroy, control or satisfy'.[107] One way is to satisfy it, so that it ceases to trouble you,[108] like the ash-smeared sādhu described by Gita Mehta, casually masturbating to reduce the rampant organ as he explains his reasons to an embarrassed interlocutor.[109] This solution, however, is never permanent. Thirst can be satisfied but never made to cease;[110] Gautama rejected extreme ascetic practices after finding that they did not achieve the required end. Another way is to dominate desire and suppress it by force of will:[111] this too is sometimes presented as a Buddhist approach, as in *Dhammapada*: 'a man may conquer a million men in battle, but the truly great thing is to conquer oneself'.[112] The third, truly Buddhist, way is to eliminate the stirring by recognition of its emptiness, and to live as simply

104. E.g., Hausner 2007, 9 and 30.

105. Quoted in Sorabji 2012, 160; cf. 63 on Epictetus.

106. Tree 2014, 260. Also Moraes and Srivatsa 2003, 311 where it is suggested that pulling the organ downwards causes its power to rise up to more noble parts of the body.

107. Strong 2001, 109.

108. Cf. Haberman 1994, 27, quoting Lacan: 'to be totally satisfied is to lack desire'.

109. Mehta 1980, 58; see also Cavafy's poem, 'Perilous Things': 'Said Myrtias . . . I shall not fear my passions like a coward. I shall abandon my body to sensual pleasures . . . Without any fear, for when I wish . . . at critical moments I shall find again my spiritual self, ascetic as before.' (Tr. E. Sachperoglou, Oxford World's Classics, 2007, 63.) Freedom from desire may come from the fulfilment of desire according to *Bṛh. Up.* 4.4.6: Ganeri 2012, 26.

110. Strong 2001, 109. However, Sati contradicts this when she says to Śiva, 'having made love to you for many years, I am satisfied, and your mind has withdrawn from these pleasures': O'Flaherty 1973/1981, 257, from the *Śiva Purāṇa* 2.2.23.7–8.

111. This was the route followed by many early Christian communities, not a few of which modelled their behaviour on that of the 'Brahmans', as they had come to be known: see Stoneman 2015.

112. Classical philosophers make the same observation: Xenophon *Ages.* 5.4–5, cf. *Mem.* 1.3.8–14; Seneca *NQ* 3 *praef.* 10: *innumerabiles sunt qui populos, qui urbes habuerunt in potestate, paucissimi qui se.* It became a standard topos enjoining self-control: e.g., Petrarch *Fam.* 4.2: Petrarch associates it with release from desires.

as possible, without needs; as Socrates expressed it, 'having the fewest wants, I am nearest to the gods'.[113] On achieving nirvana, the fiery fever of thirsting 'goes out'.[114] Haberman compares this with the Freudian 'death-instinct' – the reduction of tensions to zero.[115] It is also the way to limit karma, since 'desire is the root of all action', or as the lama put it in *Kim*, 'all action is evil'.[116] 'Happiness is the removal of anxiety', as the narrator says in Anand's novel *Private Life of an Indian Prince*[117] – a neat expression of the Hellenistic ideal of *ataraxia*.

Much of what we know of Pyrrho's life and teaching recalls these key lines of Buddhist practice. His way of life seems to have resembled that of a sādhu: he was celibate, would withdraw from society and seek solitude, or would go wandering, he would deliver philosophical discourses even when there was no audience present, and, as Diogenes Laertius records, 'on being discovered once murmuring (*lalōn*) to himself, he answered, when asked the reason, that he was training to be good'.[118] This looks suspiciously like a description of a man engaged in meditation, murmuring a mantra. His pupil Philo also had the habit of talking to himself, either murmuring a mantra or internally conducting an argument.[119] The propensity to give lectures even when no audience is present (apart from being a symptom of academic dutifulness) is also observable in the discourse of Dandamis in Palladius' *De Bragmanibus*, where the philosopher keeps talking even after Alexander has bidden him farewell and left the scene. (But this may just be literary ineptitude on the part of Palladius.)

Another pupil, Timon, was an 'urban(e)' philosopher, and taught his son medicine.[120] Buddhists, too, engaged with the world to the extent of giving medical assistance to their fellows.[121] Indeed, Buddhist philosophy is a kind of psychic medicine,[122] while for Epicurus too philosophy has a therapeutic purpose.[123]

113. D.L. 2.27. Similarly Seneca *Ep.* 2: 'being poor is not having too little, it is wanting more'.

114. Panaioti 2013, 133.

115. Haberman 1994, 28.

116. Haberman 1994, 160; Kipling 1987, 212. A drink from the well Venukup, 'the Flute Well', in the village of Bhandiraban, is said to quench all desires: Haberman ibid. 204.

117. Anand 1953/2008, 344. So it is an Indian commonplace, not just a Buddhist one.

118. D.L. 9.64.

119. Ibid. 9.69, Beckwith 2015, 94.

120. Ibid. 9.109–10, Beckwith 2015, 94.

121. Naqvi 2011; ch. 5 above.

122. Gowans 2010; Ganeri 2010, 122.

123. Tsouna 2009.

Withdrawal from the world or *apragmosyne* is in keeping with the injunction in the *Dhammapada* to 'cherish disengagement';[124] wandering is the duty of the renunciant, as many of the Saṁnyāsa Upaniṣads make clear: 'Observing the duties proper to him, let a mendicant yogin at all times wander in a pure region, looking always at the ground ... Regarding all beings as himself, let a mendicant wander about the earth, as if he were blind, hunchbacked, deaf, mad and dumb.'[125] As a modern-day Jaina nun expressed it to William Dalrymple, 'as wanderers, we monks and nuns are free of shadows from the past. This wandering life, with no material possessions, unlocks our souls.'[126] A whole tribe, the Mirigans, has apparently adopted a similar way of life, of abstinence and chastity: 'they have no desires ... they walk about talking of God in his heaven, they sleep.'[127] Pyrrho withdrew from the world because 'he had heard an Indian reproach Anaxarchus, telling him that he would never be unable to teach others what is good while he himself danced attendance on kings in their courts.'[128]

Pyrrho defined his own mission as διαγωνίζεσθαι πρὸς τὰ πράγματα, the struggle against *pragmata*.[129] The word means 'things, matters' and the phrase can easily be unpacked to connote the refusal to recognise any outer realities. Pyrrho was famous for his absolute suspension of judgment, so that his friends, according to a perhaps invented anecdote, had to prevent him from walking over precipices by accident.[130] According to another anecdote, Anaxarchus once fell into a bog, and Pyrrho ignored him.[131] Another anecdote tells how he preserved his calm when the ship he was travelling on was in danger of being wrecked by pointing to a pig that was also on board, that paid no attention to the commotion around it.[132] (On this occasion Pyrrho displayed more calm than the Buddhist monks described by Milinda, who ran away when a mad elephant was bearing down on them: Milinda uses this episode as a way to attack the idea of Buddhist freedom from fear.)[133] *Dhammapada*

124. *Dhammapada* 5.75.

125. *Nāradaparivrājaka Up.* 159, Olivelle 1992, 187.

126. Dalrymple 2009, 19.

127. Lewis 1991, 191.

128. D.L. 9.63.

129. Ibid. 9.68.

130. This is the sort of scepticism of which Wittgenstein wrote, 'Scepticism is not irrefutable but obviously nonsensical': *Tractatus* 6.51.

131. D.L. 9.63.

132. Ibid. 9.68.

133. *Milindapāñha* 4.4.44.

states, 'among humans who are restless do we dwell without restlessness'.[134] One thinks too of the adoption by Epicureans of the pig as the symbol of untroubled life.

The pig anecdote shows well how the philosophical position of holding no tenets or opinions serves the moral aim of freedom from anxiety. Diogenes Laertius' account of Pyrrho concludes by noting that in order to live in the everyday world one may adopt habits, and observe rules and customs. Behaving 'as if' is a way of coping when there is 'no self.'[135] The *Madhyamika* also accepts cause-and-effect for everyday practical purposes in the phenomenal world.[136] 'According to some authorities the end proposed by the Sceptics is insensibility; according to others, gentleness'.[137] Much the same quandary occurs when one encounters a sādhu.

This suspension of judgment has something in common with existentialism, with its doctrine that 'existence precedes essence', except that in the case of Buddhism or Scepticism there is no 'essence' to be revealed. The question is sometimes raised as to whether an existential world-view entails passivity. The recognition of the 'absurdity' of both metaphysical and political claims does not, however, authorise despair. In Camus's view, at least, it enjoined rebellion.[138] Thus other Hellenistic schools pursued *ataraxia* through *apragmosyne* without rejecting the evidence of the senses or common experience. Epicureanism was in some ways a rebellion.

And remember Anaxarchus' end: 'for his fortitude and contentment in life he was known as the Happy Man, but when he fell into the hands of Nicocreon, the tyrant of Cyprus, the latter put him to death for an insult made years earlier at a feast given by Alexander. The tyrant placed the philosopher in an enormous mortar and commanded him to be beaten to death with iron pestles. The philosopher uttered the apophthegm: "Pound, pound the pouch containing Anaxarchus; ye pound not Anaxarchus." Nicocreon commanded his tongue to be cut out, but Anaxarchus bit it off and spat it at him.'[139] Biting off the tongue is another method of mortification sometimes practised by sādhus, so maybe Anaxarchus too had learnt something from the Indian phi-

134. *Dhammapada* 15.199.

135. Ganeri 2012, 122 and 201; at 164 he describes the Middle Way between eternalism and nihilism, according to which the 'self' is 'real like a stream'.

136. Matilal 2005, 120–1.

137. D.L. 9.108.

138. Zaretsky 2013, 19 and 177.

139. D.L. 9.59. Cf. Plu. *De tranq. an.*, *Mor.* 475e on the similar attitude of Socrates.

losophers. But he was no Buddhist, for he was sure that his self would survive the destruction of its bodily shell; also, biting off the tongue is forbidden by the Buddha.[140] The Dandamis of Palladius has a similar faith: 'If Alexander takes away my head he will not destroy my soul, but only my head which will fall silent.'[141] Dandamis here is modelled on (or is perhaps a model for) Christian martyrs, but the idea of his beheading by the tyrant presumably goes back to the riddle-contest in the Berlin papyrus and Plutarch, where the king threatens to put to death whoever answers worst.[142] Though neither would have put it thus, Dandamis and Anaxarchus were both in their way engaged in 'the struggle against *pragmata*'.

Cynics and Naked Philosophers

Hephaestion: The Indian's faith may soar as high as heaven:
His pride is narrow as the Cynic's tub.
Alexander: You hate Calanus.

—AUBREY DE VERE, 'ALEXANDER THE GREAT' 4.2

Our earliest information about the naked philosophers of Taxila comes from Onesicritus, as described in the first section of chapter 11 above. Onesicritus called himself a 'hearer' of Diogenes,[143] and thus Diogenes Laertius describes him as a 'student' (*mathetes*) of the Cynic. It has therefore been supposed that Onesicritus brought to his meeting with Mandanis/Dandamis and the other naked philosophers a certain philosophical baggage which may have influenced his understanding and presentation of their doctrines. I myself thought that this was likely when I first wrote about it in 1995. In the discussion of the matter in chapter 11 above, I conclude that most of what Onesicritus, and indeed the *Alexander Romance*, tell us about the philosophers is observably genuine Indian detail.

However, the episode as presented in the *Alexander Romance* was quickly adopted by a Cynic writer in Greece as the basis for a *diatribe*, most of which is preserved on a papyrus dating from the mid-second century CE.[144] The papyrus also contains a fragmentary text about Heracles, whom Cynics regarded

140. Timmer 1930, 79.
141. Pall. *De Brag.* 2.17.
142. See Stoneman 2012, xxxii, 77–8.
143. Str. 15.1.65 = Onesic. F 17a. Brown 1949, ch. 2 discusses the matter.
144. Geneva papyrus 271, published by Martin 1959. Translation in Stoneman 2012, 78–83.

as a hero and exemplar for their way of life. The diatribe or sermon of Dandamis in the papyrus covers much the same ground as his discourse in the *Romance*, but at much greater length. He praises the solitary ascetic life, devoted to religious contemplation:

> We rejoice in solitude, sitting among the trees. We apply our minds to god, so that our souls may not, by associating with men, turn their eyes from God ... God made the forest and mountains as a home for us ... I do not wear soft clothing: this is slavery for an Indian ... [145] We are poor and are amazed at nothing ... Why do you force yourselves to be filled only to force yourselves to empty yourselves again, combing offence with disease? Wait for nature to fill you with what she wishes, and you will serve yourselves correctly.

This ascetic creed caught the imagination of later writers, not least the Christian writer Palladius (b. 364), who adapted it further to include an attack on Roman wild beast shows and, perhaps, to incline men's minds to a life of Christian monasticism.[146] The utopian aspect of the dialogue was influential in the centuries directly following Alexander's visit to Taxila, in the creation of several utopian texts by Hellenistic writers (see chapter 9 above). A number of actual breakaway groups with an ascetic mode of life took shape in the period, not least the Jewish sect of the Therapeutae, near Alexandria, whose life bears comparison with that of the 'Brahmans'.[147] In fact the Greek philosopher Clearchus regarded the Jewish people as a people of philosophers, 'descended' from the Calani, by which he seems to mean the naked philosophers (see further below, on Clearchus). The Cynic way of adapting the utopian vision is exemplified by Crates, who described a utopian island called 'Pera'. The word means 'knapsack', and the clear implication is that the Cynic carries his utopia with him wherever he goes. A man without a *polis* must be either a beast or a god, as Aristotle said,[148] and the Cynic becomes a beast (in this case a dog, *kuon*) in order to become a god. Cynics did not form societies. Citizens of no city, they are citizens of the universe, *kosmopolitai*.

The 'dog-like' way of life espoused by the Cynics, beginning with the founding father of the 'philosophy', Diogenes, entailed living without possessions –

145. Cf. *Buddhacarīta* 11.36. Most of the eleventh book is on this theme.

146. See the discussion in Stoneman 2012, xxv–xxvii.

147. Stoneman 2015 offers a longer discussion of these and others.

148. Arist. *Pol.* 1253a, 4–5, 25–9.

Diogenes threw away his cup when he saw a dog lapping from a stream – including all but the most minimal clothing, and leading a life entirely in the open. Thus Diogenes famously slept in a large storage jar, and a well-known anecdote describes an encounter with Alexander, who asked him what he could do for him, to which the philosopher replied, 'Stand out of my sunshine'. The pose is recognisably similar to that of Dandamis, and of many real-life sādhus today. Their life is one of 'perpetual liminality',[149] a position from which they are able, and perhaps entitled, to judge their fellow-men and their fallibility. Another anecdote describes Diogenes going about with a lantern 'looking for a good man'.

But Cynics also had a more extreme side than this genial rejection of 'bourgeois' values. Christian writers, who often admired Cynics, rated their own co-religionists much higher: the Cynics, unlike Christian 'athletes of virtue', 'do what they do for the sake of glory, not virtue'.[150] There can be little doubt that Diogenes was a show-off. Many sādhus, too, are regarded by laymen as charlatans or misfits.[151] Diogenes and Crates certainly drew attention to themselves by their insistence on performing all bodily functions in the open, like dogs: not only excreting, but masturbating and having sexual intercourse in public places.[152]

This last aspect is not one that is associated with all Indian sādhus (though some 'graze like deer').[153] However, there is at least one Indian sect that makes a point of shamelessness: these are the Pāśupatas. In 1962 Daniel Ingalls published a detailed comparison of the practices of the Cynics and the Pāśupatas, focusing on shamelessness and the deliberate seeking of dishonour. He stops short of suggesting influence in either direction, but regards them as parallel phenomena of 'sects of men who performed beast-vows'. The word 'Pāśupata' means a worshipper of Śiva Pāśupati, 'lord of the beasts', and Ingalls saw both groups' behaviour as being derived from shamanic practices. The latter idea is not convincing, at least in the case of the seemingly highly rational Cynics, but the connection of the two movements deserves further consideration. Pāśupata itself may have a wider significance, since Verrier Elwin notes that the Baiga regard themselves as 'the true Pashupati, the lords of all wild animals;

149. Hausner 2007, 199.

150. Theodoret, *Cure of Pagan Maladies* 12.32, cited in Stoneman 2015, 59, with other examples.

151. Hausner 2007, 20–1.

152. Sextus Empiricus *PH* 3.200 says that Indians have sex in the open, 'like Crates'.

153. *Buddhacarīta* 8.3.

the magical protection of the forest is their charge; they have derived their material sustenance from it for hundreds of years'.[154]

The seeking of dishonour is key to both groups. Antisthenes is said to have taught that dishonour, *adoxia*, was a good thing and, along with poverty and exile, the mark of a true Cynic.[155] The German philosopher Peter Sloterdijk, in his *Critique of Cynical Reason*, identifies 'cheekiness' as the characteristic posture of the Cynic, as well as of the cynic.[156] Pāśupatas are enjoined in the *Pāśupata Sūtra* to 'engage in open action' (such as snoring), to limp as if deformed, to play the lecher (by staring at length at pretty girls) and to act and speak improperly (without decorum) 'so that he may come to be ill-treated'. When those around him condemn him for these deliberate acts of shamelessness, 'he receives merit and gives demerit and so becomes purified'.[157]

The Pāśupatas traced their origin to Śiva the Lord of the Beasts and believed that their sect was founded by Lakulīśa, a manifestation (the twenty-eighth and last avatar) of Śiva, to whom the *Pāśupata Sūtra* is attributed. Śiva as lord of the beasts may be related to the horned god of the Indus valley culture.[158] This god is apparently ithyphallic (though there is dispute about the interpretation of the iconography), and Lakulīśa in older representations is commonly ithyphallic, though modern images are less explicit. Indeed, he sometimes appears as *dvilingi Lākuliśa*, Lakulīśa with two penises. This emphasis on the lustful and abandoned side of Śiva is well expressed in the injunction to 'behave like a lecher', mentioned above, which clearly recalls the behaviour of Śiva in the pine forest, when 'by his erotic appearance and gestures (his nakedness and his dancing) he excites the women and infuriates their husbands, but he does not actually *do* anything'.[159]

Even more than his unusual phallic endowment, a constant feature of the iconography of Lakulīśa is his club. This is associated with him in the earliest representations, dating from about the second century BCE (for example, a relief in the Mathura museum), and to a classicist's eye this instantly recalls

154. Elwin 1964, 115.

155. D.L. 6.11, 8.16.

156. Sloterdijk 1987, 103–6.

157. All these details are from *PS* 3, of which an English translation is given in Ingalls 1962, 285–91.

158. Hartsuiker 1993/2014, 21. But for doubts about this identification see ch. 3 above, *Dionysus*.

159. O'Flaherty 1973/1981, 183.

Heracles, the hero of the Cynics. Before Gregory of Nazianzus fell out with his friend Maximus the Cynic, he described how

> It was a great thing for me that this dog should patter
> Through my hall and worship Christ instead of Heracles.[160]

Apuleius explains the connection: Crates is a kind of Heracles, because of his devotion to *ponos*, 'toil', and his lifelong 'combat against anger, envy, greed, and lust, and all other monstrous and shameful urges of the human soul'.[161] One of the pseudonymous 'Letters of Diogenes' enjoins, 'Regard your cloak as the lion skin, your staff as the club, your knapsack as the earth and sea wherewith to nourish yourself; for thus will the fortitude of Hercules stand by you, which is above all turns of fortune.'[162] In Lucian's *Auction of Lives*, Diogenes is asked, by a prospective buyer, whom he emulates, and the philosopher replies, 'Heracles ... like him I'm fighting a campaign against pleasure, not at anyone else's bidding, but of my own free will, since I've made it my purpose to clean up human life'.[163] Sloterdijk thinks Heracles can also be regarded as an example of shamelessness, and illustrates a famous Roman statue of the hero pissing ostentatiously. 'This "dirty" materialism', he writes, 'is an answer not only to an exaggerated idealism of power that undervalues the rights of the concrete ... Urine in the academy! That would be the total dialectical tension, the art of pissing against the idealist wind.'[164]

Be that as it may, the resemblance of the names is also food for thought. Lakulīśa may in fact be a Sanskritisation of the name 'Heracles', in a region of India where /l/ regularly replaces /r/ (as in the word *laja* for *raja* in Aśoka's inscriptions).[165] The founder Lakulīśa, if he existed, is probably to be placed no earlier than the second or first century BCE, the time when representations of him begin to appear. This seems to be a case where an Indian sect may have learnt something from Greek 'philosophers', and not the other way around at all.

160. Greg. Naz. *De vita sua*, 2.1.975, tr. Carolinne White ('Concerning his own life') in White 1996.

161. Apul. *Flor.* 22.

162. Diog. *Ep.* 26, quoted by Ingalls 1962, 293.

163. Luc. *Vitarum Auctio* 1.

164. Sloterdijk 1987, 105.

165. The connection is made by Ingalls 1962, 296 n. 30. See Bloch 1950/2007, 46–7.

Smoke and Fire: Logic and Materialism between Indians and Greeks

Indian philosophy is commonly divided into six schools: *Nyāya*, founded on logic and the exposition of a system of 'right reasoning'; *Vaiśeṣika*, similarly logical and based on an atomistic physical theory; *Saṁkhya*, a rationalistic metaphysical system with a dualist basis, said to have been developed by Kapila as early as the seventh century BCE; *Yoga*, a rule of meditation to develop contemplation; *Mīmāṁsā*, a ritualistic code that lays down the principles of *dharma* or right living, and is intimately rooted in Hindu practice; and *Vedānta*, again a strictly Hindu philosophy of life, founded on the Upaniṣads which, in the form of *Advaita Vedānta* (non-dualist Vedanta), is the dominant philosophic outlook of modern Hinduism.[166] These constitute the *astika* schools (the 'it is'-ers); there are also the *nastika* schools (the 'it is not'-ers), loosely translated as 'heretics'. These are the traditions that reject the Vedas and include (chiefly) the Buddhists, Jains and Lokāyatas or Cārvākas. The last is said to originate from a *Lokāyata Sūtra* composed by one Bṛhaspati. The author may be mythical and the sutra has not survived. The doctrines developed by its adherents are essentially materialist and atheist, and make heavy use of sceptical arguments about the primacy of sense-perception and the rejection of many forms of inference such as were developed by the Nyāyas.[167]

Both Nyāya and Lokāyata exhibit interesting parallels with Greek thought. An ancient critic of Bṛhaspati wrote that 'everywhere the sutras of Bṛhaspati have the sole purpose of questioning (the opinions or doctrines) of others'.[168] One is reminded of the mission of Socrates to question the opinions of others in pursuit of greater clarity through dialectic. The use of quibbling and destructive arguments was developed into an art-form by the Megarian philosophers, to the irritation of their fellows,[169] while Lokāyata materialists were famous for captious arguments.[170] But it would be mere fantasy to connect this similarity with the alleged visit of an Indian to Socrates in Athens, reported by Aristoxenus: the Indian is said to have mocked Socrates for his

166. See for example Nehru 2004, 192–200; Singh 2009, 425–8; King 1999.

167. Gokhale 2015 is an intricate exploration of the varieties of Cārvāka philosophy. See also Chattopadhyaya 1959/1973.

168. Gokhale 2015, 23–4.

169. Stoneman 1995, 113.

170. Waley 1952, 54 and 271 n.

quest to discover about human life, on the grounds that this was impossible if he did not know about divine matters.[171] An Indian who said such a thing was clearly not a Cārvāka, at any rate.

Lokāyata materialism and scepticism relate interestingly to Buddhist positions. While the date and origin of the Lokāyata doctrines is quite uncertain, since no original texts survive, it is plausible to imagine such beliefs arising in the same circles as Buddhist ideas which reject the authority of the Vedas and insist on a materialistic and atheistic position. Both philosophies also make extensive use of sceptical arguments. The Buddhist commentator Nāgārjuna, like Bṛhaspati, was sometimes called a *vaitaṇḍika*, one who argues for the sake of argument only, and whose sole concern is the destruction of the opponent's view.[172] Much Cārvāka thought is devoted to identifying the legitimate sources of knowledge: Cārvākas insist on the primacy of the senses and debate hotly the role of inference. The standard example is 'Smoke and Fire'. On seeing smoke, one may infer that there is a fire. But is this a necessary truth? It may be possible for smoke to exist without fire: it may not be a law of nature that the two go together. In fact, there may not be laws of nature: Cārvākas deny essentialism.[173] They do not even admit the logical relation of cause and effect.[174] It is easy to see how this position meshes with the Buddhist doctrine of no-self: the chariot is no more than the sum of its parts, not a thing in itself.

The forms of argument that are subjected to scrutiny here are associated with the Nyāya school. The Nyāya Sūtras were composed by Akṣapada at some date between the sixth and second centuries BCE, and focus on sixteen categories of *pramāṇa* (the word means 'means of right knowledge'). These include, besides both discussion and disputation, such topics as fallacies, quibbles and futile rejoinders. Nyāya, as an *astika* school, is opposed to materialists, including Buddhists, in important particulars: for example, Nyāyas believe in the existence of universals, Buddhists do not. The positive means to knowledge include forms of reasoning, among them inference and syllogism, that are familiar to Western readers from Aristotle, especially the *Prior Analytics*. It has from time to time been proposed that Akṣapada acquired his explanation of the various structures of the syllogism from a study of this

171. Aristox. F 53 Wehrli = Eus. *PE* 11.3.

172. Matilal 2005, 27.

173. Summarised from Gokhale 2015, 52–6 and 61–6.

174. Cf. Garfield 1990, 292 and 299, comparing Hume and Nāgārjuna.

work of Aristotle.[175] This is in principle possible, if Akṣapada lived towards the end of the period suggested, since by the second century BCE there is no difficulty in imagining a fairly extensive traffic between Greeks and Indians through the Bactrian and Indo-Greek kingdoms. But it does not seem to be a necessary conclusion; and even if Akṣapada had read Aristotle, he was certainly not copying him or adopting his doctrines.

Very frequently in reading Indian philosophy one is struck by the thought that similar issues are being addressed as were also addressed by the Greeks with whom we in the West are more likely to be familiar. For example, the philosopher Diṅnāga, who is usually described as a Buddhist idealist, deals with the distinction between conventional reality and ultimate reality by questioning whether we can refer to the unique particular in language without resorting to concepts or universals.[176] 'The only way a name can identify, or refer to, a particular is through negation and elimination of other concepts.' This last move is very specific to the Indian philosopher; but the general problem resembles the one which induced Plato to conceive of the world of Forms, absolutes by which one can recognise the individual particulars. At the same time, the distinction between showing and saying that lurks here is not only very Buddhist, but also looks forward to the famous closing line of Wittgenstein's *Tractatus*, 'Whereof one cannot speak, thereof one must be silent.' Philosophers read each other's works, but they use them as building blocks for their own ideas. I cannot imagine that Plato was aware of the Buddha, or that Diṅnāga was aware of Plato, but I am sure that if Diṅnāga had been able to read Wittgenstein he would have used his work too.

All in all, the case of logic and epistemology shows only that both Greek and Indian philosophers were beginning to think about similar issues at the same time. It is also worth stressing the point made by B. K. Matilal in 1971, that Western views of Indian philosophy have been coloured by the emphasis, of both the founding fathers of Indology and some of the first leaders of independent India, on the spiritual side of the matter, to the exclusion of the very rigorous systems of logic and epistemology that belong to the tradition from, it appears, the sixth century BCE onwards.[177] This may have led some to suppose that, where technical philosophical argument occurs in Indian writers, they must have borrowed it from the Greeks. Atomism, for example,

175. Vidyabhusana 1918, cited with approval by Jairazbhoy 1963, 83. Matilal 2005, 98 refers to similarities between the syllogism structures of Aristotle and Indian logic.

176. In this discussion I am indebted to Matilal 2005, 17–19.

177. Matilal 2005, xiii, from the preface to the first edition of 1971.

can be cited as a theory that appears in both Indian and Greek thought at about the same time. But Indian atomism stops at the level of reflection on what things are made of, and does not develop a systematic physical theory comparable with that of Democritus and Epicurus. For example, it never investigates perception.[178]

There is no difficulty in accepting that Greek science became very influential in India some time later, in the early centuries CE, but the search for Greek influence on philosophy in the third and second centuries BCE appears fruitless. At this time, any interchange seems to have been more at the level of lifestyle. I am sure that Pyrrho modelled himself in some way on Buddhist attitudes, and it is quite conceivable that Paśupatas adopted aspects of the Cynic way of life. But detailed verbal and thematic exchange came later.

The Questions of King Milinda: Debate and Disputation.

One of the most accessible works of ancient Buddhist philosophy, written as most of them are in Pali, is *The Questions of King Milinda* (*Milindapāñha*).[179] Milinda is Menander, the Indo-Greek king who ruled from 155–130 BCE, from a capital at Sagala (Sialkot).[180] There is little doubt that the king himself was a Buddhist, and when he died his relics were treated with a reverence comparable to those of the Buddha, being distributed among stupas across his realm. As Plutarch writes (incorrectly making him a king of Bactria),

> When a certain man named Menander, who had been a good king of the Bactrians, died in camp, they celebrated his funeral as usual in other respects, but in respect to his remains they put forth rival claims and only with difficulty came to terms, agreeing that they should divide the ashes equally and go away and erect monuments to him in all their cities.[181]

Menander became a familiar name in Buddhist history, as an anecdote in the Tibetan author Tāranātha's (1575–1634) *History of Buddhism in India* makes clear:

> There lived in the country called Thogar [Sagala?] a king named Mi-nar. In this country, everybody worshipped the sky-god. Besides this, they knew no distinction between virtue and vice. During their festivals, they

178. For an outline see Gangopadhyaya 1980.
179. A useful recent survey of scholarship on this work is Kubica 2014.
180. Perhaps identical with Euthydemia: Jairazbhoy 1963, 51.
181. Plu. *Praecept. reip. gerend.* 821d. See also Coloru 2009, 69–79.

> worshipped the sky-god with great smoke by burning grains, clothes, jewels and fragrant woods. Along with his five hundred *arhat* followers, *arya* Dhitika once flew through the sky, appeared at the place of their worship and took his seat at the altar there. They took him as the sky-god, bowed down at this feet and worshipped him elaborately. When, however, he preached the Doctrine, about one thousand people – including their king – were led to the realization of the truth.[182]

The *Questions* is set in Sagala, where the king poses a series of questions to the monk Nāgasena on matters of Buddhist doctrine. The fact that a king is posing questions has led some to suppose that there is a model for this long work in the short encounter of Alexander with the naked philosophers in the *Alexander Romance*, and the fact that the debate leads to the development of philosophical ideas has also led to the suggestion that the dialogue was influenced by the model of the Platonic dialogue.[183] It has even been proposed that the work is a translation from a lost Greek original. This is unlikely in the extreme, since it contains nothing that would remind one of Greek philosophy. Nor does it resemble the Platonic model of dialogue with its continuous application of Socratic dialectic: in the first two books the king poses philosophical problems to Nāgasena, which the sage answers with a variety of good and bad arguments, but in the rest of the work the king's questions simply act as prompts for Nāgasena to deliver a series of sermons on Buddhist doctrine. Our text is certainly not the oldest version, dating probably from the fifth century CE or later, when Buddhaghoṣa was aware of it, while versions exist in Chinese from as early as the third century CE.[184] Tarn and Derrett both settle on a date of composition about 150 CE, when Menander had been dead for more than two hundred years and had become a legend.

This judgment may be supported by a consideration of the history of dialogue and debate in Indian philosophy. The question presented itself already in connection with the question-and-answer session conducted by Alexander with the naked philosophers in the *Alexander Romance*. While it would be

182. Tāranātha 1970, 46.

183. Tarn 1951, 414–36; Derrett 1967; Stoneman 1995 leaves the question open. See also Bussagli 1996; Coloru 2009, 69–79. Lloyd 2014, 43 is persuaded by Bronkhorst 1999 that there is Greek influence on the *Milindapāñha*. Kubica 2016 is firm for the dialogue's Indianness, and I am persuaded by her.

184. R. Gombrich, in a lecture given at King's College London, 5 March 1999. Hinüber proposes a Gandhārī original: see Kubica 2014, 190.

stretching terminology to call this series of riddles a 'debate' – it is more like a catechism – it does have points in common with Indian philosophical texts, and looks likely to be based on a genuine discussion with some Indians.[185] It quickly moves on to a sermon by Dandamis, and this takes pride of place in later rewritings of the episode, the Cynic diatribe in the Geneva papyrus, and the *De Bragmanibus* by Palladius which is based on the diatribe; but the latest rewriting from antiquity, the *Correspondence of Alexander and Dindimus*, reverts to the dialogue or debate form.[186]

Plato is usually given the accolade, by classical scholars, of inventing the dialogue form, but G.E.R. Lloyd has emphasised the significance, in the matter of recognition of 'experts' in a field, of debate, in both India and Greece (or at least Athens; and also in China). The forms of validation differ, however: while in Greece arguments are weighed up for the strength and persuasiveness to a large audience, in India, Lloyd points out, victory in philosophical debate often belongs to the guru who reduces everybody else to exhausted silence.[187] A rare papyrus find from Ai Khanum (admittedly a heavily Hellenised corner of 'India') contains part of a philosophical dialogue about Plato's Forms, which might suggest that the Greek dialogue-form influenced the Indian.[188] But this proposition cannot be sustained in face of the Indian evidence.

The debate of philosophers as a public spectacle, before a king or the general public, is a well-established form in Indian philosophy.[189] It probably explains the enthusiasm of Bindusara, who asked to be sent some figs from Greece, and a philosopher.[190] The Upaniṣads, the earliest-known philosophical texts from India, some of them dating to the very end of the Vedic age and even preceding the rise of Buddhism in the fifth century BCE, largely consist of series of questions and answers. Sometimes the same subjects arise as in the debate in the *Alexander Romance*: where the latter poses the insoluble question, 'Which came first, the night or the day?', the *Bṛhadāraṇyaka Upaniṣad* provides the information, 'The day, clearly, was born afterwards to be the sacrificial

185. See previous chapter.

186. Steinmann 2012, with my review in *Gnomon* 87 (2015), 658–60; translations of all these texts are in Stoneman 2012.

187. Lloyd 2014, 21. There is a helpful survey of the similarities and differences between Greek and Indian forms of debate in Matilal 1986, 8–93.

188. Lerner 2003.

189. Bronkhorst 2011, 176–87.

190. Athen. 14.67 (652–3 C).

cup placed in front of the horse, and its womb is in the eastern sea. The night was born afterwards to be the sacrificial cup placed behind the horse, and its womb is in the western sea.'[191] The Indian text is not pellucid, but the concern over the order of creation of night and day is present in both.

The Upaniṣads, too, contain a great deal of posing of difficult questions and attempts by the other participant to answer. In the *Bṛhadāraṇyaka Upaniṣad*, probably the earliest of the genre, it is the king of Videha who initiates a series of questions to the sage Yājñavalkya,[192] all of which elicit replies stressing the importance of Brahman priests for solving the problems of the universe. For example,

> Yājñavalkya, tell me – when this whole world is in the grip of death, when it is overwhelmed by death, how can the patron of a sacrifice free himself completely from its grip?
>
> Yājñavalkya replied: By means of the Hotṛ priest – that is, by means of the fire, by means of speech. [Etc.].

As the chapter proceeds, however, a series of other sages pose questions to Yājñavalkya: it is not the king who leads the discussion throughout, as in the case of Alexander. One of the sages, or novices, is a young woman, Gārgī, who begins with the baffling question, 'Since this whole world is woven back and forth on water, on what, then, is water woven back and forth?' 'On air, Gārgī.' 'On what, then, is air woven back and forth?' And the questions continue (eleven altogether) until Yājñavalkya tells her, 'Don't ask too many questions, Gārgī, or your head will shatter apart!'[193] Gārgī has been credited with thus exposing the philosophical problem of the infinite regress. No such philosophical achievement can be ascribed to the passage in the *Alexander Romance*, but it is hard not to imagine that a debate of the kind represented by this Upaniṣad could have influenced the structure (and some of the content) of the interview with Dandamis.[194]

Debates and debating competitions play an important role in Indian philosophy, and indeed in the education of the young. The Brahmānas describe many such contests, and the use of question-and-answer, referred to there as

191. *Bṛh. Up.* 1.2, tr. Olivelle 1996.

192. Ibid. 3.1.

193. Ibid. 3.6.

194. We shall return to the matter of philosophical debates below. For more observations and Indian parallels with the question-and-answer session, see Stoneman 2008, 93–6.

vāko-vākyam, is integral to the development of logic.[195] Wrangling and captious debate, as practised by Lokāyatas and Megarians, are mentioned in the *Sāmaññaphala Sutta*: 'some sramana-brahmanas, while living on the food offered by the faithful, engage in wrangling argumentation ... he [*sc.* the best kind] abstains from such wrangling argument'.[196]

The kind of quiz that is presented in the *Alexander Romance* also occurs in the *Mahābhārata*, where Yudhiṣṭhira is subjected to a series of questions by an invisible *yakṣa*, by answering which correctly he obtains the revival of his four dead brothers. The questions include 'What makes the sun rise?' (Brāhma), 'What is weightier than earth?' (mother), and 'Abandoning what does one become friendly, abandoning what does one not give, abandoning what does one become rich, abandoning what does one become happy?' (Pride, anger, desire, greed).[197] The teaching of Kṛṣṇa to Arjuna in the *Bhagavad-gītā* is another example.

The Buddha himself was keen on debate, surely before a Greek was ever seen in India. 'Is there anyone more enlightened than our Lord?', asked the disciple Śāriputra, intending a compliment: the Buddha turned it into a debating point.[198] The Chinese pilgrim Yijing described a visit to the monastery at Nalanda, 'where brilliant scholars of outstanding talent assemble in crowds to discuss questions of right and wrong.... When they take part in a debate, they always win the case and sit on double mats to show their unusual intelligence. When they carry on arguments to refute [heretics], they render their opponents tongue-tied in shame.'[199] In the Pali story of the Buddha's miracle at Sravasti, the Buddha realises that the only person who is capable of conducting a serious debate with him is himself, and so he creates a double of himself in order to be sure of getting a sensible answer to every question. (As a result, two hundred million onlookers were brought to a comprehension of the *dharma*.)[200]

Questions similar to those of Yudhiṣṭhira's adversary are preserved among the sayings attributed to Pythagoras, such as 'What is the wisest?' (number),

195. Basu 1969, 46 and 243–4.

196. *Sāmaññaphala Sutta* 53 (Bodhi 1989, 34). Some characteristically intransigent gambits include 'I'm being consistent. You're inconsistent', and 'Your doctrine has been refuted. You're defeated'.

197. *Mbh.* 3.297–9, tr. van Buitenen; discussed in Stoneman 2008, 95–6.

198. Strong 2001, 166–7.

199. Li 2000, 150.

200. Strong 2001, 142.

and 'What is the most truly said?' (human beings are bad). Such questions hover on the borderline between religious catechism and philosophical speculation; they are designed to make you think and reflect, often on moral questions. It is questions like these that Milinda seeks answers to in the early books of the *Questions*.

Milinda is presented as a king like no other. 'As a disputant he was hard to equal, harder still to overcome; the acknowledged superior of all the founders of the various schools of thought'.[201] One day, after completing a review of his army, he feels the desire for a philosophical discussion. He consults his entourage of five hundred Yonakas, who suggest a range of possible interlocutors. He goes to visit one of them, Purāṇa Kassapa ('ancient Kassapa') and asks him, 'Who is it, venerable Kassapa, who rules the world?' Kassapa is ready with a reply: 'The Earth, great king, rules the world!' But this is not good enough for Milinda, who has a further question: 'But, venerable Kassapa, if it be the Earth that rules the world, how comes it that some men go to the Aviki hell, thus getting outside the sphere of the Earth?' Kassapa is reduced to sulky silence, since he can 'neither swallow the puzzle, nor bring it up'.[202] Milinda gives up on Kassapa and tries a second sage, Makkhali Gosala, with no better result.

Milinda's procedure here reminds one of that of Ajatasattu (Ajataśatru) in the *Sāmaññaphala Sutta*, who likewise tries the doctrines of the same sages, and, like Milinda at the end of the debate, is converted. But it is too late, because he had killed his father. 'If this king had not taken the life of his father ... then in this very spot there would have arisen in him the dust-free, stainless eye of *dhamma*.[203]

After reflecting on his quandary for some time, Milinda's advisers come up with the idea of introducing him to the Arahat Nāgasena: an Arahat, it is explained, is a member of the (Buddhist) Order who, while yet alive, has attained Nirvana.[204] Nāgasena was endowed with 'instantaneous and varied power of repartee',[205] and proves to be a match for Milinda. The king sends his messenger Devamantiya (the name may represent Demetrius) to request an audience, which Nāgasena grants. The ensuing debate covers some six hundred pages of the English translation, and begins in book 2 with a key question

201. *Milindapāñha* 1.9.
202. Ibid. 1.10
203. *Sāmaññaphala Sutta* 101 and 104 (Bodhi 1989, 50–1).
204. *Milindapāñha* 1.16.
205. Ibid. 1.40.

of Buddhist philosophy: 'If, most reverend Nāgasena, there be no permanent individuality (no soul), who is it, pray, who gives to you members of the Order your robes and food and lodging and necessaries for the sick? Who is it who enjoys such things when given?' The question continues for another half a page, and is clearly a much more thought-out criticism of a philosophical problem than those of Dandamis, or the *yakṣa* in the forest. The model is sustained for the first four books or so, and Milinda even poses a question that still exercises Buddhist dogmatists and philosophers: if there is no self, what is it that is reborn?.[206] The power of Nāgasena's arguments is such that one of Milinda's followers, Anantakaya (Antiochus), becomes a supporter of the Order:[207]

Two books later, the author sums up the achievement of the sage so far:

Master of words and sophistry, clever and wise
Milinda tried to test great Nāgasena's skill.
Leaving him not, again and yet again,
He questioned and cross-questioned him, until
His own skill was proved foolishness.
Then he became a student of the Holy writ.[208]

From this point on his questions become requests for information on doctrine rather than attempts to catch the sage out. The book as a whole becomes a comprehensive presentation of Buddhist philosophy. While this clearly has similarities to the question-and-answer session in the *Romance*, and even to Platonic dialogue, it goes far beyond the former model, and differs from the latter in turning into a sermon.

J.D.M Derrett proposed that the work's form was inspired by the question-and-answer session in the *Alexander Romance*;[209] I hope that the passages I have assembled above are sufficient to prove that there were good Indian models for all the aspects of the encounter with the gymnosophists.[210] Derrett

206. Ibid. 2.2.6. See also *Buddhacarīta* 16.81. Ganeri 2012, 173–6 also poses the question, and at 201 gives the answer as a performativist view of self, acting 'as if'. See also the discussion of rebirth earlier in this chapter. See also Siderits 2016, 81: 'The Pugalavadins ... find incomprehensible any account of rebirth that does not have it that it is a person who dies, enters the intermediate state, and is reborn'.

207. *Milindapāñha* 2.1.4.

208. Ibid. 4.1.1.

209. Derrett 1967, 45–57.

210. See also Kubica 2016, 146, summarising the results of her doctoral thesis.

admits that the *Halsrätsel* element of the Alexander text is of Indian origin, but argues that this is not integral to the colloquy, which he sees as Cynic. Unfortunately, his treatment of the recensions of the *Alexander Romance* is quite outdated, and does not support his suggestion that an early version of what he calls 'the Colloquy' was already in the alpha-recension of the *Romance*, and thus available to be consulted by the author of the *Questions*. His suggestion that Anantakaya, mentioned above, is actually an attempt by the author of *Questions* to represent 'Onesicritus' need hardly be taken seriously.[211] Though I am sympathetic to arguments for an early date for the *Alexander Romance*,[212] I think it unlikely that the author of the *Questions* needed it in order to compose his work. (Nor do I swallow Derrett's suggestion that Jesus decided he must walk on water because the Buddha had already done so.)[213]

Bronkhorst offered a variant of the argument for Greek influence. In a lecture entitled 'Why is there Philosophy in India?',[214] he distinguished the type of debate found in the Upaniṣads from 'rational inquiry', which he regards as having been introduced by the Greeks to India. Milinda is represented as questioning everything, raising difficulties with traditional Buddhist ideas, in a way that Indians had not previously done. For Bronkhorst, though there is no Greek philosophy in the *Questions of King Milinda*, the spirit of the work is Greek, at least in the early books. He writes,

> What I propose is that the Buddhists of north-west India adopted the method of rational debate and inquiry from the Greeks. They adopted this method and along with it the willingness (or obligation) to use it in areas that used to be the exclusive territory of tradition and religion, but they adopted nothing else in the domain of philosophy.[215]

This position depends on accepting that the Upaniṣads are *not* 'rational debate'. And if you are out-argued your head will no longer be 'shattered' as in the Upaniṣads. On this view the Upaniṣads are no more than conversations, and the change comes with Buddhism. He believes that the evidence of the *Questions* shows that Indians were aware of Greek debates, even though the eventual 'conversion' of Menander is not a Greek outcome. The proposal is

211. Derrett 1967, 57.

212. Stoneman 2009.

213. Derrett 1967, 37.

214. Bronkhorst 1999.

215. Bronkhorst 1999, 22–3. The argument is extended in Bronkhorst 2006, emphasising the impetus given by kings to Buddhist debating.

treated approvingly by Lloyd,[216] even as he goes on to outline the frequency of competitive debating in ancient India, for which there are also Greek parallels, which he enumerates. But the debate model, as I have shown, goes back long before the Buddhist adoption of it.[217]

There is no doubt that debate became a very popular form of philosophical (and religious) exploration in the centuries that followed, when Buddhism was in its heyday in India. Xuanzang, visiting Taxila in the sixth century CE in search of Buddhist manuscripts to collect and translate into Chinese, described how an ancient king 'summoned an assembly of different religious persons whose talents were most noted, to the number of one hundred' and set them to debate in order to put an end to disagreement and to establish the truth.[218] He could have been describing Menander, except that the latter in his humility (like Alexander, like Harṣa) went to the sages, and did not summon them. When Xuanzang reached Nalanda, he found a settlement of several thousand monks: 'those students who come here as strangers have to show their ability by hard discussion'. So popular are these discussions that the gatekeepers have to limit the numbers by posing hard questions to those who wish to attend, to see whether they are up to it.[219] Elsewhere Xuanzang describes how such discussions were so popular that traffic jams of elephants formed on the approach to the debating place.[220] On more than one occasion disputants are so determined to win that they offer to forfeit their heads if they lose the argument.[221]

So there is nothing far-fetched about Philostratus' description of Apollonius' visit to India, when he twice enters into philosophical debates with the kings he encounters. The medieval romance of *Barlaam and Josaphat*, which reprises the Buddha's life in that of the Christian saint Josaphat – the two saints are supposed to have reconverted India to Christianity after it lapsed following St Thomas's mission – also includes passages that replicate the question-and-answer model.[222] A central episode is the Great Debate, where Chaldaeans, Indians, sorcerers and Jews are all brought together before the

216. Lloyd 2014, 43.

217. See also Matilal 1986, 80–93.

218. Beal 1884, 1.107

219. Ibid. 2.170–1.

220. Waley 1952, 62.

221. Ibid., 55and 63. Forfeiting the head is a punishment for disclosing secret doctrine in *RV* 1.116.12.

222. E.g., *Barlaam* 9.67.

king:[223] Josaphat threatens to torture Nachor (who is disguised as Barlaam) if he does not win the debate. 'With mine own hands', pronounces the Christian saint, 'I will quickly tear out thy heart and thy tongue, and throw them with the residue of thy carcase to be meat for the dogs.'

The habit of debating seems to have been ineradicable in India. Amartya Sen entitled his book of essays *The Argumentative Indian*, and stressed the love of debate that characterises the country. Mughal emperors were impressed by this enthusiasm: Akbar held regular debates of opposing philosophical teams at his capital at Fatehpur Sikri, as part of his attempt to determine 'the truth' and to establish a 'religion for all the world' or 'religion of God', *din-e-ilahi*.[224] Akbar went so far as to propose a kind of *Halsrätsel*, suggesting that a Muslim carrying a Qur'an and a Christian carrying a Bible should both be placed on a pyre and set alight: God would save the bearer of the Truth.[225] (The proposed victims get out of it by saying that they are probably both sinners, and God might not think it worth saving either of them.) Akbar had the *Mahābhārata* and *Rāmāyaṇa* translated into Persian as part of an attempt to foster dialogue between Hindus and Muslims, while his grandson Dara Shikoh himself translated the Upaniṣads into Persian, as well as continuing the custom of religious debates.[226]

It would be nice to envisage the real Menander as being as dedicated to learning and discovery as his later successor Akbar. The legend of his debate with Nāgasena is, however, the only evidence that can be brought into play, apart from the reverence shown to his body after his death. The statement in the *Questions* that he was highly educated in the nineteen arts cannot be taken as historical evidence,[227] but if it were so it would have powerful implications for the accessibility of Greek learning and Greek texts in north-west India in the second century BCE. The following chapters will consider to what extent Greek *paideia* may have followed Greek arms into Hellenistic India, until the Scythian invasions of the 80s BCE brought the Indo-Greek kings low.

223. Ibid. 24.233ff.

224. Schimmel 2004, 113; also Gascoigne 1971, 109–10 and 145.

225. Miller 2014, 164.

226. Schimmel 2004, 113–14. See also 119: Akbar sent to Goa for a supply of philosophers – presumably with more success than met Bindusara's request to Antiochus. A more recent example is a nineteenth-century debate between a Christian missionary and a Buddhist in Sri Lanka, described by R. Gombrich 1988, 181–3.

227. *Milindapāñha* 1.9.

13

The Trojan Elephant

TWO HUNDRED YEARS OF CO-EXISTENCE FROM THE DEATH OF ALEXANDER TO THE DEATH OF MENANDER, 323–135 BCE

How many languages must you learn
Before you can understand your own?

—SUJATA BHATT, 'TRUTH IS MUTE'[1]

'I know I am only a cheechee engine driver, and my grandmother was not a princess at all; she was nobody—she may have been a loose woman, even. I know as well as you that a high-caste Indian girl would not marry a sergeant, not in those days. But that is exactly why we have to fight so hard, that is why we must pretend and keep our self-respect, even if we shut our eyes like ostriches to do it.'

—JOHN MASTERS, *BHOWANI JUNCTION* (1954), 193 (THE SPEAKER IS AN ANGLO-INDIAN, I.E., OF MIXED RACE.)

IN THE BRITISH MUSEUM there is schist relief panel depicting a horse on wheels being drawn towards a gateway by a group of men in Greek dress, while in the gateway is framed a woman, naked to the waist and clad on her lower half in a clinging skirt or perhaps pyjama, arms raised high in a gesture of seeming despair.[2] It is Gandhara work of the Kuṣān period, dated to the second or third century CE. It is difficult not to see this as a portrayal of the story

1. From *Poppies in Translation* (Manchester: Carcanet, 2015).
2. Allan 1946.

13.1 Gandhara relief depicting the Trojan horse (Trustees of the British Museum, London).

of the Trojan horse, and the woman as Cassandra, foreseeing the doom that is about to befall her city. The story found a place too in Indian literature with a not unexpected transformation of the horse into an elephant. In the parables of Buddhaghoṣa (fl. 410–32 CE) the story of Queen Samavati introduces a mechanical elephant which is used to break down the gates of a city.[3] The tale became well known, and reappears in Bāna's *Harṣacarīta* as well as in the eleventh-century *Ocean of Story*: in the first, King Mahāsena is captured by soldiers who emerge from the belly of the elephant, while in the second it is King Candramahāsena who creates the mechanical elephant and captures King Vatsaraj of Ujjain.

In fact the story of Samavati contains numerous episodes which recall moments familiar from literature and history. The princess falls for the enemy king and betrays her city, like Scylla. The captured Udema reminds us of Eumenes when he says to his captor, 'Now I am your prisoner, why don't you kill me?' And he reminds him, 'You have power over my body, but none over my mind', recalling both Dandamis' words to Alexander in the later legend, and those of Anaxarchus in the hands of Cassander's minions. Later, the escaping Udema throws down treasure to delay his pursuers, like Hippomenes

3. Buddhaghoṣa 1870, 39.

in his race with Atalanta (and like Medea, though she delayed her Colchian pursuers by throwing down, not treasure, but pieces of her younger brother, whom she had just butchered).[4]

There is little difficulty in envisaging borrowing from Greek into Indian stories by the date of Buddhaghoṣa, and we shall return to the matter in chapter 14, to suggest that some borrowing may have begun much earlier. For the moment I would like to draw attention to the capacity of the Trojan horse/elephant to stand as a symbol for the infiltration of Greek ideas and tropes into the Indian world. This is a matter on which strongly divergent opinions can be and have been held, and to achieve a judicious treatment is far from easy.

Jawaharlal Nehru, in a passage quoted above in chapter 2, referred to Alexander's invasion of north-west India as a little local skirmish with no lasting effect. In her standard history of India, Upinder Singh gives Alexander a single mention as 'background' to the rise of the Mauryas, and two pages to the Indo-Greek kings.[5] It is true that Alexander did not stay long, and his name never occurs in Sanskrit literature except for one reference in Bāna's *Harṣacarīta* (ninth century CE), where he is alluded to as a conqueror whom King Harṣa will find it easy to excel. But Alexander's legacy was not in his person alone. He founded Greek cities in Gandhara, in Swat and on the Indus, which were settled by veterans of his army and their associates: the expedition seems never to have consisted solely of military men, since we have met many of the writers, historians, philosophers, dancers and artists who came along too. Many of these must have married native women and produced progeny.

The Greek Kingdoms in Bactria and India

Alexander's departure from India was not such a clean break as Nehru implied (or would have liked).[6] Many Greeks remained behind in veteran colonies, and in the strategic garrison cities established in Central Asia and on the Indus. The Punjab was left under the rule of Porus and Taxiles as vassal kings, but Taxiles was toppled in 321 by Eudamus, whom Alexander had left

4. Ibid., 41, 40, 43. A fragmentary vase from Peshawar (*CHI* 1.646) is moreover said to bear a depiction of a scene from Antigone, though this seems harder to identify with certainty.

5. Singh 2009, 330 and 373–5.

6. The main historical treatments of the Indo-Greeks are Tarn 1951; Woodcock 1966; Narain 2003; see also Mairs 2014.

in military command of the region; Eudamus went on to assassinate Porus also, an act which opened the way for Candragupta to extend his empire to the Punjab. Another general, Peithon, ruled the Indus region until 316, when he left for Babylon; probably by 307 this had become part of Candragupta's empire. Bactria, as a satrapy of the former Achaemenid empire, remained part of the new Macedonian empire. All these territories continued to be claimed as the realm of Seleucus, ruling from Babylon. These distant regions were difficult to secure, and in 305 Seleucus led an army to the Indus and confronted Candragupta.[7] The meeting ended with a treaty by which Seleucus ceded territory to Candragupta,[8] perhaps as far west as Arachosia;[9] in exchange he received five hundred war elephants which played a decisive role at the battle of Ipsus in 301.

This kind of gift exchange continued. A bit later, Seleucus got a tiger,[10] which he sent to Athens as a present, and Candragupta also sent him some aphrodisiacs, as well as drugs with the opposite effect;[11] and his son Bindusara asked in his turn for some Attic figs, and a philosopher.[12]

The agreement of the two kings included *epigamia*:[13] this has been interpreted as the giving of a daughter of one ruler as wife to the other, and, as Seleucus is known only to have had one wife, the Iranian Apame (the only wife whose marriage lasted after the mass ceremony at Opis), it has been thought that a daughter of Seleucus (otherwise unattested) married Candragupta (or maybe his son). This would be exciting indeed, since it would make the succeeding Maurya kings half-Greek.[14] However, the alternative is just as exciting, and more probable: namely, that the agreement was regarding intermarriage of Greeks and Indians in the region.[15] There were significant numbers

7. See the systematic account in Plischke 2014, 178–95; also Karttunen 1997, 254–7. The only ancient source is Justin 15.4.20–1.

8. Probably in 304/3: Plischke 2014, 180.

9. This was certainly part of Aśoka's empire later on.

10. Cf. Ael. *NA* 15.14, on the use of 'trained' tigers as gifts to kings in India.

11. Phylarchus ap. Athen. 1.32 (18e). Such drugs were still peddled in Lahore in the early twentieth century: Nevile 2006, 10.

12. Athen. 14.67 (652–3 C).

13. Str. 15.2.1; Appian *Syr.* 55.282 (κῆδος); Plischke 2014, 190–2.

14. The *Arthaśāstra* discusses the part to be played in peace treaties by marriage exchange (7.3.26), and also by elephants (7.3.30, 2.1.25).

15. The royal marriage idea is favoured by Kosmin 2014, 33; cautiously by Thapar 1997, 17 and 20; and by Coloru 2009, 142–3; but see also Parker 2012; Sircar 1963. Right of intermarriage is preferred by Mairs 2014, 111–12; Plischke 2014, 192.

of Greeks, and they needed wives.[16] But if Indian principles of caste were strictly applied, Greeks were beyond caste; they were *mlecchas*, and you could not let your daughter marry one.[17] If this impediment was legislated away, the lives of Greeks and Macedonians in the border area would be immeasurably eased. Furthermore, a true mixed population would result, with all its attendant possibilities of cultural interaction (see further below). The agreement may have been the easier since the Maurya kings were not Brahmanical in their style, inclining to the Jains or Buddhists, who reject caste.

The satrapy of Bactria remained part of the Seleucid empire. Some fifty years after the meeting of Candragupta and Seleucus, the satrap Diodotus, 'governor of the thousand Bactrian cities' seceded from Seleucid control.[18] This took place in either about 255 or about 246, when the Seleucid king Antiochus was embroiled in the Third Syrian War: for our purpose the precise date is immaterial. Hellenistic Bactria was soon cut off from the rest of the empire by the rise of the Parthian ruler Arsaces, who created a breakaway kingdom between the two, but presently reached an understanding with Diodotus' son, Diodotus II.[19]

In about 230, Diodotus II was overthrown by Euthydemus. Twenty years later the Seleucid king Antiochus attacked the Bactrian usurper, and besieged Bactra for three years (208–6).[20] But the stand-off ended with concessions, Antiochus recognising the value of Bactria as a buffer state against the nomads of Central Asia.[21] This time it is clearly stated that Antiochus got some elephants from Euthydemus, and in exchange gave one of his own daughters to the Bactrian's son, Demetrius, and allowed Euthydemus to call himself king. Polybius goes on, 'Antiochus crossed the Caucasus (i.e., Hindu Kush) and descended into India; renewed his friendship with Sophagasenus king of the Indians; received more elephants until he had a hundred and fifty altogether'

16. Burstein 2010 argues that most Greek settlers in Bactria will have had captive wives already, and no doubt this was often the case. But it is hard to imagine that there was no contact between Greek settlers and Bactrian, or Indian, women.

17. Mehl 1986, 175, thinks that Indo-Greek marriage was possible because Greeks were outside the caste system; but this contradicts the Indian texts on the 'untouchability' of Yavanas as *mlecchas*.

18. Justin 41.4. Justin mistakenly calls him Theodotus.

19. Ibid. 41.6–10.

20. Plb. 10.49.

21. Ibid. 11.34. Strabo (11.11.2) states that the Greeks also controlled Sogdiana as far as the river Jaxartes, which separates Sogdiana from the nomads.

and then returned via Arachosia and Helmand to Iran. 'Sophagasenus' (the Indian form should be *Subhagāsena) is not otherwise heard of, and is not known as the name of any Mauryan king, so one presumes that the north-west was now under the rule of a subordinate dynasty, or perhaps a secondary Maurya line.[22] Woodcock suggested that Sophagasenus was seeking the help of Antiochus against the growing power of the Bactrian Greeks.[23]

The reign of Euthydemus saw significant expansion of the power of Bactria, both south-west to Ariana (Herat) and eastwards to India, according to Apollodorus of Artemita (quoted by Strabo).[24] Strabo is rather vague about timing, attributing conquest as far as the Himalayas and Patalene (the mouth of the Indus), as well as 'what is called the kingdom of Saraostus and Sigerdis', to either Euthydemus or his son Demetrius, or to the later king, Menander. Around this time one Heliodotus, perhaps a collateral local ruler, dedicated an inscription in elegant Greek verse to the goddess Hestia, in the region of Kuliab in Tajikistan, praying her 'to guard the greatest of all kings, Euthydemus, and his son, outstanding Demetrius, "glorious in victory"'.[25]

Here the story becomes very hard to piece together. Tarn took Strabo at this word and constructed a scenario in which Demetrius was responsible for extensive conquests to the east and south, assisted by two commanders, Apollodotus and Menander, who later issued coins in their own right as kings. Sarostros he interpreted as Saurashtra, king of Kathiawar, and stated that Sigerdis therefore 'must be' Kacch.[26] Demetrius was also supposed to have founded a city, Demetrias in Sind, which Tarn originally identified with Patala at the mouth of the Indus, though he later retracted this in response to arguments published by E. H. Johnston.[27] Apollodotus 'must have' taken control of and reorganised Ujjain (*Ozoana* of Ptolemy), and his rule extended through Kacch and Sind, including Barygaza (Broach), where the *Periplus* mentions his coins circulating. Thus all these events would belong to the period immediately following 185, when the fading Maurya dynasty was overthrown by the Śunga king, Puśyamitra.

22. Habib and Jha 2004, 88. Rawlinson 1912, 71 suggested that the name was a title of a little-known grandson of Aśoka.

23. Woodcock 1966, 77.

24. Str. 11.11.1.

25. Rougemont, Pinault and Bernard 2004; Holt 2012, 124.

26. Tarn 1951, 148 and 150.

27. Johnston 1939; Tarn 1940a.

13.2 Silver tetradrachm of Demetrius (author's collection).

Narain in 1957 rejected the whole construction, attributing all the conquests of Demetrius to a later king, Demetrius II, and placing them around 150 BCE, shortly before the death of Puśyamitra in 146. This has been generally accepted.[28] This, then, is the man who should be remembered as 'Demetrius the myhti kynge of Ynde'.[29] (Chaucer mistook his name in *The Knight's Tale*, calling him 'Emetreus king of Inde'.) This too should be the 'Demetrius Aniketos' who issued the magnificent coins depicting the king wearing an elephant-scalp headdress, symbolising his conquest of India.[30] There may be corroboration of his invasion in the Hāthīgumphā ('elephant cave') inscription outside Bhubaneshwar, created by King Khāravela of Kalinga, 'who put fear into the inhabitants of Rājagṛha (Rajgir) and sent the Yavana king Ḍimita back to Mathura'.[31] If the traditional reading of this inscription is correct, it

28. Woodcock 1966, 79–86; he suggests that Puśyamitra in his declining years had lost the vigour to resist an attack.

29. John Lydgate, *Fall of Princes* 6.1764. See Justin 41.6.

30. Woodcock 1966, 84–5.

31. Sircar 1942 1.88–9; Mitchiner 2002, 64. The damaged text is often read as *Yavānarājā … mit …*, i.e., Dimita = Demetrius. Kant 2000, 12–14, in a thorough study of this inscription, reads the words as a reference to the river Yamuna and finds the '… *mit* …' not discernible: *vipapmu(ṁ)citu Madhuraṁ apayāto Yamanā-(nadim) … Palavabhāva*. Thus there is no reference to Demetrius or to a Yavana king; he dates the battle in question near Mathura to 178 BCE, too

13.3 The inscription of King Khāravela in the Elephant Cave (Hāthigumphā), Khandagiri, near Bhubaneshwar, Odisha.

also implies that the Greeks controlled Mathura at this time. Archaeology and numismatics do not support a Greek presence in Mathura so early, so the city may have been no more than a temporary refuge for Demetrius.[32]

Demetrius I's son Agathocles (probably 190–180 BCE) became the first Greek king to rule Taxila, and also the first to mint bilingual coinage and to include images of Indian deities on his coins.[33] He was succeeded – in the most recent reconstruction by Bopearachchi – by Antimachus (185–170 BCE), while Apollodotus I ruled in Gandhara and the western Punjab and contested the Hindu Kush and Arachosia with Antimachus. Demetrius II then ruled these western regions, but lost Paropamisadae and Gandhara to Eucratides (ca. 170–45). For Strabo, Eucratides was the ruler of 'the thousand cities of Bactria';[34] Ai Khanum may be identifiable as the site of his capital Eucratidea.[35] In due course he was murdered by his son. Simultaneously Menander (155–130 BCE), apparently the son of Demetrius II, extended his conquests to the east, and thus became the ruler of the most extensive Indo-Greek territory yet – more than Alexander had ruled, as Apollodorus of Artemita remarked.[36] Much of this reconstruction is based on technical numismatic arguments, since the written sources are inadequate to provide a reliable narrative, and it is best to take refuge in a general statement that the rulers of Bactria extended their power and then divided into separate kingdoms – Bactrians and Indo-Greeks – who have left as their memorials the magnificent portraits on their coins. Each king no doubt cast a wary eye on his neighbour and regarded the other's territory as his own – a war of the successors in miniature.[37] As the forty years of warfare between Alexander's successors was at the same time one of the most culturally productive periods of Greek history, so major cultural developments could probably be attributed to this period of stasis between the Greek kings, if we knew what those developments were.

---

early for Justin's dates of 171–136 for Demetrius' reign. Caution is necessary, but certainty is probably unattainable.

32. Sircar 1972.

33. Srinivasan 1997, 215 and plate 16, 6–7.

34. Str. 15.1.3.

35. Justin 41.6.1–5: he controlled Sogdiana, Arachosia, Drangiana and Aria. Strabo (11.11.2) mentions Eucratidea. See Rapin 2017 for the identification.

36. Str. 11.11.1. The geographical information in Strabo about the course of the Ganges, deriving from Artemidorus of Ephesus, may have been acquired during Menander's campaign. Strabo (15.1.72) wrongly rejects Artemidorus' testimony: Dihle 1964, 19.

37. This is the picture accepted by Singh 2009, 375.

One moment of clarity is provided by the inscription of Heliodorus on the pillar at Besnagar, where he describes himself as ambassador of King Antialcidas who ruled in Taxila: this also makes clear the extent to which a Greek might 'go native' in India.

Going Native: The Pillar of Heliodorus

Northern India went through several major political changes in the two centuries following Alexander's invasion. Candragupta's establishment of the Maurya empire, with its capital at Pataliputra, was the first. Candragupta's rule extended north-west as far as the borders of Bactria, which continued under Greek rule. Candragupta was succeeded by his son Bindusara, and he by Aśoka, who extended Maurya territory to its greatest extent.

According to tradition, this last king was a monster of cruelty in his early years; he waged a great war against Kalinga, but after his victory was mortified by the sight of so many dead on the battlefield: he renounced violence and became, it seems, a Buddhist. In fact, he adopted Buddhism as an official religion and issued a series of Edicts preaching the *dharma*, which were inscribed on rocks in key places of the empire, as well as on seven pillars in sites from Kalinga to Kandahar. The Pali canon of Buddhist scriptures was established at a council of Aśoka in 246 BCE.[38] As a result he became a Buddhist 'saint': places associated with Aśoka are still places of pilgrimage. One such is the Rock Edict in the suburb of Delhi known as East of Kailash, which was once on a main route across north India: the short and extremely weathered inscription is protected by an ugly concrete hut, while in the small park around the rocky outcrop groups of pilgrims from Thailand engage in meditation as well as enjoying meals of hot food prepared in a travelling kitchen.

One chronicle mentions a son of Aśoka, Jalarka, who led attacks against the *mlecchas* – probably the Greeks.[39] However, Aśoka's anti-Brahman position coincided with Greek interests, so that it suited the Greeks, as their power grew, to associate themselves with Buddhist ideas.[40]

38. Orientation on Aśoka may be gained from Thapar 1997; Allen 2012; Lahiri 2015; Olivelle, Leoshko and Ray (eds.) 2012; Falk 2006. On the legend of Aśoka, see Strong 1983. It has been doubted that Aśoka was strictly a Buddhist, as opposed to a supporter of non-violence and other principles associated with the Buddha, since he never names the Buddha or refers to 'Buddhism'. But there was no word for Buddhism at this period: followers of the Buddha knew a fellow-devotee when they encountered one.

39. Kalana, *Rājataraṅgiṇī* 1.101ff.; Thapar 2013, 610–11.

40. Kubica 2013.

13.4 Aśoka's Rock Edict at East of Kailash, in Delhi is protected by a concrete shed. Buddhist pilgrims gather in the park surrounding the rock.

But soon after Aśoka's death the empire fell into the hands of the Śunga dynasty whose king was Puṣyamitra. This was the first dynasty to adopt Brahman religion and Brahman principles of kingship, rejecting the Buddhism and other ascetic sects like the Ājīvikas that had been encouraged by Aśoka.

This was the moment when the Bactrian king Demetrius invaded northwest India, and conquered territory as far as Gandhara and Taxila. He may also have gained control of Mathura and used it as a base for a campaign against King Khāravela of Kalinga.[41] His successors pushed further into the Śunga lands, and Menander became ruler of the Punjab, established his capital at Sagala (Sialkot) and penetrated briefly as far as the Śunga capital of Pataliputra (Patna). The arrival of Greek rulers in Indian lands was a momentous event, and shocking to the Brahman orthodoxy that was working to re-establish its

41. Chattopadhyaya 1974, 21. This depends on whether it is agreed that the name 'Mathurā' can be read in line 8 of the Hāthigumphā inscription: see n. 30 above. The Greek attack on Mathura may also be remembered in the story of Kālayavana, 'the Black Greek' in the *Harivaṁśa*: Hein 1989. The Surasena capital was always strongly Vedic, 'the place where Yavana ways stopped': Hein 1989, 232.

ascendancy after the powerful impact of Buddhism even in these western regions.

Greeks were settling in India from the time of Alexander's invasion onwards, even before their compatriots invaded Gandhara and the Punjab. Perhaps the largest settlement was Alexandria on the Indus – probably Uch – which is said to be the birthplace of King Menander.[42] They attracted the attention of the Maurya kings: Bindusara, as previously mentioned, upon noticing the philosophical propensities of the Greeks, sent to the Seleucid king a diplomatic mission requesting the gift of figs, wine and a philosopher: he received the reply that he could have the first two, but it was not the Greek custom to trade in philosophers.[43]

There were enough Greeks in the Maurya kingdom for Aśoka (r. 269/8–232 BCE) to be able to employ some as missionaries to spread the message of the *dharma*.[44] He writes in Rock Edict 13,

> There is no country, except among the Greeks, where these two groups, Brahmans and sramanas, are not found . . .
>
> It is conquest by Dharma that Beloved-of-the-Gods considers to be the best conquest. And it has been won here, on the borders, even six hundred yojanas away, where the Greek king Antiochus rules, beyond there where the four kings named Ptolemy, Antigonus, Magas and Alexander rule, likewise in the south among the Cholas, the Pandyas, and as far as Tamraparni . . . Even where Beloved-of-the-Gods' envoys have not been, these people too, having heard of the practice of Dharma . . . are following it.[45]

Aśoka's words were carried to Gujarat by a 'Yona' missionary with a Greek name, Demetrius, Indianised as 'Dhammarakkita',[46] while a certain Maharakkhita carried the word to 'the country of the Greeks' (i.e., Kandahar), and

42. *Milindapāñha* 3.7.4.

43. Athen. 14.67 (652–3 C). Bindusara is here called Amitrochates, which according to Jairazbhoy 1963, 62 means 'enemy-slayer'. Cf. Str. 2.1.9.

44. Thapar 1997, 125.

45. Quoted from Allen 2012, 414–15, with modifications; cf. Bloch 1950/2007, 129–30 for the variant texts. The partial Greek version from an isolated block at Kandahar does not contain this portion of the text: Falk 2006, 244–5. On the chronology of Aśoka's inscriptions, see Falk 1993, 318. Levi 1972, 110–11. also refers to this mission. See Karttunen 1997, 297 on inscriptions relating to various Yavana converts to Buddhism in the third century CE.

46. *Mahāvaṁsa* 12; O'Leary 1949, 124. On Dhammarakkhita, see Halkias 2014, 94–5. *Mahāvaṁsa* 29.39 states that Buddhist preachers were sent to nine different countries. Mahadhammarakkhita, accompanied by thirty thousand monks, went from Alasanda (i.e., Alexandria, probably on the Indus) to Anuradhapura.

Majjhantika was sent to Gandhara. How deeply the *dharma* penetrated Greek consciousness at this time is undiscoverable. It *was* presumably possible for missionaries to travel as far west as Alexandria-by-Egypt, but they have left no traces beyond a bare mention in Ptolemy.[47] Buddhism, with its insistence on travel and its need of cities as bases for mendicancy, certainly encouraged and facilitated trade, and thus the intercourse of India and the Greek world to the west.[48] It is probable that the mysterious Zarmonochegas, who burnt himself to death in Athens in the reign of Augustus – two hundred years after the death of Aśoka – was a Buddhist, perhaps a missionary, though his method of persuasion can hardly have been very effective. 'A few' Indians were seen in Alexandria in the second century CE, though whether they were Buddhists is not revealed.[49]

Indian religious ideas inevitably had more impact on Greeks living in India. The shining example, a lone figure who must stand for a putative class of persons, is Heliodorus[50] (though one should not forget Theodorus, a Buddhist meridarch who left an inscription on a pot found in Swat).[51] In about the year 110 BCE, a Greek calling himself Heliodora (with the Sanskrit masculine termination '–a'), erected a pillar at Besnagar or Vidiśā, a town on the river Bes not far from the great Buddhist stupa at Sanchi which had been constructed more than a century before.[52] Vidiśā seems to have succeeded Pataliputra as the capital of Magadha after the Śunga king Puśyamitra, having overcome the Mauryas, succeeded in repelling Menander from the walls of Pataliputra.[53] Heliodorus, born in Taxila, was an ambassador of the Indo-Greek king Antialcidas to King Kāśīputra Bhāgabhadra, 'the Saviour'. Unfortunately nothing more is known of Bhāgabadra, though Heliodorus states that he was in his fourteenth regnal year. Antialcidas ruled from about 115 to about 95 BCE. The pillar is identified by its dedicant as a 'Garuda pillar of Vāsudeva, the god of gods', and in its text, which is in Prakrit, Heliodorus identifies himself as a Bhāgavata, namely a worshipper of Viṣṇu, one of whose titles is Vasudeva. The

47. Ptol. 1.17.

48. Rawlinson 1926; O'Leary 1949, 130.

49. D.Chr. *Or.* 32.40; at 35. 22–3 he notes that 'only a few' traders from Alexandria visit India. Sedlar 1980, 79–82 collects the few data available.

50. Mairs 2014, 117–45 is a comprehensive recent presentation.

51. Tarn 1951, 388; Levi 1972, 29 also refers to a bronze vessel from Kabul in the British Museum, dated (in the second century CE) by the Macedonian month Artemisios, in Aramaic.

52. The indispensable treatment of Sanchi and its environment is Shaw 2007. She discusses Heliodorus briefly at 89–90.

53. Sircar 1963, 19–20.

13.5 The column of Heliodorus at Vidiśā (Besnagar), Madhya Pradesh.

dedication belongs to the very beginning of the development of the Bhāgavata religion, perhaps under the impetus of Śunga rulers.[54]

The nature of Heliodorus' diplomatic mission is unrecoverable. What is significant for us is that he had 'gone native', acquired the language, and adopted an Indian religious identity. Maybe he was even of mixed race. The pillar he erected stands now alone in an enclosure that still exhibits the knee-high remains of an ancient structure, probably a temple. Under a large tamarind tree some other ancient finds from the area have been assembled, notably a group of medieval sati-stones (memorials to wives who entered the fire on their husband's deaths). When first visited by a Western antiquary, Alexander Cunningham, in 1875–77, the pillar was receiving worship under the name of Khumbh-baba, Khumbh being a name for the sacred columns that are widely found in tribal villages;[55] it was thickly coated in vermilion.[56] Now it is a playground for the children of the little village of Sonpura, and cattle wander peacefully in the lane that runs by the fence, while women with lustrous hair, in dazzling and immaculate saris, come and go from the hovels alongside.

Heliodorus' was one of at least three pillars at the site, since three capitals survive. This one was topped by a sculpture of a Garuda, the bird-vehicle of Viṣṇu, as the inscription tells us; the bird has long since flown. The pillar follows the model established by Aśoka who, besides his fourteen Rock Edicts, also erected seven pillars of wisdom around his empire, including one at Sanchi. The bell-shaped lotus capital resembles those on Aśoka pillars, but the design of the column is different: instead of being cylindrical like Aśoka's, the surface is flattened into eight facets at the bottom, sixteen further up, and thirty-two at the top. The inscription is positioned somewhat above eye level. This Greek, far from home but surely not entirely alone in this rural landscape which is hard to envisage now as a royal capital, adhered to the ways of the people around him and felt himself important enough to leave a permanent memorial of his passage. We are grateful to him for this evidence of the intermingling of Greek and Indian traditions in the first century BCE. It adds colour to the evidence of the coins of the Indo-Greek kings, inscribed in both Greek and Brāhmī.

54. Doniger 2009, 260–1.

55. Examples, and explanations, may be seen in the Tribal Museum in Bhopal.

56. According to a notice at the site, it was conserved by the Gwalior archaeological department in 1921.

A crossing in the opposite direction is recorded in the inscription erected by one Sophytus in Kandahar.[57] This substantial text in elegant Greek verse records the career of an Indian whose family had fallen on hard times, but whose fortunes were restored by Sophytus' commercial journeys. The name is not Greek though its Indian form is uncertain; it has been compared with that of the ruler Sopeithes whom Alexander encountered; perhaps the merchant Sophytus was a descendant of a man who had been a king.

Greek Giants in China

Demetrius' forays to the north-east – whichever Demetrius we are speaking of – may have been equally significant. Strabo continues his narrative by saying that the kings 'extended the Bactrian empire even as far as the Seres and the Phryni'.[58] The Seres, the silk people, are the Chinese, and the Phryni may be the people of Ferghana (north-east Uzbekistan), though the *Barrington Atlas* places them in the northern Taklamakan desert, where the silk road was to develop, on the road to Ürümqi.

Archaeological finds support the presence of Greeks in this region at this time. A bronze figurine of a Greek soldier has been found north of the Tien Shan mountains and can be seen in the Xinjiang Museum in Ürümqi.[59] Some early Han bronze mirrors exhibit decorative designs that seem to recall Hellenistic art.[60] Metals from China may have been used in the minting of cupro-nickel coins of Bactria. Trade between Bactria and China was established by 126 BCE, when the explorer Zhang Qian reported that 'when I was in Daxia (Bactria), I saw bamboo canes from Qiong and cloth made in the province of Shu (territories of south-western China). When I asked the people how they had gotten such articles, they replied "our merchants go to buy them in the markets of Shendu (India [i.e., Sind])'.[61]

Greek influence on China at this time may have extended beyond statuettes and bolts of silk. A controversial theory put forward by Lukas Nickel is based on a passage in the historian Sima Qian (ca. 145–86 BCE), who relates how the First Emperor, to mark the inauguration of his new state in 221 BCE,

57. Rougemont, Pinault and Bernard 2004; Hollis 2011; Mairs 2014, 106–17 with appendix (190) for the text.

58. Str. 11.11.1.

59. Boardman 1994, 149.

60. Tarn 1951, 363–4.

61. Watson 1962, 269 (from Sima Qian *Shiji* 123: transliteration modernised).

> collected the weapons of All-under-Heaven in Xianyang, and cast them into twelve bronze figures of the types of bell stands, each 1000 *shi* in weight, and displayed them in the palace. He unified the law, weights and measurements, standardized the axle width of carriages, and standardized the writing system.[62]

Ten of these statues were melted down by a renegade general in 190 BCE, and the last two seem to have survived to the end of the Han dynasty. The *Hanshu* has more information bearing on these statues: it tells us that

> [i]n the 26th year of the Emperor, when he first brought together all-under-heaven, divided the principalities into provinces and districts, and unified the weights and measures, giants appeared in Lintao. They were five *zhang* high and had feet six *chi* long.[63]

These giants that appeared in Lintao, the westernmost outpost of China and western terminus of the Great Wall, seem to have been monumental bronze statues, and to have been the model for the First Emperor's group of twelve. Someone in Lintao had seen, or heard reports of, monumental Greek bronze sculpture; elsewhere the *Hanshu* reports that these giants were dressed in 'foreign robes'. Lukas Nickel, from whom I draw this information, has argued that this is a definite indication of influence of Greek art on China, and furthermore made the intriguing link with Alexander's twelve altars on the Hyphasis: were these accompanied by statues of the twelve Olympians, and was it these that the man from Lintao saw and described in such a way that the emperor decided he must have some too?[64] The inference is tempting. And if in China, why not in India?

Menander

Menander is the most significant of the later Indo-Greek kings. Possibly the son of Demetrius II, who ruled probably from about 155 to 130 BCE,[65] he was born near Begram, and married Agathocleia, by whom he had a son who became Strato I. As discussed in chapter 12 above, his name is remembered not

62. Sima Qian *Shiji* 240 and 256; cf. *Hanshu* (*Book of Han*), 1823, cited from Nickel 2013, 436–7.

63. *Hanshu*, 1824, Nickel 2013, 439.

64. Nickel 2013, 436–42 on the giants.

65. Woodcock 1966, 94–114.

least because of his starring role in the Buddhist work *The Questions of King Milinda*. He is probably the king who carried Greek arms as far as Pataliputra, the former Maurya capital, at the same time as Demetrius' advance to the western regions: Strabo is regrettably imprecise, referring only to 'those who after Alexander advanced beyond the Hypanis … even to Palibothra (Pataliputra)'.[66] The *Yūga Purāṇa* tells that King Puśyamitra of the Śungas died fighting against Menander in a war over a beautiful girl. This may be coloured by a memory of the Trojan War (had the Brahman author read the *Iliad*?), but the conflict of the two kingdoms is historical. Menander was probably not the first of the Greek rulers to be drawn to Buddhism: coins of his predecessor Agathocles (190–180 BCE) depict a stupa, and a tree within a railing, both typical Buddhist symbols.[67] But Menander's adoption of Buddhism may have been a way of rallying support against the Brahmanical king of the Śungas. The *Yūga Purāṇa* states that the Yavanas invaded Pataliputra in concert with the Pañcālas and Māthuras, sacked the city and left the region desolate.[68] The information is corroborated by a reference in Patañjali.[69] However, he may not have stayed long, since no Indo-Greek coins have been found at Pataliputra. The text of the *Yūga Purāṇa* reads (in the future tense, because it purports to be a prophecy):

> Once Puṣpapura has been reached, and its celebrated mud [walls] cast down, all the realms will be in disorder … In the city the Yavanas, the princes, will make this [people] acquainted with them: [but] the Yavanas, infatuated by war, will not remain in Madhyadeśa. There will be mutual agreements among them [to leave], [due to] a terrible and very dreadful war having broken out in their own realm.[70]

Possibly Menander stayed long enough to build a stupa at Pataliputra, as Buddhist tradition held.[71] The reason for the retreat is nowhere further specified, so we do not know what troubles arose at home. Could one dare to imagine a kind of conversion akin to that of Aśoka after the battle of Kalinga? Menander saw the slaughter he had caused, determined on no more, and returned to

66. Str. 15.1.27.

67. Halkias 2014, 85–90.

68. *Yūga Purāṇa* 47–8, 56–7.

69. Mitchiner 2002, 62–4. See also the discussion in Sircar 1963, and Jayaswal 1928.

70. Quoted from Mitchiner 2002, 104–5.

71. Woodcock 1966, 100.

13.6 Silver tetradrachm of Menander Soter (author's collection).

Sagala to engage in study of the Buddhist way of life. It would make a neat development. Woodcock preferred to think of a return westwards to fight a threat from Heliocles (d. 130) in Bactria,[72] and that this might explain why Plutarch refers to Menander as a king of Bactria. As noted in the previous chapter, after his death his ashes were distributed to several cities, as the Buddha's had been.[73]

Menander's reign seems to have coincided with prosperity and cultural development: Puśkalavati came to prominence, and Taxila, though no longer his capital, remained a centre of learning that attracted students and scholars from far and wide; while Sagala (Sialkot) is described in the *Milindapañha* as

> a great centre of trade, situated in a delightful country well watered and hilly, abounding in parks, gardens, groves and lakes and tanks, a paradise of rivers and mountains and woods. Wise architects have laid it out … with many and various strong towers and ramparts, with superb gates and entrance archways, and with the royal citadel in its midst, white-walled and deeply moated. Well laid out are its streets, squares, cross-roads and

72. Ibid., 103.

73. Plu. *Praecept. reip. gerend.* 821d; see also Coloru 2009, 69–79.

13.7 A cityscape as depicted in a wall painting at the Ajanta caves.

market-places ... Its streets are filled with elephants, horses, carriages and foot-passengers, and crowded by men of all sort and conditions – Brahmins, nobles, artificers, and servants.[74]

The author seems to be describing exactly the kind of busy and architecturally impressive city-scape that is depicted on several of the contemporary reliefs at Sanchi, as well as in the earliest cave-paintings at Ajanta.

Menander's reign was the apogee of Indo-Greek civilisation. As Strabo wrote, 'those kings subdued more of India than the Macedonians; that Eucratides, at any rate, held a thousand cities as his subjects' (15.1.3).[75] Strabo does not seem to distinguish sharply between the kingdoms of Bactria and of the Indo-Greeks. Both realms, at any rate, disappear almost entirely from the Greek written record after Menander (for Indian remarks see below), and a bewildering series of kings is known from coin evidence alone. The last Bactrian king, Heliocles, was killed in 130 BCE; in the course of the first century

74. *Milindapāñha* 1.2 (tr. T. W. Rhys Davids), quoted in Woodcock 1966, 109. The effusive description is very long.

75. Justin 41.1.8, 41.4.5.

BCE pressure from the north, both from the Scythian/Śaka people and from Central Asian nomads (the Yueh-chi) weakened the power of the Indo-Greeks and diminished their extent (Śakas are already mentioned by Patañjali in the second century BCE),[76] and Greek rule came to an end before the turn of the era, after a dominance in north-west India lasting close to two hundred and fifty years. That is not a long time in the span of India's immemorial past, but it is long enough to make an impact

The word for Greeks was 'Yavanas', after the Achaemenid Persian term, and it became quite widely applied to foreigners of all kinds in the north-west and west of India. From the point of view of the Brahmans who composed most of the historical sources we can rely on, such as the Purāṇas, the Yavanas, along with a number of other ethnic designations, were *mlecchas*. Greeks had stopped using the term 'barbarians' to refer to foreigners after the conquest of Persia, but the word *mleccha* has a precisely similar connotation from the Indian point of view: it was originally used to denote primitives or tribals, who are beyond caste, and you wouldn't want your daughter to marry one.[77] (According to the *Mahābhārata*, the Yonas (Yavanas) of the north-west were so-called because they were born from the *yoni* of a cow.)[78]

Nonetheless, the Greeks were very much part of the Indian scene in the period following Alexander. The *Matsya Purāṇa* makes clear how obtrusive Greeks were, well after the attack on Pataliputra:

> There will be Yavanas here by reason of religious feeling or ambition or plunder; they will not be kings solemnly anointed, but will follow evil customs by reason of the corruption of the age. Massacring women and children and killing one another, kings will enjoy the earth at the end of the Kali Age. Kings and continual upstart races, falling as soon as they arise, will exist in succession through Fate. They will be destitute of righteousness, affection, and wealth. Mingled with them will be Arya and Mleccha folk everywhere; they prevail in turn; the population will perish.[79]

76. Parasher 1991, 231.

77. I am indebted for orientation in this matter to Olga Kubica, who gave a valuable paper on the Yavanas at a conference in Reading in April 2016. Her Wrocław doctoral thesis on the subject remains unpublished; but note Kubica 2016, a summary. See in general Parasher 1991, 222–61.

78. *Mbh.* 7.87.36–7, 7.68.41–2; Hein 1989, 226.

79. *Matsya Purāṇa* 273. 25–7. See Pargiter 1913, 74; Parasher 1991, 243. Banerjee 1919, 232 thinks that the Yavana king Bhagadatta in the *Mahābhārata* is Apollodotus.

In general Greeks were seen as *mlecchas*, 'barbarians', who did not adhere to the caste system: the Buddha remarks (with approval) in the *Majjhima Nikāya*, 'Have you heard that in Yona and Kamboja and other adjacent districts there are only two castes, master and slave?'[80] Brahmans were less approving: already in the *Śatapatha Brāhmaṇa* the Punjab is the home of 'ruffians and barbarians'.[81] The Purāṇas, historical texts written in the form of prophecies and composed in the early centuries CE on the basis of oral materials, are eloquent about the disruption of traditional *mores*.

The *Mahābhārata*, in more temperate terms, heads a list of non-Arya races with the Yavanas:

> Mandhatar said: Greeks (Yavanas), Kiratas (mountain folk), Gandharas, Chinese, savages, barbarians, Śakas, Tuṣāras, Kahvas, Pahlavas (Persians), Andhras, Madrakas, Oḍras, Pulindas, the Ramaṭhas, Kācas, and mlecchas all, and men who are sons of Brahmins and kṣatriyas, and also vaiśyas, and śūdras: How can all of these who live within a kingdom do Meritorious Lawful Deeds? How can all those who live as barbarians be kept within Law by men like me?[82]

Nothing could evoke more vividly the racial mixture of northern India in the centuries following the Indo-Greek expansion, or the resentment and horror with which orthodox Brahmans regarded the religious and cultural diversity that was threatening their strict rule. (The opposition recalls that between Judaism and Hellenism in the west.) The Dharmaśāstras, too, make clear that the Yavanas are śudras, or at best a mixed caste of kṣatriya and śudra.[83] The Śungas were the first Brahman dynasty in Magadha, since of their Maurya predecessors Candragupta had been, according to legend, a Jain, while Aśoka was a Buddhist. Buddhism was a powerful presence in the north-west and west, as is evident both from the dominant position of the monastic complex

80. *Majjhima Nikāya* 2.149, tr. Horner 1954–59, 341, quoted in Mairs 2014, 129. Also Parasher 1991, 226.

81. *SB* 9.3.1.24; Witzel 2006, 485.

82. *Mbh.* 12.65.14–15, tr. Fitzgerald 2004, 328. I have adapted the translation to give the Sanskrit terms as well as the translations which Fitzgerald gives alone. See also *Mbh.* 13.35.18, tr. Ganguli: 'The Mlecchas ... the Yavanas and numerous other tribes of kṣatriyas, have become degraded into the status of śudras through the wrath of Brahmanas ... Kṣatriyas are incapable of ruling the earth without cultivating the goodwill of Brahmans.'

83. *Manusmṛti* 10.43–4; *Gautama Dhś* 4.21.

13.8 This relief sculpture is generally said to depict an Indo-Greek warrior: Queen's Cave (Ranigumpha), Khandagiri, near Bhubaneshwar, Odisha.

at Sanchi and from the selection of Menander, the *mleccha* invader, as the hero of a Buddhist treatise.

The Purāṇas' gloomy vision suggests the Buddhist allegiances of the Indo-Greek kings, and seems to take in the later Śakas and Kuṣāns in its agglomeration of violent conquerors. 'Yavana', one suspects, sometimes just means 'foreigner' – as in the present-day UK 'Paki' can be an insulting term for almost any citizen with brown skin.

It was not just a matter of political dominance. Two inscriptions from cave temples of western India refer to benefactions by Yavanas:

> Gift of two cisterns by the yavana Irila of the Gatas; gift of a refectory to the community by the yavana Cita of the Gatas.[84]

There was greater contact between India and the West. As early as the reign of Seleucus, the first tiger had been seen in Athens. Trade developed rapidly, and India became seen as a purveyor of luxury goods. Both Seleucus and Antiochus I dedicated cassia and cinnamon at Didyma.[85] Rubies had reached Babylon by the third century BCE, when some were set in the eye-sockets and navel of an ivory figurine of Ishtar, now in the Louvre. But it was not all one way: a Tamil poem mentions the 'cool and fragrant wine carried here in their excellent ships by the Greeks, and the women pour it for you out of pitchers made of gold that have been fashioned with high artistry'.[86] This poem can be no earlier than 100 BCE and is included in an anthology of 350 CE, so it does not refer to the immediate aftermath of Alexander's expedition: but the wine and the artistic goblets – as well as the light-skinned girls who poured the drinks – were making their way to Central Asia, as we know, by 100 BCE, and were clearly objects of note in south India, even though none have been found in excavations there.

Greeks were evidently a significant presence – enough to leave a handful of names and to need a word to refer to them.[87] They became sufficiently numerous to create classification problems for the orthodox Brahmans who

84. Banerjee 1919, 268, citing Burgess and Indraji, *Inscriptions from the Cave Temples of Western India*, nos. 5 and 53.

85. *DI* 424. Also Plin. *NH* 16.135; *OGIS* 214.69ff.; Wiesehöfer 1998, 228.

86. M. A. Selby, in Parker and Sinopoli (eds.) 2008, 84–5. Also Shimada 2013, 183–4, on Tamil sources regarding the Greeks.

87. Fraser 1979 and 1980 discussed some Greek names from Afghanistan. Bernard and Bopearachchi 2002 consider the prevalence of Greek heroic names (Telephus, Palamedes) among the Indo-Greeks.

were increasingly dominating Indian life. Thus the *Mahābhārata* disparages all such non-Indian residents:

> That man who is censured and cast off by the Brahmanas soon meets with discomfiture. It is in consequence of the absence of Brahmanas from among them that the Śakas, the Yavanas, the Kamvojas and other Kṣātriya tribes have become fallen and degraded into the status of Śudras.[88]

Greeks formed part of the population, and the social structure, even if not well-regarded by all their neighbours, for some two hundred and fifty years, since the Indo-Greek kingdom did not finally fall until 10 CE. Two hundred years were a sufficient time for the Norman conquerors of England to change the face of the country: architectural styles changed, the Germanic language spoken in England was deeply infused with French, political structures changed, land-holding was codified and a new legal system introduced. Two hundred years of Spanish rule in Mexico brought a new religion and a new language which completely effaced the older ones. Three hundred and seventy years of Arab rule in Spain (from Tariq ibn Ziyad's conquest of Iberia in 711 to the fall of Toledo to the Spanish in 1085) brought learning, literature and philosophy to the West, created numerous magnificent works of architecture, and infused a good many words into the Spanish language; only the vigour of the Reconquista, especially from the fall of Granada in 1492, served to expunge much of the memory of the Arab times. In Sicily (under Arab rule from 827 to 1061) the impact perhaps goes deeper, at least in the number of Arabic place names and in the inward-facing structure of many of the vernacular houses of the villages.

Such comparisons are always risky, and there is no question of the Greeks having 'taken over' local culture in the way that these dominant rulers did. For one thing, Greeks were not rulers in India, as distinct from Bactria, until the 180s BCE. But it would be surprising if they had left no impact. Apart from Megasthenes and his successor Daimachus, none of them seems to have written anything about their experiences in India, and we have only a handful of names to represent this significant Greek presence in north-west India over the next two centuries. Heliodorus has been mentioned. There is Theodorus the meridarch, a Buddhist who 'established some relics of the Buddha for the purpose of the security of many people', as he recorded on a vase found in

88. *Mbh.* 13.33.19–21, tr. Ganguli, cf. also 13.35.17–18.

Swat.[89] There are Aśoka's messengers, and those who translated his edicts into Greek to be inscribed at Kandahar. In Gandhara Greeks are perhaps easier to find: Agesilas and the surgeons of Taxila stand out:[90] Taxila was in key aspects a Hellenistic city.[91] A slave called Agisala is depicted on a casket of the age of Kanishka; one Timitra is named on a clay tablet at Besnagar; and the two Yavana benefactors named Irila and Cita, cited in inscriptions at Junnar,[92] have already been mentioned.

Some Indian historians have been concerned to deny that Greek culture left any impact at all in India: everything in India is indigenous, and probably older than anything else in the world. The attitude is not new: al-Biruni complained that Hindus had no interest in anything outside India.[93] The idea attracts its lunatic fringe, of course, but plenty of serious and rational historians too have held that the Greek period was of no importance. A. K. Coomaraswamy, for one, denied that there was anything non-Indian at all about the art of Gandhara, a view which is as unlikely to be true as that of Benedikt Niese that the entire subsequent development of India was determined by Alexander the Great.[94] R. A. Jairazbhoy, by contrast, provided an enthusiastic conspectus of spheres of influence of Greek culture on India, ranging from philosophy and literature to sculpture, painting and astronomy.[95] Even as early as Alexander, Nearchus noted Indians adopting the use of sponges, strigils and oil-flasks![96] Questions of date are crucial here, since the influence of, for example, Greek astronomy and astrology on Indian is indisputable, but it belongs to a period when contact had been established for more than two centuries.[97]

89. *CII* no. 1, dating from the first or even second century BCE; n. 37 above. Tarn 1951, 388, and 389 for some later records from the Kushan period, including a wrestler named Menander.

90. Naqvi 2011, 33 and 53.

91. Bäbler and Nesselrath 2016.

92. Banerjee 1919, 84, 87, 229.

93. Sachau 1910, 22–3. But in 1318 Amir Khusraw noted that Indians 'can speak any language of the world as fluently and efficiently as a shepherd tends his sheep': *Nuh Sipihr* 156, 53, from Nath and Faiyaz 1981, 57.

94. Cited by Banerjee 1919, 15.

95. Jairazbhoy 1963.

96. Str. 15.1.67 = Nearch. F 23.

97. *Bṛhatsaṁhitā* no. 15; Kern 1870/1875, 13: 'The Greeks, indeed, are foreigners, but with them this science [astrology] is in a flourishing state. Hence they are honoured as though they were ṛśis; how much more than a twice-born man, if he be versed in astrology.' Also al-Biruni, Sachau 1910 1.153; Jairazbhoy 1963, 69–73. Some other 'scientific' ideas also seem to have penetrated India from Greece, such as that the seed of the male is more important in conception

Greek medicine also had an impact.[98] What one would like to know is how far the limited settlement of Greeks had an immediate impact on their neighbours, and how far, if at all, they changed the direction of native Indian cultural developments. Locality is also important, since Greek rule at its greatest extent reached maybe as far south as Ujjain, and as far east as a fleeting conquest of Pataliputra; but it is to be expected that the impact will be more noticeable to the north and east of these points.

The encounter of two peoples is rarely neutral. 'Transculturation' may be simply destructive of a traditional culture, but more often sustained contact develops in what the historian Richard White, writing about North American Indians, has called the 'middle ground'. Both parties change and develop as a result of the three prime drivers of contact – war, trade and marriage. All three causes are clearly applicable here. Many of the twenty thousand Greeks and Macedonians left in garrisons by Alexander will have taken native wives, even if many of them were already provided with wives from among the women captured on campaign.[99]

In British India the mixed race population, or Anglo-Indians, became a kind of in-between class, associated with certain specific roles such as running the railways. (The theme is explored in John Masters's novel *Bhowani Junction*.[100] The 'cheechee' is at home in neither culture.) After 1947, as Tarn said of the Greeks in India, these people gradually became Indians. In Portuguese India a rather different pattern appeared with the emergence of the *moradores*, a creole bourgeoisie, who remained in close contact with the home country.[101]

Historians of British rule in India developed the concept of the 'subaltern' to refer to the adoption by the native population of the rulers' terms and attitudes. But the changes were not all inflicted on a subordinated population. Indian impact on British culture can be traced in the new lexicon that entered

---

than that of the female, an idea found not only in Aeschylus' *Eumenides* but in Aristotle: also *Manusmṛti* 9.35; *Aitreya Brahmāna* 7.33.1 (Basu 1969, 35). Parvati had the capacity to bear a son (by Śiva) who would destroy the gods, like Thetis whose offspring would be greater than his father: O'Flaherty 1973/1981, 267 and 269.

98. Jairazbhoy 1963, 73–81; Naqvi 2011.

99. See Burstein 2012. Most scholars have assumed that the settlers married native Bactrian women, but Burstein points out that in Ai Khanum 'the Greek settlers were resistant to the idea of integration' (99); and emphasises the position of the captive women: Justin 12.4.2–3.

100. Masters 1960.

101. Subrahmanyam 2017, 85.

the English language and was documented in the classic glossary of British India, *Hobson-Jobson*. It is hard to trace any similar interchange between Greece and India at the level of language, though Hesychius records a few Indian words that have entered Greek.[102] (Some of them are names of medicinal plants, and found in Dioscorides, as well as a few as early as Ctesias. *Kassiteros*, tin, from Sanskrit *kastīram*, is also known from Babylon and was already in Linear B.)[103] Greek words that entered Sanskrit are mainly related to astronomy, in which the Indians acknowledged Greek supremacy as early as the first century BCE.[104] The Greek language survived in Bactria (though Heliocles' coins exhibit poor grammar and spelling) until Kanishka ordered the use of Greek to be discontinued in favour of 'Aryan' (i.e., Bactrian); the Bactrian language continued to be written in the Greek alphabet.[105]

The archetypal exponent of colonial victimhood, Caliban, snarls at Prospero, 'You taught me language, and my profit on't is, I know how to curse.'[106] No such curses echo from the records of India in the last centuries BCE. Indian tradition was too strong and sophisticated simply to succumb to an alien invader: but it learnt where it could (astronomy), and made its allies where it could. The alliance of Greeks and Buddhists is no doubt one reason for their sidelining in the Brahminical sources that came to dominate history as Buddhism departed from India to achieve its destiny in the Far East.

The most intriguing questions relate to the possible impact of Greek traditions on art and literature; but it will be constructive first to make a few brief remarks on writing and coinage.

Writing

The existence of writing in fourth-century BCE India was touched on in the opening chapter above. Nearchus' testimony for the Indus region states that writing was in use there, while Megasthenes' for Pataliputra states that there

102. Goossens 1943. Hesychius' glosses are not always accurate.

103. Jairazbhoy 1963, 122, and 77 on Dioscorides; see also Amigues 2011.

104. Jairazbhoy 1963, 91. Astronomy-related words in Sanskrit that derive from Greek include *kendra*, compounds in *heli-*, *jāmitra* (diameter), *hrdroga* (*Hydrochoos*, the constellation Aquarius). The word *drama* (a coin) also comes from Greek. The Greek writer Yavanesvara translated the *Yavana Jātaka* from Greek into Sanskrit in the time of Rudradaman (second century CE): this work exercised a significant influence on astrology in India: Jairazbhoy 1963, 72 and 74.

105. Burstein 2010, 188. On Greek texts in the East, Schmitt 1990.

106. Shakespeare, *The Tempest* I.ii.365–6.

was no writing. Yet within two generations of Megasthenes' association with Candragupta, the latter's grandson Aśoka was using writing, both Brāhmī and Kharoṣṭhi, as well as Greek, in his pillar and rock inscriptions. In fact Brāhmī writing has been found on pottery at Anuradhapura in layers datable to the fifth century BCE, where it was perhaps employed by traders from the north.[107] Pāṇini in the fourth century is familiar with writing,[108] and any dweller in the north-west could hardly fail to be aware of the use of writing by the Achaemenid Persian administration in its satrapies which, for a time at least, included Gandhara and Sind.[109] Persian inscriptions and record tablets were in cuneiform, but the language of administration was Aramaic, and the Aramaic alphabet was certainly familiar in India, since Kharoṣṭhi derives many of its letter forms from Aramaic, though with many adaptations for the exigencies of Indian languages.[110] Brāhmī, like Kharoṣṭhi, first appears in the inscriptions of Aśoka (apart from the Anuradhapura graffiti); some scholars have assumed a connection with the Indus script of the third millennium BCE, since many shapes appear in both, but others regard it as a Maurya invention, perhaps also on the model of Aramaic.[111] The question remains open.

The next evidence for writing in India comes from coinage. The Bactrian kings issued a coinage resembling the Seleucid (though the artistic quality of the portraits on them is startlingly high, and Bactrian coins may be, in the opinion of many, the most beautiful coins ever produced). They are entirely Greek in conception. The Indo-Greek kings developed the style, and in the time of Agathocles (early second century BCE) produced coins that were hybrids of Greek and Indian motifs. Typically the portrait of the king is labelled in Greek, while the reverse depicts an Indian god and the inscription is in Kharoṣṭhi. The use of an Indian writing system for an Indian language by a Greek ruler suggests that writing was becoming familiar in India for other purposes too by the second century BCE. If texts were composed, as Nearchus tells us, on linen pages, they have left no traces for us to discover. Even the palm leaves used for the earliest Buddhist texts have only survived because they were treasured and carefully preserved; other writings, on leaves, will have gone the way of the equally ephemeral generations who produced them.

107. Coningham, Allchin, Batt and Lucy 1996.
108. *Mbh.* 4.1–10 also refers to *Yavāñilipi*, 'Greek writing': Puri 1990, 148.
109. Chattopadhyaya 1974.
110. Singh 2009, 42–6, with a table of alphabets.
111. Goyal 2006; Salomon 1998, 7–55, esp. 19 on the origin of Brāhmī.

13.9 Silver drachm of Agathocles, with Greek legend on obverse, Indian god and legend on the reverse (Classical Numismatic Group, Inc., www.cngcoins.com, GNU Free Ducumentation License).

In short, between the arrival of the Greeks and their departure, India became a literate culture. This does not mean that we have to believe literacy was very widespread in society: it does not have to penetrate to every level to be an important technological innovation. Some Indians discovered that this new technology of the invaders was useful, and employed it for their own purposes. Not least, it represented the beginning of an Indian 'coinage tradition', as Joe Cribb has demonstrated.[112]

But did these elements of 'transculturation' form the basis for anything more profound? We have already looked in the previous chapter at some possible examples of interchange between intellectuals at the philosophical level. In the following chapters I consider the possibilities of interaction and innovation in the fields of literature and the visual arts.

112. Cribb 2005.

14

Bending the Bow

KṚṢṆA, ARJUNA, RĀMA, ODYSSEUS

Greek Literature in India

The first Greek play ever performed on Indian soil may have been written by Alexander the Great. This was *Agen*, a satyr play performed, according to Athenaeus, who tells us everything we know about this play, on the banks of the river Hydaspes before Alexander's departure from India. This coincides neatly with the report in Nearchus that Alexander held *agones*, competitive games, before embarkation with his newly built fleet.[1] Greek *agones* would normally include not just athletic events, but theatrical and other spectacles; if there was any competitor to *Agen*, we hear nothing about it.

Athenaeus describes the play as a *dramation*, 'a little play, a sketch', and gives its author as Python of Byzantium or Catana, though he is aware of an alternative tradition that the king himself was the author.[2] The few lines we have make clear that it was a satire about the activities of Alexander's treasurer Harpalus, who was living like a king in Babylon with first one Athenian mistress, Pythionice, and after her death with another, Glycera, for whom he was demanding royal honours. Eventually Harpalus overreached himself, and seemed to be creating a power base in Athens by making huge donations of grain and money. After Alexander's return to Persepolis in 324 and the purge of the satraps, Harpalus felt that Babylon was getting too hot for him and fled to Athens. But here he became embroiled in a financial scandal, and decamped again, to Crete, where he was murdered not long after.

1. Arr. *Ind.* 18.12.

2. Athen. 13.68.596a.

Athenaeus says not only that the play was performed on the Hydaspes, but also that it was exhibited 'when Harpalus was flying to the seashore', after he had revolted, which would imply a date in 324. In this case Alexander would not have been on the Hydaspes, but in Ecbatana; thus many historians, beginning from Beloch, have preferred to discount Athenaeus' testimony and say that the play was performed in 324, in Susa.[3] Bruno Snell presented an alternative interpretation, keeping to the Indian setting, and demolishing the arguments of Beloch that Hydaspes might be a reference to some other, more obscure river of the same name.[4] Lloyd-Jones advanced a more broadly-based historical argument, that Harpalus was too powerful to be mocked in 326. It seems to me that if Alexander was already past the stage of killing his closest associates (Cleitus), mockery of Harpalus was not going to cause him much distress. It is at the height of a man's fortune that he is most open to malicious gossip and invective. Given the relaxed view Alexander took of Cleomenes' peculation in Egypt, he would have no need for anger at Harpalus at this juncture in his fortunes, and even his lèse-majesté could be made a joke of at this time. Harpalus was the man who kept Alexander supplied with books as he travelled further east,[5] and a literary event would be a good riposte or reprimand to a bookish subordinate who was beginning to get above himself.

There is no doubt that Alexander was closely involved with the production: it will not have come as a surprise to him when he took his seat in the theatre to see a trusted subordinate being lampooned. Kotlińska-Toma suggests that he was the *choregos*, and in a sense he must have been, since he controlled all the funds of the expedition to India. It seems probable, too, as Snell argued, that he appeared as a character in the play, if not as himself. The name *Agen* is a proper name formed from the verb *agein*, to lead, and might be boldly translated as 'the Führer'.[6] It is probable that Agen appeared at the end of the play

3. The bibliography is extensive: Beloch (see Snell); Snell 1964; Lloyd-Jones 1966; Sutton 1980; Kotlińska-Toma 2015 and 2016. See also the classic article Badian 1961 on Harpalus, which however does not discuss *Agen*.

4. Kotlińska-Toma 2015, 116, following a suggestion of J. Wikarjak, proposes that ΥΔΑΣΠΗΣ is a corruption in the MSS of ΧΟΑΣΠΗΣ, and that the play was performed at the mass weddings in Susa.

5. Plu. *Alex.* 8.

6. I wonder if there is any connection with the puzzling title of Onesicritus' book, 'How Alexander was Led'?

as a *deus ex machina* to resolve the complexities of the plot; and since any satyr play has to have a chorus of satyrs and an appearance by the god Dionysus, it is also probable that the Alexander/Agen character was a manifestation of Dionysus. Given Alexander's enthusiasm for that god, this would be very fitting.

The plot, alas, is unrecoverable. The eighteen lines we have of the play seem to come from the early part, perhaps its opening. Harpalus, under the name of Pallides, is discovered crouching by 'the harlot's temple' in grief. A group of *magoi*, or Persian priests – surely the satyrs in disguise – appear and promise to conjure up the soul of Pythionice. A little later there is a reference in a dialogue to the sufferings of Athens despite the quantities of grain that Harpalus has sent them and his honours there – a reference which must date from before the scandal of 324. And that is all we have to go on.

Harpalus was the target of satire in at least one other contemporary play, a comedy by Philemon (362–262 BCE) entitled *Babylonios*, 'The Babylonian'.[7] The one fragment promises someone that they may become queen of Babylon: 'you know about Pythionice and Harpalus'. But we know no more about it. According to Athenaeus, Alexander was informed of Harpalus' escapades,[8] particularly of the divine honours to Pythionice and Glycera,[9] which made him indignant, by a letter from the historian Theopompus.[10] After the fallout from his own attempts with *proskynesis*, this was a sensitive matter for Alexander, and Snell goes so far as to suggest it was one of the motivations for his decision to return from India to his capital to sort out the satraps. The play would thus be an element of the propaganda surrounding the disappointing decision to turn back from the search for the end of the world.[11]

If we had more of this play we might understand much better how Alexander presented his mission to the East to his companions, and even to himself. But from what we have, there seems little doubt that the spectacle combined concerns of high politics, the role of Dionysus in his conquests and comic farce, in more or less equal measure.

7. F 15 Austin (to be found in vol. 7).

8. Athen. 13.50 (586c).

9. Diod. 17.108.5.

10. *FGrH* 115 Ff 253, 254b.

11. Snell 1964, 134. Lloyd-Jones thinks that Snell takes the joke too seriously, but I am sure Alexander never did anything just 'for fun'. Kotlińska-Toma 2015, 284 regards the play as 'the official version of the scandal', and Sutton's view is similar: both however place the performance in 324, as a capstone on the events.

A second Greek play has left its mark in the Greek realm of the East. Not much can be said about it, for what little survives consists of the remains of twenty-one lines of iambic verse from Ai Khanum in Bactria. The text is preserved not on papyrus as such, but in the marks left by the ink on the papyrus when it was pressed up against a crumbled baked mud brick in the ruins of the city.[12] I offer here a translation of the complete, or more-or-less complete, words:

to wed a goddess
they seek
    or the
if I were
        ten thousand
with the proof
    into our hands

    to consider
so these things

    (of) Dionysus
            of the apparent

The lines are in good iambics and probably come from a tragedy, rather than a comedy or satyr play with their looser metrical rules. The speaker speaks in an emphatic way ('ten thousand' – a metonym for an enormous number), and there is apparently doubt about some matter or other since 'proof' is being, perhaps, sought. Right at the end, the appearance of the word 'Dionysus' brings us up short, given the importance of that god in Alexander's thinking and in the later religion of Bactria more generally.[13] It is possible that both the name Dionysus and the word 'seeming, apparent' (*dokount-*) are in the genitive, and if so they may agree with each other though separated by several other missing words. Is it a matter of someone demanding proof of a person being regarded as an impostor, a pretend Dionysus? It has also been suggested that the plot might concern one of the famous 'rejecters' of Dionysus, such as Pentheus, Lycaon, or Deriades.[14]

12. The text is published by Rapin 1987; see for discussion Hollis 2011 and also Lerner 2003.

13. On Dionysus in the plastic arts of Bactria, see especially Boardman 2014; 2015.

14. Cf. Hollis 2011, 108. Hollis also notes that the shortening of the 'i' in *hemin* is characteristic of Sophocles, so it is possible that it is a play by Sophocles.

Delightful though it is to find a god so important in Bactria mentioned in a text from Bactria, there is no compelling reason to suppose that there is any integral connection. Many Greek plays mentioned Dionysus, the presiding god of the drama, and anyone might have brought a copy of one of them to the banks of the Oxus. We need not envisage a play written for the find-spot. What the fragment does prove is that Greek drama was known and circulating as far east as the borders of India.[15]

To find such proof in the Greek city of Ai Khanum is not so amazing: it is much more remarkable when such evidence appears in the subcontinent itself. Another possible proof of such circulation is the appearance on a vase from Peshawar of a scene that has been identified as a scene from Sophocles' *Antigone*.[16] Other interpretations are possible, but if this one is right it shows that a play by Sophocles had impressed a member of the artisan population of the Punjab.

A final connection between Greek drama and India is provided by a longer papyrus find from Oxyrhynchus in Egypt. Again it takes us beyond the Indo-Greek period, as it belongs to the second century CE, when trading links between India and Roman Egypt were well established. But it is a remarkable document of interaction, since the play contains substantial passages of what has generally been identified as a south Indian language.

The play, which has been entitled *Charition* by modern scholars for ease of reference, concerns a familiar form of plot, the rescue of a Greek maiden from the clutches of Indian captors.[17] It is a burlesque of a plot familiar from tragedy, such as that of *Iphigeneia in Tauris*. Key to the rescue strategy is the plying of the Indians with large quantities of wine – a motif recalling the *Odyssey* as well as Euripides' *Cyclops*.[18] Some three columns of text survive. The style is that of farce or 'music hall' comedy. At least three speakers speak in Greek, and are answered by a character indicated in the margin as 'king', who speaks in a non-Greek language. Later several women speak in, presumably, the same

15. So was philosophy: see Lerner 2003 on the Ai Khanum philosophical papyrus, a critique of Plato's Theory of Forms. The presence of Clearchus in Ai Khanum was discussed in ch. 6 above.

16. Illustrated in *CHI* 1.646.

17. First published *POxy* 413. The earliest discussion was by Powell and Barber 1929, appendix 3 (215–22). More recent editions are by Santelia 1991 and Andreassi 2001. There is an extensive discussion of the play in Hall 2013, 118–30. See also the exposition in Varadpande 1981, 98–110, and the brief reference in Saletore 1936.

18. Andreassi (ed.) 2001, 12.

language. The non-Greek utterances extend to several lines at a time, too long to be mere nonsense words. They must represent an Indian language, and must be in a language that at least some in the audience could be expected to understand. One thinks of, for example, Shakespeare's *Henry V* or Terence Rattigan's *French without Tears,* in both of which the humour of one scene depends on the audience appreciating the protagonists' mistakes in French. Notably, two of the Greek characters also speak a few words in the Indian language: the slave at line 75 and Charition at line 124. It is a very rare thing to find a Greek text that takes cognisance in any way of a non-Greek language, and it seems to indicate an audience of Greeks and non-Greeks who, to some degree, understand each other's languages.

Oxyrhynchus is close to the main trade route from India to Rome via the port of Berenice. Indian traders have left indications of their presence in the Red Sea ports in several inscriptions,[19] and it is attractive to imagine that such traders were seated in the theatre alongside their Greek hosts to hear this play; though they will not have felt especially welcome if the boorish behaviour of the Indians in the play reflects Greek views of Indians. Towards the end of our fragment the king character breaks into Greek, describing himself as a barbarian, an offensive designation that had fallen out of use in Greek after Alexander's inroads into India:

> A boundless barbaric dance I lead, o goddess moon,[20]
> With wild measure and barbaric step;
> Ye Indian chiefs, bring the drum(?) of mystic sound.

(There are many references to the Indian drums, regarded by Greeks as making a hair-raising sound: φρικώδη βόμβον, according to the Suda.)[21]

The language has frequently been interpreted as Kannada, and translations offered on that basis.[22] More recently P. Shivaprasad Rai has proposed that the language is Tulu.[23] Whichever may be the case, the general point is estab-

19. Salomon 1991.

20. The moon is not usually a goddess in India, but a staging-post for dead souls. Bhattacharji 1970/2000, 156–7.

21. Andreassi (ed.) 2001, note on line 10.

22. See Powell and Barber 1929, 215–22, opposing an earlier treatment by Hultzsch in *JRAS* 1904. For a conspectus of interpretations see Andreassi (ed.) 2001, note on line 39. The first inscriptions in Kannada date from the fifth century CE, and thus offer an imperfect control on this text.

23. Shivaprasad Rai 1985.

lished that a Greek readership is comprehending an Indian language, and that, perhaps, Indians are also enjoying a Greek play. It is pleasing to consider this as the culmination of a process that began with the first attempts of Onesicritus to communicate with the naked philosophers of Taxila, and that must inevitably have developed, along with other interactions between the two peoples, through the centuries of Greek rule in India.

Indian Theatre

Do these fragments of interaction in the drama entitle us to consider that Greek drama became well enough known in India to have an impact on the development of indigenous Indian performance? The question has been answered by strongly held opinions on either side of the case. A. B. Keith argued at length for a deep impact of Greek drama on Indian, though 'the Indian genius has known how to recast so cleverly and to adapt what it borrowed so effectively that the traces which would definitely establish indebtedness cannot be found'.[24] M. L. Varadpande was similarly enthusiastic for a transformative influence of Greek styles on the indigenous Indian drama, while Jairazbhoy included drama in the topics of his exhaustive survey of every possible aspect of Greek influence in India.[25] Lately, Bronkhorst has reasserted it: 'The thesis of Greek influence on the Sanskrit theatre still awaits its first serious criticism'.[26]

Others have taken the opposite view. E. P. Horrwitz firmly denied any kind of influence: 'we contend that the Indian theatre is home-grown, and not a foreign graft'.[27] Sylvain Levi rejected the hypothesis of influence, but retreated from this position in later life.[28] Jawaharlal Nehru reached a firm conclusion: recognising that European scholars must have been excited at first discovering that India had a dramatic tradition to compare with the Greek, and were led to assume influence of the one on the other, he stated that 'it is now generally admitted that the Indian theatre was entirely independent in its origins, in the ideas which governed it, and in its development'.[29]

24. Keith 1924, 356.
25. Varadpande 1981; Jairazbhoy 1963, 103–9.
26. Bronkhorst 2016, 402–3.
27. Horrwitz 1912/1967, 75–8.
28. Bronkhorst 2016, 402.
29. Nehru 2004, 162; his discussion of theatre runs from 161 to 170.

How can one adjudge a controversy that has produced such conflicting opinions? To some extent it is a matter of terminology, as Nehru makes clear in referring to the 'origins' of Sanskrit drama. Clearly Greeks had nothing to do with the various forms of dramatic performance that took place in the Vedic period, and which are traced effectively by Varadpande. Did Indian drama then change as a result of Greek influence? Points can be adduced on both sides. Let us begin with those 'for'.

Plutarch says that the plays of Sophocles and Euripides were performed in Baluchistan, and Jairazbhoy supports his contention by mentioning the 'Antigone' vase from Peshawar, referred to above.[30] Jairazbhoy also refers to the familiarity of King Phraotes with Greek drama, and his ability to discuss it with Apollonius of Tyana; but that is fiction, and belongs to a period later than the Indo-Greek on which we are focusing.

One of the most striking pieces of evidence is that the Sanskrit name for the theatrical curtain is *yavanika*, the 'Greek thing'. This is not a curtain drawn across the proscenium as in a modern theatre, but a backdrop with a painted scene, perhaps on some occasions a detailed narrative painting which could be expounded by a single performer or group of performers, as in present-day Iran. Greek theatre did not use any such device, and the reference is probably to a painted cloth or maybe a tapestry, which could as well be Persian as Greek.

There is more substance in the attempt to trace similarities in the style of plots and character drawing. The parallels here are not with Greek tragedy, since Indian plays never have unhappy endings, but with New Comedy. Some plots, notably that of the classic *The Little Cart*, are supposed to involve the same kinds of characters, episodes, misunderstandings and reconciliations as the plays of Menander and Roman comedy. Indian drama does indeed present a theory of character types, tabulated in the *Nāṭya Śāstra* of Bharata, datable perhaps in the second century BCE. They include the male and female of superior and inferior type, as well as those of 'middling' type, the *viduśaka* or jester (four types), the servants, and four types of heroine, namely the goddess, the queen, the noblewoman and the courtesan.[31] Such types do indeed a ring a bell with those familiar with New Comedy.

30. Plu. *de Alex. mag. fort.* 1.328d; Jairazbhoy 1963, 104.
31. *Nāṭya Śāstra* 1988, 514–16.

Keith also noted (66) that Śiva is the patron of drama as Dionysus is of Greek drama, and that both countries had theatre festivals in the spring;[32] but he attaches little weight to this external circumstance.

Keith was keen to argue that the provisions of the *Nāṭya Śāstra* resemble those of Aristotle's *Poetics*, but it is difficult to sustain this view after even a cursory glance at the former. Though presenting itself as a 'science' of drama,[33] it is concerned to establish its credentials by its direct descent from the gods. It does not work by analysis and has no philosophical basis. Though it treats drama as an 'imitation',[34] it does not mean by this what Aristotle means. Indian drama imitates *emotions*, and the audience experiences 'not the actual emotion but an aesthetic appreciation of its *rasa* or flavour'. The eight basic emotions are love, humour, enthusiasm, anger, fear, grief, disgust and astonishment, and the corresponding flavours are the erotic, comic, heroic, furious, apprehensive, compassionate, horrific and marvellous.[35] Pity and fear, so central to Aristotle's theory, have only a small part to play! The *Nāṭya Śāstra* is concerned with pictorial effects, especially of gesture,[36] reminding us of the striking statement in the *Citra Sūtra*, the treatise on painting, that the art most resembling painting is dance. It is not a theoretical treatise, but a practical handbook of dance, mime, gesture and music. That is in fact the meaning of *nāṭya*, which is the same word as *nautch*, the term used for dancing girls under the British Raj. Much more is said of these matters than of plot or even of dialogue and speech, though characters do speak Sanskrit or Prakrit according to their social status. If we are to find similarities between Greek and Indian drama they must be found in the texts, not in the theory.

In my view it is very hard to find any real common ground between the two dramatic traditions. The roots of drama go back to the *Ṛg Veda*, which contains a number of hymns in the form of dialogues, or even scenes, as well as hymns that make use of other kinds of literary form such as the riddle and the animal fable. This is long before any Greek was seen in India. Particularly striking is *Ṛg Veda* 10.10, in which Yami tries to persuade her brother Yama to make love to her, while he manfully resists (so very unlike the content of our

32. Keith 1924, 66.
33. *Nāṭya Śāstra* 1988, 531.
34. Keith 1924, 355.
35. Bhasa 2008, xvi.
36. *Nāṭya Śāstra* 373, n.

own dear Anglican hymn books!).[37] Like the Greek drama, the Indian is part of a religious festival, and is described by the dramatist Kalidasa as 'an ocular sacrifice'.[38] 'Dancing girls' were often dedicated to temples, which suggests that the rituals included dance as well as the other things that dancing girls commonly do. The Jātakas, stories of the Buddha's previous births, contain many references to theatres and performers, though strict Buddhists frown on attending dramatic performances.[39] The *Nāṭya Śāstra* itself probably dates from the second century BCE in some form, and a work of this name – an earlier version? – is referred to by Pāṇini in the fourth century BCE. A terracotta mask from Bihar has been assigned by its stratigraphy to the fourth or third century BCE, and appears to have been used for theatrical purposes.[40]

There is thus a variety of evidence locating dramatic performance and dance in the centuries before the arrival of the Greeks. Drama in India does not derive from importation by Greeks; but did the Greek theatre have any effect on Indian practice? It may be that danced narrative and pageantry was succeeded by a more complex form of drama from the second century BCE: Keith suggests that it arose out of the Kṛṣṇa cult.[41] The name of the first dramatist, Bhasa, was already familiar in the first century BCE. At the earliest, he is late Maurya, but the thirteen plays attaching to his name are commonly dated closer to the first or second century CE.[42] His plots and themes are drawn from the repertoire of the *Mahābhārata* (six) and *Rāmāyaṇa* (two), as well as other legends: one includes a death on stage , unique in Sanskrit drama.[43] The biographer of the Buddha, Aśvaghoṣa, in the first century CE, also wrote plays, and some fragments survive of a nine-act play about the Buddha, which involves a companion who has been compared to the 'clever slave' type of New Comedy.[44] But by the time we reach the classic Sanskrit plays of the fourth/fifth centuries CE, Kalidasa's *Śakuntalā* and Viśakhadatta's *The*

37. Other hymns in dialogue form include *RV* 1.179, 10.95, 86, 108. 1.164 uses riddles, and 10.28 uses animal fables.

38. Varadpande 1981, 28.

39. Ibid., 30–2; Horrwitz 1912/1967, 121.

40. Varadpande 1981, 35 and 37.

41. Keith 1924, 45.

42. The MS was discovered in 1909.

43. 'Duryodhana' in *The Shattered Thigh*.

44. Keith 1924, 58. The title is *Śāriputra-prakaraṇa*. It was published by Lüders in 1926. Two other plays on Buddhist themes were found with it, and may be by Aśvaghoṣa. See Johnston in Aśvaghoṣa 1936/1984, xx.

Rakśasa's Ring, plots and characters have evolved to a much greater complexity. It is hard to relate the provisions of the *Nāṭya Śāstra* to plays of this kind in any detailed way.

It is easier to list the differences than the similarities between the two art forms. Perhaps most notably, Sanskrit plays are much longer than Greek ones; they have many more characters and do not observe the unities of time and place. They are never tragedies (with one exception, *The Shattered Thigh*). They do not employ a chorus. Keith points to certain plot elements, such as the occurrence of rings as recognition tokens, common to both traditions. Maybe there is a connection here, but it cannot be seen as fundamental to the art form. Tarn was dismissive of the idea that anyone would bother to bring plays by Menander to India;[45] but such plot elements can as easily be found in Euripides, whom Tarn rates more highly as an artist. Varadpande proposes that the story of Polycrates' ring was brought east by Yavana flute-girls, and thus inspired the author of *Śakuntalā*; while I fully endorse the role of women (as mothers) in passing on the stories of their native land to their offspring in a new land, I hesitate to attribute the invention of a genre to such a process.[46]

William Empson makes an interesting point about 'Far Eastern' drama which points up its difference from Greek practice and theory:

> The characters in a Far Eastern play are hardly even what we call 'types', let alone individuals. It is the situation which is typical. The situation often happens in real life, and a play about it is therefore real, and may be very moving. It is quite in order to have the whole audience in floods of tears. But in real life the situation ends in all sorts of ways, and you are not much interested in the way this one ended ... If you put in a definite ending it would be unrealistic.[47]

It would be impossible to apply such a description to any Greek drama. Actually, it does not apply very well to *The Rakśasa's Ring* either, since that is a play about historical individuals; but the observation about the predominance of situation and emotion fits with the *Nāṭya Śāstra's* remarks referred to above.

A further objection to the idea of Greek influence is that no theatre building anything like a Greek one are known in India, though there is a square

45. Quoted in Varadpande 1981, 118.

46. Lane Fox 2008 eloquently evokes the role of local women in passing on Near-Eastern myths to the children they bore to Greek traders/settlers.

47. Empson 2016, 114.

four-sided 'theatre' with banked rows of seats at Nagarjunakonda in southern India, dating from a much later period, where other Greco-Roman finds have been recorded. It may be, of course, that most Indian theatres were temporary constructions with banks of wooden seats. Such structures are described in, for example, the Tamil epic *Silappadikaram*, and pavilions with awnings are depicted in the cave paintings at Ajanta.[48]

But none of this adds up to what Varadpande terms 'a Gandhara moment' for Indian theatre. If we regard the impact of Greek theatre as slight, rather than, as Keith wished, 'deep', we should reach the same conclusion as he did (quoted above), that India adapted 'what it borrowed so effectively that the traces which would definitely establish indebtedness cannot be found'.

The situation was emphatically not comparable to what Macaulay hoped for in the nineteenth century: that English would transform Indian literature and civilisation as Greek and Latin had influenced English.[49] Nonetheless, Shakespeare did exercise a strong influence on Bengali theatre, already steeped in Sanskrit drama and myth.[50] Status is important here: people only translate, or accept influence from, a high-status language; and Brahmans would not have seen Greek as high-status, in contrast, say, to the situation in Egypt, where Egyptians learned to read and write the language of the Greeks, but not vice versa.[51] India's remained the dominant culture. As Tarn said in another context, the Greeks in India may have ultimately vanished, not because they became Eurasian, but because they became Indian.[52]

Epic

Stronger arguments can be put forward for influence of the Homeric poems on Indian poetry, particularly the *Mahābhārata* and *Rāmāyaṇa*. Ancient Greek writers seem to have suspected a connection, for Dio Chrysostom, in a critical essay on Homer, claims that

> it is said that Homer's poetry is sung even in India, where they have translated it into their own speech and tongue. The result is that, while the people of India have no chance to behold many of the stars in our part of the

48. Varadpande 1981, 86.
49. Hagerman 2013, 77.
50. Chaudhuri 1999, 53.
51. Feeney 2016, 19–21 and 31.
52. Tarn 1951, 391.

world – for example it is said that the Bears are not visible in their country – still they are not unacquainted with the sufferings of Priam, the laments and wailings of Andromache and Hecuba, and the valour of both Achilles and Hector.[53]

Aelian, a century later, says much the same:

> Note that the Indians transcribe the poems of Homer into their own language and recite them. They are not alone; the Persian kings do so as well, if we are to believe writers on these subjects.[54]

Tarn took it that Dio was referring to the *Mahābhārata* and *Rāmāyaṇa*, which have often been compared with the *Iliad* and *Odyssey*, the first as a military epic and the second as a tale of adventure and homecoming to a wife.[55] There should be no doubt that Dio's statement is incorrect insofar as there is no evidence for an actual translation of the Greek epics into any Indian language before the second century CE (or indeed much later). But a reader of the Indian epics is often struck by motifs that remind him of the Homeric ones, and related traditions: the archery contest to win the hand of Draupadi in the *Mahābhārata*, in which Arjuna is triumphant,[56] as well as Rāma's successful bending of the great bow in the *Rāmāyaṇa*; Indra's deception of Ahalya parallels Zeus' of Alcmene (but ends with the husband Gautama castrating Indra!);[57] Bhīṣma's battle with the suitors in the *Mahābhārata* also recalls Odysseus' battle in the *Odyssey*; Kṛṣṇa is overcome by being shot in his one vulnerable place, his heel, like Achilles;[58] the war to rescue Sita recalls the war over Helen at Troy; Saranyu has many features in common with Helen (even the name is cognate);[59] Ganga's systematic drowning of her sons as they are born recalls both Demeter's placing of Demophoon on the fire and Thetis' immersion of

53. D.Chr. *Or.* 53.6–7.

54. Ael. *VH* 12.48; the reference to the Persians probably comes from Dinon of Colophon, writing in the fourth century BCE (F 9 Lenfant = Athen. 14.33 (14.633ce)). A similar statement about Persia is made by Plutarch (*de Alex. mag. fort.* 328d), who also says that Bactria and the Caucasus (i.e., theHindu Kush) came to revere the gods of the Greeks because of Alexander.

55. Tarn 1951, 379; see Arora in Arora (ed.) 1991, 80. Boardman 2015, 167 seems to accept Dio's assertion, while doubting whether familiarity with a literary text could inspire artistic innovation (such as the Peshawar vase mentioned above), as suggested by Derrett 1992.

56. Doniger 1999, 162.

57. *Bālakānda Sanga* 47, 1.215; Doniger 1999.

58. Eck 2012, 221.

59. Doniger 1999, 60.

Achilles in the river Styx. Weerakkody notes the similarity of Odysseus' Sirens to the Yakśinīs of Lanka, and of his bow to Vijaya.[60] Non-Homeric Greek myths present themselves in Bhima's fight with the monster Bakasura in the *Mahābhārata* (like Perseus rescuing Andromeda); Kunti sets her son adrift on the river in what seems to be a common Indo-European kingship myth, found also in the legends of Cyrus, and similarly Nal is raised in disguise by parents of a low status;[61] the Pandavas, being chased by an angry ascetic, distract him from his pursuit by throwing down grains of rice, each of which turns into a Śivalingam, so that the ascetic is compelled to stop and worship it;[62] a similar story about Udema and Samavati was mentioned at the beginning of chapter 13. Much later, the sixteenth-century poet Tulsidas, in his rewriting of the *Rāmāyaṇa*, has Sita evade the ordeal of the fire by creating a phantom Sita; surely he was thinking of the phantom Helen of Greek tradition.[63]

What are we to make of such echoes and parallels? They need to be picked apart and classified carefully, before accepting any argument for a simple one-way traffic by which the Indian writers adopted Greek myths and re-used them.[64] A recent book by Fernando Wulff Alonso devotes nearly six hundred pages to assembling all possible parallels between the Indian epics and Greek mythology, particularly the Homeric poems, with a view to demonstrating direct influence of the Greek works,[65] and even arguing that stories told in the Indian epics can be used to assist in the reconstruction of lost Greek narratives.[66] There is no scope here for a full-scale discussion of every example in Wulff Alonso's book, and it thus seems better to try to set out some guiding principles, followed by comment upon each in turn.

60. Weerakkody 1997, 194–5.

61. Doniger 1999, 156. Other examples include Sargon, Romulus and Remus and Dara in Tarsusi's *Darabnameh*.

62. Eck 2012, 450.

63. Ibid., 428 and 450.

64. A few of these parallels are noted by Jairazbhoy 1963, 97–102. Brockington 1998, 77 even argues that Vergil was familiar with the *Mahābhārata*!

65. Wulff Alonso 2008. Though not the first such (Arthur Lillie in 1912 is mentioned by Brockington 1998, 50–1), the book is more thorough than any previous discussion, and a valuable resource. Derrett 1992 also favoured literary influence from west to east, including that of Christian texts, and the Homeric Hymns – he instances *hAp* (3) 14–18, 117–26 – on Buddhist stories, e.g., of the birth of the Buddha.

66. Wulff Alonso 2008, 506–7.

1. There may be folk-tales and elements of Indo-European traditional narratives that move freely between Indian and Greek literature, and these may explain some of the similarities between the great epics.[67]
2. The characters and story-patterns of the epics show resemblances.
3. There is direct literary borrowing.
4. Allen (2001: see below) also indicates a fourth possibility, that these stories are Jungian archetypes.

Regarding (1): some mythological patterns can surely be explained in this way – for example, the parallelism of the Dioscuri and the Aśvins; or the myth of the soma stolen from heaven by Manu and given to mankind, as Prometheus stole fire.[68] Several motifs from classical Greek literature have been recognised in the Jātakas: these Buddhist texts probably go back to soon after the lifetime of the Buddha, but were elaborated over later centuries. Thus, the story of Hippocleides dancing away his marriage (Herodotus 6.129) occurs also in the Jātakas and *Pañcatantra* 1.150;[69] the story of Artaphernes' wife who decided that she could get another husband but never another brother (Herodotus 3.18–19), which is recycled by Sophocles' Antigone (*Ant.* 909–12), is also found in *Jātaka* 67 and the *Rāmāyaṇa* 6.24.7–8;[70] the story of Rhampsinitus and the two thieves (Herodotus 2.121) which also appears as the story of Trophonius and his brother in Pausanias, is found in the Jātakas;[71] the story of the man who finds a snake coiled around the cradle of his baby, thinks his baby in danger, and in killing the snake kills the baby also (which Halliday describes as 'the Beddgelert story') is also in the Jātakas.[72]

More generally, one may consider the fable tradition, where there is no doubt that the Indian text is primary. The *Pañcatantra* rapidly acquired fame as its stories were recycled by Aesop and others, and the Sanskrit text was translated into Persian in the reign of Khosrow Anushirvan, which began its

67. The approach goes back to Rawlinson, cited in Derrett 1992, 47 n.1; see also Brockington 1998, 75–7, citing Baldick 1994.

68. *RV* 4.26, 4.27; Jamison and Brereton 2014, 42.

69. See Macan's commentary on the fourth, fifth and sixth books of Herodotus (1895), vol. 2, appendix 14, 304–11.

70. Pischel 1893; Halliday 1933, 48–9.

71. Halliday 1933, 49, unfortunately without giving the reference; Strong 2001, 20.

72. Halliday 1933, 44, again without the *Jātaka* reference. In the Welsh story, Gelert is a dog. Drew (1987, 156) claims that Gelert was originally a mongoose, so that the Indian protector from serpents becomes in the Greek one a protecting snake.

career in the languages of the Muslim world; Buddhaghoṣa's story of the Buddha consoling a grieving woman by sending her to collect grain from 'the house of one who has never known sorrow' reappears in Alexander's letter to his mother on his deathbed in the later antique versions of the *Alexander Romance* (3.33).[73] (The Biblical story of the Judgment of Solomon also appears in the Jātakas, with Buddha as the hero.)[74]

Regarding (2) above, one parallel that has been pursued in detail by N. J. Allen is that of Athena and Durga.[75] He begins with a useful conspectus of possible reasons for observed parallelism (368): they may be Jungian archetypes; they may be independent parallel inventions in similar societies; they may be due to diffusion; they may have a common origin in earlier cultures. In the case of the war goddess Athena, Allen points to several narrative motifs shared between the *Odyssey* and the *Mahābhārata*: Durga assists Yudhiṣṭhira as Athena assists Odysseus; the archery contest to win Penelope/Draupadi; Odysseus' lying accounts of his life are paralleled in the false narratives of each of the five Pandavas; as well as more subjective parallels such as the combination of the motifs of a sleeper, a tree, and hiding of a weapon, and a deity in disguise. Allen's explanation of these similarities is that they derive from Indo-European story-patterns rather than direct borrowing by one poet from another. Taken with the few examples I assembled above regarding folktales, this seems a sufficient explanation for the similarities; and it would not be hard to bring in other European epic traditions (the *Nibelungenlied* for the hero's vulnerable spot – Siegfried's back), or folktales like the Welsh tale of Gelert mentioned above. In a discussion of Saranyu, Wendy Doniger examines her resemblance to Helen (as well as the cognate name) and concludes that 'gender trumps culture': it is the nature of gender and its social construction that creates these stories in both India and Greece.[76] That is, there is a substratum of narrative which turns out similarly in the texts because of similar social constructions of gender. By analogy, the similar presentation of Indo-European tales in the Indian and Greek epics is to be explained by similar social (if not political) structures and presuppositions.

Regarding (3) above: given time, one could test this last principle on all of the parallels assembled by Wulff Alonso. Take the narrative about the bend-

73. Stoneman 2008, 192.

74. Rawlinson 1926, 11–12. Alexander also exhibits Solomonic wisdom in the Hebrew versions of the *Alexander Romance*. One great hero can be interchanged with another.

75. Allen 2001.

76. Doniger 1999, 60 and passim.

ing of the bow, which is performed by three heroes: Odysseus, Arjuna and Rāma.[77]

In the *Odyssey*,

> Ulysses viewing, ere he tried to draw,
> The famous bow, which ev'ry way he mov'd,
> Up and down turning it . . .
> With such ease drew round
> The king his bow. Then twang'd he up the string,
> That as a swallow in the air doth sing
> With no continued tune, but, pausing still,
> Twinks out her scatter'd voice in accents shrill;
> So sharp the string sung when he gave it touch,
> Once having bent and drawn it. Which so much
> Amaz'd the Wooers, that their colours went
> And came most grievously.[78]

In the *Mahābhārata*,

> Arjuna took his stand by the bow like an immovable mountain. He walked around the bow, making a solemn circumambulation, and bowed his head down to it, . . .
>
> In a twinkling of the eye he strung the bow
> And took the arrows that counted five.
> He pierced the target and brought it down,
> Hit through the hole, and it fell with a might.
>
> In the sky above there was applause,
> And great cheering in the crowd below.
> The God rained down with celestial flowers
> On the head of the Pārtha, killer of foes.[79]

In the *Rāmāyaṇa*,

> Then, as though it were mere play to him, the righteous prince [Rāma], the delight of the Raghus, strung the bow as thousands watched. The mighty man affixed the bowstring and fitting an arrow to it, drew it back. But, in so

77. See also ibid., 162.
78. Homer *Odyssey* 21.404–13, tr. George Chapman.
79. *Mbh.* 1.179.15, tr. van Buitenen.

doing, the best of men broke the bow in the middle. There was a tremendous noise as loud as a thunderclap, and a mighty trembling shook the earth, as if a mountain had been torn asunder.[80]

The story is told again later in the *Rāmāyaṇa*:[81]

Rama approached the bow. Some of the onlookers, unable to bear the suspense, closed their eyes and prayed for his success, saying, "If he fails to bring the ends of this bow together, what is to happen to the maiden?" What they missed, because they had shut their eyes, was to note how swiftly Rama picked up the bow, tugged the string taut, and brought the tips together. They were startled when they heard a deafening report, caused by the cracking of the bow at its arch, which could not stand the pressure of Rama's grip.

The atmosphere was suddenly relaxed. The gods showered down flowers and blessings, clouds parted and precipitated rains, the oceans tossed up in the air all the rare treasures from their depths ... The citizens garlanded, embraced, and anointed each other with perfumes and sprinkled sandalwood powder in the air.[82]

There is no doubt that the three epics tell, in some sense, the same story, of a hero who wins a bride by a test which involves bending a massive bow and shooting an arrow at a complex target. But the comparative method requires us not just to assemble the parallels, but to examine the differences. In all three cases, the hero accomplishes the test to show his superiority to his rivals for a bride. In the cases of Arjuna and Rāma, these are young men trying to win a bride, while in Odysseus' case the test is to prove that Odysseus is really the husband, absent for twenty years, of Penelope, and has a superior claim over those who wish her to re-marry (one of them). At first glance the Indian version looks like the primary version of the story, the hero's quest for a bride. Like Calaf winning Turandot, or Siegfried passing through the magic fire, this hero passes the test where others could not succeed.

Thus far, the 'Indo-European *Gemeingut*' explanation would seem sufficient. What of the details of the narrative? Odysseus' examination of the bow is a practical search for wormholes and cracks since he last handled it; Arjuna's

80. *Rām. 1 (Bālakāṇḍa)* 66.16–18.

81. *Rām. 2 (Ayodhyākāṇḍa)* 110.26–52.

82. *Ramayana* as retold by R. K. Narayan: 1972, 28–9.

is a circumambulation, a kind of reverential homage to the bow. Homer, as is his wont, adorns the narrative with the simile of the swallow, a type of composition not practised by the Indian poets. When Odysseus succeeds in stringing the bow, the suitors change colour and feel sick, while in the Indian narratives there is general rejoicing both on earth and in heaven. Not only is the purpose of the episode different in the Greek and the Indian epics, but the tenor of the narrative is subtly diverse. This is in no sense literary imitation of the kind one finds in, say, Vergil. And to my mind the *Odyssey* story has the air of a folktale that has been reworked with a strong feeling for realism and humour. The suitors feel queasy; there are no oceans erupting with joy in Homer. In each case, an old tale has been retold in line with the social and political circumstances of the world being described.

But what is that world? Can one regard the worlds of Homer and the Sanskrit epics as comparable, to the extent that one could imagine the Indian authors being inspired by the example of Homer to write their great epics? Many books have been written about the 'world of Homer' and the nature of Homeric poetry, and nearly as many about the Sanskrit epics. I suppose there might be general agreement that all four poems describe an ideal heroic world, based on a remembered past, but suffused with aspects of the contemporary world. This may appear in quite small details, such as the prevalence of chariots and bows in warfare in both traditions, and the significance of duels of the heroes. Wulff Alonso points to further similarities. The strife in the *Iliad* and the *Mahābhārata* is a conflict between both gods and men; there is a divine plan which is worked out, not by direct action of the gods, but through the decisions and actions of the mortal participants. Gods and men are in constant interaction. In both traditions a son of a goddess (Thetis or Ganga) takes a leading role, and there are 'dangerous women' in both.[83] The conqueror dies in his moment of triumph (though of course Achilles does not die in the *Iliad*). Wulff Alonso admits that these features are not unique to the Indian and Greek epics, and notes the example of the *Epic of Gilgamesh*.[84]

However, there are also important differences between the Indian and Greek conceptions. Most notably, the worlds of the gods and the afterlife are different in character, and, as has been mentioned before, the Indian vision is not tragic like the Greek. All turns out well in the end (after terrible suffering),

83. Wulff Alonso 2008, 147, 491 and 336–50.
84. Ibid., 532 and 538.

and one is always aware that, in the eyes of the gods, all human suffering is mere appearance.[85] No Greek author would ever rate the world beyond as more important than the here and now.

Wulff Alonso's argument, as has been indicated, requires the assumption that the Sanskrit authors were familiar not just with the two Homeric epics that we have, but with the whole cycle, including the origins of the war at Troy and the death of the leading hero. Indeed he is ready to bring in similarities between Dionysus and Kṛṣṇa, for example, to support the case, and to deploy other Indian works such as the *Bhāgavata Purāṇa* as part of the argumen.[86] He is even willing to envisage the Sanskrit authors being familiar with, and influenced by, the Hellenistic novel and the *Aeneid*,[87] and showing awareness of stories that we know only from Apollodorus; and proposes that the first fable collection was due to some Greek influence, since it was made in a region with a prominent Greek population.[88]

The modality of this transference is extremely literary: he envisages a team of authors settling down to recreate Greek epic in Sanskrit.[89] (This would, of course, be incompatible with any analysis of the Indian epics as oral compositions: but this is probably not the right model for these works.)[90] In fact he thinks the reflection of Greek in Sanskrit is so close that the Indian epics could be used to reconstruct the plots of the lost Greek epic cycle.[91] We know that Greek epic did not spring fully-formed from the brain of Homer, and it is reasonable to suppose that the Sanskrit epics similarly draw on many pre-existing narrative elements, if not 'oral' ones. (Homeric scholarship used to call them 'lays'.) This would perforce limit the individual creativity of the Sanskrit authors.

These are extreme claims, and would entail that, in important ways, Sanskrit literature could simply not have occurred without the impetus and influence of Greek literature. Wulff Alonso compares the situation of Rome, and the immense debt of Latin literature to Greek predecessors.[92] While no one

85. Ibid., 542.

86. Ibid., 402 and 431ff.

87. Ibid., 528 and 524.

88. Ibid., 538.

89. Cf. Jairazbhoy 1963, 97: 'another possibility is that some learned Indians were acquainted either directly with Greek books or through translations'.

90. Brockington 1998, 347.

91. Wulff Alonso 2008, 506–8.

92. Ibid., 517.

would dispute the importance of Greek literature to Roman, the comparison alerts at least this reader to a key difference between the two cases. The overriding theme of the *Mahābhārata* (to confine ourselves to that poem for a moment) is Brahmanical sacred monarchy. Though there are kings in Homer, in plenty, there is no theological conception of kingship to match the ideology presented at length in the *Mahābhārata*. Much of the plot hinges on Yudhiṣṭhira's confusion about his duty and his reluctance to take on the role of king rather than pursuing a quietist, non-violent way of life. The lengthy instructions of Bhiṣma in book 13 are intended to get him to snap out of this misguided piety and carry out the proper role of a kṣatriya. It has even been suggested that Yudhiṣṭhira is, in some sense, a portrait of Aśoka and an object lesson in what a king should not be like.[93] Again, the *Bhagavad-gītā*, perhaps a late element of the whole, seems to sum up this philosophy as Kṛṣṇa instructs Arjuna in the duties of a kṣatriya. Action is not to be renounced; kings must dree their weird, and that can only be done by allowing the Brahmans too to play their proper role. In putting this message across, Homer had nothing to offer.

The dating of the *Mahābhārata* is of course contentious, but the usual view would be that it was taking shape throughout the later centuries BCE and perhaps attained its finished form in the fourth century CE. Its coalescence thus runs concurrently with the resurgence of Brahmanism among, first, the Śunga kings, and later under the Guptas, following the (from a Brahmanical point of view reprehensible) Buddhist interlude represented by the Mauryas, the Indo-Greeks and the Kuṣāns.[94]

If this analysis is correct, the situation in north-west India vis-à-vis the Greeks is quite unlike that of Rome. The Roman conqueror, famously, was taken captive by the culture of the Greeks. But in India the conqueror was Greek, and lasted only a short time, and did not gain the respect of the Brahman traditionalists. The source language of a putative translation, Greek, simply did not have the status in India that it did in Rome. Yavanas were *mlecchas*. Furthermore, the Greek presence in India was associated with Buddhism. Not only did Aśoka, a Buddhist or something like it, reach out to his Greek neighbours, but the Indo-Greek king Menander went down in tradition as an enthusiast for Buddhism. Other Greek kings show signs of Buddhist tendencies,

93. McGrath 2013, 100.

94. Ibid., 42 here follows the analysis of Bronkhorst 2007, 97, that a main purpose of the *Mahābhārata* is to impose Brahmanism on the kings of the east.

and with the Kuṣāns there is no doubt of the position of the Buddha, who even appears on some of their coins. Bronkhorst has suggested (as mentioned in chapter 12 above) that philosophy in the sense of rigorous analytic argument developed among Buddhists as a result of exposure to Greek ways of arguing: not only did Buddhism infiltrate Greek philosophy, but the reverse also occurred. I have suggested that the same thing may have happened with the Paśupatas, another non-Brahmanical sect. Thus Greek ideas became associated with non-Brahmanical trends, especially Buddhism, and an attempt to impose the Brahmanical view of the world must surely turn its back on things Greek.[95] In my view, the social and political circumstances of north-west India around the turn of the era were inimical to acceptance of Greek models by the authors of the great epics.

95. However, even a Buddhist work, the *Buddhacarīta* of Aśvaghoṣa, is quite unlike a Hellenistic 'Life': Thapar 2013, 445–9.

15

Greeks and the Art of India

Faring far, wandering alone, bodiless, lying in a cave, is the mind.
Those who subdue it are free from the bonds of Mara.

—*DHAMMAPADA* 37

BETWEEN THE PERIOD of the Indus Civilisation and the earliest Maurya productions there is little that can be described as art in the Indian subcontinent. A few simple figurines and shaped bronzes, and no architectural remains to speak of since most buildings were of perishable materials. With the rise of the cities, exemplified by the excavated remains of Pataliputra, there is a marked change. 'Mother-goddesses' with bulging hips and breasts, in the form of small terracottas and a few small bronzes, *yakṣis* or apsaras or tree-spirits with opulent breasts and beatific features, fill several cases in the Patna Museum and are represented also in the collection at Mathura.[1] Their wondrous headdresses, tumbling turbans of many folds or, perhaps, an abundance of ostrich feathers, evoke an elusive stylishness at the courts of the Maurya kingdom. But the human form is still represented in a stylised, one could even say primitive form: the features of the mother-goddesses that are emphasised are breasts and hips, not facial detail, and there is no kind of harmony of form or contrapposto. There are exceptions to this generalisation, notably the over-life-size fly-whisk bearer that is the pride of the Patna Museum; though usually identified as Maurya work because of its high polish, this ascription is controversial and the piece is an uneasy fit with the more securely dated items

1. Patna and Mathura museums: see for example the illustrations in Vogel 1910, Smith 1962, Huntington 1985, Sharma 1994 and Quintanilla 2007.

(see below). A change comes in the later Maurya period with the large-scale sculptures of Sanchi and the first paintings at Ajanta, and the beginnings of Mathura sculpture in the succeeding Indo-Greek period.[2] All these belong to the period of Greek presence in north-west India, and to a Buddhist context.

The first European visitors to India in the late Middle Ages knew so little how to look at Indian art that, perhaps unavoidably, they reacted to it in terms that were familiar from Greek (and Roman) classical art. Gasparo Balbi in 1590 described Elephanta as a 'Roman temple' while at the same time claiming that it was built by Alexander the Great to mark the end of his advance into India.[3] Even Sir William Jones, the genius who rediscovered Sanskrit language and literature for Europeans, envisaged the haunts of the gods in the terms of classical poetry when he composed his 'hymns' to various Indian gods:

> What potent god from Agra's orient bowers
> Floats through the lucid air, whilst living flowers
> With sunny twine the vocal arbours wreathe,
> And gales enamour'd heavenly fragrance breathe?[4]

In truth the Horatian arbour has as little to do with the arid mountains that were the home of the Greek gods as with the scrub and jungle of the Indian plains that Jones knew well.

When European scholarship got beyond seeing Indian sculptures as 'monsters'[5] and began to discern the historical trajectory of Indian art, many were convinced that Greek art was the mainspring that got Indian sculpture going.[6] As early as 1809, Mountstuart Elphinstone (1779–1859, governor of Bombay) had visited a Buddhist stupa at Maunikyaula (now Manikyala, near Rawalpindi), and written in his *Account of the Kingdom of Caubul* (i.e., Kabul) of 1839 that it reminded him of the beehive tombs of Mycenae: 'there was nothing at all Hindoo in the appearance of this building; most of the party thought it decidedly Grecian'.[7] The chronological coincidence of Alexander's arrival in the north-west appeared to explain the sudden emergence of sculp-

2. Quintanilla 2007, 9 is of the opinion that Mathura was under Indo-Greek control from ca. 185–85 BCE, since there is no evidence of Śunga domination.

3. Mitter 1977, 37.

4. 'To Camdeo [i.e., Kama]', *Poems* 1818, 119.

5. Mitter 1977.

6. On the 'monstrous' character of Indian art, see Mitter 1977.

7. Cited from Levi 1972, 48.

ture in the Maurya lands. James Fergusson asserted that Bactria was the origin of *all* Indian art.[8]

Inevitably the sculpture of Gandhara, with its pronounced Hellenistic features, was the first to catch the eye of explorers with a background in classical art. But the art of an earlier period was quick to follow. When the Architectural Courts of the South Kensington Museum (now the Victoria and Albert Museum) opened in 1873, the European Court was balanced by an Indian Court containing a cast of the eastern gateway of the Buddhist stupa at Sanchi. The remains at Sanchi had been excavated by Alexander Cunningham and F. C. Maisey and presented in Cunningham's *The Bhilsa Topes.*[9] This included a thorough discussion of Greek sources. The archaeological surveyor for the North-West Frontier provinces (from 1868) was Henry Cole, and he wrote in the catalogue of the exhibition that 'the exceptional excellence of the Sanchi bas-reliefs suggest that Greek masons, or possibly designers, may have been called in to assist the great work. These bas-reliefs were executed between the end of the third century B.C. to [*sic*] about 78 A.D.'[10]

Next to arrive in South Kensington were painted copies of a number of the wall paintings from the Ajanta caves, the earliest of which date from the late third century BCE, while the better preserved ones are from the 460s CE. Thus all the Indian arts that received serious study at this time were of Buddhist origin, and displaced the Hindu gods with many arms that had become familiar at an earlier period, though the originals belonged to a later period than the Buddhist works. When J. Lockwood Kipling (the father of Rudyard) was appointed simultaneously the first director of the Mayo School of Industrial Art in Lahore and curator of the Lahore Central Museum – posts he held from 1873 to 1893 – his aim was to encourage the development of the indigenous arts of India through the study of the art of the past. The aim recalls that of the Society of Dilettanti, who sent Stuart and Revett to Athens in 1751 to 'improve the arts in England'. The collection Kipling assembled in the Lahore Museum is noted for its representation of Gandhara sculptures.[11] Again the Buddhist tradition is given primacy.

8. Fergusson 1868, 221; see Singh 2004, 262 and 333–4.

9. Cunningham 1854; see Singh 2004, 44–52.

10. Bryant and Weber 2017, 22–3; the quotation is from H. H. Cole, *Catalogue of the Objects of Indian Art Exhibited in the South Kensington Museum* (London: South Kensington Museum, 1874), 15.

11. Bryant and Weber 2017, 45–6. There is a charming photograph of the elementary drawing class in 1908 on p. 172.

Kipling senior's view of the purpose of the study of Indian art was not uncontested. His great opponent was Sir George Birdwood, who believed that it should be studied from a historical point of view, and preserved undamaged from the ravages of time. The past of India was, for him, a lost Golden Age to which he believed it was possible to return by a restoration of simple Indian village life. But his appreciation of the art of India was hostile, and extended to both Buddhist and Hindu traditions. As mentioned previously, he wrote in 1910, à propos a Javanese statue of Buddha,

> This senseless similitude, by its immemorial fixed pose, is nothing more than an uninspired brazen image, vacuously squinting down its nose to its thumbs, knees and toes. A boiled suet pudding would serve equally well as a symbol of passionate purity and serenity of soul.[12]

He also wrote that '[t]he monstrous shapes of the Puranic deities are unsuitable for the higher forms of artistic representation; and this is possibly why sculptures and painting are unknown, as fine arts, in India'.[13] For all that, Birdwood's ideal India was the Hindu India.[14]

Contemporaneously with the South Kensington exhibition appeared another substantial publication in Britain devoted to Indian art, namely James Fergusson's *Tree and Serpent Worship: or Illustrations of Mythology and Art in India*.[15] In a remarkably diffident preface Fergusson, who had started his Indian career as an indigo merchant, wrote that 'though fully aware of my shortcomings in a literary point of view, I felt that I probably was as competent as any other person I could name to treat of the subject of the Topes [stupas] and their sculptures from an architectural or archaeological point of view. Long personal familiarity with Indian monuments, and loving study of them, extending through half a lifetime, had given me a readiness in discriminating their peculiarities, which I am sorry to think very few possess'.[16]

Fergusson's title itself indicates that he knew (and could know) little of the historical and religious background of the Sanchi and Amaravati reliefs. Cunningham's work of 1854 on the 'Bhilsa Topes' (i.e., the stupas of Sanchi) was

12. Quoted in Smith 1962, 3.

13. Mitter 1977, 237, quoting George Birdwood, *The Industrial Arts of India* (London: Chapman and Hall, 1880), 125.

14. Bryant and Weber 2017, 16–17.

15. Fergusson 1868.

16. Ibid., vi. Fergusson's work was the inspiration for the researches of Singh 2004, which gives a sympathetic treatment.

the first serious examination of Indian Buddhism.[17] So Fergusson knew that these were Buddhist structures. But the subjects of the reliefs were only clarified through study of the comparable reliefs from Bharhut, discovered by Cunningham in 1873, which were accompanied by captions clarifying the connection with the life of the Buddha and the Jātaka stories.[18] The text of Fergusson's book is thus of merely historical interest as an exercise in anthropology, but the photographs and drawings were and are of great value as a record, and for their presentation of the gateway's complex iconographical schemes.

Fergusson, I think, makes no comment on possible Greek sources of this art, which he loved for its own sake; but Cunningham regarded the architecture of Kashmir as influenced by Greece, and he called the colonnaded style of Kashmiri temples 'the Arian Order'.

> The architectural remains of Kashmir are perhaps the most remarkable of the existing monuments of India, as they exhibit undoubted traces of the influence of Grecian art.... They cannot indeed vie with the severe simplicity of the Parthenon, nor with the luxuriant gracefulness of the monument of Lysicrates: but they possess great beauty; different indeed, yet quite their own.[19]

The presuppositions of such scholarship of the imperial period are easy to discern,[20] but they were not without historical foundation, since Greeks had been prominent, and indeed rulers, in the north-west for more than two centuries, and had extended diplomatic contacts as far as Vidiśa/Besnagar, which is only a few miles from Sanchi. (See chapter 13 above.) The emergence of Buddhist art, and of large-scale sculpture, at Mathura and elsewhere, is contemporaneous with Indo-Greek dominance. Many scholars, since Ram Raz whose monograph was published posthumously in 1834, have determinedly resisted the idea of outside influence on the arts of India.[21] Recent work (such as Quintanilla 2007) tends to play down any possibility of external influence on this newly emergent art form; yet classical scholars such as Boardman find it difficult to look at it and not to see Greek elements. Who is right?

17. Singh 2004, 44.
18. Ibid., 121.
19. Cunningham 1848, quoted in Singh 1994, 35.
20. See Hagerman 2013.
21. Singh 2004, 311–12.

The question is how far this interpretation of the origins of Indian, or at least Buddhist art, stands up to modern critical analysis. One should also distinguish between the different but related arts of architecture, figural and decorative sculpture, and painting. Within the latter two categories let us also make a distinction between style and content: techniques of carving, for example, are not the same as choice of subject matter, and choices of decorative detail lie somewhere between. Copying is not the only model: interaction and creative re-use may be more rewarding concepts. Foreigners, for example, are often represented with their distinctive features.[22] This kind of issue has arisen, for example, in the differing interpretations by John Boardman and Margaret Cool Root of the art of Persepolis, for the former sees similarities, and probably influence, in technique and style, while the latter denies influence, on the basis of pictorial content and ideological infrastructure; and both seem to be right.[23] The argument seems less developed in the case of India, and has been largely confined to generalities, and often to assertions.

Vincent Smith in 1889 argued that the art of Ajanta was impossible without Greek influence, while at the same time holding a low opinion of its quality.[24] (He might have changed his opinion after the recent cleaning and restoration of the paintings, which have led to Ajanta's inscription as a World Heritage site.) Frederick Asher, by contrast, says that 'one does not have to imagine foreign artists finally teaching the poor benighted Indians, ignorant of the potential of an image as an object of worship how to create such forms'.[25] The sarcasm may betray some unease, and he does go on to concede that the Kuṣāns (if no earlier kings) might have hired artists from distant regions thanks to the power of their empire. (In fact, Xuanzang states that Bactrian artists were employed to paint monuments under Kaniṣka, and a named Greek artist, Agiśala, is associated with the Kaniṣka reliquary from Peshawar.)[26]

A more nuanced approach arises from consideration of the appearance of life-sized sculptures of gods and mortals in India. Pāṇinī in the fourth century BCE discussed the making of images of deities for worship, and Quintanilla

22. Quintanilla 2007, 56 mentions the Phrygian caps worn by foreigners. One may think also of the 'Greek' musicians at Sanchi (fig. 15.6 below), or the 'Greek' warrior depicted at Ranigumpha Cave, Bhubaneshwar (fig. 13.8 above).

23. Cf. my brief discussion in Stoneman 2015 (173).

24. Mitter 1977, 268.

25. Asher 2006, 64.

26. Banerjee 1919, 118; Puri 2014, 321–2.

rightly takes this to show that sculpture existed before the stone tradition of Mathura. She writes, 'Once the artists at Mathura did begin to fashion architectural sculpture and iconic statues from stone, apparently during the mid-second century BCE, they did so in a style that conforms quite closely with the styles used by sculptors from other regions of the Indian subcontinent as well.' She calls this a 'pan-Indian unity of sculptural styles'.[27]

As early as the eleventh century CE, al-Biruni had observed the parallelism of the Greek and Indian employment of 'idols' in worship. After quoting at length from the *Bṛhatsaṁhitā* of the encyclopaedist Vārāhamihira (505–87 CE) on the practical instructions for making of 'idols' of particular gods, he goes on, 'the ancient Greeks, also, considered the idols as mediators between themselves and the First Cause, and worshipped them under the names of the stars and the highest substances'. He quotes from Plato and Galen on the power of idols, and concludes with a curious quotation from Aristotle:

> There is a treatise of Aristotle in which he answers certain questions of the Brahmins which Alexander had sent him.[28] There he says 'if you maintain that some Greeks have fabled that idols speak, that the people offer to them and think them to be spiritual beings, of all this we have no knowledge, and we cannot give a sentence on a subject we do not know'.[29]

Insofar as this story is anything more than a pious fiction by a pseudonymous Arab writer, it might indicate an interest among Indian thinkers in the theory of divine images. Could one imagine a Gupta craftsman seeking to understand the nature of his art through a contemplation of the power of Greek images of the gods? Vārāhamihira himself makes no such connection; however, Jawaharlal Nehru was prepared to believe that the idea of making images of the gods had come from the Greeks:

> It is an interesting thought that image worship came to India from Greece. The Vedic religion was opposed to all forms of idol and image worship. There were not even any temples for the gods ... But Greek artistic influence in Afghanistan and round about the frontier was strong and gradually it had its way.[30]

27. Quintanilla 2007, 35.

28. I do not think this treatise, which must have been one of the many attributed to Aristotle by Arab writers, is extant.

29. Al-Biruni 123–4, Sachau 1910, 11.124.

30. Nehru 2004, 161.

15.1 A *kīrtimukha* (lion-mouth) (as published in Slusser 2010).

Nehru also quotes with approval Tarn's pronouncement that 'what the Asiatic took from the Greek was usually externals only, matters of form; he rarely took the substance – civic institutions may have been an exception – and never spirit. For in matters of spirit Asia was quite confident that she could outstay the Greeks, and she did.'[31]

A symbol of this endurance might be seen in the *kīrtimukha*, the lion-face, which starts out as a Hellenistic fountainhead and becomes in Indian architecture the 'face of glory', a symbol of time, death and power: 'it is at once the work of destruction and creation, death and life, darkness and solar radiance ... a manifestation of the terrible power of the god.'[32]

If the Greek example did have something to do with the emergence of stone sculpture in the north-west, including Mathura, it is notable that Buddhist sculpture elsewhere, emerging at the same period, is comparable in style. Sanchi is already out of the Greek sphere, still more so Bharhut, Amaravati, Pitalkhora and Kanaganahalli.[33] The 'pan-Indian' unity of style observed by

31. Ibid., 160; I cannot trace these exact words in Tarn 1951, but cf. 407–8.

32. Slusser 2010, 212–15 (the quotation is from 214).

33. On these sites, see Deshpande 1959, with plates 50–66; Poonacha 2011; Knox 1992; Shimada 2013.

Quintanilla may best be explained by craftsmen travelling in a Buddhist network, all working in a style established in the north-west and Mathura.

The topics of architecture, sculpture in the round and relief sculpture, and painting should be examined separately.

Architecture

The city of Pataliputra is our only point of reference for Maurya architecture.

Pataliputra went beyond other contemporary Indian cities in including stone in its architecture. The roof of the huge audience hall was supported by eighty sandstone pillars; the one that remains exhibits the beautiful 'Maurya polish'. Most of the other structures were of wood. Nehru quoted Spooner's exclamation on the 'incredible state of preservation' of the massive wooden pillars sunk beneath the water-table, but remarked that, despite resemblance in layout to the *apadana* of Persepolis, a 'characteristically Indian artistic tradition is visible'.[34]

The question of the architectural antecedents of Pataliputra, raised here by Nehru, is a matter of debate.[35] Spooner observed the resemblance of the audience hall to the hundred-column hall of Persepolis. He also thought that the polish on the pillars was an Achaemenid technique, but the lustre of a Maurya sculpture is beyond that of anything at Persepolis, or indeed of any subsequent achievements of Indian art. Many details, however, seem Greco-Persian. In general Aśokan art displays strong Persian influence,[36] but there is Greek detail perceptible, as at Persepolis. One anta capital from the city contains Greek volutes, acanthus leaves, palmettes and a spiralling version of a key pattern, all in a rather un-Greek ensemble though the capital itself is shaped like a Corinthian one.[37] The evidence of the Sanchi reliefs for architectural styles a century after Candragupta, in the reign of Aśoka and after, is crucial. Many of these reliefs depicted trabeated buildings, with upper storeys and balconies, and arches of an Indian ogee pattern. The buildings depicted at Sanchi do not, however, look much like Greek buildings.

34. Nehru 2004, 137.

35. A valuable extensive discussion of the art of Pataliputra is Nilakanta Sastri 1957, 356–91.

36. Agrawala 1953, 70–1, quoting Sir John Marshall. The shining pillars may be echoed in *Mbh.* 2.3 in the description of the golden pillars of the Assembly Hall built for Yudhiṣṭhira by the architect Maya.

37. Drawing in Boardman 2015, 135. See further Huntington 1985, 45 on West Asiatic elements in the art of Pataliputra.

Sculpture

The picture becomes more complex when we turn to sculpture. It is not especially controversial – though still sometimes controverted – to propose Greek or Greco-Roman influence on the distinctive style of Gandhara art, broadly contemporary with the rise of the Kuṣān kingdom, from the first century CE onwards.[38] In this, classical proportions, regular features and Greek-style drapery and hairstyles bespeak a clear adoption of Greek norms, whether by Greek or Indian artists. The result is what William Dalrymple describes as a 'fusion' of Eastern and Western styles not equalled until Sir Edwin Lutyens's Delhi.[39]

My concern, however, is not so much with the art of Gandhara, as with the manifestations that preceded its rise. Large-scale art in painting and sculpture begins in India in the third or second century BCE, and Gandhara art is a later development of a style already taking shape in Mathura art, and, I would like to argue, at Sanchi and Ajanta.[40] I consider Mathura first.

Mathura

Mathura sculpture begins in the second century BCE, in the Indo-Greek period, with its heyday in the early centuries CE (the Kuṣān period). There is no archaeological evidence for urbanisation at Mathura before the third century BCE, but Megasthenes referred to it as a 'great city'.[41] Sculptures in the mottled red sandstone form the nearby Sikri quarries are found all over India, indicating that the Mathura school of sculpture was highly regarded. It was the most prominent artistic production centre from the second century BCE

38. Mortimer Wheeler in 1949 denied that the impetus to Gandhara art came from the Bactrian Greeks, and saw the influence as coming via the trade between Alexandria and Gujarat. However, no Gandhara sculptures have been found in Gujarat, and the distance from Gandhara itself is rather great. Lolita Nehru (1989) has provided a more or less conclusive discussion of the origins of Gandhara art in Greek art, and Boardman (2015, 162–7) follows this, pointing to the fact that clothing, for example, in Gandhara art is draped in the Greek not the Roman manner. For another example of Hellenistic influence on a Gandhara image, see Fischer 1987b. A useful survey with extensive illustrations is Bussagli 1996.

39. Dalrymple 1993, 84–5.

40. But note that Foucher thought Mathura art was later than Gandhara: Vogel 1910, 29. See also Banerjee 1919, 97–8.

41. Megasth. F 13a J, 50.13 Schw. Quintanilla 2007, 2 and 7 discounts the evidence of Megasthenes; but why? See also Thapar 1989.

onwards.[42] Its influence may have spread widely, since the Hāthigumphā inscription, also datable to this period (second century BCE), refers (line 12) refers to a Jina image from Kalinga.[43] Dating Mathura sculptures is not easy, though Quintanilla has established a number of criteria for stylistic development.[44] It is the earlier pieces (in her chronology) that concern us most.

Cunningham unhesitatingly saw the art of Mathura as influenced by Greece.[45] It represents a sharp break from Maurya art in scale, materials, and style. John Boardman has written, 'There is an even stronger classical element to be detected in what is otherwise a far more robustly Indian style than that of Gandhara.'[46] He judges it 'more varied' and 'more monumental'.[47] Characterising the Śunga school as a parallel phenomenon to that of Gandhara, he remarks that its human figures are 'more voluptuous even than the Hellenistic, if sometimes less anatomically plausible (a trivial point in the circumstances)'.[48] He seems to imply that the remarkably voluptuous proportioning of the female bodies is of less importance in determining the affinities of this art than the artists' concern for anatomical realism: faces, hands, postures and emotions, movement – all are there, and the fecund bosoms are perhaps just a hangover from the earlier mother goddesses. One of the most classical compositions of all, apparently a Dionysiac scene of a drunken woman from second-century BCE Mathura, still gives the woman a double-E cup size.[49] Men, by contrast, and elephants, are treated with loving attention to realistic detail and lively action.[50] Trees are instantly recognisable from their foliage. Perspective is first used soon after about 150 BCE.[51]

In addition, these sculptures include many small details of presumably Greek origin: girdles are tied in a 'Heracles knot'; the god Lakulīśa carries a club that assimilates him to Heracles. Heracles himself appears, wrestling with a lion, on a Mathura relief now in the Kolkata Museum, as well as wearing a

42. Cort 2010, 176 and 36 n. 30, quoting Quintanilla.

43. Ibid., 52; Kant 2000, 29 for the text of the inscription.

44. Cort 2010, 290 n. 14 suggests that her dates may be too precise.

45. Singh 2004, 68.

46. Boardman 1994, 137.

47. Ibid. 139.

48. Boardman 2015, 134.

49. Delhi Museum: reproduced in Smith 1992; Boardman 1994, 139 plate 4.82 and 2015, 136.

50. E.g., in a Śunga roundel, Delhi Museum.

51. Quintanilla 2007, 72 and fig. 69.

15.2 Bacchanalian group, from Mathura (National Museum, New Delhi).

lion-skin.[52] (In Gandhara, Heracles also becomes a model for depictions of Vajrapāṇi, as in a now-vanished relief from Hadda in Afghanistan, in which another of the Buddha's companions seems to bear the features of Alexander.) Bodies bend and bear their weight on one foot in a way that is first seen

52. Banerjee 1919, 95; Boardman 1994, plate 4.81.

15.3 The Heracles knot on the girdle of a Maurya statue of a *yakṣa* (Government Museum, Mathura).

in Hellenistic Greek sculptures such as the Cnidian Aphrodite. Nudity itself seems to have a different connotation from that of the mother-goddess type, and the *śālabhañjikā*s of Sanchi have a sensual allure that is absent from the Maurya figurines.

By the time of Kaniṣka, doctrinal changes in Buddhism had made it acceptable to depict the Buddha as an 'icon' and in scenes of his life and births. The process had begun at Sanchi and Kanaganahalli,[53] but is not much apparent at Mathura. Reliefs depicting narratives of the life of the Buddha, both in Mathura and in Gandhara, invite comparisons with Greek style. A key moment of the story is encapsulated in an image: the Indian tale is portrayed with 'classical restraint in the telling'.[54] It is possible that some of these reliefs may have been influenced by stage representations, or even by narrative texts of other kinds.[55] Greek influence might explain the popularity of Dionysiac

53. Infancy narratives feature, but not the Buddha's parinirvana: Quintanilla 2017, 126.

54. Banerjee 1919, 81.

55. Boardman 2015, 194 n. 441; Derrett 1992.

scenes, even though the vine was not cultivated in Mathura.[56] William Empson, in his interesting book *The Face of the Buddha*, suggests that 'the "mysticism of the East", as shown by the slim body and the half-shut eyes, seems to have been put in by the Greek artisans not by the Indians'.[57]

If Greek models did influence these artists, how did it happen? Quintanilla does not even mention the possibility of influence; the dominant mode in scholarship on Indian art is to be 'Greek-blind'. One possible model is as follows: there were Greek artists established in Bactria where they produced the dies for the beautiful coins of the Bactrian kings, from the moment of Diodotus' breakaway onwards. Their fame might have spread to the south and east and invitations might have been issued to come and work on buildings there, particularly if these artists were not employed full-time at the mint. In addition, Greeks were probably settling further south and east in India as early as the second century BCE, facilitating the advance of Greek armies when the Indo-Greek kingdoms expanded.[58]

Sanchi

The Buddhist complex at Sanchi is one of the earliest and most extensive such Buddhist settlements in central India.[59] It represents the institutionalisation of what had, to begin with, been a religion of wandering ascetics and mendicants. A mendicant order needs to settle near a city (in this case, Vidiśa/Besnagar) in order to have sufficient resources for begging; but Sanchi quickly developed into an economic centre in its own right, attracting artisans and traders in the same way as a Roman camp might do. The scale of the buildings at Sanchi dwarfs anything that had preceded them. The massive Stupa 1 dates from the third century BCE, and further stupas, temples and other buildings were added to the complex over the years. Stupa 1 is surrounded by a circuit wall with four tall gateways which are covered with a profusion of sculptural

56. Banerjee 1919, 81–2; Boardman 1994, 137. An example is the Silenus in Kolkata: Banerjee 1919, 88.

57. Empson 2016, 118.

58. See ch. 13 above.

59. It precedes Bharhut and Amaravati: Shimada 2013. Shaw 2007 is a comprehensive study. Another major Buddhist site, Kanganahalli in Karnataka, also begins in the second century BCE, and boasts a number of sculpted panels with captions in Brāhmī script, including one naming Aśoka; but the captions are of a later date (ca. 120 CE) than the images: Quintanilla 2017.The architectural depictions resemble those of Sanchi. See Meister 2007.

15.4 Aśoka swooning and supported by his two wives: relief from the south gateway, Sanchi.

decoration. Most of the relief panels depict scenes from the life of the Buddha and from the Jātakas (stories of the Buddha's previous births); others depict scenes of worship in rural settings as well as kings' processional departures from cities. One well-known scene depicts a king paying homage to a stupa; he seems to be overcome with emotion and is supported by two women, perhaps his wives. This figure is often taken to be a portrait of Aśoka, who is likely to have provided support for the foundation as he did for other śramana establishments such as the Barabar caves.[60] Fergusson wrote that 'the expression of the king's face is certainly that of a man in liquor';[61] but perhaps he has rather been overcome by religious emotion. Another intriguing scene depicts musicians. Described by local guides as 'Greek', the instruments they play include a thoroughly Greek aulos, as well as the kind of drum that may be seen in any musical performance in present-day India; they wear kilted tunics and boots. However, they also wear pointed caps which may be taken as *piloi* like those of the Dioscuri, but could perhaps also be seen as Scythian

60. His features resemble those of the figure captioned as Aśoka at Kanaganahalli: Quintanilla 2017, 122.

61. Fergusson 1868, 125 with plate xxx.

15.5 Aśoka in his chariot: relief from the south gateway, Sanchi.

15.6 Musicians, generally described as 'Greeks', from the eastern gateway at Sanchi.

15.7 Modern musicians photographed at the Craft Museum, New Delhi, 2016.
The drum is identical to that depicted on the Sanchi gateway.

pointed hats.[62] The features, too, could be interpreted as Central Asian rather than Greek.

Let us turn from the subjects depicted to the style of portrayal, and look first of all at the decorative details. The supporting columns of the buildings depicted sport capitals, echoed in the Sanchi gateways themselves, bearing addorsed lions and griffins in a very Persian style,[63] as well as extending the model to Indian creatures such as the nilgai and camel. The free-standing lions and the four addorsed lions of the 'Aśokan' capital on the Sanchi gateways – especially the details of their claws – convinced Cunningham that they were the work of Greek artists,[64] and, while one must admit that a lion is a lion is a lion, many of the details, such as the manes, do remind one strongly of Greek styles of carving. The lion, it may be observed, is essentially a West Asiatic royal beast, while the characteristic royal beasts of India are the elephant and the bull.[65] A visitor steeped in the traditions of classical art is also likely to look at the elaborate whorls on the end of some of the Sanchi beams and be reminded of Ionic volutes. The *śalabhañjikā*s (nymphs swinging from tree-branches) in the corners of some panels, here and at Bharhut, strongly resemble Greek winged victories.[66] Banerjee compares a *yakṣi* from Bharhut, about 300 BCE, with a caryatid.[67] The sculptures at Amaravati have also drawn comparisons with Greek work on account of their proportions.[68] There is, then, evidence here for detailing influenced by Greek art, often through Persian models, in the architecture of the third to second centuries BCE. Sir John Marshall, after drawing attention to such foreign motifs at Sanchi as the 'Assyrian' tree of life, the West Asiatic winged beasts, and grapes, went on to remark that 'nothing in these carvings is really mimetic, nothing certainly which degrades their art to the rank of a servile school'.[69]

62. I am not sure that the hats are tall enough for Scythians. Dhavalikar's guidebook to the site (2003, 59–60) describes the musicians as 'Śakas' (Scythians), though it seems a little early for Śakas to be prominent in this part of India.

63. Also to be seen at Ghazni: Levi 1972, 115.

64. Singh 2004, 50. Puri 2014, 321 mentions other Hellenistic motifs such as gryphons, sphinxes, tritons and erotes that appear in Buddhist art, though not all at Sanchi.

65. Huntington 1985, 45.

66. Boardman 2015, 133.

67. Banerjee 1919, 62.

68. Shimada 2013, 20, quoting Fergusson; though he entertains the possibility that influence here might have come through Arikamedu, after the establishment of trading relations with Rome.

69. Marshall 1917, 25.

15.8 Addorsed lions. Such figures are repeated several times at the stupa at Sanchi.

15.9 Griffins, from the stupa at Sanchi.

15.10 Nilgai, from the stupa at Sanchi.

15.11 An 'Ionic' volute, from the stupa at Sanchi.

15.12 *Śalabhañjikā* (tree nymph): Government Museum, Mathura.

What of the figures themselves? M. K. Dhavalikar is emphatic that there is no Hellenistic influence:

Although Marshall has inferred that these sculptures were the handiwork of artists from northwest India who were influenced by Hellenistic (Greek) art, it is apparent that they are closer in style to the Satavahana

> sculptures in Western Indian caves, and an inscription on the Southern Gateway even refers to the artist of a Satavahana king. The sculptures are clearly in the Satavahana style and there is no trace of any Hellenistic influence on them.[70]

The Sātavāhana dynasty of south India (including Kanaganahalli) originated probably in the third century BCE, though it may be later. But the point simply adds another body of evidence to the discussion. Should we see Hellenistic influence in Sātavāhana art as well?

Any assessment is bound to be subjective. I would simply like to suggest that, before these sculptures, there is no large scale sculpture in stone in India. The flexibility with which the human form is depicted is utterly different from the terracotta (and, rarely, bronze) figurines of mother goddesses and dancers that characterise the Maurya period. The one exception to this generalisation is the breathtaking life-size fly-whisk bearer from Didarganj in the Patna Museum, which is generally attributed to the Maurya period, both on account of its find-spot in the Patna district, and because of the 'Maurya polish' given to the stone of which it is made. However, Frederick Asher and Walter Spink produced forceful arguments that the statue is in fact of Kuṣān date: the polish need not be a sole prerogative of the Maurya period, and the monumentality of the figure, as well as its posture, are more reminiscent of Kuṣān art.[71] The case remains open, but there is no doubt that, if the sculpture is Maurya, it stands alone at a very great distance from all other Maurya art.

Painting: Ajanta

The earliest surviving paintings in India, apart from prehistoric stick-men and animals in the Bhimbetka caves near Bhopal, are the third- to first-century BCE wall paintings in the earliest Ajanta caves near Aurangabad (Maharashtra), especially Caves 9 and 10. The Ajanta caves were discovered for Western consideration on 28 April 1819 by a British officer, Captain John Smith. Remembered in family tradition for having bagged ninety-nine tigers, on the skins of some of which his grandchildren and great-grandchildren still played games, he was in pursuit of one of these beasts in the open jungle some sixty miles (100 km) from Aurangabad. The pursuit led him into an extensive horseshoe-shaped valley or ravine, at the apex of which he caught sight of a cave. Making

70. Dhavalikar 2003, 81. Contrast Banerjee 1919, 53.

71. Asher and Spink 1989.

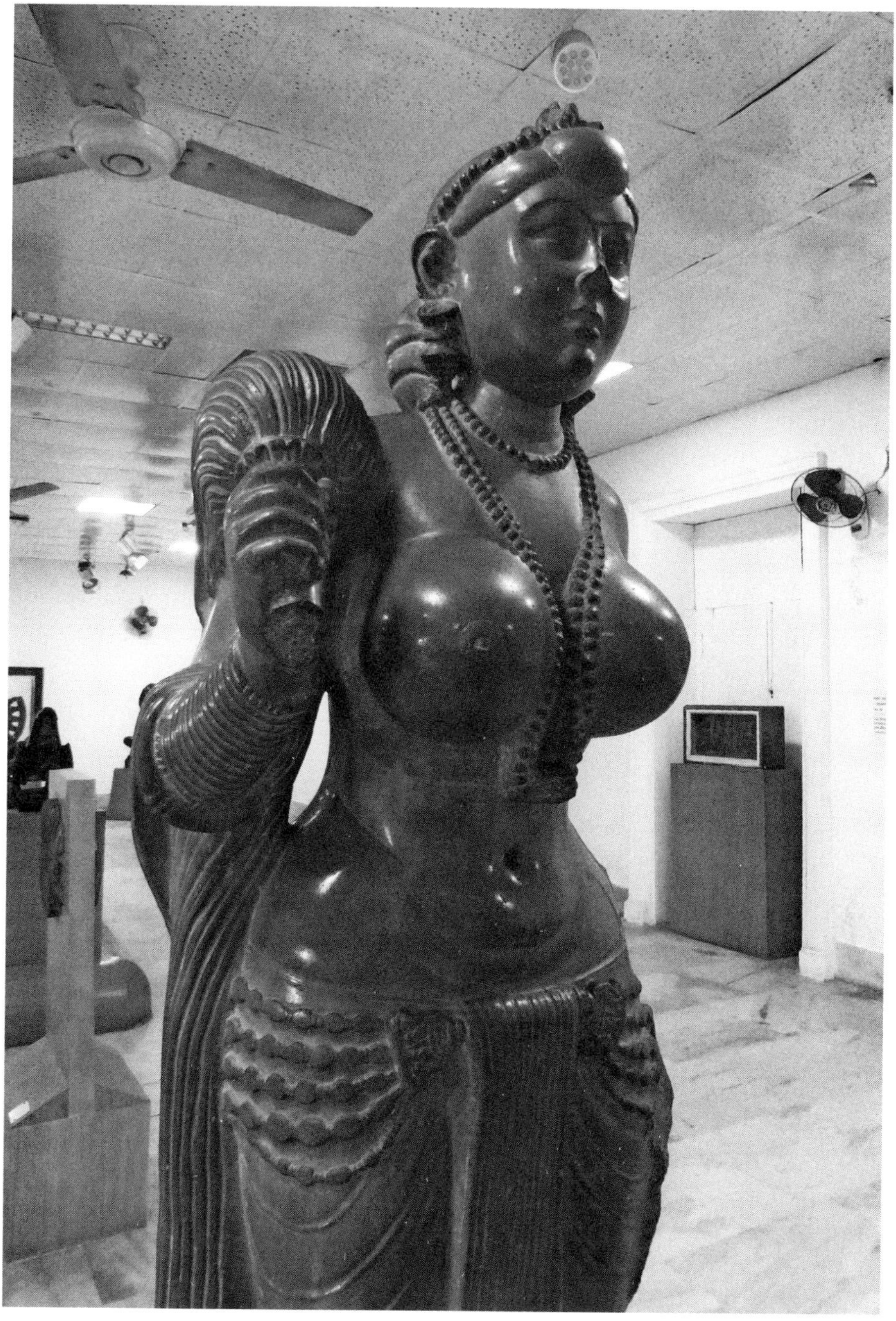

15.13 The 'fly-whisk bearer' from Didarganj (Patna Museum). This lifesize sculpture is often regarded as Maurya work because of its high polish, but may be several centuries later.

their way through the jungle of scattered trees and undergrowth, he and his companions came upon not one, but twenty-nine artificial caves. They had been hollowed out of the rock in the form of prayer-halls (*chaityagrihas*), some with colonnades and apses, all with sculptural decoration, including stupas carved from the living rock, and many with elaborately detailed wall and ceiling paintings in still vivid colours. Captain Smith carved his name in the paintwork in Cave 10: the clearly visible defacement is still pointed out to tourists.[72]

The caves quickly came to the attention of the Royal Asiatic Society, and in 1848 the Bombay Government set up the Bombay Cave Temple Commission, to undertake the clearing and preservation of the caves here and at Elephanta and in Aurangabad itself.[73] Captain Robert Gill was sent to make oil copies of the paintings for the South Kensington (now Victoria and Albert) Museum. All but five of the copies were destroyed in a fire in the Crystal Palace in Sydenham in 1866, but a second phase of copying was initiated by the Archaeological Survey of India and carried out by John Griffiths, superintendent of the Sir Jamsetjee Jeejeebhoy School of Art in Bombay, between 1872 and 1885. Griffiths regarded them as the best possible models for contemporary Indian students of art, with their 'human faces full of expression, limbs drawn with grace and action, flowers with blossom, birds which soar, and beasts that spring, or fight'.[74]

The well-watered and fertile valley had been settled by Buddhist monks from the third century BCE, and the first caves were excavated and painted in this and the following century, during the rule of the Sātavāhana dynasty (ca. 228 BCE to 224 CE). The later ones were all excavated and decorated in a brief phase of activity from 462 to 480 CE, under the rule of the Vākāṭakas.[75] All the paintings depict scenes from the life of the Buddha, and especially from the Jātakas, tales of the Buddha's previous births. Those represented include many famous stories as well as many less familiar ones, all of which have

72. My visit to Ajanta in February 2016 coincided with the arrival of a descendant of the captain, Colonel Martin Smith (who had played on the tiger-skin rug), who received a hero's welcome from the Maharashtra Government, and took the opportunity to apologise diplomatically for the vandalism: *Indian Express* 25 Feb. 2016 and *Aurangabad First*, 26 Feb. 2016.

73. Singh 2004, 56.

74. Quoted in Bryant and Weber 2017, 24; also in Banerjee 1919, 113.

75. Spink 2005–12; Singh 2012, 14–15. The most comprehensive scholarly presentations of the paintings are those by Schlingloff 1999 and Zin 2003. See also the photographic volume by Behl 2005.

15.14 A detail of one of the poorly-preserved paintings from the third century BCE in Cave 9 at Ajanta.

been identified by the scholarly labours of Walter Spink, Dieter Schlingloff and Monika Zin.[76] For example, in Cave 9 there is the story of the animals that brought gifts of food to a hermit: an otter brought fish, a jackal brought a stolen kebab, a monkey brought mangoes, but the hare had nothing to give: so he flung himself into a fire to offer his roasted body. In another painting, the king of the cuckoos lectures a relative on the depravity of the female sex. All the stories are depicted in loving detail: humans and animals are vividly and naturalistically portrayed, and the compositions are crowded with activity and large numbers of figures as well as, in later caves, architectural settings. The Cave 2 paintings (465–80 CE) are the most extensive, and the most visited and admired. Pilgrims from Thailand and Burma crowd the caves and pause for meditation.

These paintings spring into existence with no prior tradition of painting that we are aware of. They are contemporary with the Hellenistic paintings that have been emerging from the soil of Macedonia in tomb excavations in the last few decades. Is there a connection? No art historian since Vincent Smith seems to have given consideration to the matter.[77] Smith wrote that 'whoever seriously undertakes the critical study of the paintings of Ajanta and Bagh, will find, I have no doubt, that the artists drew their inspiration from the West, and I think he will also find that their style was a local development of the cosmopolitan art of the contemporary Roman Empire'.[78] In fact neither of the two phases at Ajanta is contemporary with the Roman art of the first to third centuries that Smith had in mind. Banerjee protested at the extremism of this view, arguing that 'Professor Smith … confuses the assimilation of foreign technique by Indian traditional craftsmanship with artistic inspiration'. But in fact technique is the heart of the matter. Given the connections of Greek rulers like Menander with the Buddhist movement, and the Greeks' presence in a region of India not far north of Maharashtra, it seems worth considering how the idea of adorning these caves with narrative wall paintings came about, and who the artists were who demonstrated and exercised the necessary techniques.

The Ajanta paintings are not frescoes, in the sense of paintings on wet lime plaster, as practised in the Italian renaissance. The walls are prepared with two layers of plaster followed by a thin coat of lime wash; over this the pigments

76. See also the cave-by-cave descriptions in Singh 2012.

77. Boardman 2015 does not discuss these paintings.

78. Quoted at Banerjee 1919, 118.

are applied with a binding medium of glue. The pigments used are white (lime, kaolin and gypsum), red and yellow (from ochres found nearby), black (from soot) and green (extracted from the locally-found mineral glauconite). The later paintings also employ the blue of lapis lazuli from the north-western frontier region.[79]

We are informed about the art of painting in ancient India by the *Citra Sūtra* which forms part of the *Viṣnudharmottara Purāṇa*.[80] Dating from the early centuries CE, this treatise was presumably produced for use by guilds of painters: it details the uses of colour and preparation of pigments (naming white, yellow, red, blue and black, with blue instead of the green employed at Ajanta);[81] three different ways of carrying out shading; and notes on the depiction of creatures of every kind.[82] 'Men in every land should be painted just as they are, after understanding their appearance, the way they dress and their colour'. 'Women's breasts should be beautiful, in proportion to the chest'. 'The learned [in painting] shows a city by means of various kinds of palaces of gods, palaces, shops, houses and magnificent highways'.[83] It details the nine 'sentiments' of painting: the erotic, comic, tragic, heroic, wrathful, terrible, disgusting, marvellous and tranquil (the last being suitable for ascetics).[84] Face-to-face figures in profile should be avoided.[85] Strikingly, it states that the closest art to painting is dance,[86] presumably because it depicts actions and emotions through frozen attitudes of the human form. In 1923, the ballerina Anna Pavlova performed an 'Ajanta Ballet' at Covent Garden, with choreography based on the gestures of the figures in the Ajanta caves.[87]

Tradition associates the origin of painting in India with the career of the Buddha, and the state of Bihar. A king wished to have a portrait painted of the Buddha, as a gift for another king. The painter who was assigned to the

79. Behl 2005, 34–5. White could also be made from *Ipomoea digitata*.

80. Translation: Mukherji 2001.

81. *Citra Sūtra* 40.

82. Behl 2005, 35.

83. *Citra Sūtra* 42.5, 37.4 and 42.62c–63b.

84. Ibid. 43. The range of subjects coincides neatly with those detailed in the first European (fifteenth century) handbook of art, Leon Battista Alberti's *De pictura* (*On Painting*: Alberti 1966): light, colour and perspective are deployed in the service of a lifelike depiction of movement and passions. A similar range of moods is listed in the treatise on dance and drama, the *Nāṭya Śāstra*.

85. Ibid. 43.21–22b.

86. Ibid. 35.

87. Behl 2005, 54.

task went to visit the Buddha, but was so overwhelmed by his subject's enlightened glow that he could not look at him. Instead they went to a nearby pond and the painter painted the reflection of the Buddha. The king, on seeing the portrait, understood that 'the world we see with our eyes is just a reflection of a reality that we cannot quite grasp'; though the story also shows that painting can be a route to understanding and contemplation of the ideal.[88] However, the Buddha is sometimes said to have disapproved of painting, and it was several centuries before he was ever depicted in art.[89]

No Greek text survives which discusses the techniques of painting in the manner of the *Citra Sūtra*, though such texts certainly existed.[90] Euphranor, for example, in the fourth century BCE wrote a treatise *On Colours*,[91] and there were many others, though the genre became less prevalent from the third century BCE.[92] The Peripatetic *On Colours* which survives is no kind of practical handbook, but a philosophical exploration of the physics, chemistry and physiology of colours as observed in nature.[93] To understand anything of Greek artistic theory we have to read back from the writings of critics and historians of art. From these it appears that the dominant concern of theorists is with *mimesis*, imitation, just as in Aristotle's *Poetics* a drama is an imitation of an action. Realism and naturalism, and the creation of an illusion, are to the fore. In addition, Greek criticism was concerned with the depiction of character and emotions (ἤθη and πάθη),[94] and Xenophon in a chapter of his *Memoirs of Socrates* presents a discussion of the extent to which a painter can depict 'lifelikeness' (τὸ ζωτικόν) and can convey the actions of the soul (τὰ

88. The story is told by Finlay (2002, 228–9), from whom my quotation is taken. Her source is Gega Lama, *Principles of Tibetan Art* (1983). This parable recurs many times in Sufi tradition in different forms, where it draws also on Plato's discussion of reflection and the eye of love in *Alcibiades*, and is one of the themes of Orhan Pamuk's novel *My Name is Red*; it is not the only Buddhist theme to enter Neo-Platonic tradition. (See Stoneman 2016d, with further references.) Its historicity is of course entirely debatable, but it is interesting that this Buddhist tale is the first Indian source to draw attention to the power of painting to aid contemplation. That power is amply exemplified in the paintings at Ajanta.

89. Soper 1950. *Jātaka* 4.228 forbids anthropomorphic images: see Coomaraswamy 1935.

90. A comprehensive survey of Greek painting techniques is Kakoulli 2009.

91. Plin. *NH* 35.111. Pollitt 1974, 247 – also on proportions, συμμετρία.

92. Pollitt 1974, 27.

93. Ed. C. Hampl 1811. The work may be by Theophrastus: Gottschalk 1964.

94. Cf. Plin. *NH* 35, 98.

τῆς ψυχῆς ἔργα τῷ εἴδει προσεικάζειν).[95] In more technical domains, there is a concern with *skiagraphia*, the use of line, and *skenographia*, 'scene-painting' or the depiction of large scale vistas. Vitruvius seems to be discussing perspective as an aspect of optics when he writes in *De architectura* that 'scaenographia is the semblance of a front and of sides receding into the background and the correspondence of all the lines [in this representation] to [a vanishing point at] the centre of a circle'.[96] Perspective was certainly 'discovered' and employed as early as the fifth century.[97]

Besides Pliny's history of painting in book 35 of his *Natural History*, an illuminating comment is found in Lucian's *Zeuxis*:

> As for the other aspects of the painting, those which are not wholly apparent to amateurs like us but which nevertheless contain the whole power of the art – such as drawing the lines with the utmost exactitude, making a precise mixture of the colours and an apt application of them, employing shading where necessary, a rationale for the size of figures [*sc.* perspective], and equality and harmony of the parts to the whole – let painters' pupils, whose job it is to know about such things, praise them.[98]

Philostratus in the second century CE showed a considerable interest in painting, and states that he had studied it for four years. In the preface to his *Imagines* he is concerned with imitation, light and shade and the depiction of moods and emotions:

> The invention of painting belongs to the gods – witness on earth all the designs with which the Seasons paint the meadows, and the manifestations we see in the heavens.[99]

This striking conceit is revisited in his *Life of Apollonius*, when the hero reaches India; while waiting for the king, and gazing at a series of relief panels representing the deeds of Porus, he starts a discussion with his companion Damis about art. Damis is made to propose that art is above all imitation, but when Apollonius asks whether the shapes formed in clouds are imitations made by God, Damis is abashed at the apparent conclusion that God must be

95. X. *Mem.* 3.10.5.
96. Vitruv. 1.2.2, cf. 7 *praef.* 11; Pollitt 1974, 231 and 234–5.
97. It was discovered again by Alberti: see Alberti 1966, 21 and 46–8.
98. Luc. *Zeuxis* 3, translated in Pollitt 1990, 152.
99. Philostr. *Im.* 1.1.

an artist, and admits Apollonius' alternative conclusion, that it is mankind's propensity for imitation that makes us see them thus. Imitation is thus presented as the essence of art, and can even be achieved in monochrome:

> If we draw one of these Indians with a white line, he will surely seem black; the snub nose, fuzzy hair, prominent jaws, and a look of surprise, as it were, in the eyes, lend blackness to the picture, and convey an Indian at least to an educated observer.[100]

Apollonius' vivid description of what appears to be an African physiognomy reminds us of the confusion exhibited by most ancient writers about the difference between India and Ethiopia; but the fact that it is an Indian work of art that starts Apollonius' train of thought is at least noteworthy. Apollonius returns to the subject of art when he visits Egypt,[101] asserting that the great cult statues of Greece are the result of imagination (*phantasia*) rather than imitation, while Egyptian depictions of the gods 'mock divinity rather than worshipping it'. *Phantasia* in Aristotle is 'the image-making faculty of the soul' and represents a step beyond the idea of the artist as a naturalistic copyist.[102]

Such considerations in Greek artistic theory seem at least congruent with the discussions in the *Citra Sūtra*. Whether there is any dependence of either on the other can hardly be asserted without a 'smoking gun' piece of evidence. But if Greek artists were instructing Indian artists, these are the matters they would have been discussing. Of course Italian Renaissance writers such as Cennino Cennini (fl. 1388–1427) and Leon Battista Alberti in 1435 came up with the same topics. (The Ajanta paintings have been compared with Lorenzetti, too.)[103]

Pigments, naturally, were not imported from Greece. The pigments used at Ajanta are all derived from local materials, whether earths or plants, plus lamp black. Blue, orange, brown, green and purple are the most common colours in the later Ajanta murals. The earliest ones also use considerable quantities of white (from roots of *Ipomoea digitata*, with occasional substitutes,[104] or from lime and gypsum),[105] but in these the other colours have been much

100. Philostr. *VA* 2.22.4.
101. Ibid. 6.19.
102. Arist. *de An.* 428a(ff.); Pollitt 1974, 52–5.
103. Griffiths, quoted in Banerjee 1919, 112–13.
104. See for example Nayar, Binu and Pushpangadan 1999. On Ajanta: Behl 2005.
105. Behl 2005, 34.

darkened, and are hard to study in the half-dark of the caves: reds, yellows, and browns are visible, as well as blues, so darkened now as to look black. Aided by some restoration in the last decade or so, vivid faces loom from the darkness, often topped by the voluminous turbans so typical of Maurya and Śunga figures, and shown in three-quarter profile like many of the faces in Macedonian tombs.

According to Pliny, some early Greek painters used a palette of only four colours – white, yellow, red and black – though it has been argued by Vincent Bruno that the black (*atramentum*) must actually have been a dark blue.[106] Pliny provides a detailed list of pigments used by the Greeks and Romans. Inevitably most of them are found within the region, such as Melian white, red ochre (very common) and black from soot. But he knows of Indian pigments, too; there is 'also an Indian black, imported from India, the composition of which I have not yet discovered'. Strong blues are the hardest colours to obtain in nature (lapis lazuli is the key ingredient), and Pliny has a good deal to say about indigo, 'a product of India, being a slime that adheres to the scum upon reeds. There is another kind of it that floats on the surface of the pans in the purple dye-shops, and this is the "scum of purple".'[107] Pliny shows marked distaste for this mucky but expensive substance, despite its known value also as a medicament for wounds. Later he is able to drag in Indian dyes as another illustration of his perennial theme of the moral decline of Rome caused by luxury:

> Nowadays when purple finds its way even on to party-walls and when India contributes the mud of her rivers and the gore of her snakes and elephants, there is no such thing as high-class painting.[108]

His account of indigo's production is far from accurate. It was an important dye in India – where it is called *nila* – from at least 3000 BCE. It is produced from the leaves of the indigo plant by long boiling and treading, and throughout most of its history the reducing agent used to turn it from a pigment to dye has been urine – which may explain some of Pliny's disgust, since the manufacture of indigo is certainly very smelly. (It is also very labour-intensive, and

106. Bruno 1977, 85–6, noting its use at Kazanlak; discussion of the four-colour palette at 53–9. Pollitt 1974, 111 argues for blue, and notes that blue is common on archaic Greek buildings. Croisille, comm. ad loc. suggests that it was copper sulphate, *noir de cordonnier*.

107. Plin. *NH* 35.25.43 and 35. 27.46.

108. Ibid. 35.32.50.

15.15 Wall painting of the rape of Persephone, from Tomb II at Vergina, Greece.

in 1859–60, just two years after the Indian Rebellion ['Indian Mutiny'], the conditions of near-slavery in which it was produced led to riots in Bengal.)[109]

Pigments, in short, were not imported from Greece. Their production from local materials in India will have been the result of local knowledge, and since the Indian love of clothing in bright colours was noted by the first Greek visitors to India, bright pigments must certainly have been available. Paints are easier to manufacture than dyes.

If there are conclusions to be drawn about possible influence of Greek techniques on the paintings of Ajanta they will come from considerations of technique and style, and the respective treatments of similar types of content: faces, costume and hairstyles; animals, trees and flora; architecture and the perspective of natural settings. There are, for example, architectural elements shown with 'correct' perspective, not unlike Pompeiian second- and third-style paintings. Figures mass in groups, a style not seen in the Hellenistic wall paintings known to me, though they seem to prefigure the Buddhist paintings from the caves on the Silk Road in Central Asia.

109. There is a lively account of indigo in Finlay 2002, 352–89. See also Balfour-Paul 1998. On the riots, Kling 1966.

The best comparanda for the kind of painting found at Ajanta would seem to be the very poorly-preserved paintings in the tombs at Vergina, as well as more recently discovered Macedonian tomb-paintings which have not yet all been published. Such painting began in Macedonia in the late fourth century BCE, and the artists were imported from Greece proper, from Corinth and Sicyon.[110] No doubt they then trained local artisans, some of whom could have travelled with Alexander to India. Both the hunt fresco and the Persephone fresco from Vergina are scenes of vigorous action.[111] The figures in the hunt fresco are drawn with distinct outlines, while those in the Persephone fresco make use only of light and shade to create volume: the head of Hades, for example, uses no outlining at all, though the chariot wheels are clearly delineated.[112] The Ajanta figures are all clearly outlined. Benoy Behl writes that 'there are no true shadows in the paintings, but the most subtle nuances of shading, which are achieved through the use of an almost imperceptible deepening and lightening of the same colour, persuade the eye of the roundedness and volume of forms'.[113] Behl also draws attention to the use of foreshortening, mentioned in the *Citra Sūtra*, and other aspects of perspective. The foreshortening of figures recalls that of several of the hunters in the hunt fresco; the preference for three-quarter depiction of figures and faces is also common to both the Indian and the Macedonian works. Facial features and skin colour clearly differ between the two examples, since both traditions strive for naturalism of representation. Many of the Ajanta figures are naked (as are the Vergina hunters), but the depiction of drapery seems to follow conventions similar to Greek painting. (Later Gandhara sculptures are noted for their resemblance to the drapery style of Greek art.) Gesture and movement are naturalistically evoked in both. The horses (not native to India) are Greek in style.[114] Sir John Beazley once wrote of Greek vase-painting that 'you cannot draw better, you can only draw differently': to my eye the paintings at

110. Palagia 2017.

111. A convenient presentation of the Vergina hunt is Franks 2012. There is a hunting scene at Ajanta too, in Cave 9: Schlingloff 1999, 26 no. 6. It is more crowded with figures than the Vergina example. Cf. Spink 2005–12, 2.254.

112. Incised outlines can be observed, as noted by Kakoulli, but I do not know whether similar marks have been observed at Ajanta.

113. Behl 2005, 37.

114. Moraes 1983, 198 has an anecdote about a connoisseur arguing that statuettes of horse and rider are essentially Greek or Persian.

Ajanta could have been made by a Greek (Macedonian) observing intently the Indian life around him. At present it seems impossible to do more than speculate, but the fact that wall-painting in India begins at a time when Greeks were dominant in the north-west of the country, and among Buddhists, with whom Greeks seem to have close relations, does suggest more than coincidence with regard to the origin of this Indian art.

16

Apollonius of Tyana and Hellenistic Taxila

Beyond Indus and its tribute rivers, . . .
Where ever lies, on unerasing waves,
The image of a temple, built above,
Distinct with column, arch, and architrave,
And palm-like capital, and over-wrought,
And populous with most living imagery,
Praxitelean shapes, whose marble smiles
Fill the hushed air with everlasting love.

—SHELLEY, *PROMETHEUS UNBOUND* 3.4.155–66

THIS BOOK BEGAN WITH ONE MAN who travelled to the ends of the earth, and I shall end it with another. Alexander travelled further east than anyone from Greece had done before: not only did he reach the eastern borders of the Achaemenid empire, beyond the Indus, but he was ready to travel beyond that to the end of the world, which he believed to be not far away.[1] In addition, he sent out expeditions of exploration into Central Asia, to the sources of the Nile, and perhaps to Britain.[2] According to his 'Last Plans', he was planning the conquest of Italy, of Carthage and of Arabia.

These plans which remained only dreams and were frustrated by his early death became fictional reality in the romance that began to grow up around

1. Arist. *Mete.* 1.350a.19–25.
2. Burstein 2010; on Pytheas, see ch. 1 above.

his career within fifty years of his death. In the Greek *Alexander Romance*, the hero visits the kingdom of Candace on the upper Nile, he travels far into Asia 'in the direction of the Plough', and his early campaigns include both Italy and Carthage. In a medieval Jewish story, later rewritten as a Christian tale, his journey to the East led him along the Ganges to the walls of the Earthly Paradise; and in the early modern Greek *Phyllada* it is the 'Blessed Ones' who show him the way to Paradise, though he can never get there.

In the late antique lambda-recension of the *Romance*, Alexander adds to his exploits a flight into the heavens and a descent into the sea, showing that there is no part of the universe that he has not visited and, in some sense, 'conquered'. In the thirteenth-century Persian retelling by Amir Khusraw of Delhi, the diving bell in which he descends into the ocean becomes the mirror which shows him the universe and the limitations of his mortal powers.[3]

The 'Blessed Ones', whose name is borrowed from the early Christian story of the journey of Zosimus to the land of the Blessed, are the latest incarnation of the naked philosophers of Taxila, who became the Brahmans of the *Romance* and the 'Sages of the South' of the Hebrew versions. Alexander's visit to the Brahmans is always the moral heart of his fictional career, where the man of power and action is brought face to face with contemplative quietude, and gains some inkling of that 'spiritual beauty' that Sri Aurobindo claimed no Westerner could ever understand about India.

In the first century CE the sage Apollonius, from the city of Tyana in southeastern Asia Minor, gained fame for his wisdom and his extensive travels. In the following century Philostratus wrote a fictionalised biography of the sage, in which it is scarcely possible to determine where fact ends and fiction begins. According to this biography, Apollonius travelled to the Far East and had discussions with the Brahmans of Taxila (though he declared that the true *gymnoi* actually dwelt in Egypt, and Heliodorus two centuries later relocated them even further south, in Ethiopia). Apollonius outdoes Alexander by travelling as far as Ethiopia and western Spain: even Heracles had only spanned the world from east to west. His ambit is the entire Roman empire. Like Alexander, he makes his pilgrimage to the abode of the gods, but, unlike Alexander, he achieves a divinity of his own.[4] He is the prototype of the late-antique Holy Man who channels the divine into human affairs. Unlike Alexander, who is overawed by the wisdom of the Brahmans, Apollonius as a philosopher

3. Stoneman 2016d; forthcoming b.

4. Elsner 1997.

knows that his role is to be an adviser to kings, and it is integral to the plot that not only do the kings in the East make *proskynesis* to the Brahmans, and that Apollonius holds his own and more in discussion with the Brahmans, as well as being looked up to by the king, Phraotes,[5] but that on his return to the West he faces down the emperor of Rome. The sage, like the king, is an intermediary between gods and men.[6]

Though presented as a second, 'holy' Alexander by Philostratus, Apollonius is also important as a historical 'witness' for Hellenistic Taxila. How we judge this importance depends on our assessment of the historicity of Philostratus' account. Did Apollonius actually go to India? Is the character Damis, whose book was given to him by his patron Julia Domna, and who provided Philostratus with most of his information, a genuine person or a figment of Philostratus' imagination? If genuine, were his memoirs fiction?[7] Did Philostratus have access to a description of Taxila, from whatever source? Is his description of historical value? These questions have been variously answered, answers to the last ranging from the generally accepting (Anderson; Charpentier)[8] to the completely sceptical.[9] The most recent assessment, by Balbina Bäbler, concludes that Philostratus was working with an actual description of contemporary Taxila, but adapted it for his fictional purposes. His historical and topographical coordinates are more accurate than those of, say, St Luke's Gospel,[10] but fall short of the meticulous positioning of Tolstoy's *War and Peace*. He cites some earlier sources, such as Scylax,[11] and is clearly deriving most of his information from other written sources, many of which we can identify (see below). There is little to suggest the eyewitness, unlike, say, Achilles Tatius' account of Alexandria in *Leucippe and Clitophon*.

Achaemenid Taxila, the city that Alexander visited (and which I, alas, have not), was without doubt one of the larger cities in the eastern Achaemenid realm and an altogether exceptional place by Indian standards. The ruins today cover an area of more than twelve square miles (31 km^2).[12] The name

5. Philostr. *VA* 2.27.

6. Flinterman 1995, 178–9, quoting Porphyry *Quaestiones Homericae*.

7. So Smith 1914.

8. Charpentier 1934, c: 'mostly trustworthy' in book 2, while book 3 is valueless. Cf. Drew 1987, 89 on the Temple of the Sun.

9. Smith 1914: 'all demonstrably false'.

10. Lane Fox 1991.

11. Philostr. *VA* 3.47.

12. Dani 1986, 79. The plentiful illustrations in Nadiem 2008 are also helpful.

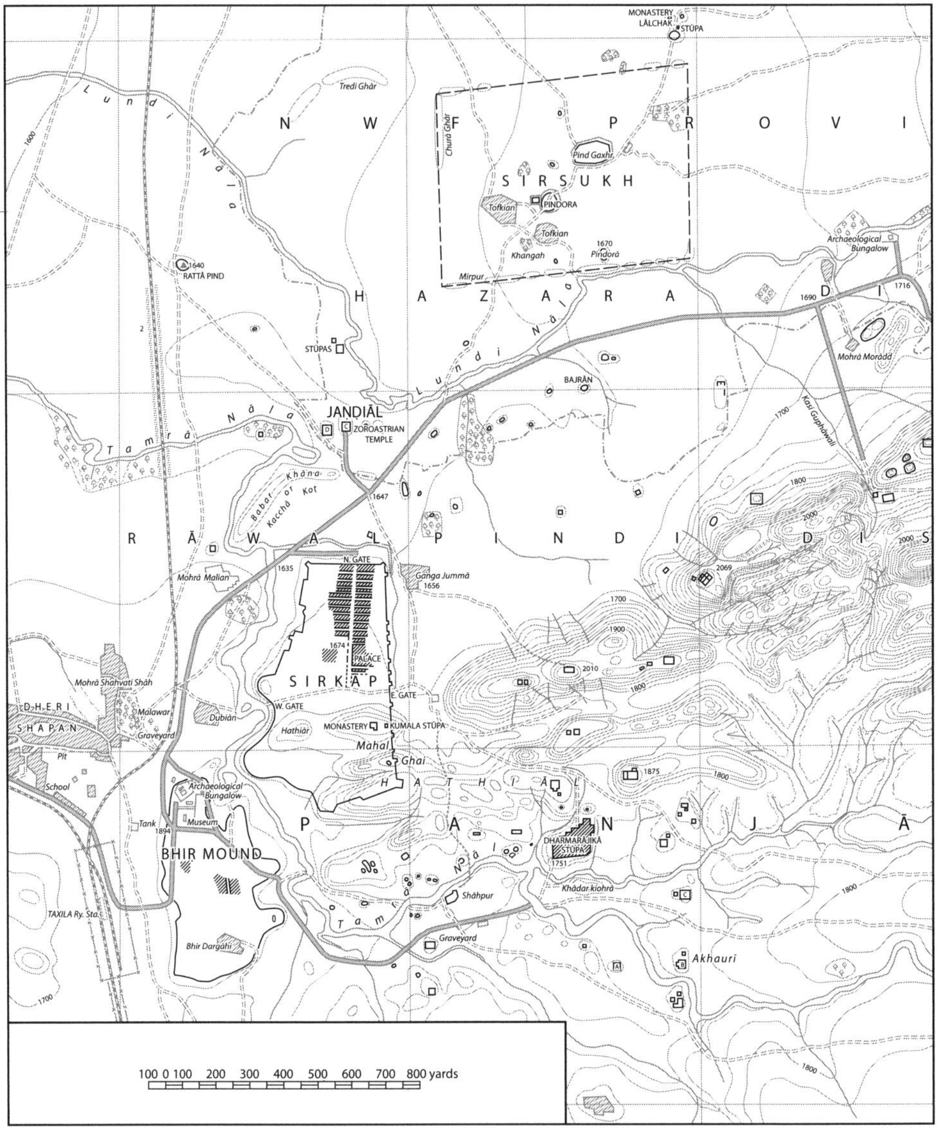

16.1 Plan of Taxila (after Marshall 1960).

Takshasila may derive from Taksha, a Naga king (*sila* means 'hill'), and there is evidence of settlement on the site from 3000 BCE. It stands at the junction of three trade routes.[13]

Arrian calls it 'a great and prosperous city, the largest of all between the Indus and the Hydaspes':[14] it was under the control of a *hyparch* or governor, though by Alexander's time it was ruled not by a Persian satrap but by a subordinate of King Omphis (as the Greeks called the ruler of Taxila). This Achaemenid city was located by its first excavator, Sir John Marshall, on Bhir mound. Excavation has uncovered levels from the sixth and fifth centuries BCE, with a few Achaemenid objects. There is one straight street, while the rest are 'meandering' (Dani). Dani locates the Achaemenid city on Hathial mound B, however.[15] This settlement has been variously described by modern excavators as 'unplanned' in the oriental style (Dani) and 'a shambles' (Mortimer Wheeler).[16]

In the second century BCE a new Greek city with a Hellenistic grid plan was built at Sirkap on the Hathial hill, bounded by the Gau rivulet to east and north.[17] The city was extended by the Śakas, and some scholars, following Erdosy, have preferred to date it all in the Śaka period, from the first century BCE onwards. Tarn attributed the building of this city to Demetrius, but remarked that the only Greek thing about it was the grid plan, which is also described by Philostratus (most of the houses had basements, but did not rise to more than one storey above ground);[18] for otherwise it lacked any of the typical Greek buildings of a *polis*, and even the circuit wall was only of mud until the Śakas built a stone one. 'The transference of the population of Old Taxila, even to their University and their gods, seems to have been so complete that there was no real break in the continuity of the city's life.'[19]

Subsequent research has deepened our understanding of Hellenistic Taxila,[20] with work at Hathial mound turning up some Indo-Greek coins (but more

13. Dar 1984, 1–6; on trade routes see Lahiri 1992; Singh 2009, 288–91, 407; ch. 5 above.

14. Arr. *Anab*. 5.8.2.

15. Bäbler and Nesselrath 2016, 63.

16. Dani 1986, 80 and 83.

17. Ibid., 88.

18. Philostr. *VA* 2.23.

19. Tarn 1951, 179. Fussman too regards Sirkap I as basically Indian in appearance: cited in Callieri 1995, 295–7.

20. Dar 1984; Dani 1986; Callieri 1995; Rapin 1995.

Śaka ones).[21] Several monumental buildings belong to the Sirkap I period. First is the apsidal temple in the city centre.[22] Second is the temple at Jandial C, further north than Sirkap, which has a Greek plan and peristyle, and thus resembles that in Philostratus' description (see below).[23] This is the only peristyle temple in all of the subcontinent. Another temple, slightly to the west of this one, remains a puzzle.[24] A third major temple, at the village of Moḥrā Madiārān, just west of the city walls, is to be dated after ca. 50 BCE: it is on a Near-Eastern courtyard plan with six Ionic columns in the sanctum. 'But it is a debased Ionic order more like the local version of the original. The bases . . . are otherwise true Attic'.[25] It has been plausibly interpreted as a Zoroastrian structure.

An earthquake in Taxila in about 20–30 CE destroyed many buildings,[26] including, according to Dar, the Jandial C temple, which would therefore not have been in existence when Apollonius visited, if he did, in the mid-first century CE. Dar thinks that he visited the later temple at Mohra Madiārān.[27] At all events, if Apollonius visited Taxila, it was Sirkap II (post-earthquake) to which he came.[28]

The Sirkap II period has yielded a number of Greco-Roman finds: amphorae, silver tableware with Dionysiac scenes, ivory handles depicting Indian gods in Greek clothing.[29] Such finds are quite typical of Parthian sites: Parthian rule displaced the Śakas early in the first century CE. King Gondopharnes can be dated to about 20–46 CE. Around the end of the first century, the Parthians were displaced by the Yueh-chi nomads, of whom the dominant group were the Kuei-shang, better known as the Kuṣāns, who continued to rule parts of north-west India well into the third century CE.[30]

There is no doubt that Taxila was an important city throughout these centuries, and that if Apollonius had gone to India he would have visited it, not just for its associations with Alexander and the naked philosophers, but be-

21. Dani 1986, 96.

22. Colliva 2007.

23. Philostr. *VA* 2.20; Dani 1986, plate 30.

24. Dar 1984, 30–3.

25. Ibid., 109–10, quoted at Dani 1986, 114.

26. Marshall 1960, 29; Dani 1986, 95.

27. Dar 1984, 60–2; Rapin 1995, 282–4.

28. Bäbler and Nesselrath 2016, 69.

29. Ibid., 71–2.

30. A thorough recent treatment is Puri 2014.

cause of its still-flourishing reputation as a university town. When the Chinese pilgrim Xuanzang visited it in the sixth century CE (he called it Chu-cha-shi-lo) it was dominated by its Buddhist monastery; this will have developed partly as a result of Kuṣān enthusiasm for Buddhism, and no doubt has something to do with the form (in our sources)[31] of the story of Candragupta's being sent there to study by Canakya. But in the first century CE Buddhism is likely to have been just one element of intellectual life in Taxila.

The questions that arise regarding Apollonius' visit to Taxila – and indeed the rest of Philostratus' account of his life – are, first, whether Apollonius went there; second, what the status is of his companion Damis, whose diary Philostratus claims to be following; and third, whether Philostratus make use of another account of Taxila, if not Damis', to construct his description. The enigmatic Damis has often been met with complete scepticism by modern scholars, and as a corollary any historicity in the visit of Apollonius to Taxila is denied. Fussman, Rapin and Bernard all regard the visit as fiction. Various proposals have been made to explain how Philostratus came by the alleged work of Damis: either he is an invention by Philostratus himself, or his account was a forgery by which Philostratus was more or less taken in. Bowie has suggested that his name may conceal that of Philostratus' preceptor Flavius Damianus of Ephesus, who might have given Philostratus some information about Apollonius, though it is impossible that he could have accompanied him.[32] Anderson is reluctant to dismiss Damis as entirely fictional, though his existence remains problematic.[33]

It is very intriguing that the names of Apollonius and Damis, and also of Iarchas and Phraotes, their Eastern hosts, appear in a Sanskrit work of uncertain date, the *Āgamaśastra* of Gauḍapāda, under the names Apulunya and Damīśa. This is reported in the biography of the sage Gauḍapāda (perhaps sixth century CE) in the *Jagadgururatnamālāstava* of Sadaśiva-brahmendra,[34] in which he is described as 'the preceptor of mystics including *apalūnyadamīśādyaparāntyayogibhiś ca*', that is, 'Apollonius accompanied by Damis'. It also says 'his feet were adored' by Ayārcya, who seems to be the Greek Iarchas;

31. Mainly Hemacandra: see ch. 5 above.

32. Bowie 1978, 1670, 1681 and 1687; mentioned with approval by Dzielska (1986, 28).

33. Anderson 1986, 169. C. M. Wieland, in his novel about Apollonius *Agathodämon* (1799), had his narrator exclaim, 'So dumpf und idiotisch Damis war, so wäre doch zu wünschen, wir hätten sein Buch noch gerade so von Wort-zu-Wort wie ers geschrieben.'

34. This work is the earliest exposition of Vedanta-Veda, influenced by Buddhism. See Bhattacharya 1943, lxxii–iv.

and the Phraotes, king of Taxila, whom Philostratus names, appears in the Sanskrit text as Prāvrti.[35] This proves at least that Philostratus' work was known in India some time after its appearance: to regard it as independent evidence for the visit of Apollonius and Damis to Taxila would be extravagant.

But the existence of Damis is irrelevant to our main question: whether Philostratus' description of Taxila can be regarded as in any way historical. Philologists have perhaps been more enthusiastic about its possibilities than the archaeologists, while displaying a proper caution.[36] Philostratus describes a 'symmetrically fortified' Greek city, containing a palace where the ruler lived. 'In front of the walls' was a temple, slightly less than one hundred feet (30 m) in length and built of limestone with shells embedded in it. It had many columns, and the interior walls were adorned with bronze panels illustrating the deeds of Alexander and Porus. 'On them, in brass, silver, gold and dark bronze, there are depicted elephants, horses, soldiers, helmets and shields, with spears, javelins, and swords all in iron.' Somewhat later, Philostratus mentions also a 'shrine of the Sun', where there stood statues of Alexander and Porus. The walls of the shrine are said to be of red stone, while 'the image itself was of mother-of-pearl, made in the symbolic shape that all barbarians use for their holy objects'.[37]

Marshall believed that the remains of the royal palace could be identified on Hathial hill, at the far southern end of Sirkap's main street, but Bernard rejected this hypothesis: the building does not resemble a palace, and could be, for example, a mint or administration centre.[38] If Bernard is right, there is no other candidate for a palace, and Philostratus' statement is invention. The temples too are enigmatic. Philostratus' classical-style temple seems at first glance to be a description of the Jandial C temple, which is rectangular and has a peristyle, though of pilasters rather than free-standing columns.[39] The dimensions of this temple are somewhat larger than Philostratus' 'one hundred feet'; but *hekatompedon* denotes a style of temple rather than necessarily its exact dimensions, and this imprecision may be allowed to pass. However, there are no reliefs such as Philostratus describes associated with this temple.

35. This reference was first noted by Bowersock et al. (1985, 657), and briefly discussed by Dzielska (1986, 29). Apollonius also features in Sasanian literature: Manteghi forthcoming.

36. Bäbler and Nesselrath 2016 provides a valuable up-to-date survey.

37. Philostr. *VA* 2.2.20–4.

38. Dani 1986, 93.

39. Rapin 1995, 287–9.

The second temple, at Mohra Madiārān, does contain fragments of reliefs, which Dar believed were the basis for the description of the bronze panels in Philostratus:[40] he proposed that these were actually Buddhist reliefs depicting the attack on the Buddha by the army of Mara, and further that the temple contained an image of the Buddha.[41] Philostratus calls this second temple a temple of the Sun, which Dar finds plausible: a statue of the Sun god was in fact found at Sirkap.[42] The term could also denote a Zoroastrian temple, since classical writers generally believed that Persians worshipped the sun. But if it was a Zoroastrian structure, it can have contained no image of any kind, as Philostratus says it did, but should instead have contained an eternal flame (which perhaps a classical author would not bother to mention). It may be that an earlier Zoroastrian temple was redeployed for Buddhist worship; Philostratus might then be reporting on both phases of the temple simultaneously.

There would be no surprise in finding Zoroastrians at Taxila, or Buddhists, though perhaps not both in the same temple at the same time. In support of Zoroastrian citizens, Bäbler draws attention to the absence of burials at Taxila, but this could be explained, not just by Zoroastrian exposure of the dead, but by Indian cremation and disposal in the river. Recall that Alexander's first question to the naked philosophers in the *Romance* is, 'Do you have no graves?'[43]

In short, Philostratus' information looks as if it is based on an actual account of the buildings of Taxila, but he has freely adapted it to create a description that fits the requirements of his narrative and his presentation of Apollonius. He cannot be used as independent historical evidence.

The same principle seems to apply to the other details of Apollonius' Indian sojourn, such as the name of Phraotes. No such king is known, but Tarn suggested that the word is actually a title of Gondopharnes, *aprahita*, 'unconquered'. This was rejected by Bernard, but Bäbler prefers to admit its possibility.[44] Greeks often seem to have interpreted titles in this region as actual names; one thinks of 'Taxiles' in the Alexander historians, and 'Mories' for the Maurya prince Candragupta. Bäbler reminds us that even Aśoka is not that ruler's actual name.[45]

40. Dar 1984, 61–2.

41. See Bäbler and Nesselrath 2016, 79–88.

42. Dani 1986, plate 36.

43. *AR* 3.6.

44. Tarn 1951, 341; Bäbler and Nesselrath 2016, 88–9.

45. Bäbler and Nesselrath 2016, 89.

Later, Philostratus describes the altars that Alexander erected on the Hyphasis. These have been discussed above, in chapter 2. Again, the description seems devised to reflect a particular image of the East as it relates to Apollonius: it is not a historical account of Alexander's constructions. The dedications are chosen to fit Alexander's known interests – Ammon, Apollo, Heracles and Olympian Zeus; the Cabiri of Samothrace because his parents met there (or because they are identified with the Dioscuri, with their dynastic connection with the Macedonian royal house); Athena Pronoia may recall the Pronoia, the 'Providence Above' of the *Alexander Romance* (though Bäbler regards this title as another Delphic detail, recalling the temple of Athena Pronaia there).[46] The dedication of the last altar, to Helios, is invented, according to Bäbler, in line with Apollonius' own devotion to the Sun.[47] Once again it is clear that we are dealing with a fictional construction by Philostratus, not a historical account.

If we cannot use Philostratus' descriptions as evidence for the history and appearance of Hellenistic Taxila, that does not diminish the importance that Apollonius' sojourn holds in the plot of the *Life* as a whole, nor its importance as a kind of summation of the Greek experience of India.

What Apollonius Learned in Taxila

India dominates the action of the *Life of Apollonius* throughout the second and third of its eight books. The geographical setting is enhanced by the introduction of many from the repertoire of strange and wild animals and creatures, largely from the Alexander historians but also from the *Romance*, which must, it seems, have been circulating in some form when Philostratus was writing. Elephants, of course, make an early appearance (2.12–16).[48] Since their first encounter with Westerners in Alexander's army, elephants had become quite familiar to the Greek and Roman world, and Philostratus gives Apollonius the opportunity for a discourse on some of their remarkable characteristics, some of which may raise an eyebrow now. The great size of the Indian elephant in comparison with the Libyan (i.e., the small African elephant, now extinct)[49] is noted, as well as its use in battle: not only does it carry a

46. Ibid., 92–4.
47. Philostr. *VA* 2.28, etc.
48. Ibid. 2.12–16.
49. Scullard 1974.

howdah occupied by up to fifteen warriors,[50] but it uses its trunk as a hand for throwing its own supply of javelins. Elephants were famed for longevity, so it is not surprising that Apollonius and Damis encounter one in Taxila, named Ajax, which had taken part in the battle of Porus against Alexander some 350 years earlier. In chapter 13 Philostratus displays some of his own learning about elephants, derived from a book by King Juba of Mauretania, but in the following chapter Apollonius draws his own lessons from the behaviour of the elephants, their intelligence, their care for their offspring (which he finds remarkable, even though it is shared, as he goes on to expound, with the rest of the animal kingdom), and their capacity for rational behaviour in their method of crossing rivers. (The smallest goes first, and if that gets over safely, the rest know they will have no trouble.)

The elephant topos disposed of, the narrative moves on to the giant snakes and dragons of the river Acesines, for which Philostratus cites two Alexander historians, Nearchus and Orthagoras. Crossing the Indus, the pair observe many hippopotamuses and crocodiles,[51] and flowers that resemble those that grow in the Nile (i.e., lotuses). Arrival in Taxila ensues, with a brief memoir of Porus and an episode in which Apollonius and Damis conduct a quasi-Socratic dialogue about the art of painting (see chapter 15 above). They are then invited to the palace of the king. The fact that the palace is no more splendid than any of the other houses in Taxila is explained by the king's quality as a philosopher: 'our customs are modest, and I observe them even more modestly', he tells the sage. 'I have more than any human, but need little, considering most things to belong to my own friends.' (If Dandamis lived in a palace, this is how he would speak.) His diet consists of vegetables, 'the pith and fruit of date palms, and everything that the river nourishes'. Soon the king reveals himself as a speaker of Greek, and addresses Apollonius in that language. In Alexander's time, of course, it was only the trees that could speak Greek, but three centuries of Greek presence have made the attainment common in these parts. The king also explicitly acknowledges the sage as his superior,[52] a reaction Dandamis failed to elicit from Alexander.

Over dinner, at which the guests are offered not only fish and fowl but whole lions and roast loin of tiger, and during which they are entertained by

50. Trautmann 2015, 230–3, notes that the use of the howdah or tower came in with Pyrrhus, and it is possible that India adopted it from the Hellenistic armies. Whether it would normally carry as many as fifteen warriors is unknown.

51. Philostr. *VA* 2.19.1.

52. Ibid. 2.27.2.

acrobats, the king explains to Apollonius the exceptional interest of Indians in philosophy, which among other peoples is 'something filched from others, which people wear like an ill-fitting garment', while in fact they are devoted to gluttony, sex and fine clothing. (It might be the protagonist of the *Correspondence of Alexander and Dindimus* speaking.) In Taxila, by contrast, those who show an inclination to philosophy and are of good character are sent off across the river Hyphasis to 'the men whom you are seeking', later described as 'the sages' (*sophoi*).[53]

It seems that the king is describing the naked philosophers encountered by Alexander, and Apollonius says so; but the king contradicts him. 'Those were Oxydracae, and that tribe is always claiming its freedom and preparing for war. They say they are conversant with philosophy, but they know nothing about virtue. The true Wise Men are situated half way between the Hyphasis and the Ganges, in territory which Alexander did not even approach.'[54] At one stroke Philostratus presents an Apollonius who is on the point of trumping Alexander completely: for he will achieve a journey to these Sages, who fend off attackers by hurling thunder and lightning at them, which Alexander did not even attempt. Furthermore, Alexander, it is made plain, got the wrong lot of philosophers: there was no chance of his learning wisdom from them. It is notable that these inadequate philosophers are named by Phraotes as Oxydracae, for that name is first applied to the naked philosophers in the *Alexander Romance*: in the historians, the Oxydracae are simply a warlike tribe to the south.[55]

The next day finds the king dispensing justice. The justice of the Indians had been a commonplace of Greek writing since Ctesias, and the king's duty to dispense it is stated in the *Laws of Manu*, though the Greek authors do not refer to courts as such.[56] This gives the opportunity to introduce the conundrum of the man who sold another some land that contained a hidden treasure. The problem is familiar from Plato's *Laws*, and becomes a problem for Alexander to solve in the Hebrew *Alexander Romances*, where it gives him the opportunity to show his Solomon-like wisdom in deciding difficult legal cases.[57] Had the episode become attached to Alexander before the time of

53. Ibid. 2.32.1.

54. Ibid. 2.33.1.

55. Cf. Stoneman 1995.

56. *Manusmṛti* 7.12–18; Stoneman 2016b.

57. Stoneman 2008, 121.

Philostratus? We do not know, but at any rate Apollonius' solution is quite different from that of Alexander. The traditional answer is that the offspring of the two men should marry each other, and thus re-unite the property and the treasure in one family; Apollonius decides it according to the 'virtue' of the two parties, and the buyer wins on grounds of goodness and piety. Virtue and wisdom trump royal power and everyday justice, as Apollonius shows himself greater than Alexander.

Book 3 begins with our doughty pair crossing the river Hyphasis. Again the local flora and fauna are described, but apart from the monkeys, pepper and cinnamon, they are more or less magical in quality. The river-worm that produces an inextinguishable oil, valuable in siege warfare, is not observed by Apollonius (nor does it appear in any earlier source), but the sage is impressed by his first sight of a unicorn, though quite unfazed by an encounter with a woman whose head and breast are white while the rest of her is black: for she is a servant of Aphrodite.[58] The appearance of these unfamiliar creatures signals that Apollonius has crossed a border into a magical land. Like the children in *The Lion, the Witch and the Wardrobe* who enter Narnia through a wardrobe, Apollonius and Damis do so by crossing the Hyphasis.[59]

Narnia, is, of course, a place where one's religious consciousness is expanded. In chapter 10 the pair reach the dwelling of the Wise Men, and the episode seems like a reprise of the themes of this book. The sages are described as advisers to the king (as in Megasthenes), and it turns out that everybody in this region speaks Greek. Their overall philosophical position is described as Pythagorean, as in Onesicritus.[60] 'They claim to inhabit the centre of India, and regard the peak of this hill as its navel':[61] this looks like a reminiscence of the Hindu cosmology with Mount Meru at its centre (see chapter 5 above). Apollonius identifies these sages as 'Brahmans', and writes of them, 'I saw the

58. The next parti-coloured person in literature, as far as I know, appears in Wolfram von Eschenbach's *Parzival*: the son of a black man and a white woman naturally comes out striped.

59. So Reger 2015, 150, noting that the arrival of Apollonius at the true naked philosophers of Ethiopia is also achieved by going beyond a limit set by Alexander. See also 152: 'Whenever Apollonios passes in the East beyond the point where Alexander stopped, he enters a world of mystery, wonder, enchantment. Griffins, ants that guard gold, precious goods left unguarded on the road, Indian philosophers who can levitate, 300 year-old elephants, naked Ethiopian wise men, satyrs tamed by inebriation – such are the marvels Apollonios sees'.

60. Philostr. *VA* 3.10–12; Onesic. F 17ab.

61. Philostr. *VA* 3.14.3.

Indian Brahmans living on the earth and not on it, walled without walls, owning nothing and owning everything':[62] this is rather a good description of a typical Indian renouncer, a sādhu.

The sages have a leader, Iarchas, who expounds their philosophy in a friendly way and with none of the antagonism shown by the philosophers to Onesicritus and to the Alexander of the *Romance*. After a short interlude of mass levitation, the sage explains that their philosophy begins from self-knowledge (which is the end of philosophy for the Greeks); he states the doctrine of rebirth, which he points out Pythagoras had transmitted to the Greeks, 'and we to the Egyptians'. (He does not seem to say that Pythagoras got it from the Indians.) Later, he speaks of the nature of justice:[63] justice had been a theme of Greek accounts of India since Ctesias (see chapter 8 above), and Iarchas points out the key to understanding this idea, that avoidance of wrong is not the same as justice. Justice is also observed in the variable number of the philosophers.[64] Apollonius cannot understand why there are eighteen of them, since this is not a perfect number on Pythagorean principles; the point is that there might at some time be a different number of virtuous persons in existence, and it would be unjust to exclude any of them from the philosophers' number.

The sage confirms, as we would surely expect, that the philosophers, and even their king (who bows to their superiority), stick to a vegetarian diet.[65] When the king arrives for dinner, magical urns bring forth food – 'dried fruits, loaves, vegetables, and seasonal morsels' – while two more urns flow with wine, and one with cold water, one with permanently warm water. The cups and decanters are made from precious stones, emphasising that we are still in fairyland. The dinner concludes with more mass levitation at midnight.[66]

The following day, Iarchas continues his exposition of their beliefs with a discourse on the nature of matter: everything is made of the five elements standard in Indian belief.[67] (Apollonius is surprised at the existence of the fifth, ether). Furthermore, the universe is hermaphroditic, creating all beings

62. Ibid. 3.15.1.

63. Ibid. 3.25.

64. Ibid 3.30.

65. Ibid. 3.26.

66. Ibid. 3.33.

67. *Aitareya Up.* 3.3; discussed by Keith 1909. Later Indian philosophy, including the atomist tradition, thinks in terms of four elements: Gangopadhyaya 1980.

by intercourse with itself. This is close to the process described in *Bṛhadāraṇyaka Upaniṣad* 1.4.1 and 3:[68]

> In the beginning this world was just a single body shaped like a man ... He wanted to have a companion. Now he was as large as a man and a woman in close embrace. So he split his body into two, giving rise to husband and wife ... He copulated with her, and from their union human beings were born.

The universe is explained as an intelligent being on the analogy of a ship with many gods as steersmen: the obscurity of this analogy may suggest that Philostratus is summarising some source on the subject, and not simply offering a Stoic allegory.

Apollonius brings the conversation back to earth by asking one of the sort of questions that Alexander had posed to the sages of Taxila: 'Is the sea or the land greater?' Iarchas' sophistic reply goes beyond the clarity of Dandamis' answers to the riddles of the *Romance*, but we are spared an extension of the riddle dialogue by the arrival of a messenger with people needing healing from diseases both physical and psychic. The expertise of the Sarmanes in healing is mentioned by Megasthenes, so this is in character for the sages. A father complains that his sons had died as soon as they began to drink wine: Iarchas replies with a harsh compassion worthy of the Buddha, that if they had lived they would certainly have gone insane;[69] to protect future sons, a diet of lightly boiled owls' eggs will dispel for ever the craving for wine. 'Apollonius and Damis were amazed at their Eminences' unlimited wisdom'.[70]

The final discussion is about prophecy, stated to be the role of the Brahman advisers to the king by Megasthenes).[71] Again Philostratus' information is accurate and his source is plain to see.

In the four months which the philosophic pair spend in the sages' *phrontisterion* (might we interpret as ashram?), Damis cannot be diverted from more mundane interests, and asks also for accounts of the manticore, the stream of gold, the magnetic stone that attracts rubies and the people who use their feet as umbrellas. Iarchas tells Damis that it is up to him to describe such matters.

68. *Bṛh. Up.* 1.4.1, 1.4.3.

69. Philostr. *VA* 3.40. On 'being cruel to be kind', see Panaioti 2013, last chapter.

70. Philostr. *VA* 3.41.

71. Diod. 2.40.2–3: see ch. 8 above.

Such things, we presume, are beneath the dignity of a sage to discuss, and it is for Western writers to decide if they wish to bother with such matters. He does flatly deny the existence of the Shadow-feet and the other strange races described by Scylax.[72] He has a prosaic explanation for the 'ant-gold', but admits the existence of griffins: 'Indian artists who portray the Sun god show his statue drawn by four of them'.[73] This seems to be an invention by Philostratus, though griffins often figure in the arts of Central Asia.[74] Finally, the phoenix, the bird engendered by the Sun, which visits Egypt every five hundred years, spends the intervening time flying about in India.[75]

This symbol of the sun and of resurrection is Iarchas' last word from India. The travellers now make their way back west, to the Red Sea, following a route which as described by Philostratus makes no sense, since they keep the Ganges on their right and the Hyphasis on their left, which, as a glance at a map will show, would lead them towards the Himalayas.[76] But then, the way back from Narnia was through a wardrobe, and anything is possible in fairyland. On the way, Philostratus includes a disquisition on pearls,[77] deriving from the accounts in Nearchus and Megasthenes.

If we try to summarise Philostratus' presentation of India in his fiction, several things become apparent. First, the picture he presents of the sages closely resembles that given by Onesicritus and Megasthenes, both in general atmosphere and in the detail and selection of topics. As Albrecht Dihle has made clear, Megasthenes' description of India quickly became a classic, and no later author tried to add any significant new data to it.[78] A second point is that Philostratus outdoes these sages later in his book by having Apollonius encounter a superior group of wise men in Ethiopia, who are actually the 'true

72. Philostr. *VA* 3.47.

73. Ibid. 3.48.

74. The Sun's chariot is drawn by seven horses at *RV* 1.50.8–9, 4.13.3, 5.45.9. The Aśvins' chariot is drawn by birds, bulls, or horses: 1.119.4, 4.45.4, 1.118.4: Jamison and Brereton 2014, 48.

75. The phoenix was known to live at the ends of the earth (Hdt. 2.73; Ach.Tat. 3.25.6; *una est quae reparet, seque ipsa reseminet, ales: Assyrii Phoenica vocant:* O. *Met.* 15.392–3. Though not mentioned in the *Alexander Romance*, it did make an appearance in *Sesonchosis*, a work certainly related in some way to the *Romance*. See *POxy* 5263, F 2 col. 2.30, and Trnka-Amrhein forthcoming.

76. Pliny's enumeration of the tribes of India, probably following Artemidorus, takes an almost equally puzzling course: down the Ganges, around India, up the Indus and then down again. A writer at his desk might be forgiven for getting confused.

77. Philostr. *VA* 3.57.

78. Dihle 1964.

sages'. Philostratus cannot add new marvels either to the Indian scene or to the achievements of the philosophers. In order to create a further stage of wisdom, at which Apollonius can excel, he invents a new group of philosophers beyond another limit of Alexander's explorations, at the fringes of the Roman empire.[79] Apollonius boxes the compass of that empire.[80] He visits Gadeira as well as crossing the Hyphasis. Reaching not only the furthest west and south, he also encompasses the Far East by visiting India and discovering that it is not only familiar, but not so remarkable after all. This is a political dimension to his travels, in which India, now known to Rome through many trading links and its productivity of grossly expensive luxuries, is no longer 'other'. Everyone there seems to speak Greek! India is an exotic part of this world, not another world as it was for Alexander's contemporaries. That was the result of three centuries of Greek settlement, language connections and other interactions. On the intellectual plane, India is now somehow 'understood', albeit that understanding might seem faulty to us today, or even to medievals like al-Biruni and Babur. A philosopher needs an other-worldly plane to play out his connections with the gods above, and that for Philostratus is found in the fairyland beyond the Hyphasis. India became known, but it still represented the unknown. There is only one phoenix, and that is where it lives, and recreates itself incessantly.

79. Reger 2015, cited above, n. 59.
80. Elsner 1997.

APPENDIX

Concordance of the Fragments of Megasthenes

Schwanbeck	Jacoby	Jacoby	Schwanbeck
1	4	1	48
2	5	2	28
3	–	3	42, 43
4	6	4	1
5	6	5	2
6	6	6	4, 5, 6, 8
7	–	7	9, 10, 20
8	6	8	11
9	7	9	X
10	7	10	21, 22, 23
11	8	11	–
12	21	12	–
13	21	13	15, 50, 51
14	21	14	50c
15 (15b)	13 (–)	15	29
16	22	16	–
17	24	17	–
18	*Anhang* 10	18	25, 26
19	25	19	32, 33
20 (20b)	9 (–)	20	36, 37, cf. 38
21	10	21	12, 13, 14
22	10	22	16
23	10	23	39
24	–	24	17
25	18	25	19
26	18	26	50b
27 (27b, c, d)	32 (–, –, –)	27	29
28	2	28	30
29	27, cf. 15	29	30

Schwanbeck	Jacoby	Jacoby	Schwanbeck
30 (30b)	28, 29 (29)	30	31
31	30	31	34
32	19	32	27
33	19	33	41
34	31	34	44, 45
35	–		
36	20		
37	20		
38	Cf. 20		
39	23		
40	–		
41	33		
42	3		
43	3		
44	34		
45	34		
46	*Anhang* 3		
47	–		
48	1		
49	–		
50 (50b), 50c	13 (26), cf. 14		
51	13c		
52 (doubtful)	–		
53 (doubtful)	–		
54 (doubtful)	– but cf. 33, 34		
55 (doubtful)	–		
56 (doubtful)	–		
57 (doubtful)	–		
58 (doubtful)	–		
59 (doubtful)	*Anhang* 18		

BIBLIOGRAPHY

Abdullaev, K. 2005. 'Les motifs dionysiaques dans l'art de la Bactrie at de la Sogdiane', in Bopearachchi and Boussac (eds.) 2005, 227–57.

Achaya, K. T. 1994. *Indian Food: A Historical Companion.* Delhi: Oxford University Press.

Achaya, K. T. 1998. *A Historical Dictionary of Indian Food.* Delhi: Oxford University Press

Agrawala, Vasudeva Sharma 1953. *India as Known to Panini: A Study of the Cultural Material in the Ashtadhyayi.* Lucknow: Lucknow University.

Agrawala, V. S. 1965. *Studies in Indian Art.* Varanasi: Vishwavidalaya Prakashan.

Aitken, Bill 1992. *Seven Sacred Rivers.* Gurgaon: Penguin India.

Alberti, Leon Battista 1966. *On Painting,* tr. and ed. John R. Spencer. New Haven, CT: Yale University Press.

Albinia, Alice 2008. *Empires of the Indus.* London: John Murray.

Allan, John 1946. 'A *Tabula Iliaca* from Gandhara'. *JHS* 66, 21–3.

Allchin, F. R. 1979. 'India: The Ancient Home of Distillation'. *Man* 14, 55–63.

Allchin, F. R. 1995. *The Archaeology of Early Historic South Asia: The Emergence of Cities and States.* Cambridge: Cambridge University Press.

Allen, Charles 2012. *Ashoka. The Search for India's Lost Emperor.* London: Little, Brown.

Allen, N. J. 2001. 'Athena and Durgā: Warrior Goddesses in Greek and Sanskrit Epic', in S. Deacy and A. Villing (eds.), *Athena in the Classical World.* Leiden: Brill, 367–82.

Almagor, Eran 2012. 'Ctesias and the Importance of his Writings Revisited'. *Electrum* 19, 9–40.

Almagor, Eran and Skinner, Joseph (eds.) 2013. *Ancient Ethnography: New Approaches.* London: Bloomsbury.

Amigues, Suzanne (ed. and tr.) 2006. *Théophraste. Recherches sur les Plantes, tome V, livre IX.* Paris: Les Belles Lettres.

Amigues, Suzanne 2010. *Théophraste: Recherches sur les plantes.* Paris: Belin.

Amigues, Suzanne 2011. 'La flore indienne de Ctésias: un document historique.' *Journal des Savants* Jan.–June, 21–76.

Amigues, Suzanne 2015. 'Le tarandos de Théophraste, un animal reel à l'origine d'une créature de fantaisie'. *Journal des Savants,* Jan.–June, 3–24.

Anand, Mulk Raj 1953/2008. *Private Life of an Indian Prince.* London: Bodley Head/pbk edn: HarperCollins.

Anderson, Graham 1986. *Philostratus.* Beckenham: Croom Helm.

André, Jacques and Filliozat, Jean 1980. *Pline l'Ancien: Histoire naturelle. Livre VI, 2e partie.* Paris: Les Belles Lettres.

André, Jacques and Filliozat, Jean 1986. *L'Inde vue de Rome. Textes latins de l'Antiquité relatifs à l'Inde*. Paris: Les Belles Lettres.

Andreassi, Mario (ed.) 2001. *Mimi greci in Egitto: Charition e Moicheutria*. Naples: Palomar.

Andronikos, Manolis 1984. *Vergina: The Royal Tombs and the Ancient City*. Athens: Ekdotike Athenon.

Anon. 1904. *Chandragupta's Marriage with Alexander's Granddaughter*: Bareilly: Warman & Nephew.

Arnold, David 2005. 'Envisioning the Tropics: Joseph Hooker in India and the Himalayas, 1848–1850', in F. Driver and L. Martins (eds.), *Tropical Visions in an Age of Empire*. Chicago: University of Chicago Press, 137–55.

Arnott, W. G. 2007. *Birds in the Ancient World from A to Z*. London: Routledge.

Arora, U. P. 1981. *Motifs in Indian Mythology: Their Greek and other Parallels*. New Delhi: Indika.

Arora, U. P. (ed.) 1991. *Graeco-Indica: India's Cultural Contects* [sic] *with the Greek World*. Delhi: Ramanand Vidya Bhawan.

Arora, U. P. 1991–92. 'The *Indika* of Megasthenes – an Appraisal'. *Annals of the Bhandarkar Oriental Research Institute*, 72/73 (Amrtamahotsava 1917–1992 vol.), 307–29.

Arora, Udai Prakash 2005. 'The Fragments of Onesikritos on India – an Appraisal'. *Indian Historical Review* 23, 35–102.

Asher, F. and Spink, W. 1989. 'Maurya Figural Sculpture Reconsidered'. *Ars Orientalis* 19, 1–25.

Asher, Frederick M. 2006. 'Early Indian Art Reconsidered', in Olivelle (ed.) 2006, 51–66.

Aśvaghoṣa 1936/1984. *Buddhacarita*, tr. E. H. Johnston. Delhi: Motilal Banarsidass.

Auberger, J. 1995. 'L'Inde de Ctésias', in J.-C. Carrière et al. (eds.), *Inde, Grèce ancienne. Regards croisés en anthropologie de l'espace*. Paris: Les Belles Lettres, 31–59.

Audouin, Remy and Bernard, Paul 1974. 'Trésor de monnaies indiennes et indo-grecques d'Ai Khanoum (Afghanistan)', *Revue numismatique* 16, 6–41.

Aurobindo, Sri 1947. *Heraclitus*. Calcutta: Arya.

Bäbler, Balbina and Nesselrath, Heinz-Günther 2016. *Philostrats Apollonios und seine Welt*. Berlin: De Gruyter.

Badian, Ernst 1961. 'Harpalus'. *JHS* 81, 16–43; also in Badian, *Collected Papers on Alexander the Great*. Abingdon: Routledge, 2012, 58–95.

Bailey, Greg and Mabbett, Ian 2003. *The Sociology of Early Buddhism*. Cambridge: Cambridge University Press.

Baldick, Julian 1994. *Homer and the Indo-Europeans: Comparing Mythologies*. London: IB Tauris.

Balfour-Paul, Jenny 1998. *Indigo*. London: British Museum Press.

Bali, V. 1879–88. 'On the Identification of Animals and Plants of India which were Known to Early Greek Authors'. *Proceedings of the Royal Irish Academy – Polite Literature and Antiquities* 2, 302–46.

Baltrušaitis, J. 1981. *Le moyen âge fantastique*. Paris: Flammarion.

Bāna 1897. *The Harṣa-Carita*, tr. E. B. Cowell and F. W. Thomas. London: Oriental Translation Fund.

Banerjee, Gauranga Nath 1919. *Hellenism in Ancient India*. London: Butterworth.

Banerjee, Pompa 2003. *Burning Women. Widows, Witches and Early Modern Travelers in India*. London: Palgrave.

Bar-Kochva, Bezalel 2010. *The Image of the Jews in Greek Literature: The Hellenistic Period*. Berkeley: University of California Press.

Basham, A. L. 1951. *History and Doctrines of the Ajivikas: A Vanished Indian Religion*. London: Luzac.

Basham A. L. 1954. *The Wonder that was India*. London: Sidgwick and Jackson.

Basu, Jogiraj 1969. *India of the Age of the Brahmanas*. Calcutta: Sanskrit Pustak Bhandar.

Beagon, Mary 1992. *Roman Nature: The Thought of Pliny the Elder*. Oxford: Oxford University Press

Beal, Samuel (tr.) 1884. *Si-yu-ki. Buddhist Records of the Western World* (2 vols.). London: Trübner.

Beckwith, Christopher 2015. *Greek Buddha*. Princeton: Princeton University Press.

Behl, Benoy K. 2005. *The Ajanta Caves. Ancient Paintings of Buddhist India* (revised edn). London: Thames and Hudson.

Berlekamp, Persis 2011. *Wonder, Image, and Cosmos in Medieval Islam*. New Haven, CT: Yale University Press.

Bernabé, Alberto and Mendoza, Julia 2013. 'Pythagorean Cosmogony and Vedic Cosmogony. Analogies and Differences'. *Phronesis* 58, 32–51.

Bernard, Paul 1985. 'Le monnayage d'Eudamos, satrape grec du Pandjab et "maître des éléphants"', in G. Gnoli and L. Lanciotti (eds.), *Orientalia Iosephi Tucci Memoriae Dicata*, vol. 1. Rome: Istituto Italiano per il Medio ed Estremo Oriente, 65–94.

Bernard, Paul and Bopearachchi, Osmund 2002. 'Deux bracelets grecs avec inscriptions grecques trouvés dans l'Asie Centrale hellénisée'. *Journal des Savants*, 237–79.

Berve, Helmut 1926. *Das Alexanderreich auf prosopographischer Grundlage*. Munich: Beck.

Bett, R. 2000. *Pyrrho, his Antecedents and his Legacy*. Oxford: Oxford University Press.

Bhagat, M. G. 1976. *Ancient Indian Asceticism*. New Delhi: Munshiram Manoharlal.

Bhāgavata Purāṇa. *See* Bryant 2003.

Bhasa 2008. *'The Shattered Thigh' and Other Plays*, tr. with intro. A.N.D. Haksar. New Delhi: Penguin.

Bhattacharji, Sukumari 1970/2000. *The Indian Theogony. Brahma, Viṣṇu and Śiva*. Cambridge: Cambridge University Press; repr. Penguin.

Bhattacharya, Ramkrishna 2000. 'Uttarakuru: The (E)utopia of Ancient India'. *Annals of the Bhandarkar Oriental Research Institute* 81, 191–201.

Bhattacharya, Vidhushekara 1943. *The* Āgāṁaśāstra *of Gauḍapāda*. Calcutta: University of Calcutta Press.

Bichler, Reinhold 2016. 'Herrschaft und politische Organisation im älteren Indien-Bild der Griechen und in der klassischen Alexander-Historie', in Wiesehöfer, Brinkhaus and Bichler (eds.) 2016, 5–26.

Biffi, Nicola 2000. *L'*Indike *di Arriano: Introduzione, testo, traduzione e commento*. Bari: Edipuglia.

Bigwood, J. M. 1978. 'Ctesias' Description of Babylon'. *AJAH* 3, 32–52.

Bigwood, J. M. 1980. 'Diodorus and Ctesias'. *Phoenix* 34, 195–207.

Bigwood, J. M. 1989. 'Ctesias' *Indica* and Photius'. *Phoenix* 43, 302–16.

Bigwood, J. M. 1993a. 'Aristotle and the Elephant again'. *AJP* 114, 537–55.

Bigwood, J. M. 1993b. 'Ctesias' Parrot'. *CQ* 43, 321–27.

Bigwood, J. M. 1995. 'Ctesias, his Royal Patrons and Indian Swords'. *JHS* 115, 135–40.

Bloch, Jules 1950/2007. *Les Inscriptions d'Asoka*. Paris: Les Belles Lettres.

Boardman, John 1994. *The Diffusion of Classical Art in Antiquity*. London: Thames and Hudson.

Boardman, John 2014. *The Triumph of Dionysos*. London: BAR.

Boardman, John 2015. *The Greeks in Asia*. London: Thames and Hudson.

Bodhi, Bhikkhu 1989. *The Discourse on the Fruits of Recluseship. The* Sāmaññaphala Sutta *and its Commentaries*. Kandy: Buddhist Publication Society.

Bolton J.D.P. 1962. *Aristeas of Proconnesus*. Oxford: Oxford University Press.

Bopearachchi, O. and Boussac, M.-F. (eds.) 2005. *Afghanistan: ancient Carrefour entre l'est et l'ouest*. Turnhout: Brepols.

Bopearachchi, Osmund and Flandrin, Philippe 2005. *Le Portrait d'Alexandre le Grand: Histoire d'une découverte pour l'humanité*. Monaco: Editions du Rocher.

Bosworth, A. B. 1980–. *A Historical Commentary on Arrian's History of Alexander* (vol. 1, 1980: books 1–3; vol. 2, 1995: books 4–5; vol. 3, forthcoming: books 6–7). Oxford: Oxford University Press.

Bosworth, A. B. 1988a. *Conquest and Empire: The Reign of Alexander the Great*. Cambridge: Cambridge University Press.

Bosworth, A. B. 1993. 'Aristotle, India and the Alexander Historians'. *Topoi* 3, 407–24.

Bosworth, A. B. 1996a. *Alexander and the East: The Tragedy of Triumph*. Oxford: Oxford University Press.

Bosworth, A. B. 1996b. 'The Historical Setting of Megasthenes' *Indica*'. *CPh* 91, 113–27.

Bosworth, A. B. 1998. 'Calanus and the Brahman Opposition', in W. Will (ed.), *Alexander der Grosse. Eine Welteroberung und ihr Hintergrund*. Bonn: Rudolf Habelt, 173–203.

Bosworth, A. B. 2002. *The Legacy of Alexander. Politics, Warfare and Propaganda under the Successors*. Oxford University Press.

Bosworth, A. B. 2003. 'Arrian, Megasthenes and the Making of Myth', in J. A. López Férez (ed.), *Mitos en la literatura griega helenistica e imperial*. Madrid: Clásicas, 299–320.

Bosworth, A. B. and Baynham, E. 2000. *Alexander the Great in Fact and Fiction*. Oxford: Oxford University Press.

Bowersock, Glen 1994. 'Dionysus as an Epic Hero', in Hopkinson (ed.) 1994, 156–66.

Bowersock, G. W., Innes, D. C., Bowie, E. L. and Easterling, P. E. 1985. 'The Literature of the Empire', in P. E. Easterling and Bernard M. W. Knox (eds.), *The Cambridge History of Classical Literature*, vol. 1. Cambridge: Cambridge University Press, 642–713.

Bowie, E. L. 1978. 'Apollonius of Tyana: Tradition and Reality'. *Aufstieg und Niedergang der römischen Welt* 2.16.2, 1652–99.

Bretzl, Hugo 1903. *Botanische Forschungen des Alexanderzuges*. Leipzig: Weidmann.

Briant, Pierre 2002. *From Cyrus to Alexander. A History of the Persian Empire*. Winona Lake: Eisenbrauns.

Briant, Pierre 2016. *Alexandre. Exégèse des lieux communs*. Paris: Gallimard.

Bridgeman, Timothy P. 2005. *Hyperboreans. Myth and History in Celtic-Hellenic Contacts*. New York: Routledge.

Brinkhaus, Horst 2016. 'Zum aktuellen Stand der Arthaśāstra-Forschung: Kann Kautilya noch als Kronzeuge für Megasthenes gelten?', in Wiesehöfer, Brinkhaus and Bichler (eds.) 2016, 27–36.

Brockington, J. L. 1998. *The Sanskrit Epics*. Leiden: Brill

Bronkhorst, Johannes 1999. *Why is there Philosophy in India?* Amsterdam: Royal Netherlands Academy of Arts and Sciences.

Bronkhorst, Johannes 2006. 'Systematic Philosophy between the Empires: Some Determining Features', in Olivelle (ed.) 2006, 287–313.

Bronkhorst, Johannes 2007. *Greater Magadha. Studies in the Culture of Early India.* Leiden: Brill.

Bronkhorst, Johannes 2011. *Buddhism in the Shadow of Brahmanism.* Leiden: Brill.

Bronkhorst, Johannes 2016. *How the Brahmins Won: From Alexander to the Guptas.* Leiden: Brill.

Bronkhorst, J. and Deshpande, M. M. (eds.) 1999. *Aryan and Non-Aryan in South Asia.* Harvard: South Asia Books.

Brown, Truesdell S. 1949. *Onesicritus: A Study in Hellenistic Historiography.* Berkeley: University of California Press.

Brown, Trusedell S. 1955. 'The Reliability of Megasthenes'. *AJP* 76, 18–33.

Brown, Truesdell S. 1973. *The Greek Historians.* Lexington, MA: D. C. Heath.

Bruno, Vincent J. 1977. *Form and Colour in Greek Painting.* London: Thames and Hudson.

Bryant, Edwin 2003. *Krishna: The Beautiful Legend of God.* Śrīmad Bhāgavata Purāṇa, *Book X.* London: Penguin.

Bryant, Julius, and Susan Weber (eds.) 2017. *John Lockwood Kipling. Arts and Crafts in the Punjab and London.* New York: Bard Graduate Center Gallery and Yale University Press.

Buddhaghoṣa 1870. *Buddhaghosha's Parables, Translated from Burmese by Captain T. Rogers.* London: Trübner.

Bunbury, E. H. 1879. *A History of Ancient Geography* (2 vols.). London: John Murray.

Burley, Mikel 2016a. 'Rebirth and "Ethicisation" in Greek and South Asian Thought', in Seaford (ed.) 2016, 220–34.

Burley, Mikel 2016b. *Rebirth and the Stream of Life.* London: Bloomsbury.

Burstein, Stanley (ed.) 1989. *Agatharchides of Cnidus: On the Erythraean Sea.* London: Hakluyt Society.

Burstein, Stanley 2010. 'New Light on the Fate of Greek in Ancient Central and South Asia'. *AWE* 9, 181–92.

Burstein, Stanley 2012. 'Whence the Women?: The Origin of the Bactrian Greeks'. *AWE* 11, 97–104.

Bussagli, Mario 1996. *L'Art du Gandhāra.* Paris: Le Livre de Poche.

Buzurg ibn Shahriyar 1928. *Book of the Marvels of India,* tr. L. Marcel Devic and into English by Peter Quennell. London: Routledge.

Callatay, François de 2013. 'Pourquoi le "distatère en or au portrait d'Alexandre" est très probablement un faux moderne'. *Revue Numismatique* 170, 127–89.

Callieri, P. 1995. 'The North-west of the Indian Subcontinent in the Indo-Greek Period. The Archaeological Evidence', in Invernizzi (ed.) 1995, 293–308.

Carey, John 1999. *The Faber Book of Utopias.* London: Faber.

Carlisle, Clare and Ganeri, Jonardon (eds.) 2010. *Philosophy as Therapeia.* Cambridge: Cambridge University Press.

Carter, Martha L. 1982. 'The Bacchants of Mathura: New Evidence of Dionysiac Yaksha Imagery from Kushan Mathura'. *Bulletin of the Cleveland Museum of Art* 59, 247–57.

Carter, Martha L. 1992. 'Dionysiac Festivals and Gandharan Imagery', in R. Gyselen (ed.), *Banquets d'Orient,* Res Orientales 4, 51–9.

Carter Martha L. 2015. *Arts of the Hellenized East. Precious Metalwork and Gems of the Pre-Islamic Era*. London: Thames and Hudson.

Casson, Lionel (ed. and tr.) 1989. *The* Periplus Maris Erythraei. Princeton: Princeton University Press.

Chanana, Dev Raj 1960. *Slavery in Ancient India*. New Delhi: People's Publishing House.

Chandra, Pramod 1985. *The Sculpture of India 3000 BC–1300 AD*. Washington, D.C.: National Gallery of Art.

Charpentier, Jarl 1934. *The Indian Travels of Apollonius of Tyana*. Uppsala: Almqvist & Wiksell/Leipzig: Harrassowitz.

Chatterjee, Upamanyu 1988. *English, August: An Indian Story*. London: Faber.

Chattopadhyaya, Debiprasad 1959/1973. *Lokāyata. A Study in Ancient Indian Materialism*. New Delhi: People's Publishing House.

Chattopadhyaya, Sudhakar 1974. *The Achaemenids and India* (2nd edn). New Delhi: Munshiram Manoharlal.

Chaudhuri, Sukanta 1999. *Translation and Understanding*. New Delhi: Oxford University Press.

Chowdhury, M. K. 2005. 'The Totos', in S. K. Chaudhuri and S. S. Chaudhuri (eds.), *Primitive Tribes in Contemporary India*, vol. 1 Delhi: Mittal, 143–59.

Chuvin, Pierre 1994. 'Local Traditions and Classical Mythology in the *Dionysiaca*', in Hopkinson (ed.) 1994, 167–76.

Clark, Stephen R. L. 1977. *The Moral Status of Animals*. Oxford: Oxford University Press.

Clarke, Katherine 1999. *Between Geography and History: Hellenistic Constructions of the Roman World*. Oxford: Oxford University Press.

Cohen, Getzel 2012. *The Hellenistic Settlements in the East from Armenia and Mesopotamia to Bactria and India*. Berkeley: University of California Press.

Collins, Brian 2014. *The Head beneath the Altar. Hindu Mythology and the Critique of Sacrifice*. East Lansing: Michigan State University Press.

Collis, John Stewart 1937. *An Irishman's England*. London: Cassell.

Colliva, Luca 2007. 'The Apsidal Temple of Taxila: Traditional Hypotheses and Possible New Interpretations', in Hardy (ed.) 2007, 21–9.

Coloru, Omar 2009. *Da Alessandro a Menandro: il regno Greco di Battriana*. Pisa: Giardini.

Coningham, R.A.E., Allchin, F. R., Batt, C. M. and Lucy, D. 1996. 'Passage to India? Anuradhapura and the Early Use of the Brahmi Script'. *Cambridge Archaeological Journal* 6, 73–97.

Coomaraswamy, A. K. 1935. *Elements of Buddhist Iconography*. Cambridge, MA: Harvard University Press.

Coomaraswamy, A. K. 1993. *Yakṣas: Essays in the Water Cosmology* (new edn). New Delhi: Indira Gandhi National Centre for the Arts.

Cooper, Ilay and Dawson, Barry 1998. *Traditional Buildings of India*. London: Thames and Hudson.

Cort, John E. 2010. *Framing the Jina*. Oxford: Oxford University Press.

Cowell, E. B. (ed.) 1895–1913. *The Jātaka, or Stories of the Buddha's Former Births. Translated from the Pali by Various Hands* (7 vols.). Cambridge: Cambridge University Press.

Crane, Peter. 2013. *Ginkgo*. New Haven, CT: Yale University Press.

Cribb, Joe 2005. *The Indian Coinage Tradition*. Anjaneri: IIRNS Publications.

Cribb, Joe 2017. 'The Greek Contacts of Chandragupta Maurya and their Relevance to Maurya and Buddhist Chronology', in *From Global to Local: Papers in Asian History and Culture: Prof. A. K. Narain Commemoration Volume* (3 vols.), vol. 1. Delhi: Buddhist World Press, 3–27.

Cribb, Joe and Herrmann, Georgina (eds.) 2007. *After Alexander: Central Asia before Islam.* Proceedings of the British Academy 133. Oxford: British Academy/Oxford University Press.

Cunliffe, Barry 2001. *The Extraordinary Voyage of Pytheas the Greek.* London: Allen Lane.

Cunningham, Alexander 1848. 'An Essay on the Arian Order of Architecture, as Exhibited in the Temples of Kashmir', *Journal of the Asiatic Society of Bengal* 17, 241–327.

Cunningham, Alexander 1854. *The Bhilsa Topes.* London: Smith, Elder.

Dąbrowa, E. 1998 (ed.). *Ancient Iran and the Mediterranean World.* Kraków: Jagiellonian University Press.

Dahlquist, Allan 1962. *Megasthenes and Indian Religion: A Study in Motives and Types.* Stockholm: Almqvist & Wiksell. 1962; repr Delhi: Motilal Banarsidass, 1977.

Dalby, Andrew 2003. *Food in the Ancient World from A to Z.* London: Routledge.

Dale, Stephen F. 2004. *The Garden of the Eight Paradises. Bābur and the Culture of Empire in Central Asia, Afghanistan and India (1483–1530).* Leiden: Brill.

Dalrymple, William 1993. *City of Djinns. A Year in Delhi.* London: Harper Collins.

Dalrymple, William 1998. *The Age of Kali. Indian Travels and Encounters.* London: Harper Collins.

Dalrymple, William 2009. *Nine Lives. In Search of the Sacred in Modern India.* London: Bloomsbury.

Dani, Ahmed Hasan 1986. *The Historic City of Taxila.* Tokyo: Centre for East Asian Cultural Studies.

Daniélou, Alain 1992. *Gods of Love and Ecstasy. The Traditions of Shiva and Dionysus.* Rochester, VT: Inner Traditions.

Danino, Michel 2010. *The Lost River: On the Trail of the Sarasvatī.* New Delhi: Penguin India.

Dar, S. R. 1984. *Taxila and the Western World.* Lahore: Library and Information Management Academy.

De Lazzer, Alessandro, Calderón Dorda, Estéban and Pellizer, Ezio (eds.) 2003. *Pseudo Plutarch: Fiumi e monti.* Naples: M. D'Auria.

Derrett, J. Duncan M. 1967. 'Greece and India: The *Milindapañha*, the *Alexander-romance* and the Gospels.' *Zeitschrift für Religions- und Geistesgeschichte* 19, 33–64.

Derrett, J. Duncan M. 1970. 'Greece and India again: The *Jaimini-Aśvameda*, the *Alexander-romance* and the Gospels'. *Zeitschrift für Religions- und Geistesgeschichte* 22, 19–44.

Derrett, J. Duncan M. 1992. 'Homer in India: The Birth of the Buddha'. *JRAS* ser. 3.2, 47–57.

Deshpande, M. N. 1959. 'The Rock-cut Caves of Pitalkhora in the Deccan'. *Ancient India* 15, 66–93.

Devahuti, D. 2001. *The Unknown Hsüan-Tsang.* Delhi: Oxford University Press.

Devi, Gayatri 1976. *A Princess Remembers: The Memoirs of the Maharani of Jaipur.* Philadelphia: Lippincott.

Dewey, Clive 2014. *Steamboats on the Indus: The Limits of Western Technological Superiority in South Asia.* Oxford: Oxford University Press.

Dhavalikar, M. K. 2003. *Sanchi: Monumental Legacy.* New Delhi: Oxford University Press.

Diels, H. and Rehm, A. 1904. 'Parapegmenfragmente aus Milet', *Sitzungsberichte der königlich preussischen Akademie der Wissenschaften* 3, 1–20.

Dihle, Albrecht 1964. 'The Conception of India in Hellenistic and Roman Literature'. *PCPS* 190, 15–23.

Dihle, Albrecht 1987. 'Dionysos in Indien', in Pollet (ed.) 1987, 47–58.

Diller, Aubrey 1952. *The Tradition of the Minor Greek Geographers.* Lancaster, PA: American Philological Association.

Dillery, John 2015. *Clio's Other Sons: Berossus and Manetho.* Ann Arbor: University of Michigan Press.

Djurslev, Christian Thrue 2016. 'The Figure of Alexander the Great and Nonnus' *Dionysiaca*' in Nawotka and Wojciechowska (eds.) 2016, 213–21.

Doniger, Wendy 1981. *The Rig Veda.* Harmondsworth: Penguin.

Doniger, Wendy 1999. *Splitting the Difference: Gender and Myth in Ancient Greece and India.* Chicago: University of Chicago Press.

Doniger, Wendy 2009. *The Hindus.* Oxford: Oxford University Press.

Doniger, Wendy 2016. *Redeeming the* Kamasutra. Oxford: Oxford University Press.

Doniger, Wendy and Kakar, Sudhir (trs.) 2002. *Kamasutra.* Oxford: Oxford University Press.

Doniger, Wendy, and Smith, Brian K. (ed. and tr.) 1991. *The Laws of Manu.* Harmondsworth: Penguin.

Dougherty, Carol 2001. *The Raft of Odysseus: The Ethnographic Imagination of Homer's Odyssey.* Oxford: Oxford University Press.

Dragona-Monachou, M. 1994. 'Divine Providence in the Philosophy of Empire'. *Aufstieg und Niedergang der römischen Welt* 2.36.7, 4417–90.

Drew, John 1987. *India and the Romantic Imagination.* Delhi: Oxford University Press.

Dreyer, Caren 2011. *Albert Grünwedel. Zeichnungen und Bilder von der Seidenstrasse im Museum für Asiatische Kunst.* Berlin: Museum für asiatische Kunst.

Ducoeur, Guillaume and Muckensturm-Poulle, Claire (eds.) 2016. *La transmigration des âmes en Grèce et en Inde anciennes.* Besançon: Presses universitaires de Franche-Comté.

Dudley, Donald R. 1937. *A History of Cynicism: From Diogenes to the Sixth Century.* London: Methuen.

Dumont, Louis 1980. *Homo Hierarchicus: The Caste System and its Implications*, tr. Mark Sainsbury, Louis Dumont and Basia Gulati. Chicago: University of Chicago Press.

Dzielska, Maria 1986. *Apollonius of Tyana in Legend and History.* Rome: L'Erma di Bretschneider.

Eck, Diana L. 1983/1992. *Banaras, City of Light.* Princeton: Princeton University Press/New Delhi: Penguin India.

Eck, Diana L. 2012. *India: A Sacred Geography.* New York: Harmony.

Ede, Piers Moore 2015. *Kaleidoscope City: A Year in Varanasi.* London: Bloomsbury.

Edwards, Mark 2006. *Culture and Philosophy in the Age of Plotinus.* London: Duckworth.

Eggermont, P.H.L. 1993. *Alexander's Campaign in Southern Punjab.* Leuven: Peeters.

Elsner, John 1997. 'Hagiographic Geography: Travel and Allegory in the *Life of Apollonius of Tyana*'. *JHS* 117, 22–37.

Elwin, Verrier 1947. *The Muria and their Ghotul.* Oxford: Oxford University Press.

Elwin, Verrier 1955. *The Religion of an Indian Tribe.* Bombay: Oxford University Press.

Elwin, Verrier 1964. *The Tribal World of Verrier Elwin.* Oxford: Oxford University Press.

Empson, William 2016. *The Face of the Buddha.* Oxford: Oxford University Press.

Engels, D. W. 1978. *Alexander the Great and the Logistics of the Macedonian Army.* Berkeley: University of California Press.

Enright, Kelly 2008. *Rhinoceros.* London: Reaktion Books.

Falk, Harry 1991. 'The Seven "Castes" of Megasthenes', in Arora (ed.) 1991, 48–56.

Falk, Harry N. 1993. *Schrift im alten Indien: Ein Forschungsbericht mit Anmerkungen.* Tübingen: Gunter Narr Verlag.

Falk, Harry 2006. *Aśokan Sites and Artefacts. A Source-Book with Bibliography.* Mainz: Philipp von Zabern.

Faure, Paul 1987. *Parfums et aromatiques de l'antiquité.* Paris: Fayard.

Feeney, D. C. 2016. *Beyond Greek: The Beginnings of Latin Literature.* Cambridge, MA: Harvard University Press.

Fehling, Detlev 1989. *Herodotus and his Sources: Citation, Invention and Narrative Art.* Liverpool: Cairns.

Ferguson, John 1975. *Utopias of the Classical World.* London: Thames and Hudson.

Fergusson, James 1868. *Tree and Serpent Worship or Illustrations of Mythology and Art in India.* London; repr. Delhi: Indological Book House 1971.

Filliozat, Jean 1963. 'La mort volontaire par le feu dans la tradition bouddhique', *Journal Asiatique* 251, 21–51.

Filliozat, Jean 1967, 'L'abandon de la vie par le sage et les suicides du criminel et du héros dans la tradition indienne'. *Arts Asiatiques* 15, 65–88.

Finlay, Victoria 2002. *Colour. Travels through the Paintbox.* London: Hodder and Stoughton.

Fischer, K. 1987a. 'Icons of Heracles and Alexander in the Eastern Parts of the Latter's Empire', in Pollet (ed.) 1987, 59–66.

Fischer, K. 1987b. 'Why has a Gandharan Sculptor Depicted the Nagaradevatā Semi-nude in the Abhiniṣkramana Scene?', in Yaldiz and Lobo (eds.) 1987, 61–6.

Fitzgerald, James L. 2004. *The Mahabharata.* 11: *The Book of the Women.* 12: *The Book of Peace, Part One.* Chicago: University of Chicago Press.

Flinterman, Jaap-Jan 1995. *Power, Paideia and Pythagoreanism: Greek identity, Conceptions of the Relationship between Philosophers and Monarchs and Political Ideas in Philostratus'* Life of Apollonius. Amsterdam: Gieben.

Flintoff, E. 1980. 'Pyrrho and India'. *Phronesis* 25, 88–108.

Flower, Michael A. 1994. *Theopompus: History and Rhetoric in the Fourth Century BC.* Oxford: Oxford University Press.

Fogelin, Lars 2015. *An Archaeological History of Indian Buddhism.* New York: Oxford University Press.

Forster, E. M. 1940. *Abinger Harvest.* London: Edward Arnold.

Forster, E. M. 1953. *The Hill of Devi.* London: Edward Arnold.

Forsyth, James 1871. *The Highlands of Central India.* London.

Francis, Matthew 2008. *Mandeville.* London: Faber.

Franks, Hallie M. 2012. *Hunters, Heroes, Kings. The Frieze of Tomb II at Vergina.* Princeton: Princeton University Press.

Fraser, P. M. 1979. 'The Son of Aristonax at Kandahar'. *Afghan Studies* 2, 9–22.

Fraser P. M. 1980. 'Palamedes at Bağlan'. *Afghan Studies* 3–4, 79–80.

Fraser, P. M. 1994. 'The World of Theophrastus', in S. Hornblower (ed.), *Greek Historiography*. Oxford: Oxford University Press, 167–92.

Fredricksmeyer, Ernst 2000. 'Alexander the Great and the Kingdom of Asia', in Bosworth and Baynham (eds.) 2000, 136–66.

French, R. and Greenaway, F. (eds.) 1986. *Science in the Early Roman Empire: Pliny the Elder, his Sources and his Influence*. London: Croom Helm.

Frenkian, Aram M. 1957. *Scepticismul grec şi filozofia indiană*. Bucharest: Academiei Republicii populare romîne: see the German summary review in *Bibliotheca Classica Orientalis* 4 (1958), 212–49.

Friedman, J. B. 1981. *The Monstrous Races in Medieval Art and Thought*. Cambridge, MA: Harvard University Press.

Fuchs, Stephen 1973. *The Aboriginal Tribes of India*. New Delhi: Macmillan.

Fulińska, Agnieszka 2014. 'Dionysos, Orpheus and Argead Macedonia. Overview and Perspectives'. *Classica Cracoviensia* 17, 43–68.

Fuller, J.F.C. 1960. *The Generalship of Alexander the Great*. New Brunswick, NJ: Rutgers University Press.

Fürer-Haimendorf, Christoph von 1967. *Morals and Merit*. London: Weidenfeld.

Fussman, G. 1987–88. 'Central and Provincial Administration in Ancient India: The Problem of the Maurya Empire'. *Indian Historical Review* 14, 41–72.

Futre Pinheiro, Marília P. and Montiglio, Silvia (eds.) 2015. *Philosophy and the Ancient Novel*. Groningen: Barkhuis.

Ganeri, Jonardon 2010. 'A Return to the Self: Indians and Greeks on Life as Art and Philosophical Therapy'. In Carlisle and Ganeri (eds.) 2010, 119–36.

Ganeri, Jonardon 2012. *The Concealed Art of the Soul. Theories of Self and Practices of Truth in Indian Ethics and Epistemology*. Oxford: Oxford University Press.

Gangopadhyaya (or Ganguli), Mrinalkanti 1980. *Indian Atomism: History and Sources*. Calcutta: K. P. Bagchi.

Garfield, J. L. 1990. 'Epoché and Śūnyatā: Skepticism East and West'. *Philosophy East and West* 40, 285–308.

Garfield, Jay 1995. *The Fundamental Wisdom of the Middle Way. Nagarjuna's* Mūlamadhyamakakārikā. *Translation and Commentary*. Oxford: Oxford University Press.

Garland, Robert 1995. *The Eye of the Beholder: Deformity and Disability in the Greek and Roman World*. London: Duckworth.

Gascoigne, Bamber 1971. *The Great Moghuls*. London: Cape.

Gaur, Albertine 1975. *Indian Charters on Copper Plates*. London: British Museum.

Gell, Simeran Man Singh 1992. *The Ghotul in Muria Society*. Chur: Harwood Academic.

Gethin, Rupert 2008. *Sayings of the Buddha*. Oxford: Oxford University Press.

Ghosh, A. 1973. *The City in Early Historical India*. Simla: Indian Institute of Advanced Study.

Gilmour, David 2002. *The Long Recessional: The Imperial Life of Rudyard Kipling*. London: John Murray.

Ginsberg, Allen 1970/1996. *Indian Journals*. New York: Grove Press (orig. edn San Francisco: City Lights).

Glancey, Jonathan 2011. *Nagaland: A Journey to India's Forgotten Frontier*. London: Faber.

Gokhale, Pradeep P. 2015. *Lokāyata/Cārvāka. A Philosophical Inquiry*. New Delhi: Oxford University Press.

Gold, Daniel 2015. *Provincial Hinduism. Religion and Community in Gwalior City*. Oxford: Oxford University Press.

Gombrich, Richard 1988. *Theravada Buddhism*. London: Routledge.

Gombrich, Richard 2013. *What the Buddha Thought*. Sheffield: Equinox.

Gómez Espelosín, F. J. 1994. 'Estrategias de veracidad en Ctesias de Cnidos', *Polis* 6, 143–68.

Goossens, Roger 1943. 'Gloses indiennes dans le lexique d'Hesychius'. *Antiquité Classique* 12, 47–55.

Gottschalk, H. B. 1964. 'The *De coloribus* and its Author'. *Hermes* 92, 59–85.

Gowans, Christopher W. 2010. 'Medical Analogies in Buddhist and Hellenistic Thought: Tranquillity and Anger', in Carlisle and Ganeri (eds.) 2010, 11–34.

Goyal, S. R. 1985. *Kautilya and Megasthenes*. Meerut: Kusumanjali.

Goyal, S. R. 2000. *The Indica of Megasthenes: Its Contents and Reliability*. Jodhpur: Kusumanjali.

Goyal, S. R. 2006. *Brahmi Script: An Invention of the Early Maurya Period*. Jodhpur: Kusumanjali.

Graf, Fritz and Johnston, Sarah Iles 2007. *Ritual Texts for the Afterlife. Orpheus and the Bacchic Gold Tablets*. Abingdon: Routledge.

Grainger, John D. 1990. *Seleukos Nikator: Constructing a Hellenistic Kingdom*. London: Routledge.

Greenblatt, Stephen 1991. *Marvelous Possessions: The Wonder of the New World*. Chicago: University of Chicago Press.

Gruen, Erich 2011. *Rethinking the Other in Antiquity*. Princeton: Princeton University Press.

Gunderson, L. 1980. *Alexander's Letter to Aristotle about India*. Meisenheim am Glan: Anton Hain.

Haberman, David 1994. *Journey through the Twelve Forests: An Encounter with Krishna*. New York: Oxford University Press.

Haberman, David 2006. *River of Love in an Age of Pollution: The Yamuna River of Northern India*. Berkeley: University of California Press.

Haberman, David 2014. *People Trees. Worship of trees in Northern India*. Oxford: Oxford University Press.

Habib, Irfan and Jha, Vivekanand 2004. *Mauryan India* (*A People's History of India*, vol. 5). New Delhi: Tulika Books.

Habib, Irfan and Habib, Faiz 2012. *Atlas of Ancient Indian History*. Delhi: Oxford University Press.

Hagerman, C. A. 2013. *Britain's Imperial Muse: The Classics, Imperialism, and the Indian Empire, 1784–1914*. Basingstoke: Palgrave Macmillan.

Hale, W. E. 1986. *Asura in Early Vedic Religion*. Delhi: Motilal Banarsidass.

Halkias, Georgios T. 2014. 'When the Greeks Converted the Buddha: Asymmetrical Transfers of Knowledge in Indo-Greek Cultures', in Peter Wick and Volker Rabens (eds.), *Religions and Trade: Religious Formation, Transformation and Cross-Cultural Exchange between East and West*. Leiden: Brill, 65–115.

Hall, Edith 2013. *Adventures with Iphigeneia in Tauris*. Oxford: Oxford University Press.

Halliday, W. R. 1933. *Indo-European Folktales and Greek Legend*. Cambridge: Cambridge University Press.

Hamilton J. R. 1969. *Plutarch,* Alexander*: A Commentary*. Oxford: Oxford University Press.
Hamilton, J. R. 1994. 'The Start of Nearchus' Voyage'. *Historia* 43, 501–4.
Hamilton, Sue 2000. *Early Buddhism: A New Approach. The I of the Beholder.* Richmond: Curzon.
Hansen, G. C. 1964. 'Alexander und die Brahmanen'. *Klio* 43–45, 351–80
Hardy, Adam (ed.) 2007. *The Temple in South Asia*. London: British Association for South Asian Studies.
Hardy, Gavin and Totelin, Laurence 2016. *Ancient Botany*. Abingdon: Routledge.
Hartman, S. S. 1965. 'Dionysos and Heracles in India according to Megasthenes: A Counter-argument'. *Temenos* 1, 55–64.
Hartsuiker, Dolf 1993/2014. *Sadhus. Holy Men of India*. London: Thames and Hudson.
Hausner, Sondra L. 2007. *Wandering with Sadhus: Ascetics in the Hindu Himalayas.* Bloomington: Indiana University Press.
Hawley, John Stratton (ed.) 1994. *Sati. The Blessing and the Curse.* Oxford: Oxford University Press.
Heckel, Waldemar, 2008. *The Conquests of Alexander the Great.* Cambridge: Cambridge University Press.
Heckel, Waldemar 2015. 'Alexander, Achilles, and Heracles', in Wheatley and Baynham (eds.) 2015, 21–34.
Heckel, Waldemar and Yardley, John 1981. 'Roman Writers and the Indian Practice of Suttee'. *Philologus* 125, 305–11.
Heesterman J. C. 1985. *The Inner Conflict of Tradition: Essays in Indian Ritual, Kingship and Society.* Chicago: University of Chicago Press.
Heesterman, J. C. 1993. *The Broken World of Sacrifice: An Essay in Ancient Indian Ritual.* Chicago: University of Chicago Press.
Hein, Norvin 1989. 'Kālayavana, a Key to Mathura's Self-Perception', in Srinivasan (ed.) 1989, 223–35.
Hemacandra 1998. *Lives of the Jain Elders*, tr. R. C. Fynes. Oxford: Oxford University Press
Hennig, R. 1930. 'Herodots "goldhütende Greifen" und "goldgrabende Ameisen": Ein Kapitel zur Klarstellung antiker Wirtschaftsgeographie'. *RhMus* 79, 330–2.
Herzfeld, Ernst 1968. *The Persian Empire.* Wiesbaden: Steiner.
Hollis, A. S. 2011. 'Greek Letters from Hellenistic Bactria', in D. Obbink and R. Rutherford (eds.), *Culture in Pieces: Studies Presented to Peter Parsons.* Oxford: Oxford University Press, 104–18.
Holt, Frank L. 2003. *Alexander the Great and the Mystery of the Elephant Medallions*. Berkeley: University of California Press.
Hoover, Oliver D. 2013. *Handbook of the Coins of Baktria and Ancient India*. Lancaster, PA: Classical Numismatic Group.
Hopkinson, Neil (ed.) 1994. *Studies in the* Dionysiaca *of Nonnus.* Cambridge: Cambridge Philological Society.
Hornblower, Jane 1981. *Hieronymus of Cardia*. Oxford: Oxford University Press.
Horrwitz, E. P. 1912/1967. *The Indian Theatre: A Brief Survey of Sanskrit Drama* (reprint). New York: Benjamin Blom.
Horten, H. 1912. 'The Mouthless Indians of Megasthenes'. *Journal of the Asiatic Society of Bengal*, n.s. 8, 291–301.

Hourani, George F. 1995. *Arab Seafaring in the Indian Ocean in Ancient and Early Medieval Times*. Princeton: Princeton University Press.

Howe, T., Müller, S. and Stoneman, R. (eds.) 2016. *Ancient Historiography on War and Empire*. Oxford: Oxbow.

Huntington, Sheila 1985. *Art of Ancient India*. New York: Weatherhill.

Huttner, U. 1997 *Die politische Rolle der Heraklesgestalt im griechischen Herrschertum*. Stuttgart: Steiner Verlag.

Ibn Battuta 1929. *Travels in Asia and Africa 1325–1354*, tr. and ed. H.A.R. Gibb. London: Routledge and Kegan Paul.

Ingalls, Daniel H. H. 1962. 'Cynics and Pāśupatas: The Seeking of Dishonor'. *Harvard Theological Review* 55, 281–98.

Invernizzi, Antonio (ed.) 1995. *In the Land of the Gryphons: Papers on Central Asia in Antiquity*. Florence: Le Lettere.

Inwood, Brad 2001. *The Poem of Empedocles. Text and Translation with an Introduction*. Toronto: Toronto University Press.

Ions, Veronica 1967. *Indian Mythology*. London: Paul Hamlyn.

Irwin, Robert 2006. *For Lust of Knowing: the Orientalists and their Enemies*. London: Allen Lane.

Jacobs, Bruno 2016. 'Megasthenes' Beschreibung von Palibothra and die Anfänge der Steinarchitektur unter der Maurya-Dynastie', in Wiesehöfer, Brinkhaus and Bichler (eds.) 2016, 63–77 with plates 78–83.

Jacobs, Julian (et al.) 2012. *The Nagas. Hill Peoples of Northeast India* (2nd revised edn). New York: Thames and Hudson.

Jairazbhoy, R. A. 1963. *Foreign Influence in Ancient India*. New York: Asia Publishing House.

Jamison, Stephanie 1991. *The Ravenous Hyenas and the Wounded Sun*. Ithaca, NY: Cornell University Press.

Jamison, S. and Brereton. J. 2014. *The Hymns of the Ṛg Veda*. Oxford: Oxford University Press.

Jansari, Sushma and Ricot, Richard 2016. 'Megasthenes and the *Astomoi*: A Case Study', in Wiesehöfer, Brinkhaus and Bichler (eds.) 2016, 85–96.

Jātakas. *See* Cowell 1895–1913.

Jayaswal, K. D. 1928. 'Historical Data in the Garga Saṃhita and the Brahmin Empire'. *Journal of the Bihar and Orissa Research Society* 14, 397–421.

Jha, Satyendra Kumar 1998. *Beginnings of Urbanization in Early Historic India*. Patna: Novelty & Co.

Johnston, E. H. 1939. 'Demetrias in Sind?'. *JRAS* (no vol. no.), 217–40.

Jones, Sir William 1995. *Selected Poetical and Prose Works*, ed. M. J. Franklin. Cardiff: University of Wales Press.

Jurewicz, Joanna 2016. *Fire, Death and Philosophy. A History of Ancient Indian Thinking*. Warsaw: Dom Wydawniczy Elipsa.

Kak, Subhash 1996. 'A Note on Caste'. *Annals of the Bhandarkar Oriental Research Institute* 77, 235–40.

Kakoulli, Ioanna 2009. *Greek Painting Techniques and Materials from the Fourth to the First Century BC*. London: Archetype.

Kalana 1900. *Rājataranginī. A Chronicle of the Kings of Kaśmir*, tr. M. A. Stein. Westminster: Constable.

Kalota, Narain Singh 1978. *India as Described by Megasthenes*. Delhi: Concept.

Kant, Shashi 2000. *The Hāthīgumphā Inscription of Khāravela and the Bhabru Edict of Aśoka*. New Delhi: DK Printworld.

Karttunen, Klaus 1984. 'ΚΥΝΟΚΕΦΑΛΟΙ and ΚΥΝΑΜΟΛΓΟΙ in Classical Ethnography'. *Arctos* 18, 31–6.

Karttunen, Klaus 1989. *India in Early Greek Literature*. Helsinki: Finnish Oriental Society.

Karttunen, Klaus 1991. 'The *Indica* of Ctesias and its Criticism', in Arora (ed.) 1991, 74–85.

Karttunen, Klaus 1997. *India and the Hellenistic World*. Helsinki: Finnish Oriental Society.

Kautilya 1992. *The Arthashastra*, ed., rearr., tr. and intro. L. N. Rangarajan. New Delhi: Penguin India.

Kazis, Israel J. 1962. *The Book of the Gests of Alexander of Macedon*. Cambridge, MA: Medieval Academy of America.

Keay, John 2000. *A History of India*. London: Harper Collins.

Keay, John 2001. *India Discovered. The Recovery of a Lost Civilization* (3rd edn). London: Harper Collins. (Orig. edn 1981, with different pagination.)

Keith, A. B. 1909. 'Pythagoras and the Doctrine of Transmigration', *JRAS* (no vol. no.), 569–606.

Keith, A. B. 1924. *The Sanskrit Drama in its Origin, Development, Theory and Practice*; repr. Delhi: Motilal Banarsidass 2015.

Kent, Eliza F. 2013. *Sacred Groves and Local Gods: Religion and Environmentalism in South India*. Oxford: Oxford University Press.

Kern, H. 1870 and 1875. 'The *Brhat-Sanhita*; or Complete System of Natural Astrology of Varaha-mihira. Translated from Sanskrit into English.' *JRAS* 4, 430–79 and 7, 81–134.

Khilnani, Sunil 2016. *Incarnations: India in 50 Lives*. London: Allen Lane.

Khusraw, Amir 1999. *Lo specchio alessandrino*, ed. and tr. A. M. Piemontese. Catanzaro: Rubbettino.

Kienast, Dietmar 1965. 'Alexander und der Ganges'. *Historia* 14, 180–8.

King, Richard 1999. *Indian Philosophy. An Introduction to Hindu and Buddhist Thought*. Edinburgh: Edinburgh University Press.

Kipling, Rudyard (1987). *Kim*, ed. A. Sandison. Oxford: Oxford University Press.

Kipling, Rudyard (1919). *Letters of Marque*, in *From Sea to Sea*, vol. 1. London: Macmillan.

Kirfel, Willibald 1967. *Die Kosmographie der Inder*. Hildesheim: Olms.

Kling, Blair B. 1966. *The Blue Mutiny: The Indigo Disturbances in Bengal, 1859–1862*. Philadelphia: University of Pennsylvania Press

Knox, Robert 1992. *Amaravati: Buddhist Sculpture form the Great Stupa*. London: British Museum Press.

Koehler, Jeff 2015. *Darjeeling*. London: Bloomsbury.

Koestler, Arthur 1960. *The Lotus and the Robot*. London: Hutchinson.

Konaris, Michael 2011. 'Dionysos in Nineteenth-Century Scholarship', in R. Schlesier (ed.), *A Different God? Dionysos and Ancient Polytheism*. Berlin: de Gruyter.

König, Roderich and Hopp, Joachim 1994. *Plinius: Naturkunde*. Zurich: Artemis & Winkler.

Kosmin, Paul 2014. *The Land of the Elephant Kings. Space, Territory and Ideology in the Seleucid Empire*. Cambridge, MA: Harvard University Press.

Kotlińska-Toma, Agnieszka 2015. *Hellenistic Tragedy: Texts, Translations and a Critical Survey*. London: Bloomsbury.

Kotlińska-Toma, Agnieszka 2016. 'On his Majesty's Secret Service – Actors at the Court of Alexander the Great'. In Nawotka and Wojciechowska (eds.) 2016, 273–86.

Krishen, Pradip 2005. *Trees of Delhi*. New Delhi: Dorling Kindersley.

Krishna, Nanditha and Amirthalingam, M. 2014. *Sacred Plants of India*. Gurgaon: Penguin India.

Kubica, Olga 2013. 'Edicts of King Piyadassi (Aśoka) in the Context of Ethnicity'. *European Scientific Journal*, special edn 2, 723–33.

Kubica, Olga 2014. 'Beyond Influence. A Reflection on the History of Research on the *Milindapañha*, with a Comparison of the Text to the *Kitab al Khazari*'. *Eos* 101, 187–206.

Kubica, Olga 2016. 'Greek Literature and Cultural Life East of the Euphrates. The Greeks and Buddhism'. *Eos* 103, 143–7.

Kuhrt, Amélie and Sherwin-White, Susan 1993. *From Samarkhand* [sic] *to Sardis. A New Approach to the Seleucid Empire*. London: Duckworth.

Kuiper, F.B.J. 1969. Review of Dahlquist 1962. *Indo-Iranian Journal* 11, 142–6.

Kumar, Manoj 2013. *Chanakya and Chandragupta. The Mentor and the Prodigy*. Delhi: Vijay Goel.

Kuzminski, Adrian 2008. *Pyrrhonism. How the Greeks Reinvented Buddhism*. Plymouth: Lexington Books.

Lahiri, N. 1992. *The Archaeology of Indian Trade Routes up to 200 BC*. Delhi: Oxford University Press.

Lahiri, Nayanjot 2015. *Ashoka in Ancient India*. Cambridge, MA: Harvard University Press.

Lakhnavi, Ghalib and Bilgrami, Abdullah 2007. *The Adventures of Amir Hamza*, tr. M. A. Farooqi. New York: The Modern Library.

Lane Fox, Robin 1973. *Alexander the Great*. London: Allen Lane.

Lane Fox, Robin 1991. *The Unauthorized Version: Truth and Fiction in the Bible*. London: Allen Lane.

Lane Fox, Robin 1996. 'Text and Image: Alexander the Great, Coins and Elephants'. *BICS* 41, 87–108.

Lane Fox, Robin 2008. *Travelling Heroes. Greeks and their Myths in the Epic Age of Homer*. London: Allen Lane.

Lane Fox, Robin 2011. 'The First Hellenistic Man', in A. Erskine and L. Llewellyn-Jones (eds.), *Creating a Hellenistic World*. Swansea: Classical Press of Wales.

Lassen, Christian 1847–61. *Indische Alterthumskunde* (2 vols.). Bonn: H. B. Koenig.

Laufer, Berthold 1908. 'Die Sage von den goldgrabenden Ameisen'. *Toung Pao* 9, 429–52; repr. in *Kleinere Schriften* (1976–1992), vol. 2, 1271–94.

Law, Bimala Churn 1954. *Historical Geography of Ancient India*. Paris: Société Asiatique.

Lawrence, James Henry 1811. *The Empire of the Nairs, or, the Rights of Women; An Utopian Romance, in Twelve Books*. London: Hookham.

Lee, H.D.P. 1948. 'Place Names and the Date of Aristotle's Biological Works'. *CQ* 42, 61–7.

Leick, Gwendolyn 2001. *Mesopotamia: The Invention of the City*. London: Penguin.

Lenfant, Dominique (ed. and tr.) 2004. *Ctésias de Cnide: la Perse, l'Inde, autres fragments*. Paris: Les Belles Lettres.

Lerner, Jeffrey 2003. 'The Ai Khanoum Philosophical Papyrus'. *ZPE* 142, 45–51.

Leroi, Armand Marie 2014. *The Lagoon*.

Le Strange, G. (ed.) 1919. *The Geographical Part of the* Nuzhat-al-qulub *(740/1340)*. Leyden: Brill.

Levi, Carlo 2007. *Essays on India*. London: Hesperus.

Levi, Peter 1972. *The Light Garden of the Angel King: Travels in Afghanistan.* London: Collins.

Lewis, Norman 1991. *A Goddess in the Stones. Travels in India.* London: Cape; repr. London: Eland 2017.

Li, Rongxi (tr.) 2000. *Buddhist Monastic Traditions of South Asia. A Record of the Inner Law Sent Home from the South Seas, by Śramana Yijing.* Berkeley, CA: Numata Centre for Buddhist Translation and Research.

Li, Rongxi 2002. *Lives of Great Monks and Nuns.* Berkeley, CA: Numata Centre for Buddhist Translation and Research.

Lightfoot, J. L. 2014. *Dionysius Periegetes: Description of the Known World.* Oxford: Oxford University Press.

Lloyd, G.E.R. 2014. *The Ideals of Inquiry. An Ancient History.* Oxford: Oxford University Press.

Lloyd-Jones, Hugh 1966. Review of Snell 1964. *Gnomon* 38, 12–17.

Long, A. A. and Sedley, D. 1987. *The Hellenistic Philosophers.* Cambridge: Cambridge University Press.

Lovejoy, Arthur O. and Boas, George 1935. *Primitivism and Related Ideas in Antiquity.* Baltimore: Johns Hopkins University Press.

Lüders, H. 1926. *Bruchstücke der Kalpanāmaṇḍitikā des Kumāralāta.* Leipzig.

Ludvik, Catherine 2007. *Sarasvatī. Riverine Goddess of Knowledge. From the Manuscript-carrying Vīṇā-player to the Weapon-wielding Defender of the Dharma.* Leiden: Brill.

McClish, Mark and Olivelle, Patrick 2012. *The Arthashastra: Selections from the Classic Indian Work on Statecraft.* Indianapolis: Hackett.

McCrindle, John W. 1901. *Ancient India as Described in Classical Literature.* London; repr. Delhi: Munshiram Manoharlal 1979.

McCrindle, John W. 1926. *Ancient India as Described by Megasthenes and Arrian.* London; repr. Delhi: Munshiram Manoharlal 2000.

McCrindle, John W. 1927. *Ancient India according to Ptolemy.* London; repr. New Delhi: Munshiram Manoharlal 2000.

Macdowall, D. W. 2005. 'The Role of Demetrius in Arachosia and the Kabul Valley', in Bopearachchi and Boussac (eds.) 2005, 197–206.

McEvilley, Thomas 2002. *The Shape of Ancient Thought. Comparative Studies in Greek and Indian Philosophies.* New York: Allworth Press.

McGrath, Kevin 2013. *Heroic Kṛṣṇa. Friendship in Epic Mahābhārata.* Boston and Washington: Ilex Foundation and Center for Hellenic Studies. Distributed by Harvard University Press.

Mackintosh-Smith, Tim 2002. *The Travels of Ibn Battutah.* London: Picador.

Maggi, Daniele 2016. 'Perspectives sur la transmigration des âmes dans l'aire indo-européenne: L'histoire indienne d'Urvaśī et Purūravas', in Ducoeur and Muckensturm-Poule (eds.) 2016, 27–43.

Magnone, Paolo 2016. 'Soul Chariots in Indian and Greek Thought: Polygenesis or Diffusion?', in Seaford (ed.) 2016, 149–67.

Mahāvaṃsa, The Great Chronicle of Ceylon 1950, tr. William Geiger. Colombo: Ceylon Government Information department. (Orig. edn 1912.)

Mairs, Rachel 2014. *The Hellenistic Far East: Archaeology, Language and Identity in Greek Central Asia.* Berkeley: University of California Press

Majumdar, B. K. 1960. *The Military System in Ancient India.* Calcutta: Mukhopadyay.

Majumdar, Bimalendu 1998. *The Totos: Cultural and Economic Transformation of a Small Tribe in the Sub-Himalayan Bengal*. Calcutta: Academic Enterprise.

Majumdar, R. C. 1958. 'The *Indika* of Megasthenes'. *Journal of the American Oriental Society* 28, 273–6.

Majumdar, R. C. 1960. *The Classical Accounts of India*. Calcutta: Mukhopadyay.

Mallinson, James (tr.) 2007–09. (Somadeva's) *The Ocean of the Rivers of Story* (2 vols.). New York: New York University Press.

Mandeville, Sir John 1983. *Travels*, tr. with intro. C.W.R.D. Moseley. Harmondsworth: Penguin.

Mann, Richard D. 2012. *The Rise of Mahasen. The Transformation of Kanda-Kārttikeya in North India from the Kuṣāna to Gupta Empires*. Leiden: Brill.

Manteghi, Haila forthcoming. 'The King and the Wizard: Apollonius of Tyana in the *Iskandarnama* of Nizami Ganjavi (1141–1209)', in Stoneman, Nawotka and Wojciechowska (eds.) forthcoming.

Manusmṛti (*The Laws of Manu*). *See* Doniger and Smith (ed. and tr.) 1991.

Manuel, Frank and Manuel, Fritzie 1979. *Utopian Thought in the Western World*. Cambridge, MA: Harvard University Press.

Markstrom, Kurt Sven 2007. *The Operas of Leonardo Vinci, Napoletano*. Hillsdale, NY: Pendragon Press.

Marshall, John 1917. *The Monuments of Sanchi*. Bombay.

Marshall, John 1960. *A Guide to Taxila*. Cambridge: Cambridge University Press.

Martin, Victory 1959. 'Un recueil de diatribes cyniques: Papyrus Genève inv. 271'. *Mus. Helv.* 16, 77–115.

Masters, John 1960. *Bhowani Junction*. Harmondsworth: Penguin.

Matilal, Bimal Krishna 1986. *Perception. An Essay on Classical Indian Theories of Knowledge*. Oxford: Oxford University Press.

Matilal, Bimal Krishna 2005. *Epistemology, Logic, and Grammar in Indian Philosophical Analysis*. New Delhi: Oxford University Press.

Maugham, W. Somerset 1944. *The Razor's Edge*. London: Heinemann.

Mayor, Adrienne 2000. *The First Fossil-Hunters: Palaeontology in Greek and Roman Times*. Princeton University Press.

Mehl, A. 1986. *Seleukos Nikator und sein Reich*. Leuven: Peeters.

Mehta, Gita 1980. *Karma-Cola*. London: Minerva.

Meister, Michael W. 2007. 'Early Architecture and its Transformations: New Evidence for Vernacular Origins for the Indian Temple', in Hardy (ed.) 2007, 1–20.

Menon, Subhadra 2000. *Trees of India*. Hong Kong: Local Colour.

Michell, George and Antonio Martinelli 1994. *The Royal Palaces of India*. London: Thames and Hudson.

Miller, B. S. 1977. *Love Song of the Dark Lord. Jayadeva's Gītagovinda*. New York: Columbia University Press.

Miller, Sam 2014. *A Strange Kind of Paradise: India through Foreign Eyes*. London: Cape.

Milns, R. D. 1989. 'Greek Writers on India before Alexander'. *Australian Journal of Politics and History* 35, 353–63.

Miquel, André 1967. *La géographie humaine du monde musulman*, vol. 1. Paris: Éditions de l'École des hautes études en sciences sociales.

Mirza, Mohammad Wahid 1935. *The Life and Works of Amir Khusrau*. Delhi: Idarah-I Adabiyat-I Delli.

Mitchiner, John E. (ed. and tr.) 2002. *The Yuga Purāṇa* (2nd revised edn). Kolkata: The Asiatic Society.

Mitter, Partha 1977. *Much Maligned Monsters. A History of European Reactions to Indian Art*. Chicago: University of Chicago Press.

Molina Marín, Antonio Ignacio 2010. *Geographica: ciencia de espacio y tradición narrativa de Homero a Cosmas Indicopleustes*. Murcia: Universidad de Murcia.

Momigliano, Arnaldo 1975. *Alien Wisdom: The Limits of Hellenization*. Cambridge: Cambridge University Press.

Montaigne, Michel de 2014. *Shakespeare's Montaigne: The Florio Translation of the Essays – A Selection*, ed. Stephen Greenblatt and Peter G. Platt. New York: NYRB.

Mookerji, Radha Kumud 1966. *Chandragupta Maurya and his Times*. Delhi: Motilal Banarsidass.

Moraes, Dom 1983. *Answered by Flutes: Reflections from Madhya Pradesh*. Bombay: Asia Publishing House.

Moraes, Dom and Srivatsa, Sarayu 2003. *The Long Strider. How Thomas Coryate Walked from England to India in the Year 1613*. New Delhi: Penguin India.

Mørkholm, Otto 1991. *Early Hellenistic Coinage, from the Accession of Alexander to the Peace of Apamea (336–186 BC)*. Cambridge: Cambridge University Press.

Morton, A. G. 1986. 'Pliny on Plants. His Place in the History of Botany', in French and Greenaway (eds.) 1986, 86–97.

Moyer, Ian S. 2011. *Egypt and the Limits of Hellenism*. Cambridge: Cambridge University Press.

Muckensturm, Claire 1993. 'Les gymnosophistes étaient-ils des cyniques modèles?', in M. O. Goulet-Cazé and Richard Goulet (eds.), *Le Cynisme ancient et ses prolongements*. Paris: PUF, 225–39.

Mukherji, Parul D. (ed. and tr.) 2001. *The* Citrasutra *of the* Viṣṇudharmottara Purāṇa. New Delhi: Indira Gandhi National Centre for the Arts.

Müller, Sabine 2014. *Alexander, Makedonien und Persien*. Berlin: trafo Verlag.

Munson, Rosaria V. 2001. *Telling Wonders: Ethnographic and Political Discourse in the Work of Herodotus*. Ann Arbor: University of Michigan Press.

Muntz, Charles E. 2012. 'Diodorus Siculus and Megasthenes'. *CP* 107, 21–37.

Muntz, Charles E. 2017. *Diodorus Siculus and the World of the Late Roman Republic*. Oxford: Oxford University Press.

Murphy, Trevor 2004. *Pliny the Elder's* Natural History. Oxford: Oxford University Press.

Murray, Oswyn 1970. 'Hecataeus of Abdera and Pharaonic Kingship'. *JEA* 565, 141–71.

Murray, Oswyn 1972. 'Herodotus and Hellenistic Culture'. *CQ* 22, 200–13.

Nadiem, Ihsan H. 2008. *Taxila in Buddhist Gandhara*. Lahore: Sang-e-Meel Publications.

Nagarjuna. *See* Garfield 1995 *and* Siderits and Katsura 2013.

Naipaul, V. S. 1964. *An Area of Darkness*. London: André Deutsch.

Naqvi, Nasm H. 2011. *A Study of Buddhist Medicine and Surgery in Gandhara*. Delhi: Motilal Banarsidass.

Narain, A. K. 2003. *The Indo-Greeks. Revisited and Supplemented*. Delhi: B.R. Publishing.

Narasimhan, Sakuntala 1990. *Sati. A Study of Widow Burning in India*. New Delhi: Viking.

Narayan, R. K. 1972. *The Ramayana. A Shortened Modern Prose Version of the Indian Epic.* Harmondsworth: Penguin.

Nath, R. and Faiyaz 'Gwaliari' 1981. *India as Seen by Amir Khusrau in 1318 AD.* Jaipur: Historical Research Documentation Programme.

Nāṭya Śāstra of Bharatamuni 1988. Translated by a Board of Scholars. Delhi: Sri Satguru Publications.

Nawotka, Krzysztof and Wojciechowska, Agnieszka (eds.) 2016. *Alexander the Great and the East: History, Art, Tradition.* Wiesbaden: Harrasowitz.

Nayar, T. S., Binu, S., and Pushpangadan, P. 1999. 'Uses of Plants and Plant Products in Traditional Indian Mural Paintings'. *Economic Botany* 53, 41–50.

Nehru, J. 2004. *The Discovery of India.* Gurgaon: Penguin India. (1st edn 1946; also many others, with different paginations).

Nehru, Lolita 1989. *Origins of the Gandharan Style: A Study of Contributory Influences.* Delhi: Oxford University Press.

Nesselrath, H. G. 1995. 'Herodot und die Enden der Erde'. *Mus. Helv.* 52, 20–44.

Nevile, Pran 2006. *Lahore: A Sentimental Journey.* Gurgaon: Penguin India.

Nichols, Andrew 2011. *Ctesias on India.* London: Bristol Classical Press.

Nickel, Lukas 2013. 'The First Emperor and Sculpture in China'. *Bulletin of SOAS* 76, 413–47.

Nilakanta Sastri, K. A. 1950. *History of India. Part 1 – Ancient India.* Madras: S. Viswanathan.

Nilakanta Sastri, K. A. 1957. *A Comprehensive History of India*, vol. 2. *Mauryas and Satavahanas.* Bombay: Orient Longmans.

Nilakanta Sastri, K. A. (ed.) 1967. *Age of the Nandas and Mauryas* (2nd edn). Delhi: Moltilal Banarsidass.

Nīlakaṇṭha 1931. *The Elephant-Lore of the Hindus*, ed. and tr. Franklin Edgerton. New Haven, CT: Yale University Press.

Nippel, Wilfried 1996. 'Facts and Fiction: Greek Ethnography and its Legacy'. *History and Anthropology* 9, 125–38.

Nussbaum, Martha 1994. *The Therapy of Desire. Theory and Practice in Hellenistic Ethics.* Princeton: Princeton University Press.

Obeyesekere, Gananath 2002. *Imagining Karma: Ethical Transformation in Amerindian, Buddhist and Greek Rebirth.* Berkeley: University of California Press.

O'Flaherty, Wendy Doniger 1973/1981. *Śiva, the Erotic Ascetic.* Oxford: Oxford University Press.

O'Flaherty, Wendy Doniger 1980. 'Dionysus and Śiva: Parallel Patterns in Two Pairs of Myths'. *History of Religions* 20, 81–111.

O'Flaherty, Wendy Doniger (ed.) 1980. *Karma and Rebirth in Classical Indian Traditions.* Berkeley: University of California Press.

O'Leary, De Lacy 1949. *How Greek Science Passed to the Arabs.* London: Routledge and Kegan Paul.

Olivelle, Patrick (tr.) 1992. *Saṃnyāsa Upaniṣads: Hindu Scriptures on Asceticism and Renunciation.* New York: Oxford University Press.

Olivelle, Patrick (tr.) 1996. *Upaniṣads.* Oxford: Oxford University Press.

Olivelle, Patrick (tr.) 1999. *Dharmasūtras. The Law Codes of Ancient India.* Oxford: Oxford University Press.

Olivelle, Patrick (tr.) 2004. *The Law Code of Manu*. Oxford: Oxford University Press.

Olivelle, Patrick (ed.) 2006. *Between the Empires: Society in India 300 BCE to 400 CE*. Oxford: Oxford University Press.

Olivelle, Patrick, Leoshko. Janice and Ray, Himanshu Prabha (eds.) 2012. *Reimagining Aśoka. Memory and History*. New Delhi: Oxford University Press.

O'Sullivan, Lara 2015. 'Callisthenes and Alexander the Invincible God', in Wheatley and Baynham (eds.) 2015, 35–52.

Otto, W. F. 1965. *Dionysos*. Bloomington: Indiana University Press.

Pal, Ranajit 2002. *Non-Jonesian Indology and Alexander*. New Delhi: Minerva.

Palagia, Olga 1980. *Euphranor*. Leiden: Brill.

Palagia, Olga 2017. 'Highlights of Greek Figural Wall Paintings', in S.T.A.M. Mols and E. M. Moorman (eds.), *Context and Meaning*. Leuven: Peeters.

Palagia, Olga forthcoming. 'Visualising the Gods in Ancient Macedonia', in P. P. Iossif and W. van de Put (eds.), *Greek Iconographies: Methodological Approaches in Ancient Greek Imagery*. Leiden: Brill.

Panaioti, Antoine 2013. *Nietzsche and Buddhist Philosophy*. Cambridge: Cambridge University Press.

Panchenko, Dimitri 1998. 'Scylax' Circumnavigation of India and its Interpretation in Early Greek Geography, Ethnography and Cosmography, I'. *Hyperboreus* 4, 211–42.

Panchenko, Dimitri 2002. 'Scylax in Philostratus' *Life of Apollonius of Tyana*'. *Hyperboreus* 8, 5–12.

Panchenko, Dimitri 2003. 'Scylax' Circumnavigation of India and its Interpretation in Early Greek Geography, Ethnography and Cosmography, II'. *Hyperboreus* 9, 274–94.

Paranavitana, Senarat 1971. *The Greeks and the Mauryas*. Colombo: Lake House Investments.

Parasher, Aloka 1991. *Mlecchas in Early India: A Study in Attitudes towards Outsiders up to AD 600*. New Delhi: Munshiram Manoharlal.

Parfit, Derek 1984. *Reasons and Persons*. Oxford: Oxford University Press.

Pargiter, F. E. (ed. and tr.) 1913. *The Purana Text of the Dynasties of the Kali Age*. Oxford: Oxford University Press

Pargiter F. E. 1922. *Ancient Indian Historical Tradition*. Oxford: Oxford University Press.

Parker, Grant 2008. *The Making of Roman India*. Cambridge: Cambridge University Press.

Parker, Grant 2012, 'Aśoka the Greek, Converted and Translated', in Olivelle, Leoshko and Ray (eds.) 2012, 310–26.

Parker, Grant and Sinopoli, Carla M. 2008. *Ancient India and the Wider World*. Ann Arbor: University of Michigan Center for South and Southeast Asian Studies.

Parker, Robert 2017. *Greek Gods Abroad: Names, Natures and Transformations*. Berkeley: University of California Press.

Parkin, Robert 1992. *The Munda of Central India*. Delhi: Oxford University Press.

Parmar, Y. S. 1975. *Polyandry in the Himalayas*. Delhi: Vikas Publishing House.

Parpola, Asko 2002. 'Πανδαίη and Sītā: On the Historical Background of the Sanskrit Epics'. *JAOS* 122, 361–73.

Parpola, Asko 2015. *The Roots of Hinduism: The Early Aryans and the Indus Civilization*. Oxford: Oxford University Press.

Paz, Octavio 1989. *The Monkey Grammarian*. London: Peter Owen.

Paz, Octavio 1997. *In Light of India*. London: Harvill Press.

Pearson, Lionel 1960. *Lost Historians of Alexander the Great*. Philadelphia; repr. Chico, CA: Scholars Press 1983.

Peissel, Michel 1984. 'The Ants' Gold: The Discovery of the Greek El Dorado in the Himalayas. London: Harvill Press. (*See too* Peissel, 'The Land of the Gold-Digging Ants'. *Geographical Journal* 150, 145–6.)

Penzer, N. M 1924. *The Ocean of Story: Being C. H. Tawney's Translation of Somadeva's* kathā sarit sāgara (10 vols.); repr. Delhi: Motilal Banarsidass 1968.

Pfister, Friedrich 1961. 'Das Alexander-Archiv und die hellenistisch-römische Wissenschaft'. *Historia* 10, 30–67.

Pischel, R. 1893. 'Zu Soph. *Ant.* 909–912'. *Hermes* 28, 465–8.

Pleij, Herman 2001. *Dreaming of Cockaigne: Medieval Fantasies of the Perfect Life*. New York: Columbia University Press.

Plischke, Sonja 2014. *Die Seleukiden und Iran*. Wiesbaden: Harrassowitz.

Pollet, G. (ed.) 1987. *India and the Ancient World*. Leuven: Peeters.

Pollet, G., Van Damme, G. and Depuydt, F. 2014. *Corpus Topographicum Indiae Antiquae III. Indian Toponyms in Ancient Greek and Latin Texts.* (atlas volume). Leuven: Peeters.

Pollitt, J. J. 1974. *The Ancient View of Greek Art. Criticism, History, and Terminology*. New Haven, CT; Yale University Press.

Pollitt, J. J. 1990. *The Art of Ancient Greece. Sources and Documents*. Cambridge University Press.

Polo, Marco 1903. *The Book of Ser Marco Polo*, ed. Henry Yule and Henri Cordier. London; repr. Delhi: Munshiram Manoharlal 1993.

Poonacha, K. P. 2011. *Excavations at Kanaganahalli (Sannati), Taluk Chitapur, Dist Gulbarga, Karnataka.*. New Delhi: Chandu Press.

Possehl, G. L. 2002. *The Indus Civilization: A Contemporary Perspective*. Walnut Creek, CA: AltaMira Press.

Powell J. U. and Barber, E. A.1929. *New Chapters in Greek Literature*, vol. 2. Oxford: Oxford University Press.

Prakash, Buddha 1964. *Political and Social Movements in Ancient Panjab*. Delhi: Motilal Banarsidass.

Primo, Andrea 2009. *La storiografia sui Seleucidi da Megastene a Eusebio di Cesarea*. Pisa: Fabrizio Serra.

Puri, B. N. 1971. *India as Described by Early Greek Writers*. Varanasi: Indological Book House.

Puri, B. N. 1990. *India in the Time of Patanjali* (3rd edn). Delhi: Munshiram Manoharlal.

Puri, B. N. 2014. *Kuṣānas in India and Central Asia*. Delhi: Munshiram Manoharlal.

Puskás, Ildikó 1996. 'Magasthenes [*sic*] and the Indian Gods Heracles and Dionysos'. *Mediterranean Studies* 2, 39–47.

Quintanilla, Sonya Rhie 2007. *History of Early Stone Sculpture at Mathura*. Leiden: Brill.

Quintanilla, Sonya Rhie 2017. 'Transformations of Identity and the Buddha's Infancy Narratives at Kanaganahalli'. *Archives of Asian Art* 67, 111–42.

Rāmāyaṇa (*of Vālmīki*) 1 (*Bālakāṇḍa*); 2 (*Ayodhyākāṇḍa*); 3 (*Araṇyakāṇḍa*); 4 (*Kiṣkindhākāṇḍa*). *See* Vālmīki.

Rapin, C. 1987. 'Textes littéraires d'Ai Khanum'. *BCH* 111, 225–66.

Rapin, Claude 1992. *Fouilles d'Ai Khanoum VIII: la trésorerie du palais hellénistique d'Ai Khanoum.* Paris: Boccard.

Rapin, Claude 1995. 'Hinduism in the Indo-Greek Area. Notes on Some Finds from Bactria and on Two Temples in Taxila', in Invernizzi (ed.) 1995, 275–91.

Rapin, Claude 2017. 'Alexandre le Grand en Asie Centrale. Géographie et stratégie de la conquête des Portes Caspiennes à l'Inde', in C. Antonetti and P. Biagi (eds.), *Moving East and Back to West: With Alexander in India and Central Asia.* Oxford: Oxbow, 37–121.

Rawlinson, H. G. 1912. *Bactria. The History of a Forgotten Empire*; repr. Yardley, PA: Westholme 2013.

Rawlinson, H. G. 1926. *Intercourse between India and the Western World. From the Earliest Times to the Fall of Rome.* Cambridge: Cambridge University Press.

Ray, Himanshu P. 'Interpreting the Mauryan Empire: Centralized State or Multiple Centers of Control?', in Parker and Sinopoli (eds.) 2008, 13–51.

Ray, Satyajit 2004 [1987]. *The Unicorn Expedition and Other Stories.* New Delhi: Puffin India.

Raz, Ram 1834. *Essay on the Architecture of the Hindus.* London: The Royal Asiatic Society of Great Britain and Ireland.

Reese, Wilhelm 1914. *Die griechischen Nachrichten über Indien.* Leipzig: Teubner.

Reger, Gary 2015. 'Apollonios of Tyana and the *Gymnoi* of Ethiopia', in Futre Pinheiro and Montiglio (eds.) 2015, 141–58.

Rice, E. E. 1983. *The Grand Procession of Ptolemy Philadelphus.* Oxford: Oxford University Press.

Robinson, Andrew 2015. *Lost Civilizations: The Indus.* London: Reaktion Books.

Rocher, Ludo 1975. Review of Paranavitana 1971. *JAOS* 95, 141.

Roller, Duane W. 2010. *Eratosthenes' Geography: Fragments Collected and Translated.* Princeton: Princeton University Press.

Roller, Duane W. 2014. *The Geography of Strabo.* Cambridge: Cambridge University Press.

Rollinger, Robert 2013. *Alexander und die grossen Ströme: Die Flussüberquerungen im Lichte altorientalischer Pioniertechniken.* Wiesbaden: Harrassowitz.

Rollinger, Robert 2014. 'Aornos and the Mountains of the East: The Assyrian Kings and Alexander the Great', in S. Gaspa, A. Greco, D. M. Bonacossi, S. Poncha and R. Rollinger (eds.), *From Source to History: Studies on Ancient Near Eastern Worlds and Beyond. Dedicated to Giovanni Battista Lanfranchi* […]. Münster: Ugarit Verlag, 597–635.

Romm, J. S. 1989. 'Aristotle's Elephant and the Myth of Alexander's Scientific Patronage'. *AJP* 110, 566–75.

Romm, James S. 1992. *The Edges of the Earth in Ancient Thought.* Princeton: Princeton University Press.

Romm, James S. 2008. 'Geography as Eschatology: Greek Alexander Lore and the Eastern Limits of India', in Parker and Sinopoli (eds.) 2008, 93–105.

Romm, James S. (ed.) 2012. *The Landmark Arrian.* New York: Pantheon.

Rougemont, G, Pinault, G.-J. and Bernard, P. 2004. 'Deux nouvelles inscriptions', *Journal des Savants*, 333–56.

Roy, Kumkum 1994. *The Emergence of Monarchy in North India: 8th–4th centuries BC, as Reflected in the Brahmanical Tradition.* New Delhi: Oxford University Press.

Roy, S. N. 1972. 'Textual and Historical Analysis of the Puranic Chronology relating to the Maurya Dynasty'. *Purana* 14, 94–106.

Ruffing, Kai 2011. 'Ktesias' Indienbilder', in J. Wiesehöfer, R. Rollinger and G. Lanfranchi (eds.), *Ktesias Welt = Ctesias' World*. Wiesbaden: Harrassowitz.

Russell, Robert Vane and Hiralal, Rai Bahadur 1916. *The Tribes and Castes of the Central Provinces of India* (4 vols.) London: Macmillan.

Sachau, Edward C. 1910. *Alberuni's India*. London: Kegan Paul, Trench and Trubner; repr. Delhi: Munshiram Manoharlal 1992.

Sachse, Joanna 1981. *Megasthenes o Indiach* (in Polish with summaries in English and German). Wrocław: Wydawnictwo Uniwersytetu Wrocławskiego.

Sacks, Kenneth S. 1990. *Diodorus Siculus and the First Century*. Princeton: Princeton University Press.

Said, Edward 1978. *Orientalism*. New York: Pantheon.

Saletore, B. A. 1936. *Ancient Karnataka*. Poona: Oriental Book Agency.

Salomon, Richard 1991. 'Epigraphic Remains of Indian Traders in Egypt'. *JAOS* 111, 731–6.

Salomon, Richard 1998. *Indian Epigraphy*. New York: Oxford University Press.

Santelia, Stefania (ed.) 1991. *Charition liberata (P. Oxy. 413)*. Bari: Levante Editori.

Sanyal, Charu Chandra 1973. *The Meches and the Totos*. Darjeeling: University of North Bengal.

Sayce, A. H. (ed.) 1883. *The Ancient Empires of the East: Herodotus I–III, with notes introduction and appendices*. London: Macmillan.

Schiern, F. 1873. *Über den Ursprung der Sage von der goldgrabenden Ameisen*. Copenhagen: Ursin.

Schimmel, Annemarie 2004. *The Empire of the Great Mughals*. London: Reaktion Books.

Schlingloff, Dieter 1999. *A Guide to the Ajantā Paintings*, vol. 1: *Narrative Wall Paintings*. Delhi: Munshiram Manoharlal.

Schlingloff, Dieter 2012. *Fortified Cities of Ancient India*. London: Anthem Press.

Schmitt, Rüdiger 1990. 'Ex occidente lux: Griechen und griechische Sprache im hellenistischen Fernen Osten', in. P. Steinmetz (ed.) *Beiträge zu hellenistischer Literatur*, 41–58.

Schoff, Wilfred H. (ed. and tr.) 1914. *'Parthian Stations' by Isidore of Charax. An Account of the Overland Trade Route between the Levant and India in the First Century B.C.* Philadelphia: Commercial Musuem; repr. Chicago: Ares 1989.

Schwanbeck, E. A. 1846. *Megasthenis Indica*. Bonn: Pleimes.

Schwarz, F. F. 1968. 'Mauryas und Seleukiden', in M. Mayrhofer, F. Lochner-Huettenbach, and H. Schmeja (eds.), *Studien zur Sprachwissenschaft und Kulturkunde. Gedenkschrift für W. Brandenstein*. Innsbruck: Amoe, 223–30.

Schwarz , F. F. 1975. 'Arrian's *Indike* on India: Intention and Reality'. *East and West* 25, 181–200.

Schwarz, F. F. 1982–83. 'The Itinerary of Jambulos – Utopianism and History', in G.-D. Sontheimer and P.K. Aithal (eds.), *Indology and Law: Studies in Honour of Professor J. Duncan M. Derrett*. Heidelberg 1983, 18–55.

Scott, Paul 2005. *The Jewel in the Crown*. London: Arrow (orig. edn Heinemann 1966).

Scullard, H. H. 1974. *The Elephant in the Greek and Roman World*. London: Thames and Hudson.

Seaford, Richard (ed.) 2016. *Universe and Inner Self in Early Indian and Greek Thought*. Edinburgh: Edinburgh University Press.

Seaford, Richard forthcoming. *Atman and Psyche. How did Philosophy begin in India and Greece?*.

Sedlar, Jean W. 1980. *India and the Greek World: A Study in the Transmission of Culture*. Totowa, NJ: Rowman and Littlefield.

Sedlar, Jean W. 1982. *India in the Mind of Germany*. Washington, D.C: University Press of America.

Seligman, Hilda 1940. *When Peacocks Called*. London: John Lane.

Sen, Colleen Taylor 2015. *Feasts and Fasts: A History of Food in India*. London: Reaktion Books.

Sergeant, David 2013. *Kipling's Art of Fiction, 1884–1901*. Oxford: Oxford University Press.

Sethna, K. D. 1989. *Ancient India in a New Light*. New Delhi: Aditya Prakashan.

Settis, Salvatore 2008. *Artemidoro. Un papiro dal I secolo al XXI*. Turin: Einaudi.

Shamsie, Kamila 2014. *A God in Every Stone*. London: Bloomsbury.

Shand, Mark 1991. *Travels with my Elephant*. London: Cape.

Sharma, J. P. 1968. *Republics in Ancient India*. Leiden: Brill.

Sharma, R. C. 1994. *Splendour of Mathura: Art and Museum*. New Delhi: D.K. Printworld.

Sharma, R. C. 1995. *Buddhist Art: Mathura School*. New Delhi: Wiley Eastern.

Sharma, R. S. 1959. *Aspects of Political Ideas and Institutions in Ancient India*. Delhi: Motilal Banarsidass.

Sharma, R. S. 2009. *Rethinking India's Past*. Delhi: Oxford University Press.

Shastri, Ajay Mitra 1996. *Varahamihira's India* New Delhi: Aryan Books International.

Shaw, Julia 2007. *Buddhist Landscapes in Central India: Sanchi Hill and Archaeologies of Religious and Social Change, c. Third Century BC to Fifth Century AD*. London: British Association for South Asian Studies.

Shimada, Akira 2013. *Early Buddhist Architecture in Context*. Leiden: Brill.

Shipley, Graham 2011. *Pseudo-Skylax's Periplous: The Circumnavigation of the Inhabited World*. Exeter: Bristol Phoenix Press.

Shivaprasad Rai, P. 1985. '*Sariti*: A 2000 Year Old Bilingual Tulu–Greek Play'. *International Journal of Dravidian Linguistics* 14, 320–30.

Siderits, Mark 2016. *Studies in Buddhist Philosophy*. Oxford: Oxford University Press.

Siderits, Mark and Katsura, Shōryū 2013. *Nagarjuna's Middle Way*. Mūlamadhyamakakārikā. Somerville, MA: Wisdom Publications.

Singh, Rajesh 2012. *An Introduction to the Ajantā Caves*. Vadodara: Harisena.

Singh, S. D. 1965. *Ancient Indian Warfare*. Leiden: Brill.

Singh, S. D. 1978. *Polyandry in Ancient India*. New Delhi: Vikas.

Singh, Upinder 2004. *The Discovery of Ancient India. Early Archaeologists and the Beginnings of Archaeology*. Delhi: Permanent Black.

Singh, Upinder (ed.) 2006. *Ancient Delhi* (2nd edn). New Delhi: Oxford University Press.

Singh, Upinder 2009. *A History of Ancient and Medieval India. From the Stone Age to the 12th Century*. London: Pearson/Delhi: Dorling Kindersley.

Singh, Upinder 2017. *Political Violence in Ancient India*. Cambridge, MA: Harvard University Press.

Sircar, D. C. 1935. 'Yavana and Parasika'. *Journal of Indian History* 14, 34–8.

Sircar, D. C. 1942. *Select Inscriptions Bearing on Indian History and Civilization*, vol. 1. Calcutta: University of Calcutta; repr. Delhi: Facsimile Publisher 2017.

Sircar, D. C. 1947/1971. 'Gangā and the Gangaridae'. *Proceedings of Indian Historical Congress*. Bombay: 91ff.; repr. in Sircar 1971, 213–24.

Sircar, D. C. 1963 'The Account of the Yavanas in the *Yuga Purana*', *JRAS* (no vol. no.), 7–20

Sircar, D. C. 1971. *Studies in the Geography of Ancient and Medieval India* (2nd edn). Delhi: Motilal Banarsidass.

Sircar, D. C. 1972. 'Indological Notes 15: The Yavanas and Mathura'. *Journal of Ancient Indian History* 6, 168–73.

Skinner, J. E. 2012. *The Invention of Greek Ethnography: From Homer to Herodotus*. Oxford: Oxford University Press.

Skurzak, Ludwik 1954. 'Études sur les fragments de Mégasthène. Βραχμᾶνας–Σαρμάνας'. *Eos* 47, 95–100.

Skurzak, Ludwik 1979. 'En lisant Mégasthène. (Nouvelles observations sur la civilisation indienne)'. *Eos* 67, 69–74.

Sloterdijk, Peter 1987. *Critique of Cynical Reason*. Minneapolis: University of Minnesota Press. (Orig. German edn: *Kritik der zynischen Vernunft*. Frankfurt: Suhrkamp 1983.)

Slusser, Mary Shepherd 2010. *The Antiquity of Nepalese Wood Carving*. Seattle: University of Washington Press.

Smith, Alison, Brown, David Blayney and Jacobi, Carol 2015. *Artist and Empire: Facing Britain's Imperial Past*. London: Tate Publishing.

Smith, Vincent 1901. *Aśoka, the Buddhist Emperor of India*. Oxford: Oxford University Press.

Smith, Vincent A. 1914. 'The Indian Travels of Apollonius of Tyana'. *ZDMG* 68, 329–44.

Smith, Vincent A. 1962. *A History of Fine Art in India and Ceylon* (3rd edn, revised and enlargd by Karl Khandalavala). Bombay: Taraporevala.

Snell, Bruno 1964. *Scenes from Greek Drama*. Berkeley: University of California Press.

Soper, Alexander Coburn 1950. 'Early Buddhist Attitudes toward the Art of Painting'. *Art Bulletin* 32, 147–51.

Sorabji, Richard 2012. *Gandhi and the Stoics*. Oxford: Oxford University Press.

Spink, Walter 2005–12. *Ajantā – History and Development* (6 vols.), ed. J. Bronkhorst) Leiden: Brill.

Srinivasan, Doris Meth (ed.) 1989. *Mathura: The Cultural Heritage*. New Delhi: Manohar.

Srinivasan, Doris Meth 1997. *Many Heads, Arms, and Eyes*. Leiden: Brill.

Staal, J. F. 1965. 'Euclid and Panini'. *Philosophy East and West* 15, 99–116.

Stadter, Philip 1980. *Arrian of Nicomedia*. Chapel Hill: University of North Carolina Press.

Stafford, Emma 2012. *Heracles*. Abingdon: Routledge.

Stannard, Jerry 1965. 'Pliny and Roman Botany'. *Isis* 56, 420–5.

Starr, S. Frederick 2013. *Lost Enlightenment: Central Asia's Golden Age from the Arab Conquest to Tamerlane*. Princeton: Princeton University Press.

Stein, Aurel 1929. *On Alexander's Track to the Indus*. London: Macmillan; repr. New Delhi: AES 1996.

Stein, Otto 1921. *Megasthenes und Kautilya*. Vienna: Hölder.

Stein, Otto 1932. 'Megasthenes' *RE* 15, 230–326.

Steinmann, Marc 2012. *Alexander der Grosse und die 'nackten Weisen' Indiens. Die fictive Briefwechsel zwischen Alexander und dem Brahmanenkönig Dindimus*. Berlin: Frank & Timme.

Stern, S. M. 1968. *Aristotle on the World State*. Oxford: Oxford University Press.

Stoneman, Richard 1994a. 'Who are the Brahmans?' *CQ* 44, 500–10.

Stoneman, Richard 1994b. 'Romantic Ethnography'. *Ancient World* 25, 93–107.

Stoneman, Richard 1995. 'Naked Philosophers'. *JHS* 115, 99–114.

Stoneman, Richard 2004. *Alexander the Great* (Lancaster pamphlet; 2nd edn). London: Routledge.

Stoneman, Richard 2008. *Alexander the Great: A Life in Legend*. New Haven, CT: Yale University Press.

Stoneman, Richard 2009. 'The Author of the *Alexander Romance*', in M. Paschalis, St. Panayotakis and G. Schmeling (eds.), *Readers and Writers in the Ancient Novel*. Groningen: Barkhuis.

Stoneman, Richard 2012. *Legends of Alexander the Great* (2nd edn). London: IB Tauris.

Stoneman, Richard 2013. 'Alexander, Philotas and the Origins of Modern Historiography'. *Greece and Rome* 60, 296–312.

Stoneman, Richard 2015. 'Tales of Utopia: Alexander, Cynics and Christian Ascetics', in Futre Pinheiro and Montiglio (eds.) 2015, 51–63.

Stoneman, Richard 2016a. 'The Trees of the Sun and Moon in the *Alexander Romance*: Genuine Indian Detail?', *Eos* 103, 89–98.

Stoneman, Richard 2016b. 'The Justice of the Indians', in R. Seaford (ed.), *Universe and Inner Self in Early Indian and Early Greek Thought*. Edinburgh: Edinburgh University Press.

Stoneman, Richard 2016c. 'How the Hoopoe Got his Crest: Reflections on Megasthenes' Stories of India', in T. Howe, S. Müller and R. Stoneman (eds.), *Ancient Historiography on War and Empire*. Oxford: Oxbow, 188–99.

Stoneman, Richard 2016d. 'Alexander's Mirror', in Nawotka and Wojciechowska (eds.) 2016, 329–43.

Stoneman, Richard 2016e. 'The Struggle against *Pragmata*'. Review of Beckwith 2015. *CR* 66, 487–8.

Stoneman, Richard forthcoming a. 'The Alexander Romance and the Rise of Paradoxography', in Stoneman, Nawotka and Wojciechowska (eds.) forthcoming.

Stoneman, Richard forthcoming b. 'Plato's Advice to Alexander: Amir Khusraw's *Mirror of Alexander* (1299)'.

Stoneman, Richard, Erickson, Kyle and Netton, Ian (eds.) 2012. *The* Alexander Romance *in Persia and the East*. Groningen: Barkhuis.

Stoneman, Richard, Nawotka, Krzysztof and Wojciechowska, Agnieszka (eds.), forthcoming. *The* Alexander Romance*: Literature and History*.

Strachan, Michael 1962. *The Life and Adventures of Thomas Coryate*. Oxford: Oxford University Press.

Strong, John S. 1983. *The Legend of King Aśoka. A Study and Translation of the* Aśokāvadāna. Princeton: Princeton University Press; repr. Delhi: Motilal Banarsidass 2008.

Strong, John S. 2001. *The Buddha: A Beginner's Guide*. Oxford: Oneworld.

Subrahmanyam, Sanjay 1998. *The Career and Legend of Vasco da Gama*. Cambridge: Cambridge University Press.

Subrahmanyam, Sanjay 2017. *Europe's India: Words, People, Empires 1500–1800*. Cambridge, MA: Harvard University Press.

Sugiyama, Koichi 1969. *A Study of the Mundas. Village Life in India*. Tokyo: Tokai University Press.

Sulimani, Iris 2011. *Diodorus' Mythistory and the Pagan Mission. Historiography and Culture-heroes in the First Pentad of the* Bibliotheke. Leiden: Brill.

Sutton, Dana F. 1980. *The Greek Satyr Play*. Meisenheim am Glan: Anton Hain.

Szalc, A. 2011. 'Alexander's Dialogue with Indian Philosophers: Riddle in Greek and Indian Tradition'. *Eos* 98, 7–25.

Szalc A. 2012. 'In Search of Water of Life: The Alexander Romance and Indian Mythology', in Stoneman, Erickson and Netton (eds.) 2012, 327–38.

Szalc, Aleksandra 2016. 'The Metamorphoses of Pseudo-Callisthenes' Motifs concerning India in the Persian Alexander Romances', in Nawotka and Wojciechowska (eds.) 2016, 287–302.

Tambiah, Stanley 1976. *World Conqueror and World Renouncer.* Cambridge: Cambridge University Press.

Tāranātha 1970. *History of Buddhism in India*, tr. Lama Chimpa and A. Chattopadhyaya, ed. D. Chattopadhyaya. Simla: Indian Institute of Advanced Study.

Tarn, W. W. 1940a. 'Demetrias in Sind?'; with a reply by E. H. Johnston. *JRAS*, 179–89 + 189–93.

Tarn , W. W. 1940b. 'Two Notes on Seleucid History'. *JHS* 60, 84–94.

Tarn, W. W. 1951. *The Greeks in Bactria and India* (2nd edn). Cambridge: Cambridge University Press.

Thackston, Wheeler M. 2002 (tr.). *The* Baburnama. *Memoirs of Babur, Prince and Emperor.* New York: Modern Library.

Thapar, Romila 1987. *The Mauryas Revisited. S. G. Deuskar Lectures on Indian History 1984*. Calcutta: K. P. Bagchi for the Centre for Studies in Social Sciences.

Thapar, Romila 1989. 'The Early History of Mathura', in Srinivasan (ed.) 1989, 12–18.

Thapar, Romila 1997. *Aśoka and the Decline of the Mauryas* (2nd edn). Delhi: Oxford University Press.

Thapar, Romila 2002. *Early India: From the Origins to AD 1300*. London: Allen Lane.

Thapar, Romila 2013a. *Readings in Early Indian History*. New Delhi: Oxford University Press.

Thapar, Romila 2013b. *The Past before Us. Historical Traditions of Early North India*. Cambridge, MA: Harvard University Press.

Thompson, D'Arcy Wentworth 1936 (2nd edn). *A Glossary of Greek Birds*. Oxford: Oxford University Press.

Thompson, Edward 1928. *Suttee: A Historical and Philosophical Inquiry into the Hindu Rite of Widow-burning.* London: Allen and Unwin.

Timmer, Barbara C. J. 1930. *Megasthenes en de indische maatschappij*. Amsterdam: H. J. Paris.

Toynbee, A.J. 1961. *Between Oxus and Jumna*. Oxford: Oxford University Press.

Trautmann, Thomas 1971. *Kautilya and the* Arthashastra*: A Statistical Investigation of the Authorship and Evolution of the Text.* Leiden: Brill

Trautmann, Thomas 1982. 'Elephants and the Mauryas', in S. N. Mukherjee (ed.), *India, History and Thought: Essays in Honour of A. L. Basham*. Calcutta: Subarnarekha,, 254–81.

Trautmann, Thomas R. 1998. 'The Lives of Sir William Jones', in Alexander Murray (ed.), *Sir William Jones 1746–94: A Commemoration*. Oxford: Oxford University Press; 91–121.

Trautmann, Thomas R. 2015. *Elephants and Kings. An Environmental History.* Chicago: University of Chicago Press.

Tree, Isabella 2014. *The Living Goddess*. London: Eland.

Tribulato, Olga and Olivieri, Luca Maria 2017. 'Writing Greek in the Swat Region: A New Graffito from Barikot'. *ZPE* 204, 128–35.

Trnka-Amrhein, Yvona forthcoming. 'Interpreting *Sesonchosis* as a Biographical Novel'.

Tsouna, Voula 2009. 'Epicurean Therapeutic Strategies', in J. Warren (ed.), *The Cambridge Companion to Epicureanism*. Cambridge: Cambridge University Press, 249–65.

Vālmīki 1984. *The Rāmāyaṇa of Vālmīki. An Epic of Ancient India.* 1: *Bālakāṇḍa*, tr. Sheldon I. Pollock, ed. Robert P. Goldman; intro. and annot. Robert P. Goldman and Sally Sutherland. Princeton: Princeton University Press.

Vālmīki 1986. *The Rāmāyaṇa of Vālmīki. An Epic of Ancient India.* 2: *Ayodhyākāṇḍa*, tr., intro. and annot. Sheldon I. Pollock, ed. Robert P. Goldman. Princeton: Princeton University Press.

Vālmīki 1991. *The Rāmāyaṇa of Vālmīki. An Epic of Ancient India.* 3: *Araṇyakāṇḍa*, tr., intro. and annot. Sheldon I. Pollock, ed. Robert P. Goldman. Princeton: Princeton University Press.

Vālmīki 1994. *The Rāmāyaṇa of Vālmīki. An Epic of Ancient India.* 4: *Kiṣkindhākāṇḍa*, (tr., intro. and annot. Rosalind Lefeber, ed. Robert P. Goldman. Princeton: Princeton University Press.

Van Buitenen, J.A.B. 1968. *Two Plays of Ancient India*. New York: Columbia University Press.

Varadpande, M. L. 1981. *Indian and Indo-Greek Theatre.* New Delhi: Abhinav.

Vasunia, Phiroze 2013. *The Classics and Colonial India.* Oxford: Oxford University Press.

Vegad, Amrit Lal 2008. *Narmada: River of Beauty.* Delhi: Penguin.

Vidyabhusana, S. C. 1918. 'Influence of Aristotle on the Development of the Syllogism in Indian Logic'. *JRAS* 50, 469–88.

Vogel, J. P. 1910. *Catalogue of the Archaeological Museum at Mathura.* Allahabad: Government Press, United Provinces.

Waley, Arthur 1952. *The Real Tripitaka.* London: Allen and Unwin.

Wallace, Shane 2016. 'Greek Culture in Afghanistan and India: Old Evidence and New Discoveries'. *Greece & Rome* 63, 205–26.

Watson, Burton 1958. *Ssu-ma Chi'en: grand historian of China*. New York: Columbia University Press.

Weerakkody, D.P.M. 1997. *Taprobane. Ancient Sri Lanka as Known to Greeks and Romans.* Turnhout: Brepols.

Welles, C. B. 1934. *Royal Correspondence in the Hellenistic Period.* New Haven, CT: Yale University Press.

West, M. L. 1964. 'Megasthenes and the Astomi'. *CR* 14, 242.

Wheatley, Pat. 2014. 'Seleucus and Chandragupta in Justin XV.4', in H. Hauben and A. Meeus (eds.), *The Age of the Successors and the Creation of the Hellenistic Kingdoms.* Leuven: Peeters; 501–16.

Wheatley, Pat and Baynham, Elizabeth (eds.) 2015. *East and West in the Empire of Alexander the Great.* Oxford: Oxford University Press.

Wheeler, R.E.M. 1949. 'Romano-Buddhist Art: An Old Problem Revisited'. *Antiquity* 23, 4–19.

White, Carolinne (ed. and tr.) 1996. *Gregory of Nazianzus: Autobiographical Poems.* Cambridge: Cambridge University Press.

White, David Gordon 1991. *Myths of the Dog-Man.* Chicago: University of Chicago Press.

Wiesehöfer, Josef 1998. 'Geschenke, Gewürze, Gedanken. Überlegungen zu den Beziehungen zwischen Seleukiden und Mauryas', in Dąbrowa (ed.) 1998, 225–36.

Wiesehöfer, J., Brinkhaus, H. and Bichler, R. (eds.) 2016. *Megasthenes und seine Zeit/Megasthenes and his Time*. Wiesbaden: Harrassowitz.

Willekes, Carolyn 2016. *The Horse in the Ancient World: From Bucephalus to the Hippodrome*. London: IB Tauris.

Williams, J. H. 1950. *Elephant Bill*. London: R. Hart-Davis.

Willson, A. Leslie 1964. *A Mythical Image: The Ideas of India in German Romanticism*. Durham, NC: Duke University Press.

Wilson, H. H. (tr.) 1840. *Vishnu Purāna* London: Oriental Translation Fund.

Winiarczyk, Marek 2011. *Die hellenistischen Utopien*. Berlin: de Gruyter.

Wirth, Albrecht 1894. 'The Story of the King's Daughter in the Besieged Town'. *American Anthropologist* 7, 367–72.

Wittgenstein, Ludwig 1993. 'Remarks on Frazer's *Golden Bough*', in J. C. Klagge and A. Nordman (eds.), *Philosophical Occasions, 1912–1951*. Indianapolis: Hackett, 118–55.

Wittkower, Rudolf 1942. 'Marvels of the East: A Study in the History of Monsters'. *JWCI* 5, 159–97.

Witzel, Michael 1999. 'Aryan and Non-Aryan Names in Vedic India. Data for the Linguistic Situation, c. 1900–500 B.C.', in Bronkhorst and Deshpande (eds.) 1999: 337–404.

Witzel, Michael 2006. Brahmanical Reactions to Foreign Influences and to Social and Religious Change', in Olivelle (ed.) 2006, 457–99.

Wöhrle, G. 1985. *Theophrasts Methode in seinen botanischen Schriften*. Amsterdam: Grüner.

Wood, Frances 1995. *Did Marco Polo Go to China?* London: Secker and Warburg.

Woodcock, George 1966. *The Greeks in India*. London: Faber.

Wriggins, Sally H. 2004. *The Silk Road Journey with Xuanzang*. Boulder, CO: Westview Press.

Wu, Anthony C. 2006. *The Monkey and the Monk*. Chicago: University of Chicago Press.

Wulff Alonso, Fernando 2008. *Grecia en India: el repertorio griego del Mahabharata*. Madrid: Ediciones Akal.

Yaldiz, M. and Lobo, W. (eds.) 1987. *Investigating Indian Art*. Berlin: Museum für indische Kunst.

Yardley, John C. and Heckel, Waldemar 1981. 'Roman Writers and the Indian Practice of Suttee'. *Philologus* 125, 305–11.

Zambrini, Andrea 1982. 'Gli *Indika* di Megastene I'. *ASNP* 12, 71–149.

Zambrini, Andrea 1985. 'Gli *Indika* di Megastene II'. *ASNP* 15, 781–853.

Zaretsky, Robert 2013. *A Life worth Living. Albert Camus and the Quest for Meaning*. Cambridge, MA: Harvard University Press.

Zhmud, Leonid 2012. *Pythagoras and the Early Pythagoreans*. Oxford: Oxford University Press.

Zin, Monika 2003. *A Guide to the Ajantā Paintings*, vol. 2: *Devotional and Ornamental Paintings*. Delhi: Mushiram Manoharlal.

Zysk, K. 1998. *Asceticism and Healing in Ancient India*. Delhi: Motilal Banarsidass.

INDEX

The pages of illustrations are indicated by italic type

A NOTE ON THE TYPE

This book has been composed in Arno, an Old-style serif typeface in the classic Venetian tradition, designed by Robert Slimbach at Adobe.